THE COMPLETE WRITINGS OF

H. A. MAXWELL

WHYTE

THE COMPLETE WRITINGS OF

H. A. MAXWELL

WHYTE

WHITAKER
HOUSE

This book is not intended to provide medical advice or to take the place of medical advice and treatment from your personal physician. Readers are advised to consult their own doctors or other qualified health professionals regarding the treatment of their medical problems. Neither the publisher nor the author takes any responsibility for any possible consequences from any treatment, action, or application of medicine, supplement, herb, or preparation to any person reading or following the information in this book. If readers are taking prescription medications, they should consult with their physicians and not take themselves off medicines to start supplementation without the proper supervision of a physician.

THE COMPLETE WRITINGS OF H. A. MAXWELL WHYTE

Includes the following books:

The Power of the Blood	*Hidden Spirits*
Demons & Deliverance	*How to Receive the Baptism of the Holy Spirit*
The Kiss of Satan	*Is Mark 16 True?*
Bible Baptisms	*The Prophetic Word*
The Body Is for the Lord	*Pulling Down Strongholds*
Charismatic Gifts	*Return to the Pattern*
Divine Health	*The Working of Miracles*
The Emerging Church	*Where Is the Antichrist?*
Fear Destroys	

ISBN: 978-1-62911-941-0
eBook ISBN: 978-1-62911-942-7
Printed in the United States of America
© 2018 by Michael Whyte

Whitaker House
1030 Hunt Valley Circle
New Kensington, PA 15068
www.whitakerhouse.com

Library of Congress Cataloging-in-Publication Data (Pending)

1 2 3 4 5 6 7 8 9 10 11 ᰃ 25 24 23 22 21 20 19 18

CONTENTS

THE POWER OF THE BLOOD

CONTENTS

FOREWORD

It has been a great joy to read this book, and a delight to accede to the request of the author that I write a foreword.

Every fresh outpouring of the Spirit of God begins with a praying group, or with praying groups. There were two such groups in the British Isles in 1907—doubtless more, but the writer knows of these two. One group of five women met every Saturday in a small home in London to pray for an outpouring of the Spirit; the other group of five men met each Saturday night in the Episcopal rectory in Sunderland, England. The cry of both groups was for a Pentecostal outpouring in the British Isles.

The Lord came to the London group first. Catherine Price, a humble housewife, was preparing her dinner when she was constrained by the Spirit to leave everything and go to wait upon the Lord. As she waited, Jesus came to her in person. As she magnified and glorified Him, her English was taken away and she began to praise Him in a new language.

A few days later she was led to go to a meeting in London, organized by the Keswick group, a people who stood for the highest spiritual life in those days. The service began with a song, but there seemed to be no heart in the worship. The Spirit of the Lord fell upon Catherine Price, a very timid woman, and she cried out, "Oh, how can you sing so listlessly, so apathetically, so carelessly about the blood of Jesus Christ!" Immediately she began to speak in another tongue as the Spirit gave utterance.

The effect upon the audience was tremendous. Some fell upon their faces before God; others rushed out of the building in fear. A number were deeply impressed that this was truly a manifestation of the Spirit of God, and they inquired for the address of this woman. From that day there came to her home many who desired to know more about this, and they were baptized in the Spirit. Her home was opened for meetings in which the one theme was *"Behold! The Lamb of God"* (John 1:29, see also verse 36), for by the out-poured blood of the Lamb, the gift of the Holy Spirit was purchased. And so the outpouring of the Spirit began in London.

Soon the Spirit was out-poured in Sunderland; and there, as in London, the blood of Jesus Christ was extolled. As they reverently pleaded the blood of Jesus, many were filled with the Holy Spirit.

Incidentally, there was another group praying in Valparaiso, Chile, South America, in a Methodist church; the Lord poured out His Spirit upon Dr. Hoover and his Methodist brethren—a group of five who met every day for prayer. The theme of that revival was also the blood of Jesus Christ.

They greatly honored the blood in those days and constantly sang,

Under the blood, the precious blood;
Under the cleansing, healing blood;
Keep me, Savior, from day to day,
Under the precious blood.

It seemed that there was no end to the revelations of the power and the preciousness of the blood of Jesus Christ.

Now, once again, the Lord is bringing the power of the blood to the attention of the church. Let us honor and plead the blood of the Lamb very reverently, for through the blood we have power over all the might of the enemy. To those who plead the blood of the Lamb—not mechanically, but in true holy reverence—there will be a restoration of all that the locust, the cankerworm, the caterpillar, and the palmerworm have eaten. (See Joel 2:25.)

—*Stanley H. Frodsham*
Ontario, Canada
August 1959

PREFACE TO
THE SEVENTH EDITION

This seventh edition of *The Power of the Blood* has been revised and enlarged. Since the book was originally written in 1959 we have seen a great increase in New Testament revival, especially among the more formal churches. God is showing that He is no respecter of persons or denominations. One of the great truths which is being recovered in this revival is that regarding the power of the blood of Jesus.

Everywhere it has been the privilege of the author to minister, the message on the blood has been received with gladness, and many have thereby been healed and filled with the Holy Spirit. On every hand it seems that God has again revealed to Christians that they should "plead the precious blood of Jesus."

—*H. A. Maxwell Whyte*

1

LIFE IS IN THE BLOOD

Pastor Whyte, will you pray for my eyes?" Betty asked me one day. She was a young girl of sixteen who worked in a Fish 'n' Chips store in Toronto.

"Why, certainly, Betty," I replied. "Let's just believe God together and plead the blood of Jesus." I looked at her for a moment and felt the great compassion of Jesus stirring within me. She was totally blind in her right eye, and her left eye was wandering so that it was very difficult for her to focus at all. She was wearing very, very thick glasses—the thickest she could get.

I began to pray for her, pleading the blood strongly and emphatically. Instantly, the Lord restored the sight of her right eye.

"Oh, praise the Lord!" she exclaimed. "I can see!" We rejoiced together at the mercy of the Lord.

Over a period of weeks, the wandering eye began to focus, and in a matter of months, she had 2020 vision. That was twenty years ago, and she is still healed.

A MYSTERIOUS SUBSTANCE

This is but one example of hundreds upon hundreds of stories that I could relate to you that demonstrate the power of the blood of Jesus. Each story is thrilling and convincing. But first, let me share with you some of the basic teachings of the Bible about the blood.

Blood is a strange and mysterious substance. A small, unimaginative boy gazing into a slaughterhouse can watch the blood of animals running down a drain without flinching; but the same boy when grown older, with a bit more imagination, may pass out in a dead faint at the sight of blood.

On the other hand, excited men and women may clap and cheer when their favorite boxer causes blood to flow in a boxing match. It seems that the baser side of man likes to see blood; it excites him. But the nobler side of man is repulsed by blood, and sympathy is expressed at the suffering of those whose blood has been shed in accidents and war. Yes, blood is a mysterious substance.

In the Scriptures we begin to get some understanding of this amazing substance. While the Bible does not tell us about the chemical composition of the red and white corpuscles, it does tell us something that is absolutely basic to the mystery: The life of a living creature is in its blood. Thus, in Leviticus 17:11 we read, *"For the life of the flesh is in the blood."*

But *life* is as mysterious as blood, and very little is understood about it. We do know that man cannot create or copy life, even though he tries to do so in laboratories. The well-known story of Frankenstein and his monster claims to portray how life came from an electric storm into a corpse made of human tissue; but, of course, this is pure fiction. It is best that we accept the fundamental truth that both electricity and life come from the Author of all life, God Almighty.

In the second chapter of Genesis, we read how God created man. It is important that we understand that man can never create man. Man is God's greatest creative achievement on earth and was made in His likeness. The Bible teaches that man is *"fearfully and wonderfully made"* (Psalm 139:14), far more wonderfully made than the angels—at least in respect to the idea that angels have no blood in them, for they have no flesh. Angels are spirit beings and have only spiritual life. This is the way God made them.

BLOOD, THE CARRIER OF LIFE

When God made man, He formed a body from the dust of the ground, from the substances and chemicals of this planet. Then He breathed into this body the breath of life. In other words, He breathed into this composition of inert chemicals some of His own spiritual life, and that life was held in the complex substance we call blood.

So, you see, blood is not life, but it *carries* life. This becomes quite clear by observing what happens at death. Immediately after expiration, the person's body is still warm and will remain so for a brief time. Yet that person is dead because life has mysteriously departed from the blood. The life of man is carried in his bloodstream. Life itself is spiritual, but it must have a physical carrier, and this carrier is the blood.

However, to me, the most amazing thing about blood is its capacity to carry the life of God. The point of contact between the Divine and the human rests in the bloodstream. No wonder we say that blood is a mysterious substance! It contains something that no scientist can explain—it contains the life of God. In the not too distant past, it became possible to draw blood from a person's veins, seal it in special containers, and store it in newly created blood banks, where the life that alone comes from God could be kept in refrigerators much below the normal temperature of blood in a human body. Blood can even be frozen, but the life that is in it is unaffected by this freezing process.

Apart from the compatibility factor of the various blood types, it doesn't matter if the blood of a woman is given to a man, if the blood of a black donor is put into the veins of a white person, or if a skid-row bum receives a transfusion from a wealthy person. Blood does not determine the sex, the color of the skin, or the culture of the person; it simply carries the life that comes from God. There would be no chemical difference between dead blood and live blood of the same type, apart from the life that God put in it and took away from it.

It is possible for a person who has been seriously wounded to literally bleed to death as the heart pumps the life-giving blood out of the wound. As soon as the blood has gone, the life has gone, for the life is in the blood! One can fill the veins with chemicals, dress up the corpse, and lay it in a casket for all to see—but the corpse is still a corpse, for there is no blood in the veins and thus no life in the body.

THE UNIQUENESS OF JESUS'S BLOOD

This discussion quite naturally leads to some consideration of the unique nature of Jesus's blood. I am deeply grateful to Dr. William Standish Reed of the Christian Medical Foundation of Tampa, Florida, for his thoughts on the matter of the supernatural conception of Jesus in the womb of Mary. The female ovum itself has no blood, and neither has the male sperm; but it is when these come together in the fallopian tube that conception takes place and a new life begins. The blood cells in this new creation are from both father and mother, and the blood type is determined at the moment of conception and is thereafter protected by the placenta from any flow of the mother's blood into the fetus.

The Bible is explicit that the Holy Spirit was the Divine Agent who caused Jesus's conception in the womb of Mary. This, therefore, was not a normal conception but a supernatural act of God in planting the life of His already existent Son right in the womb of Mary, with no normal union of a male sperm with a female ovum from Mary. As the blood of the Son of God was of an entirely separate and precious nature, it is inconceivable that Mary could have supplied any of her Adamic, unregenerate blood for the spotless Lamb of God. All the Child's blood came from His Father in heaven by a supernatural creative act of God. Jesus's blood was without the Adamic stain of sin.

The idea held by many that Mary supplied the ovum and that the Holy Spirit supplied the spiritual sperm would mean that Jesus would have been conceived with mixed blood, part of Adam and part of God, which is repugnant to God's plan of salvation for a fallen human race. Such an erroneous idea also lends encouragement to the view held by some in the metaphysical cults that Jesus had no existence prior to His conception in the womb of Mary.

The fact of the matter is that God says in the Bible that He prepared a body for His Son. "*Therefore, when He came into the world, He said: 'Sacrifice and offering You did not desire, But a body You have prepared for Me'*" (Hebrews 10:5). It was *that* body that was implanted in Mary's womb. Jesus knew before His birth at Bethlehem that His Father would build and prepare a body for Him, which He later described as the temple of God. (See John 2:21.) He simply came down from heaven and entered into the newly created body in the womb of Mary, His earthly mother. This body had blood created by His Father. There was no Adamic intermixing.

Jesus was *"the only begotten of the Father"* (John 1:14), and His body was formed and fashioned wonderfully in the womb of Mary, His mother. But the life that was in Jesus Christ came uniquely from the Father by the Holy Spirit. Therefore, this life that flowed in the veins of the Lord Jesus Christ came from God alone. No wonder He said, *"I am...the life"* (John 14:6). God imparted His own life into the bloodstream of Jesus. Adamic blood is corrupt and was carried by Mary, who declared that Jesus her Son was *"God my Savior"* (Luke 1:47). Mary was the chosen carrier of the body of her Son, but all of His blood came from God.

BLOOD TYPES

A limited number of categories or types of human blood have been catalogued by medical science (A+, B+, AB+, O+, O-, AB-, B-, and A-), but I am certain that the blood "type" of the Lord Jesus Christ was entirely different. The blood that flowed in His veins was perfect since it was not contaminated by Adam's sin, which brought sin and sickness into human blood.

If Adam had not sinned, he would not have died. But by his sin, he introduced death into the human family. The human body, therefore, became subject to corruption and decay, and death ultimately comes to each one of us. It is at the moment of death when the life that is in the blood takes its departure from the physical body, along with the spirit and soul of man.

Jesus Christ had no sin in His body, but He allowed Himself to die for the sins of a sinful humanity. He gave the perfect life that was in His perfect blood to redeem imperfect mankind—whose bodies carry death because of sin—in an exchange of pure blood for contaminated blood, life for death, *"for the life...is in the blood."* This is why Jesus is described as the last Adam. God sent Him to earth in the *likeness* of sinful Adam, but with pure, uncontaminated blood in His veins. God sent Him so that He might shed that pure blood of His for the life of humanity.

It is very important for us to understand that the blood of Jesus is in a completely different category from ours. Peter rightly described it as *"precious blood"* (1 Peter 1:19). It is not possible to assess the value of Jesus' blood in human terms. It is priceless. It is God's price for the redemption of the whole human race.

SPIRITUAL TRANSFUSIONS

Stretch your imagination for a moment. Wouldn't it be wonderful if Jesus' blood could be kept in the blood banks of our hospitals? Don't you see that everyone who could obtain a transfusion of Christ's blood would actually be receiving God's eternal life in pure blood? Of course, God never meant to administer salvation by blood transfusions! But a miracle just as great takes place when a man trusts in Jesus and accepts Him as his personal Savior. Immediately, a great cleansing takes place, and the sin that is in the bloodstream is purged. *"For I will acquit them of the guilt of bloodshed, whom I had not acquitted; for the LORD dwells in Zion"* (Joel 3:21).

When we receive Jesus, the Bible expresses the idea that the *heart* is cleansed by the blood of Jesus. (See, for example, 2 Chronicles 30:18–19; Hebrews 9:14; 1 John 1:7.) This may be more literal than some would dare to believe. If the sin and corruption in our bloodstream is purged and all spiritual filth is washed out, then certainly the very heart that pumps the blood may be spoken of as being cleansed. By the miracle of salvation, we receive both eternal life and the divine health of the Son of God. The greatest disinfectant in the world is the blood of Jesus Christ. It carries the eternal life of God in it.

DEAD BLOOD, LIVE BLOOD

In this connection it is interesting to note that Satan's nickname *Beelzebub* means "Lord of the flies," or "Prince of the flies." Dead blood will quickly attract flies, which will breed corruption in the coagulating blood. However, the blood of Jesus has exactly the opposite effect: it repulses Beelzebub and all his demons. When you put the blood of Jesus on something by faith, Satan will flee because the blood of Jesus is alive. The life is in the blood.

The devil hates the mention of the blood of Jesus. This is very evident in our deliverance ministry when demons talk to us. I have heard some demons actually wail, "Don't say that; don't say that," when we mentioned the blood of Jesus. Another demon said accusingly, "You said that!" as though we had said some terrible thing.

One time we were praying for a woman who was insane. "Jesus," I said, "we plead Your precious blood!" Immediately, a strange voice came out of the woman's throat. "Don't say that," the voice growled. "I don't like that!"

But we persisted. "We plead the blood!" we cried. Finally the demon gave up. "All right, you can say it—I don't mind," it said. "Anyway, it's all dried up; it's all dried up!" With that, the demon went out, and the woman was restored to sanity. Again we rejoiced at the power of the blood.

DELIVERANCE TO LIFE

So do not underestimate the power of the blood of Jesus. In Leviticus 17:11, we read, *"For the life of the flesh is in the blood, and I have given it to you upon the altar to make atonement for your souls; for it is the blood that makes atonement for the soul."* The apostle, therefore, made no mistake when he wrote, *"Without shedding of blood is no remission"* (Hebrews 9:22).

2

ATONEMENT BY THE BLOOD

Imagine, if you can, the scene at Calvary. No artist has ever pictured the Calvary scene as it really was. It would be too repulsive to paint on any canvas. It is doubtful that the Romans left Jesus even the courtesy of a loincloth. He became as exposed as the first Adam in the garden so that He might cover His own nakedness with His own precious blood—not even a linen cloth to contaminate or spoil the type.

In turn, we may cover our nakedness with His precious blood—a perfect atonement or covering indeed! We cannot even offer a convenient loincloth or fig leaf to hide our sins; we must divest ourselves of everything and appear destitute of all covering in His presence. Then He will give us His own blessed robe of righteousness after we have accepted the cleansing of His precious blood. A glorious truth indeed!

THE ULTIMATE BLOOD SACRIFICE

The crown of thorns was then put upon His head, not gently but roughly. Many thorns—perhaps a dozen or more—up to one-and-a-half inches long, were jabbed into His scalp, producing such serious wounds that trickles of blood spurted out and ran into His hair and beard, matting both in dark red. The spikes were driven into the wrists of His hands, and His blood coursed down His arms and sides. Spikes were also driven through His feet and more blood ran down the sides of the cross on behalf of the sins of the whole world. Later a spear was thrust into His side, and His blood spilled out (see John 19:34) and ran down the cross onto the ground beneath.

His bones were out of joint. (See Psalm 22:14.) His face was dreadful to look upon. There was "*no beauty* [in Him] *that we should desire Him*" (Isaiah 53:2). God gave His best, His Son, His perfect sacrifice. Even in death, there was no blemish in Him, for He was already dead when the soldiers arrived to break His legs; therefore, not a bone of Him was broken. (See Psalm 34:20; John 19:36.) Those who looked on Him saw only blood. It was a spectacle of blood. His hair and beard were soaked in His own blood. His back was lacerated from the thirty-nine stripes and was covered with His own blood. The cross was covered with blood, and the very earth was soaked. It was blood, blood, blood everywhere.

It is important for us to grasp the fact that complete atonement is provided for us through the blood of Christ. The word *atonement* is a beautiful word, and one that is, unfortunately, sometimes misunderstood. One group has offered the suggestion that the word *atonement* means "at-onement." The best we can say for this is that it is an apt play on words, but not the literal meaning. The word *atonement* simply means "a covering." *"Where sin abounded, grace abounded much more"* (Romans 5:20), for with grace came the blood of Jesus, which, freely given in love, covers all our sins. (See Proverbs 10:12.)

THE FAMILY BOMB SHELTER

The effectiveness of the covering by the blood of Jesus was made very real to Mrs. Whyte and me during World War II when we were living in England. We often experienced dangerous air raids, during which buzz bombs were flying everywhere. But we were able to lie down with our children and sleep through much of the peril.

The protection afforded by the blood of Jesus was so real that it seemed as if we were sleeping in a strong shelter. In fact, we used to speak of the blood as the "best air-raid shelter in the world." However, we never took this shelter for granted. Instead, every night before we went to sleep, we would cover ourselves, our home, and our children with the blood of Jesus. One night thirteen bombs landed within a three-quarter-mile radius from our home. And they were big blockbusters. Yet aside from some minor damage to the house, we were all kept safe.

GOD'S LOVE COVERS OUR SINS

If we can clearly understand the meaning of the word *atonement*, we have discovered tremendous truth. God has provided a substance by which we can cover things we no longer want; God guarantees not even to see our sins after we reckon by faith that the blood of Jesus has covered them. Why is this? Because when God sees the blood of the Lamb, He does not see sin.

We are told in Leviticus that not only is the life in the blood, but the blood is the only substance that can make an atonement, or covering, for our souls.

> *For the life of the flesh is in the blood, and I have given it to you upon the altar to make atonement for your souls; for it is the blood that makes atonement for the soul.* (Leviticus 17:11)

The sinner, therefore, upon accepting a substitute—in Old Testament times, it was a clean animal—sees the substitute dying in his place. In this way, a blood covering is provided for the sinner.

"FIG-LEAF" RELIGIONS

At the beginning of creation, God commanded that living creatures, greatly beloved of Adam, must be slaughtered by him and their blood must be shed to supply a covering for Adam and Eve's obvious nakedness. Fig leaves were insufficient. So animals were slaughtered, and after the blood was shed, Adam and Eve were covered with the skins. The principle of a life for a life runs throughout the Bible. No other garments would sufficiently cover Adam and Eve except those that involved the shedding of blood. If man is left to himself, he usually invents a religion that does not require the shedding of blood—a "fig-leaf" religion.

This is why it is exceedingly important that, in observing the Lord's Supper, we partake of both the bread and the wine. To take of the bread only, as some groups do, would be equivalent to a bloodless offering, for there is no life in the flesh without blood.

IN PERFECT HARMONY

In 1 John 5:8, we read, *"And there are three that bear witness on earth: the Spirit, the water, and the blood; and these three agree as one."* In the Scriptures, water is often a symbol of the Word of God; it is what washes us continually, as we see in Ephesians 5:26. But the Word without the blood is ineffectual, for the life of Jesus, who is the Word of God, is in the blood. Therefore, in the Lord's Supper, it is not proper to receive the bread alone. We are to receive both bread and wine, which speaks of Jesus, the crucified Word of God, and the blood that He willingly shed.

The Holy Spirit is also in complete agreement with the water and the blood. For this reason, when we honor the blood of Jesus, the Holy Spirit immediately manifests His life on our behalf. The Holy Spirit agrees with the Word of God and with the blood of Jesus, and all three are in agreement with the others. They are triunely one.

GOD'S EQUATIONS

As recounted by the author of Hebrews, on the Day of Atonement in the Old Testament, Moses *"took the blood…and sprinkled both the book itself and all the people"* (Hebrews 9:19). Why? Because the book is a lifeless book to the reader unless the blood is first applied. Both the book (the Word of God) and the people were sprinkled with the blood. This too, was fulfilled on Calvary. Jesus, who is the living Word of God, was sprinkled with His own blood.

There are some who tell us that it is enough that we have the name of Jesus, but I beg to differ. We need the name *and* the blood, for the life is in the blood. There is power in the name of Jesus only because He shed His own blood and offered it to His Father, who then gave His power and His authority to His Son. (See Matthew

28:18.) That same power and authority is given to all believers (see Luke 10:19), but it only becomes operative as we honor His blood.

IN OUR PLACE

The death of Christ is often spoken of as being substitutionary. Jesus died in our place for us. Referring to the Old Testament will give abundant evidence that sins could only be forgiven by God on the grounds of shed blood—a life for a life—and we are informed of this fact in the New Testament as well: *"Without shedding of blood is no remission"* (Hebrews 9:22).

When Jesus died upon the cross, He, as God's High Priest, shed and sprinkled His own blood on behalf of the people. He was crucified at the time of the feast of the Passover, the feast the Jews kept to remember the time when God said, "When I see the blood, I will pass over you and will not allow the destroyer to attack you." (See Exodus 12:23.) At the very time when the Jews were celebrating the first exodus, Jesus was making atonement for the second exodus. To all who will believe in this sacrifice and the efficacy of His precious blood, there is an exodus from sin and the penalty of sin, which includes sickness.

FORESHADOWING FULFILLED IN CHRIST

Every type and symbol of the atonement in the Old Testament was fulfilled in Christ. When Jesus' shed blood covered the cross, Himself, and His garments, the following events that foreshadowed His atoning work were completed:

1. blood sprinkled on the altar (Exodus 24:6–8);
2. all around on the altar (Exodus 29:12, 16; Leviticus 7:2);
3. on the high priest and his garments (Exodus 29:20–21);
4. sprinkled seven times, the number of perfection or completion (Leviticus 4:6);
5. at the base of the altar (Leviticus 4:7);
6. on the side of the altar (Leviticus 5:9);
7. sprinkled before the tabernacle seven times (Numbers 19:4).

This last was fulfilled in that the cross and the hill of Calvary were within sight of the temple in Jerusalem, for Calvary was outside the city wall.

All these Old Testament types were fulfilled in the crucifixion of Jesus, who made Himself our Passover, our High Priest, our Savior, and our blood sacrifice. His blood alone covers our sins.

JESUS BORE OUR GUILT

When we consider the great load of sin and guilt that Jesus carried on Calvary, is it any wonder that He cried out in agony, not so much of body, but of soul, *"My God, My God, why have You forsaken Me?"* (Psalm 22:1; Matthew 27:46). But why had the Father forsaken the Son? Because it is written that God cannot look upon sin. (See Habakkuk 1:13.) When Jesus was bearing the sins of the world in His body on the cross, the Father could not look at His Son. Jesus had become sin for us. (See 2 Corinthians 5:21.)

Since Jesus was bearing the guilt of *"our sins in His own body"* (1 Peter 2:24), it was not possible for the Father to look upon Him until Jesus had covered His own body with His blood. Only then could the Father turn and gaze again upon His only begotten Son. He had been *"obedient to the point of death, even the death of the cross"* (Philippians 2:8), and now our sins were atoned for, or covered, with His own precious blood. His life for our life—that is what the Father demanded. After it was accomplished, the Father then looked, not on our sin, but on His Son's blood. That was enough; His Son had offered His life in His blood for all mankind. The Father had respect for the pure offering, and our redemption was made complete.

If we honor the blood of Jesus Christ, the Father will smile upon us with forgiveness and cleansing. However, this must not be a dull theological formality, but an active, vital embracing of His blood. We do not offer our own works; we offer only His blood. When God sees the blood of His Son, which we offer as our covering, pardon, and plea, God does not see our sin at all; He can see only the covering, the precious blood of Jesus. Therefore, we understand that *"it is the blood that makes atonement for the soul"* (Leviticus 17:11).

3

THE BLOOD SPEAKS

When Lester Sumrall ministered deliverance to a demon-possessed girl in the Philippine Islands a number of years ago, the demon in the girl spoke in the purest English, although the girl herself spoke only a local dialect. This demon spirit first cursed the Father, then the Son, then the Holy Spirit, and then the blood of Jesus, in that order. I heard Brother Sumrall say at the 1957 Full Gospel Businessmen's Convention in Chicago that the way the demon cursed, it almost seemed that the demon believed the blood of Jesus was alive.

DEMONIC REACTIONS

Remembering that the life of God is in the blood of Jesus, I am not surprised at the reaction of these strong demon spirits. As soon as any Christian takes the precious blood of Jesus on his tongue and sings it, talks it, or pleads it, the devil gets terribly disturbed. The devil understands the power of the blood of Jesus, and he has done everything possible to blind Christians to this truth. Many people who are Christians in name only will have nothing to do with what they call "a slaughterhouse religion." Theirs is a religion without the life of God in it, and the devil has no objection to them participating in this kind of religion. But as soon as we honor the blood of Jesus in an active sense, we stir up demons to a fever pitch. It is like fire in a hornet's nest.

It is surprising that so little has been taught about the blood and so little is known about the activity of demon spirits, even within the Christian church. No wise Christian would dare try to cast out demons without faith in the blood of Jesus. I have been used of God many times to deliver people from demon powers, both in soul and body, but never without a conscious pleading of the blood of Jesus and a knowledge that I have been literally covered by His blood. In such cases, Jesus' promise that *"nothing shall by any means hurt you"* (Luke 10:19) and the promise in Isaiah 54:17 that *"no weapon formed against you shall prosper"* find their complete realization.

THE CRY OF JESUS'S BLOOD

The protection afforded us by the blood rests in the fact that Jesus' blood says something to God. The blood cries out to God, "Sin is covered! The penalty is paid!"

In fact, there is abundant evidence in the Bible that all shed blood speaks to God. After the murder of Abel by his brother Cain, we read in Genesis 4:10, *"And* [the Lord] *said, "What have you done? The voice of your brother's blood cries out to me from the ground."* It is clear from this Scripture that the life that was in Abel's blood did not cease after his murder, but cried out for vengeance. This may be difficult for us to grasp, but there is no doubt that God is telling us that innocently shed blood cries out to Him for vengeance.

In Hebrews 12:24, the writer referred to the blood of Jesus by contrasting it with Abel's blood and calling it *"the blood of sprinkling that speaks better things than that of Abel."* Whereas Abel's blood cried out for vengeance, Jesus' blood cries out for mercy. This is what was symbolized in Old Testament days when the mercy seat within the Holy of Holies was sprinkled with the blood of bulls and goats when the high priest went within the veil once a year. (See Hebrews 9:25.)

WITHIN THE VEIL

The result of such sprinkling was that God manifested His *shekinah* glory and spoke to the high priest from between the two cherubim that overshadowed the mercy seat. (See Exodus 25:22.) It is interesting to note that the glory was *seen* and the voice *heard* only when the blood was used. It was not sufficient that the high priest had faith in the blood for the atoning of the sins of Israel for the past year; he had to use it. It is exactly so today. None of us can enter into this holy place (heaven itself) except

> *…by the blood of Jesus, by a new and living way which He consecrated for us, through the veil, that is, His flesh, and having a High Priest over the house of God, let us draw near with a true heart in full assurance of faith, having our hearts sprinkled from an evil conscience and our bodies washed with pure water.* (Hebrews 10:19–22)

When the high priest in the Old Testament went into the Holy of Holies, he would have been stricken dead had he not offered blood. So he carefully offered nothing else but blood. Today in Christian circles, we find many offering other things—works, emotion, strange fire (see Leviticus 10:1–2), and various kinds of worship—but we must be aware that if we are to enter into *"heavenly places in Christ Jesus"* (Ephesians 2:6), we can only do so as we consciously offer the blood of Jesus as our only plea.

To plead the blood of Jesus is to confess to God that we are depending wholly on His mercy. As the wonderful old hymn says,

Rock of Ages, cleft for me,
Let me hide myself in Thee.
Let the water and the blood,
From Thy wounded side which flowed,
Be of sin the double cure,
Save from wrath and make me pure.

Nothing in my hand I bring,
Simply to Thy cross I cling;
Naked come to Thee for dress,
Helpless look to Thee for grace;
Foul I to the fountain fly,
Wash me Savior or I die.

When we plead the blood of Jesus, it immediately pleads for us, because it is speaking blood. It speaks mercy from the mercy seat in heaven where Jesus is seated with His Father. This is why we plead the blood of Jesus.

We are convinced that the whole church has yet to learn the value of using the blood of Jesus. To those who have discovered this secret, the whole realm of God's power is opened, and all the angels in heaven come to help and rescue the child of God who honors, uses, and pleads the blood of Jesus. Truly, as the songwriter Charles Wesley penned in the old hymn, *Arise, My Soul, Arise*, "The Spirit answers to the blood."

4

THE PASSOVER

The book of Genesis teaches us that the ancient patriarchs offered animals as sacrifices. Abram offered a ram instead of his son Isaac (see Genesis 22:13), and Noah built an altar after the flood and offered some of every clean beast and fowl that had been safely delivered through the flood (see Genesis 8:20). These animals were costly; nothing cheap was good enough.

Many would have suggested that it was wasteful for Noah to kill and offer valuable animals that God had delivered from drowning. Why not just kneel down and offer a prayer of thanksgiving? Similarly, many today suggest that we would be better off to have less emphasis on the blood and more on worship and prayer. And in this, Satan has deceived us. If we would offer the blood of Jesus more and cut some of our long prayers down in size, we might get better answers and have less fear in our hearts! God can only receive us and our praise and thanksgiving on the basis of the blood of His Son. There is no other way into God's presence.

REQUIRED BLOOD SACRIFICES

The children of Israel knew this in Egypt. Although they had no codified law, yet the word had been passed down from generation to generation that God required blood. The Israelites knew about blood because their forefather Abraham had taught them that they owed their very existence as a nation to God's mercy in supplying a ram for sacrifice in place of the life of Isaac. Had Isaac not been spared, there would have been no nation of Israel, for Isaac was Abraham's only son of promise. So Isaac was a miraculously delivered child, saved by the blood of a substitute sacrifice. Every Israelite had been taught this story and understood the importance of the blood.

God taught them this even more dramatically when He delivered them from Egyptian bondage. God had visited nine terrible plagues upon Egypt, but still Pharaoh would not let the children of Israel go. It took blood to turn the battle in favor of God's people.

God said to Moses and Aaron, "*Speak to all the congregation of Israel, saying: 'On the tenth of this month every man shall take for himself a lamb…a lamb for a household'*" (Exodus 12:3). It was to be a lamb without blemish, the most expensive one in the flock, nothing cheap or second rate. It was to be the best. Each house was to have a lamb, and that lamb would count for the whole house—one lamb for about fifteen people. There is tremendous truth here for Christian families. God wants to save whole families, and all Christians ought to claim the salvation of their households!

Beginning in verse seven, further instructions are given:

> *They shall take some of the blood and put it on the two doorposts and on the lintel of the houses where they eat it…. For I will pass through the land of Egypt on that night, and will strike all the firstborn in the land of Egypt, both man and beast…. Now the blood shall be a sign for you on the houses where you are. And when I see the blood, I will pass over you; and the plague shall not be on you to destroy you…. And you shall take a bunch of hyssop, dip it in the blood that is in the basin, and strike the lintel and the two doorposts with the blood that is in the basin. And none of you shall go out of the door of his house until morning. For the LORD will pass through to strike the Egyptians; and when He sees the blood on the lintel and on the two doorposts, the LORD will pass over the door and not allow the destroyer to come into your houses to strike you.*
>
> (Exodus 12:7, 12–13, 22–23)

THERE'S SAFETY IN OBEDIENCE

Several things are to be noted here. First, if any Israelite made a mockery of these unusual orders given by God through man, or if anyone claimed that Moses and Aaron were mad and not capable of leading them anymore, then they would have perished with no second chance. Second, had they decided to "go to another church" where such "rubbish" was not taught, they would have perished. Third, if they had decided to venture out in the middle of the night to see what was going on, even for one brief second, they would have perished, for they would not at that time have been "under the blood." Fourth, if they had decided to offer their own righteousness and not sprinkle the blood, they would have perished. Finally, had they sprinkled tinted water or red paint or some other substance, it would not have been good enough; they would have been smitten dead.

If similar orders were given by God's servants today, very few would even consider obeying! Blood is not a pleasant substance to handle; it is unhygienic in hot weather, attracting flies and germs. No modern sanitary department would agree to such action today. A more practical, sensible, desirable way would need to be found, but surely not blood.

OVERCOMING THE DESTROYER

Notice also that when God surveyed the scene, He would not permit the *"destroyer"* to enter into their homes to visit them with death. Who is this destroyer made helpless by blood? The answer is found in Revelation:

> And they had as king over them the angel of the bottomless pit, whose name in Hebrew is Abaddon, but in Greek he has the name Apollyon.
>
> (Revelation 9:11)

Both *Abaddon* in Hebrew and *Apollyon* in Greek mean "a destroyer." So the great destroyer is none other than Satan, the king of the demons of the bottomless pit.

It is important to understand that Satan is the destroyer. Nothing good or constructive ever comes from him. He is the author of death and misery. But the Bible assures us that God is supreme and that Satan cannot bring destruction and trouble to anyone unless it is permitted by God. And even if God should grant such permission to the destroyer, still He will work out even that for your blessing if you are a Christian. (See Romans 8:28.) Righteous Job was given boils by Satan. It was Satan who took the lives of his children, destroyed his cattle, and burned up his home—but only with God's permission. Yet God worked it out for Job's good in the end: *"And the* Lord *restored Job's losses when he prayed for his friends. Indeed the* Lord *gave Job twice as much as he had before"* (Job 42:10).

Satan is both the ruler of this world and the prince of the upper atmosphere that surrounds this earth. (See John 12:31; Ephesians 2:2.) It is only the mercy of God that keeps us from the incredible power of the wicked destroying angel, Satan. It is only faith in the blood of Jesus that comes between us, the devil, and his demon spirits.

SAVING ENTIRE HOUSEHOLDS

If it had not been for the blood sprinkled on the lintels and doorposts of the homes of the Israelites, the firstborn in every family would have perished. Even the cattle were saved by blood. What a wonderful truth for faithful tithing farmers today! If you reckon by faith that the blood of Jesus avails for your home and your cattle, it will do so, and the angel of death will just as surely be kept away from you and yours!

We have been told that it is not scriptural to pray for cattle, but we have seen cows and even dogs healed with the laying on of hands! It was somewhere around 1910 that the late John G. Lake was challenged to pray for a horse bleeding to death in the streets of Johannesburg, South Africa. He accepted the challenge and began to rebuke the flow of blood. Immediately the blood stopped, and the horse got up to its feet and lived. How was this miracle brought about? By pleading the blood of Jesus.

It all gets back to the word *atonement*, which means "a covering." When the Israelites used the blood, taking hyssop and splashing the blood upon their lintels and doorposts (see Exodus 12:22), God would not permit Satan or his demon spirits to enter their homes. The Israelites were completely covered. Satan, that teeth-gnashing creature, was bound in fury by God because the Israelites used blood. I believe the reason that so many Christians are feeble, sick, and fearful today is because they have not been taught to use the blood of Jesus as a covering.

PENTECOSTAL REVIVAL EXPERIENCES

In the early days of the Pentecostal revival, between 1908 and 1912, much was heard about "pleading the blood." Mrs. Woodworth-Etter, in her great deliverance campaigns in Los Angeles and Chicago, used to stand with hands raised and by living faith sprinkle the blood of Jesus upon the crowds. The results described in her book are fantastic. People would come rushing to the front of the auditorium and fall prostrate; many were healed before they reached the front; many fell down speaking in other tongues. Such songs as "We Are under the Blood" were sung frequently in those days.

In the early days of the outpouring of the Spirit in Great Britain, such marvelous baptisms of the Spirit were experienced through pleading the blood that people came from all over the world to receive their baptism.

It is recorded in Pastor Kent White's book, *The Word of God Coming Again* (now out of print), that the reality of using the blood by speaking it or pleading it came by sovereign revelation of the Holy Spirit to hungry seekers. Previous to that time, not much was known about the importance of pleading the blood. Even a young girl of tender years was heard pleading the blood earnestly under a table! No one had taught her about this; it came to her as a revelation from the Holy Spirit. As soon as this truth was discovered by more people, the number of those receiving true baptisms in the Spirit increased greatly.

One of the best-known places where such experiences were received was in the Parish Hall of St. Mary's Church near Sunderland, England, where the Church of England vicar, A. A. Boddy, was conducting Holy Spirit meetings. Smith Wigglesworth received his baptism of the Spirit there. Nonetheless, after some time, the practice of pleading the blood for the baptism died out, to be replaced by praising and other methods. However, it was recorded that the number receiving the baptism dropped off considerably, until a brother from a Scottish assembly in Kilsyth came down and urged them to honor the blood in their seeking once again. Immediately the power of God fell afresh, and people were prostrated under the power of God, speaking in tongues. Even Vicar Boddy was stricken under the power of God.

Is it any wonder that mighty miracles were commonplace in those days? Is it any wonder that divine healing came in as a tremendous revelation? When folks started to plead the blood, the devil just had to leave. Satan cannot stand before the blood of Jesus when it is honored.

THE ULTIMATE WEAPON

I am convinced that when people cannot receive a good clear baptism in the Holy Spirit, it is because they are bound by Satan. In such cases, the best and most scriptural way of obtaining release is to go into the presence of God boldly pleading the blood of Jesus out loud, opening one's whole soul to the incoming of the Spirit.

Some may argue that this is not a scriptural practice for New Testament Christians. But let me refer you to Hebrews where we read that *"we have come…to the blood of sprinkling"* (Hebrews 12:22, 24). This does not refer back to the past, but is a present-tense experience, *"we are come."* It is our privilege now as New Testament priests of the *"church of the firstborn"* (verse 23) to sprinkle the blood of Jesus—not merely to believe that Jesus did it for us in the past (which He certainly did), but to do it now. We must now battle the principalities and powers and wicked spirits of the devil (see Ephesians 6:12); thus we sprinkle that precious blood once shed for us, and Satan and his demon powers must give ground. They may be stubborn, but Christians should be even more stubborn. We possess the winning weapons!

Because the enemy is tenacious, the victory does not always come easily. Sometimes we need to battle with the weapon of the blood in prayer for weeks and months. But victory is certain. In Revelation 12:11, we read of saints who overcame Satan *"by the blood of the Lamb and by the word of their testimony."* No hint is given of the possibility of failure. *"They overcame."* And they accomplished this by the blood and by their testimony.

Peter also gave some good teaching on this subject. We are *"elect…for obedience and sprinkling of the blood of Jesus Christ"* (1 Peter 1:2). It is not a passive faith in the blood that brings victory, but an active sprinkling of it in faith by each elect believer. Peter continued the theme by telling us that, as holy priests, we are *"to offer up spiritual sacrifices acceptable to God through Jesus Christ"* (1 Peter 2:5). As the priests offered up daily blood sacrifices on behalf of the people in Old Testament times, so also today in New Testament times we offer the blood of Jesus Christ to God as our plea on behalf of ourselves, our children, our loved ones, and even our livestock!

EMERGENCY PROCEDURES

Mrs. Nuzum, a Pentecostal author of the early part of the twentieth century, wrote much on the subject of covering our loved ones with the blood of Jesus. I can tell you that even in my own family this practice has been most useable and effective during the past twenty years. And there are many others who likewise testify of its effectiveness. Great peace of mind and wonderful answers to prayer have come to those who practice using the blood as a covering.

The destroyer cannot get in under the bloodline where it has been placed. But, unfortunately, too many have been loosely taught that Satan cannot ever get through the bloodline. They have not been informed that Satan can and does get through if the bloodline is let down. And how do we let it down? By our disobedience.

We can hardly claim to be under the blood of Jesus if we are walking in deliberate disobedience. Peter stated that we are *"Elect…for obedience and sprinkling of the blood of Jesus Christ."* Sprinkling or pleading the blood of Jesus without obedience to the Word of God will avail us nothing. If an Israelite had come out of his home for a moment during the night of the Passover, he would have died within sight of the blood simply because it was not covering him at that instant! He would have believed in the blood all right, but he would not have been honoring it in obedience. In like manner, the New Testament makes it clear that we must sprinkle the blood of Jesus in faith and with obedience.

5

THE SCARLET THREAD

In the second chapter of Joshua, the story of the harlot Rahab and the two Israelite spies in the city of Jericho is a remarkable account of deliverance through blood. The scarlet thread was a token of blood.

Israel was commanded to go in and take the wicked city because it was wholly given over to sin. It is perhaps difficult for us in Western cities to appreciate how low and debauched some cities became in early Bible times. For instance, the city of Sodom, which was eventually destroyed, was so base that even angels were accosted by the men of the city for purposes of moral perversion. We have no reason to believe that Jericho was much better. The two spies found shelter in a harlot's house, and it seems probable that this woman supported her father, mother, brothers, and sisters by prostitution. It is also highly probable that her brothers were "pimps" and that her sisters engaged in the same traffic. So these two children of God found refuge in the best place they could find—a brothel! Is it any wonder that God desired to wipe the memory of such a wicked city from the face of the earth? And He chose His people Israel as the instruments for that purpose.

REPENTANCE AND FAITH

As soon as the two men of God arrived, Rahab began to feel the need of repentance. Her conscience began bothering her a great deal. She had heard of the fame of the God of Israel, and upon being faced with her guilt, she began to confess her faith in Him: *"For the LORD your God, He is God in heaven above and on earth beneath"* (Joshua 2:11). She asked them to help her stay alive, for she knew by revelation of the Spirit that Israel would surely win the battle and destroy Jericho. She wanted to be left alive with her whole house. But how could it be done? *"Give me a true token"* (verse 12), she said.

It didn't take her long to find out that God is always willing to reveal Himself to those who really want to know Him. She was willing to comply with the instructions of the two children of God. She was willing to start living a new life of faith in God. So the two spies promised, by the God of Israel, that they would indeed save her life, and her father, mother, brothers and sisters—in fact, all who were inside that house on the walls of Jericho.

Because of Rahab's faith, the Lamb of God slain from the foundation of the world became efficacious for this poor harlot and her sinning family. Perhaps it seems strange to you that such a woman should be saved, but God's dealings with sinners are always quite unbelievable! Jesus has no appeal to the worldly-wise and the self-righteous. He came to those who have need of a physician. (See Mark 2:17.) Here was a poor woman who knew that she had need of God, and He was ready to forgive her immediately!

STAY INSIDE AND FOLLOW DIRECTIONS

The two spies remembered that the blood that had been sprinkled on the lintels and doorposts of their homes in Egypt had been given to them as a token. (See Exodus 12:13.) It spoke of the blood of Jesus, already shed in the mind of the Father. (See Revelation 13:8.) Had they been able, I am sure those two spies would have slain a lamb and sprinkled its blood on Rahab's home. But there was no time for that. The king of Jericho, who knew of their presence in the city, was searching for them. They had no time to slay a lamb and do what Moses had done, so they said to Rahab, in essence, "We will give you a token; take this scarlet cord and tie it in your window." (See Joshua 2:18.) They told her that if she would do this, symbolically honoring the blood, that her whole house would be preserved and her loved ones would walk out alive, even if everyone else in Jericho perished. But there was one condition. "Stay in your house," they said. "If any go out, their blood will be on their own heads." (See verse 19.) But absolute safety was promised to those who would stay in the house, under the protection of the blood.

This showed amazing faith on the put of the two spies, who were able to prophetically promise such a remarkable thing. They had faith in the blood! And the Bible tells us that she did what she was told in complete faith and simplicity: *According to your words, so be it…. And she bound the scarlet cord in the window*" (Joshua 2:21). Yes, there is a bloodline, and the great destroyer cannot get through it; but have you put it there?

We know the story so well. The Israelites, led by their singers, walked around the walls of Jericho for seven days. On the seventh day, they walked around seven times. Then God did His part. Never expect God to do His part until you have done what you know to do! God sent the earthquake. It broke down the walls of the city. The

Israelites then entered in and set fire to it, killing right and left; but the section of the wall on which Rahab's house was built remained intact. Her house was untouched. With her whole family, she walked out alive and joined God's people. Gentiles were permitted into the house of Israel by faith in Israel's God, and the blood of Jesus availed for them even then.

Note particularly that if Rahab had not been obedient in the details given by the spies, she and her family would have perished. It was the token of the bloodline that saved them; for when God saw this scarlet thread, He passed over the house and did not suffer the destroyer to enter in. A miracle indeed! Rahab used the blood, not in passive faith, but in active faith that gets results.

DEDICATION FOR THE PRIESTHOOD

Even many years before this, when the high priest and his sons were ordained to the priesthood, part of their ordination included putting blood upon (1) the lobes of their right ears; (2) the thumbs of their right hands; and (3) the big toes of their right feet. (See Leviticus 8:23–24.) Thus, in type, Israel was taught that the blood cleanses and sanctifies all that enters into a man's ear, everything he puts his hand to do, and wherever he goes in the course of his duties. Even if he walks into a den of vice (not to partake of it!), the blood will keep Satan away from his thought life, his work life, and wherever he goes.

Remembering the teaching given by the apostle Paul that our bodies are temples of the Holy Spirit (see 2 Corinthians 6:16) and that we are not to deliberately touch any unclean thing, it is interesting to realize that as sons of the High Priest Jesus, we can also apply His precious blood to our ears, thumbs, and toes and know that our whole lives—spirit, soul, and body—will *be preserved blameless at the coming of our Lord Jesus Christ*" (1 Thessalonians 5:23).

ACTIVATE YOUR FAITH IN THE BLOOD

I repeat, I am convinced that the reason so many Christians are living such miserable lives, with sickness and recurring sin, is because they have not realized that we must turn our passive theological faith in the blood into a vital, active faith that uses it, sprinkles it, pleads it, and recognizes that it is just as effective today when applied in faith as it was in the days of Moses and Joshua.

When the blood covers us and we know it—and we have placed it by faith upon our hearts, lives, homes, and loved ones—then we have created a condition where Satan cannot get through. So keep under the blood! This is one substance that all the devils in hell cannot penetrate. But, it is not there automatically. Salvation is not automatic. Healing for the body is not automatic. No promise of God is obtained automatically, but all the promises are obtained through faith and maintained by continuing in that faith. We are not to let down our faith in the blood. There is more power in the blood than anyone has ever imagined.

EMERGENCY CIRCUMSTANCES

In 1945, our third son was born. As a baby, he was fed on a kind of thin, hot porridge that my wife prepared for him. This was heated to a temperature of boiling water (212° F). As she was taking this upstairs, carrying the cup in one hand and a large jug of boiling water in the other, in her haste she tripped on a step. Thinking first to save her legs from the boiling water, she managed to place the jug on a step safely. But in so doing, she spilled the hot cereal, and it spread over her arm, settling in the crook of her elbow. It is obvious that boiling porridge would produce a bad burn on such a sensitive spot and cause the skin to peel off and inflammation to set in. When the porridge was wiped off, her arm was red and painful. However, the baby had to be bathed and fed, and there was no one to help. So my wife began to plead the blood of Jesus out loud several times, believing that it was applied to her injured arm. After a few minutes, the pain left, and she was able to bathe and feed the baby. That same evening, all that could be seen was a small red mark about the size of a dime where the center of the burn had been. By the next morning, no trace of red could be seen at all. Her flesh and skin were perfectly whole.

We must realize that Satan is the author of all damage to the body. Demons try to attack any injured part of our body and permit germs, which are always around us, to impinge on the injured flesh and do their work of destruction and poisoning. But when the blood of Jesus is applied in faith, it acts as a covering that prevents Satan from attacking us with germs. Therefore, the natural healing processes in our body quickly do their work because they are not hindered by Satan. The blood of Jesus is the finest covering and disinfectant in the world. It is perfect.

WITHOUT A SCRATCH

The power of Jesus' blood was vividly demonstrated one day when we were traveling in Canada. We had as passengers a young married couple whom we were bringing back to Toronto with us. We had told them about the wonderful truths concerning pleading the blood of Jesus. Little did we know, as we drove along in the rain, that God had a plan whereby we were going to demonstrate this truth to save our lives. Coming over a rise on the road, we hit some bad potholes. The back wheels, which were under coiled springs, went into a bounce. The car literally jigged and skidded to the wrong side of the road, completely out of control. Before us we could see three cars approaching us at about 60 M.P.H., and we were powerless to avoid a terrible crash. Immediately we started to plead the blood of Jesus out loud.

Our friends in the back seat, who had been sound asleep, suddenly awoke, realizing that something was wrong. It seemed that an angel of the Lord then took over.

The back wheels suddenly gripped and stopped bouncing, and the car returned to the right side of the road and went off the pavement with the front wheels down in a grassy ditch. We thought we could possibly pull out of the ditch and back onto the road. But the grass was too soft due to the rain, and we found that we were stuck.

What now? We were safe, we were alive, but we were stuck. So God still had more to do on behalf of His servants. He had said, *"Call upon Me in the day of trouble; I will deliver you, and you shall glorify Me"* (Psalm 50:15). So we did this, and almost immediately two men drove up in an old car. We said nothing, but one of them said, "We will pull you out." They put action to their words and pulled a chain out of the trunk, attached it to our car, and pulled us safely out of the ditch. We were safely delivered from death, without a scratch on our bodies or our car. Why? The blood of Jesus covered us because we put it there by faith!

6

THE VALUE OF THE BLOOD

Any attempt to appraise the value of the blood of Christ would be impossible. It is priceless! We learn from 1 Corinthians 6:20 and 7:23 that we are *"bought at a price,"* and that price is the blood of Jesus, which Peter called *"precious."* Don't you remember how he said, *"You were not redeemed with corruptible things, like silver or gold…but with the precious blood of Christ"* (1 Peter 1:18–19)?

AT THE TEMPLE DEDICATION

When the temple was dedicated on Mount Moriah, the actual count of animals slaughtered was amazing. Before the Ark of the Covenant was brought in, it is recorded that the sacrificing of sheep and oxen *"could not be counted or numbered for multitude"* (1 Kings 8:5; 2 Chronicles 5:6). Scripture further tells us that a peace offering was later made on behalf of the whole nation of Israel, and it is recorded that 22,000 oxen and 120,000 sheep were sacrificed, and *"so the king and all the children of Israel dedicated the house of the LORD"* (1 Kings 8:63). Furthermore, we must remember that only the best animals were accepted for sacrifice by the Levites. No "seconds" were good enough. Doesn't this seem to be a ridiculous, senseless waste? Wouldn't one sheep or a small inexpensive lamb have been enough? Surely, if God wanted to keep the symbolism right, one little lamb would have been enough to typify the Lamb of God who took away the sins of the world!

But, no, 22,000 oxen, worth hundreds of dollars apiece, and 120,000 sheep had to die. By this, I believe God is trying to impress upon us that the value of the blood cannot be measured in dollars, cents, or gallons. No amount of blood of animals in the Old Testament could have atoned for your sins and mine. On the Day of Atonement, the brook Kidron was fed with the blood of the animal sacrifices that flowed continually for days, reminding the inhabitants of Jerusalem that when God caused His Son to die, He opened a fountain that would flow forever and ever. (See

Zechariah 13:1.) This is described as a river, a continually flowing river into which we may plunge daily to wash away our sins and sicknesses and sorrows. This stream ever flows before Satan and all his host; and as we honor it, sing about it, talk about it, and plead it out loud, the blood of Jesus pleads mercy, forgiveness, pardon, healing, protection, deliverance, and multiplied joy and peace.

DAILY SACRIFICES

It is not enough to believe in the historic blood of Calvary. It is necessary that we believe in the fountain now, and by faith avail ourselves of its power and life. Love is only a word until it is demonstrated; and in like manner, blood is only a word until it is used. Ammunition in an arsenal is useless. It must be taken and *used* to bring terror to the enemy. The army of the Lord is powerless until it uses its weapons, which are *"mighty in God for pulling down strongholds"* (2 Corinthians 10:4). The primary weapons are the sword of the Spirit, which is the Word of God, and the blood, for we read in Revelation 12:11, *"They overcame him [Satan] by the blood of the Lamb and by the word of their testimony."* We need the Word and the blood.

We must remember that the sacrifices of blood made by King Solomon did not end the sacrifices. There were daily sacrifices, to remind the people of the present power and efficacy of the blood. Yesterday's leftovers could not be accepted.

We get the same thought with the manna, which speaks of the Word of God. Only what was picked up that day was sweet and suitable for use. In like manner, the blood of Jesus is fresh and sweet today—not dead and coagulated. The daily shedding of blood should bring home to us the tremendous value that God puts on blood: *"Without shedding of blood there is no remission"* (Hebrews 9:22).

THE SYMBOLISM OF THE OLD COVENANT SACRIFICES

The blood offerings were tremendous, and they should prove to us the tremendous meaning and value of the blood of the Lamb of God. The great Day of Atonement, held annually, with the scapegoat taken off into the wilderness, had great meaning as a type of Christ, who took the condemnation and curse of sin upon Himself, and carried it off into an uninhabited desert place, to be seen no more. (See Leviticus 16:10, 21–22.)

The sin offering represented the broken covenant between God and man, caused by man's original fall into sin. Again we see that God and man can only be reconciled by blood. There were daily and evening sacrifices, with a double burnt offering on the Sabbath, as well as the burnt offerings on the great festivals or special Sabbaths. All these foreshadowed Jesus Christ, who made a full surrender of His life by pouring out His blood—a perfect sacrifice in our stead, consumed in the fiery heat of His great sufferings for us.

The value of the blood is also taught by the great number of lambs slaughtered in the annual observance of the Passover. In this annual event, the head of each family would bring a lamb for sacrifice unto the Lord. According to Josephus (*Wars* VI, 9, 3), ten people was the least number and twenty the greatest permissible number of individuals who could partake of a single Passover lamb. If one lamb was slain for fifteen people on an average throughout the nation, then for the 2.5 million people at the time of the Exodus, over 160,000 lambs were slain on that historic night when the bonds of Egypt gave way before the blood.

In the time of Solomon, the population had increased to five or six million, so the great slaughter of lambs, by all who were able to take part, may be estimated to be around 400,000. What would our hard-pressed farmers say today if such a large number were required for sacrifice annually? But thank God, we read in 1 Corinthians 5:7 that *"Christ, our Passover, was sacrificed for us."* No longer are we expected to take a lamb for fifteen people and offer its blood for our sins and sicknesses, for Christ took our place and became our Passover Lamb. We now accept His singular, pure, perfect sacrifice (see Hebrews 10:9–14) and offer His blood by faith.

If every Christian who names the name of Jesus would plead His precious blood every day—out loud—we believe that the result would be catastrophic in Satan's kingdom and that great deliverance would be felt in the church and in the nation.

GUARDING YOUR BLOOD-BOUGHT DELIVERANCE

However, I need to emphasize the fact that any deliverance brought about through pleading of the blood can only be maintained as the parties concerned meet the conditions for keeping that deliverance. An arresting example of this fact took place in Cadillac, Michigan, where I was conducting special services. One evening, a compassionate Christian woman brought with her a four-year-old girl whose eyes were badly crossed.

"Brother Whyte," she said, "this little girl's parents are unbelievers. Will you pray for her eyes? Perhaps if God heals this child, her parents will be awakened."

So we removed the child's glasses and prayed for her. I removed the curse by pleading the blood. Immediately her eyes straightened out, to the amazement of everyone present. Needless to say, there were many tear-filled eyes in that congregation as the little girl, who had previously seen only double, toddled around the church saying, "I see one! I see one!"

However, when the kind Christian woman took her back to her unbelieving parents and told them what had happened, they refused to believe it.

"You get those glasses back on!" her father said to her. "We're not having any of that nonsense around here!" And they forced the girl to wear the glasses. By their unbelief, they destroyed the faith of the little child, and through time, her eyes became crossed again.

So it is clear that no deliverance can be maintained without keeping under the blood. But as long as we stay under the blood by faith and obedience, Satan cannot penetrate the bloodline. No wonder we say that the blood of Jesus is of such infinite value!

A SINGULAR OFFERING

It is impossible to compute the amount of blood that was shed in the 1,500 years of Israel's history under the old covenant. Nothing could be obtained from God except on the basis of blood sacrifice, nor can anything be obtained today except on the basis of the blood of Jesus, which flows as a healing stream for the spirit, soul, and body of man.

Very shortly after the resurrection of Jesus, He appeared to Mary before He appeared to anyone else and said to her, *"Do not cling to Me, for I have not yet ascended to My Father"* (John 20:17). In the law of Israel, a high priest could not be touched by the people just before he entered into the Holy Place with the blood of animals; it was only after he had offered blood and been accepted before the mercy seat that the common people could touch him. In like manner, Jesus the High Priest could not be touched with human hands until He had ascended to His Father and offered His blood at the throne of God. We assume this was done sometime soon after appearing to Mary, for when He appeared to the other disciples a few days later, He said, *"Behold My hands and My feet, that it is I Myself. Handle Me and see, for a spirit does not have flesh and bones as you see I have"* (Luke 24:39). So apparently, the sprinkling of His blood had been accomplished by that time.

ENTER BOLDLY

We know that the high priest entered once a year into the Holy Place with blood. (See Hebrews 9:7–14.) If he had entered into the Holy of Holies without blood he would have been stricken dead instantly. However, the offering and sprinkling of the blood on the mercy seat caused the miraculous *shekinah* glory of God to light up the darkened room, and God then communed with the high priest above the mercy seat. (See Exodus 25:22.)

To fulfill this type, we read of Jesus who *"not with the blood of goats and calves, but with His own blood He entered the Most Holy Place once for all, having obtained eternal redemption"* (Hebrews 9:12). Just how Jesus transported His own precious blood from Calvary to heaven is not understood by mortal man, but the Scripture shows that He fulfilled the type, and therefore He must have sprinkled His own blood upon the mercy seat (the throne of God) in heaven. This blood was accepted. No other sacrifice would have been sufficient except His precious blood.

Now you and I can enter right into the Holy Place of heaven itself any time we want to. Any time we have a need, whether of deliverance or of the baptism of the Spirit, we can enter into the Holy Place of heaven itself. But how? Without blood? A thousand times no! We can only come with the precious blood of Jesus.

> *Therefore, brethren, having boldness to enter the Holiest by the blood of Jesus,...*
> *let us draw near with a true heart in full assurance of faith, having our hearts*
> *sprinkled....* (Hebrews 10:19, 22)

ARISE, MY SOUL, ARISE

BY CHARLES WESLEY

Verse 1

Arise, my soul, arise,
Shake off your guilty fears;
The bleeding sacrifice,
In my behalf appears;
Before the throne my Surety stands,
Before the throne my Surety stands,
My name is written on His hands.

Verse 2

He ever lives above,
For me to intercede;
His all redeeming love,
His precious blood, to plead;
His blood atoned for every race,
His blood atoned for every race,
And sprinkles now the throne of grace.

Verse 3

Five bleeding wounds He bears,
Received on Calvary:
They pour effectual prayers,
They strongly plead for me:
"Forgive, him, oh, forgive," they cry,
"Forgive, him, oh, forgive," they cry,
"Nor let that ransomed sinner die."

Verse 4

The Father hears Him pray,
His dear Anointed One
He cannot turn away.
The presence of His Son;
The Spirit answers to the blood,
The Spirit answers to the blood,
And tells me I am born of God.

Verse 5

My God is reconciled;
His pardoning voice I hear;
He owns me for His child;
I can no longer fear
With confidence I now draw nigh,
With confidence I now draw nigh,
And "Father, Abba, Father," cry.

7

HOW TO PLEAD THE BLOOD

At the beginning of the outpouring of the Holy Spirit in Great Britain around 1908 or 1909, many independent Pentecostal assemblies sprang up. In these meetings, there were many evidences of new spiritual life and power. Since there was no legislative organization tying these assemblies together, individual Christians learned to rely solely on the moving of the Spirit and His various gifts and operations. The Holy Spirit began to move in an unusual way, since there was no council or review board to enforce any limitations on those Christians.

Many of the believers, so recently baptized in the Spirit and with the *shekinah* glory resting upon them, used to plead the blood of Jesus in strong repetition for all that was burdening their hearts: unsaved relatives, troubles in the home, troubles in the nation. Realizing that they had access to the throne of God, they went in boldly with the blood of Jesus. Seekers for the baptism in the Holy Spirit were especially helped by doing this. And it was believed by many that the pleading of the blood was a very powerful weapon against evil spirits that would oppose answers to prayer.

DOING BATTLE

"Is this latter point scriptural?" you ask. Well, we must not forget that as soon as Daniel began to pray for the liberation of his people, it took three weeks of "knee battle," while the archangels Michael and Gabriel were battling it out in the heavenlies with the princes of evil. Likewise, today we must often battle with unseen demonic forces before we can get answers to our prayers. The pleading of the blood will cause consternation and confusion to the opposing evil spiritual forces that often delay God's answers. I believe that pleading the blood has a primary place in all intercessory prayer.

Rest assured, when one begins to plead the blood of Jesus out loud, there will be those who will rise up in opposition. Pleading the blood stirs up the backslider and

46

offends the uncrucified flesh of the carnal believer. But in spite of opposition, the use of the blood will clean up any church or prayer group and make way for the operation of the gifts of the Spirit. Oh, the power of the blood of Jesus!

INFUSIONS OF LIFE

Since the life of Jesus is in His blood, if we plead, honor, sprinkle, and sing about it, we are actually introducing the life of the Godhead into our worship. Our prayers and requests become charged with the life and power of Jesus. No wonder Satan will do all he can to suppress practical teaching on the blood. He hates it more than anything else.

Perhaps you have noticed that unbelievers, controlled by evil spirits, often speak the name of Jesus in blasphemy. But have you ever heard a person under the influence of demons blaspheme the blood? Probably not. This is because demons cannot and will not speak of the blood. I have found through practical experience that when a person is unable to plead the blood of Jesus audibly, it is a sign that that person needs strong prayers of deliverance because they are hindered by a binding spirit that will not permit them to say "the blood of Jesus."

I would like to especially emphasize the importance of pleading the blood for the baptism in the Spirit. I feel constrained to do this because there are so many different procedures prescribed by so many different groups, yet many hungry seekers have tried all the methods and still haven't received. Isn't it strange that we have all but forgotten that we can receive *nothing* from God apart from His mercy and Jesus's shed blood?

Pastor A. A. Boddy of Sunderland, England, on a return trip from the early Pentecostal outpouring in Norway, said that nowhere in Europe where he had been had he seen people receive the baptism of the Spirit so easily and beautifully as by the pleading of the blood of Jesus. This method was therefore introduced in Boddy's meetings in Parish Hall, and people would even travel across the Atlantic to receive the Pentecostal experience by the pleading of the blood—whereas they had failed to receive the Spirit by other means employed at that time.

GOING TO EXCESS

I realize that many unscriptural methods of receiving the baptism in the Spirit have been introduced by enthusiastic, well-meaning people. Some have suggested that the more noise we make, the more power we will get; others have stressed great fleshly excitement and the thumping of pews, chairs, or even the floor as a means of attracting God's attention. Some have thought that God would be pleased if they deliberately rolled on the floor. These are some of the excesses that have brought great reproach upon the work of the Holy Spirit. We admit, however, that the coming of the Spirit will frequently cause people to drop to the floor "under the power of God," but this is quite different from deliberately throwing oneself to the floor as a means to the baptism! We have been told that the longer one waits, prays, agonizes, and begs for the baptism, the better it is for the supplicant, since it works out something in him that no other spiritual exercise can do. But in so reasoning, aren't we forgetting that the baptism is a free gift?

Now, let's examine the scriptural teaching about this matter. Who gives the baptism in the Spirit? None other than Jesus Himself. (See Matthew 3:11.) And where is Jesus? Why, He is in heaven at the Father's right hand. (See 1 Peter 3:22.) So, obviously, if we are to receive this free unmerited gift (Greek *dorea*, which means a free, unearned gift or present), we must go to the One who earned it for us and who will give it to all who ask in faith, without any waiting, at any time. If there is any waiting, it is on our part, not on His. Our approach is completely wrong when we think that we have to wait. The Bible teaches us that all believers are now kings and priests (see Revelation 1:6) and that we can enter in whenever we desire. There is no waiting list, but we must enter in with His blood.

SIMPLICITY IS BEST

Let me share with you a simple method for receiving the baptism in the Holy Spirit, which I share with seekers everywhere. First of all, it is important for you to relax every muscle in your body. Let all tenseness and uncertainty depart. The baptism in the Holy Spirit is Jesus' work, and there is no reason for you to be tense. Then close your eyes and lift up your hands in adoration and worship; be comfortably seated, and take the precious blood of Jesus on your lips and speak it with your tongue, making it your insistent plea. Be positive and believing in your approach.

Of course, you must do this in simple, reverent faith, having an awe of a holy God who will receive us in the presence of His Son only if we plead His blood. The result of this method of approach is marvelous. Within seconds and minutes, the Holy Spirit begins to answer to the pleadings of the blood. Opposing and binding spirits begin to draw back, a way is made between heaven and earth, and soon the person becomes bathed in the glory of God. The most natural thing for them to do at this point is to turn their vocal cords loose and speak in other tongues as the Spirit gives utterance. (See Acts 2:4.)

When the revelation of the pleading of the blood was first given and practiced, there was no teaching on it such as has been given in this book. There was no preaching or exhortation or remarks of any kind on the subject. The practice commenced spontaneously under the strong, compelling power of the Holy Spirit. God desired to manifest His power, but it could only come forth as the blood was honored, for His life is in the blood.

So today, honoring and wielding the precious blood of Jesus clears the way for the power of God to be revealed anywhere men and women are pressing in for the gifts of the Spirit, or for miracles and healings. Receiving the baptism in the Spirit by pleading the blood has been so marvelously easy that some have doubted the result, for there were no fleshly manifestations. It is sometimes forgotten that when the Spirit descended on Jesus after He had been baptized in water, He descended in the shape of a dove, quietly, reverently, without outward showiness—and immediately the voice of God was heard. Jesus made no fleshly noises or jerking. And that is the way it should be today. The person who goes into the Holy Place pleading the blood will find that God will manifest His *shekinah* glory as He did in the Holy Place of Solomon's Temple, and he will commune with God with the voice of other tongues.

Where the blood of Jesus is not honored in this way, and where *"strange fire"* (Leviticus 10:1 KJV) is offered instead of that fire that comes in answer to the blood, we have the danger of fanaticism creeping in, with fleshly manifestations that detract from the true moving of the Spirit of God. The Spirit cannot operate on the basis of fleshly offerings, but where the blood of Jesus is offered, then the true move of the Spirit can be expected.

In Romans, we read of Jesus being *"set forth as a propitiation by His blood, through faith, to demonstrate His righteousness, because in His forbearance God had passed over the sins that were previously committed"* (Romans 3:25). We are required to exercise faith in His blood. To plead the blood without faith or with our hearts full of fear is both repulsive and ineffective. When we plead the blood audibly, care should always be taken to do so in simple believing faith; then it will avail.

ANTIDOTE FOR POISON

A pastor of our acquaintance, who was at one time a naturopathic doctor, once contracted ptomaine poisoning. He placed his hands upon his own body and for twenty minutes pleaded the blood of Jesus, saying, "I plead the blood of Jesus," over and over again. The result of this attack upon Satan's effort to destroy him was that he was completely healed. Others find that the simple repetition of the one word *blood* is sufficient. There are no rules; it is the simple offering of the blood of Jesus in faith, as New Testament priests, that brings results. God will hear the blood-cry and will respect what it has purchased for us. We can obtain all the blessings of the redemption of Christ that we need.

PROPERTY LINES

This truth was brought home to one of my friends, Rudy Peterson, of Detroit, Michigan, a preaching railroad man. Rudy went down to preach in a little mission station in the Bahamas. It had previously been impossible for any missionary to stay and preach because the local natives, whipped up by the devil, used to make terrible noises with tin cans and cries, so as to make worship impossible. When Rudy and a friend of his arrived at the mission station, they walked around the perimeter of the mission, pleading the blood of Jesus out loud. This was done several times, and after that no further trouble was experienced. Rudy, by faith, had put a bloodline right around the chapel.

PLEADING THE BLOOD BRINGS DELIVERANCE

You can always count on deliverance when you plead the blood.

+ The Israelites sprinkled blood in Egypt, and it brought deliverance.

+ Rahab used the bloodline token, and it brought deliverance.

+ The High Priests of the Old Testament sprinkled blood, and it brought forgiveness.

+ Jesus sprinkled His own blood and purchased salvation for all mankind!

+ We, the New Testament priests serving under our High Priest Jesus, may now sprinkle blood for forgiveness, salvation, redemption, healing, protection, and victory!

Lest anyone should think that the sprinkling of the blood was for the Old Testament saints only, and that the practice ceased when Jesus sprinkled His own precious blood on our behalf, I would remind you of God's command in Exodus 12:24: *"And you shall observe this thing as an ordinance for you and your sons forever."* If blood must be sprinkled today, then it must be the New Testament priests who do it—and we are those priests if we believe in the Son of God.

8

THE APPLICATION OF
THE BLOOD

One dark night many years ago, I went out to my garage to get the car. There was no light in the garage, and I forgot that someone had partially driven a nail into one of the walls. As I walked hastily to the car, my forehead was grazed by the protruding nail. I pulled my head away quickly, realizing what had happened, but it was too late—there was a nasty wound on my head. Immediately I began to plead the blood of Jesus. In half an hour, there wasn't a mark on my head! So, you see, pleading the blood is a very practical thing.

Most of the questions directed to me regarding this matter have to do with how to apply the blood of Jesus in practical form to any situation that may be controlled by Satan. The crucial question is one of practical usage rather than the theological concept. Theology teaches that Jesus shed His blood once for the sins of the world, and that is all there is to say about it! The danger lies in allowing this to become a historical, lifeless fact rather than a present, potent reality.

DISINFECTING WOUNDS

So let's talk about how to apply the blood. In the natural world, we would have no difficulty understanding how to apply disinfectant to an infection. We would take the disinfectant and sprinkle or pour it on the infection, and the result would be that all germs and living organisms present in that infection would die.

Now we should have no difficulty in doing the same thing spiritually. Wherever Satan is at work, we must apply the only corrective antidote there is—the blood of Jesus. There is absolutely no alternative, no substitute. Prayer, praise, worship, and devotion all have their part in our approach to God, but the blood of Jesus is the only effective counteragent to corruption.

This is why Satan has always tried to take the blood out of our churches. If there is no disinfectant, then his demons are free to continue their deadly work of destruction in spirit, soul, and body.

Having concluded therefore that the blood of Jesus is our only remedy, how are we to obtain it and use it? In the Old Testament, the priest took a bunch of hyssop, dipped it into the blood, and then sprinkled or daubed it upon the lintels and doorposts of the houses of the Israelites. But in the spiritual realm, we take the blood by faith and then speak it, which is really a form of intercessory prayer. Each time we plead the blood, we are offering the only plea that can bring any results in intercession.

Think of it this way. The word *blood*, spoken in faith once, could be likened to one drop of blood splashed upon the evil, corruptive situation with which we have to deal in prayer. Obviously, no one putting disinfectant upon corruption at the bottom of a garbage container would use only one drop, would they? So the more we plead the blood, the more power we are bringing to bear against this evil situation.

However, let me warn against rote repetition. Obviously, pleading the blood mechanically in vain repetition is ineffective and foolish, especially to the unbeliever. But for the child of God who pleads the blood in faith, it quickly brings wonderful results. The whole approach is so simple and obvious to the spiritual mind that we are often amazed that so many people miss it.

PHYSICAL AND SPIRITUAL SACRIFICES

In Old Testament times, the priests offered physical sacrifices of animals. The flesh was burned with fire, but the blood was drained into basins and was used by being sprinkled. In New Testament times, we are priests who *"offer up spiritual sacrifices acceptable to God through Jesus Christ"* (1 Peter 2:5). Spiritual sacrifices are the New Testament counterparts of the Old Testament physical sacrifices. As New Testament believer-priests, we are to take the living blood of Jesus and "sprinkle" it before the Lord by repeating the word *blood*. Immediately, we begin to bring Satan's work into captivity and nullify his evil workings.

The blood of Abel spoke vengeance, but the blood of Jesus speaks peace, pardon, and reconciliation for all who are bound by Satan. As we speak the word *blood*, we must remember that the blood of Jesus carries all the power, Spirit, and life that is in Jesus. As the blood of a human carries his life, so does the blood of Jesus carry the life of the Son of God. Each time we say the word *blood* in faith, we are bringing the creative life force of the universe to bear upon the destroying power of Satan.

HOW OFTEN IS NECESSARY?

I do not mean to suggest for a moment that the blood does not avail for you at all times, and that therefore you must continually plead the blood to keep yourself covered. I remember a young man who approached my wife after one of my teaching sessions and said in grave earnestness, "Sister Whyte, how often do you think we should plead the blood? Should we, for instance, plead it every half hour?"

Mrs. Whyte said later with some amusement that she could just see him standing there with a stopwatch saying, "Well, now, I must plead the blood!" Of course, such an idea is ridiculous. No, the point I am trying to make is that in every situation where you sense that you are under the attack of Satan or needing special protection, that is the time to plead the blood. By so doing, you are reminding God that you are trusting in His mercy, you are reminding Satan that he cannot touch you a long as you are under the blood, and you are reminding yourself of the ground of your confidence in Christ.

VALIDATION OF TONGUES

Pleading the blood is also a good way to test the validity of many spiritual manifestations. We are frequently asked the question, "If Satan can speak through us in tongues, how can I know that my tongue is of God?" This is an important and valid question. I have already said that a person who is bound in some area by Satan will find it difficult or impossible to plead the blood. If a person speaks in a demonic tongue, he will not be able to plead the blood. So this is a good way to test the reality of your tongues-speaking experience.

To receive the baptism in the Holy Spirit with the evidence of tongues, I always teach seekers to plead the blood out loud in faith. They might start haltingly, but as the Spirit of God descends upon them, and the inner cleansing begins to take effect, they find that their tongues are beginning to enjoy this practice in faith, and the word *blood* begins to tumble out of their mouths in great boldness.

Seekers usually receive such an anointing of the Spirit in answer to the cry of the blood that words of an unknown tongue begin to be manifested and a torrent of *glossolalia* flows. In this case, there can be no doubt whatsoever that the tongues spoken are truly a manifestation of the Holy Spirit.

ABANDONING SELF-WILL

Some, however, are far more hesitant and find it difficult to abandon their wills to God; they are uncertain, fearful, and cautious in their approach to Him. On the other hand, they may have been taught that they already had the fullness of the Spirit when they were converted; this teaching can be a stumbling block to many.

We must always bear in mind that speaking in tongues is an evidence of overflow, not of static fullness. We can become confused about these two distinct experiences. John the Baptist was full of the Holy Spirit before Pentecost, and he would have overflowed in the upper room had he been there. Similarly, since Mary was in the upper room, she did overflow, and out of her mouth came a torrent of worship in unknown tongues.

BANISH YOUR FEARS

Hesitant people who are full of fears and doubts are a little more difficult to help, but experience has shown that great progress can be made if we can just get them to begin pleading the blood. They usually begin very quietly though, almost in a whisper, and we have to encourage them to go on with more determination and holy abandon.

As they do so, they gradually begin to disperse their fears and new words begin to be spoken, sometimes haltingly, mixed up with pleading the blood. Sometimes they will revert to saying, "I can't," which is an expression of the spirit of fear stirred up by the pleading of the blood. Nevertheless, they are urged to start pleading the blood again. It usually becomes easier as doubts and fears are driven out, and soon they begin to speak in other tongues, often to their astonishment and joy.

It will be readily seen that this method of receiving the baptism in the Spirit is very effective. In fact, in my many years of ministry, I have rarely seen it fail. Many chronic seekers who have not been able to receive the baptism in the Spirit by other means have quickly "come through" by pleading the blood. When people have asked for the baptism in the Holy Spirit in prayer lines in many countries of the world, I have simply instructed them to start repeating the word *blood*, and within a matter of seconds they have begun to speak in tongues. Usually I then call over another worker and suggest that he or she praise God with those who are being baptized so that they do not stop speaking in tongues. They are now entering another spiritual dimension, and it is wonderfully strange! It is important that they do not begin to doubt at this point. I then go on to the next one in line and begin all over again.

Where there are many to receive the baptism in the Spirit, I find it most effective to teach them a little about the significance of pleading the blood of Jesus. When we actually begin to plead the blood, we often have twenty or more seekers pleading together. Very soon, one by one, the Spirit enters fully into them and they overflow in tongues. The blood of Jesus has great power when spoken in faith!

PRACTICAL APPLICATIONS

When the children were small, we often had to plead the blood over their scratches and scrapes! One day in particular when little Stephen was in the kitchen with my wife, he got badly burned. It was a cold day, and we had opened the oven to help circulate a little extra heat through the house. Stephen accidentally backed into the oven lid, which was quite hot, and got a bad burn across the back of his legs. Instantly, Olive and I began pleading the blood.

"It will be all right," I said. "The blood has never lost its power!"

That night when we were going to bed, I said, "By the way, Stephen, how are your legs?"

Olive and I looked, and there wasn't the faintest trace of a burn.

The Word of God teaches, *"When I see the blood, I will pass over you; and the plague shall not be on you to destroy you"* (Exodus 12:13). Paul told us that Jesus is our Passover. (See 1 Corinthians 5:7.) He became our Passover by shedding His own precious blood. There is nothing more precious to believers than this!

9

PROTECTION THROUGH THE BLOOD

As I have already explained earlier, the word *atonement* means "a covering." We as believers can be protected with an impervious covering that keeps us safe from the enemy.

THE KEEPING POWER OF THE BLOOD

This is why the apostle John taught us that *"the wicked one toucheth him not"* (1 John 5:18). The qualification for this state of protection, however, is that *"he that is begotten of God keepeth himself."* This means basically that believers must keep themselves consciously and consistently under the blood. Unconfessed sin is never under the blood; only when it is confessed and forsaken are we covered and protected.

I have received letters from many parts of the world telling of spectacular deliverances taking place when people have audibly pleaded the blood after reading an earlier edition of this book. Of course, not only do we actually plead the blood against the devil and his demons, but we also command Satan to loose his grip in the name of Jesus. The actual pleading of the blood must generally be used in conjunction with the command given in the name of Jesus. This is especially important when we are ministering to others. We need to plead the blood to keep ourselves safe from any satanic kickback while the sufferer is being released from his terrible bondage.

Testimony after testimony can be given by those who dare to oppose Satan in his dealings with humanity and minister to others through the power of the blood. My experience shows, however, that even many Christians are cruelly bound and oppressed by demons; in fact, it is Christians who are seeking deliverance today far more than unbelievers.

PROTECTION ON THE ROAD

In the winter of 1971, I had taken a party of fourteen young people to skate on Lake Simcoe, Ontario. I was driving a station wagon that had rather bald front tires. On our return on an icy road, the front of the vehicle went out of control and ran into a snow bank. As it left the road, I pleaded the blood out loud, and the car came to rest in a snow bank about eighteen inches from a telephone pole. One can imagine what might have happened had we hit the pole head-on. The blood saved us! Soon we were dragged out by a tow truck, and we proceeded on our way, rejoicing.

Unknown to us, my wife was ahead of us on Highway 400, which was also ice-covered. Suddenly, her car also went completely out of control, spinning in a circle. My wife pleaded the blood out loud and the car came to rest, facing the other way against a snow bank. On the other side of this bank was a twenty-foot drop! Once again, she was saved by the blood. Satan had made a determined attack upon us both, but we opposed him by wielding the blood of Jesus.

SECURITY CHECKS

A more unusual testimony comes from Reverend W. G. of Phoenix, Arizona. He decided one day to sprinkle the blood of Jesus over his paycheck; within a short time he received an increase in salary! One of the Christian ladies known to him then did the same thing and received an unexpected bonus in cash. I know that such testimonies are scorned by carnal-minded Christians. However, carnal Christians will never enter into any fight against Satan's bindings, much less in the matter of salary and possessions!

Always be quick to plead the blood when you realize that Satan is attacking you, either physically or emotionally. Blue Mondays turn into days of rejoicing for those who cover themselves with the blood. But you must use it; you must sprinkle it by faith.

PROTECTIVE SERVICES

At the end of January, 1908, in Westport Hall, Kilsyth, Scotland, there was a visitation of the Holy Spirit that began spontaneously by the pleading of the blood. A brother named John Reid, sitting in the middle of the prayer group, suddenly raised his hand and started to plead the blood, saying, "Blood, blood, blood!" Immediately the Spirit descended upon the group, and thirteen young people went to their knees and began to speak in other tongues. It was the pleading of the blood that brought the outpouring.

It was around this same time that Mrs. Woodworth-Etter was holding her great meetings in Los Angeles and Chicago. She used to hold her arms aloft and say to the people, "I sprinkle the blood of Jesus upon you," and she made a motion with her hands as if she were actually doing it. People would come running to the front of the auditorium, and many fell prostrate, speaking in tongues and receiving healing.

The pleading of the blood was an accepted revelation of the Holy Spirit in the early days of the Pentecostal outpouring. However, like many other divine revelations, it was lost as man's organizations came in to replace the supernatural workings of the Spirit. Yet wherever this message is preached today, it is still received with gladness. And when the blood is used, it brings astounding results. Truly we are *"more than conquerors"* (Romans 8:37) through the blood. (See Revelation 12:11.)

One of the early pioneers in Scotland, Pastor Andrew Murdoch of Kilsyth, received the baptism in the Spirit in early 1908. His wife received a vision of the blood running as a waterfall in her bedroom, and she was frightened. She cried out, "Blood, blood, blood!" and called for her husband. He assured her that this vision was of God. The same day she received the baptism in the Holy Spirit, speaking in other tongues. The Niagara of blood continued in her vision for a time, though, reminding her of the mighty stream that flows from Calvary, washing away sin and all uncleanness. The Holy Spirit gave these supernatural experiences to awaken God's people to the reality of the blood and its vital connection with the baptism in the Spirit.

OVERSIGHT AND OUTPOURING

In February 1908, a certain William Macrea was praying in his house in Kilsyth, and God made known to him by a revelation that two men were coming from Glasgow, intent on overseeing a church service. Neither of these men had received their Pentecostal experience. The Holy Spirit spoke and said that they were to be prevented from going to the platform. However, when the time for the meeting arrived, it was not easy to put this into effect, and the men were permitted to oversee the service.

Macrea kept the elders and deacons in a back room and asked them to plead the blood. While they did so, the Lord revealed all that was taking place in the meeting hall. One of the men from Glasgow got up to sing, but the Spirit revealed to the praying men that he was just showing off his voice! The elders and deacons continued to plead the blood, believing the Lord to work in the meeting. Within a few days, both men received the baptism in the Holy Spirit. In addition, forty-three were baptized in the Spirit that same weekend by the pleading of the blood. This is the way the outpouring of the Spirit began in Scotland in early 1908.

About this same time, several people journeyed from the United States to Kilsyth to receive the baptism. These people had been prayed for many times by the laying on of hands, but nothing had happened. But when they came to Scotland and began to plead the blood, they all received quickly. No wonder John told us that the Spirit and the blood agree! (See 1 John 5:8.)

OVERCOMING UNHOLY INHERITANCES

I well remember the very first time I began asking for the Holy Spirit baptism in 1939. My mother and her family had been deeply involved in spiritism, which had affected our whole family. Many tragedies took place in our family because of this, although my mother was unaware of the cause. I suppose I was contaminated with this spiritism more than I realized, for spiritual filth spreads rapidly, and only the blood can cleanse it away. However, I was unaware of this contamination; I only knew that I needed the baptism in the Holy Spirit. I remember so clearly how I knelt down by a chair and began to pray. On and on I prayed, but never once did I plead the blood. I was in need of deliverance but did not know it.

Others were pleading the blood aloud, however, and suddenly I had a most amazing experience. A creeping rigidity took possession of my body, and I stiffened up and fell prostrate on my face as stiff as a rod. After a while, the stiffness left me, and I stood up, feeling quite embarrassed. An evil spirit had left me that I did not even know I had! No doubt it had entered me when I had experimented with table-turning as a boy of twelve, in the company of my aunts and uncles who thought it was a great parlor game. (Many think this of the Ouija board, but it is highly dangerous.)

A week later, I was even hungrier for the baptism in the Spirit and readily knelt down again. This time I started to plead the blood with enthusiasm. It was not long before I began to speak in tongues and have been doing so until this day.

TRAVELING MERCIES

I have never known the active, audible pleading of the blood to fail. I travel much by car and much by air and have never failed to arrive at my destination on time to keep the Lord's engagement. I cover the car or the plane with the blood. As one blesses one's food by prayer, so we also protect our vehicles by pleading the blood.

I remember a brother in England years ago who, when faced with a motor that would not start in his car, just pleaded the blood because be knew nothing about automobiles. It started! When you find that difficulties are piling up against you or your family, just start pleading the blood and watch Satan's plans dissipate. It is surefire!

THE FAMILY PROTECTION ACT

In the early days of the outpouring of the Spirit in this century, Mrs. Nuzum of California used to teach her listeners in her Pentecostal meetings to sprinkle the blood upon their loved ones, their children, and all that God had given them. Didn't the children of Israel actually splash blood on their buildings? Is there any limit to using the blood in faith against satanic powers and the darkness of the world? Wouldn't it be good if congregations of Christians were to stand united in pleading the blood of Jesus against the demonic forces now trying to take over our cities and our young people?

I believe that the church has yet to discover the deeper dimension of spiritual warfare through pleading the blood. Great miracles can take place if we learn this secret. There is wonder-working power in the blood!

DEMONS & DELIVERANCE

CONTENTS

PREFACE

My first experience with the ministry of deliverance involved a man who had suffered from chronic asthma from birth. Before he came to us for prayer, he had been prayed for by the orthodox methods known to the church at that time, but nothing at all happened. When we changed from the prayer of petition to a prayer of forceful command, the results were astounding.

As soon as we *commanded* the asthma to leave in Jesus' name, the spirit of infirmity causing the asthmatic symptoms began to come out. In an hour and a half, he was completely and permanently healed.

To say that my wife and I were astonished is an understatement. We had not done this by knowledge of theology, for what does theology teach us about casting out demons? We did it experimentally, willing to try any method or system that would bring release to the afflicted.

This first clear-cut case of healing by deliverance brought us a glimmer of understanding on a subject about which we knew practically nothing. This formed a basis of experimentation, and during the next three decades we were to have some intensely interesting cases and many marvelous deliverances. God taught us progressively by His Holy Spirit as we were willing to tackle each case presented to us.

I took the simple position of knowing nothing—but I was willing to learn by successes and mistakes. We made many errors, but we saw some wonderful deliverances. Fortunately, I had not been taught that a Christian cannot "have" a demon. In fact, I had been taught *nothing* for or against demons: I was just plain ignorant.

More and more suffering people approached us over the years as news leaked out that we were involved in the "deliverance ministry." Most of them seemed to be completely, or at least partially, delivered. Some were untouched, even though we were willing to spend much time in trying to dislodge the demons that were troubling them. We rejoiced at the successes but continued to ask the Lord about the failures. The Lord gradually taught us, and our percentage of successes increased.

We learned many things, but there is so much more to know. The whole ministry of deliverance seems to be an inexhaustible well of God's love to set the captives free.

I would urge the reader to consider the author not as an expert, but merely as a servant of God whom the Lord has brought into a degree of knowledge of this vital subject. Because of this ministry, thousands have been set free and are still being set free.

This is not a theoretical theology, but a practical, down-to-earth Bible approach to the needs of people—and it works!

—*H. A. Maxwell Whyte*

PART 1:
DOMINION OVER DEMONS

1

SATANIC REALITIES

While I was preaching in the auditorium of the City Hall in Hamilton, Bermuda, a Scottish lady in the crowd listened intently to the message of healing and deliverance. Several months later she visited our church in Toronto and asked for prayer for her arthritis. I had been informed, however, that this lady regularly attended a spiritist church and had no connection whatsoever with the Christian faith. Her desperate need for healing, however, made her a sincere inquirer.

I explained that I must be frank and asked her if it was true that she was attending spiritist services and séances.

"Yes," she said, "and I have received so much benefit from the meetings. I have found God in a much closer way, and He has helped me so much."

I gently explained to her that all forms of the occult are expressly forbidden in the Scriptures. God said that all who participate in these activities will actually be cut off or severed from His presence—which was quite the opposite of her testimony about how close she felt to God.

"Would you like me to show you in the Bible where all forms of spiritism are expressly forbidden by God?" I asked.

"Yes, please show me." Her openness indicated that the Holy Spirit was at work. I turned to the following Bible passages:

Give no regard to mediums and familiar spirits; do not seek after them, to be defiled by them: I am the LORD your God. (Leviticus 19:31)

And the person who turns to mediums and familiar spirits, to prostitute himself with them, I will set My face against that person and cut him off from his people. (Leviticus 20:6)

And when they say to you, "Seek those who are mediums and wizards, who whisper and mutter," should not a people seek their God? Should they seek the dead on behalf of the living? To the law and to the testimony! If they do not speak according to this word, it is because there is no light in them. (Isaiah 8:19–20)

Those passages quickly convinced her. She immediately renounced all forms of occultism and necromancy. This woman had *no idea* that God had forbidden these practices, and she was very humble about the whole matter.

When I prayed for her, the Lord instantly healed her of all arthritis, stiffness, and pain, and she kept her healing. A week after her deliverance, she returned to the church and was mightily baptized in the Holy Spirit, speaking in tongues. She wrote to me regularly from Scotland, and her faith remained firm.

WEIRD DEMONIC POWERS

Those who practice spiritism and the occult have produced amazing, verifiable signs and wonders. To deny their power is foolishness. Things can be made to appear and disappear.

Levitation of inanimate objects is a reality. Articles such as vases and drinking glasses can sail across a room and be dashed in pieces against a wall. Tables can be made to walk up walls, and voices, including "other tongues" can be heard through trumpets and other objects.

I remember speaking to a Jewish friend who had been in the company of several men in Newcastle, Australia, one of whom practiced the occult arts. He boasted that he could cause anything to appear in the room where they were sitting.

My friend immediately asked him to "materialize" a tuna fish out of the Southern Ocean. No sooner had the wish been made known, than a great, flapping, wet tuna was right in the middle of the room.

How did it get there? How can a fish appear out of nowhere? How are inanimate objects levitated, defying the natural laws of gravity? Are all these lying signs and wonders so much "hocus pocus," or are they real?

The answer, my friends, is that *they are real, but they are not of* God. They are brought about through demon powers. The demons, being invisible, carry the glasses, support the walking tables upon the walls, and transport such things as a tuna fish out of the sea into a room. They have laws that we do not know and understand. Anyone who opens their lives, through disobedience to God's Holy Word, can become the servants of these same demon powers.

The two magicians in Pharaoh's court, Jannes and Jambres, like modern African witch doctors, had limited power—but power nonetheless. Moses' rod turned into a serpent, and theirs appeared to do likewise. (See Exodus 7:10–12.)

But we must remember that Satan has no power to create. Only God can and does create by His Word. Satan can create nothing except confusion and havoc by taking the things of God and prostituting them to his own ends.

We do not believe that Jannes and Jambres created serpents; we believe they merely used demon powers to transport them from the forests into Pharaoh's court. The serpent created by God then ate up the natural-born serpents, showing that God is greater than the devil and his demon powers.

GOOD AND BAD SPIRITS?

Man communicates with demons, and he thinks it's merely a parlor game or harmless fun. Many people believe in "white magic" and "black magic" and distinguish between "good spirits" and "bad spirits." The truth is that many bad spirits pretend to be good in order to deceive. All demons are bad, even if they transform themselves into angels of light. (See 2 Corinthians 11:14.)

People have many misconceptions regarding spiritist mediums and what actually happens at séances. Regardless of what they claim, spiritist mediums do not communicate with the dead. Instead, they communicate with demon spirits who imitate those who have died.

Imagine a person being inhabited by a demon for years. On his death, this demon roams around in a disembodied state looking for another person who will not resist his efforts to gain entrance. This demon knows many intimate things that happened in the life of the departed person. If some medium is willing to communicate with this familiar spirit, naturally the spirit can simulate the dead person and fool the assembled gullible gathering.

Many people also have misconceptions about haunted houses. Some think that the ghosts of departed people live in such houses, but this is not true.

Demons haunt houses and can cause thumps and bangs at any time of the night or day. These happenings are real, but a Christian need not fear them because he has the name of Jesus and His shed blood with which to expel these demon powers.

INCREASED SATANIC ACTIVITY

I read recently that every American high school has its witch or witches. In the Bible, men who dabble in the occult are called wizards. Both male and female witches are possessed by a "familiar spirit" which is expressly forbidden by Scripture.

There shall not be found among you anyone who makes his son or his daughter pass through the fire, or one who practices witchcraft, or a soothsayer, or one who interprets omens, or a sorcerer, or one who conjures spells, or a medium, or a spiritist, or one who calls up the dead. For all who do these things are an abomination to the LORD.

(Deuteronomy 18:10–12)

Spiritism is now openly practiced on every American campus. Witchcraft is widespread in Britain, and Brazil faces an epidemic of occultism. Why is there such an increase in satanic activity? Because people are departing from God and His Word, and the vacuum created in the human spirit is being filled by "other spirits."

A beautiful sixteen-year-old girl once approached me for prayer. She seemed the type you would meet at church, but Satan is an arch deceiver. This girl first told me that she had been on drugs. Then she confessed that she had also been acting as a witch at school. Apparently she had two demons.

I laid my hands upon her head, rebuked the demons, and commanded them to come out in Jesus' name.

Immediately they started to scream, for they realized their impotency before the name of Jesus and His shed blood. They screamed and choked her for nearly an hour. Many surprised Christian students began to intercede for her until she was completely delivered.

I asked her if she would like to be filled with the Holy Spirit. She readily agreed, and she was taught to plead and honor the blood of Jesus in prayer. Soon the Holy Spirit entered into her, and she began to speak in a beautiful unknown tongue! I marveled at the wonderful change that Jesus brought to her countenance.

IN NEED OF DELIVERANCE

I realize that some of these accounts may shock those *"who are at ease in Zion"* (Amos 6:1). While the bridegroom delayed, the church slumbered, slept, and lost many of these great truths. (See Matthew 25:5.) Today, however, God is bringing deliverance. Precious secrets that were unknown for years are being revealed by the Spirit of God.

How many Christians are indeed wrestling against demon powers? How many are arrayed in their gospel armor? Our churches look more like social clubs than military barracks! We neither know our enemy, nor the weapons that God gives us to fight him. We don't want to fight the forces that oppose the kingdom of God; we prefer to dream about going to heaven.

Many people attending our churches today are themselves in need of deliverance. Many are bound and oppressed, and some of their peculiar mannerisms may be due to demonic influence.

One Sunday morning, I was ministering in a full gospel church in Brooklyn, New York. The pastor and his wife had recently graduated from a Bible school in

Lima, New York. He was leading a song service, when suddenly a woman in the congregation began to sway from side to side with a look of contortion and agony spread across her face. She started to bump into those on either side of her, and it was obvious to me that she was in torment.

Turning to the pastor, I commented, "See that woman down there? That's a first-class case of a religious demon operating."

"What should we do?" the startled young pastor asked.

In a situation like that, the gifts of the Spirit are indispensable. The Lord impressed upon me to walk down the aisle and speak to the woman. At that point, however, I did not know what God wanted me to say to her. I encouraged the pastor to continue the singing while I addressed the situation.

"Sister, you are tormented," I said to her.

"Yes," she replied, "I know."

Then I offered to pray for her during the time of ministry that followed the service. Before returning to the front, I told her to sit down and behave in the name of the Lord, which she did.

At the end of the service my wife and I approached the lady and asked her if she wanted us to pray for her. She did, so I began to rebuke the religious demon in Jesus' name. Immediately, it started to scream with an unearthly sound. I quickly circled the sanctuary and closed every window. It was summertime, and the church members—not to mention their next door neighbors—were astonished at what was happening.

By the time I returned from this chore, my wife laid her hands on the woman's shoulders and held her from being hurled to the floor. The demons in this woman were greatly agitated. After about ten minutes of screaming and violent coughing, she was delivered.

After experiencing a glorious release from demonic bondage, she immediately asked, "Why hasn't anyone ever done this for me before?" What a pathetic question—and yet how appropriate. Why?

The ministry of deliverance, or casting out demons, has been neglected by the Christian church for a number of reasons. Many ministers and churches shy away from it because they fear the unknown. God is restoring scriptural teaching on deliverance to equip people for this ministry in the latter days.

Many people lack knowledge of the nature and operation of demons. Most Christians know that angels are ministering spirits sent to those who are the heirs of salvation. (See Hebrews 1:14; Psalm 91:11.) Unfortunately, we often forget about the opposing spiritual forces in the world. Evil angels—those who fell from their previous high estate as the trusted servants of Jehovah—were defeated in their rebellion and cast out of heaven with Lucifer, the son of the morning, or Satan himself.

> *So the great dragon was cast out, that serpent of old, called the Devil and Satan, who deceives the whole world; he was cast to the earth, **and his angels were cast out with him.*** (Revelation 12:9)

The Bible also teaches that the Lord used these fallen angels to visit suffering upon those who deliberately disobeyed Him.

> *[God] cast on them the fierceness of His anger, wrath, indignation, and trouble, by sending **angels of destruction** among them.* (Psalm 78:49)

The next verse implies that these evil angels caused a deadly plague that brought God's judgment. These fallen angels are *"reserved in everlasting chains under darkness for the judgment of the great day"* (Jude 6). At the coming of the Lord Jesus Christ, Satan himself will be bound for one thousand years and cast into the bottomless pit. (See Revelation 20:1–3.)

When Satan was cast out of heaven with his legions, he was given authority over mankind and all creation. In fact, he is able to influence everything that has life. And he has a very definite effect on the very atmosphere that surrounds the earth. The apostle Paul called him the *"prince of the power of the air"* (Ephesians 2:2).

This beautiful, created being was at one time called *Lucifer*, which means "shining one." (See Isaiah 14:12.) He held the greatest position among the created angelic hosts but tried to usurp God's throne. Lucifer proudly made a five-fold declaration:

> *I will ascend into heaven, I will exalt my throne above the stars of God; I will also sit on the mount of the congregation on the farthest sides of the north; I will ascend above the heights of the clouds, I will be like the Most High.* (Isaiah 14:13–14)

Lucifer did not lose his power or authority when he was cast out of heaven. By divine permission he uses it today among the earthly creation. His power, therefore, is second only to Jesus Christ and is infinitely greater than many people imagine.

In the end, however, Satan will meet a resounding defeat. That same passage of Scripture goes on to describe the judgment of Lucifer.

> *Yet you [Lucifer] shall be brought down to Sheol, to the lowest depths of the Pit. Those who see you will gaze at you, and consider you, saying: "Is this the man who made the earth tremble, who shook kingdoms, who made the world as a wil-*

derness and destroyed its cities, who did not open the house of his prisoners?"
(Isaiah 14:15–17)

WICKED SPIRITS

Christians must remember that Satan is neither omnipresent nor omniscient. His power is limited. In order to carry on his insidious work of maintaining curses upon the world, he uses a great company of wicked spirits, or fallen angels, to do his bidding. Without a doubt these wicked spirits are governed by well-disciplined angelic orders of generals and captains.

We do not know the number of these wicked spirits. There seems little doubt that they are far more numerous than mankind. The poor demoniac of Gadara had a legion in him. We read in *Smith's Standard Bible Dictionary* that a legion consists of about six thousand men and expresses any large number with the accessory ideas of order and subordination. (See Matthew 26:53; Mark 5:9.)

There seems little doubt that many accidents, misfortunes, quarrels, sicknesses, diseases, and unhappiness are the direct result of the individual work of one or more wicked spirits. Spirits are just as much *beings* as humans, except that they have no physical form. This is why they seek to indwell humans or animals (as in the case of the swine into which the Lord cast the legion from the demoniac of Gadara). They may even seek to re-enter a body when the spirit of that person ceases to resist their forces. (See Matthew 12:43, 45.)

WHO FILLS THE EMPTY SPACE?

Dr. Lawrence Hammond, a born-again nuclear scientist, tells of an experience that changed his thinking about demonic power:

> One sun-drenched day in voodoo-infested Haiti, an old hag violently attacked me. Her face was a horrible Halloween mask, her teeth fangs, her fingers clutching claws. Nobody had to tell me that she was oppressed by demons. Through the power of the blood of Jesus, and the authority of His name, the Holy Spirit enabled me to cast the demons out of her.
>
> I had never heard of anyone practicing deliverance today. Furthermore, I knew that many Christians totally rejected the existence of demons. But face to face with the satanic power expressed through this violent woman, I learned—much to my amazement—that a Christian who believes he has received power over the enemy can cast out evil spirits in the name of Jesus.
>
> But I had a lot to learn. For weeks I puzzled over how that woman could be so oppressed by demons.

As a scientist, I knew the emptiness of the atom, whose electrons are so small that only one millionth part of that atomic volume is occupied. I also knew that the human body is composed of such "empty" atoms, and that you and I are actually 999,999,999,999 parts empty space!

Lee Chesnut, former nuclear science lecturer and author of The Atom Speaks and Echoes the Word of God, pointed out that this emptiness must be filled with something: either the Spirit of God or the spirit of Satan. As he said, "You and I must decide between Satan and the Lord Jesus Christ, and which is to occupy and fill our lives."

OPPRESSED, OBSESSED, OR AFFLICTED

When evil spirits gain entrance into a person's body, we speak of demon oppression. These demons use the body of the afflicted person to work their wicked acts. Demons delight in actually controlling humans and speaking through them.

Demons can worry, tempt, or distract believers. This would be another example of *demon oppression*. They might cause us to get "out of victory," or lose our temper, a condition in which no Christian need ever be.

If evil spirits control a person's mind, this is called *demon obsession*. Someone who thinks he has committed the unpardonable sin is plagued by demon obsession. Upon questioning, however, he is unable to tell you what constitutes the unpardonable sin!

Demons also cause many afflictions from which mankind suffers. The spirits described in the Scriptures are foul, wicked, evil, deaf, dumb, infirm, unclean, and seducing.

Many believe that cancer is nothing more than a work of evil spirits which, when cast out in the mighty name of Jesus, shrivel up and die. Who disputes the possibility that arthritis, tumors, deafness, and dumbness may not be the actual work of demons in portions of the body? We do not say that such a person is "demon possessed," but we do suggest that they are sorely afflicted by demons.

We believe that the primary cause of all sickness is spiritual. Symptoms may be treated by natural means, yet if we use the name of Jesus Christ and His shed blood as a weapon against Satan in faith, then certainly we will see manifestations of divine healing because the sickness is destroyed at the root.

DEAL WITH DEMONS FIRST

Are healing and deliverance the same? Jesus didn't think so. He distinctly differentiated between divine healing and deliverance from demons. Let's look at His last discourse to His disciples. He taught them to expect five signs to prove the ministry of the Word of God.

> And these signs will follow those who believe: in My name they will cast out demons; they will speak with new tongues; they will take up serpents; and if they drink anything deadly, it will by no means hurt them; they will lay hands on the sick, and they will recover. (Mark 16:17–18)

The first sign was casting out demons in His name. This particular sign is mentioned *before* the sign of physical healing. We do not know whether this order is accidental, but we suspect that Jesus had a reason for listing deliverance first because He always dealt with primary issues first. If we first cast out demons, we would frequently have no need to pray for the sick; deliverance from the demon would bring all the healing needed.

It is interesting to note that the very first recorded act of public ministry by Jesus was to cast out a devil.

> Now there was a man in their synagogue with an unclean spirit. And he cried out, saying, "Let us alone! What have we to do with You, Jesus of Nazareth? Did You come to destroy us? I know who You are—the Holy One of God!" But Jesus rebuked him, saying, "Be quiet, and come out of him!" And when the unclean spirit had convulsed him and cried out with a loud voice, he came out of him. Then they were all amazed, so that they questioned among themselves, saying, "What is this? What new doctrine is this? For with authority He commands even the unclean spirits, and they obey Him." (Mark 1:23–27)

Many in the church today are asking these same questions. What is deliverance? Is this some new doctrine? Is every believer called to deliver people from evil spirits? Are there dangers in getting involved in deliverance?

This ministry raises many questions in the minds of Christians. Can a bornagain Christian be oppressed by demon powers? Are physical and mental sicknesses caused by demons? Where has this ministry of deliverance been throughout the ages? Can a Christian cast demons out of himself? How does a person come under demon influence?

The time has come to answer the questions Christians are asking today. Not so we can formulate more doctrine and theology, but so we can start setting people free!

If this ministry was so important to Jesus, should it be any less important to us?

2

THE STRANGE WORLD
OF SPIRITS

Y ou foul spirit of fear, come out of her in Jesus's name!" I commanded. I knew that
nothing else would help her.

At the close of a home prayer meeting in Florida, a few people had decided to
stay for the prayer of deliverance. A fearful woman who had been troubled with a
stiff neck for many years was among those in need of ministry. I began to pray by
commanding the spirit of fear to come out of her. Immediately we witnessed a reaction, and for the next few minutes this spirit began to choke out of her until peace
returned.

Then God reminded her how she had been afflicted with this miserable condition in the first place. When she was five years old, her father frequently told her scary
bedtime stories. One night he outdid himself in horror fiction. The details were so
vivid and frightening that she began to scream in terror. The mother rushed in and
commanded her well-meaning husband to leave the room. She tried to comfort her
terrified daughter, but it was too late; the damage had been done. When her mother
left the room, the little girl buried herself beneath a patchwork quilt, completely pet-
rified with fear at the memory of her father's gruesome story.

As a result of this terrifying experience, a spirit of fear entered this young girl.
This foul spirit remained for fifty years and also brought a spirit of tension, causing
stiffness in the neck. She experienced great relief when we cast that demon out of her.

MAN–A SPIRITUAL BEING

The ministry of deliverance is difficult for some people to understand. Let's turn
to the Scriptures to explain the spiritual realm.

The apostle Paul prayed, "*Now may the God of peace Himself sanctify you completely; and may your whole spirit, soul, and body be preserved blameless at the coming of our Lord Jesus Christ*" (1 Thessalonians 5:23). Man is triune. First spirit, then soul, then body. Man is, therefore, primarily and essentially a spiritual being.

In the beginning, God fashioned a human body out of the dust of this earth, and then breathed into this lifeless body the breath of life. I do not believe that God merely expanded Adam's lungs with fresh air. Obviously, it would take more than this to cause him to live. I believe that God literally breathed into man His own life. He breathed spirit into him, for God is Spirit.

Man is first a spiritual being. God did not create man to use his mind apart from his spirit. Unfortunately, our modern educational systems appeal only to the development of the mind. The mind of man teaches the mind of man, but the spirit of man is completely ignored. In fact, unregenerate men simply do not comprehend their spiritual needs at all. As the Scriptures say,

> *The natural man does not receive the things of the Spirit of God, for they are foolishness to him; nor can he know them, because they are spiritually discerned.*
> (1 Corinthians 2:14)

The mind can understand only the things of the mind, and likewise the spirit the things of the Spirit. An old adage states that "Birds of a feather flock together." Like always goes with like.

A church that ministers to the needs of the human spirit will attract spiritual people. But most religion simply caters to the carnal man. The body, with its five senses, prefers to produce a substitute for true worship. But Jesus said that God is looking for those who will worship Him "*in spirit and truth*" (John 4:23).

We cannot worship God with our minds or intellects with the efforts of soulish religion. Long ago Job asked, "*Can you search out the deep things of God?*" (Job 11:7). The answer is No. We cannot find God or understand anything about God with our minds or our bodies. That's why God made man a spiritual being.

THE DOOR TO THE SPIRITUAL REALM

Like goes to like. "*Deep calls unto deep*" (Psalm 42:7). If man wishes to find God, he must seek Him through his spirit. If we want to listen to a radio program, we must tune the frequency of our receiver to exactly the same frequency as that of the transmitter. In this way, we can get perfect reception if we are in range. In like manner, the spiritual part of our triune nature can communicate with God when we are tuned in through the working of the Holy Spirit.

When we commune with God, we do so with our spirits. Only then do we begin to understand the mind of God. We begin to realize that God gives us some of His mind. (See 1 Corinthians 2:16.) We begin to think as God thinks, but only in part, of course. Our minds become actuated by our regenerated spirit in communion with God.

This actuating of our minds becomes quickened when we are baptized in the Holy Spirit. We begin to understand how God imparts such gifts as words of wisdom or knowledge, discerning of spirits, tongues, interpretation, and prophecy. These come from the Spirit of God through the human spirit—not through the mind.

If spiritual gifts came through our minds, then it could be said that "we just thought them up." But since they come down from God, we do not think them up at all; we simply receive them through our spirits. Any so-called gift that comes only from the human mind is a counterfeit gift.

On either side of the spirit of man are two spiritual powers vying for his attention. On the one hand, God and the angels exert a holy influence on man. On the other hand, Satan, who left his state of perfection to become the devil, tempts men to sin. Many believe that he took with him one-third of all the created angelic beings, and that these now constitute the demons that torment and afflict all mankind. Lucifer and God's angels became Satan and his demons.

Once a man experiences the new birth and learns the secret of using his spirit instead of his mind, he opens the door into the spiritual realm. He may now communicate with other spiritual beings—and this is spiritual dynamite! By the operation of his own free will, he may freely converse with Almighty God. Some Christians have even experienced visitations from the angels.

SATANIC VOICES

Man, being essentially a spiritual being, can hear the voice of God's Spirit or the voice of Satan and his evil hordes. Many clear-minded, Holy Spirit-baptized Christians have been disturbed at the suggestions that evil spirits place in their minds. In fact, those who excessively dwell on such thoughts have even suffered nervous breakdowns. Other believers who are not firmly grounded in the Word of God have doubted their salvation and ultimately lost their minds because of this mental torment.

The moment we open the door of our spirit to the spiritual realm, we can receive whatever voice we tune into. For example, a short-wave radio receiver does not differentiate between Russian stations or American stations; it simply hears what it tunes into. The human spirit acts in the same way. But with a radio, we can tune out radio

Moscow if we do not like the propaganda. Similarly, Christians can tune out the unwanted satanic voices and tune into God's frequency by an act of their will.

Many Christian people have told us about the evil, unrighteous, and lustful ideas that Satan injects into their thought life. Other believers report that Satan says they are not saved. But the Word of God says just the opposite. Which are we to believe? The Spirit of God bears witness to the Scriptures that say we are saved by faith. On the other hand, Satan protests, "Oh no, you're not!" Isn't this the same strategy the devil used in the garden of Eden? "Has God said...?" What a liar he is!

Remember, hearing a satanic voice is not wrong. Sin comes only in obeying that voice. Never become obsessed with the voice of the enemy. People who continue to listen to Satan are rapidly on their way to becoming demon obsessed. Believers must deal quickly and decisively with the lies of the enemy. Arm yourself with the Word of God and refuse to believe anything contrary to its teaching.

DECEIVED BY SATAN

Unless a believer maintains his integrity and his righteous standing before God, he can easily be seduced by an angel of light. (See 1 Timothy 4:1–2; Corinthians 11:13–15.) These evil spirits attempt to woo Christians in much the same way as an immoral woman would endeavor to win the affections of a married man.

The difficulty is that Satan doesn't always tell lies. An angel of light may actually tell the truth, but its unholy inspiration comes directly from Satan. Many Christians who attend church regularly are being deceived by these angels of light and are sources of grave trouble to their pastors.

The New Testament records one such incident that Paul and Silas encountered in Philippi.

> Now it happened, as we went to prayer, that a certain slave girl possessed with a spirit of divination met us, who brought her masters much profit by fortune-telling. This girl followed Paul and us, and cried out, saying, "These men are the servants of the Most High God, who proclaim to us the way of salvation." And this she did for many days. (Acts 16:16–18)

Notice that the slave girl's declaration was correct—Paul and Silas were God's messengers who preached salvation. Many unwary people in full gospel churches today would have applauded such an utterance as being of the Holy Spirit. After all, it was *true*, wasn't it? But Paul, being greatly annoyed, turned and said to the spirit, "*I command you in the name of Jesus Christ to come out of her*" (verse 18). And he came out that very hour.

No wonder Jesus told His disciples to be *"wise as serpents and harmless as doves"* (Matthew 10:16). We continually need to be one step ahead of Satan so that his seducing spirits do not deceive us.

TESTING THE SPIRITS

Many questionable teachings are floating around in the church during these last days.

Beware of doctrines that throw doubt on the reality of heaven and hell and God's judgments; doctrines that tell us no one lives again until the resurrection day. These doctrines are not revealed by the Holy Spirit, whom Jesus said would guide us into all truth. Such doctrines are revealed by other spirits.

> *Now the Spirit expressly says that in latter times some will depart from the faith, giving heed to deceiving spirits and doctrines of demons.*   (1 Timothy 4:1)

> *And when they say to you, "Seek those who are mediums and wizards, who whisper and mutter," should not a people seek their God? Should they seek the dead on behalf of the living? To the law and to the testimony! If they do not speak according to this word, it is because there is no light in them.* (Isaiah 8:19–20)

Let us always weigh everything carefully against the written Word of God. To depart from God's standard is the quickest way to fall into error and deception.

This raises the question, "How can we know the source behind a spirit?" The answer can be found in the New Testament.

> *Beloved, do not believe every spirit, but test the spirits, whether they are of God; because many false prophets have gone out into the world.*   (1 John 4:1)

The apostle John also gave the early church some specific instructions on trying the spirits:

> *By this you know the Spirit of God: every spirit that confesses that Jesus Christ has come in the flesh is of God, and every spirit that does not confess that Jesus Christ has come in the flesh is not of God. And this is the spirit of the Antichrist, which you have heard was coming, and is now already in the world.*
>
> (verses 2–3)

Every Christian should heed Jesus' warning for this day.

> *For false christs and false prophets will rise and show great signs and wonders to deceive, if possible, even the elect.*   (Matthew 24:24)

In the current revival of the supernatural, we need to be very careful to check every miracle with the Word of God.

If we carelessly accept everything as coming from God, we will be easily deceived. A sign or a wonder does not necessarily come from God. It can come from Satan.

God has given discerning of spirits to the church, and I do not believe that He intended this gift to be used by the pastor only. This gift is for all children of God, although the pastor is sent by the Holy Spirit to administer the truths of the Spirit to the people.

Once in Erie, Pennsylvania, at a convention where I was speaking, a man stood up and shouted that a certain evangelist was a man of God and that the people should give heed to him. This he did three times, disturbing the meeting. Several men endeavored to quiet him, but he would not keep quiet.

I discerned that this was a demon at work and not the spirit of the man. I arose from my seat, discerning the evil spirit, and commanded it to be silent in the name of Jesus. This man caused no further disruption.

For the protection of the church, pastor and layman alike must know how to discern evil spirits and how to deal with them.

EMOTION OR ANOINTING?

Anything goes in many churches. Hollywood evangelism thrives, and signs and wonders take place in large meetings without scriptural warrant or foundation, and the people are delighted and deluded! We need God's gift to discern spirits now more than ever.

Should we accept every supernatural event as coming from the Holy Spirit? Not everything that happens in a full gospel meeting is orchestrated by the Holy Spirit. As God increasingly manifests His power in the ministry of deliverance, Satan also steps up his lying signs and wonders. (See Matthew 24:24.)

When a person becomes born again and filled with the Holy Spirit, he may experience intense emotion. The degree of emotion is usually in proportion to the make-up of the person. A Scot might feel less emotion than a Frenchman, or a Pennsylvania Dutchman less than a Texan. The baptism in the Holy Spirit is not given to us to perpetuate feelings but to enable us to fight the devil in faith whether we feel good or not.

Unfortunately, Satan has been very clever in diverting thousands of Holy Spirit-baptized Christians into an orgy of feelings and emotions. The gospel owes nothing to the human emotions; it is based on faith in God's Word.

Many sincere Christians are deceived. When they manifest the gift of tongues or prophecy, they feel they must draw attention to themselves by waving their arms, jerking their bodies, or using falsetto voices in order to impress others with the "tremendous anointing of the Spirit" that they feel. All of these fleshly additions are unnecessary and are caused by the work of a deceiving spirit. The message may be of God, but the manifestation is of the flesh.

I remember casting a religious demon out of a lady who kept on crying "Hallelujah" in an unnaturally high voice. After the demon came out, she collapsed in a heap and couldn't utter a word. The church is swarming with religious demons today who are simulating holy things.

Not everything that happens in a Pentecostal meeting is inspired by the Holy Spirit. Many occurrences are of the *human* spirit that has not been correctly disciplined. Other disturbances are the work of *evil* spirits who have taken control of the person.

WHAT ABOUT SPEAKING IN TONGUES?

If the devil can simulate religious things, then speaking in tongues may not necessarily be a sign of the indwelling Holy Spirit! This presents a problem in the minds of many people, but I believe the answer is simple.

Long before God created man, the angelic beings that fell from their high estate in heaven were cast out to the earth with their leader, Satan. (See Revelation 12:7–8.) Imagine a demon gaining possession of a Chinese man centuries ago. That demon would learn to speak Chinese by indwelling that man. At the Chinese man's death, the demon would seek to inhabit another human body. This time he might enter an Indian and learn his language. Over the years, he might inhabit men and women of many different nationalities. In time he would learn all of their languages.

Imagine this multilingual demon entering an English-speaking man who came to one of our Pentecostal churches. If he raised his hands and spoke in Chinese, Indian, French, or Hottentot, we would receive him without question! Many would say the man had been baptized in the Holy Spirit!

In a deliverance session held by the Reverend Lester Sumrall, a demon spoke perfect English through an ignorant girl who could not speak her own Philippine dialect properly. When the demon was cast out, the girl could not speak in English anymore.

In my own experience, when delivering people, I have heard demons actually sing and prophesy before being cast out. In such cases, the face of the person is usually contorted in horrible shapes, but the utterances can deceive.

DON'T BE GULLIBLE!

Where large crowds are gathered, religious demons love to "show off." Christians must not be gullible. Just because a person may fall down under the power of God, we shouldn't assume that all falling down is of God.

For instance, in the case of the demoniac son whom Jesus delivered, we read that *"the spirit cried, and rent him sore, and came out of him: and he was as one dead; insomuch that many said, he is dead"* (Mark 9:26). Sometimes when an afflicted person comes into the presence of someone who casts out demons, the demon will throw him to the ground, convulse him, or cause some other physical manifestation.

I remember ministering to a girl in New York State who had just received a glorious baptism of the Spirit and had spoken in tongues. While magnifying God, her left arm oscillated violently, and we noticed this and inquired about it. A well-meaning bystander informed us that her tremors were caused by "the Holy Spirit" for every time she started to praise God her left arm started to oscillate.

We kindly pointed out that the Holy Spirit does not cause peoples arms to oscillate violently like that. We then learned that this seventeen-year-old girl had epilepsy. In fact, her parents planned to have brain surgery performed on her when she reached the age of twenty-one. Doctors recommended such an operation to relieve the pressure on the left top side of the brain. In spite of this dire medical prognosis, I informed the people present that this girl needed deliverance.

As we began to constantly rebuke Satan's power, her arm started to oscillate violently. During the next fifteen minutes, the oscillation progressively decelerated. After thirty minutes, it ceased all movement.

We looked her in the eye and exclaimed, "Sister, we believe you are healed!" She started to weep for joy, telling us that the Lord had relieved all brain pressure. Later she testified in her own church of being healed by the power of God. No operation at the age of twenty-one was necessary. The demon had been cast out.

WHAT MAKES THE DIFFERENCE?

We underestimate the power of demonic forces. Demons try to keep us in ignorance, for we are not taught in our churches about these things. No matter how glorious your past experience has been, no matter how often you have spoken in tongues and prophesied, no matter how exemplary your life has been in the past, you can still backslide and permit a demon to gain a foothold in your life.

The gifts of the Spirit are gifts of God, but they will not prevent you from letting in other spirits. Once we have opened our lives to the spirit world, we must be careful that only the Holy Spirit possesses us, and that we are kept under the precious blood of Jesus.

Although Satan can speak in tongues through a person, everyone truly baptized in the Spirit can also speak in tongues as the Holy Spirit gives the utterance. (See Acts 2:4.) But how may we know the difference?

Jesus gave the answer: *"You will know them by their fruits"* (Matthew 7:16). If a tongues-speaking Christian does not manifest the fruit of the Spirit (see Galatians 5:22–23) in his life, he must be suspect in the assembly.

I believe that a pastor has God-given authority to insist that an unruly member keep silent in the church lest he give an utterance from an evil spirit or from his own human spirit instead of the Holy Spirit. And such an occurrence is altogether possible if a Christian does not walk in close fellowship with God.

This fact throws some light on the words of Jesus:

> *Many will say to Me in that day, "Lord, Lord, have we not prophesied in Your name, cast out demons in Your name, and done many wonders in Your name?" And then I will declare to them, "I never knew you; depart from Me, you who practice lawlessness!"*   (Matthew 7:22–23)

How could these people cast out devils, prophesy, and perform signs, wonders, and miracles? Surely, like Judas Iscariot, they must have been in right relationship with God at one time. But what happened to them? They yielded to pride, power, avarice, lust, and jealousy, and Jesus had no place for them in His kingdom. Tongues didn't save them; prophesying didn't save them. *"You will know them by their fruits,"* said Jesus. (See Matthew 7:16.)

Paul focused on the balance between the fruit and the gifts of the Spirit in his epistles.

> *Though I speak with the tongues of men and of angels, but have not love, I have become sounding brass or a clanging cymbal. And though I have the gift of prophecy, and understand all mysteries and all knowledge, and though I have all faith, so that I could remove mountains, but have not love, I am nothing.*
> (1 Corinthians 13:1–2)

> *Pursue love, and desire spiritual gifts.*   (1 Corinthians 14:1)

Paul exhorted the Corinthians to seek both the fruits included in the all-embracing fruit of love, as well as the nine spiritual gifts mentioned in that same epistle.

The gifts without the fruit profit no one, including the user. Fruit without the gifts are beautiful, but lack power. We need nine gifts and nine fruit working in symmetry and harmony in this last-day revival of the supernatural.

3

HOW TO PROTECT YOURSELF

One hot August day in Huntingdon Beach, California, I addressed a group of charismatic believers and preached on the ministry of Jesus in healing the sick and casting out demons. When I finished, I explained that Jesus wanted to touch people in the same way today. As I began to pray for people with various needs, many coughed, choked, and showed the usual manifestations of deliverance that happen each time I minister.

One Christian man suffered from a locked spine. He walked upright but had not been able to bend over for twenty years because his spine was "frozen." After explaining to him that his affliction was probably caused by a— spirit of infirmity, I reminded him of the woman in the Bible who had a similar condition:

> *And behold, there was a woman who had a spirit of infirmity eighteen years, and was bent over and could in no way raise herself up. But when Jesus saw her, He called her to Him and said to her, "Woman, you are loosed from your infirmity." And He laid His hands on her, and immediately she was made straight, and glorified God.* (Luke 13:11–13)

I emphasized that the woman's condition was caused by a demon—by a "spirit of infirmity." I then laid hands on the man, rebuked the spirit of infirmity, and commanded it to come out of his spine.

"Now," I said to the man, "Just start bending your back, and keep on bending until you can touch your toes."

He looked at me somewhat startled. "I have not been able to do that for twenty years!"

But he acted in faith, and slowly but surely, each time he bent down, his fingertips stretched a little bit closer to his toes. After eight minutes, he started to shout.

He had touched his toes! Jesus had healed twenty years of crippling in only eight minutes!

CONTINUALLY CLEANSED

Many Christians are offended by the idea that they might have a "spirit of infirmity" or be oppressed by some other demon. Some people get infuriated when we tell them that Satan may deceive them, visit sickness on them, entice them to backslide, or seduce them.

They reply, "Satan cannot bother me. I'm a Christian." We have met thousands who refuse to believe that Satan can worry, afflict, oppress, suppress, depress, frustrate, speak to, or lie to a child of God.

If Christians cannot be afflicted by Satan and his demonic hordes, why did several New Testament writers warn the early church about the enemy's deceptive tactics? We need to read these admonitions carefully and put them into practice in our daily lives:

> *...nor give place to the devil.* (Ephesians 4:27)

> *Be sober, be vigilant; because your adversary the devil walks about like a roaring lion, seeking whom he may devour. Resist him, steadfast in the faith.*
> (1 Peter 5:8–9)

> *Resist the devil and he will flee from you.* (James 4:7)

The apostles Paul, Peter, and James addressed Holy Spirit-baptized Christians who had opened their lives, minds, and hearts to the Holy Spirit. Once they were empowered by the Holy Spirit, they could expect Satan to try to afflict or hinder them from doing God's will.

A HOLE IN THE HEDGE?

We are all familiar with the Book of Job. This righteous man, Job, had a nice, protective hedge around him. Satan used to prowl around this hedge day and night waiting for a hole to appear. And one day a hole did appear.

How did that happen? Job's fear tore down God's defenses. Remember what Job said? *"For the thing I greatly feared has come upon me, and what I dreaded has happened to me"* (Job 3:25).

God had not torn down the hedge. But Job had *created* a hole in the hedge *by his own fear.* God's protection could no longer operate because faith cannot exist where fear is present. Satan caused job great distress and nearly destroyed his life.

Realizing these truths will help us to understand why some Christians get sick in body and mind. Why are some Christians in mental homes? This is not the fault of the gospel, for Jesus came *"to proclaim liberty to the captives"* and *"to set at liberty those who are oppressed"* (Luke 4:18).

Whose fault is it that Christians succumb to physical and mental afflictions? Could it be that those who have received Christ by faith begin to listen to the temptations of Satan and fall into his snare, thereby ignoring God's clear commands?

There is nothing automatic about salvation or any of the promises of God. They must be embraced by faith continually; we must resist the devil daily. If we do not, it is not God's fault that our protective hedge crumbles to give the destroyer access to our lives.

NO GUARANTEES

The classic case of demon possession involves Judas Iscariot, whom Jesus had chosen as an apostle and disciple. It seems unthinkable that Jesus would have chosen a wicked man to heal the sick and cast out devils! Judas must have been sincere in his faith at one time, even as many in the church are today.

In John 13:2, we read of how Satan tempted Judas to do his foul deed:

And supper being ended, the devil having already put it into the heart of Judas Iscariot, Simon's son, to betray Him.

The first act of the devil was to speak to Judas and *put the thought into his heart,* the innermost seat of his affections. Judas decided to obey Satan, and therefore turned his back on God and His Word. Judas, the disciple, was first oppressed, but finally he was possessed! *"After the piece of bread, Satan **entered** him"* (verse 27).

If Judas Iscariot could end up being possessed of the devil, how much more can we today? Satan knows that his time is short, and he is working harder than ever to destroy the work of God that is transforming lives today. Being saved and filled with God's Spirit is not an automatic guarantee that you will continue in the faith.

Many sincere Christians maintain the unscriptural attitude that once they are born again and washed in the blood of Christ, Satan can never again touch them. Unfortunately, this teaching works in reverse and instead of providing protection makes many believers vulnerable to attack. Why? Because God's protection is not automatic!

PROTECTED BY THE BLOOD

In the same way that a child needs to wash daily with soap and water, we need the continual cleansing of the blood of Christ. We do not take the Lord's Supper once after conversion and then never come together to take it again, do we? Then why should we regard the cleansing of the blood of Christ in this way? We need continual cleansing. What do the Scriptures say?

> But if we walk in the light as He is in the light, we have fellowship with one another, and the blood of Jesus Christ His Son cleanses us from all sin.
>
> (1 John 1:7)

Notice that *"cleanses"* is in the present tense. This means that it *continually* cleanses—not once in the past, but progressively now and in the future.

Every child of God must keep himself consciously covered and washed in the blood of Jesus Christ every moment of every day.

The blood of Jesus Christ is our greatest safeguard. Those involved in the ministry of deliverance should use the blood in faith to test all that they receive from the spiritual realm. Evil spirits are greatly agitated at the mention of the blood of Jesus.

A so-called Christian lady threw a real tantrum one day and rebuked me severely. But I determined that I was not going to be rebuked by a backslidden woman! I therefore commanded the demon to come out of her. It did—at least one of them did— and caught me by the throat and started to strangle me.

I cried, "The blood!" three times, and the demon went back into her.

But while it tried to choke me, the demon in the lady said, "There you are, *you* have a demon!" But it was a lie of Satan. And, through the blood, I overcame the demon.

On another occasion I experienced a demonic attack while I slept. In the middle of the night, I awoke to realize that the life had nearly been choked out of me. My heart was strongly oppressed. I felt as if life was almost gone.

I cried, "The blood!" three times. The demon departed rapidly, and the rest of the night was spent in peace. The next night at the same time, the same experience happened to my wife, and the same usage of the blood brought instant deliverance. No demon can get through the blood, but it has to be in place by faith.

A fellow minister told me the following story He had gone down to the Bahama Islands to preach in a church. No pastor had ever been able to stay there because the unfriendly natives would come out from the bush beating their drums and shouting obscenities, which made worship impossible.

Our friend accepted the challenge and decided to claim that area for Christ. He walked around the perimeter of the church property, pleading the blood of Jesus aloud for Satan to hear and God to honor. Once was enough. Now there is peace.

The disturbing evil spirit has departed, and a new missionary plans to take over the church. Now God's work will go on.

We do not speak enough of the blood of Jesus in our worship, our praying, and our attacks on Satan's strongholds. I am sure that if Christian assemblies everywhere would magnify the blood of Jesus, we would see carnal members stirred up and tremendous blessings poured out in new life for the church.

POWER OF THE BLOOD

Medical science teaches that germs cause many sicknesses. Small parasitic creatures can breed in a portion of the body, multiply, and cause great distress. Other sicknesses, however, do not appear to be caused by germs.

Does God have some way of protecting His people from these germs? God is omnipotent, and nothing is beyond His power. Certainly, He can send His ministering spirits to protect us and to prevent evil spirits from putting germs into our bodies, if we pray for protection and keep God's laws.

Remember that nothing happens by "chance" or luck, but all is ordered by God. Germs are part of the curse that will be destroyed at the coming of Jesus Christ, and demons are merely agents in the hands of Satan to do his work at his bidding in the same way that soldiers obey their officers.

In our experience we have positively proved this fact. When boiling water spilled on a man's arm, we immediately prayed, acknowledging the power of the shed blood of Jesus Christ over the injury. Amazingly, no inflammation occurred. This shows clearly that demons cannot visit the injured part of the body with germs when we recognize and use the blood of Jesus.

The same is true of cuts or scratches. We recently rebuked the flow of blood from a deep scratch in a child's forehead, and it immediately stopped. The wound was pinched together, and the next day the child was running around as if nothing had happened. The finest disinfectant in the world is the blood of Jesus Christ, applied by faith, because it keeps all unclean spirits away.

The only way we can protect ourselves from these terrible powers is by constantly keeping ourselves covered by faith in the blood of Jesus, which speaks defeat to these demon spirits. This is the blessed position of dwelling "*in the secret place of the Most High*" and abiding "*under the shadow of the Almighty*" (Psalm 91:1). We can trust no other protection or "shadow" than the covering of the precious blood of Jesus Christ.

ANGELIC PROTECTION

God's angels also protect us from the small mishaps of life that are directly caused by demon spirits. Let's look at a tremendous promise in the Word of God:

Because you have made the LORD, who is my refuge, even the Most High, your dwelling place, no evil shall befall you, nor shall any plague come near your dwelling; for He shall give His angels charge over you, to keep you in all your ways. In their hands they shall bear you up, lest you dash your foot against a stone.

(Psalm 91:9–12)

Isn't it wonderful to think that God's children, by faith in Jesus Christ, are the object of angelic care?

God's angels also bring answers to prayer. A spiritual battle in the heavens hindered the answer to Daniel's prayer and fasting.

Then [the angel] said to me, "Do not fear, Daniel, for from the first day that you set your heart to understand, and to humble yourself before your God, your words were heard; and I have come because of your words. But the prince of the kingdom of Persia withstood me twenty-one days; and behold, Michael, one of the chief princes, came to help me, for I had been left alone there with the kings of Persia."

(Daniel 10:12–13)

The demonic forces over that geographic area opposed God's messenger during the three weeks that Daniel fasted and prayed. When Michael joined the battle, the forces of God prevailed. Daniel finally received his answer.

TAKE YOUR AUTHORITY

Some of the experiences I've been describing may scare the timid soul from entering fully into his inheritance. But I would like to remind you that Jesus' promise still stands:

Behold, I give you the authority to trample on serpents and scorpions, and over all the power of the enemy, and nothing shall by any means hurt you.

(Luke 10:19)

Satan's great weapon is fear. We must not succumb to dread or be paralyzed by fear. We must be bold in the strength of our Savior, who has told us to fear nothing. There is nothing to fear. Satan is a defeated foe.

Remember that some demons long ago said, *"Jesus I know, and Paul I know; but who are you?"* (Acts 19:15). Demons recognize that the man of God bears the same authority as Jesus—if he exercises the power and authority that Jesus has given him.

In Acts 1:8, we read that power comes upon us when we're filled with the Holy Spirit. Many people today are looking in vain for a demonstration of the power of God. No car goes forward until it is put into gear.

In like manner, no Holy Spirit filled Christian will produce any power until faith is exercised—until we determine that we are going to put an end to this evil oppression right now through Christ. Christians who take action get results.

The praying Christian who battles on his knees can attack the devil's stronghold with great effect. *"Every place that the sole of your foot will tread upon I have given you"* (Joshua 1:3). We must place our foot on Satan's neck, take him by the tail, and cast him out.

WHAT SHOULD WE DO?

The more a nation departs from God and His love as shown in Jesus Christ, the more that nation opens itself to control by demonic powers. This same principle holds true for individuals.

A drunken man opens himself to demon possession because of his lack of control. One who loses his temper is also similarly exposed. Unregenerate sick people who are weakened by suffering are also vulnerable unless someone prays for them by faith. And anyone who has anything to do with spiritism, occult sciences, or bloodless cults is almost certain to be affected.

How should we respond to the demonic forces that surround us? God's Word gives us the answer:

> *Resist the devil and he will flee from you.* (James 4:7)

Resistance involves being on guard, being covered with the blood of Christ, and keeping ourselves under control.

The apostle Paul wrote about spiritual warfare being necessary to change situations in the natural realm.

> *For we do not wrestle against flesh and blood, but against principalities, against powers, against the rulers of the darkness of this age, against spiritual hosts of wickedness in the heavenly places.* (Ephesians 6:12)

These demon powers control the rulers of darkness and live in the first heaven of the earth's atmosphere. They do not live in heaven, for it was from there they were ejected.

The apostle Paul also listed the spiritual armor that Christians need to resist and fight the true enemy who opposes our interests on earth.

> *Therefore take up the whole armor of God, that you may be able to withstand in the evil day, and having done all, to stand. Stand therefore, having girded your waist with truth, having put on the breastplate of righteousness, and having shod*

your feet with the preparation of the gospel of peace; above all, taking the shield of faith with which you will be able to quench all the fiery darts of the wicked one. And take the helmet of salvation, and the sword of the Spirit, which is the word of God. (Ephesians 6:13–17)

If we do not follow his advice, then we are exposed to demon powers and we must not blame God. He has made every provision for our protection.

4

UNIQUE
DEMON PERSONALITIES

Demons have distinct and unique personalities just like human beings. No two demons are the same. I have witnessed very peculiar demonic personalities manifesting themselves through people.

I made an unusual discovery about demon personalities in Bogota, Colombia, South America. A Colombian pastor had asked me to go to the city hospital to pray for a lady who was dying. When we entered her hospital room, we saw a pathetic sight.

The woman was unconscious, and a rubber tube was inserted into her windpipe. She drew oxygen from a bottle, and her nose and mouth were taped shut. Her relatives had not left the room for four days. Hour by hour, they had stayed there weeping, which hardly charged the atmosphere with faith. The doctors informed me that she had but two hours to live.

I had been called to help, but what could I do? I hadn't the faintest idea, but I knelt by the bed and asked God to help me. Suddenly, an unearthly peace descended into that room—even all the relatives felt it. The Spirit of God enveloped us. I took the young lady's hand, laid my other hand on her forehead, and said, "Death, I rebuke you in Jesus' name." The next day I learned that the young lady had rapidly regained consciousness. Within one week she was released from the hospital.

The Colombian pastor who had accompanied me to the hospital was astonished by this good report. He asked me to meet with him in his office. With his head hanging, he admitted that he felt ashamed of his church because no one had been able to do this.

"Yes," I said, "but it was Jesus who healed her, not me."

"Yes," he replied, "but you *rebuked death*. I've never heard anyone do that before."

Jesus probably would have done the same in this situation because death is a spirit. This healing impacted the church in Colombia and opened them up to the working of the Holy Spirit among them.

INTELLIGENT BEINGS

Remember that neither Satan nor his demon spirits are *things*. Neither should they be taken lightly. Demons are *beings* who possess malign intelligence, and each one desires to express himself through a body. A demon is not happy unless he has a body. Because they do not possess physical bodies of their own, demons seek to inhabit or use the bodies of humans or animals.

Many sicknesses are actually caused by demons, and they should be treated as such. Let's look at a scriptural example where this actually happened.

> Now [Jesus] *from the synagogue and entered Simon's house. But Simon's wife's mother was sick with a high fever, and they made request of Him concerning her. So He stood over her and rebuked the fever, and it left her. And immediately she arose and served them.* (Luke 4:38–39)

If this fever was only a physical problem, then how foolish to rebuke it! It makes no sense whatsoever to rebuke an inanimate thing. One can only rebuke something having intelligence, and Jesus knew that a spirit caused this fever. The fever left Peter's mother-in-law because it had to obey Jesus' authoritative command.

CALLING THE ENEMY BY NAME

When you're engaged in spiritual warfare, it's important to know your enemy. The following evil spirits, demons, or devils are mentioned in the Scriptures. Each one is a personality, and the word used expresses their nature:

1. spirit of infirmity or weakness (Luke 13:11)
2. mute spirit (Mark 9:25)
3. dumb spirit (Mark 9:25)
4. distressing spirit (1 Samuel 16:14)
5. foul spirit (Revelation 18:2)
6. unclean spirit (Matthew 10:1)
7. spirit of divination (Acts 16:16)
8. spirit of bondage (Romans 8:15)
9. spirit of error (1 John 4:6)
10. spirit of the world (1 Corinthians 2:12)

11. deceiving spirits (1 Timothy 4:1)

12. jealous spirit (Numbers 5:14)

13. lying spirit (2 Chronicles 18:21)

14. familiar spirit (Deuteronomy 18:11 KJV)

15. spirit of the antichrist (1 John 4:3)

16. spirit of fear (2 Timothy 1:7)

17. perverse spirit (Isaiah 19:14)

18. sorrowful spirit (1 Samuel 1:15)

19. spirit of deep sleep (Isaiah 29:10)

20. spirit of harlotry (Hosea 4:12)

21. different spirit (2 Corinthians 11:4)

Satan, their undisputed overlord, exercises absolute control over his invisible hordes. His names reveal his variable characteristics:

22. Lucifer (Isaiah 14:12)

23. prince of the power of the air (Ephesians 2.2)

24. ruler of the demons (Matthew 12:24)

25. destroyer (1 Corinthians 10:10)

26. angel of light (2 Corinthians 11:14)

27. serpent of old (Revelation 20:2)

28. great dragon (Revelation 12:9)

29. devil (Revelation 12:9)

30. wicked one (Matthew 13:19)

31. father of lies (John 8:44 KJV)

32. murderer (John 8:44)

Is it any wonder that we are continually afflicted, frustrated, oppressed, perplexed, worried, and tormented by these disembodied beings? They swarm around us like mosquitoes. Once we are filled with the Holy Spirit and empowered to tear down the enemy's kingdom, we become special targets for their evil intentions.

OPPRESSION AND DEPRESSION

The most common form of attack is *oppression*. Oppression is a spiritual "pressing down" that leads to depression. Christians tolerate this condition, then something worse may develop. For instance, if we entertain an idea that is contrary to the Word of God, we become *obsessed* by that wrong idea or doctrine. Many false prophets today are demon obsessed.

Satan's goal in afflicting people with oppression, depression, or obsession is to lead them to a more dangerous state—possession. We must differentiate between possession of part of the body—as in epilepsy—and possession of the soul that leads to eternal separation from God. Even a Christian may end up in this latter kind of possession.

Many stubborn believers have disobeyed God for so many years that they have succumbed to demonic powers. In many cases, these tormented individuals need to be delivered by their pastors. Unspiritual members who yield to Satan's demons cause more trouble in local churches than we are willing to admit. Such people are probably only oppressed, but even oppression is a dangerous state in which to remain. A church split is always the work of a grinning demon.

Many years ago I tried the following approach on our two oldest boys who were quarreling. We rebuked this disturbing spirit and commanded it to stop troubling them. The boys instantly were released and stopped their disputing.

CONFESSION BEFORE DELIVERANCE

No sin can be forgiven unless it is confessed and covered by the blood of Jesus. Scripture gives this stern admonition to all who return to the fleeting pleasures of sin:

> For if we sin willfully after we have received the knowledge of the truth, there no longer remains a sacrifice for sins, ²⁷ but a certain fearful expectation of judgment, and fiery indignation which will devour the adversaries.
>
> (Hebrews 10:26–27)

Nothing will alter God's judgment unless that willful disobedience is confessed and put under the blood of Jesus.

I learned this lesson well in Caxton Hall, Westminster, London, England, when an insane girl walked in to be prayed for. When her turn for ministry came, the friend who brought her explained that she had been taken from a mental institution in order to come to this meeting.

I did not inquire as to the type of insanity but laid my hands on the woman's head and started to rebuke the demon spirits. Nothing happened. I noticed that her face had the strained look of one in torment. The Spirit of God showed me that her trouble was caused by a persecution complex. This woman thought that everyone was against her and gossiped about her. When I confronted her with this revelation, she admitted that it was true.

I then explained that this was a sin that she must confess to God before she could expect to be delivered. She seemed quite surprised, but agreed, and prayed with me before the assembly, asking God to forgive her for thinking such ridiculous thoughts.

When I laid my hands on her head and prayed a second time, the spirit of insanity immediately left. Her face began to radiate with a bright smile of understanding and joy. I told her to turn around and face the congregation. A time of great rejoicing erupted as she praised the Lord for His healing power.

I learned an important principle from this case. People seeking release from bondage should ask God for forgiveness of their sins *before* we pray for deliverance. Confession must first be made unto salvation. Jesus cannot forgive us or deliver us until we say we are sorry. Stubbornness and pride have kept many people from receiving total freedom in Christ.

FREEING FINANCES

Can the enemy afflict believers with financial loss or poverty? We believe he can, but the following testimony demonstrates that God is greater than Satan in this realm, too. One of our church members owned a store, and above her business she rented a fine apartment. The owner was distressed because she could not rent it. As a result, she had lost over one thousand dollars. The Lord showed us that Satan was attempting to frustrate, impoverish, and withhold money from this fine Christian woman.

We visited the apartment with the owner, and together agreed for this restraining, evil power to leave. We pleaded the blood of Jesus in every room and cupboard and commanded the evil spirit to go. Then a word of prophecy declared that the apartment would be rented within a week. Within two days a tenant signed the lease.

The evil presence that had been cast out then descended into the store below, and business started falling off for no reason whatsoever. Adjusting price levels created no more business. Staff troubles, disputes, and unpleasantness added to the problems. Persistent, special prayer was made, and that malign spirit eventually left. Now both the apartment and the business are flourishing!

A DISTRACTING DEMON

Some of the demons I have encountered are so extraordinary that I hesitate to put the stories into print. The "music demon" is one such case.

During a stay with friends in Dunedin, Florida, I visited the wife of a member of the Full Gospel Businessmen's Fellowship. I asked her to explain her trouble. Everywhere she went, her head was filled with music. In fact, this phenomenon was so distracting that she could scarcely concentrate on what she was doing. Frankly, her plight amused me. What was wrong with a built-in radio playing all the time? I even asked her if it was classical music or rock and roll.

"No," she said, "it's not rock and roll; it's good music."

This puzzled me. If it had been rock and roll, I might have quickly said that the devil instigated her problem. But good music? What should I say?

Then she looked me squarely in the eye and said, "You're a man of God. Tell me, is it a demon?"

I was on the spot! This is one of those cases where you quickly pray, "Lord, show me! Lord, help me!" And as soon as I inquired of the Lord, the reply came back loud and clear.

"Yes," the Holy Spirit said, "this is a demon."

So I told the lady that it was a demon, but at this point I had no idea of its name. As we began to pray together, the Lord revealed to me that this was a *distracting demon. As* soon as I commanded this spirit to come out in Jesus' name, it coughed out, a most common form of ejection. In about one minute she was delivered of a distracting music spirit and has remained free since that day.

BINDING SPIRITS OF MURDER

I encountered another demon personality in Dallas, Texas, at a meeting held by a Bible school. A certain woman came for prayer, and as usual, I asked, "What do you want from Jesus?" She replied that she was afraid of destroying herself and her three children. Satan's intention was to wipe out the whole family.

I then began to bind and command these murder demons to leave. I was not surprised when she began to scream in a loud voice, for I knew that Jesus had encountered this kind of demonic reaction many times. (See Luke 4:33–34.) It was not a pleasant experience. The demons manifested themselves in a frenzy of rage and then started to vomit out.

These murder demons were somewhat stronger than most of the demons with which we deal. Strong demons usually vomit out, often bringing mucus with them and sometimes even the poison that surrounds them. This is quite an operation! The very hand of Jesus, the Divine Physician, reaches right inside them and brings salvation and healing. I have seen many expensive operations done by Jesus for free, and the results are often left on the floor or in buckets. Gruesome and horrible, but true.

This deliverance took about half an hour. Then we began to pray for this woman to be baptized in the Holy Spirit. We taught her to plead the blood of Jesus out loud. Jesus gave her a new tongue, and she began to speak as the Spirit gave utterance.

The vessel that had been filled with murder now overflowed with love. What a transformation!

The name of Jesus casts out every foul spirit, and the applied blood of Jesus cleanses the vessel. This paves the way for the Holy Spirit to come in and do His work.

These experiences taught me many lessons. We must not stop wrestling. We must never stop fighting. Many people receive prayer for deliverance but quit resisting when they do not get instant relief.

Christians should never stop resisting the devil for even a moment. We can cast him out of our lives, homes, offices, and factories. We are sons of God. We have been given dominion over every creature, including demons. We have dominion in the name of the Lord.

5

DELIVERANCE
THAT LASTS

Our first experience with deliverance happened in our Toronto church and involved a fine, converted, Catholic man who attended regularly. He had suffered from chronic asthma since birth and was also a heavy smoker. Although we prayed for him and anointed him with oil, he was no better. The asthma continued to plague him, and he could not quit smoking.

A woman suggested to me what seemed to be a preposterous idea. "Do you suppose this is a smoking demon?"

At that time, I had never heard of a smoking demon. Many Christians refuse to hear of them even today. If you had told me about an asthma demon, I wouldn't have believed it either. After all, wasn't asthma a nervous disease and smoking merely a dirty habit? Demon? Devil? Evil spirit? How could it be? The Spirit of God was leading and teaching me many things I could never have learned in Bible school!

First, I prayed with this man to receive everything from God, but he still remained bound. He had developed asthma as an infant and had not been able to work until he was twenty-six. For the next fourteen years he spent his hard-earned money on doctor bills, hoping to find a little relief.

I prayed with him, and he was marvelously baptized in the Holy Spirit with the evidence of speaking in tongues. Despite receiving this blessing from God, he was still afflicted with asthma and bound by nicotine.

Many Christians, who have been taught that the Holy Spirit will not enter an unclean vessel, refused to believe his experience. We learned that the Holy Spirit is given, like every other gift of God, on the basis of grace and faith—not because of our worthiness or holiness.

"COME OUT!"

One day I said to this brother, "We think you may be afflicted by a smoking demon. How do you feel about having it cast out?"

He wasn't shocked at my suggestion that he needed deliverance. Because of his Roman Catholic background, he had learned to accept what the priest said as true. I suppose this is a great lesson for rebellious Protestants to learn!

Before praying, we led him to the church kitchen in the basement because we had read that demons sometimes come out crying with a loud voice. At that time, my wife and I had no firsthand experience in these matters, but we took precaution nonetheless.

My wife and I sat down, and our friend sat in front of us. I knew nothing except what Jesus had told me—and that is always enough! He had said, *"In My name they will cast out demons"* (Mark 16:17). 1 also remembered the teaching I had received about using the blood of Jesus in the presence of the destroyer.

We started to sing some choruses about the blood never losing its power. Then we launched an attack! "In the name of Jesus, come out!" As we gave persistent commands and pressed the battle hard, the demons of asthma and smoking started to cough out and vomit out.

After one hour and twenty minutes a huge pile of handkerchiefs soaked with sputum were on the floor. But our friend was gloriously healed! He stood up, inhaled deeply, and exclaimed, "Praise God! I am healed! I can breathe properly for the first time in my life!"

What had we done? As the apostle Paul said, *"We do not wrestle against flesh and blood, but against principalities, against powers, against the rulers of the darkness of this age, against spiritual hosts of wickedness in the heavenly places"* (Ephesians 6:12).

We cast out the spirit of infirmity that caused this man's asthma. Although asthma affects the breathing and nervous system, we learned that a demon could cause this affliction.

This brother is still healed today, and his heart was pronounced strong five years after the healing. He no longer needs to smoke because Jesus set him free. God uses him in the gift of tongues, interpretation, and prophecy in the assembly.

A SPIRIT OF SUICIDE

Two days later, another man telephoned us. This Christian brother, who had been a deacon in a full gospel church, was battling a strong urge to commit suicide. Could it be that a Holy Spirit-baptized man—a deacon in a full gospel assembly— could be demon possessed?

What would our Bible schools say? What would the pastor of his church say? What would anyone say? Who cares what they say! I quickly told the afflicted man that demons were probably the source of his torment. Being desperate, he asked what he could do. Remembering the recent deliverance session where the asthmatic was gloriously set free, I felt I was ready for anything.

"There is one thing we can do," I said. "We can cast out these suicide demons."

"When?" he asked.

"Tonight," I replied, full of faith and the joy of the Lord! I was learning that I was seated in heavenly places in Christ and had been given authority over demonic forces.

My wife again came down into the basement kitchen with us. We sat on one side of the room, and this despondent man sat on the other side with his wife. The kitchen became an arena of spiritual conflict.

We began by singing choruses about the blood of Jesus because we didn't want these demons to attack us. There is nothing like a fresh reminder of the power of Jesus' blood. The demons knew they had no power over us. Then we gave the command.

To my astonishment, this man shot into the air about one foot off his chair. He landed with a thud, and his head shook to and fro as if he were a toy in a dog's mouth.

We doubled our forceful commands in the name of Jesus and ordered every foul suicide demon to come out. After one hour, many unclean spirits had come out moaning, coughing, vomiting, and writhing. Then they started to speak. We had read about demons who spoke to Jesus, but we didn't know anyone who heard demons speak today. We know differently now.

We asked the spirits how many more remained in our brother, and they replied, "Twenty." We counted them as they came out, paused at each fifth one, and asked again. Amazingly, they told the truth, although they argued and sometimes refused to answer. But our pressing commands in Jesus' name caused them to tell the truth.

"Fifteen." "Ten." "Five." The last demon put up a twenty-minute fight, but the name of Jesus and an authoritative command expelled him. Finally set free from demonic bondage, this brother threw his head back and spoke in tongues, magnifying God.

He then made a pact with God; he said that if he was truly delivered, he would like God to give him the gift of prophecy. And the next Sunday around the communion table, this cleansed vessel brought forth a beautiful prophetic word that edified the entire church.

SIN NO MORE

Such deliverances are spectacular. Seeing captives set free by the power of God exhilarates me. Manifesting Satan's defeat builds faith to tremendous heights. But deliverance is in no way automatic. Keeping your new freedom is dependent on maintaining a very close walk with God.

The apostle Paul simply wrote, *"Work out your own salvation with fear and trembling"* (Philippians 2:12). The apostle James tells us that *"faith without works is dead"* (James 2:26).

Some people who have been delivered in a most spectacular manner have returned to their old ways. Why the disheartening relapse? The demons have returned with a vengeance, and the outcome is usually worse than before. Epileptics have been gloriously delivered and released from their seizures. But because they did not walk more closely to the Lord than before, the demons returned.

We have ministered deliverance to people again when demons gain access to their lives through sin, rebellion, or simple carelessness. We must realize that demons entered into their lives only because of a previous weakness. Unless that gap is closed after deliverance, the same trouble will befall the person again.

Jesus warned a paralytic who had just been healed, *"See, you have been made well. Sin no more, lest a worse thing come upon you"* (John 5:14). Jesus indicated that his previous sin had caused his lameness. The remedy after deliverance was to sin no more. When we realize that the scriptural definition of sin is *"lawlessness"* (1 John 3:4), we are reminded that we can no longer do as we please. The walk with God after deliverance is very narrow.

Too many Christians have only a vague idea of what it means to follow Jesus. To them, He is a sentimental Lover with whom they can be as perverse as they feel inclined, and they think that Jesus will understand. They interpret being under grace but not under law as an excuse to do what pleases them, and they will not be tied to Scripture.

These careless, carnal Christians are likely to get sick and stay sick. *"Sin no more, lest a worse thing come upon you"* needs to be the text of all deliverance churches today.

"IS THERE HOPE FOR ME?"

Perhaps the best Scripture on this subject details the story of the man whose house was garnished, swept, and cleansed after the evil spirit had gone out. This demon was not so easily defeated. He wandered around, waiting for a convenient moment to return. Finally, the man backslid, and the demon did return and brought with him seven other spirits worse than himself. (See Matthew 12:43–45.)

To say that this man was not saved is to misuse the plain meaning of words. Obviously, he was saved, delivered, and cleansed in the blood; but he chose to backslide and consequently returned to his previous habit, and seven other demons came to plague him. The frightful possibility of such a relapse was made very real to me a number of years ago.

The telephone rang. "Is that you, Pastor Whyte?" The same man who had been delivered from twenty demons in our church kitchen seven years before was on the line.

"Yes," I replied. "What can I do for you?"

"Are you in the same place?"

"Yes."

"Do you still have the same ministry?"

"Yes."

He sighed with relief, saying that God had directed him to call me. He was trapped in the pit of sin again. "Do you think there's any hope for me?" he sighed. "I'm in a terrible mess."

I assured him that there was indeed hope, for the mercies of God are new every morning. So he came to my office.

His story was very sordid but a warning to us all. After his spectacular deliverance, he had moved out of the area and into the suburbs. The new church he attended did not believe the full gospel and did not teach or practice healing or deliverance.

One rainy day, as he drove downtown to his business in Toronto, he noticed a man at a bus stop. With compassion, he invited the man to get into his car. This worldly man offered our friend a cigarette. His offer opened a wonderful opportunity for our friend to witness about the salvation and deliverance available in Christ. But no. Instead, he took the cigarette, which proved to be his first step to hell on earth.

Each day he picked up this man, and each day they smoked. Soon they talked about drinking together. Their sin escalated from the tavern to the race track where they bet on the horses. Finally the new found friend said to our brother, "I love you."

As I listened to this man's story, I could hardly believe it. He had a beautiful wife, four wonderful children, and a good home. I had often visited them. What power drove a good Christian man to become a homosexual, leave his wife and family, and live in one room with another man? Psychology cannot explain this. It was the devil working through indwelling demons.

WORSE OFF THAN BEFORE

Theology explains that no Christian can have a demon. But I remembered how God had delivered this dear brother from a suicide demon seven years before. How could this Spirit-filled man have gotten a suicide demon in the first place? And what about the demons that were in him now?

I knew there was only one answer. He had arrived at this miserable state by disobeying the words of Scripture, *"...nor give place to the devil"* (Ephesians 4:27). He had allowed the devil to occupy territory that had previously been occupied by the Holy Spirit.

The broken man slumped into a chair after his agonizing confession. He had scraped the bottom of the barrel of sin but was ready to be rescued again.

Without further delay, we gave the command. "Come out, in the name of Jesus! " The man was ready. The filthy demons began to pour out of him with almost continual coughing and choking. Without any asking on my part, they willingly named themselves as they came out. Lust, filth, uncleanness, perversion, cursing, etc. In twenty minutes he was completely free again.

When it was all over, I realized that I had seen a fulfillment of Jesus' words:

When an unclean spirit goes out of a man, he goes through dry places, seeking rest, and finds none. Then he says, "I will return to my house from which I came." And when he comes, he finds it empty, swept, and put in order. Then he goes and takes with him seven other spirits more wicked than himself, and they enter and dwell there; and the last state of that man is worse than the first.

(Matthew 12:43–45)

This explained what had happened to the man. After his first deliverance, his "house" had been cleansed, swept, and put in order. But he had not kept it filled with the new Visitor, the Holy Spirit. His house had been left empty, so the suicide spirit came back. But he also beckoned to seven of his filthy friends, and they came in also. What a mess a Christian can get himself into by backsliding! But thank God, deliverance is available to all who bend the knee to Jesus and ask Him to forgive their sins and enter into their lives.

Seven years later, I met this same brother again in a certain church. Immediately I asked how he was doing. He joyfully told me that after his second deliverance, he returned home and made a full confession to his wife and family. They forgave him and took him back. God then began to prosper his business, and he bought a better home. Now he was keeping his house clean with the blood of Jesus, and the demon had permanently left.

HOW TO STAY DELIVERED

God is restoring His power to the church to drive out demons, but the suffering person, whether a Christian or unbeliever, *must be willing to be delivered.*

Although moral perverts, alcoholics, and drug addicts say that they want deliverance, in their hearts they may want only temporary relief and not real deliverance to serve a living God. They are ashamed but unrepentant. Let me warn you that these *cannot* be delivered even if we spend hours with them. Many searching questions and discerning of spirits will be necessary.

Willing cooperation by the sufferer is of greatest importance in achieving a lasting deliverance. This is especially true with drug addicts and alcoholics. If they do not go on with God after the demons have been cast out, the demons will quickly come back. (See Matthew 12:43–45.)

This ministry does not rest on sentimentality. We may feel sympathetic for people, but unless they are willing, they cannot be helped. Even if we were to cast demons out of them (which is possible), these evil entities would only re-enter them when our back was turned.

People must be willing to be delivered and stay delivered. The hole in the hedge that gave Satan access must be closed after he has been cast out. We must refuse to succumb to the enemy's scare tactics. After deliverance we must live in close fellowship with God. Only then can we guarantee that deliverance will last.

6

SETTING PEOPLE FREE

When this ministry began, I frequently spent from one-half to two hours in prayer for the oppressed. This became very exhausting and demanding on my time and strength. Over the years I began to see that deliverance could and should be speeded up. Quick and effective deliverance depended on two factors:

1. Our understanding of our powerful authority in Christ

2. The willing collaboration of the one in need of deliverance

In prayer we began to tell Satan that he was not going to stall. When we commanded him to come out *immediately*, he obeyed. Deliverances that previously took an hour now were completed in minutes. We began to pray for many afflicted individuals, and within minutes evil spirits came out coughing, choking, and screaming. Many people fell to the ground and then rose to their feet praising God, *free!*

I refused to talk to demons any more, nor did I encourage them to speak, or confess their names or presence. The Holy Spirit showed me all I needed to know. Jesus commanded demons to be quiet and come out. This seemed to be the scriptural pattern. We did the same, and they obeyed. We learned that if we were uncertain, Satan and his demons took advantage of us, and put on a show by either refusing to come out or coming out only very slowly while we fought.

Every week in our church in Scarborough, a suburb of Toronto, Ontario, many came for release and the infilling of the Spirit. People who were afflicted with arthritis, heart troubles, lung troubles, and throat troubles sought and found healing with deliverance. Those who were bound by jealousy, anger, hatred, self-pity, murder, suicide, smoking, drinking, unlawful sex, and drugs were gloriously set free.

People with such problems came in a steady stream to us, and God, through our prayers, brought permanent deliverance to most of them. Immediately after their deliverance, we asked them if they would like the Holy Spirit to fill all the areas previously occupied by unclean spirits. Most agreed, whether they understood much or not, for they were hungry. In many cases, those who had no prior instruction on the baptism in the Holy Spirit began to speak in tongues much to their astonishment. What a change on their faces!

Thousands of afflicted and tormented people need this ministry in our churches today. Arguing whether these afflicted people are truly "saved" or not is pointless. They need help in whatever spiritual condition they find themselves in. God delivers today as He did in Jesus' day. The ministry of deliverance is meeting the deep spiritual needs of people like never before.

DEFEATED DEMONS

The apostle James tells us that *"even the demons believe—and tremble!"* (James 2:19). Christians need to understand their tremendous authority over demons in the name of Jesus. We should deal with them as defeated foes.

An unusual experience helped me to realize this truth. One day I was talking with another minister in our sanctuary. A drunk man unexpectedly lurched into the church and began to insult us. Realizing that I was face to face with a demon, I rebuked it in Jesus' name and commanded it to be subject to me. The results were extraordinary.

The man jumped up and down and cursed the name of Jesus. He pulled off his jacket and tossed it into the air. Then he tore off his shirt and threw it away, too. He dug his hands into his pockets, pulled out all his change, and scattered the coins all over the sanctuary. During his antics I continued to bind and rebuke Satan.

Next, the drunk staggered toward this minister and me and became quite contentious, arguing that he knew more about religion than we did. I continued to rebuke and bind the demons. Finally, he fell to the floor and started to spin like a top.

Suddenly the man stopped spinning, stood up, walked over to his shirt, put it on, and began to pick up his scattered coins. I helped him retrieve as many as I could. Then, after I had helped him on with his jacket, he sauntered out of the church very peacefully.

That instance dramatically demonstrated the power we have over demons. I knew that I would never again need to be afraid of anything or anybody. Jesus has given us practical protection against the powers of darkness that are continually arrayed against us.

POWER OVER INSANITY

I witnessed another demonstration of this power over demons in dealing with a spirit of insanity. Mary had been oppressed by demonic forces and incarcerated in a mental hospital in Ontario. For part of each month, however, she returned to sanity. But with the approach of her menstrual cycle, she became violently insane.

Mary's mother, who was a Christian Scientist, took her daughter from the hospital for a few days each month but was warned to get her back to the hospital well before the next seizure.

When the mother heard about our ministry of casting out demons, she approached me to see if I could help. As a Christian Scientist, she knew nothing whatsoever about the ministry of deliverance. This woman's church taught that her daughter was not really sick—it was just "all in her mind."

Mary's mother arranged to bring her to the church office. She had apparently waited a little too long, however, for on the way to the church the mother realized that she was in a very dangerous predicament. Mary was losing her mind!

As soon as Mary got out of the car, she started shouting, "I'm not going in there!" Her mother tried to calm her, but Mary was furious. She turned and ran into traffic. Naturally, her mother was extremely disturbed, but I assured her that we could take dominion over this demon and command Mary to return. We did not phone the police; we called on Jesus instead. And sure enough, Mary returned in ten minutes. But she still refused to enter the church.

"Mary," I said in a stern voice, "I command you in the name of Jesus to go inside." And immediately she obeyed.

Once we were inside, I commanded her to enter the office. Then I commanded her to sit down. She was very obedient to every command. I was learning in a practical way that we do indeed have power over the enemy.

Her mother explained to me that Mary often became very violent and might try to push her hands through glass windows. Having been warned about this, I began to command these insane demons to come out of her. We engaged in a long battle, possibly because her mother was present and was not exercising real faith.

After about an hour, Mary uttered some terrible screams as some demons came out of her. At that point, however, other demons became greatly agitated. Mary rose to her feet, intending to push her hands through the glass windows. I remembered that a punch to the solar plexus would knock the wind out of a person temporarily. To stop her self-destructive behavior, I gave her a sharp blow in this area, and she immediately collapsed back into a chair and began screaming. I am neither recommending this treatment nor defending my actions, but in this case it worked.

Mary calmed down somewhat but obviously was out of her mind and still greatly agitated. It was now about 2:00 a.m. on Sunday morning, and we decided to take her back to the mental hospital.

"He'll never arrive," she growled. "I'll jab my cigarette in his neck while he is driving."

As we started, I again rebuked the spirits and commanded them to be silent. In a short time Mary fell asleep beside her mother in the back seat. My wife rode with me in the front seat and prayed continually. Soon, we safely returned her to the hospital.

The next day, Mary exhibited the worst spell of raging insanity she had ever had. For her own safety and the protection of others, orderlies placed her in a special padded room. Interestingly enough, Mary never suffered another attack after this one. The demons had yielded to our authority. The last we saw of Mary some years later, she was a counselor in a Billy Graham Crusade.

DELEGATED AUTHORITY

I was not surprised that the demons obeyed our commands. When Jesus sent out His twelve disciples, He commissioned them to *"heal the sick, cleanse the lepers, raise the dead, cast out demons"* (Matthew 10:8). Later Jesus also sent out seventy others two by two into every city and place where He intended to go. (See Luke 10:1.)

When they returned from their first missionary journey, the disciples exclaimed with joy, *"Lord, even the demons are subject to us in Your name"* (Luke 10:17). After hearing this good report, Jesus gave a wonderful promise to His disciples. In fact, this promise will strengthen any believer who engages in warfare against the enemy:

> *Behold, I give you the authority to trample on serpents and scorpions, and over all the power of the enemy, and nothing shall by any means hurt you. Nevertheless do not rejoice in this, that the spirits are subject to you, but rather rejoice because your names are written in heaven.*   (verses 19–20)

God's Word assures us that we can cast out demons in His name, and they will not hurt us, for He has given us complete *power* or *authority* over all the power of the devil.

Cases of anemia, asthma, high blood pressure, colitis, and heart trouble have positively been healed by commanding the spirits of infirmity to leave the body, which they do with open manifestations. Some even see "dark shadows" leave them and feel a tremendous sense of relief.

CARTWHEELS IN CHURCH

One day a lady visited our church in Toronto. She had heard our radio broadcast and was fascinated by the healing power of God in our midst. She suffered from degeneration of the spine, which would lead ultimately to being confined to a wheel chair.

Because this woman was an accomplished swimmer and swimming instructor, she was greatly concerned about the outcome of her life. I took dominion over the destructive spirit of infirmity that was at work in her spine, and immediately she received heating.

Quite understandably, this miracle of healing completely changed her whole understanding of New Testament Christianity. This woman wanted to share her newfound faith with her daughter who had severely injured her ankle doing gymnastics at school. The girl had been taking cortisone for some months to kill the pain, but her ankle hadn't improved.

One day Gail came to church, limping and carrying a cane. At the end of the service when everyone else had gone, she remained behind with her mother and shyly asked for prayer. Naturally, I agreed but was greatly surprised when she asked, "Can I do a hand spin after prayer?"

"Cartwheels in church?" I asked, laughing. "Why not, if Jesus is in the act!"

We laid hands on Gail and prayed in faith. Then, without further ado, she turned on her hands and feet *in church*, proving that Jesus had healed her. That experience completely changed her whole life, and she and her mother soon received the baptism in the Holy Spirit. Later on she was delivered from other emotional problems, and finally married my son Stephen. Gail graduated from the University of Toronto with a degree in physical education.

What a story! From my radio broadcast to a bride for my son. We never know what the Lord has in store for those who love Him.

CONFESSION, DELIVERANCE, AND HEALING

Another example of this power over demons concerns the mother-in-law of my oldest son. David married a fine Christian girl from Northern Ireland. Unfortunately, Genevieve's mother suffered from bursitis and ever-worsening arthritis in her right arm. In fact, she had been unable to raise her arm for three years. She knew nothing of divine deliverance, but Genevieve asked me to visit her and pray for her mother's debilitating condition.

I discovered that this kind Irish lady couldn't lift her arms very much. Even her hands were knotted and full of pain. She was able to get about only with much difficulty. Obviously, she would eventually be confined to a wheelchair if God didn't intervene.

I explained that my prayer would be different from that which she had previously known. I was not going to ask Jesus to heal her, but I would pray the way He told His disciples to pray. I also explained that in certain diseases, self-examination is often necessary to see if criticism, grumbling, or self-pity is a hindrance to healing. If these sins have taken root in the heart of an afflicted person, they must be confessed and forsaken. This she did.

Then she sat down, and I began to rebuke the binding spirits in Jesus' name. As I continued to take authority in the situation, she broke into a sweat and exclaimed, "I've never heard anyone pray like that before!"

I continued praying this way for about ten minutes. Sensing that a work of healing had begun, I told her to lift her arm above her head. She found this very painful, so I gently helped her, and together we got the arm up. The effort left her crying with pain and sweating profusely. Despite the difficult beginning, by the time I left her home she was able to raise her arm above her head. All the pain had left her hands, and she was able to move them freely.

What had happened? I had cast out a spirit of bondage that was binding her joints. This happens in hundreds of cases of arthritis. Now this lady testifies to everyone about the power of God and demonstrates her healing. Oh, the glorious liberty of the children of God! (See Romans 8:21.)

NEW TESTAMENT PATTERNS

The ministry of deliverance was quite obvious in the early church after Pentecost. Philip, the evangelist, was credited with working miracles.

> *And the multitudes with one accord heeded the things spoken by Philip, hearing and seeing the miracles which he did. For unclean spirits, crying with a loud voice, came out of many who were possessed; and many who were paralyzed and lame were healed.* (Acts 8:6–7)

Was there just one way to accomplish deliverance in the life of an afflicted person? No! God moved through the apostle Paul in ways that were previously unheard of:

> *Now God worked unusual miracles by the hands of Paul, so that even handkerchiefs or aprons were brought from his body to the sick, and the diseases left them and the evil spirits went out of them.* (Acts 19:11–12)

Other Scriptural examples exist, but we want to focus on *today*. The ministry of casting out evil spirits is a glorious reality *today*. We have witnessed many wonderful deliverances. People have been set free from suicide demons, epileptic demons, arthritic demons, cancer demons, insane demons, asthma demons, foul demons, sex demons, religious demons, and even spirits of fear and jealousy.

These have frequently come out crying with a loud voice, sometimes accompanied by vomitings, spittings, coughings, and writhings. Demons have argued back and refused to come out, but ultimately have obeyed the authority that God gives to His people. It is impossible to classify all these cases, but they all come out at the command of faith *in the name of the Lord Jesus*.

Deliverance is always certain, although it can be delayed and take a period of time. In fact, you may have to engage in more than one period of spiritual warfare before final deliverance is obtained for the victim. But victory is certain.

SET FREE FROM LUST

One beautiful deliverance took place when my good friend, Dr. Russell Meade, of Chicago Bible College, brought a young college graduate for prayer.

This young man had a great need. Without going into unwholesome details, it is sufficient to say that he was bound by a spirit of lust. Naturally, I asked if he was married, and he replied that he was. Certainly, it would be a very unpleasant thing for a wife to have a husband bound by a lust spirit, and so I asked no more questions. I commanded the spirit of lust to come out in Jesus' name. Immediately, we saw the familiar choking ejection through the throat. After ten minutes all deliverance ceased, and by his countenance I knew he had been set free.

Some months later we met Dr. Meade in Chicago, and he referred to this young man. Apparently his wife had approached Dr. Meade and asked, "Where did you take my husband?"

"To Toronto," he said, "to Brother Whyte's church."

"Well, what did you do?" she inquired.

"We prayed for him," he replied.

"Well," she said, "I don't know what you did, but I would like you to know that I have a completely changed husband." A wife should know, shouldn't she?

Thousands are bound by a spirit of lust. This tormenting demon takes many beastly forms and shackles many with misery. But this is the day of the visitation of God's love. You *can* be delivered.

WHAT ABOUT YOU?

If you believe that the Lord Jesus Christ was anointed to proclaim *"the opening of the prison to those who are bound"* (Isaiah 61:1), we urge you to stand on Jesus's promise, *"In My name they will cast out demons"* (Mark 16:17). Put away timidity and uncertainty, knowing that *"nothing shall by any means hurt you"* (Luke 10:19).

We must remember that the ministry of deliverance requires faith. Some experimenting, unbelieving Jews experienced disastrous results when they tried to cast out demons by using the name of Jesus without faith. (See Acts 19:13–16.)

Before beginning this ministry, cover yourself by faith in the precious blood of Jesus and keep under its shadow. Enter the battle with the full gospel armor. You don't need to shout at demons; they hear quite well and will obey you. Your faith will rise as never before as you behold the wonderful deliverances that can be wrought today in the mighty name of Jesus.

PART TWO:
QUESTIONS AND ANSWERS

7

DEMONS AND DELIVERANCE

1. WHAT IS A DEMON?

The word *demon* comes from the Greek *daimon*, which means "an evil spirit." *Daimon*, in turn, comes from a root which means "a shadow." Satan, the supreme commander of all demons, sends these evil spirits upon people to bring shadows—darknesses—over the spirit of man.

Anyone who cannot believe in spirits will certainly have trouble believing in God. Beginning in Genesis, Scripture teaches that personal spirits exist. First, the Spirit of God Himself *"moved upon the face of the waters"* (Genesis 1:2 KJV). The same Spirit was breathed into lifeless Adam, and *"man became a living being"* (Genesis 2:7).

Many other references to the Spirit (or breath) of God refer to a *personal* Being. If the Spirit of God is a personal Being, then so are all other spirits.

FALLEN ANGELS

Demons are actually fallen angels. One-third of all the angels were expelled from heaven because of the original rebellion of Satan against Jesus Christ. Let's examine the scriptural basis for their origin.

> *And another sign appeared in heaven: behold, a great, fiery red dragon…. His tail drew a third part of the stars [angels] of heaven, and threw them to the earth.* (Revelation 12:3–4)

> *And war broke out in heaven: Michael and his angels fought with the dragon; and the dragon and his angels fought, but they did not prevail, nor was a place found for them in heaven any longer. So the great dragon was cast out, that*

119

serpent of old, called the Devil and Satan, who deceives the whole world; he was
cast to the earth, and his angels were cast out with him.   (Revelation 12:7–9)

The rebellious angels were cast down to the earth as disembodied spirits. And they are still here—whether we believe they are or not!

Certain liberal theologians have dismissed the reality of demons by the "accommodation theory." Since the common people superstitiously believed that demons caused sickness, Jesus "accommodated" Himself to their superstitions. Not wanting to upset them in their simplicity, He "went along with them," and cast out demons that really didn't exist! Anyone who believes the Bible to be the Word of God cannot possibly accept this theory.

Evangelical theologians generally accept biblical statements about Satan— although some of them fail to understand that Satan *maintains* his curse upon humanity through his hordes of demons. Satan finds this necessary because he is not omnipresent, as the Spirit of God is. But Satan has no shortage of help. The number of wicked, fallen spirits swarming on earth cannot be counted. They swarm like flies. In fact, the name Beelzebub, which is often applied to Satan, means "the lord of flies."

For the sake of simplicity, let us state that blessings come from God by His Holy Spirit, and cursings come from Satan by his unholy spirits. To fail to recognize demons is to fail to recognize the fundamental reason for the sufferings of humanity.

2. HOW DOES A PERSON COME UNDER THE INFLUENCE OF DEMONS?

Demonic influence occurs in many ways. In certain cases, people have been born with demons. Years passed before I was persuaded by events and the Holy Spirit that an infant could be born with an evil spirit in him. Initially that thought seemed to be preposterous and revolting.

But so strong was the testimony of the Scriptures that the Lord is a jealous God, *"visiting the iniquity of the fathers upon the children to the third and fourth generations"* (Exodus 20:5), that I began to look into the matter more closely.

I found many young babies who were extremely irritable and frequently wore out their mothers. Only when we prayed for them, they were delivered. Babies and young children rarely have any noticeable reactions during deliverance. The demon probably has not sunk deeply into the personality of the child, and therefore yields easily to an authoritative command in the name of the Lord.

Demons may also enter young children. Many adults have testified that a terribly frightening experience as a young child gave opportunity for the evil spirit to come in. Having entered, the spirit will not leave readily, especially when a person waits fifty years before seeking deliverance.

During this period of time, the spirit digs in more and more tenaciously and may bring other symptoms such as fear, pains, arthritis, and stomach disorders. To prevent such demonic attacks in childhood, Christian parents should ask God's protection for their children each night and ask for a covering of the blood of Jesus.

OPEN TO OPPRESSION

Obviously, if a person gives place to the devil, as in drinking alcohol to excess or taking illicit drugs, a door may be opened for a wicked spirit to enter.

Any tampering with the occult—any "playful" experimentation with Ouija boards, card playing, fortune telling, reading horoscopes, or the more obviously sinful practices of yoga, hypnotism, or spiritist seances—almost certainly exposes a person to demon oppression. Oppression, in turn, leads to obsession, and may ultimately lead to total possession and death. Those who seek deliverance should destroy all idols and occult literature in their homes.

Ephesus was filled with many idol worshipers who were converted through the preaching of the apostle Paul and the special miracles that God worked through him. How did these new believers forsake their former way of life?

And many who had believed came confessing and telling their deeds. Also, many of those who had practiced magic brought their books together and burned them in the sight of all.   (Acts 19:18–19)

AVOID BACKSLIDING

Some Christians open themselves to demonic attack by backsliding. If a Christian backslides or grows cold in his allegiance to Christ, Satan first tempts him to do wrong. If he sins, he opens himself for a spirit to enter and take control. The spirit doesn't come in immediately for God is very merciful. But if sin is continually indulged in and not forsaken after professed conversion, then such a person is wide open to demonic oppression in its many forms.

One classic case I dealt with many years ago involved a man who was delivered of suicide demons, which made a great noise as they came out. This man later backslid and became a homosexual. He returned to the Lord, weeping and confessing his sin; but by this time seven other spirits had entered in. (See Matthew 12:45.)

Once again he was completely delivered. The spirits named themselves without my asking them to do so. It was a real give-away of information on their part. Afterwards, this brother told me he had no power to stop these spirit voices speaking through him. But this time he was permanently delivered. This should be a very great lesson to all Christians to avoid backsliding.

3. HOW CAN YOU KNOW WHEN YOU HAVE A DEMON?

Any person who is periodically attacked by a compulsion to act in a way that is contrary to his basic nature and alien to his own personality should suspect demon activity.

Whereas God visits mankind by His Spirit, Satan visits mankind by sending his demons. The result of such a demonic visitation is almost unbelievable. The object of attack demonstrates behavior that "can't be him." It isn't. Actually, the personality of the demon spirit manifests through him.

Such a person may be himself at times but sooner or later reverts to strange behavior that is totally uncharacteristic of him. Another name for this problem is "split personality," or *schizophrenia*. Seeing that schizophrenia could be caused by demonic interference was quite a revelation to me!

Spirits of infirmity may cause weakness or sickness in the human body. Spirits of lust incite people to commit adultery, homosexuality, or similar deviations.

COMPULSIVE BEHAVIOR

Whatever the manifestation, knowing that we can really bring pleasure to demon spirits by allowing them the use of our bodies for their own purposes should cause us considerable horror. What does Scripture say about our responsibility to consecrate our bodies to the Lord?

> *Or do you not know that your body is the temple of the Holy Spirit who is in you, whom you have from God, and you are not your own? For you were bought at a price; therefore glorify God in your body and in your spirit, which are God's.*
> (1 Corinthians 6:19–20)

> *For this is the will of God, your sanctification: that you should abstain from sexual immorality; that each of you should know how to possess his own vessel in sanctification and honor.*
> (1 Thessalonians 4:3–4)

If we are plagued by compulsive behavior or demonic oppression, we should confess our sins and submit ourselves to deliverance. Jesus came to break Satan's bondages and to proclaim release to captives. In the authority of His name, we can experience power over oppression.

4. WHAT IS DELIVERANCE?

Deliverance is the practice of expelling demons by an authoritative command in the name of Jesus. If you have a demon or suspect that you have one, I strongly recommend that you submit yourself to the ministry of deliverance. Ask a man or woman of

God to cast the demon out in the name of Jesus Christ—after you have professed that Jesus Christ is your Savior and that you want to be rid of that particular evil spirit.

In general, the ministry of deliverance can best be explained as a forceful, commanding prayer given in the name of Jesus against sickness of spirit, mind, or body. Man is an inseparable trinity made up of body, soul, and spirit. If he is under attack in one area, he often feels the reaction in all three areas.

In the past, the church has generally confined itself to a simple prayer of petition, asking God, through His Son Jesus, to heal, restore, and deliver—and many wonderful answers have been granted; but many who received prayer were *not* delivered.

WHO IS TO CAST OUT DEMONS?

Did Jesus instruct His disciples to ask *Him* to cast out demons? Let's look at who was supposed to minister deliverance to the oppressed.

> *These twelve Jesus sent out and commanded them, saying: …Heal the sick, cleanse the lepers, raise the dead, cast out demons. Freely you have received, freely give.* (Matthew 10:5, 8)

Jesus commanded *them* to heal the sick and cast out devils! They were expected to exercise their delegated authority in Christ.

Similarly, the apostle James instructed the elders of the churches to pray *over* the sick, not *for* the sick.

> *Is anyone among you sick? Let him call for the elders of the church, and let them pray over him, anointing him with oil in the name of the Lord. And the prayer of faith will save the sick, and the Lord will raise him up.* (James 5:14–15)

The word "over" suggests that the one who prays *takes dominion over* the sickness and commands it to leave in the authority of Christ. The same kind of command is to be issued when we are dealing with demons. When this is done, the results that follow are often startling.

5. CAN ANYBODY CAST OUT DEMONS?

No. Casting out demons is no parlor game for the curious. In fact, tangling with demons can be quite dangerous if you are not properly qualified.

What are the qualifications? Primarily, that you believe in Jesus Christ as your Lord and Savior and trust in His power. Jesus said, "*These signs will follow* **those who believe**: *In My name they will cast out demons*" (Mark 16:17).

No human being has the power to cast out demons without Christ. Therefore, be very sure that Jesus Christ abides in you. If He is in you, you are more than a conqueror through His power and His name. (See Romans 8:37.) Any born-again Christian can cast out demons.

I am fully aware that the word "exorcist" has been used outside of Christian circles. Witch doctors often try to drive evil spirits out of people, but this must not be confused with Christian deliverance. No matter what a witch doctor might claim, he cannot cast out demons.

> *How can Satan cast out Satan? If a kingdom is divided against itself, that kingdom cannot stand. And if a house is divided against itself, that house cannot stand. And if Satan has risen up against himself, and is divided, he cannot stand, but has an end.* (Mark 3:23–26)

NO OTHER POWER

Some spiritist mediums claim power to expel demons. This is impossible. Sometimes, though, they persuade the demon to go into temporary hiding, and the person who has been "exorcised" by a medium thinks that he has been set free. But, sooner or later, the demon manifests himself again, usually with worse effects than before. No other power drives out demons except the power of Jesus Christ.

What happens if someone who does not know Christ tries to cast out demons? Scripture records an incident where this actually happened.

> *Then some of the itinerant Jewish exorcists took it upon themselves to call the name of the Lord Jesus over those who had evil spirits, saying, "We exorcise you by the Jesus whom Paul preaches." Also there were seven sons of Sceva, a Jewish chief priest, who did so. And the evil spirit answered and said, "Jesus I know, and Paul I know; but who are you?"* (Acts 19:13–15)

These Jewish exorcists had no personal faith in Jesus, but they had observed how the apostle Paul had successfully dealt with demons in the name of Jesus, so they thought they'd try it, too. What happened?

> *Then the man in whom the evil spirit was leaped on them, overpowered them, and prevailed against them, so that they fled out of that house naked and wounded.* (verse 16)

That's what can happen if you start playing at deliverance, but if you know Jesus Christ, you have nothing to fear. Take the authority that is yours, and cast out the demons in Jesus's name!

8

DEMONS AND THE BELIEVER

1. CAN A CHRISTIAN BE POSSESSED BY A DEMON?

The very phrasing of this question is unfortunate. The question is usually asked in a derogatory manner by those who totally reject the idea that a born-again Christian could ever be troubled or afflicted by a demon.

The problem revolves around the use of the word *possessed*, a word that suggests the demon totally inhabits and owns the sufferer with no area free and with free will absolutely blocked.

I do not believe a born-again Christian can be possessed by a demon. The very idea of a Christian who loves the Lord being *owned* and *controlled* by a demon is totally abhorrent and unacceptable. If Christians would abandon the use of this confusing word "possessed" and speak of demon problem in terms of "oppressions," "vexations," or "bindings," believers would avoid a lot of confusion.

The matter may be made even clearer by considering whether a Christian can be totally possessed of the Holy Spirit. From a theoretical point of view, we might be tempted to answer a hasty "yes" based on the following verse:

> Do you not know that your body is the temple of the Holy Spirit who is in you, whom you have from God, and you are not your own? For you were bought at a price. (1 Corinthians 6:19–20)

In a certain sense we are the rightful property of the Holy Spirit, yet even He can only *possess* us in practical terms as we consciously *yield* ourselves to Him.

To speak of any Christian as being totally possessed by the Holy Spirit implies that he is, at all times and in all places, controlled by the Holy Spirit in all that he says and does. But we know by experience that this is not so! Many other factors enter in. The will of the person may cause him to do something quite contrary to the known Word of God. We must not make a Christian a puppet in the hands of God. But suppose we fail to obey God? Is the Holy Spirit then possessing us? He may be in us, but we are not giving Him His rightful place at that moment of disobedience.

In like manner, a demon may trouble or afflict a Christian in any number of ways. But we are not suggesting for a moment that such a Christian is "demon-possessed."

2. IF NOT POSSESSED, IS THERE ANY CHANCE THAT A CHRISTIAN MIGHT "HAVE" A DEMON?

Yes, certainly. But first, let us consider what we mean by the word "have." What do we mean if we "have" a visitor in our home (perhaps an unwelcome one)? What about having a mouse in our home or even a flea in our clothing?

We are not *possessed* by these visitors, but we may be embarrassed by them. We may even be irritated by them and try to get then out of our house or clothing as conveniently as possible.

In like manner, Christians may receive unwelcome demonic visitors. Take one of Jesus' disciples, for instance. Peter started to rebuke the Son of God, no doubt with good intentions, because he could not understand that Jesus *had* to be killed. Jesus replied to him in the same forceful manner as He had replied to Satan in the wilderness: "*Get behind Me, Satan!*" (Mark 8:33).

Peter meant well; he was sincere; but in trying to save Jesus from Calvary, he became an instrument of Satan at that moment. Was Peter "possessed of the devil"? Certainly not. But in his ignorance he gave *place* to the devil, who used his mind and voice.

Some might feel that Jesus was rather unloving by rebuking Peter, but His motive became quite clear when Jesus said to Peter,

> *Satan hath desired to have you, that he may sift you as wheat: but I have prayed for thee, that thy faith fail not.* (Luke 22:31–32 KJV)

Satan was trying to "*have*" Peter, and when Peter gave place to him, Peter "had" Satan. If we entertain Satan in our thoughts or lives, we "have" him. Only as we expel him in the name of Jesus do we get rid of him and his terrible, gripping powers.

Jesus knew that Satan sifted Peter in the same manner that he had sifted Job many years before. The struggle became so intense that Peter, an apostle, openly denied his Lord before a young girl! Despite being a believer, he cursed and lied. Why did he cave in under stress? Because Satan attacked him and Peter gave place to him in his thoughts and words.

After Pentecost, Peter was a changed man. He had repented in bitter tears and learned to resist the devil. He was filled with the Holy Spirit.

DECEIVED AND DEVOURED

Could it be that Satan tries to sift some of us? Why do some Christians feel constrained at times to curse God, or destroy without reason, even to murder or commit adultery? Many a person in a police court has said to the judge, "I don't know why I did it, but something made me." Who is the "something"?

The apostle Paul warned the Corinthian church *"lest Satan should take advantage of us"* (2 Corinthians 2:11)—and we must remember that the Corinthian church was made up of Spirit-filled Christians.

The apostle Paul also warned this church about the possibility of receiving *"another spirit"* (2 Corinthians 11:4 KJV). Obviously, then, Spirit-filled Christians can receive a spirit from Satan. Of course, this could happen only if they deliberately gave place to such a spirit.

The apostle Paul wrote,

> But I fear, lest somehow, as the serpent deceived Eve by his craftiness, **so your minds may be corrupted** from the simplicity that is in Christ.
> (2 Corinthians 11:3)

Corruption of the mind of a Spirit-filled Christian can only be accomplished by demonic invasion. The corruption that comes from Beelzebub, the prince of decay, is implanted in the mind. "Mind corruption" in a Christian is a very serious matter, and a Christian who is under this kind of satanic attack is not helped by being told he "cannot have a demon." He needs counseling and the prayer of deliverance.

Worse than being corrupted is to be devoured by the enemy. Peter, who learned from his experience of being sifted, exhorted the early believers,

> Be sober, be vigilant; because your adversary the devil walks about like a roaring lion, seeking whom he may devour.   (1 Peter 5:8)

The apostle Paul warns us *"that in the latter times some shall depart from the faith, giving heed to seducing spirits, and doctrines of devils"* (1 Timothy 4:1 KJV). Scripture indicates that a spirit can seduce a Christian.

If a man seduces another man's wife, and the once faithful spouse ceases to be faithful, she is obeying another spirit in committing adultery (which is also a spirit). Similarly, Satan may come as a charming personality and literally seduce a believer into spiritual adultery with demons.

If we do not control our fleshly nature and appetites, which are God-given, then Satan will tempt us to yield them to him. We are the ones who control the situation, not Satan. He has no power over one who keeps himself unspotted from the world, the flesh, and the devil. (See 1 John 5:18.)

PHYSICAL AFFLICTIONS

Sometimes, Christians may contact demons that cause terrible physical problems—such as epilepsy. No intelligent person would even suggest that epilepsy was from God, or that God ever intended that any of His children should suffer from such a terrible and embarrassing sickness. But we must not compound distress by suggesting that such a person is demon possessed. This will not help at all.

According to the Scriptures, these foul sicknesses are from Satan. We must recognize his influence in our fight of faith against all sicknesses of mind and body. When the sufferer manifests an attack of epilepsy or some other form of extraordinary behavior, we should recognize that a demon is exercising control upon a certain part of the body and to be dislodged by the prayer of deliverance given in Jesus' name.

One of the first persons to be delivered in our early ministry was a woman who had been experiencing attacks of nocturnal epilepsy. She has been healed ever since. This Christian woman had been dedicated to the Lord since childhood. She certainly was not possessed by a demon. After the commanding prayer of faith, the demon that was *vexing* her left, and she was permanently healed.

Yes, a Christian can "have" a demon, but he can also be set free if he confesses it to the Father and seeks his freedom in Christ.

3. WHERE DOES THE BIBLE SAY THAT A CHRISTIAN CAN HAVE A DEMON?

People who ask such questions often demand that we show them exact chapter and verse to support our beliefs.

Obviously, no quotation in the Bible says, "A Christian *can* have a demon." Neither will you be able to find an exact reference that says, "Thou shalt not smoke marijuana nor take cocaine!"

Actually, Christians in the Bible not only "had" demons, but also had them cast out. Scripture records the story of a woman who had been afflicted for years and was in need of deliverance:

There was a woman who had a spirit of infirmity eighteen years, and was bent over and could in no way raise herself up. But when Jesus saw her, He called her to Him and said to her, "Woman, you are loosed from your infirmity." And

He laid His hands on her, and immediately she was made straight and glorified
God.   (Luke 13:11–13)

Jesus described this woman as *"a daughter of Abraham"* (verse 16), meaning she
was a true believer. She was walking in the faith of Abraham. Scripture does not even
hint that she was guilty of any particular sin. But she had been afflicted by a demon
for eighteen years, even though she was a believer!

FORCED INTO THE OPEN

A Spirit-filled Greek Orthodox priest informed me that all new converts go
through deliverance before being water baptized in his church. This is exactly what
Justin Martyr, Polycarp, Clement, and Iranaeus—the early church fathers—tell us
in their writings. All new converts automatically went through deliverance whether
they asked for it or not. Church leaders dealt with spiritual contamination and filth
before immersing new converts in water.

All those who come for deliverance in our meetings are professing Christians.
Many have already been baptized in the Spirit. Although they praise God in tongues,
bondages may still hinder their lives. In fact, I am inclined to believe that these
demons are often brought to light *because* these people have been baptized in the
Spirit. In other words, the presence of the Holy Spirit stirs up the other spirits that
are in hiding. They are forced into the open by the Spirit of God where they can be
dealt with and cast out in Jesus's name.

4. HOW COULD A DEMON AND THE HOLY SPIRIT DWELL IN THE SAME PERSON AT THE SAME TIME?

This question is based on the assumption that "when Jesus comes in, Satan goes
out." Certain holiness churches teach a "second work of grace," or "sanctification,"
which eradicates all traces of the sin nature in the believer.

Experience contradicts such an extreme doctrine, therefore we are forced to conclude that Christians frequently do things that are not consistent with the life of
Christ *in* them. This does not mean that *every* willful act on the part of a believer is
motivated by a demon; but many Christians *are* cruelly bound and need deliverance.

To say that such people are not believers is ridiculous. How many Christians are
bound by habits? How many demonstrate temper and jealousy? Saying these people
aren't Christians is easier than admitting believers can be troubled by evil spirits.

A well-known and respected minister in Toronto said that a Christian is like a
hotel with many rooms. Only some of the rooms are surrendered, while others are
still filled with spirits other than the Holy Spirit. Jesus only comes in where He is
invited.

Some people take many months or years to realize all is not well in their lives; only after much inner turmoil have they reluctantly sought help. Although the Holy Spirit needed months to convince these people that rooms in their lives were still not filled with God, the prayer of faith brought immediate deliverance.

Upon conviction, they asked Jesus to come into the rooms—but Satan had to be expelled first, with their wills desiring it. We must be wary of a theoretical theology, lest we miss the blessing and remain bound.

SATAN FILLED THEIR HEARTS

The case of Ananias and Sapphira is interesting. Few would dispute that they were members of the apostolic church in Jerusalem. This couple had witnessed great miracles and healings in the first century church. Yet Scripture records that they were influenced by demonic forces to be dishonest in their giving.

> But a certain man named Ananias, with Sapphira his wife, sold a possession. And he kept back part of the proceeds, his wife also being aware of it, and brought a certain part and laid it at the apostles' feet. But Peter said, "Ananias, **why has Satan filled your heart to lie to the Holy Spirit** and keep back part of the price of the land for yourself?" (Acts 5:1–3)

Even though they were Spirit-filled Christians, that did not prevent Satan from filling their hearts. The negative drove out the positive; the unholy drove out the holy; and they died as a result.

We have found by experience that many young people who have experimented with drugs and have been on psychedelic "highs" still suffered torment or mental bondage *after* receiving Jesus as Savior and *after* being baptized in the Holy Spirit. These troubled young people have come to us and asked for deliverance from this bondage. As soon as we have rebuked these tormenting spirits, the demons have responded by coming out.

In our churches today, there are many believers who need deliverance; but the church has not practiced this ministry. In our generation God is restoring the ministry of deliverance to set the oppressed free.

5. IF CHRISTIANS CAN HAVE DEMONS, HOW CAN WE BE SURE THAT ANY CHRISTIAN'S MANIFESTATION OF THE HOLY SPIRIT IS GENUINE?

This question is often asked in particular reference to the manifestation of tongues. Suppose a Christian prays for the baptism in the Holy Spirit and then speaks in tongues. How do we know that this is a genuine working of the Holy Spirit? Couldn't it also be a demonic manifestation?

We need to remember the words of Jesus in reference to the Holy Spirit:

If a son asks for bread from any father among you, will he give him a stone? Or if he asks for a fish, will he give him a serpent instead of a fish? Or if he asks for an egg, will he offer him a scorpion? If you then, being evil, know how to give good gifts to your children, how much more will your heavenly Father give the Holy Spirit to those who ask Him! (Luke 11:11–13)

Jesus clearly said that we need not fear getting something we didn't ask for, or something evil. If you ask for bread, you'll get bread. If you ask for an egg, you'll get an egg. If you ask for the Holy Spirit, you'll get the Holy Spirit. No one has ever asked the Father for the Holy Spirit and received an unholy spirit. God is faithful and good, and He'll give you what you ask for.

Do you think, then, that a Christian could earnestly ask for the power of the Spirit and receive an unholy, devil-inspired tongue? Certainly not!

I cannot emphasize too strongly the importance of the blood of Jesus. What right have we to claim any of the blessings of Christ apart from the covering of His blood? The person who asks for the baptism of the Spirit should also say, "I plead the blood of Jesus." What other plea do we have? How else can we presume to ask God for blessings we don't deserve? But if you plead the blood, you can be assured of protection from the deception of demons, and you'll receive a genuine baptism in the Spirit.

BY THEIR FRUITS

We do find, however, that some people who receive the baptism in the Spirit may still have a latent evil spirit in hiding, waiting to be cast out. The incoming of the Holy Spirit may not always drive out the unwelcome spirits, although demons do sometimes leave as the Holy Spirit enters.

In cases where demons remain in hiding, how are we to know when that Christians "spiritual manifestations" are genuine? Very simply.

You will know them by their fruits. Do men gather grapes from thornbushes or figs from thistles? Even so, every good tree bears good fruit, but a bad tree bears bad fruit. (Matthew 7:16–17)

Similarly, the Holy Spirit brings forth holy fruit, but an evil spirit brings forth evil fruit.

If a particular manifestation is good and glorifies Christ, we may be assured that the Holy Spirit is in control.

6. WAS PAUL'S THORN IN THE FLESH A DEMON?

This question is a real hot potato! To many, the very thought that the apostle Paul could have "had a demon" is so revolting that it cannot be entertained. To get around this difficulty, many Bible teachers say that Paul had defective eyesight, caused by his ill treatment when he was stoned at Lystra. (See Acts 14:19.)

The difficulty is most easily resolved, it seems to me, by looking at the passage and accepting what it very plainly says.

> *And lest I should be exalted above measure by the abundance of the revelations, a thorn in the flesh was given to me, a **messenger of Satan to buffet me**, lest I should be exalted above measure.* (2 Corinthians 12:7)

The grammatical construction in this passage is very interesting. Anyone who understands the most simple principles of English construction knows that the words in italics "*...a messenger of Satan to buffet me*" are used *in opposition* to the words, "*thorn in the flesh.*" In other words, the second expression explains the first. The apostle Paul explains his thorn in the flesh by saying it was "*the messenger of Satan to buffet me.*"

The word "*messenger*" is a translation of the Greek word *aggelos*, which is usually translated "angel." Since demons are nothing more than fallen angels, we can conclude that Paul's thorn in the flesh was a demon who continually buffeted (struck, battered) him.

This "battering" is probably more literal than most people think. At Lystra, the apostle Paul was stoned until the people thought he was dead. Paul also describes his "batterings" in the following passage:

> *In labors more abundant, in stripes above measure, in prisons more frequently, in [at the point of] deaths often. From the Jews five times I received forty stripes minus one. Three times I was beaten with rods; once was I stoned; three times I was shipwrecked; a night and a day I have been in the deep; in journeys often, in perils of waters, in perils of robbers, in perils of my own countrymen, in perils of the Gentiles, in perils in the city, in perils in the wilderness, in perils in the sea, in perils among false brethren; in weariness and toil, in sleeplessness often, in hunger and thirst, in fastings often, in cold and nakedness.* (2 Corinthians 11:23–27)

God permitted all these experiences of adversity because of the abundance of the revelations given to Paul, to *keep him humble*. The agent of this distress and woe was an angel of Satan—a powerful demon.

Have you ever wondered why things sometimes seem to go wrong when you are serving the Lord to the best of your ability? King David was hunted and persecuted despite his integrity and uprightness before God. How did David view his circumstances?

> *Many are the afflictions of the righteous, but the* LORD *delivers him out of them all.* (Psalm 34:19)

Who sends these afflictions? Satan afflicted Job—but only with God's permission. Are we any different? Was Paul any exception?

Apparently, persecution is one kind of demonic oppression that no Christian can avoid. But we need not be depressed about it. Every Christian can claim an inner deliverance from demonic depression—Paul obviously had that kind of deliverance and was full of the joy of the Lord.

7. HOW CAN A CHRISTIAN RESIST DEMONIC INFLUENCES?

Resisting the enemy is both positional and practical. Scripture records that "*he who has been born of God keeps himself, and the wicked one does not touch him*" (1 John 5:18).

First, notice that the verse pertains to "*he who has been born of God.*" By spiritual rebirth (as taught by Jesus in John 3:3–5 and John 1:12), a sinner becomes elevated to sonship in Jesus. He becomes an adopted son of God—a member of the royal family of heaven. His elder brother is Jesus, and all other born-again Christians are his brethren.

Second, we are told that this child of God "keeps himself." He accomplishes this by keeping himself clean and spotless from the world, thinking and practicing pure thoughts, and keeping himself under the blood of Jesus.

Then, providing he fulfills part two, he is in a position to rebuke the devil, resist him, and put him to flight. Not only can the wicked one not touch him, but Satan will flee from his presence for he manifests the sweet savor of Christ. (See 2 Corinthians 2:15.)

Spiritually speaking, the believer smells like the Rose of Sharon and the Lily of the Valley. All his garments smell of myrrh and aloes and cassia. As Satan's "odor" is completely offensive to the Christian, in like manner the Christian's sweet "fragrance" is offensive to Satan; it reminds him of the total defeat he suffered when Jesus shed His blood on the cross to cleanse us from sin.

While the born-again Christian rejoices that "the wicked one does not touch him," let me quickly point out that this promise is conditional on his obedience. Some people try to hide behind this verse and claim that Satan cannot touch them or oppress them. Unfortunately, some Christians are professing (theologically) a freedom that they do not have in practical reality.

ARE YOU SUBMITTED TO GOD?

Our churches are full of disobedient Christians whom Satan has cruelly bound. Submitting to deliverance to rid yourself of affliction or oppression is far better than acting as though bondage does not exist in your life. Once you are at peace on the inside, you will then be able to resist the demonic attacks that come to you from the outside.

James gives us an important key to resisting demonic influences. He says,

Therefore submit to God. Resist the devil and he will flee from you.

(James 4:7)

If your heart is not yielded to God, you will have difficulty resisting the enemy's temptations and oppression.

Peter had been sifted and used as a tool of Satan. What advice did he pass on to other believers who would face similar battles with such a cunning enemy?

Humble yourselves under the mighty hand of God, that He may exalt you in due time.... Be sober, be vigilant; because your adversary the devil walks about like a roaring lion, seeking whom he may devour. Resist him, steadfast in the faith.

(1 Peter 5:6, 8–9)

If we first humble ourselves before God and then before our brothers and sisters in Christ, we are in a position of strength. Remember that God actively opposes the proud. (See 1 Peter 5:5.) Without humility, we will be quite unable to overcome Satan. We are warned that he desires to "devour" us—so we need to be careful to resist the devil with all our might.

While we have no strength of our own to fight the devil, we can claim the strength of Christ. We can say as the apostle Paul said, "*I can do all things through Christ who strengthens me*" (Philippians 4:13). With strength like that, the devil is a defeated foe!

8. HOW TO KEEP FROM GIVING A "PLACE" TO THE DEVIL?

First, recognize that you can have practically no resistance at all to demons without Jesus. The apostle Paul said, "*I can do all things through Christ who strengthens me.*"

The natural man, without Christ, is spiritually weak and highly susceptible to infestation by demons. If Christ is not dwelling in him, a natural man can't do much about fighting off demons. If you do not know Christ, I urge you to turn from sin to

Christ, and receive Him as your Lord and Savior. If you ask Him to come into your life, He will keep His promise and come in.

> *Behold, I stand at the door and knock. If anyone hears My voice and opens the door, I will come in to him.*   (Revelation 3:20)

But that is only the first step. Once you have received Christ and become a born-again Christian, then you must make it a habit to give no place to the devil. (See Ephesians 4:27.) You might as well face the fact that any part of your body can become a place for a demon. A demon will take anything he can get!

If we yield to our fleshly nature and give a hand, an eye, or an ear, a demon spirit with a particular characteristic may take hold of that particular part and occupy it. The spirit of lust may occupy the eye, for instance, and you may find yourself compelled to stare with lust at pornographic magazines or X-rated movies. The demon may compel you, even against your better judgment, to continue more and more in these practices.

One particular scriptural exhortation is certainly worthy of close attention.

> *He who has been born of God* [that is, the born-again Christian] *keeps himself, and the wicked one does not touch him.*   (1 John 5:18)

"Keeping ourselves" means steady abstinence from the wickedness of the world, continual walking in the Spirit, and keeping ourselves consciously under the blood of Christ.

By following the Holy Spirit, we can receive the strength to maintain continual fellowship with Jesus. Anybody who maintains that kind of fellowship with Him will certainly not give place to a demon!

9

KINDS OF DEMONS

1. ARE THERE DEMONS THAT CAUSE SICKNESS?

Indeed there are. The real forces behind our physical world are spiritual in nature. God spoke matter into existence. He framed the worlds so that *"the things which are seen were not made of things which are visible"* (Hebrews 11:3). He created atoms and molecules. Our bodies are *"fearfully and wonderfully made"* (Psalm 139:14). Only when demonic forces invade our marvelous, God-created bodies are we afflicted with mental and physical sicknesses.

One passage of Scripture makes this especially clear.

> *God anointed Jesus of Nazareth with the Holy Spirit and with power, who went about doing good and healing all who were oppressed by the devil, for God was with Him.* (Acts 10:38)

In Greek, the word translated as *"oppressed"* means "to overcome" or "to overpower" and suggests that the people healed by Jesus were set free from their sicknesses because an "overpowering" spirit left at the command of faith.

Look again. The verse says Jesus healed all that were oppressed (overcome) by the devil. In other words, Satan was the agent who caused their sicknesses. We must remember that Satan is the supreme commander of all demonic forces. As he gives the orders, his swarms of demons will invade, attack, and oppress human beings—and that includes afflicting us with sickness, disease, discouragement, depression, anxiety, and despair.

THE REAL CAUSE

The sick person, not understanding the cause of his condition, observes his symptoms and seeks medical treatment. I praise God for doctors, but Christians should understand that the real cause of some sickness is neither mental nor physical—it's spiritual. That's why Jesus rebuked the fever in Peter's mother-in-law. (See Luke 4:38–39.) As soon as the spirit behind the fever was expelled, the fever left and she was healed.

The chief objection to this teaching is the automatic revulsion that comes upon a Christian when someone suggests that a demon has invaded him and put a sickness on him. No one likes to hear bad news. Discovering we might have cancer or some other horrible disease is bad enough. But to be informed that we may have an infestation of invisible, living spirits in our body is so repulsive that we mentally reject it as being impossible. But rejection of the idea doesn't eject the demons!

I read of a missionary in South America who became so depressed that she left the mission field with chronic ill health. The Spirit of God finally revealed the cause of her problem: demons. She decided to fast. Every half hour she would kneel down, rebuke Satan and his demons, and claim victory. She continued doing this for one whole day. At the end of the day, she was totally delivered and restored to complete health.

2. WHEN A PERSON IS SICK, SHOULD YOU ALWAYS CAST OUT A DEMON?

God never planned for His people to be sick! In that sense, we can say that Satan is responsible for sickness. Who would think of blaming it on God?

Latent in the human body are natural recuperative powers. Tissue renews itself, and antibodies work to repulse the incursion of germs—but Satan is ever trying to prevent these processes. Prayer is very effective in these instances.

When any sickness persists over a period of time and does not respond to fervent prayer, we should consider casting out the binding spirit. This is true in cases of arthritis, bursitis, and other sicknesses of a similar nature. Constriction of the heart muscles, which we call angina of the heart, may well be caused by the activity of a binding spirit.

Are congenital defects always the result of sin? Scripture reveals God's perspective on just such an incident.

> Now as Jesus passed by, He saw a man who was blind from birth. And His disciples asked Him, saying, "Rabbi, who sinned, this man or his parents, that he was born blind?" Jesus answered, "Neither this man or his parents sinned, but that the works of God should be revealed in him." (John 9:1–3)

We are often asked to explain the case of the man born blind whom Jesus healed. The disciples assumed incorrectly that he or his parents must have sinned, but Jesus told them that the weakness existed so that He might reveal the healing power of God in restoring the man's sight.

We must not hide behind this story and believe that every congenital weakness or deformity is the will of God because it's not. The consequences of our forefathers' sins are still passed on to third and fourth generations. Neither can we say that the man "had a demon" because he was blind, but we could correctly say that Satan was the original cause of the blindness.

But even though Satan caused this man's condition, Jesus did not cast out a demon. He simply performed a creative miracle and gave the man his sight.

In like manner, when we are asked to pray for sick people, we do not always "cast out the devil." Instead, we often pray for a miracle, and God mercifully responds with astonishing signs and wonders.

3. IF A PERSON IS SET FREE FROM A DEMON THAT HAS CAUSED SICKNESS, SHOULD HE IMMEDIATELY GIVE UP ALL MEDICATION?

The whole ministry of praying for the sick is very closely connected with the ministry of deliverance. Jesus *"cast out the spirits with his word, and healed all that were sick"* (Matthew 8:16 KJV). In many cases where people suffer from physical maladies, the spirit of infirmity behind the physical manifestation can be instantly cast out.

But even after deliverance removes the primary cause of infirmity, certain symptoms may remain. The pain and soreness may still be very evident, the inflammation may still be visible, the headaches and the actual germs or viruses may still be active.

If such is the case, what should the sufferer do? Should he give up all medication in evidence of his faith? Not necessarily—and certainly not without divine guidance in the matter.

Many have discovered, to their sorrow, the terrible results of plunging ahead without direction from God. In cases of diabetes, it would be pure presumption to give up taking insulin until the pancreas reverts to its normal production.

Even after a healing, restoring the body tissues and readjusting to good health may require time. Taking medication during this period is not wrong, especially where viruses are still active. If the healing has been so extensive that medication is not needed, that fact will soon become evident.

Some believers may find that an instantaneous healing removes all their symptoms. Others may experience a more progressive restoration to full health. In fact, this latter circumstance is far more prevalent than the instantaneous miracle.

WHAT ABOUT TAKING MEDICINE?

Taking medication is not a sin. When Hezekiah was sick, he was healed—but apparently with the help of medication.

> Then Isaiah said, "Take a lump of figs." So they took and laid it on the boil, **and he recovered.** (2 Kings 20:7)

Isaiah the prophet *ordered* this medication to draw out the poison from the boil.

Many would ask, "Why did Isaiah resort to medicine after he prayed?" Apparently because this was the revealed will of God in that situation. God told Isaiah to tell the king that He would heal him—but not without the fig remedy.

In some cases, such a procedure may be within the will of God for us today. The Word of God clearly states, "*they* [believers] *will lay hands on the sick, and they will recover*" (Mark 16:18). But this does not rule out the use of God-given medication. To refuse to take medication *can* be presumption, not faith.

Christians who scorn taking medication point to King Asa, who died because he went to the physicians. This is really a misstatement, for King Asa had been previously visited by the prophet Hanani, who rebuked him for trusting in his Syrian allies, instead of trusting in the living God. King Asa was so enraged that he put Hanani in prison—hardly a suitable attitude for receiving healing from the Lord. (See 2 Chronicles 16.)

After Asa rejected the man of God, God rejected Asa. Like Saul who went to a witch for counsel, Asa went to his physicians for help and died. Had Asa been a godly man who received the prayers of Hanani and accepted his correction, he would no doubt have recovered whether he used the services of the medical profession or not.

Seeking help from doctors is not a sin. God has been good to give them an understanding about medicine, and there are many fine Christian doctors who can help us.

WHOM SHOULD WE SEEK?

I believe the proper procedure in cases of mental or physical sickness is clear. First, we are to seek God. Second, if the sickness persists, we ought to also seek the help of the medical profession. I do not recommend seeking a doctor and not seeking God in prayer.

In many cases, the prayer of faith with the laying on of hands *does* bring permanent and instantaneous healing and deliverance, and no further help or medication is necessary. But Jesus Himself said, "*Those who are well have no need of a physician, but those who are sick*" (Matthew 9:12). This seems to be a clear statement supporting the legitimate work of the medical profession, rather than a condemnation.

Many believers who take the extreme position of "no medication and no doctors" must reverse their stance in later years, when the body grows more frail. Some have died because they scorned all medication. Their refusal is not faith—otherwise they would not have died. At best, their extreme position is unwise enthusiasm bordering on presumption; at worst, it is plain fanaticism. God does not get the glory in cases like these.

Many natural curative drugs are found in the vegetation around us. Modern science will often manufacture these drugs synthetically instead of processing them from vegetation. Digitalis, for example, which comes from the foxglove plant, greatly strengthens weak hearts.

In recent years the connection between certain diseases and our lifestyles has come to light. We need to get enough sleep, exercise regularly, and eat a balanced diet. Using common sense and taking preventative measures can greatly reduce our incidence of illness and disease. If we do happen to get sick, we can come to God in faith for the healing He has provided through Jesus Christ.

Long experience has shown me that most people do not have as much faith as they think they have, or should have. They think they insult God by taking medicine. If you have been prayed for and you still carry symptoms, then by all means seek medical advice and get a prescription that can help you. Ultimately, God is the One who will heal you anyway—if you believe.

4. ARE THERE DEMONS THAT CAUSE EMOTIONAL DISTURBANCES, OR ARE SUCH PROBLEMS MERELY PSYCHOLOGICAL?

We must understand that God wants to deal with us as whole people. Thinking of any problem as being psychological rather than spiritual is probably a mistake. It is more likely to be both!

Education has conditioned us to believe that a psychiatrist ought to be consulted for an emotional disturbance. To the humanist, the concept that the primary cause of blessing or cursing is spiritual makes no sense at all.

Doctors examine the body, psychiatrists probe the mind, and ministers deal with the spirit. But some professionals have noticed the relationship between these areas. Spiritual problems can bring on physical problems, and vice versa.

Unfortunately, many ministers work mostly in the intellectual realm, completely neglecting the spirit of man. The church desperately needs men who are "spirit specialists," who can minister to the spiritual needs of the people. If the spirit of man is oppressed by spirits of darkness, then his mind will be dark, his emotions will be disturbed, and his body may even become sick.

Intellectual men may call emotional problems by certain psychological names and try to deal with them on the level of the human mind; but the primary cause is often the operating of in evil spirit in the area of the human spirit, affecting both the emotions and the body.

Many negative emotions come from the working of evil spirits. For instance, *"God has not given us a **spirit** of fear, but of power and of love and of a sound mind"* (2 Timothy 1:7). Just as a spirit of fear can afflict a person with terror or dread, the Holy Spirit can impart attributes of power, love, and a sound mind.

5. ARE THERE CERTAIN KINDS OF DEMONS THAT MAY CONTAMINATE US THROUGH EXPERIMENTATION WITH THE OCCULT?

If a person plays with a skunk, he will most certainly end up smelling like one! Occult involvement always contaminates the spirit.

If a person participates in a spiritist séance, inevitably that person will absorb a measure of evil from the evil spirits present. The Bible calls these spirits *"familiar spirits"* (Deuteronomy 18:11; 1 Samuel 28:7–19 KJV), because they are the pet spirits who work through the medium. These spirits are designated in the Scriptures as being foul or unclean. As soon as such a spirit is contacted, and we act in a friendly way toward it, we come under its malign influence.

Similarly, if we read horoscopes, play with Ouija boards, take part in levitation or table turning, or indulge in any form of water or mineral divining, spiritual contamination begins. It is a spiritual law.

If a parent engages in any regular form of occult involvement, the children of the family may suffer as well. Recently, a British advertiser produced a billboard that showed a pregnant woman smoking. The advertisement warned that her unborn child would almost certainly be contaminated physically and mentally. In like manner, a pregnant woman who contaminates her mind by seeking after evil spirits will almost certainly bring some form of mental or physical contamination to her unborn child.

Spiritual contamination may lead to sickness, mental torments, and disgusting behavior patterns—especially those dealing with erotic sex, homosexuality, and general vulgar acts. Before we can experience deliverance from such bondage, we must confess our sins (even of ignorance), renounce them, and put them under the blood of Jesus. Then the prayer of command can cast out the contaminating demons.

History shows that when people depart from the Christian faith, the vacuum is filled up with other spirits. Heathen nations are full of demons and cruelty. When the Bible was banned from American schools, an open door was made for occult spirits to take over—and now most American high schools have at least one witch!

Our generation is experiencing a heightened interest in the occult. Unless God sends a true New Testament outpouring of the Holy Spirit, Satan will ultimately triumph and destroy many nations. The reverse is coming to pass, however, for God has promised to pour out His Holy Spirit upon all flesh—and that is happening today.

6. ARE THERE DEMONS THAT CAN COME TO US THROUGH OUR ANCESTORS?

Yes, there are, but that's no reason for us to keep them forever! Deliverance is available for all congenital weaknesses that are caused by demons. Such problems generally fall into two categories:

1. Physical abnormalities caused by an unfortunate combination of genes.

2. Emotional or spiritual weaknesses received by heredity.

While we would not suggest that physical malformations or malfunctions are caused directly by demons, some emotional and spiritual weaknesses can be demonic in origin.

Unfortunately, the sins of the parents are often visited upon the children up to the third and fourth generations—that is, from eighty to one hundred years. (See Exodus 20:5.) The rebellion and disobedience of our forefathers are not our fault, but we carry the mental and spiritual scars nevertheless.

Infants of drug-taking mothers often die at birth, or they may need to he kept alive by a small dosage of some lesser drug because they have become addicted in the womb. Women who smoke can give birth to yellow-skinned babies who need a whiff of tobacco to soothe them and cause them to stop crying. They are already addicted. These babies have to be weaned from drugs at birth.

Venereal diseases can be transmitted through the bloodstream to unborn children, terribly affecting the eyes and other vital organs. A child can be born with a spirit of temper or a destroying spirit. The demon is literally transmitted from the woman to the unborn child while yet in the womb.

Many years ago, an experiment was carried out. The children of certain God-fearing parents were followed to see how they would fare in life. Their descendants became clergymen, lawyers, teachers, and people who made a positive contribution to society. Researchers also traced the children and grandchildren of a criminal family for comparison. Their descendants were found to be robbers, sex perverts, racketeers, and unemployables.

If your family history is less than exemplary, is this cause for despair? No! If you have been born with inherited demons, you can take heart in the knowledge that they can be cast out in Jesus' name!

7. COULD THERE BE SUCH A THING AS A "DORMANT DEMON" THAT MIGHT NOT MANIFEST ITSELF UNTIL A CERTAIN TIME IN A PERSON'S LIFE?

We believe that many children born of godless or rebellious parents—especially those who have indulged in forbidden occult practices—are already infested with demons. These demons may remain dormant or manifest themselves in strange behavior only at certain times.

I remember being told of a man who was prayed for in a church in northern Ontario. One of the spirits that was identified was named a "nicotine spirit." When challenged, this spirit was ejected through the throat, accompanied by a strong smell of tobacco. Amazingly, the man had never actually indulged in tobacco smoking!

How could this be? I believe he had a latent demon, which would have completely overpowered him had he given it the slightest toehold. But he resisted the temptation.

Let's look at a passage on temptation and sin.

Blessed is the man who endures temptation; for when he has been approved, he will receive the crown of life which the Lord has promised to those who love Him. Let no man say when he is tempted, "I am tempted by God"; for God cannot be tempted by evil, nor does He Himself tempt anyone. But each one is tempted when he is drawn away by his own desires and enticed. Then, when desire has conceived, it gives birth to sin; and sin, when it is full-grown, brings forth death.

(James 1:12–15)

Notice what James says here. If one gives way to temptation, there is a "conception"—which means "the creation of a new life." If a person has a latent demon, and he yields to temptation, I believe this would actually cause a new demonic life-activity in him—an activity which, like a fetus, would grow, develop, and ultimately be born in that person's life.

The man who had the "nicotine spirit" within him had never yielded to it. But if he had not resisted the temptation to smoke, the nicotine habit would have developed to monster proportions.

A person having a latent spirit within him from birth may be brought up in a disciplined Christian home and ultimately make a decision to become a practicing Christian. He might not discover this demon until many years later. But once discovered, a latent spirit can be cast out.

Even after a person has been delivered from a known, recognized spirit, it may still be possible for other spirits to remain hidden until the Holy Spirit brings them to the surface. Then a second session of deliverance will be necessary. A commanding prayer in the name of Jesus can drive the latent spirit out.

8. ARE SOME DEMONS STRONGER THAN OTHERS?

The Bible teaches that some demons have more authority than others. If several spirits are binding a person, a "captain in charge" may lead the oppression. When delivering a man from suicide, my wife and I had a strong feeling that this demon was the "captain" who remained behind until all the lesser ones were ejected.

Some people use the expression "ruler spirit." This expression is based on the following passage:

> *For we do not wrestle against flesh and blood, but against principalities, against powers, against the rulers of the darkness of this age, against spiritual hosts of wickedness in the heavenly places.* (Ephesians 6:12)

The categories of demons mentioned in this verse include:

1. principalities
2. powers
3. rulers of the darkness of this age
4. wickedness in heavenly places

There are two words in the Greek language for demons that rule nations. One is *daimon*, and the other is *daimonion*. The first word is usually associated with the powerful demons. The second word is a diminutive form denoting the lesser ranks. Those who teach about the existence of "ruler spirits" base their teaching on this passage in Ephesians.

Actually, that considerably weakens the teaching, since the context indicates that the authority of a "ruler spirit" extends to rulers, kings, despotic dictators, or governors. In other words, the work of a "ruler spirit" involves the actual rule of a nation or territory. Hitler or Stalin were no doubt controlled by such "ruler spirits."

While certain demons seem to be stronger than others, it probably is not wise to refer to any demon in the average person as a "ruler spirit." Maybe the thought would be more correct if believers used another word such as "captain" or "sergeant"!

Some teach that the one ministering deliverance must first challenge this "captain spirit" and cast him out, and then his minions will follow meekly after the boss has gone. We must remember, however, that some of these practices and methods were "discovered" in an actual dialogue with demons. Any information gained from demons should be open to serious question!

I do not recommend that we try to compel demons to speak and name themselves. Jesus commanded them, saying, "*Be quiet, and come out of him!*" (Mark 1:25).

Demons are all liars and will use the most nonsensical statements in order to confuse the unwary and the novices in this ministry.

A demon, when challenged, might say, "I am the ruler spirit," thereby boasting of a rank that he does not have—and this statement could be enthusiastically received by those wanting to "prove" they have power to cast out a real, high-ranking demon.

I do not recommend forming doctrines based on the word of a lying spirit. I do not, as a general rule, hold any dialogue with these foul entities. I despise them and you should, too.

9. IS IT SAFE TO LISTEN TO WHAT DEMONS SAY?

Although some people who practice the ministry of deliverance often get into arguments with demons, I see no reason for this. Attempting a conversation with demons is neither good nor scriptural.

Once an evil spirit voluntarily told us the correct number of demons left in a despondent, suicidal man—and they were all successfully cast out. But we must remember that Satan is the father of lies, and his demons are liars, too. If you ask a demon to identify himself, or tell how he got into the person, his answer probably can't be trusted anyway. That's why you shouldn't talk to them.

Sometimes people will try to force a demon to tell the truth in the name of Jesus. But even then, demons find it almost impossible to tell the truth, and they will hedge and argue rather than tell the truth.

Furthermore, we are expressly commanded in the Bible not to communicate with evil spirits.

> There shall not be found among you anyone…who practices witchcraft, or a soothsayer, or one who interprets omens, or a sorcerer, or one who conjures spells, or a medium, or a spiritist, or one who calls up the dead. For all who do these things are an abomination to the Lord.   (Deuteronomy 18:10–12)

Scripture exhorts us to "resist the devil," not talk with him! (See James 4:7.) Don't forget that King Saul lost his life by disobeying God's law and seeking information from a demon-possessed witch. (See 1 Samuel 28:7–19.)

The practice of seeking after those with familiar spirits is condemned throughout the Scriptures.

> And when they say to you, "Seek those who are mediums and wizards, who whisper and mutter," should not a people seek their God? Should they seek the dead on behalf of the living? To the law and to the testimony! If they do not speak according to this word, it is because there is no light in them. (Isaiah 8:19–20)

Talking with demons is highly dangerous, even if you are only arguing with them. Demons are completely unreasonable anyway, and you'll never win the argument!

Our goal is to cast out demons quickly, giving no place to them, and refusing to make any agreement with them at all. We demand unconditional surrender. That is why Jesus commanded the spirits to be silent and come out. If a spirit can start arguing, he can delay his expulsion.

WHOSE VOICE DO DEMONS USE?

We must remember that demons are invisible, spiritual beings who have no physical organs of their own. They have no voice box, no lips, no mouth.

Jesus made a revealing statement about the nature of demons.

When an unclean spirit goes out of a man, he goes through dry places, seeking rest, and finds none. (Matthew 12:43)

This verse seems to indicate that every demon craves expression through a physical body. When a demon cannot find a body to occupy, he is without rest. Demons of profanity and obscenity, for instance, crave human lips and voices so they can give expression to their blasphemous thoughts.

Most demons do not talk—but when they do, they simply use the natural vocal cords of the person whose voice they are controlling. Usually the tone is different, though—not the normally recognized tone of the individual involved—but a totally different kind of voice. But anyone can hear it.

After many years in the ministry of deliverance, we've found that demons do not speak very often. We simply ask the person about his need; after his confession of sin, we start commanding the demon to leave in the name of Jesus. As the spirit leaves, the person seeking deliverance may cough, sigh, or shake—but sometimes no outward manifestation occurs at all.

Occasionally, though, demons will argue with us, refuse to come out, or tell us to "shut up." In cases where demons want to talk, I do as Jesus did, who commanded, *"Be quiet, and come out of him!"* (Mark 1:25).

10

THE MINISTRY
OF DELIVERANCE

1. WHY MUST DEMONS LEAVE WHEN A CHRISTIAN GIVES THE COMMAND?

I sn't it incredible that Jesus Christ shares His authority with us! We usually have no difficulty believing that Jesus has authority over evil spirits, but sometimes it is hard for us to grasp that He has now delegated that authority to us. Jesus said to His disciples,

> *All authority has been given to Me in heaven and on earth. Go therefore and make disciples of all the nations, baptizing them in the name of the Father and of the Son and of the Holy Spirit.* (Matthew 28:18–19)

Somehow, that isn't quite the way we would expect Jesus to say it. We would more naturally expect Him to say, "All authority has been given to Me in heaven and on earth. *I* will go therefore...." But that isn't what He said. Rather, He said, *"All power is given unto me...go ye therefore"* (KJV). Why did He say that? Because He had received power, and He has now delegated it to us.

If all demon spirits are subject to Jesus, then they are also subject to Jesus' people because we have His power. When Jesus died on the cross and shed His blood, He also stripped Satan and his demons of their power. Scripture says, *"Having disarmed principalities and powers, He [Christ] made a public spectacle of them, triumphing over them in it"* (Colossians 2:15).

We should not be surprised at this. Even before Calvary, Jesus gave His disciples power over demons—and it worked! They came back and reported, *"Lord, even the demons are subject to us in Your name"* (Luke 10:17).

IN JESUS'S NAME

The name of Jesus carried great authority when He walked the earth, and today we are rightful bearers of His delegated authority. When we cast out demons in His name, we are doing it as His representatives. No demon can ignore the command of faith given by a child of God. He must obey, just as though Jesus Himself were speaking.

After the disciples had expressed their elation over discovering their newly found power over the enemy, Jesus said, *"I saw Satan fall like lightning from heaven"* (Luke 10:18). Apparently, Jesus saw the casting out of demons by His disciples as an indication that Satan was about to be defeated at Calvary and would fall as lightning to the earth.

Satan and his demons have no legal rights over a Christian. Demons must be absolutely subject to any Christian who knows and uses his authority.

2. SHOULD INEXPERIENCED PEOPLE TRY DELIVERANCE?

Anyone who tries anything new is obviously inexperienced, but experience comes by working at it. I was totally inexperienced when I began this ministry, and what I have learned has been learned the hard way.

How are we to become experienced unless we try? No one has ever done anything worthwhile in life without making mistakes. Jesus didn't tell His disciples to wait until they became experienced, or until they understood all the pitfalls. He told them to *do* it. They did it, and it worked.

The ministry of deliverance *does* attract a minority of very enthusiastic but immature people who rush in without quite knowing what is going on. Novices generally cause confusion without bringing deliverance. They may stir up the devil, but that's all.

Since more and more people are practicing the ministry of deliverance, and since some good books are available, I feel that newcomers should be encouraged to work with more experienced people. Novices should humble themselves under the instruction of the more experienced.

People who need deliverance often come to our prayer room following our Sunday evening service. I recently observed a situation where two newcomers came in and quite brazenly pushed aside a more experienced elder who was ministering to a young girl. After telling her that she had a "murder demon" they proceeded to "cast it out" and informed her that she might have killed someone someday if they had not had "discernment"!

PRIDE VS. HUMILITY

Usually, all deliverance should begin with personal confession. The genuine gifts of the Spirit are not substitutes for personal confession and renunciation. If a suffering person comes to be freed from bondage, he (and not I) will express the particular need. I always encourage him to tell me, in the simplest language possible, what his need is—always remembering that confession is good for the soul.

Such sins as homosexual activity, adultery, and fornication need to be confessed, as well as "lesser sins." They need to be forsaken in prayer. Asking for God's forgiveness is a necessary prerequisite to receiving deliverance from bondage. If the person feels too embarrassed to acknowledge his sins, he will not wholeheartedly enter into his deliverance. Confession is therapeutic.

The novice may find it more exciting to rely on the gifts of the Spirit to tell the person what is wrong. But whenever we are ministering, we must be sure that we have the mind of the Spirit and not our own mind, which is quite frequently in error. All of us have heard sincere people say, "The Lord told me!" Among inexperienced people this is frequently not the Spirit of God but the mind of a proud person.

I remember an elder who announced that the Lord had revealed to him that his sister-in-law would die that very night. That was fifteen years ago. He himself died a few years later, but his sister-in-law is still alive!

I recently heard of another man who declared that God had revealed to him that he would not die until Jesus returned. He has been dead for ten years, and Jesus has not yet come back. What makes people say such things?

EXPERIENCE COUNTS

To get back to our question—I think that inexperienced people should be permitted to enter into the ministry of deliverance, but they should also be willing to serve with the more experienced.

I find that the gifts of the Spirit do operate through me, but usually after I have begun to tackle a known, confessed problem. In the interest of safety, ask any others present if they have also had the same revelation in the Spirit.

Unfortunately, some evangelists have made capital out of their ministry by "putting a demon on" a person in order to "cast it out." The sufferer may have no knowledge whatsoever of the "revelation" but in faith gratefully believes that he has been delivered of intended suicide, murder, or cancer, when in actual fact the whole idea came out of an enthusiastic (let's not say malicious) human mind.

Those inexperienced in the ministry of deliverance may get the demon stirred up into frenzied activity, but then they don't know how to use their authority to cast it out. Many times I've had to come to the rescue and command the demons to stop "acting up" and putting on a show.

Knowing how to handle strange manifestations comes only by experience. Novices should be encouraged to get that experience by working with mature, seasoned Christians who have been used in the ministry of deliverance.

3. SHOULD ANY CHRISTIAN ATTEMPT TO CAST DEMONS OUT OF OTHERS BEFORE HE HAS BEEN BAPTIZED IN THE HOLY SPIRIT?

I am answering this question on the assumption that we are speaking of receiving the infilling of the Holy Spirit and manifesting it by the outflowing of *glossolalia*, or "other tongues," from our innermost parts.

We must remember that the practice of deliverance is not peculiar to the days after Pentecost. Even the seventy disciples practiced this, much to their astonishment. (See Luke 10:1–20.) They were operating under Christ's delegated authority even though the Holy Spirit had not yet fallen on any of them!

Obviously, then, any born-again Christian can cast out demons. The great commission to the whole church begins with the statement that all believers should cast out demons.

> *These signs will follow those who believe: In My name they will cast out demons; they will speak with new tongues; they will take up serpents; and if they drink anything deadly, it will by no means hurt them; they will lay hands on the sick, and they will recover.* (Mark 16:17–18)

The ministry of deliverance is not restricted to a select few, nor even to the Spirit-filled, but rather to every active member of the Body of Christ. Naturally certain people will become leaders and teachers in deliverance and other ministries of the church.

I am not suggesting, though, that the baptism in the Spirit is unimportant. I believe that Jesus intended all New Testament believers to not only speak in tongues, but also to exercise the other gifts of the Spirit.

WORKING MIRACLES

The casting out of demons is equated with the gift of miracles in the following passage:

> *Now John answered Him, saying, "Teacher we saw someone who does not follow us casting out demons in Your name, and we forbade him because he does not follow us." But Jesus said, "Do not forbid him, for no one who **works a miracle** in My name can soon afterward speak evil of Me."* (Mark 9:38–39)

Therefore any humble (and the more humble, the better!) believer *may* and *should* cast out demons, and thereby perform a miracle. If the born-again believer can perform such a miracle, then how much greater will the miracles be when he is Spirit-filled!

The church has been so weak and feeble that such plain teaching may cause dismay to many powerless church "leaders." They would rather not face up to the increased demonic activity of our day, instead retreating into theological formulas and dispensational nonsense. They reason that if miracles do not occur in their denomination, then they should not, or cannot, occur in others.

Any born-again Christian ought to desire all of God's power he can get. Not only should a believer be filled with the Spirit, but he should also be active in the ministry of casting out demons—not apart from the Body of Christ, but working under the guidance and direction of elders.

No one should ever tangle with this ministry unless he has a spiritual leader. No married woman should enter into this supernatural realm who does not acknowledge her husband as her head, or who does not attempt to have her children in subjection. Deliverance is a powerful ministry and needs people whose lives are in order and submitted to God.

4. IS FASTING NECESSARY FOR SUCCESSFUL DELIVERANCE?

No, fasting is not necessary, but in certain circumstances it may be helpful. Let's examine a passage of Scripture where an unsuccessful attempt at deliverance is mentioned with a lack of prayer and fasting.

> *And when they had come to the multitude, a man came to Him, kneeling down to Him and saying, "Lord, have mercy on my son, for he is an epileptic and suffers severely; for he often falls into the fire and often into the water. So I brought him to Your disciples, but they could not cure him." ...And Jesus rebuked the demon, and he came out of him; and the child was cured from that very hour. Then the disciples came to Jesus privately and said, "Why could we not cast him out?" So Jesus said to them, "Because of your unbelief; for assuredly, I say to you, if you have faith as a mustard seed, you will say to this mountain, 'Move from here to there,' and it will move; and nothing will be impossible for you. However, this kind does not go out* **except by prayer and fasting.***
> (Matthew 17:14–16, 18–21)

The King James Version describes this boy as being *"lunatic"* (verse 15). Whatever the modern medical term might be, the boy frequently fell into the fire or water. He may have been a spastic or subject to epileptic seizures. The disciples prayed to the best of their ability, but they lacked power to bring the needed results.

When Jesus "rebuked the devil," the demon that had caused his affliction departed from him. The disciples were very embarrassed and asked Jesus privately why they had not succeeded.

FASTING OR FAITH?

He replied that their unbelief caused their failure. They did not have the necessary faith for this deliverance. They were fearful. Most of us can react quite sympathetically to this. How many times have we had the same experience!

Jesus said that this kind of demon comes out only by *"prayer and fasting"* (verse 21). A more detailed account of the same story is given in Mark 9. Jesus did not cast out the demon until the father of the boy cried out, *"Lord, I believe; help my unbelief"* (Mark 9:24), showing that *someone* had to believe before the miracle was done.

This mention of fasting is one of the few cases in the Bible where a word may have been inserted by a copying monk in past centuries. He made the annotation, probably from his own thoughts, but later copyists put it into the text. In the minds of most Bible scholars, a real question hangs over verse 21.

If we dismiss verse 21, then we are driven to the conclusion that the real reason that the demon could not be cast out was their unbelief. To me, this seems more reasonable than to say that lack of fasting was the reason. If we were to go on a fast for everyone seeking deliverance today, we would have no time or strength left to pray for the multitudes of people who are now seeking help.

WHAT'S OUR MOTIVATION?

A few minutes before writing this, I spent an hour counseling and praying with an alcoholic. The demon of alcohol was visibly and definitely cast out of him. But I did not fast in preparation for this deliverance session. I had just eaten a light supper. I don't mean to discourage fasting. If a person is bound and in need of deliverance, it may be a good idea for him to have a mild fast, or to miss one or two meals before coming for prayer.

Fasting does not "twist God's arm" or earn deliverance from a "mean" God, but it does show the Lord the earnestness and seriousness with which the suppliant comes for healing. Fasting proves that the spirit of the man aspires to be stronger than the flesh. Denying the flesh also weakens the body against any resistance to the expulsion of the spirit behind the sickness.

Fasting was very popular among monks in the middle ages. This was a work of supererogation—or performing more than is required by duty or obligation. At the time of the Reformation, Martin Luther, together with hundreds of monks, left their cloistered solitude and gave up these practices, coming out into the freedom that

Jesus gives us. The person who practices fasting is not bound by legalism, but our fasting should be led by the Spirit.

The disciples of Jesus were rebuked on one occasion for not fasting. Their freedom was contrasted with the Pharisees who fasted often while the disciples didn't fast at all! Obviously, this was a simple case of self-righteous criticism by the Pharisees! Jesus said they had no need to fast while they had the Bridegroom with them. We might ask ourselves the question, "Do we indeed have the Bridegroom with us?"

No doubt that fasting may be indicated in certain circumstances when someone is seeking deliverance. In general, however, there seems to be no need for the Christian to fast before praying for the bound and tormented.

5. DO CHRISTIANS HAVE AUTHORITY TO SEND DEMONS TO THE PIT OF HELL?

This is a very popular question, probably because Christians hope that the offending spirits can be confined to some kind of spiritual "garbage dump," so they'll not be troubled again! Many people have also asked where demons go when they are cast out. I'll try to answer both of these questions.

No passage of Scripture directs us to send demons back into the pit of hell. In fact, the opposite seems to be the case. In the story of the Gadarene demoniac, the demons begged to be sent into a nearby herd of swine because they feared that Jesus would torment them before their time. (See Matthew 8:28–34.)

We can infer that the ultimate torment for demons is to be cast into the pit, or "lowest hell." The demons knew that hell was prepared for *"the devil and his angels"* (Matthew 25:41), but as long as they were in the demoniac, they were safe from the pit. When the demons recognized Jesus, they feared meeting their ultimate destiny and requested the next best alternative—to go into the swine. The pigs plummeted over the precipice into the sea and drowned! The demons should have had more sense, but this proves how stupid they really are.

According to Scripture, the fate of Satan and his demons is sealed.

And the devil, who deceived them, was cast into the lake of fire and brimstone where the beast and the false prophet are. And they will be tormented day and night forever and ever. (Revelation 20:10)

Until this final act of Jesus, demons have a certain "legal" right to inhabit this planet. As long as they're here, they'll always be looking for the body of a man or beast as a vehicle to manifest their foul, evil natures. That's why demons inhabit the earth.

The earth has always been Satan's domain (even before he fell), and he still claims it as his kingdom. That's why, when Satan tempted Jesus, he showed Him all the kingdoms of the world in a moment of time and said,

> All this authority I will give You, and their glory; for this has been delivered to me, and I give it to whomever I wish.　　　　　　　　　(Luke 4:6)

The apostle Paul also refers to Satan as *"the god of this world"* (2 Corinthians 4:4 KJV).

The insane demons that left the Gadarene demoniac knew they faced a horrible fate, even if they were not immediately sent to the pit. Jesus taught His disciples what happened once an unclean spirit was cast out of a person.

> When an unclean spirit goes out of a man, he goes through dry places, seeking rest; and finding none, he says, "I will return to my house from which I came."
> 　　　　　　　　　(Luke 11:24)

Demons would be forced to wander around, seeking to reenter the body from which they were ejected, or to inhabit another body.

Spirits, having been forced out of a body by the death of that person, have been known to cling to the building and haunt it. Family members and visitors may hear or see apparitions or sense their presence.

A Christian family moved into such a house in Oshawa, Ontario, some years ago, and the haunting spirits walked up and down the halls, opening and closing doors until the new owner called me to cast them out. This was done in about half an hour by audibly pleading the blood of Jesus in every room and closet, and then loudly commanding them to depart in Jesus' name—which they did. No more trouble was experienced.

Where do these demons go? Why, they just take off to find some other person to inhabit! As long as demons can live in a human being, they are happy; they will go to extreme measures to entice a person to sin. Satan tempted Judas Iscariot to sell Jesus for money, and later entered into him. First the temptation, then the overcoming of the person, who becomes bound until set free by prayer.

The whole strange teaching of "astral plains" taught among spiritists—the "seven stages" where departed humans go after death—is based on the fact that demons actually do stay close to this earth, perhaps in degrees or plains, but all "earth-bound."

This doctrine, believed so implicitly by necromancers (those who communicate with the dead), comes from demons. In the pit, demons will never again have human bodies in which to dwell and manifest themselves. Imagine a sex demon having no body to use in hell! That will *be* hell for the demon!

A human who was driven by this demon and never repented will face a horrible eternity.

> But the cowardly, unbelieving, abominable, murderers, sexually immoral, sorcerers, idolaters, and all liars **shall have their part** in the lake which burns with fire and brimstone, which is the second death. (Revelation 21:8)

This place or pit was not prepared for humans, but for the devil and his angels. But if any human insists on permitting one of these foul spirits to govern his life, he will go *along with the demons* to the same place. Is it worth it?

Jesus offered forgiveness and deliverance to the tormented soul that fell at His feet. Christ set the Gadarene demoniac free to live in holy joy in this life and to enjoy the glories of heaven at death. He could have gone to hell, but he repented of his sins and his hideous condition. The demons will go to the pit, but not the demoniac. He is no longer bound by demons. He is a child of God forever.

6. WHAT DID THE APOSTLE PAUL MEAN WHEN HE WROTE, *"GOD...WILL CRUSH SATAN UNDER YOUR FEET SHORTLY"* (ROMANS 16:20)?

The word *"shortly"* means "with speed." The apostle Paul taught the Romans that they should expect to quickly tread on Satan's head, as David quickly beheaded Goliath after robbing him of his sword. Jesus, the fulfillment of David, took the terrible "sword" away from Satan (which speaks of his lying word), and put another "sword" in our mouth, which is the Word of God.

After the fall, God prophesied that the seed of the woman would bruise the serpent's head. (See Genesis 3:15.) The apostle Paul borrowed his metaphor from this ancient prophecy. All Christians may exercise their authority in Christ and put their feet on the neck of the defeated (but not yet dead) enemy, Satan, and render him powerless.

Not only did Jesus (the seed of the woman) bruise the head of Satan, but we, the continuing seed of the virgin bride (the church) are expected to bruise Satan's head by treading upon it daily in Jesus' name.

Christians ought to claim the following promise:

> You shall tread upon the lion and the cobra, the young lion and the serpent you shall trample under foot. (Psalm 91:13)

So few have tried. No doubt the people in the church at Rome were also fearful, but the apostle Paul promised them that they would indeed trample Satan under their feet as a normal, daily exercise of faith.

Obviously, if Satan and his demons are safely under our feet, they cannot attack our minds or bodies. This is the only spiritually healthy stance for a Christian. Let us be careful lest, in our fearfulness or timidity, we depend on someone else to do the treading for us. There is no scriptural provision for this. Another Christian may cast a demon out of your life, but you must put your foot on him. If you do not, he may try to attack you again!

This is why Jesus admonished a man who had been healed of his paralysis, *"Sin no more, lest a worse thing come upon you"* (John 5:14).

The full meaning of Romans 16:20 is dramatized for us in Joshua 10, where the five kings who were determined to destroy the Gibeonites were themselves destroyed. Gibeon had seen the advancing Israelite army destroy Ai and Jericho, and so they wisely decided to throw in their lot with Israel and accept the leadership and protection of Joshua.

Later on, as Joshua moved forward quickly to defend the Gibeonites against the five kings, God sent hailstones to kill the armies of these kings. When the kings themselves saw that the battle was lost, they ran away and hid themselves in a cave, which was to become their tomb.

> So it was, when they brought out those kings to Joshua, that Joshua called for all the men of Israel, and said to the captains of the men of war who went with him, "Come near, put your feet on the necks of these kings." And they drew near and put their feet on their necks. Then Joshua said to them, "Do not be afraid, nor be dismayed; be strong and of good courage, for thus the LORD will do to all your enemies against whom you fight." (Joshua 10:24–25)

Then Joshua himself struck them and killed them, and hanged them on five trees. At sundown they cut them down from the trees, threw their bodies back into the cave, and blocked it up with heavy stones.

In the spiritual realm, God wants his children to face up to any demonic attack that might be launched against them—whether it be in the form of despair, shame, sickness, poverty, or famine. Demonic forces are constantly seeking to oppress us. We must never run from them, but face right up to them and put our feet squarely on the problem.

7. SHOULDN'T DELIVERANCE BE DONE PRIVATELY, AWAY FROM THE EYES OF PEOPLE WHO MIGHT NOT UNDERSTAND?

Obviously, the best way to deal with each individual would be to take them into a private room and counsel them. This also provides an opportunity to allow the Spirit of God to help us understand the problems of the sufferer. Following the time of counseling and listening to them, we can agree for the prayer of deliverance to take place. The evil spirits will soon be ejected, and whether they are noisy or quiet makes little difference.

Obviously, the actual and the ideal are often worlds apart. What should we do when confronted with a situation similar to the one that Philip faced?

> Then Philip went down to the city of Samaria and preached Christ to them. And the multitudes with one accord heeded the things spoken by Philip, hearing and seeing the miracles which he did. For unclean spirits, crying with a loud voice, came out of many who were possessed; and many who were paralyzed and lame were healed.
> (Acts 8:5–7)

Philip was right out in the open air, and as he preached Christ to the people, the demons started to react very noisily.

What should he have done? Should he have taken them to a room in the City Hall? Should he have told them to keep quiet? Should he have taken each one aside for separate counseling and prayer? Obviously, this was not possible, and so it was necessary to have a mass deliverance service.

We are living in times when we may encounter such a grew amount of demonic activity that there may be nothing else to do but stand by the microphone and publicly rebuke every alien spirit in the place, binding them and commanding them to come out. I have been in services where I have had to deal with hundreds of cases all at the same time.

I've met some people who think that this is a terrible thing to do in a public place—but what is our alternative when hundreds are seeking relief from oppression? In many places, it is not possible to deal with individuals privately because so many are seeking deliverance.

In our church in Scarborough, Ontario, we have tried to cope with this problem. The assistant pastor, the elders, and trained workers gather in our prayer room after the evening service. Some people receive counseling while others confess their needs privately. Then we lead them to renounce their sins and agree to put them away forever.

After this, we openly rebuke the demons in Jesus' name, while the workers gather around and pray in groups with each individual. I supervise and help in cases where difficulties may arise or where demons are stubborn and want to show off. People are delivered and filled with the Holy Spirit during these times of ministry each Sunday evening.

I know of no other way to avoid the possible confusion that might arise from a public deliverance service. If there are not trained workers, then we are compelled to handle the matter in whatever way we can. Deliverance is not an extra to the preaching of the gospel—deliverance is the very center of the gospel.

Jesus came that He might destroy the works of the devil and set the captives free. If people remain bound in our churches, then we are not fulfilling the great commission. Jesus said these signs shall follow those who believe in Him: "*In My name they will cast out demons*" (Mark 16:17).

8. IS IT NECESSARY TO SPEND HOURS TRYING TO SET A PERSON FREE FROM DEMONS?

In our earlier experiences with deliverance, we were sometimes trapped by clever demons into spending much time and much energy, trying to budge the recalcitrant spirits. Some people have exhausted themselves by staying up all night but without bringing the sufferer to complete deliverance. Satan knows how to wear out the saints!

Sometimes, though, there are reasons for excessively long deliverance sessions. If a sufferer is seeking deliverance for wrong motives, we often find that the demons are hard to cast out. We must realize that demons claim a "legal right" to occupy a person who has given place to him and does not want to serve the Lord fully.

Someone may stir up a demon to great activity but fail cast him out of a person. All we do is get him shaken up but not out. The demon may play with us and put on show for hours so that we believe we are getting somewhere. When I encounter this situation, I immediately take charge, command the spirit to be silent, and order him to come out immediately. He usually does.

READY AND WILLING?

Before beginning the prayer of deliverance, find out whether the one who is bound really wants to serve the Lord. Discover if any known sins are unconfessed. The sufferer should seek forgiveness for the sin or weakness that allowed the spirit to enter in the first place.

Long, drawn-out deliverance sessions are not scriptural. If I don't begin to get positive results within several minutes, I'll stop and inquire whether the person is sincere.

In one case, a woman informed my wife and me that she was a lesbian. We implored her to seek the Lord's forgiveness and forsake this sin, which is so highly condemned in Scripture. To our astonishment, she admitted that she wasn't sure she could do it since she felt the experience was rather beautiful. This woman wanted to be set free from the stigma of her sin, but she didn't want to forsake it. No amount of prayer would have budged this unclean spirit. The demon had a right to stay there and manifest its unclean nature.

When a person is ready and willing, the time of prayer can be very exhilarating; but where unwillingness is present, it can drag the strength out of you because you are fighting an impossible battle.

We must remember, too, that more time may be required if a person has more than one demon. Even after a person has been delivered of one spirit, another may surface, and you may need to have a second or third session—or even more in some cases!

9. MUST CHRISTIANS FORCE DEMONS TO NAME THEMSELVES BEFORE CASTING THEM OUT?

A more basic question needs to be asked, and that is, Can you trust demons to tell the truth anyway? If you must call a demon by name in order to expel him, the demon could stall a long time by giving you one false name after another.

I am aware that there are many sincere people who feel this is the right way to go about it. They do not attempt to cast out any demon until they first get its name. This idea is based on one incident in the life of Jesus: His encounter with the Gadarene demoniac.

The incident is related in three gospels, but it will be sufficient to look at Luke's version. After Jesus had commanded the unclean spirit to come out of the man, the next verse says, *"Jesus asked him, saying, 'What is your name?' And he said, 'Legion,' because many demons had entered him"* (Luke 8:30).

That *does* say that Jesus asked the name of the demon, doesn't it? But look again. I don't think it does. You'll notice that whenever Luke refers to the *man*, he uses the pronoun "he" or "him." Look closely at the following passage:

> When **he** [the man] *saw Jesus,* **he** *cried out, fell down before Him, and with a loud voice said, "What have I to do with You, Jesus, the son of the Most High God? I beg You, do not torment me!"*   (verse 28)

But when Luke refers to the *demons,* he uses the plural pronoun "they" or "them." Keep reading that same passage.

> And **they** [the demons] *begged Him that He would not command* **them** *to go out into the abyss.*   (verse 31)

What should we conclude then? Why, simply, that when Jesus asked *him,* "What is your name?" He was asking the *man,* not the demons. And it was the *man* who said his name was Legion, for he apparently *knew* that he was full of demons!

Since no other place in the Bible instructs us to ask *anything* of demons, I conclude that we have no scriptural basis for asking demons to give their names.

In my own ministry, I have not found it necessary to get any kind of information from demons. Frequently, however, the Spirit of God will reveal by a word of knowledge the name and nature of the demon, and then we cast it out before it has any opportunity to lie.

10. ARE DEMONS ALWAYS EXPELLED THROUGH THE MOUTH?

In the ministry of deliverance, a belief has arisen that demons must always be disgorged through the mouth. Apparently, this conclusion is based partly on the several cases of deliverance in the Bible where people cried out with loud voices, and partly on the experiences of people who have become nauseated during deliverance and have actually vomited out strange substances.

While many demons *are* cast out with these manifestations (and we are not to be alarmed if this takes place), experience shows that we can by no means expect that this will always happen. (I cannot imagine anyone actually *wanting* to see such things!)

With the increase of this ministry, we are learning to proceed with each case individually, with no preconceived notions about what will happen. Many demons leave with no visible manifestations at all—although in such cases, we usually get a strong inward witness that the demon has gone. The person involved also receives a deep peace, and their torment disappears.

I think we should do all that we can to *stop* any unpleasant demonic manifestations. Some are unavoidable, to be sure, but we certainly shouldn't encourage demons to make a show of themselves. Some people have mistakenly asked the demon to manifest himself. I tell him to be quiet and come out!

11. I'VE HEARD THAT THERE ARE SOMETIMES UNPLEASANT MANIFESTATIONS DURING DELIVERANCE. WHAT ARE THEY? ARE THEY NECESSARY?

I want to guard against any teaching that would cause afflicted or tormented individuals to expect unpleasantness, and thus shy away from a greatly needed deliverance. If you are plagued by demons, let *nothing* hold you back from getting rid of that which troubles you! If the process turns out to be unpleasant or distasteful, just remember that hospital operations are also unpleasant—but often very necessary!

In my own ministry, I have been able to cast out demons with a minimum of unpleasantness. By binding the demon in the name of Jesus, and commanding the spirit to be quiet and come out, I usually see little outward manifestation.

But there are exceptions. In some cases, the person may tremble all over for a few seconds or longer; this is usually indicative of the demon's unwillingness to leave. In other cases, the person may fall to the floor.

This is what happened when a boy bound by a mute spirit was brought to Jesus.

> *And when he saw Him, immediately the spirit convulsed him, and he fell on the ground and wallowed, foaming at the mouth.*   (Mark 9:20)

Apparently the boy suffered from a case of epilepsy caused by demon oppression. Jesus rebuked this foul spirit, saying,

> *You deaf and dumb spirit, I command you, come out of him, and enter him no more.*   (Mark 9:25)

In other cases, the expelling of the demon may be evidenced by weeping, crying out, or even screaming.

> *Then the spirit **cried out**, convulsed him greatly, and came out of him.*
> (Mark 9:26)

> *But Jesus rebuked him* [the unclean spirit], *saying, "Be quiet and come out of him!" And when the unclean spirit had convulsed him and **cried out with a loud voice**, he came out of him.*   (Mark 1:25–26)

Let no one think that he *must* cry or scream in order to receive deliverance, though. Such manifestations are caused by the departing demon, who certainly needs no help in expressing himself. But sometimes, in spite of the person's efforts to squelch unpleasantness, it happens anyway.

Occasionally we encounter extreme cases where the departing demon causes violent coughing, nausea, or vomiting. We must not draw back in astonishment or embarrassment from the one for whom we are praying if that happens. We must press on in our commands until the last spirit is expelled.

12. WHY DO SOME PEOPLE EXPERIENCE ONLY A PARTIAL DELIVERANCE WHEN DEMONS ARE EXPELLED?

People are not totally delivered for several reasons. First, God delivers a person only up to the "ceiling" of his confession. If several demons are present and only one is confessed, then most likely only this demon will be ejected. As I pray for a person, the Holy Spirit often reveals another type of demon; when this demon is named and challenged, it will often react very suddenly and come out.

Sometimes people are not totally set free because they are not aware of all the areas in their lives that need deliverance. The Holy Spirit may gradually reveal their areas of need over a period of days or weeks. On the other hand, we can sometimes discover which demons are present through a word of knowledge.

Another reason why complete deliverance eludes some people is because their own faith is weak, or they may be quite unsure about this whole ministry anyway. Because of fear, they may not be fully cooperative.

If we succeed in dislodging a spirit after a strong fight, we then encourage the person to go home and ask God to reveal to them any other arms where they may be needing help. In this way, their own faith deepens, and they become more cooperative. Better results may occur in a second or third session than in the first one.

There may be any number of other reasons for partial deliverances. Sometimes, as we grow in grace, we find that latent weaknesses begin to show up more and more. A quick temper or jealousy, which has not troubled us very much in the past, may now begin to upset our Christian life. This has been my own experience, but when I asked for prayer, the spirit left me, never to return.

SUBMITTING TO ONE ANOTHER

Many of us may need to ask a brother or sister to pray for us. As we humble ourselves and submit ourselves one to another, God works mightily in our lives. Confessing our sin and asking for prayer may be very difficult, but humility may be the key to a more complete deliverance and healing. *"Confess your trespasses to one another, and pray for one another, that you may be healed"* (James 5:16).

If some well-meaning person approaches me and says, "Brother Whyte, the Lord has showed me that you have a spirit of _____ and need to be delivered," I do not brush him off as a "nut." I gladly submit myself, saying, "Very well, then you pray for me that I might be delivered." If his "discernment" is false (it may be caused by zeal without knowledge), then he will back off. But if his leading is from God, our spirits will witness to its truth. We should gladly submit to prayer.

At a meeting of charismatic ministers in 1973, a humble Episcopalian clergyman asked me to pray for his hasty temper. I took him aside, and we prayed together; he wept for joy as the evil spirit left him.

Submitting ourselves one to another knocks all pride out of us. God is looking for those with a humble and contrite spirit whom He can use to set others free from oppression.

13. IF A CHRISTIAN HAS BEEN DELIVERED OF A DEMON, IS THERE ANY GUARANTEE THAT THE DEMON WILL NOT RETURN?

I think the answer to this question boils down to a matter of self-control. Unfortunately, many people who have experienced valid deliverances return to their old ways because of discouragement, pressure from relatives, or even business problems. The danger of backsliding after deliverance is very real, and if it takes place, the devil usually gains a much stronger foothold the second time.

This belief is supported by the following passage of Scripture:

When an unclean spirit goes out of a man, he goes through dry places, seeking rest, and finds none. Then he says, "I will return to my house from which I came." And when he comes, he finds it empty, swept, and put in order. Then he goes and takes with him seven other spirits more wicked than himself, and they enter and dwell there; and the last state of that man is worse than the first.

(Matthew 12:43–45)

This teaching of Jesus should be sufficient motivation to keep all "cleaned up" Christians following hard after the Lord in their lives and their worship.

Peter also put it very plainly:

*For if, after they have escaped the pollutions of the world through the knowledge of the Lord and Savior Jesus Christ, they are again entangled in them **and overcome**, the latter end is worse for them than the beginning.*   (2 Peter 2:20)

In verse 22, Peter likens this behavior to a dog returning to lick up its vomit. A revolting analogy!

In my ministry, I have encountered a number of people who have been delivered, only to return to their own ways. Ultimately, their problems became worse than they were before deliverance. We need to understand that temptation is very real, even after deliverance. But the devil is not stronger than Jesus. We do not have to give place to Satan.

Experience has taught me that at no time in my Christian experience am I in the final place of maturity and perfection. There is always room for more of Jesus; there are always deeper recesses in my spirit that need to be purged and invaded by the presence of Jesus. Because this is true, there is the ever-present possibility that demons may get control (or keep control) of some area of my life.

Keeping ourselves in the love of God, under the blood of Jesus, and unspotted from the world will prevent an evil spirit from returning. This was John's recommendation. (See 1 John 5:18.) Any born-again Christian can do this.

11

OBJECTIONS TO DELIVERANCE

1. ISN'T IT DANGEROUS TO CAST OUT DEMONS?

Possibly. Driving a car on a modern highway can be dangerous if you ignore the rules!

We must remember that the kind of New Testament Christianity taught by the apostle Paul is not practiced in many of our churches today. Paul exhorted the early church to be soldiers, clad in protective armor, with a sword and a shield in their hands, battling against monstrous demon forces called principalities, powers, rulers of darkness, and wicked spirits.

> *Finally, my brethren, be strong in the Lord and in the power of His might. Put on the whole armor of God, that you may be able to stand against the wiles of the devil.* (Ephesians 6:10–11)

> *For though we walk in the flesh, we do not war according to the flesh. For the weapons of our warfare are not carnal but mighty in God for pulling down strongholds.* (2 Corinthians 10:3–4)

What resources for ordinary Christians! Why were these spiritual weapons necessary for the early believers? Because their enemies were powerful demon spirits controlling nations and organizations of men, evil spirits ruling in the dark places of the earth, and enormous numbers of evil spirits that attempted to harass them daily.

THE PROTECTION OF THE BLOOD

Is war dangerous? Only if you have improper equipment! If our armor is not worn properly, there will be chinks in it, and Satan will shoot his fiery darts through them. If we don't hold the shield of faith at the right angle, it will not avail. If we aren't familiar with the sword of the Spirit, which is the Word of God, then we have no offensive weapon. We are sitting ducks!

God has not only given us a protective armor that is impervious to Satan's attacks, but He has also given us the blood of His Son. I cannot recommend too strongly that those who enter into this battle deliberately cover themselves by faith in the blood of Jesus. Satan cannot get through the bloodline—but it is up to us to put it in place.

Before God released the children of Israel from Egyptian slavery, the blood of lambs had to be sprinkled on the lintels and side-posts of all Israelite homes before the angel of death passed over. If no blood had been used, death would have come to the first-born in every family. (See Exodus 12.)

Obviously, Satan will launch a counterattack when you become a nuisance to him. But it is better to go in and win than to sit on the sidelines and lose. The best form of defense is attack. That is why Jesus tells us,

> *Behold, I give you the authority to trample on serpents and scorpions, and over all the power of the enemy, and nothing shall by any means hurt you.*
>
> (Luke 10:19)

WHAT ABOUT LAYING ON OF HANDS?

There has been a very common objection to the laying on of hands in connection with deliverance. Many have said that we should not put our hands on anyone with an evil spirit, lest it enter us!

This may have some basis in common sense, especially in cases where the sufferer is oppressed to the point of insanity and violence. But I do not believe there is any danger of a "kick-back" from the demon or that the wicked spirit can get into us through the laying on of hands. The power of the Holy Spirit in us is infinitely greater than the power of Satan.

I usually begin deliverance sessions by praying for the person without laying my hands on them. If the sufferer begins to show signs of distress, I then use the laying on of hands to bring the force of the Holy Spirit to bear upon him. I often think of this as being similar to connecting a battery charger to the terminals of a dead battery. The power of the Holy Spirit flows into the demon-oppressed person and helps to drive out the evil spirit.

If you are inexperienced and uncertain about the whole matter of deliverance, then I suggest that you keep your hands off. Better wait until you've gained some experience.

To those who battle under the blood without fear, there is absolutely no danger. Satan and his demons are in danger. Jesus conquered them all at Calvary. With millions of people waiting to be delivered, let us arise, put our armor on, and begin to make war against Satan.

2. SHOULDN'T WE JUST PREACH THE GOSPEL AND NOT CONCERN OURSELVES WITH THE MINISTRY OF DELIVERANCE?

This is a favorite question with those who do not understand. The Bible says that Israel limited God by their unbelief:

> *They turned back and tempted God, and **limited** the Holy One of Israel.*
>
> (Psalm 78:41)

They believed as much about God as was convenient for them in their way of life. Many of these people fill both the pulpit and the pews of our churches today. To them, the gospel of salvation is *limited* to John 3:16.

Now I am certainly not objecting to sermons preached on John 3:16! Every sinner needs to be born again and believe on the Lord Jesus Christ for salvation. But the church has been commissioned to do more than preach John 3:16. What instructions were given along with the great commission?

> *Go into the world and preach the gospel to every creature. He who believes and is baptized will be saved; but he who does not believe will be condemned. And these signs shall follow those who believe: In My name they will **cast out demons**; they will **speak with new tongues**...they will **lay their hands on the sick** and they will recover.* (Mark 16:15–18)

Jesus equipped His twelve disciples and later the seventy with much more than a simple gospel proclamation when He sent them out.

> *Then He called His twelve disciples together and gave them power and authority over all demons, and to cure diseases. He sent them to preach the kingdom of God and to heal the sick.* (Luke 9:1–2)

> *After these things the Lord appointed seventy others also, and sent them two by two before His face into every city and place where He Himself was about to go....Then the seventy returned with joy, saying, "Lord, even the demons are subject to us in Your name."* (Luke 10:1, 17)

Christ delegated complete authority to His followers to cast out demons. This is the first sign that Jesus mentioned would be given to prove the authenticity of genuine Christianity.

Philip the evangelist, because he did not preach a limited Christ, saw God confirm His Word with signs following.

Then Philip went down to the city of Samaria and preached Christ to them. And the multitudes with one accord heeded the things spoken by Philip, hearing and seeing the miracles which he did. For unclean spirits, crying with a loud voice, came out of many who were possessed; and many who were paralyzed and lame were healed. (Acts 8:5–7)

If a clergyman minimizes any part of the plan of salvation, he undersells his congregation on the meaning of salvation. In New Testament Greek, salvation means "to be made whole" or "to be delivered." The salvation of the Lord means soundness for man's spirit, soul, and body.

PREACHING THE FULL GOSPEL

I once spoke on a Toronto radio station about the miracles of lengthening legs and straightening twisted spines that God had performed in our Midst. After hearing how God miraculously touched specific cases, an inspired listener wrote about having a crooked spine and one leg shorter than the other. He decided to come to our church, and said he had faith that our prayers would cure his condition.

I was on the spot! Should I have kept my mouth shut? Was I treading on dangerous ground?

When the man showed up in church one Sunday and later went to the prayer room, I knew the "moment of truth" had come! Asking him to sit in a chair, I held his two legs and discovered that his right leg was five-eighths of an inch shorter than his left leg. I prayed and asked Jesus to heal the man. Immediately, the right leg grew out before our eyes until it matched the left one, and his spine became straight!

He wrote several days later, saying he had tried every test he could think of and the miracle held firm. He later returned to have a spirit of fear cast out. The man was gloriously healed and set free! I was glad that I had a full gospel to present to that man!

Should we leave out any part of the good news of salvation? Should we have the joy of seeing sins forgiven, but put up with being afflicted with physical sickness and mental torment? I admit that not everyone we pray for is healed or delivered—and there may be many reasons why—but that is no reason for failing to preach a *whole* gospel.

DEBATING WITH SKEPTICS

During a TV appearance in Toronto, I appeared side-by-side with a liberal, unbelieving minister. He thought that the first eleven chapters of Genesis were pure myth, and he didn't believe in demons at all.

I explained that the Bible spoke clearly about demons and how Jesus dealt with them by casting them out. I showed how Satan entered into Judas Iscariot and how the disciples also cast out demons. This liberal minister replied that demons were the "interpretations" of the men who wrote the gospels and the book of Acts. He wanted proof.

I told him about people who had been bound in mind or body and who were permanently set free when we cast out the demons in Jesus' name. What further proof did he need? Then I asked the liberal minister what came out of these afflicted people when they cried or fell to the ground.

His reply was surprising. "I have no doubt that you healed them!" he remarked. I corrected him and pointed out that I was only an instrument in the hands of Jesus. How could people receive miraculous healings and deliverance if demons do not exist? He had no answer.

Today Jesus is restoring all the gifts and offices of the Holy Spirit that the church might preach a whole gospel as Philip did. As we walk in faith and obedience, we can expect the same experiences and results to follow our preaching.

Remember, casting out demons is at the top of the list of signs that should follow our preaching. (See Mark 16:17.) Deliverance is not something we can sweep under our theological rug and forget. God is restoring the ministry of deliverance as an essential part of the gospel to be carried to all nations.

3. ISN'T IT MENTALLY UNHEALTHY TO BECOME TOO "DEMON CONSCIOUS"?

Those who are engaged in the ministry of deliverance are often accused of being more interested in demons than in the Holy Spirit. Some assume we are unhealthy in our attitude, thinking everyone involved in this ministry goes around "witch-hunting" and "looking for demons" behind every tree or circumstance.

We admit freely that some in this ministry do blame demons for everything, instead of blaming themselves. Some, pretending to have "discerning of spirits," make a bad guess and say, "You have a spirit of _____," and then proceed to "cast it out"—or claim to do so, anyway.

This kind of behavior may impress some but offend others. We must *know for certain* that demon activity is present before we start rebuking it and casting it out.

In every true move of the Spirit of God, enthusiastic people want to help without having the proper experience behind them. We must admit, however, that no one will ever learn anything unless he begins somewhere. Let's not be too hard on these enthusiasts. Novices should be involved under the direction of more experienced Christians.

Christians who are involved in the ministry of deliverance are not *looking* for demons. They are looking to bring healing and release to the thousands who are oppressed.

EXPOSING THEMSELVES

When the Lord first opened my eyes to the reality of demons, I was *not* looking for them. My only motivation was to bring healing to a man who was chronically sick. Someone had advised me to change my method of praying. Instead of asking Jesus to heal the man, this person suggested that I might get better results by rebuking the sickness in Jesus' name.

The results were astonishing. I came face to face with demons immediately. But I was not *looking* for them. They reacted when challenged in the mighty name of Jesus. Many Christians, fearing the unknown, prefer to do nothing about demons. Our ignorance and inactivity allows them to remain hidden as they happily continue their evil work.

Demons always react when Jesus is preached in His fullness. Evil spirits often deceive people into believing they don't exist. Demons may hurl criticism or condemnation upon those who are casting them out.

During a worship service in Brooklyn, New York, a religious demon started to manifest itself by praising God in a falsetto voice. The face of the person was contorted in distress. I recognized the demon and cast it out at the end of the service. I was not looking for it. But the worship of God flushed it out of its hiding place and caused this demon to try to simulate praise.

What happened when Jesus went into the synagogue at Capernaum? Was He looking for demons? No, He was merely teaching doctrine when suddenly an unclean spirit cried out.

> *But Jesus rebuked him, saying, "Be quiet, and come out of him!" And when the unclean spirit had convulsed him and cried out with a loud voice, he came out of him.* (Mark 1:25–26)

The evil spirit obeyed. The people in the synagogue were undoubtedly astonished by those unusual events. Maybe if Jesus had been more refined and diplomatic, He would have avoided such an "unpleasant reaction" in the house of God!

No, we don't look for demons; but they are hiding until we address them and cast them out—or until the presence of the Lord stirs them up and they manifest themselves.

4. CAN'T DEMONS BE HANDLED MORE EFFECTIVELY BY SIMPLY PRAISING GOD AND IGNORING THEM?

In the move of the Holy Spirit today, the necessity to praise God is emphasized in many teachings. Biblical praise and worship have been sadly lacking in the historic, denominational churches. But where true rejoicing is being practiced, worshipers are discovering that *"a merry heart does good, like medicine"* (Proverbs 17:22).

Are there any limits to our being thankful in this life?

In everything give thanks; for this is the will of God in Christ Jesus for you.
(1 Thessalonians 5:18)

Giving thanks always for all things to God the Father in the name of our Lord Jesus Christ. (Ephesians 5:20)

Scripture tells us to give thanks *in* everything and *for* everything. Demonstrating such an attitude in the face of adversity will result in having a joyful spirit. By praising God, we can certainly prevent evil spirits of despondency, jealousy, and criticism from robbing us of the victory of Calvary.

The doctrine of praise, however, does not replace the doctrine of deliverance. The two are distinctly separate, yet complimentary. In many cases, a person may be bound by a *"spirit of heaviness"* (Isaiah 61:3), and this must be replaced by the spirit of joy. Praising God from the heart is difficult if one is bound by a spirit of heaviness.

Heaviness and depression are characteristics of a demon spirit, while joy is a characteristic of the Holy Spirit. Heaviness must be cast out in the name of Jesus before the Holy Spirit can be prayed in. After the Holy Spirit comes in, the formerly afflicted person will find it much easier to worship God.

NO SUBSTITUTE

Let me add this warning. Praising God with a loud voice or with raised hands can be done in the energy of the flesh, and not from the inner recesses of the heart. This exercise will produce nothing except weariness. A display of fleshly effort will certainly not cast out spirits from one's person.

First, we must get to the point of thanking God *in* our suffering. Then we must resist any temptation to be sorry for ourselves and begin to praise God in the unpleasant situation; then we will encourage our spirits and minds to believe God for the ultimate deliverance.

Although I've ministered to charismatic groups who have been taught to praise, I've still had to cast out the binding spirits from them. Praise is no substitute for deliverance, although praise certainly makes it easier to resist Satan.

The first reaction after deliverance is almost always a strong desire to praise God. Sometimes, the person may be so overcome with emotion that their praising is seen in weeping—which is a little hard for unsaved people to understand!

Praise is good, but it's not a substitute for deliverance. If you are afflicted, start praising God and seek the help you need to be free from demonic oppression. We need to experience deliverance from bondage and freedom in worship if we are to be whole in body, mind, and spirit.

5. DOESN'T THE MINISTRY OF DELIVERANCE MAGNIFY THE DEVIL RATHER THAN JESUS CHRIST?

On the contrary, the ministry of deliverance demonstrates the defeat of the devil more plainly than any other ministry I know! When we cast out wicked spirits in the name and authority of Jesus, Jesus is magnified, certainly not Satan and his evil hordes.

When you "magnify" anything, you make it look bigger or greater. How does *casting out* demons make them look greater than Jesus Christ? If we can order demons to leave in the name of Jesus, and they obey, doesn't that demonstrate the *power* of Jesus and the *lack of power* of the devil?

Where do we get the idea that defeating demons and casting them out gives *any* glory to the devil? Strange kind of glory *that* is! Is it any glory to a man when he is fired from his job? Is it any glory to demons when they are expelled in the name of Jesus? Far from it, casting out demons shows what miserable, weak creatures they really are!

This question is usually asked by Christians who attend churches where the biblical command to "cast out devils" is not being obeyed. These believers have not been taught that Jesus defeated demons, sickness, and disease at Calvary. These uninformed Christians go through life believing that they are "bearing their cross" when oppression comes. How the devil must enjoy our appalling ignorance of the power of the gospel!

THE HEART OF THE GOSPEL

What does Scripture say about Jesus' very purpose for coming to earth?

For this purpose the Son of God was manifested that He might destroy the works of the devil. (1 John 3:8)

God anointed Jesus of Nazareth with the Holy Spirit and with power, who went about doing good and healing all who were oppressed by the devil. (Acts 10:38)

> *Through death He [Jesus] might destroy him who had the power of death, that is, the devil, and release those who through fear of death were all their lifetime subject to bondage.*　　　　　　　　　　　　　　　　　(Hebrews 2:14–15)

The very heart of the gospel is Jesus' power to deliver suffering humanity from the cruel oppression of the devil. This is to be done through the preaching of the Word, casting out demons, and healing the sick.

The gimmicks, contests, and "giveaways" used by many churches today to encourage Christian people to "win souls" are certainly not based on the Bible. Yet those who "play at the gospel" with such unscriptural means of reaching the lost scoff at those of us who take the command of Jesus seriously to "cast out devils"!

One of the early demonstrations of Jesus' power took place when He cast a demon out of a man at Capernaum. (See Mark 1:23–27.) Later, He gave His twelve disciples authority over all demons and power to cure all diseases. (See Luke 9:1.) Finally, He passed on this ministry of deliverance to the entire church, saying, "*These signs will follow those who believe: In My name they will cast out demons*" (Mark 16–17).

The ministry of deliverance is not an unpleasant addition to the gospel. Casting out demons is one of the very essential ministries of those who preach the gospel. Praise God that the whole ministry of deliverance is being rediscovered in this present outpouring of the Holy Spirit! More and more Spirit-filled Christians are entering into the battle, and thousands are being set free.

6. WHY BLAME THE WORKS OF THE FLESH ON DEMONS?

Obviously, the temptations of the flesh are different from oppression by demons. If your problem is due to the weaknesses of the flesh, you can gain victory by dying to the desires of the flesh, trusting Jesus, and walking in the power of the Holy Spirit. But if your problem refuses to be conquered, then you may suspect the activity of demons.

These two kinds of problems are to be handled in two very different ways. The flesh is to be *crucified*, but demons are to be *cast out*. You cannot crucify a demon.

The Bible teaches us to bring the works of the flesh into subjection to Jesus Christ. We must "reckon" that our old Adamic nature, which is corrupt, is nailed to the cross of Jesus. This is a daily "reckoning."

> *Reckon yourselves to be dead indeed to sin, but alive to God in Christ Jesus our Lord. Therefore do not let sin reign in your mortal body, that you should obey it in its lusts. And do not present your members as instruments of unrighteousness to sin, but present yourselves to God as being alive from the dead, and your members as instruments of righteousness to God.*　　　　　(Romans 6:11–13)

Jesus can only live His life in a Christian's mortal body as He is given daily permission. But if that Christian gives his old fleshly nature back to Satan after reckoning it to be dead, then Satan will gladly take it again (or any portion of it). We must not blame the devil for our backslidings. We must blame ourselves.

COMBATTING THE WORKS OF THE FLESH

The apostle Paul clearly warned the Galatians about the works of the flesh.

Now the works of the flesh are evident, which are: adultery, fornication, uncleanness, lewdness, idolatry, sorcery, hatred, contentions, jealousies, outbursts of wrath, selfish ambitions, dissensions, heresies, envy, murders, drunkenness, revelries, and the like; of which I tell you beforehand, just as I also told you in time past, that those who practice such things will not inherit the kingdom of God.
(Galatians 5:19–21)

The solution for combatting the works of the flesh is found in that same chapter. "*I say then: Walk in the Spirit, and you shall not fulfill the lust of the flesh*" (Galatians 5:16). Christians need to replace sinful behavior or habits with Spirit-led activity. Instead of stealing, a person needs to labor with his hands. Unwholesome speech needs to be replaced by words that edify. (See Ephesians 4:28–29.)

The apostle Paul also exhorted the early Christians to give "*no place to the devil*" (Ephesians 4:27 KJV). If we surrender any part of our old nature to the devil after conversion, he immediately takes what he can and plots to "install" a demon to continue the work of evil.

This is what happens when a Christian backslides. In cases where chronic backsliding has occurred, the tormented individual may need to call for the elders of the church to pray the prayer of faith and set him free from these demonic powers.

I am not saying that a Christian becomes oppressed by demons the moment he backslides and partakes of fleshly activity. But he is certainly making a way for Satan to occupy an area of his life. There is no other protection from demonic oppression except repenting immediately, pleading the blood of Jesus, and being restored to full fellowship with Jesus. Maintaining a close walk with God is essential to keeping your deliverance.

7. IF THE MINISTRY OF DELIVERANCE IS VALID AND SCRIPTURAL, WHERE HAS IT BEEN THROUGHOUT THE CHURCH AGE?

The writings of some of the early church fathers, such as Iranaeus, Polycarp, Justin Martyr, and Clement, indicate that each new convert normally experienced deliverance at conversion before being baptized in water. Ancient writings of the

Roman Catholic Church reveal that certain priests had a ministry of deliverance, with coughing and manifestations similar to those we see in this ministry today.

Unfortunately, the church fell into apostasy with the passing of time. Despite losing its grip on many of the precious ministries and gifts of the Holy Spirit, the church began to recapture these truths through Martin Luther, the Wesley brothers, and other great evangelical leaders of the past century.

God continued to gradually restore forgotten truth. Justification by faith, baptism by immersion, and translating the Word of God into the language of the common people brought tremendous upheaval and change. At the turn of the twentieth century, the outpouring of the Holy Spirit revived speaking in tongues, prophesying, and the ministry of divine healing.

Halfway through this century, Christians began to realize that demons cause mental and physical sicknesses. Following the scriptural pattern of Christ and His disciples, we proceeded to cast demons out of afflicted individuals who sought relief from oppression. Deliverance meetings were met with scorn, especially by those groups that did not understand this ministry.

CLEANING UP THE CHURCH

Great opposition accompanied speaking in tongues at the turn of the century, but God still moved forward. Despite misunderstanding and opposition to the ministry of deliverance, God will still continue to move forward in victory.

Jesus Christ is preparing His church—His bride—to be without spot or wrinkle and to be prepared for His return. The bride needs a whole lot of "working over." Jesus is not returning for a Roman Catholic bride or a Protestant bride. He is returning for one church, composed of blood-washed men and women who are filled with the Spirit. Like the parable of the five wise virgins, He is looking for those whose lamps are full of oil and burning brightly.

The day of denominations has ended. The only "world church" will be the true one that Jesus is now building in every nation. This is the day of cleansing—and that is why God is restoring the ministry of deliverance to the church.

Many Christians need deliverance from satanic oppression. We need not be fearful of exercising our rightful authority in Jesus Christ to set the captives free. Let us use it to prepare the body of Christ for the last phase of the church age.

8. WOULDN'T IT BE BETTER TO CAST THE DEMONS OUT OF OURSELVES, RATHER THAN WORRYING ABOUT THE DEMONS IN OTHERS?

Some of the people who ask this question feel that "demon" is a dirty word, and that deliverance is such an embarrassing and private matter that they would far rather "deliver themselves" than ask for the prayers of someone else!

On the other hand, some people are concerned about the whole question of deliverance from another standpoint: they ask themselves, "How will it affect my attitude toward my Christian friend if I begin to believe that he is oppressed by a demon? Won't that block fellowship? Won't that make me unnecessarily wary of him? Wouldn't it be better for me not to entertain such thoughts, and just keep my own backyard clean?"

Let's address the second question first. If a friend of yours is obviously being oppressed by a demon, you do him no favor by ignoring his problem and acting like it doesn't exist!

If you truly love him as a brother in Christ, then you ought to spend time with him in prayer and fellowship until he comes to an understanding of his problem. When he is ready for deliverance, you ought to be the first to extend the helping hand, either by casting out the demon yourself or by taking him to a man or woman of God who practices this kind of ministry.

Another Christian should never be excluded from your fellowship just because he is being oppressed by a demon. Despite being under attack by Satan, he is a brother who also has the Holy Spirit in him. If there ever is a time when a person needs fellowship, it's when he's being oppressed by the devil. Don't sin against your Christian brother by ignoring his problems. Reach out in love and set the captive free in the name of Jesus.

DELIVERING YOURSELF?

Let me answer the first question about "delivering yourself." I agree that Christians can deliver themselves of demonic oppression—and many have done so. For some people, however, it *may* be a disturbing experience.

We know one lawyer in Michigan who heard teaching on deliverance and decided to try it on himself while driving home. As soon as he verbally rebuked the spirits in himself and commanded them to come out in Jesus' name, he immediately became nauseated. Not expecting that, he zipped into his driveway just in time, tumbled out of the car, and vomited on his front lawn! Later on, when he shared his experience with us, I reminded him that having someone else minister to him might have been much easier!

If submitting yourself to the ministry of deliverance seems somewhat embarrassing, just remember that this may be exactly the kind of humility that some of us need in order to be set free. Perhaps this is the reason the apostle James tells us to "*Confess your trespasses to one another, and pray for one another, that you may be healed*" (James 5:16).

Notice that confession of sin, which is a difficult if not embarrassing thing to do, precedes praying for one another. Once we have confessed our needs and our faults to one another, it is much easier to pray the prayer of faith. Remember, the prayer of *faith*, not the prayer of uncertainty, brings results.

9. IF THE GREAT ARCHANGEL MICHAEL DARED NOT REBUKE SATAN, WHO ARE WE THAT WE MAY DO SO?

This question is frequently asked by those who do not understand our amazing authority in Christ. Let's look at the passage upon which this argument is based.

> *Yet Michael the archangel, in contending with the devil, when he disputed about the body of Moses, dared not bring against him a reviling accusation, but said, "The Lord rebuke you!"* (Jude 9)

If this great archangel, who is the helper of all Christians (see Daniel 12:1), dared not bring any criticism or accusation against Satan, how is it that *we* can openly and pugnaciously rebuke the devil?

In the beginning, God made man after His own image—but a *little lower* than the angels. (See Psalm 8:5.) When Jesus, made in the likeness of sinful man, took man's place on the cross and died for the whole world, He defeated Satan completely and totally for all time.

Any person who trusts in Christ automatically becomes a son of God, raised to a much higher level than was possible in Old Testament days. In Old Testament times, the angels were higher than men; but after the cross, believers were elevated higher than angels, including Satan himself.

THE AUTHORITY OF THE BELIEVER

God the Father raised Jesus from the cross to the position of supreme conqueror, and put Him at His right hand on His throne. Christ is seated in heavenly places "*far above all principality and power and might and dominion, and every name that is named, not only in this age but also in that which is to come*" (Ephesians 1:21). All the defeated enemies are now under Jesus' feet.

Positionally, we are in Christ, and therefore we share in His victory. According to the words of Jesus, we may also put *our* feet on these angelic and demon powers.

> *Behold, I give unto you power [exousia: authority] to tread on serpents and scorpions, and over all the power [dunamis: ability] of the enemy: and nothing shall by any means hurt you.* (Luke 10:19 KJV)

Jesus was raised to sit in heavenly places by His Father, and is authorized to elevate us also, as we abide in Him. We may exercise His power and authority without any fear of reprisals from our adversary, the devil.

Most people are unaware of this authority vested in Christians and, therefore, do not use it. Others are aware of it, but may be afraid to exercise it lest they get a "kick back." Their fear and inactivity allows Satan to continue his dirty work unopposed.

Too often we pray but do not take our authority. Jesus did not tell us to pray for Him to rebuke the devil. He did that on the cross. He tells us to rebuke the enemy in His name. We become an extension of Jesus on earth as members of His Body—flesh of His flesh and bone of His bone. (See Ephesians 5:30.)

Jesus did not die for angels. He died for humans. Angels have become our servants to help us exercise the ministry of Jesus here on earth. (See Hebrews 1:14.) If He cast out demons (fallen angels), we may do the same.

We now possess His power of attorney, and we must do as He commanded us:

And as you go, preach, saying, "The kingdom of God is at hand." Heal the sick, cleanse the lepers, raise the dead, cast out demons. Freely you have received, freely give. (Matthew 10:7–8)

The work of every minister of the New Testament gospel is summed up in this commission. If we preach without healing and casting out demons in His name, we are simply saying, to our everlasting shame, that we know a better way to preach the gospel.

THE KISS OF SATAN

CONTENTS

1

THE LAW OF OPPOSITES

It seems that there is a universal law of opposites. One seems to counterbalance the other. If we find a positive, we must expect a negative. Darkness is the absence of light, and when light is manifested it dispels the darkness.

In the study of the principles of electricity, we find that there is a positive and a negative, and without these two opposite poles there can be no flow of current. Instead, a condition of static immobility would result. And when we consider the behavior of alternating current, we find that the positive peak is equal to the negative peak; but the negative component may be rectified (or converted) and made positive. We can use this as an analogy of the workings in the world of spirits, both holy and unholy.

The whole of creation is held together by the Holy Spirit of God. God is the original Creator of all matter and spirit and without His eternal being there would be nothing. But matter and spirit are extensions of His mind, for He spoke and "it was so" and God saw that it was good. In the New Testament this is taught by Paul in Colossians 1:16–17 where we read that "all things" both physical and spiritual were created by Jesus (the spoken Word of God), and they were created for Him, and thereafter are maintained by Him. In Hebrews 11:3, we read that the worlds were framed by the Word of God and were made of invisible things. Thus, spiritual forces of God created visible matter, and the very composition of these elements in their atomic form is maintained by the Spirit of God alone.

The bridge between the tangible and the intangible is real. There is a vital link between matter and spirit. It is impossible to understand the workings in the physical realm without understanding the sustaining force of God; but there is a negative force which interrupts this state of well-being, and this force is also personal. God is the eternal person, but Satan is the opposite—a created person. God creates; Satan destroys. God heals; Satan makes sick.

The biblical picture of the Christian Church is a composition of men and women filled with the Holy Spirit and thus receiving blessings of health, strength, joy, and peace. This church, called the body of Christ, is to show forth and demonstrate His saving grace to all who are activated by "other spirits" and to deliver them from the thralldom of these spirits, converting them to faith in Christ so that they also may be filled with God's Spirit. Using the electrical analogy, God desires to transform the individual from the negative cycle to the positive cycle. The Bible actually uses the word *transform*: "...*do not be conformed to this world, but be transformed by the renewing of your mind*" (Romans 12:2). The power of God completely changes the whole nature of the individual by rectification of the spirit of man through the Holy Spirit. The negative personality becomes positive in action and behavior. The mentally and spiritually bound becomes liberated as a transformation takes place.

In the law of opposites, day cannot be fully appreciated unless we have been through the night. We venture to suggest that vigorous health cannot be enjoyed to the fullest without the opposite experience of sickness and disease. The realization of the holiness and greatness of Almighty God cannot be appreciated in the right perspective, unless man is faced with an alternative. Man being a creature of free will is therefore faced with two opposites: good and evil. These are ever around him. He has to make a choice between the two each day.

Long ago Joshua challenged God's holy people by saying, "*Choose for yourselves this day whom you will serve, whether the gods which your fathers served that were on the other side of the River, or the gods of the Amorites, in whose land you dwell. But as for me and my house, we will serve the* LORD" (Joshua 24:15). The choice here is between God and gods: God, represented to a Christian as the triune God (Father, Son and Holy Spirit), or a multiplicity of gods.

As the Trinity works in unison, so does Satan and his gods. As God the Father manifests His Son on earth by the Holy Spirit, so does Satan, the Prince of this world, manifest his evil powers by his unholy spirits. The image of a heathen god is but the outward symbol of the evil spirit behind it. The real god is not the idol of wood or stone, but the powerful demon inhabiting the idol and its associated worship.

The word *occult* basically means "hidden." Thus, the danger of the occult will be hidden from natural eyes and understanding and can only be revealed by the Spirit of God through the operation of the charismatic gifts. The fact that the spirit world is invisible does not mean it does not exist; in fact, as we have explained, the physical is in fact the manifestation of the spiritual; and where the laws of God are upset, as in the case of breakdown in mental or physical health, we must look for another spirit, an evil spirit, which will be invading and upsetting the perfect balance created by God. God gives us His health; Satan steals it from us and then tells us a lie by saying we have no right to expect to be healthy. He is the Father of Lies. When

Jesus rebuked the wind and the waves, He was not rebuking air and water but the spirit behind these elements which Satan was using for destruction. Water is good to drink and to swim in, but not to drown in. The same air we breathe for life can be so whipped up by satanic fury that it can blow our house down and kill us. What matters, then, is the agent behind the storm. Though we cannot see the occult agent, yet we can feel and experience his power in the destructive elements.

Deuteronomy 28 clearly gives us the choice of two ways. It contains the law of spiritual opposites and the effects which happen according to our choice. If we obey God, then a whole catalogue of blessings are promised in health, work, occupation, and farm stock. Blessings overtake us. We do not seek after them; they follow us like the signs enumerated in Mark 16:16–18. On the other hand, if we do not obey, then a very long list of curses will automatically follow us. There will be no avoiding them. These curses, the opposite of the blessings, come from Satan through his unholy spirits. The blessings come from God by His Holy Spirit.

The natural man with his rationalizations and philosophies will never understand the cause of his problem. It is "occult," that is to say, "hidden" from view. We pray to God, and the Holy Spirit comes to our aid with ministering angels sent by God. Both the Holy Spirit and the angels are outside the realm of natural understanding or comprehension. If we do not pray to God in faith for help, then we do not release the positive forces of good on our behalf, but we maintain a state of unbelief in which the negative forces of evil operate automatically to our hurt and destruction. We can see the evidence of faith or absence of faith, but we cannot see the primary cause which is spiritual. Only with our spiritual eyes shall we see and understand these mysteries.

The spirit of an unconverted person is totally dark. It is only when the Light of the World, Jesus, shines into our spirits that we become new creatures, and the candle of the Lord is lit within us. "*The spirit of a man is the lamp of the* Lord, *searching all the inner depths of his heart*" (Proverbs 20:27); but we also read that "*there will be no prospect for the evil man; The lamp of the wicked will be put out*" (Proverbs 24:20). In the case of the righteous man, the candle is shining and illuminating the very inner recesses of the personality; but in the case of the disobedient man, the candle is put out. The result is total darkness and complete lack of understanding which often leads to early physical death and insanity. When we allow Jesus to shine into our beings and reveal the Word of God to us, then we realize how much darkness there is. As we turn from darkness to light, conversion takes place. We are transformed.

On one side of us there is eternal life and light; on the other is eternal death and darkness. We are in the middle. The decision of which way we go, the broad path that leads to destruction or the narrow way that leads to life (see Matthew 7:13–14), is ours alone. No one can make it for us. Satan ever seeks to capture and blind us by telling us he alone is the angel of light. *"For Satan himself transforms himself into an angel of light. Therefore it is no great thing if his ministers also transform themselves into ministers of righteousness"* (2 Corinthians 11:14–15). Notice in this case that Satan, who is a spirit, transforms himself; but we are transformed by an operation of the Holy Spirit. Satan by his demon spirits transforms his own ministers as angels of light to deceive us. They appear in many guises but are always controlled by an occult spirit. They can minister in churches claiming to be Unitarian, Modernistic, Theosophic, or any of the Christ-denying cults that deny the efficacy of the Blood of Jesus to cleanse. They can come as false prophets and false christs (see Matthew 24:24), or they can come as sheep in wolves' clothing, but inwardly they are as ravening wolves (see Matthew 7:15), and we are told to beware of them. They come as angels of light, as sheep to be accepted of the unwary, but the spirits operating in and through them are demonic and destructive. These are occult spirits.

There are men who creep into churches and pray for the sick, and miracles seem to take place, but they are operating in the strength and revelation of the occult spirits, deceiving many. Jesus said, *"You will know them by their fruits"* (Matthew 7:16). They often put on a false front of "love" to deceive, and the evil spirit shows in their faces. As someone has described it, it has the appearance of a "plastic face"—an unreal mask; but challenge them and plead the blood of Jesus and their spirit will soon be revealed for what it is: an occult, deceiving, religious spirit.

Beware of false prophets.

2

PERSONAL EXPERIENCES

If God intends to use a man in a positive way, He may first give him some education of the negative way. We learn by contrast. As a child I grew up in a nominal Christian home and went regularly to the Scottish Presbyterian Church, but my mother was enmeshed on her side of the family in spiritism and variations of the occult. I was led to understand that the family was really communicating with the human spirits of departed people and that these people desired to get in touch with us through the agency of a medium. My Aunt Esther was such a medium. My eldest uncle, Walter, was a professor at Leeds University in England and was one of the first to practice hypnotism clinically in Leeds Infirmary. Another uncle, Aubrey, was a medical doctor and studied occult practices of various kinds. Uncle Harry claimed to be a pantheist, i.e., one who disavows the personality of God but sees the universe and God as the same thing. Aunt Daisy was a Theosophist of high rank, believing in the equality of Buddha, Mohammed, Confucius, Jesus Christ, etc., but not in salvation through the blood of Jesus Christ.

You can see that our whole family was one big mess of occultism in its various manifestations. They believed in reincarnation, astral plains, and communications with the dead (necromancy). No one except my mother, who later was truly converted, believed that Jesus was the Son of God and the Savior of the world. They attended séances, saw trumpets floating around the room, experienced levitation, heard the voices of spirits, enjoyed table rapping, and took part in both spirit writing and spirit drawing. My aunt Esther used to draw the internal anatomy of humans with uncanny accuracy, and these were checked by both of my uncles who were medical doctors. Mother used to hold a pencil in her hand and watch the controlling spirits write in large writing all kinds of nonsense (and some sense). I was always taught that this "proved" that life existed after death.

Hour after hour, I listened as my medium Aunt talked incessantly to my mother about these things. I saw "spirit photographs," pictures of "fairies," and was taught about ectoplasm and the materialization of spirit forms. Let me explain. When a spirit medium is in a deep trance and under the control of the familiar spirit, it is possible for this spirit to take some of the physical matter of the medium's body and use it to materialize a form, sometimes the face of the departed person.

Recently a man told me that he had been to a trumpet séance. As the speaking trumpets would "sail" round the room, he asked the spirit if he might shake hands, so the spirit offered the trumpet as a hand. This man told me that he insisted on shaking hands with the spirit purporting to be the spirit of a departed person. Immediately this man felt three clammy cold fingers of ectoplasm in his hand which he described as dead cow's udders. He was disgusted.

I was familiar with clairvoyance, psychometry, and all the paraphernalia that goes along with the occult. As a child of twelve, I took part in the experiment of a heavy dining room table walking up the wall of my grandfather's house in Beckenham, Kent, England. I have heard my uncles speaking to the spirits, who replied with one knock for "yes" and two knocks for "no"—a kind of demonic Urim and Thummim. I have seen them using the ouija board, or planchette, and the spirit behind the board would spell out their answers. Today a whole generation of our young people can purchase these ouija boards and "play" with them for kicks, not realizing the danger involved.

When I was a young man, one of my friends who, like myself, had recently got married, was encouraged by a third friend to try "spirit writing." My friend, coming from a God-fearing Anglican home, knew nothing of this at all. He simply took a pencil, waited, and the spirit began to take control and started writing. Various questions were asked, such as, "Who are you?"—to which the spirit replied by writing the name of an Italian. My friend Don had never heard of this name before, but he went with his wife to the library to check; and sure enough, it was the name of a sixteenth century Italian painter. He was immediately afraid and dropped the practice.

But how could this spirit know about this Italian painter? Could it indeed have been the actual human spirit of the artist? No, it was a demon spirit that lived in the mind and body of the artist and knew his intimate, evil life. Demons do not die; they do not sleep. They wander naked seeking the house of another body through whom they desire to manifest their evil nature and characteristics. All we have to do is open the door to them. The door of occultism in any form is that which they seek. No wonder Paul said, "...*nor give place to the devil*" (Ephesians 4:27).

I have seen my uncles and aunts put their fingers under the armpits of another person and lift. By levitation of the spirits human bodies are lifted. In cases of spiritist experts, the mediums can be lifted right up to the ceiling by the spirits. Objects in haunted houses can suddenly sail across the room to be dashed senselessly against the wall.

It is easy to say, "I don't believe these things." Did not Paul speak of unbelief when he wrote, *"For what if some did not believe? Will their unbelief make the faithfulness of God without effect?"* (Romans 3:3). This Scripture, of course, applies strictly to belief in the works of the Holy Spirit; but as we are trying to show that we learn by contrasts, many who refuse to believe in God also refuse to believe in the negative supernatural of Satan and his demons.

Many who investigate the evidence of both the Holy Spirit in healings, miracles, tongues, prophecy, etc., and the supernatural happenings in the occult, cannot explain these things at all. So they try to make a science of it and create university courses called "parapsychology," where young people are led to study the workings of demons. Many young people become enmeshed in dangerous occult practices through such studies.

In my own family, disaster struck time and time again. Without mentioning names, there has been adultery and sudden deaths among my cousins. Husbands have left wives with children, and then to seek solace, they have gone to false cult religions instead of Jesus, who heals, forgives, and cleanses by His blood. Marriages have broken up, and one in particular has become a wastrel and an immoral man. The mark of Cain is on the family.

We cannot play with sin and escape contamination. There is no doubt in my mind that everyone, who has in times past been contaminated by occultism in any form, has also been polluted by evil spirits, either in their minds or bodies. The effect seems to be cumulative, and the older the person, the more the evil spirits dig down deep into the personality, binding and destroying like a spiritual cancer. Senility may often be traced to occult involvement in times past or in the history of our parents. Cancer and other foul diseases may also be traced. There seems to be an occult line which is very tenacious and has to be confessed, forsaken, and forgiven before it can be broken by the prayer of faith given in the name of Jesus.

When I first sought the baptism in the Holy Spirit in 1939, I knew nothing of these things. My friends urged me to "plead the blood of Jesus," but I refused. I could not. They joyously did so, and of course the effect was immediate. I stiffened out like a board from a kneeling position and fell flat on my face, wondering what was happening! It was years later when I realized that, at that moment, an evil spirit of occult contamination had left me, by honoring of the blood of Jesus. It was cast out of me by the power of God that answered to the cry of the blood. Satan is always defeated by any mention of the blood of Jesus whether in song or prayer. A week later I went to another "seeking meeting," as they were called then, and was quickly filled with the Holy Spirit, because this time I was freely able to plead the blood. I heard myself begin speaking in a heavenly language as the Holy Spirit came in. The occult spirit had gone out.

My mother was a great student of the writings and prophecies of Johanna Southcott, a last century medium. She made many false prophecies which were published and which led to the forming of a society. We pleaded with her to burn them, but she said she had been helped so much by these writings that she refused to destroy them. Although she followed me into the truths of the baptism in the Holy Spirit and received an experience of "speaking in tongues," she never had too much liberty. When I first started telling her about the gifts of the Holy Spirit, especially the true gift of prophecy, she said, "I know all about these things!" What she really meant was that she was familiar with Satan's counterfeits. She was unable to discern the true from the false.

So many people in our historic churches are unable to understand that healings are indeed practiced in spiritist churches with "messages." When they hear of gifts of healing being practiced in New Testament churches which honor the blood of Jesus, they think of all supernatural happenings as coming from the same source—God. Tongues, interpretation, and prophecy are what they have in séances! Satan is a good counterfeiter.

So many in spiritism say that the evidence of the supernatural and the friendliness of the people have drawn them closer to God, and they are not willing to depart from their spiritual harlotry.

3

THE "APPEARANCE" OF SAMUEL

In 1 Samuel 28:7–25, we have an amazing story of spiritism at its worst. The witch of Endor had a familiar spirit—that is to say, she was possessed and motivated by an evil spirit who "divined" messages from the unseen occult state. The demon spirits in her, in favorable circumstances such as a trance, would communicate their thoughts through the mouth of the human witch.

It is strongly emphasized among spiritists, who now claim the title "Christian Spiritualists," that this account is a classic case of a medium bringing Samuel back out of the unseen state, and that the whole story illustrates the "truth" that it is possible not only to communicate with dead persons but also to see them in bodily manifestation. The wording of the Scripture would seem to bear this out. Saul said to the witch, *"Bring up Samuel for me"* (verse 11). And when the woman saw Samuel, she cried with a loud voice and said, *"An old man is coming up, and he is covered with a mantle"* (verse 14). And Saul perceived that it was Samuel. And Samuel said to Saul, *"Why have you disturbed me by bringing me up?"* (verse 15), to which Samuel replied, *"So why do you ask me, seeing the LORD has departed from you and has become your enemy?"* (verse 16).

If Samuel really did appear and speak to Saul, then the laws of God would have been set aside. God would have contradicted what He already said and spoken through Samuel when he was alive. This is an impossible contradiction. In 1 Samuel 28:6, we read that Saul inquired of the Lord and the Lord answered him not. The three major means whereby God would speak to Saul were closed: dreams in the night to his spirit, Urim and Thummim in the breastplate of the High Priest, and the voice of His prophets. Saul was literally cut off from God and all means of communication with Him. In desperation he sought another means forbidden by God—a voice from the pit. It was an absolute impossibility that God would speak to him, and we will endeavor to prove this.

In the law we read, *"And the person who turns to mediums and familiar spirits, to prostitute himself with them, I will set My face against that person and cut him off from his people"* (Leviticus 20:6). The law was clear. Saul disobeyed it; therefore, in going to a woman who had a familiar spirit (a demon), he received the reply of that demon, because all communication with God by His Holy Spirit was severed. Saul himself was no longer considered a child of God, and he was cut off from among his own Israelite people. As we read later, Jesus spoke of a branch of the vine being pruned or cut off the tree; it then died and was burned. (See John 15.) This was the inexorable fate of King Saul. It was not Samuel who spoke to Saul; it was a demon spirit impersonating Samuel, and this spirit could be materialized since this possibility exists even in advanced spiritism. The witch of Endor was a very powerful medium.

Saul confessed to the demon impersonating Samuel that God would not speak to him anymore, either by dreams or prophets. (See verse 15.) How then could this be a prophet speaking to Saul when he already confessed that the voice of the prophets was silent? It could only be an impersonator.

This seems to be made very clear in the final account of the tragic death of King Saul. *"So Saul died for his unfaithfulness which he had committed against the LORD, because he did not keep the word of the LORD, and also because he consulted a medium for guidance. But he did not inquire of the LORD; therefore He killed him"* (1 Chronicles 10:13–14). The reason for his untimely death was because he inquired of an evil spirit. God would not have allowed him to die if he inquired of God. It is clearly stated that the communication was with a demon spirit, because all communication with God by the Holy Spirit had been completely and finally severed. Saul did not speak to Samuel. He spoke to an evil occult spirit impersonating Samuel, and God had no alternative under the dispensation of the law but to cause His judgment to operate. Saul died.

It is very important to remember that Saul did not seek the Lord; he went to seek a woman that had a familiar spirit. (See 1 Samuel 28:7.) Saul already sought the Lord but only received silence. The ministry of Samuel was to be a prophet, a mouthpiece of God. God spoke to Saul and others through Samuel. No other voice came through him because he was filled with the Holy Spirit. The Apostle Peter makes it clear that the ancient prophets spoke as they were moved by the Holy Spirit: *"For prophecy never came by the will of man, but holy men of God spoke as they were moved by the Holy Spirit"* (2 Peter 1:21). Even when Balaam tried to prophesy for financial gain, the only words that came out of his mouth were from the Holy Spirit.

Assuming that Saul did indeed see and talk to Samuel in the witch's home, no words would have come out of his mouth, for God had already shown that He would never speak to Saul again by a prophet. The genuine Samuel would have been silent like his God. All that Saul hoped to gain was supernatural information from a source other than God; therefore, he went to inquire of a familiar spirit, which is specifically mentioned as one of the sins of Israel in Isaiah 8:19, where inquiring of the dead by the agency of familiar spirits is contrasted with seeking after God. It seems we have the other side of the prophetic coin here. One side enables us to communicate with God by His Holy Spirit, and the other with evil spirits simulating the dead.

When the witch was using her occult powers, she was alarmed when she saw what appeared to be Samuel, plus other spirits referred to as "gods" ascending from the earth. We have already explained that when God commands us not to serve "other gods," He had in mind that we should not serve the demons behind the idols of the heathen. The first commandment, "*You shall have no other gods before* [or instead of] *Me*," is immediately followed by the second commandment which is a logical corollary of the first: "*You shall not make for yourself a carved image*" (Exodus 20:3–4).

It is impossible to worship an unseen occult spirit without some visible manifestation to represent the deity behind that image. This is why some idols are so hideous, especially in China, for the worshippers have actually seen the appearance of the gods they worship. Witch doctors, swamis, holy men, and high priests are merely the mediums through whom the demons manifest themselves. All heathen religions of any form are of the occult. It is unfortunate that the practice of making "holy images" crept into the Church at the time of Constantine, when he forced everyone of note in the pagan Roman Empire to be baptized by decree to become "Christians." The heathen succeeded in bringing their idols into the Church by giving them Christian names.

There is a good reason why the Bible teaches us that no man has ever seen God. He is the invisible God and the only way we are going to "see" Him is by seeing the Son. (See John 14:9.) Jesus is the express image of the invisible God (see Colossians 1:15), and no stone or wooden statue will portray God Almighty! The Bible says that Hezekiah had to destroy the brazen serpent which Moses put up on a pole, because after people were healed by looking on it (for it typified Christ) it became an idol worshipped by the Israelites. As soon as we start to worship the creation rather than the Creator, we are into the world of the occult. (See Romans 1:21–25.)

In Deuteronomy 18:11, one of the forbidden practices was that of consulting with familiar spirits. As we have said, Saul had no intention of consulting with God. His intention was clear; he sought out a witch with a familiar spirit.

The evil spirit impersonating Samuel would, of course, have known Samuel's way of life and many details that occurred in his life. Where demons appear in spiritist séances and communicate "messages," it is highly probable that they actually lived in the departed person, and so could actually speak the language and accent of that person. We are not suggesting that this was so in the case of Samuel. He was a servant of God and therefore a much feared enemy of Satan. No doubt Satan and his demons watched his every move for many years. Given the right circumstances, demons can speak in other languages as well as prophesy through spiritist mediums. These demons will prophesy through false prophets—right in our churches—and in Deuteronomy 13:1–3 we read that their instruction would be to serve "other gods."

God permits these poor deluded souls to be in our midst, for He said that He wants to test *"you to know whether you love the* Lord *your God with all your heart and with all your soul"* (Deuteronomy 13:3). Here we get the contrast approach, learning the positive from the negative. If we never hear a false prophecy or come into contact with a false prophet (or prophetess), then how will we recognize the true one? The spirits that inhabit these prophets are called "lying spirits" in the Bible, and we are counseled to test the spirits whether they are of God. *"Beloved, do not believe every spirit, but test the spirits, whether they are of God; because many false prophets have gone out into the world"* (1 John 4:1).

Any prophecy that detracts from Jesus and advertises man is the utterance of a demon. The Holy Spirit is only sent to *"glorify [Jesus]"* (John 16:14). Saul came under the bondage of a lying spirit after he rebelled against God, and this spirit obviously enticed him to go to the witch.

Having identified the demon spirit that personified Samuel, we then find that he gave himself away to Saul. The final message that he gave was, *"Tomorrow you and your sons will be with me"* (1 Samuel 28:19). The spirit was "brought up" by the witch out of the pit called Sheol, or the place of departed spirits. Samuel was in Abraham's bosom, not in torment but at rest, and nothing would disturb his sweet rest in the abode of the righteous dead.

There is a great gulf fixed between these two places, as we read in the parable of Lazarus and the rich man. Lazarus was carried by the angels to Abraham's bosom, but the rich man died, was buried and went to hell! (See Luke 16:19–26.) If we wish to enter into the eternal state of bliss, we must cross over the bridge of this great gulf by accepting the sacrifice of Jesus. And we must do this now. It is too late after death. Any teaching which is contrary to this simple truth is out of the pit, from a seducing spirit, and is a doctrine of demons. (See 1 Timothy 4:1.) There are many specious cults that deny the simple truths of the duality of the gospel. Universalism, for example, teaches that all go to heaven ultimately. This is the teaching of an occult spirit.

The only known case of a man being brought back from Abraham's bosom was that of Moses, who appeared on the Mount of Transfiguration. (See Matthew 17:1–18.) We are distinctly told, however, that this was an act of God, not of a demonized witch or wizard. God is omnipotent and can do as He wills. If we try to imitate Him by interfering with the underground world of demons, we shall be "cut off" and probably die before our time in sickness or mental disease.

In praying for the sick today we have been amazed at the numbers who have been engaged in some forbidden occult practice in past times. If we give our minds and bodies to these cruel spirits, they will take the place we give them, will refuse to leave, and will multiply in our minds and bodies like germs. They have to be confessed, forsaken, and cast out in the Name of Jesus before any release and healing can take place.

4

OCCULT PRACTICES

In Deuteronomy 18:10, we have a command forbidding the heathen practice of making sons or daughters to pass through fire. Some interpret this as the human sacrifice practiced in sonic heathen religions as mentioned in Deuteronomy 12:31: *"...for they burn even their sons and daughters in the fire to their gods."* The command in Deuteronomy 18:10, however, refers to going through fire, and coming out unharmed.

In the most interesting book *From Witchcraft to Christ*, Doris Irvine tells how she achieved the great distinction of actually walking into a great fire on Dartmoor in England during a great conclave of European witches and warlocks. Miss Irvine testified that when she was actually in the fire, Satan himself would be there, would hold out his hand to her and see her safely through. This actually happened as she foretold, and she was promoted to Queen of witches for Europe for one year. She suffered no harm in the fire and even the smell of smoke was not on her black witch's gown. Doris Irvine was saved during Evangelist Eric Hutchings' campaign and was later delivered from the occult demons through the ministry of a Baptist minister in the west of England.

We knew of the case of a Spirit-filled minister who went to Indonesia, and while watching heathen witch doctors walk on live hot coals and stones, was challenged to do the same in the power of his God. He accepted the challenge and actually walked on hot stones with no harmful results. We feel that this was unwise and was presuming on God's goodness, for we are told not to tempt God. His protections operate for us, as in the case of the three Hebrew youths who were thrown into the fiery furnace because of their testimony. They declared that God would deliver them, and He did, without the smell of smoke on their garments.

We see here the positive and negative principle again. Both Satan and God can protect in fire. In like manner, God promises that if we drink poison we shall not be harmed, but we must not tempt God by experimenting.

Similarly, in Mark 16:18, believers are told that they can take up serpents without harm, but this should not be done deliberately to prove God and tempt Him. Many have died in so doing. Serpents typify Satan and his demons, and we are supposed to keep as far away from them and their spells as we can! When a viper bit Paul on the back of his hand on the island of Malta, he shook it off back into the fire and never gave it another thought. He knew about God's protection. (See Acts 28:3–5.)

We understand that it is possible for a person to be so hypnotized and put into a trance that a surgeon can perform an operation without using an anesthetic. We have even heard of demon-possessed warlocks operating on a human body without the incision of a knife, and then closing up the wound with no remaining scar. This may sound like a very tall story, and we cannot prove it, but we have read that it does happen in certain heathen cultures. There are areas of the occult that are terrifying without knowledge of the protection of the blood of Jesus.

When heathen priests have their ritualistic orgies, working themselves into frenzy and inviting demons into their lives, they can freely demonstrate their ability to walk in fire, live coals, and hot stones. This is done in India, Indonesia, Africa, and dark areas of the world, and proves that the power of spirit is stronger than matter. It also shows us by contrast the incredible power of the Holy Spirit to keep us from harm if we abide in the secret place of the most high. (See Psalm 91:1, 10–14.) The promise is that no evil shall befall us, and the angels of God will have charge over us to keep us in all our ways. We shall tread on the lion and the adder, just as Jesus assures us in the New Testament. *"I give you the authority to trample on serpents and scorpions"* (Luke 10:19). The trouble with us is that we find it easier to run than to tread! But the promise still stands!

In India, heathen priests and holy men have the ability to lie on beds of nails or drag carts with hooks in the flesh of their backs with no sign of blood. Spears pierce their flesh and spikes pierce their noses, but no blood appears—no pain is felt. Why is this? They have given their bodies over to the power of Satan, and he works these miracles to show them his great power. They know nothing of the greater power of Jesus or the cleansing power of His blood. How much more, if we give our minds and bodies to the Lord Jesus Christ, will He keep us from harm and danger?

The black art of divination is also mentioned in Deuteronomy 18:10–12. This is mystic insight into the future in its many forms such as reading palms, reading Tarot cards or teacups, and crystal ball gazing. It can include water or mineral divining by rod or twig over land or maps. A good illustration of this is the well-known case of the young girl in Acts 16:16–18 who had a spirit of divination. She was a young witch and prophesied correctly that Paul and his friends were servants of the Most High God. This was true and Satan knew it. Satan will advertise God for his own ends. Paul took dominion over this spirit of divination and cast it out. Simon Magus in

Acts 8 was another well-known man in Samaria for his satanic miracles—known as "the great power of God." There is a man called Harry Edwards in London, England, who can fill the Royal Albert Hall with seven thousand people and can heal and do miracles, but he openly admits that his power is from the spirit world. A miracle is a sign of a spirit working, but not necessarily the Holy Spirit! Again, we see the principle of the negative in contrast to the positive.

If anyone tries to get their fortune told, they are automatically entering into the world of spirits and are attracting demonic power and ability to themselves. Their minds receive the "messages" given by these demons. In many cases, these messages seem non-sensible, but at other times, surprising shafts of truth come through. Demons cannot foretell the future; this belongs alone to God, the Great I Am. But demons are very intelligent and make some surprising deductions from known facts in fortune telling.

Let me say right here that it is even dangerous to ask a Holy Spirit filled person to prophesy over you, for this reduces the gifts of the Spirit to "private fortune telling," and however sincere the child of God may be, they may attract to themselves another spirit if they disobey God in the proper use of the gifts of the Holy Spirit which are for the edification of the Church. (See 1 Corinthians 14:12.) It is a different matter if God by the Spirit reveals something to a minister of the Lord. Many times God uses a person for the ultimate blessing of a brother or sister. This often happens in healing lines where the sick are being prayed for. The revelation is not sought after. It is word of knowledge given by God.

The elders of Moab and Midian approached Balaam with the reward of divination. (See Numbers 22:7.) They were not interested in a pure word of prophecy. They wanted an occult spirit to put a curse on Israel. Balaam tried so hard to earn this fortune telling money, but the Spirit of God would not respond, and so Balaam gave a blessing instead. A fortune teller will usually ask a price! Because of Israel's refusal to obey the law we read that *"caused their sons and daughters to pass through the fire, practiced witchcraft and soothsaying, and sold themselves to do evil in the sight of the LORD, to provoke Him to anger. Therefore the LORD was very angry with Israel, and removed them from His sight"* (2 Kings 17:17–18). Ten tribes were banished from God's presence into the hands of the cruel Assyrians because they preferred to practice occultism for gain, rather than to serve the Lord for blessing. Do we not see this across the world again in our day? Why should any of God's people prefer witchcraft to God? It is because of the "kicks." Fire walking and fortune telling can be very entertaining, but Satan has the last kick. We shall get kicked out!

When the Ark of the Covenant had been in the land of the Philistines for seven months, the priests of Israel brought in the diviners to ask their advice in getting it back! (See 1 Samuel 6:1–2.) Is this not the same among some of the priests of our old-line denominational churches who encourage spiritistic practices and give their Sunday school children Ouija boards to play with? The priests of Israel thought God let them down when He punished them. No doubt King Saul did as well. They went to the negative source for information. They offered the opinion that maybe "*it happened to* [them] *by chance.*" (1 Samuel 6:9). The very wording of their pronouncements was not of God. We don't get "lucky chances" with God. We get positive blessings if we believe. There were plenty of false prophets in Israel who prophesied lying pronouncements. They were fortune tellers. And we still have them today!

5

DELUSIONS

In May, 1973, a young teenage girl in Ontario was held for the slaying of a person with a butcher knife in a "ritualistic slaying." Her cult in California demanded a human blood sacrifice, although the sacrifices of animals are quite common among satanist cults. Usually some of the blood is mixed with human blood obtained from incisions in the arm and then is drunk. We see a most revolting opposite of using blood in their sacrificial offerings as compared to the blood of Jesus Christ which He offered for the sins of the world on the cross, and which we may use by faith and drink in the communion service.

Before any young person arrives at the rite of drinking blood in a black mass, he will first be introduced to drugs in varying forms, because it is while the human mind is thus exposed that demons enter in and stay. The more a person subjects himself to drugs, the more the demons take over progressive control of the mind, until the spirits become the dominant factor in the human behavior pattern. Thus, any kind of atrocious crime can be committed, because the motivating force will be demonic and not human. Demons seek bodies in which their evil nature can be manifested. I admit that this seems quite an impossible truth for the "intellectually wise" to face up to; but owing to the terrible growth of occultism in our society, especially in high schools, people are being forced to notice something which they have previously screened from their minds.

As I am writing this I have a letter from some people in California who tell me that they have been "forced into a ministry of deliverance." They did not seek it; neither did they want it, because, they explained, it was "too controversial!" Young people came to them for help, so when they prayed for them in the name of Jesus, demons would start manifesting themselves by speaking, arguing, and then violently ejecting through the throat. When God called me into this ministry back in 1947, I was not "looking for demons." I was trying to help people and was not really aware that the cause of their troubles might be demons. In fact, I honestly knew nothing about evil spirits. Since those days literally thousands have been set free by a commanding prayer given in Jesus' name and the efficacy of His precious blood claimed against these terrible destructive personalities.

Our modern "civilization" is being forced to take note that things are happening today of which no previous generation had detailed knowledge. We have buried our heads in the sand, or preached that these things could be swept under the rug of "parapsychology." No one really understood the meaning of the word. The Bible tells us the whole sordid story. To play with any form of occultism will force you into the hands of evil demonic forces from which you will not be able to extricate yourself. God will cut you off from His protection and Satan will progressively bind your mind and body until you die. Some do this in the guise of a religion that "helps them." Oh, the pity of it all!

Again referring to Deuteronomy 18, the next category on the list for consideration is the "observer of times." Manasseh, King of Judah, was one who consulted with familiar spirits and observed times. God said, "*I will wipe Jerusalem as one wipes a dish, wiping it and turning it upside down*" (2 Kings 21:13). The King led the people into sin. Had there been newspapers, radio and television in those days, they would have had horoscopes, fortune telling columns, charts of the heavens, and zodiac symbol charms. These things would have been done by the King and people in direct rebellion against the known laws of God. Is it any wonder that Canada, the United States, and other freedom-loving nations are suffering such terrible happenings? Is it any wonder that we finally have to face up to the unpalatable fact that the politics of these countries are basically rotten? A rotten politician represents a rotten people until both grow tired of their rottenness. It is then that God promises to "*sprinkle clean water on* [us]" (Ezekiel 36:25).

This cleansing from on high is overdue, but it is coming. Without a spiritual renewal, these nations would be wiped clean like a plate. Do we not sweep up garbage and burn or bury it? What will God do with the pornography and the mental and spiritual garbage in America today? If He leaves it too long, the whole nation would be irredeemably polluted with mental and physical sickness.

An observer of times is a prognosticator—one who attempts to foretell future events by means of supernatural powers for personal gain. Some people will not even plan their day without consulting their horoscopes. They arrange their marriage day and business appointments by observing times. Thank God that we read, "*My times are in Your hand*" (Psalm 31:15). This means that as He is the eternal "I Am," we do not have to observe times, but just trust Him at all times! Jesus said, "*Therefore do not worry about tomorrow, for tomorrow will worry about its own things. Sufficient for the day is its own trouble*" (Matthew 6:34).

Another evil practice mentioned in Deuteronomy 18 is the art of enchantment. This is the practice of magical arts by magicians. We have a wonderful contrast between the real power of God and the enchantments of Jannes and Jambres in Pharaoh's court. Pharaoh was not amazed when God's man, Moses, threw his rod to the ground and it was instantly changed into a writhing serpent. He called for his own (a) wise men, (b) sorcerers, (c) and magicians; these highly paid false prophets and religious leaders of Egypt used their enchantments. They cast down their rods and each rod became a small serpent. Now how did they do this? It is obvious to all Christians that God can do any miracle and create matter for His own purposes, but can magicians do this? No, but they can counterfeit the miracle-working power of God. Demons were dispatched to the desert at lightning speed by the satanic powers working with these men, and exchanged serpents from the desert rocks for the priests' sticks. This is levitation as used in spiritist séances. As glasses and other objects can be made to sail across a room, so were serpents supernaturally transported into Pharaoh's court, and Pharaoh had no doubt that the magicians could do such a trick. It was in fact a demonic sleight of hand.

But God showed His superior power because Moses' serpent swallowed up the lesser serpents. The same magicians made water appear as blood (see Exodus 7) and made frogs appear all over the land of Egypt. They counterfeited God's miracles, but when Moses came to the fourth plague of lice on the land, it is written, *"Now the magicians so worked with their enchantments to bring forth lice, but they could not"* (Exodus 8:18). Satan's power, though great and fascinating to the unwary, is yet limited before God's ultimate power and judgments.

In Isaiah 47:9–11, we have an account of God's ultimate judgment descending on a rebellious people. The basic cause of the terrible punishment was because of their sorceries and enchantments. The result was loss of children and widowhood which came upon them suddenly; punishments and blessings often come suddenly. On the day of Pentecost, the Holy Spirit came suddenly, causing them to speak in other languages, much to their astonishment. This present renewal of the church is uncovering many incredible hidden truths and practices, both good and bad. Blessings and curses in abundance—which do you want?

So many play with the occult "just for kicks." They are storing up God's judgments to suddenly visit them in suffering, sickness or sorrow. And when it happens we say, "Wasn't I unlucky?" The ancient Egyptian goddess of good fortune was named "Luk," from which the modern word *luck* is derived. Yes, we do get what these gods give us. We get what we deserve! *"For rebellion is as the sin of witchcraft"* (1 Samuel 15:23). Play with witchcraft and you get the curse of witchcraft.

A few years ago there was an article in *Reader's Digest* about a famous French spiritist who levitated from his chair in a sitting position to the ceiling where he remained suspended in the air without visible means of support or suspension. How? This is an enchantment. If two people put two fingers under the armpits of a consenting person, "they" can lift him easily. How? The demons in each case lend their strength for the levitation.

Nebuchadnezzar also had magicians in his court. It was the normal heathen practice at this time. These "wise men" were the mystics, the prophets of heathendom. Daniel and his three friends, however, were the real prophets of God in a heathen setting. They were the positive in the negative. It was written of them, *"God gave them knowledge and skill in all literature and wisdom; and Daniel had understanding in all visions and dreams. …And in all matters of wisdom and understanding about which the king examined them, he found them ten times better than all the magicians and astrologers who were in all his realm"* (Daniel 1:17, 20).

It is instinctive in a man to want to know his future, and God has provided His people with true prophets and teachers. He has given us the gifts of the Holy Spirit, including prophecy, the word of wisdom and knowledge, and the gift of interpretation. Why do people need to go to Satan instead of God? Isaiah tells us why. *"It is because there is no light in them"* (Isaiah 8:20). If we walk in darkness, we grope in darkness and hear nothing except empty demonic pronouncements. Much of the church in times past has been spiritually dead and sterile. It has had little to offer in the way of the supernatural, and so Satan has won an easy victory with many who have sought the mystical among the demons. But the whole pattern is changing. God is switching on the Light of the Spirit upon the church in our day, and many are awakening to understanding. *"Should not a people seek their God? [instead of]…the dead on behalf of the living?"* (Isaiah 8:19).

6

WITCHES AND WARLOCKS

The term *witch* is usually applied to females, whereas a male is a *wizard* or a *warlock*. Their ministry of evil is the same. So serious did God consider this demonic practice that His law said that a witch should be put to death. (See Exodus 22:18.) This law was not carried out strictly, because King Saul was able to consult with a witch. She was afraid when she realized who he was because she thought he had come to put her to death. He promised her life in direct contradiction to God's Word.

Witch doctors in Africa are demon-possessed practitioners and are, in fact, practicing mediums. By rites and incantations they are supposed to heal the sick and put curses on people. Those who are cursed often die, for the familiar spirit kills them. When sickness leaves a person, through the incantations of a witch doctor, it is not cast out as when a Christian prays in Jesus' name to cast out a demon. It is simply removed temporarily from the part of the body that is affected. It is usually driven deeper into the inner personality only to reappear at a later time as a worse sickness of the mind or body, or to return to in its original form.

Deliverance in Jesus' name is much different. In many cases where spirits of infirmity are rebuked in Jesus' name, the spirits move around, and the person claims to feel their presence, pressure or pain in various parts of the body, until they ultimately leave, often through the throat with a cough or cry.

A medical doctor recently examined the strange rites and results of witch doctors in Africa and reported that healings did indeed take place, not only of the body but also of disturbed minds. This doctor claimed that they were "doing a good work" among their native tribes and should be encouraged to continue, especially where the medical services were lacking!

In Africa today, reports are coming in from many countries that witch doctors are turning to Christ, burning their fetishes and jujus, and being delivered of their familiar spirits. I learned firsthand in Nigeria that witch doctors who used to be so greatly feared by the primitive peoples are now in turn fearing the native Spirit-filled ministers who are proliferating in the present charismatic outpouring of the Holy Spirit.

In more sophisticated countries however, we do not have witch doctors, but we have the more refined hypnotists. Briefly, one who practices hypnotism is a witch! What actually happens is that the familiar spirits controlling the hypnotist take over the mind of the person being hypnotized. Of course, the patient must be willing to be hypnotized; otherwise it doesn't work! He must surrender his mind and will utterly to the hypnotist. It is not a question of one mind controlling another, or of one mind being stronger; it is simply a manifestation of a powerful, familiar, evil spirit taking over the subjected mind of the patient, who is temporarily forced into a trancelike state. The spirit invades the victim. In hypnotism, it is possible to hypnotize oneself, and the familiar spirit then reveals hidden secrets that may have been forgotten by the mind, but which are resident in the mind nevertheless. One goes into a trance and the evil spirits will speak. The classic case in recent times was Edgar Cayce of Virginia Beach, Virginia, who diagnosed sickness in others by the evil spirit within him as he was in a deep trance.

There is a more subtle form of witchcraft in church circles. This concerns the false prophet with false occult gifts. They creep into churches manifesting the supernatural; but they are healing by "the spirits" and not by the Holy Spirit. They preach a very light message with very little scriptural backing, and then healings occur which charm the people (literally) and they conclude that he must be "a man of God." He is in reality a wizard! This is a religious spirit and when cast out has been known to reveal itself as a "spirit of witchcraft." I heard one friend who is a pastor explaining that their faces seemed to have a "plastic look," and this exactly describes their mask-like, unnatural "holy" look! It reveals the seducing spirit inside. It is false and it simulates the things of God by counterfeit.

The classic case, of course, is Simon the sorcerer in Acts 8:9–11. He used sorcery in Samaria to bewitch (because he was a witch) the people, and stated by self-advertisement that he was a "great one." Because of the healings, all the people readily agreed that he was "the great power of God." It is stated that he bewitched them for a long time with his sorceries. Simon was astonished when one greater than he came to the city: Philip the Evangelist. He manifested the gift of miracles and healings, and Simon knew at once that Philip had superior power and tried to buy it with money! The whole occult realm relies on money—from the greased palm of the palmist to the charges of practitioners from the bloodless cults.

On the Island of Paphos, Paul and Barnabas received a visit from a Roman deputy named Sergius Paulus, who was described as a prudent man. He inquired about the way of salvation. In the same place was a sorcerer named Bar-Jesus, which means son of Joshua. Here was a "son of Joshua"; surely he would rejoice at Sergius Paulus coming to Paul and Barnabas to inquire about Jesus. Not so. Although he had such a fine spiritual name, he was a warlock who operated by other spirits and withstood the men of God. This is one of the great signs of a false prophet today. They withstand the obvious truths of the Word of God, especially those that deal with the whole salvation purchased by Jesus for all mankind, and substitute their religious formulas; however, they claim to represent Jesus!

When Elymas (for that was Bar-Jesus' other name) started his negative opposition, Paul looked hard at him and said to this supposed "man of God":

> O full of all deceit and all fraud, you son of the devil, you enemy of all right-
> eousness, will you not cease perverting the straight ways of the Lord? And now,
> indeed, the hand of the Lord is upon you, and you shall be blind, not seeing the
> sun for a time. And immediately a dark mist fell on him…. Then the proconsul
> believed, when he saw what had been done, being astonished at the teaching of the
> Lord. (Acts 13:9–12)

What a remarkable story! His blindness was caused by his activity in witchcraft, but the judgment brought salvation to another man.

Who can tell how many sicknesses are the direct or indirect result of occult involvement in the family? Did Paul make Bar-Jesus blind? No. Paul knew by a word of knowledge from the Holy Spirit that this would happen. In the same manner, Peter did not cause the death of Ananias or his wife in Acts 5:1–10. He simply spoke the word of God with boldness and God did the rest. Those who get involved with demonic activities today, even if disguised in a Christian garb, may tremble at what God is doing today as the Word of God is preached in the power of the Spirit and confirmed by signs, wonders, and miracles.

We read that the demons believed in God and trembled. (See James 2:19.) No wonder witch doctors are now trembling in Africa at the outpouring of the Spirit and the preaching of the Word of God. I have seen demon-possessed men and women cry out when they have seen me, "Don't you touch me," visibly trembling with terror written all over their faces. We have nothing to fear (see Psalm 27), but Satan has everything to fear. No wonder we read that Jesus will destroy the wicked by the brightness of His coming. (See 2 Thessalonians 2:8.) This is the day of the reappearing of the Word of God in the power of the Spirit, who will consume the wickedness of the occult as well as those who tangle with it. At the same time, His mercy is extended to all who confess, forsake, and ask forgiveness for their wicked ways. Hell was not prepared for humans, but for the devil and all his angels, including the whole occult family. (See Matthew 25:41.)

Now, let me say just a word about the "evil eye." Paul was well aware of the subtle dangers surrounding the early Christians. He wrote to the Galatians, *"O foolish Galatians! Who has bewitched you that you should not obey the truth...?"* (Galatians 3:1). The Greek word for *"bewitched"* is *baskaino,* which literally means to "smite with the eye." This is an occult practice similar to hypnotism and referred to in the Bible as an "evil eye." As Paul, filled with the Spirit, bore his eyes into Elymas and brought blindness, so the eye of a witch or warlock can bore into the very soul of a gullible person and bring a curse into their lives. When praying for the sick, false prophets will literally bore their eyes right through a person, and that person will often fall to the ground supposedly "under the power of God."

This must not be confused with the laying on of hands by Spirit-filled servants of God, which may cause a person to collapse because of the "jolt of the Spirit." The Galatians were suffering from the operation of some false prophet with a seducing spirit, and as he talked to them, he would bore them through and through with his eyes and bring them into a state of spiritual subjection. His seducing spirit would then take over, as in the case of hypnotism, and destroy the pure doctrine of God.

Hypnotism is often performed through the use of the evil eye. It is often very easy to detect demon-possessed people by the narrow pupils of their eyes. They seem to have a "hypnotic effect." This same narrowing takes place when a person is under the influence of drugs. A demon has entered, and even if the drug addict turns to Christ, he or she may still have to be exorcised from them.

Today we must do what John instructed of us: to *"test the spirits, whether they are of God"* (1 John 4:1). We must not let any false prophet lay hands on us, for he might impart a wrong spirit. We must not let him look into our eyes. We must have nothing whatever to do with him. John says that if any of them, whom he describes as "antichrists" or false christs, come to our door, we must not let them into our household. (See 2 John 1:10.) They do not come advertising themselves as false prophets, but as true ones. The burden is on us to prove them.

7

THE DANGERS OF OCCULTISM

A few years ago I received a letter from the brother of an old friend in England. He wrote inquiring about our healing ministry. I wrote him, sending a tract I had written entitled *Divine Healing*, and explained that we laid on hands, prayed in the name of Jesus, and pleaded the precious blood of Jesus for healing and cleansing. He wrote back saying that he was quite interested in what I told him, but he did not understand what I meant when I referred to the Holy Spirit, for he prayed and asked the spirits, whom he called angels, to help him get well. He also failed to see why we had to use the blood of Jesus. This made no sense to him at all.

This was obviously a case of spiritism. I wrote and told him that, warning him of the great dangers. He replied that he was a "Christian spiritualist" and he believed God healed, even as I did. It seems that it was just our approach that was different! He sent me a tape to listen to. For a while I forgot about it, but some months later found it and decided I ought to listen to it to see what more he had to say about his version of "spiritual or faith healing." He explained how he ministered healing. The spirits and angels did the healing while he went into a trance. He said that on the reverse side of the tape, I would hear his voice change as the spirit took control. This should have been enough for me, but curiosity got the better of my knowledge of the dangers, so I listened to the whole tape. While listening I had a horrible feeling of evil, although I was playing the tape in our church.

Within two weeks I was stricken with a very bad attack of bronchitis, which bordered on bronchial pneumonia. It knocked me out, and I would cough up black-looking mucus. My wife was concerned. Was this coincidence? I trusted the Lord for healing and after about six weeks I was fully delivered, but it was a real battle of faith. It was a horrible tenacious attack of Satan, for sickness is an oppression of the devil. (See Acts 10:38.) I fully believe that I gave a place to Satan because I deliberately entertained him in a recording of a séance in my own church! By listening to the workings of Satan on a magnetic tape, I was stricken with sickness, even though I was a Spirit-filled believer!

When Oral Roberts first started praying for the sick on the radio, his radio messages and prayers were made on tapes, and many objected saying "How can God's healing power be transmitted through a tape?" But it was, and the Holy Spirit would confirm the word preached electronically and people would be healed listening to their radios. In like manner, by the law of opposites, Satan's cursing power can be transmitted electronically.

Consider that today the television screens of North America are carrying interviews with witches; séances have even been conducted on radio, and discussions on parapsychology and the occult have been openly made. Can this affect our health if we deliberately look or listen? Certainly. We can be afflicted through the ear-gate or the eye-gate. Paul distinctly wrote, "...nor give place to the devil" (Ephesians 4:27). I believe that I gave my ears and mind to the devil when I listened to the séance recording. I got what I deserved. Some deliberately take university courses on the occult for which they obtain credits. The devotees of the cults are trying to make it a respectable science and popular for the masses.

In considering the bloodless cults, we find that Mrs. Mary Baker Eddy used to go into trances to get her revelations that she taught under the name "Christian Science." Helena Petrovna, a Russian girl, married N. B. Blavatsky in 1848 and became a spiritist medium. She founded the Theosophical Society in New York in 1875. The Unity Church was founded by Franz Anton Mesmer, a German physician who started the practice of Mesmerism, a form of hypnosis. Mesmer spoke of his "magnetic fluid." It was something that flowed from him. We understand, of course, that this was simply the powerful familiar spirit in him bringing the other person's mind into subjection.

Quimby took up his teachings and became a pioneer "spiritual healer." Mormonism was started by an illiterate man named Joseph Smith, who claimed to have seen an angel named Moroni. This "angle" showed him where certain golden plates were buried in New York State. Supernatural ability was supposed to be given to Smith to interpret the hieroglyphics. We do not doubt the appearance of this supernatural being, but as the teachings of Mormonism do not agree with the Word of God, we must assume that it was an evil angel, a deceitful spirit. Smith nearly died afterwards.

Jehovah Witnesses deny the pre-existence of Jesus Christ, and John states positively that this is the teaching of a false prophet. (See 1 John 4:1–3). Russellism is anti-Christian by definition.

The relatively new cult of Armstrongism is having a revival. It also belongs to the tares of the field—*"An enemy has done this"* (Matthew 13:28, see also verse 39). We are in the harvest time of the age, and all anti-Christian cults in the world are coming to their full fruition, as is also the wheat of Jesus' planting. It is a most interesting and challenging age in which to live. These cults are opposed to Jesus Christ and are repulsed by any mention of His blood. They are well described by Paul when writing to Timothy. *"Now the Spirit expressly says that in latter times some will depart from the faith, giving heed to deceiving spirits and doctrines of demons, speaking lies in hypocrisy…"* (1 Timothy 4:1–2).

These false cults, which have proliferated like tares, are demonic in origin and teaching. If we give our minds to their evil teachings and practices, we shall receive their spirits which are woven in the whole texture of their cults. These are occult societies, with occult spirits operating and hidden from man's view. They can only be detected by the discerning of spirits, which is one of the nine charismatic gifts of the Holy Spirit mentioned in 1 Corinthians 12:8–10. Those who have been enmeshed by these cults can turn to Jesus and ask for His forgiveness and cleansing blood, but they will probably need the strong prayer of exorcism to deliver them from the evil spirits that will have probably taken up residence in them by "[giving] *place to the devil*" (Ephesians 4:27). We cannot blame God if we lose our health, our minds, or even our loved ones. Being involved in the occult is like taking a viper to our bosoms. It will give us the kiss of death.

I am constantly receiving letters in my office telling me of cases of people bound in wheel chairs because their mother or father (or both) were involved with the occult in some form or another. The sins of the fathers are indeed brought upon the third and fourth generations of those who disobey God. This warning is given to us in Exodus 20:5 in the Ten Commandments, and it is directly related to the command forbidding the making of graven images and worshipping them. Disobedience on these matters goes straight into Satan's occult camp. The results of such activity are suffering, sickness, sorrow, despair, and often, early death unto the third and fourth generation, from grandchildren to great grandchildren. Are you willing to take this risk?

There is forgiveness and deliverance in Jesus Christ. He is very merciful toward those who repent of their sins and turn to Him. One must make open renunciation and repudiation of these occult sins; only then can forgiveness and cleansing be received. Through faith in Jesus Christ and His blood, the occult line that runs through a family can be broken.

8

HOROSCOPES AND CHARMS

This chapter deals first with horoscopes. They should really be called horror-scopes, however, for by reading them and digesting their contents, a person opens himself to the horrors of the devil.

Most of our newspapers today carry a column for horoscopes, called monthly prognostications in the Bible, and lay out the pretended things that will happen to the readers each day of the month. This is not a new practice; it is as old as mankind.

In Daniel's day, he and his friends were included among the "wise men" who were magicians, astrologers, and soothsayers. Where Jesus is not honored and the presence of the Holy Spirit enjoyed, mankind will automatically degenerate into the negative cycle of dealing with demon powers and inquire of them for information about the future. This is especially done on those days in the monthly calendar which may be considered favorable for certain activities. Astrology must not be confused with the legitimate science of astronomy; the basic idea behind astrology is that the stars themselves influence the conduct of human affairs.

The worship of the sun and moon has been recognized by mankind since earliest times. The sun would represent the supreme deity and the moon, a female deity owing her allegiance to the sun god. The stars became the lesser gods, all of which in the overall picture affect humanity for good or evil. They had to be worshipped and horoscopes were made according to their prognostications. This is pure heathen practice with the demon-gods operating behind the heavenly facade.

In 1935, I was employed by a large oil company in London, England, and my boss at the head office informed me that he "wrote horoscopes." With my history of occult involvement, I became quite enthusiastic and asked him if he would write mine. I got the nearest time and date of my birth (this is extremely important) and he made me my very own horoscope. The contents certainly seemed to explain some of the behavior patterns of my life, which were basically known to my boss as well as the demons! It was really quite an intriguing transcript and I showed it to my fiancée Olive. She agreed it was a fairly accurate portrait of myself. I returned to my boss's office and asked him if he would consider writing a horoscope for my fiancée. At first he was not too keen because he was a cynic as far as women were concerned, but he finally agreed. I got Olive's time and date of birth as near as we could compute them.

My boss wrote the horoscope, which was not as good as mine. Then he cast the two together and rather horrified us with the definite statement that we were not temperamentally suited and should not consider marriage! He assured us it would never work! You can see what you get into when you start inquiring of the devil!

We both lost confidence in this method of "fortune telling" or soothsaying and decided to ignore it, going along marriage plans anyway. Up to the time of this writing, we have been happily married for thirty-nine years! We have both been used by the Lord in the ministry of deliverance, healing the sick, and casting out demons. Is it possible Satan might have had some pre-cognizance of what would have happened to his kingdom if he did not stop us teaming up against him? Pre-cognizance is one of the occult gifts! Clairvoyance is another. Could he have seen, however dimly, what would happen? All we can say is—it is possible.

But suppose we were involved more deeply in this business of astrology and reading horoscopes? Suppose we had no faith in God at that time? Thank God we had a little, which seemed to be enough to sustain us and bring us back to the realization that anyone who allows their life to be governed by astrology is a fool. We might have been trapped by the lies of the devil. The "stars" said we must not marry; we were incompatible. But instead of listening to the stars, we listened to God and believed He brought us together. Olive prayed most sincerely about our relationship, and when I proposed, she felt a strong pressure from the Holy Spirit to accept the proposal.

How many lives have been ruined by foolish people who listen to the demons behind the horoscopes instead of trusting the Lord who promised to bless us with uncounted blessings if we serve Him?

Perhaps the saddest part of this story is that my boss died three years later of cancer that disfigured his face.

Israel, God's chosen people, His church of the old covenant, pursued every type of occult practice they saw among their Gentile neighbors. They learned more easily about other gods than they did about the true God. Along with their elders, they faithfully promised to have no other gods before Jehovah. God lovingly told them what would happen, but they refused to listen. He said,

> *Therefore shall evil come upon you.... You will not be able to put it off. And desolation shall come upon you suddenly.... Stand now with your enchantments and*

the multitude of your sorceries…. Let now the astrologers, the stargazers, and the monthly prognosticators stand up and save you from what shall come upon you. Behold, they [their gods] shall be as stubble, the fire shall burn them; they shall not deliver themselves from the power of the flame. (Isaiah 47:11–14)

All the worship of heathen gods, all the money they poured into the coffers of the heathen temples, all their time and devotion to a lost cause would not save them from total, irrevocable calamity. It happened just as He said it would, and my friend, it will happen to you if you persist in your practice of reading the daily horoscope. My wife was trying to explain to a lady that it was literally playing with death to read horoscopes, but her reply was typical: "When I come to the part called 'Horoscopes,' I just go on reading. It is entertaining and fun. What's the harm anyway?"

You would have a better chance of not being harmed if you played Russian roulette and a rattlesnake as a pet, than by dabbling in the forbidden practices of the occult. The hidden demon spirits are lurking to trap and destroy you.

Destroy? How? How can reading a daily horoscope kill me? How can reading tea leaves, reading cards, having my palm read, and carrying a lucky charm hurt me? Friend, it can kill you. We have uncovered time after time that the primary causes of such death-dealing sicknesses as cancer, heart failure, and arthritis were associated in the past with some of these "innocent practices." By seeking knowledge from these sources, we can open ourselves to demons that may cause arthritis and other crippling diseases.

The church has been silent, not warning people. Ministers of large denominations have even encouraged their members to go to spiritist séances because they "prove" that life after death exists! They have served on committees for the investigation of psychic phenomena. In some Protestant churches, healing orders have been literally shot through and through with metaphysical teachings and spiritual healing by other means than Jesus Christ.

On one occasion, I was invited to speak on spiritual healing at a retreat in Ontario, twenty miles north of Toronto. I did my best. I spoke about how Jesus healed and how He was still healing through His servants. I spoke of the power of the blood of Jesus. I did not know that the other speaker after me was a "Christian spiritualist." In fact, I did not even know that "Christian Spiritualists" existed! I thought they were all of the devil! She relied on a tape recording to give her the right type of music so that she could slip into a trance. When she switched on the tape recorder, it would not work! She tried everything in her power to get it to work, but nothing. Another tape recorder was produced and connected up, but it also failed to work. She was never able to minister. Jesus and His blood had made both tape recorders fail to work. What a good thing the Lord had me bat first!

The present outpouring of the Holy Spirit is stirring up the demonic powers to a frenzy, and is flushing out all things of the occult. The same fire of the Holy Spirit will soon begin burning up their powers, even as it stopped the tape recorders. Jesus prophesied this when He said in Matthew 13:30, 40 that He would send messengers who would burn up these tares. In the present church renewal, many will be delivered from occult bondages and brought to salvation in Jesus Christ and the subsequent infilling with His Holy Spirit. Instead of following false spirits, many will be guided by the Holy Spirit, who has gifts such as the word of knowledge, the word of wisdom, tongues and the interpretation of tongues, and prophecy. Everything we need to know will be given to anyone who inquires of the Lord.

Jesus said,

> *However, when He, the Spirit of truth, has come, He will guide you into all truth; for He will not speak on His own authority, but whatever He hears He will speak; and He will tell you things to come.* (John 16:13)

We do not need Satan's lies. We need the God's truth.

Another subject about that the church has been strangely silent about is the distribution and wearing of the so-called "good luck" charm. But why should we be silent about it when God spoke so plainly of it in Deuteronomy 18:10–11? "*There shall not be found among you any one that maketh his son or his daughter to pass through the fire, or that useth divination, or an observer of times, or an enchanter, or a witch. Or a charmer…*" (KJV).

A *"charmer"* is someone who performs a ritual over some object, and then recommends that it be worn around the neck or carried close to the heart. It is believed that a talisman will bring "luck" to the user. This is an ancient practice which was brought into the church by unconverted heathens in the days of Constantine, when he decreed Christianity the official religion of the Roman Empire. So strong is the grip of this demonic superstition that millions even today believe in "lucky charms." For this reason, we urge all those who are wearing charms to carefully reexamine the whole subject.

If any object whatsoever is revered above the Word of God and the name of Jesus, it must be suspect and put away. Many missionaries returning from foreign fields bring back heathen charms which may be likenesses of demons, or the actual idol that was worshipped. Always remember that there is a demon lurking behind every idol or charm.

Witch doctors use all kinds of material substances, such as feathers, dried manure, bones, skin, etc., to put in containers that are worn about the neck. Such charms are supposed to bring healing, deliverance, or blessing to the ignorant. Demons will oblige in many cases.

Even in more "civilized" countries, it is sad to see the remnants of such superstition still hanging on. Indeed, it was absolutely pathetic to see the number of young men flying aircraft during World War II who carried charms such as rabbits' feet, Kewpie dolls, and teddy bears to bring them "luck."

Time and time again, it has been proven that after one destroys these charms, he experiences the real help and blessing of Jesus.

9

THERE IS DELIVERANCE

I have tried to show in this book the danger of experimenting with occult powers. Man was made by God to have fellowship with Him, to be free, healthy and wise; but if man does not serve God, then the spiritual vacuum will automatically be filled by Satan. Man is not a completely free agent, but is free to choose. He is made to serve God, but if he will not, he will serve the devil. Paul made this very clear when he wrote, *"Do you not know that to whom you present yourselves slaves to obey, you are that one's slaves whom you obey, whether of sin leading to death, or of obedience leading to righteousness?"* (Romans 6:16). If God is not your Master, then Satan become s your slave master.

If we obey God, we worship Him because we love Him, but if we do not obey God, we worship Satan, and it is in the various occult forms that we find our spiritual contact with Satan and his demons. This is why Moses instructed Israel to have no other gods before Him. The issue is clear. You will either serve God or gods. You will either worship the Father, the Son and the Holy Spirit, or you will worship Satan and his evil spirits. Satan will serve you, answer your prayers, delude you and finally give you the reward—*"for the wages of sin is death"* (Romans 6:23).

I have tried to show that the many "gods" or demons of Satan manifest his evil in many subtle ways. The moment a person, however sincere, contaminates himself with the occult, be it teacup reading or the grosser forms of spiritist séances, he puts himself in the vulnerable position of being subjected progressively by a demon spirit. This evil spirit will not stop at a small bridgehead, but will progressively work its way into one's mind and body like cancer.

As this door is opened wider, other spirits will also enter—some to give delusions in the mind, others to cause erratic behavior, still others to send sickness upon the body. It results in degeneration as the person ages, until their last days when they may be totally senile and crippled. Always remember that God's norm is a long life with abundance and satisfaction. (See Psalms 91:16.) God gives regeneration, not degeneration. Regeneration is not only a fact at our spiritual rebirth (see John 3:3–5), but it is a progressive daily experience. The fact is that many who become Christians by rebirth find their health progressively improving over the years. This has been true in my own case.

What can we do for these millions of people—including many professing Christians—who have contaminated themselves with the demons behind the many occult mysteries? Can we find healing for them to rid them of their infestations? Yes, in Acts 10:38 we are told that Jesus, anointed of the Holy Spirit, went around among the people healing all that were oppressed by the devil. This means that He took the people from their spiritual subjection and brought them into the glorious liberty of the sons of God. (See Romans 8:21.) The word "oppressed" means to be overpowered or overcome; in other words, it means to be brought to a place of captivity and bondage, as in a prison. However, Jesus came to set us free, for *"if the Son makes you free, you shall be free indeed"* (John 8:36).

In the present charismatic move of God among churches, "The Deliverance Ministry" has arisen. It has been found that when Christians take their rightful authority in Christ against sin, sickness, and suffering and openly rebuke it in His name, the demons behind the troubles react and come out, often quite violently as we read in Mark 1:25–26. This is frequently a very astonishing experience and will increase your faith in God and His Word tremendously! The number of people who are using this forceful and scriptural approach in prayer is rapidly increasing, in spite of the opposition of some fearful people!

This is the day of the revelation of God's power that was manifest in the life of Jesus when He delivered the captives and set them free. The concept that emotional problems and physical bondages can actually be precipitated by occult involvement is so alien to Christian thinking that it is hard for people to understand. Of course we know that those in psychiatry and the medical profession know nothing about these dangers or the causes. This is a brand new field of understanding in healing. It is a fulfillment of the words of Jesus who referred to the Isaiah's prophecy: *"He has anointed Me to preach the gospel to the poor; He has sent Me to heal the brokenhearted, to proclaim liberty to the captives and recovery of sight to the blind, to set at liberty those who are oppressed"* (Luke 4:18).

Priests of heathen religions will explain to visitors from Western countries that there are spirits behind their idols, and it is these spirits who answer their prayers. The average tourist may think this is "funny" or just superstitious foolishness, but it is dreadfully and fearfully true. We have shown that not only are demons behind idols, but there are holes in the back of some Asian temples which demons use to go in and out. He goes in when some sacrifice or oblation is made to him. We have shown that demons can inhabit the physical matter of these idols. In the Bible, the Holy Spirit is likened to water, because water is fluid, and evil spirits are likewise fluid and will actually flow over us and into us if we give them place. Paul said to *"give no place to the devil"* (Ephesians 4:27). If we do, we actually create a "hole" in which Satan can flow in and out with his spirits. As the pure water of the Holy Spirit can flow in and out of us in the operation of charismatic gifts (see John 7:38), so can unclean spirits flow in and out of us, manifesting their filth in false prophecies, false teachings, and evil words.

When people visit us for special prayer at our Toronto Church, we ask them if they have had any form of occult involvement; a surprisingly large number realize that they have been involved in such things in times past. Due to the ignorance of parents and friends, many have been seduced into communicating with demons, from the "amusing" Ouija board to the equally entertaining Chinese fortune cookies given to us at Chinese restaurants. Many have read their horoscopes as well as books about the occult religions of Unity, Theosophy, Parapsychology, etc. Many have invited evil thoughts from evil personalities into their minds, and the resulting mental or physical bondage has caused many people to seek prayer. However, prayer is ineffectual unless the cause is understood, confessed, and forsaken. Resentments, criticisms, and pride must also be confessed; bring these out into the open, and then forsake them as something hideous and unclean. Forgiveness must be sought from the Savior and His cleansing blood. The occult line can then be quickly broken, the continuing curse in our life can be lifted, and we can be set free as the demons are commanded to come out in Jesus' name.

To "do business" with Satan may be entertaining for a while. The trinity of Satan (the world, the flesh, and the devil) may appear satisfying for a season, but what a collective price we must pay for this lifestyle! It has been my privilege in recent times to pray for quite a few young witches, who at first certainly did not appear to be evil; but through time, even their very faces would change and their bodies would be twisted as a result of twisted minds. In all cases, demons quickly responded. In some sessions of prayer, the demons threw their subject to the floor and spoke back, but finally came out, screaming and coughing, being ejected through the witch's throat. The longer a young witch practices evil ways, the greater the control the familiar spirit exercises over her. The older the witch, the more violent the deliverance, for trouble compounds with time.

Our young people go in for the occult because they say it gives them power over their peers. In truth, it does give them power. When Philip came to Samaria in Acts 8, he exercised a much greater power than Simon the Sorcerer. Previous to Philip's visit, the whole city believed that Simon had the ultimate power. He bewitched the people with sorceries. But when Philip's power manifested, Simon quickly saw that his power was much weaker than Philip's, and he attempted to buy it with money.

When we minister deliverance to witches and spiritists, we always lead them into receiving the baptism in the Holy Spirit. As they begin to speak in other languages as the Holy Spirit gives them utterance (see Acts 2:1–4), a stronger power flows through them—a power that can heal the sick, raise the dead, and cast out demons.

If you are looking for power, the Holy Spirit can give you the power you need. All people need power; all people crave power. This is why an unbeliever seeks self-aggrandizement and works himself to death in trying to be top dog. But when God makes you a son, He gives you the potential to act like a son and do the works of the Son of God. You can have His power over sin, sickness, and evil in any form. You can have power over evil men and those who attack you. You can sit in the driver's seat— the seat of authority in Christ. You can become the head and not the tail. You can have the dynamic power which Christ gives to those who ask. (See Acts 1:8.)

If you have been involved in any form of the forbidden occult, confess it and contact someone in your area who can pray the commanding prayer of faith that will set you free. Start afresh with Jesus the Son of God, and go out and do His works. (See John 14:12.)

This is the day of the full restoration of the body of Christ. *"In My name they will cast out demons"* (Mark 16:17). Jesus promised it.

10

GOD'S ALTERNATIVE

Not only does occult involvement lead to sickness, slavery, and death—it is also unnecessary. There is no reason to seek power and knowledge from Satan, since the Lord provides everything we need. Indeed, His provision for us is greater than we can possibly imagine. Jesus told us *"I am the way, the truth, and the life"* (John 14:6). In this triad we have the recipe for a life of dominion over the world, the flesh, and the devil. There is not a created being, be it an elephant or a germ, that can harm us, unless we permit it to harm us by lack of faith! Once we fully understand the authority vested in us by God through Christ, we can proceed to take our place as invincible creatures of faith, and not conquerable captives of fear. Paul wrote, *"We are more than conquerors through [Christ]"* (Romans 8:37). We are not just conquerors; we are more than conquerors.

Jesus is the way out of our captivity, our bondage, our sorrows, and our feebleness. He blazed a trail clean out of captivity. He was manifest and anointed with the Holy Spirit at Jordan that He might heal the brokenhearted, proclaim liberty to the captives, open the prison doors to those who are bound in chains, and set them free. This fullness of salvation does not have to be repeated. We are saved, and set free once and for all, that we might enjoy fullness of blessing in the kingdom of God on earth— restored paradise indeed. The salvation of the soul is the way into the new life, with healing of the mind and body, so that we might enjoy divine health and strength. The prison door is not opened that we might come and go back in a week's time because we got so used to "being cared for by the devil."

It was said that many slaves who were emancipated in the days of Abraham Lincoln continued to work for their old masters, rather than venture into an unknown world. Truly the kingdom of God is an unknown world to most people; unfortunately, few Christians today experience Jesus' blessings. They would rather live like other churchgoing people than to act as sons of God. Being of the royal family of

God sets them too far apart from members of their own families, who remain in sin and ignorance. They dare not be different. However, the Bible teaches us that we are different—completely different and separate from the world. It is as we learn to live and act differently that we begin to experience divine power, authority, and blessing that amazes us and demonstrates God's glory.

Jesus said, "*I am the truth.*" The Bible teaches that once we have accepted the way, we must walk in the light as He is in the light. (See 1 John 1:7.) We no longer walk by traditions taught to us by others, even if these traditions sound sensible and were taught by church leaders. In Jesus' day, there were many rabbis and a powerful church, but Jesus said that these figures made the Word of God of no effect by their traditions. In plain language, this means that they threw the Bible out the window. They had church, ceremonies, religion, priests, and services but no truth. Once a son of God enters the kingdom of God, he must adjust his life, his thinking, his speech, and his bearing, realizing that "*perfect love casts out fear*" (1 John 4:18). What a challenge. The more our lives become readjusted to His truth, the more authority we will exercise over Satan. Though all men may laugh at you, it is better to obey God than man.

Jesus said, "*I am the life.*" Christianity is not a monastic life suppressing natural desires and appetites. It is a life of abundance for spirit, soul, and body. Jesus said that He came to give life and to give it more abundantly. He came to take that tired, bound, captive life and fill it with His overwhelming abundance.

Can we imagine Adam being sick, depressed, miserable, weak, and fearful in the garden? Jesus came to give us back everything that Adam lost, and as we shall see, even more under the new covenant in His blood. Abundant life means just what it says for every child of God; everyone who approaches the mercy seat will have available to him every blessing in the Bible immediately, and there are thousands. Abundant life, including joy, peace, strength, health, and prosperity are laid to your account in heaven by Jesus Christ. "*My God shall supply all your need according to His riches in glory by Christ Jesus*" (Philippians 4:19).

Unfortunately, when a child of God ventures into the bank of heaven after knocking timorously, he cautiously and apologetically approaches one of the tellers and proffers a check with a small amount and wonders whether it will be honored. This is not an exaggeration concerning the approach in prayer of the average child of God. We might just as well write "million" as "two" because it belongs to an heir of God anyway. Let us therefore go boldly into the holiest place by a new and living way, and plead the blood of Jesus as our reason for expecting fantastic blessings. The world uses the word "pay off." Our "pay off" includes every good thing the moment we dare to enjoy it by faith. The blood of Jesus purchased every redemptive blessing for us.

"But I am not worthy of His blessings," some might say. Who said so? The opposite is the truth; this is a lie of Satan. *"You have a few names…who have not defiled their garments; and they shall walk with Me in white, for they are worthy"* (Revelation 3:4). Jesus makes us worthy in Him. As long as we abide in Him, and permit His Word to abide in us, then we will continue to be worthy of all His abundant blessings. Though these wonderful blessings were made available to us at the cross, each promise must be appropriated by our personal faith—not that of another; no promise of God is automatically bestowed on us. It must be appropriated by faith.

The story is told of a soldier son who faithfully sent his uneducated mother a monthly check, enough to keep her in comfort, health, and happiness. The mother could not read; so when she received her son's letters, she would stuff the money under her mattress over a period of years. She died in abject poverty, bringing early death upon herself due to lack of proper food. Had she not the means? Were the checks no good? Was not the son faithful in all that he did? Had she understood the ways of the bank and her son, she wouldn't have died in misery. She was worthy for she was his mother. We are worthy of these blessings because we are sons.

Many Christians fail to appreciate the significance of their sonship, believing that Jesus only vested His authority in the twelve apostles. It is true that these men were the foundation of the New Testament church and that they were built on Jesus, the cornerstone. However, the church —the body of Christ—is composed of many members, and these are supposed to exercise His authority each day in their lives. This is so that the church shall arrive at a point of having no spot or wrinkle, no sickness or disease, no defeat or frustration, and no oppression of Satan. We are told to go onto perfection!

Before Jesus left this earth He gave a last commission to His church, which was not a limited dispensational commission, but binding for the whole Christian age or dispensation, which ceases only at His second coming. In Matthew 28:18, Jesus told His disciples that He gave all power in heaven and upon earth. He earned this power by His death and the shedding of His blood. The whole power of the universe was vested in one Man who rose from the dead.

Because of the death of the testator, the new covenant came into operation, as in the case of common earthly testaments, or wills. God in Christ died, reconciling the world to Himself, and in this manner, ushering in the new covenant when Jesus shed His blood and gave up the Spirit on the cross, crying, *"It is finished!"* (John 19:30). Because God died in the person of Christ, it became legally possible for His Son to possess all things. And because He possesses all things, He has a free hand to give them to whomever He wishes.

It was this thought that was in His mind when He gave seventy men His power, for this was His right to give. When they dared to use it in faith—it worked! This should not surprise any of us, for we have a demonstration of higher authority every day in the police force of any nation or city. When the policeman holds up his hand in traffic, the vehicles grind to a halt because the authority of the head of state is vested in that policeman's hand! In the British Commonwealth, that authority belongs to the Queen or King and is known as the authority of the crown. When we accept Jesus as Savior, we accept the authority of the crown, for we are a royal priesthood. We are kings and priests; we are a royal family; we enforce the law of Calvary! His crown covers our authority and when we hold up our hands before Satan, he also must grind to a complete stop. Indeed, we can give Satan a ticket!

It is in keeping with the Gospel that we should all understand that we have His authority and that we can use it daily.

> *These signs will follow those who believe: In My name they will cast out demons; they will speak with new tongues; they will take up serpents; and if they drink anything deadly, it will by no means hurt them; they will lay hands on the sick, and they will recover.* (Mark 16:17–18)

To whom does *"they"* refer to? It refers to those who believe and are baptized— every child of God born into the kingdom of God by the Holy Spirit. The same authority that was vested in the seventy is now vested in all who believe. Hallelujah! We are to cast out demons, heal the sick, and handle serpents as harmless things, just as Moses handled a serpent in Exodus 4:4. Moses' ministry was to deliver the people, and the ministry of Jesus was also to deliver the people, and He handed on His mantle to the church on the day of Pentecost to continue the same ministry so that people might be delivered today. *"Let My people go"* is still God's cry to us today. Are we doing it or making excuses? We have the authority and the power—all that is now required is that we go forth and use it.

Jesus gives us a parable in Luke 11:21–22. He speaks of a strong man being armed and keeping his palace. Satan is this strong man, and he is described as the Prince, or ruler, of the present world in which we live. He certainly does a good job at keeping this world bound in sin, sickness, sorrow, and suffering. But Jesus said that when a stronger man comes, he binds the strong man and delivers him of his captives and takes his house and possessions. Jesus did this at Calvary, and He hands on the keys of the kingdom to all who will take them and go into Satan's strongholds to set the people free. Greater is He who is in you than he who is in the world. (See 1 John 4:4.) This is such a tremendous truth! We do not call on Jesus to do this for us; this is apologetic unbelief, for He is in us and so we go forward in Him and do it in His name. Jesus did not tell His disciples to pray for Him to heal the sick or cast out devils. Instead, we read,

As you go, preach, saying, "The kingdom of heaven is at hand." Heal the sick, cleanse the lepers, raise the dead, cast out demons. Freely you have received, freely give. (Matthew 10:7–8)

We are on the receiving end to give to those who are in need.

As we hold on to the right hand of the Lord, who has the victory, then we take from Him the healings, deliverances, and blessings that He commands us to give to others. When Jesus fed the five thousand, He broke bread and gave it to the disciples, who in turn gave it to the hungry. The same call to *"give them something to eat"* (Mark 6:37) still echoes from heaven today. We do not try to be religious and kneel down, piously asking Him to do the giving for us. This is unbelief in action. We take and we give; there will be many basketfuls left over after our ministry, so that we have a never decreasing supply to give to everyone who is hungry for God and His blessings. While we are busy giving bread, we can eat as much as we like ourselves, so both the giver and the receiver are blessed, healed, and restored.

Don't limit God. Limiting God is why Israel failed to go into a land that flowed with milk and honey. In Psalm 1, we are told that a child of God will prosper in everything he does. This means material prosperity, mental and emotional prosperity, and spiritual prosperity. We shall have all that we need from the bank of heaven. This is a land that flows with milk and honey; and there is much milk and so much honey that the cruse of God's blessings will never dry up, the barrel of meal will never cease to supply our needs. Whatever we do shall prosper! But in order for this to happen, we must be planted by the river of life that flows through the paradise of God. We must feed upon Him who died for us.

And so the disciples *"went out and preached everywhere, the Lord working with them and confirming the word through the accompanying signs. Amen"* (Mark 16:20). Notice the gospel ends with "Amen," which means "let it be." God desires an opportunity to do His part by confirming His Word that is preached by us. These signs will be the casting out of demons, healing the sick, and taking dominion over every evil sin and sickness, handling them as dead serpents and scorpions. We preach, and the signs will follow. Amen.

11

JOINT HEIRS

To fully appreciate the incredible blessings which we receive from God through Jesus Christ, we must consider the amazing teachings of apostle Paul in Romans chapter 8.

> *For as many as are led by the Spirit of God, these are sons of God [Greek: huios—mature sons]. For you did not receive the spirit of bondage again to fear, but you received the Spirit of adoption by whom we cry out, "Abba, Father." The Spirit Himself bears witness with our spirit that we are children of God [Greek: teknon—new born ones], and if children, then heirs—heirs of God and joint heirs with Christ.* (Romans 8:14–17)

Paul starts by telling us that as mature sons of God, we can, and should be led by the Holy Spirit. This is quite different from being led by the wisdom of man, for being led of the Holy Spirit is the daily experience of a son of God that has grown out of the milk stage to the meat stage. God expects us to be led of His Spirit, which is a continual operation of the gifts of the Spirit in our daily lives. He goes onto explain that if we fear, we are not receiving that from God. It is an evil spirit—a demon—sent by Satan, not of God. What God gives us is the Holy Spirit that adopts us into His family.

Just as a natural born child and a legally adopted child in a family would have the same name, the same privileges, the same standard of living, the same education, and share the same estate of the father, we are adopted into the family of God in the same manner. Jesus becomes our elder brother, and He is the only begotten of the Father. But although He is the begotten son and we are adopted out of every tongue, we still become sons of God and are reckoned to have all the privileges, favors, and blessings that belong by legal right to the Son of God. He does not withhold anything from those that walk uprightly. He is more anxious to bestow His favors on us than we are to receive them. We cannot imagine or understand such blessings, such prosperity, and such health. We are as one in a dream, but the Word of God is true, "*if children, then heirs—heirs of God.*" As Jesus became the rightful possessor of all His Father's estate, so also do we become heirs of this estate through faith in Christ. We become heirs of the same estate that was given to Jesus, due to His obedience unto the death of the cross. He paid for all these blessings with His own blood. They are His and they are ours.

Does He share them with us? No! They are just as much ours as His. Now we find that we have become joint heirs with Christ. A joint heir is one who has as much of a right to the estate as the other joint heir. Now notice that it does not matter how many children apply for the blessing of this New Testament estate, for the riches in glory never dry up. To borrow from John Bunyan's *The Pilgrim's Progress*, "The more we give away, the more we have." There is room at the cross for you, my friend, even though millions have already come. You will never exhaust the riches of glory. They are unlimited.

Jesus taught us that He inherited all things in heaven and on earth. All power is His—the silver, the gold, the cattle, all are His by right of inheritance because the testator died. His death established, ratified and probated the New Testament. All the promises of the Old and New Testaments are ours today and forever. He does not share or give us handouts; He is the Good Shepherd of the sheep, and we can go in and out of the pasture, knowing the wolf shall not touch us. He is our brother; we are His brethren. What is His is ours and all we have to give is ourselves. He multiplies our station and our prosperity, making us into kings and priests. We are transformed from commoners to royalty in one rebirth; no wonder so many find it hard to appreciate such riches and such glory. It seems to take us so many years to lay hold on this prosperity; we are so used to being stupid, fearful, and poor, that it takes time to realize what the expression "riches of grace" really means!

Some may argue that these promises are only to make us spiritually rich, but physically poor. Let us remind you that Jesus told us He became poor to make many rich. (See 2 Corinthians 6:10.) We must be careful not to seek riches as an end, but only to seek Jesus and His righteousness. Then He will become our prosperity in spirit, soul, and body. We shall lack nothing, and this is riches indeed. Let us not indulge again in apologetics, but enter into His riches in glory by Christ Jesus. John knew this when he wrote, "*Beloved, I pray that you may prosper in all things and be in health, just as your soul prospers*" (3 John 1:2).

David, in Old Testament times, put no division between the blessings of health related to both the spirit and the body. We have two feet to tread upon the two curses of Satan, the scorpion of sin and the serpent of sickness. "*Bless the LORD, O my soul, and forget not all His benefits: who forgives all your iniquities, who heals all your diseases"* (Psalm 103:2–3). His power and authority are sufficient, for if He puts all things under His feet, then they are under ours also. For our feet become His feet on earth, and our hands His hands, for our bodies are the temples of the Holy Spirit through which God wishes to manifest the Son through the Holy Spirit in us.

The amazing truth of our adoption is given a double witness in Galatians 4. Paul begins by reminding us that we were in bondage before we found liberty in Christ, but Jesus redeemed us, or purchased us, from this bondage into the glorious liberty of the sons of God. It was as if we were slaves to Satan. Jesus came and paid the price of His own blood and we were set free from the power of Satan, for *"if the Son makes you free, you shall be free indeed"* (John 8:36). Thus, we are completely free from want, fear, poverty, suffering, and sickness. This all is a free gift, and is called the good news of the kingdom of God.

The redemption price at Calvary introduced the law of adoption. By believing with our whole hearts that Jesus paid the penalty of our sins, we were reckoned to have been adopted by God into His family. We may not have been aware of this, nor of the amazing blessings that accrue to us, but God reckoned it nevertheless. It is as we become aware of this truth that we enter into a greater degree of blessing as we exercise our faith; and our faith comes through reading and believing the Word of God. Paul concludes, therefore, by telling us that we are no more servants, but sons, and if sons, then heirs of God through Christ. It is all through our elder brother.

Now notice the tremendous change that takes place when Jesus incorporates us into His royal family. We are no longer a little below the angels, but now lifted up into heavenly places in Christ. (See Ephesians 2:6.) It is always necessary to remember that as we abide in Christ, we are where He is. He is the new creation, and we also are reckoned to be a new creation in Him. If He is far above all principality, power, might, dominion, and every name that is named, not only in this world, but also that which is to come (see Ephesians 1:21), then we also are positionally the same when we learn to abide in Him. No wonder Jesus told His disciples that they had power over all the power of Satan. Jesus obtained that power through the cross, and now we are joint heirs with Him in His reigning position at the right hand of God, set down in heavenly places. This truth is so amazing that it alarms the timid who think more of their unworthiness than His worthiness. *"Worthy is the Lamb,"* the angels cried.

Paul understood this truth when he reminded us that "we do not wrestle against flesh and blood, but against principalities, against powers, against the rulers of the darkness of this age, against spiritual hosts of wickedness in the heavenly places" (Ephesians 6:12). This verse enumerates the various degrees of satanic spiritual wickedness. These are not earthly powers; they are satanic spiritual powers that control earthly kingdoms, dictatorships, political systems, and religious systems opposed to God. Every evil or foul demon working for Satan is mentioned in the categories; now

Paul says we wrestle with them! Is this a hopeless wrestling match? Are the odds one hundred to one against us? Do we go into the ring doomed to be pulverized by these powers? No, a thousand times no. We go in to win, to defeat the enemy by commanding, through prayer, our very attitude of victory.

The very moment Satan sees us enter the ring, he knows that he is defeated. He will certainly put up stiff and stubborn opposition, but he knows he is defeated. It is only a matter of time before he throws in the towel and declares that he can no longer oppress us in the way he tried so hard to do. Therefore, our faith must never waiver. The battle may be long and fierce, but *"I can do all things through Christ who strengthens me"* (Philippians 4:13). Defeat is not in the dictionary of heaven unless it speaks of Satan and his demons. For the Christian, there is only victory.

Why is this? It is because our lives are hid in Christ, and the wicked one touches us not. *"Resist the devil and he will flee from you"* (James 4:7).

When ministering in Uruapan, Mexico, we met a Christian man who was a cotton grower with a farm given to him by the Mexican government. The surrounding cotton farmers resented his faith, for they were fanatical religionists stirred up by their priests. They commanded this man to leave his faint, but he refused. They came again and ordered him to run, threatening that they would shoot him if he stayed. He refused to run and told them he would stay where God put him. Then an enraged fanatic said he would shoot him where he stood, so he said, "Go ahead and shoot, but I'm not quitting." A strange thing happened at that moment: the man began to tremble violently and turned away. This is a true story, for the man gave me his sombrero as a memento of a New Testament story. Resist the devil steadfastly in the faith. Sometimes we do not wrestle long enough. We give up and Satan wins, whereas he was only supposed to lose and run!

We once had an objection raised to the teaching of our authority in Christ. How could we command Satan when even the great and mighty archangel Michael dared not rebuke Satan, saying, *"The Lord rebuke you!"* (Jude 9). This is a wonderful and marvelous revelation. Before Calvary, man was a little lower than the angels, including Michael the archangel; but after Calvary, we were elevated far above all principalities and powers. Now an angel becomes a ministering spirit to those who are heirs of this salvation. This is where our position of being joint heirs with Christ is rightly understood. Now Michael and other angels become our ministering spirits; now we are re-created in Christ to be above them—not a little lower, but now far above. Michael has never sinned and therefore, does not need a Savior. It was the fallen angels who sinned, who were divested of their spiritual bodies and position. They were cast out into the earth. (See Revelation 12:9–10). However, Michael is still an archangel and is still subject to obedience of rank. Satan was created the greatest and the most powerful of all the angels, and Michael was next in rank with others like

Gabriel. Therefore, Michael could not rebuke his superior officer, even if his superior officer had sinned. He still carries his rank, for the callings of God are not to be repented of. Satan now uses his rank to break down God's heritage instead of helping to build it up by ministering to it, as Michael does. Satan was created as the supreme commander-in-chief of all angelic forces. Before the cross he even entered heaven to give an account of himself as we read in Job 1 and 2. He correctly reported that he was walking to and fro in the earth, for that was his domain, as Prince of this world. Although Satan fell heavily at the cross and lost his right of entry into heaven, he never lost his rank. (See Luke 10:18.) Michael cannot rebuke Satan, but Jesus did; therefore, we can do so today in His name! This is why we cast out demons in the name of Jesus; we heal the sick in the name of Jesus; we can do all things in the name of Jesus, even commanding a mountain to be cast into the sea. If we do not doubt in our hearts, these things will happen! Try it and see!

Thus, we find in God's Word that He is imploring us to understand our high calling in Christ.

> *That the God of our Lord Jesus Christ…may give to you the spirit of wisdom and revelation in the knowledge of Him, the eyes of your understanding being enlightened; that you may know what is the hope of His calling, what are the riches of the glory of His inheritance in the saints, and what is the exceeding greatness of His power toward us who believe, according to the working of His mighty power which He worked in Christ when He raised Him from the dead and seated Him at His right hand in the heavenly places, far above all principality…power… might…dominion…name…. And…put all things under His feet.*
>
> (Ephesians 1:17–22)

This is the position of Jesus Christ today. God put Him there after He raised Him from the dead and as we abide in Him and are *"found in Him"* (Philippians 3:9), we can exercise all the power and authority that He vests in us, His brothers and sisters.

In Romans 8:11, Paul records that "if the Spirit of Him who raised Jesus from the dead dwells in you, He who raised Christ from the dead will also give life to your mortal bodies through His Spirit who dwells in you." The quickening power of the Holy Spirit will continually restore our mortal body to health and strength for every time of need in our victorious battle against Satan. Finally, when it is God's time (and not Satan's time) for us to go to be with the Lord, He will quicken our bodies so completely that we will have a body which is from heaven. (See 2 Corinthians 5:1–2). Every punch that Satan puts to us—in suffering, sickness, frustration, and sorrow— will be repulsed by the quickening power of the Spirit of God in our mortal bodies if we resist it. Perhaps this is what Paul had in mind when he wrote that if a believer speaks in tongues he edifies himself, for in so doing, he would cause the Spirit of God to move mightily in his mortal body. Paul also told Timothy to stir up the gift that was in him. Christians today are far more likely to let the devil stir them up, kick them around, and stamp them, rather than to take the initiative and stir up the Holy Spirit in themselves, charging into Satan like a quarterback and knocking him down. It may seem a crude thing to say, but either Satan is going to kick you around, or you are going to kick him around. Choose which position you want to play!

BIBLE BAPTISMS

CONTENTS

FOREWORD

Even as the mind of man is incapable of reconciling "One God" with the three Persons of the Holy Trinity, so also does it encounter difficulty in attempting to cope with the variety of baptisms of the Bible as so ably dealt with in *Bible Baptisms*. This is especially true in the light of the *"one baptism"* of Ephesians 4:5. So God admonishes us to become as little children in eternal matters. And a little child simply believes and receives the blessings.

The principle of the "unity of many," which was so perfectly demonstrated on the day of Pentecost, has become more understandable to me through the teachings embodied within the context "I am the Potter; you are the clay." (See Jeremiah 18:6.) Here God illustrates the underlying relationship in which we are the vessels in the process of being made *"useful for the Master"* (2 Timothy 2:21). And as I read through the pages of *Bible Baptisms*, God spoke to my heart through my own experience as an amateur potter.

The production of a vessel of any type begins with a lump of mud and an idea in the mind of the potter. And as no two vessels are ever identical, so the potter makes each of His vessels an individual masterpiece, whose ultimate purpose is known only to Himself.

After properly preparing the mud ball and forming it into a rounded shape, the potter throws it onto the wheel and starts it rotating at just the right speed. Then by proper application of pressure inside and out, the vessel comes forth under the skilled hands of the potter and is laid aside to dry. It has now been changed from a mud ball into a fragile shell of dried clay—dull, weak, unattractive, and useless. Literally a useless "once-born" piece of raw material "possessing a form of usefulness but lacking the power thereof." (See 2 Timothy 3:5.) During this formative stage of life, the vessel has nothing to do but "sit and let it happen." Any attempt on the part of the pot to assist the potter in any way will cause complete collapse of the pot and it must be removed from the wheel and destroyed.

After reaching the dry, or "greenware," state, the vessel is now ready for its first baptism of fire in the kiln of the potter. This first firing will literally transform the clay into a new creation by changing its structure from a mixture of loosely combined minerals, oxides, vegetation, and miscellaneous impurities into a vessel of great strength, toughness, durability, and beauty. Numerous firings will be necessary to impart all these qualities and the first or "regenerating" fire simply places the vessel in a position to receive further processing by the potter. Prior to the first firing, the slightest shock would cause the pot to crumble into dust. The final firing will find the vessel strong, muscular, and impervious to external circumstances, provided the potter is permitted to have his way without restriction.

The first or regenerating fire seems to me to be analogous to our entrance into the body of Christ by the operation of the Holy Spirit, which makes us new creatures in Christ Jesus, and which God describes in 2 Corinthians 5:17 and Romans 6:3. Then the new creatures, weak, crumbly, and ineffective, must undergo the baptism of Jesus in the Holy Spirit—the first of numerous "maturing" fires designed to impart qualities not previously present in their lives. Then with the gifts of the Holy Spirit available for us to deliver into the lives of the needy all about us, we are *on the way* to becoming finished products.

If the final result is to be a piece of porcelain or fine china, it must undergo many exposures to fires of varying degrees of intensity, called "maturing fires." Each "baptism" will contribute something to the final result so that the masterpiece, when completed, will be able to endure great strain through exposure to extremes of hot and cold, but must also be able to absorb stresses and shocks brought about through everyday contact with other vessels. No amount of "pushing around," being dropped, or otherwise mistreated by the happenings of life will have any noticeable effect on the vessel in its finished state of usefulness.

The initial exposure to fire has caused the pot to shrink in physical size to about eighty percent of its original stature through removal of elements and impurities of which it was totally unaware. Subsequent firings will further refine its texture and add other qualities so necessary for that perfection which will bring joy to the heart of the potter. While the ancient Chinese master potters added their personal signatures only to vessels in completed form and which met the most exacting standards of perfection, our God puts His mark upon us at the beginning and gives us the witness of the Spirit that *"He who began a good work in you will continue until the day of Jesus Christ [right up to the time of His return], developing [that good work] and perfecting and bringing it to full completion in you"* (Philippians 1:6 AMPC)

The second exposure to fire, when Jesus baptizes us in the Holy Spirit, equips us according to His promise in Acts 1:8 with power to begin our *"ministry of reconciliation"* (2 Corinthians 5:18) in witnessing to Him and becoming deliverers of Himself to others.

Further exposure to fire through the "baptisms of suffering" will produce in us that supernatural quality whereby we are impervious to circumstances so that we along with the apostle James can *"count it all joy"* (James 1:2 KJV) in whatever state we find ourselves and can "praise the Lord *anyhow.*" At the same time we will have acquired an understanding of what the other person is going through so that we may be ministers of deliverance, healing, and transformation through the *"God's love… poured out in our hearts through the Holy Spirit"* (Romans 5:5).

"Though He was a Son, yet He learned obedience by the things which He suffered" (Hebrews 5:8). Many of life's experiences are not meant for us for corrective reasons so much as to perfect our ministry of Jesus into the lives of others through the understanding of affliction which comes only through personal experience.

The fire of full maturity is reached when the vessel becomes invisible in the white-hot atmosphere of the kiln—where "God is all in all" (see 1 Corinthians 15:28) and we the vessel are incandescent—completely aglow with the fire of the Holy Spirit—literally on fire for Jesus.

The final or decorating fire, executed at a much lower temperature, may appear to be entirely superfluous to the vessel. Without it, however, that delicate gold banding around the lip of the cup would be impossible. If we are certain that *"all things work together for good"* (Romans 8:28) in the lives of the Master Potter's children, then will we *"in everything give thanks; for this is the will of God in Christ Jesus for you"* (1 Thessalonians 5:18). And each time of testing will be known for what it is; simply another step in the coming forth of that perfect state where we shall hear Jesus our Master Potter say, *"Inasmuch as you did it to one of the least of these My brethren, you did it to Me"* (Matthew 25:40).

May you be blessed as I was through prayerful reading and rereading of *Bible Baptisms.*

—*Harold E. Hill*
Towson, Maryland
April 1967

1

OLD TESTAMENT BAPTISM

The practice of water baptism in the New Testament has its roots deep in the Old Testament, and New Testament baptism is a fulfillment of the Old Testament rite. If we are to understand the antitype, we must understand the type, and its purpose in the ordinances of Israel worship.

When John the Baptist came baptizing in the Jordan River, he introduced no new thought to the Jews. They understood perfectly what he was doing. When he baptized Jesus there was no conflict of thought or theological practice. John's baptism was a logical fulfillment of what the writer to the Hebrews called *"various washings, and fleshly ordinances"* (Hebrews 9:10). Briefly stated, the whole ordinance of *"various washings"* that preceded New Testament baptism was the act of washing away dirt, which had the symbolic implication of washing away of sins.

The concept of washing was introduced by God through Moses to the children of Israel on the occasion of their "marriage" to Jehovah. In Exodus 19:7–14, we find that the children of Israel, through the elders or representatives of the people, promised faithfully, as in a wedding ceremony, that they would faithfully obey all the words that were spoken to them by Moses. Moses then returned their promises to God on their behalf; thus we see that Moses was a type of Christ, a minister standing between God and the church.

Following the agreement by Israel to obey and serve God, Moses at once told them to "sanctify themselves and wash their clothes," (See verse 10.) This ordinance of national sanctification was to be a three-day ceremony, so that the people could have impressed upon them the importance of becoming clean, remaining clean, and continuing clean, *after* they had promised to serve God. On the third day another symbolic baptism occurred, that of the Holy Spirit; for God said that He would come down in the sight of all the people upon Mount Sinai. In verse 16 it is recorded,

Then it came to pass on the third day, in the morning, that there were thunderings and lightnings, and a thick cloud on the mountain; and the sound of the trumpet was very loud, so that all the people who were in the camp trembled. ... Now Mount Sinai was completely in smoke, because the LORD descended upon it in fire. (Exodus 19:16–18)

Thus in symbol and type water baptism was immediately followed by the baptism with the Holy Spirit and fire. (See Matthew 3:11.) We draw attention to the fact that as soon as God came down upon Mount Sinai (typical of the church), His voice was heard speaking. *"Moses spoke, and God answered him by voice"* (Exodus 19:19).

It is inconceivable that the children of Israel did not wash their bodies before putting on clean, newly washed clothes. Clothing in the Bible is a type of the righteousness of Christ which He puts upon us as a bride, when we accept Him as Savior and Lord. His righteousness (or right living) is only given to us to put on lives which have been changed and cleansed in the blood of Jesus Christ. The whole teaching of the apostle Paul is that Jesus imputes to us righteousness as a perfectly fitting garment to cover our nakedness. Thus we see here a perfect type of elementary baptism immediately following regeneration and marriage as a bride to her bridegroom. What bride will ever go to her bridegroom unwashed? Will she not rather wash and be sanctified only for him?

The Jews would understand when we read in Hebrews 10:22, "Let *us draw near with **a true heart** in full assurance of faith, having our hearts sprinkled from an evil conscience and **our bodies washed with** pure water.*"

When it came time in God's unfolding plan of salvation to set aside a certain people as priests or ministers to His people, He chose Aaron as High Priest and his sons as serving priests. Before this time Moses had stood and judged God's people, now God was sanctifying men who would spend their lives in Bible reading, meditation, and ministering to the people, who would pay tithes for their support. This principle would still seem applicable to the church of the New Testament, for although all believers are priests, i.e., sons of the High Priest Jesus, as Aaron's sons; yet God puts a special anointing upon certain men to be apostles, prophets, evangelists, pastors, and teachers. In 1 Corinthians 12:28, we read that *God has set* these. It is not the work of man, who can only ratify by the laying on of hands that which it is obvious that God has already set.

When these priests were set in office Moses, as a type of Jehovah-God, took both Aaron the High Priest (a type of Christ the Son) and his sons (types of all believers) and washed them in water. (See Leviticus 8:6.) This was done first before the oil (typical of the Holy Spirit) was poured upon them. "[Moses] *poured of the anointing oil on Aaron's head and anointed him, to consecrate him*" (Leviticus 8:12). This anointing oil was no symbolic mark on their foreheads, but a deliberate pouring from a sacred vessel upon their heads and this oil ran right down to the very bottom of the skirts of their priestly robes. (See Psalm 133.) All parts of Aaron and his sons were immersed in oil. This in type was a baptism in the oil of God's Holy Spirit. There was no question of a sprinkling or a chrismal symbolic mark. The oil flowed right down to the feet.

Throughout the book of Leviticus we read that *"various washings"* were a regular part of demonstrating continual cleanliness. When the sins of Israel were imparted to the scapegoat in chapter 18, he was led away to a distant place, even as Jesus carried our sins and sicknesses and was led away to Calvary, a horrible hill called Golgotha or the place of a skull! This meant that our sins were taken to a place once and for all and nailed to the cross. When we accept this fact, we must also do what the children of Israel were commanded to do: *"And he shall wash his body with water in a holy place, put on his garments"* (Leviticus 16:24). Again in Leviticus 17:15–16: *"He shall both wash his clothes and bathe in water.... But if he does not wash them or bathe his body, then he shall bear his guilt."* Jesus said, *"He who believes and is baptized will be saved."* The converse was also spoken: *"he who does not believe will be condemned"* (Mark 16:16). These ordinances or washings were, of course, only for those who could understand and obey. There is no record that babies washed and put on new garments for ceremonial purposes.

We next come to a further out-calling, that of the whole tribe of Levi, who were chosen to serve as a priestly tribe, and do no manual work, because they had volunteered in a time of national rebellion to serve the Lord, when all the tribes were revolting and Moses challenged them. Because they volunteered they were chosen, but before they could be used by God, they had to be ceremonially sanctified or set apart by a religious ceremony. Moses was instructed to *"Take the Levites from among the children of Israel and cleanse them ceremonially.... Sprinkle water of purification on them...and let them wash their clothes, and so make themselves clean"* (Numbers 8:6–7). No man can serve God unless he is clean, and in Old Testament times this was a ceremonial washing, clean bodies and clean garments for clean service.

There was yet another ordinance called the "water of separation." The priest was commanded to wash his clothes in water and bathe his flesh in water. This was called "water of separation" and was a purification for sin. (See Numbers 19.) When a Christian is baptized on confession of faith in Jesus as his Savior—the Lamb of God—then he is indeed "separated from sin" to serve the Lord in holiness. As we shall see later on in this book, a Christian is so separated that he is buried in the water as a type of watery grave. It should not be necessary to bury him again; otherwise Christian baptism loses all meaning.

Those who care to read through the books of Leviticus and Numbers will see that the Old Testament abounds with teachings concerning *"various washings,"* all of which speak of ceremonial washing of uncleanness. All have sinned, therefore all need cleansing.

This chapter would not be complete without reference to the Red Sea deliverance and the crossing of the Jordan River in the escape of Israel to the Promised Land.

The apostle Paul wrote to the Corinthian Christians as follows:

Moreover, brethren, I do not want you to be unaware that all our fathers were under the cloud, all passed through the sea, all were baptized into Moses in the cloud and in the sea. (1 Corinthians 10:1–2)

It seems clear that in type both water baptism and the baptism in the Holy Spirit are referred to in this passage. The whole nation of Israel passed safely through the waters of the Red Sea which opened wide to them, the ground even becoming "dry land," and when they were safely across, men, women, and children, the Egyptians who attempted to pursue were drowned. Thus were the children of Israel delivered through death to resurrection life under Moses, but the Egyptians, who knew no circumcision or faith in God, were drowned by the same waters. There was no other way to life than through death, which this national baptism portrayed so vividly. In the desert, the Holy Spirit was a pillar of fire by night and a *shekinah* cloud by day, so that they were always made aware visibly of the presence of the Holy Spirit to protect and guide them.

In spite of their continual rebellions, it was God's determined intention to bring them into the Promised Land, and so He allowed a rebellious generation to die out, and then brought in the new generation, who all had to be circumcised, and then they had to follow their priests through the Jordan River. Two cairns of twelve stones were erected, one in the middle of the river bed to signify the old life buried, and the other on the Promised Land side of Jordan, to signify the resurrection of the twelve tribes. There we are planted together in the likeness of His death, so that we might also be in the likeness of His resurrection on the Promised Land side of Jordan. (See Romans 6:5.) The whole Old Testament church of the wilderness thereby was twice delivered by a miracle to enjoy the wonders of salvation in a land that flowed with milk and honey.

We are also delivered through death unto life to enjoy the blessings of the New Testament kingdom of God on earth. This kingdom is overshadowed by the Holy Spirit, who indwells those who believe.

We have to come out to go in. We have to die to live.

2

JOHN'S BAPTISM

For over four hundred years the Jews had had no prophet to exhort them to holy living. The nation and their priests were utterly corrupt. Jesus used words that no preacher would dare to use today—He called the clergy whited sepulchers, full of dead men's bones. He told them they were twofold more the children of hell than the proselytes that they made to their religion. They failed to recognize Him as their Messiah, Deliverer, and Savior, and yet they were the custodians of the Holy Scriptures and should have known Him when He commenced to minister. When He revealed God's love in healing the sick and raising their dead, they reviled Him and crucified Him saying, *"We will not have this man to reign over us"* (Luke 19:14), and again, *"His blood be on us and on our children"* (Matthew 27:25)! Has this not been terribly fulfilled? Many ask today why six million Jews perished during World War II. Others ask why God did not intervene and prevent it. God cannot break His own laws. We will either accept the blood of God's Son for salvation or for condemnation. The Jews accepted it for condemnation. We all have our choice today. Life or death. Blessing or cursing. Health or sickness. God lets us make our choice.

Into such a situation John the Baptist came. Conceived miraculously in his mother Elizabeth's womb when she was past the age of child bearing and was looked upon as barren (see Luke 1:36), John came as a "voice crying in the wilderness" (see John 1:23). He was to preach the truth of repentance from sins and faith toward God. He was the climax of the Old Testament, being the greatest of all the Old Testament prophets. His message was simple—it was not preached in the synagogues, but the people were ready to hear it, and it is written, *"Then all the land of Judea, and those from Jerusalem, went out to him"* (Mark 1:5). This is a big statement, and it is obvious that huge crowds went out into the wilderness just outside Jerusalem to hear this man of God. Naturally the priests were jealous and came to see what was going on, and we suspect to see where their congregations were straying! *"But when* [John] *saw many of the Pharisees and Sadducees coming to his baptism, he said to them, 'Brood of vipers! Who warned you to flee from the wrath to come?'"* (Matthew 3:7).

We have our fundamental Pharisees today and our liberal Sadducees who deny teaching of the rebirth, water baptism, and the baptism in the Spirit. We have the same problems as John had—no wonder God is helping us by pouring out the Holy Spirit again today in convicting power. Only when we have the Holy Spirit dwelling in us in fullness can we understand fully the plan and purposes of God. We need many Johns today, in fact we read that before the great and terrible days of the Lord should come, He would raise up again unto us—Elijah, which translated means "The Lord is God" or "God Himself"; as John the Baptist came in the spirit and power of Elijah (see Matthew 11:14; 17:10–13), so God is raising up men today in the same Spirit and power, with the same ministry and the same baptism.

It is clear from a simple reading of the Scripture that John took his disciples down into the water of the Jordan River and baptized them. When the Bible was translated from the Greek there was a great difficulty in arriving at a suitable word for "baptism"! Those bishops of the Church of England appointed by King James were in a dilemma, because the practice of the Established Church was to "christen" babies, which had been carried over from the Roman Catholic Church. The word *baptize* was a created word from the Greek *baptizo*, which simply means to "dip into and out again." Its root is *bapto-*, which simply means "to dip." The word *baptize* carried the meaning of taking the penitent and dipping him, or immersing him, into water. By no stretch of imagination can it be twisted to mean making a sign of a cross on a baby's forehead. John simply took the penitent Jews into the Jordan River where there was enough water to submerse them, therefore symbolically washing the whole of their bodies with water and their garments also!

In the Church of Ireland prayer book of the Established Church in Southern Ireland, there is a note that tells us in the plainest terms that it was the intention and desire of the leaders of this reformed church to throw out "infant baptism" and substitute it by the scriptural practice or ordinance of infant dedication. After all, Mary the mother of Jesus brought Him into the temple, gave Him into the arms of the priest who *presented* Him to the Father. (See Luke 2:21–22.) This request was turned down by Queen Elizabeth I, who stated that she felt the reformation had gone far enough, and it should not be the purpose of the church to take away from the simple people things they held as sacred and proper, and so the leaders bowed to Royal Command (instead of the Word of God) and failed to obey God's leading! All the reformed churches still "baptize" babies, in common with the Roman Catholic Church, whose stand is that a baby cannot inherit eternal life unless it is baptized! This of course, is adding to the perfect work of Jesus on the cross, who as the Lamb of God finished the work that the Father had sent Him to do; to save us from our sins and the penalty of our sins. As we shall see later, water baptism is an agreement, or a ratification, of what Jesus did for us, not an addition.

We must remember that the New Testament dispensation sealed in Christ's blood did not come into existence until Jesus gave up His spirit on the cross and cried, *"It is finished"* (John 19:30). One of the last great acts of the Old Testament and a fulfilling of a "divers washing," was the baptism of Jesus by John in the Jordan River. Not only did Jesus come to be our Savior, but also a perfect example. He kept the law perfectly, and if He was to identify Himself with sinful man, He must also be baptized as a sinful man for all sinful men! He humbled Himself right down to this act. Many today are too proud even to be baptized by total immersion, hiding behind an act that took place when they were too young to remember! Neither parents nor "godparents" can confess our sins for us. Each must do that for himself and then "[arise] *and* [be] *baptized"* (Acts 9:18).

Jesus, in identifying Himself with sinful man, said to a sinful man, "John, I want you to baptize me!" (See Matthew 3:14.) The Baptist's reaction was immediate. He forbade Jesus and said that if anyone needed to be baptized it was John by Jesus, not the other way around! Sinful man recognized the sinless Man, but Jesus insisted and said, *"'Permit it to be so now, for thus it is fitting for us to fulfill all righteousness.' Then he allowed Him"* (Matthew 3:15). Notice please that both were blessed; Jesus because He was obedient to His Father in identifying Himself with sinful man, and John because He was obedient to the living Word of God. *Both* fulfilled, or filled up, righteousness; in, other words, both did the right thing at the right time in the right way. Obedience pays!

The pattern of the Old Testament was faithfully being fulfilled again as Jesus washed His body all over with water—"a divers washing" fulfilling all the types of cleansing which we have considered, and the Holy Spirit descended and lighted upon Him in the bodily shape of a dove. As the Spirit of God descended upon Mount Zion, and as the oil came down on Aaron and his sons, so also did the Holy Spirit descend upon Jesus, the fulfillment of Aaron. As God spoke audibly to Moses at Sinai when Israel promised to obey and serve God, so the voice of God again was heard at the banks of Jordan saying, *"This is My beloved Son, in whom I am well pleased"* (Matthew 3:17).

The pattern is clear, first water washing, second Spirit immersion, and third the voice of God heard audibly. Do we stretch truth if we suggest that this is the reason that all who receive a true New Testament baptism in the Holy Spirit should speak in other tongues? It is the supernatural miraculous voice of God speaking from heaven, telling us the same thing for *"a voice came from heaven, 'You are My beloved Son, in whom I am well pleased'"* (Mark 1:11). The voice of God coming again in the charismatic gifts of the Holy Spirit will always glorify the Son—His beloved Son.

Glossolalia is not gibberish. It is God's voice glorifying the Son. Perhaps we have to have spiritual ears as well as spiritual eyes to perceive this!

John's baptism was a Jewish washing. It symbolized the washing away of past sins *after* they had been confessed. John baptized or immersed "*for the remission of sins*" (Matthew 26:28). There was no doubt in any one's mind who came out from Judah, Jerusalem and the regions round about what John meant when he haled them into the river. The Jewish priests understood perfectly. Is it not strange that Satan has so confused the issue that thousands cannot see the truth! This is brainwashing.

3

INFANT BAPTISM

The case for infant baptism by the reformed churches is made out on a false assumption.

In the Old Testament, which supplies the truth roots of all that grew into fruition in the New Testament, circumcision of the foreskin of the male child was primarily a ceremonial cutting away, as well as a hygienic operation. It spoke to the people of God that as the foreskin was cut away from the male organ which produced life, in like manner God would circumcise their hearts from wrong fleshly appetites and desires and give them His abundant life.

After God had in mercy restored the two tables of stone with the ten commandments to Israel, Moses said to them, *"therefore circumcise the foreskin of your heart"* (Deuteronomy 10:16) and again if Israel would continue to serve God in truth and holiness, Moses promised them that *"the LORD your God will circumcise your heart and the heart of your descendants, to love the LORD your God with all your heart and with all your soul, that you may live"* (Deuteronomy 30:6). It seems clear that circumcision of the foreskin was to impress the truth upon the Israelites that God Himself would circumcise their hearts by a divine operation. To suggest that infant circumcision has been replaced by infant baptism is to contradict the plain meaning of these two terms. Water baptism is a fulfillment of many washings, but circumcision is another matter, for the apostle Paul in Romans 2:29 wrote, *"Circumcision is that of the heart, in the Spirit, not in the letter."* Paul made it very clear in his epistles that circumcision of the foreskin profits nothing as an act of itself, other than hygiene.

The whole teaching, which the Jews found so difficult to understand, was that unless the heart is circumcised there can be no rebirth. Neither circumcision of the flesh nor baptism of a baby can do anything for the child if it is considered as an addition to the work of Jesus on the cross. We would hasten to state, however, that if a baby is presented to the Lord as Jesus was by His mother Mary, then it at once becomes clear that God is bound by His Word to bless the child and give His angels charge over it keeping it from harm. If a child is dedicated in a house of God with the agreement of the parents, who will have understanding of the solemnity of this simple act of faith, God must accept the responsibility of keeping the child safe until it reaches an age of understanding and accountability, so that it can then with understanding of the Scriptures, which are able to make us wise unto salvation, make the decision to follow the Lord. (See 2 Timothy 3:15.) Timothy experienced this, having a godly grandmother and mother who taught him the Bible. He chose and he chose well. Do we suppose that Timothy was "baptized as a baby," or do we believe he was dedicated by his mother Eunice, with his grandmother Lois looking with smiling approval. Are we to believe that there were godfathers and godmothers present? The Scriptures do not teach us so.

Perhaps we should not be surprised that Jesus said of the priests in His day that they had made the Word of God of none effect by their traditions. We believe it could be said of many of our denominations today that they have wrested Scripture and introduced traditional teachings which cannot be substantiated from Scripture. Is not this what Martin Luther fought in AD 1517? We cannot believe the reformation, which began then, has yet been completed. There is great evidence that the reformation is coming to a climax in our day. Infant baptism must give way to believers' baptism.

The author was married in an Anglican Church in the county of Kent in England in 1934. This church did not receive the testimony of my wife when she was baptized in the Holy Spirit in 1940. It was therefore with great delight that we learned that the Rector of this Church of England was baptized in the Holy Spirit and spoke in tongues in 1964, and we had the joy and privilege of meeting him in his rectory, and he told us of many in his parish who were similarly receiving this marvelous baptism and speaking in tongues. He was on fire for God and a very honest man. Once he was indwelt by the Holy Spirit according to the experience of Acts 2:4, the Spirit began to teach him and show him that infant baptism was nowhere to be found in Scripture. He spoke to his Bishop, who was evangelical, and to others who held high office in the Church of England who were known to him as friends. He told them he could no longer "baptize" little babies, but could only dedicate them in the house of God. There was no way out, no compromise could be found. Priests of the Church of England are empowered by state law to make the sign of the cross in the water of christening, and if an ordained priest for conscience sake cannot do so he must leave the church! He therefore left and is now working as an independent evangelist and Bible teacher. After all, Martin Luther did not cease to minister, even after he was excommunicated! Truth always divides because it is the Sword of the Spirit, which is sharper than any two-edged sword. Incidentally, it is the same Sword of the Word of God that circumcises our hearts! Heart circumcision is a divine miracle which can only be done by the divine surgeon Jesus, using the divine scalpel of the Word of God.

We understand that there has been a great stirring within the ranks of the priests of the Church of England on this issue of water baptism for infants. The press has carried articles on the subject, but the Church of England cannot reform in this practice without an act of Parliament at Westminster. There are many in the Reformed Dutch Church also who are disturbed about the practice. We believe that there will be a great turning away from this tradition by many priests and we pray that God may help them contend for the truth in their preaching and practice.

No wonder God is pouring out His Spirit to renew the church!

In our study on the baptisms of the Bible, we must remember that the "doctrine of baptisms" is a fundamental of the doctrines of Christ (see Hebrews 6:2), and we are convinced that when God reveals the baptism in the Spirit to members of reformed churches, and baptizes them in the Spirit as He did the early church at Pentecost, then it will be necessary for us to have a new appreciation of all the implications of the plurality of baptisms. It seems quite obvious to us that a rereading of the Bible with the new anointing of the Holy Spirit will reveal with absolute clarity that water baptism for believers is scriptural and that water baptism for babies is unscriptural and will show that there is no conflict between circumcision and dedication. The two are separate experiences.

Jesus explained that evil actions proceed from the heart, *"For **out of the heart** proceed evil thoughts, murders, adulteries, fornications, thefts, false witness, blasphemies. These are the things which defile a man"* (Matthew 15:19–20). Circumcision of the foreskin will not cut these out of the heart, neither will infant sprinkling. It takes a real work of the Holy Spirit, using the Word of God as a sharp scalpel, to cut away all the fleshly appetites of our fallen nature. Jesus called this a rebirth by the Spirit of God. When this has happened, then we are candidates for water baptism.

Let us not forget that Jesus was dedicated, and He waited another thirty years to be baptized. We must dedicate our children to God's service in life and believe for them and teach them the Word of God. When they are able to understand and appreciate the teachings of Jesus, we are happy to baptize them by immersion.

4

BELIEVER'S BAPTISM

It is so interesting to notice the gradual progression of truth in the Bible. The roots of these progressive truths are deep in the Old Testament, and the revelation grows throughout the Bible, especially as we enter into the New Covenant in Christ's blood. From early washings of clothes and bodies, we progress to John's *"baptism of repentance for the remission of sins"* (Mark 1:4); but this is not a final fulfillment by any means. We suggest that it is an interim baptism.

Jesus began to teach His apostles and early disciples that water baptism must follow personal faith in Christ and His finished work on Calvary. He said, *"He who believes and is baptized will be saved"* (Mark 16:16). We must not deduce from this that water baptism adds anything to Calvary, but we certainly can understand that it is incumbent on all believers to obey and be baptized! There are denominations who believe that unless we are baptized we cannot be saved. In fact this thought lies at the very root of regenerative baptism as practiced on babies by the reformed churches as well as the Roman Catholic Church. Some of these denominations do not like to be reminded that they do in fact teach that there is no salvation without water baptism, whether adult or infant, but it is still true that the very basis of the desire to sprinkle water on infants lies in this misconception of truth. The Roman Catholic Church, which originated this practice, will go to the extreme of injecting water into the mother in the hospital so that the unborn child may be sprinkled in cases where it is feared the mother or baby will die. It is commonly taught that unless this extreme action is taken with the help of a nurse or doctor, the child if it dies will not enter heaven, but go to an imaginary place called "limbo." This place is described in a standard dictionary of the English language as "an indefinite border region in the intermediate state, nearer hell or heaven according to the class of souls there awaiting the judgment," from the Latin *limbus* meaning "edge." It is said that millions believe this unscriptural nonsense because they neither have the Bible nor the Holy Spirit.

God is changing this, for the Holy Spirit baptism is being given to many Roman Catholics as well as Reformed Protestants.

Jesus said of little children, *"for of such is the kingdom of heaven"* (Matthew 19:14). We must become as little children to have any hope of the kingdom of heaven, and a child cannot be judged by God according to His law, if they are too young to obey the law. Therefore all children are in a legal state of innocence before a just God, and neither circumcision nor infant baptism can affect them at all spiritually. It is not until a child reaches an age of accountability, which varies with different children, that he or she can accept Jesus as Savior from sin, having been first brought to Christ by the law which is described by Paul as a schoolmaster. (See Galatians 3:24.) It is in such a case that water baptism becomes a duty of loving obedience for the penitent saved sinner.

We have noted that Jesus said that water baptism should occur after we have believed. Similarly, the apostle Peter taught this on the day of Pentecost, *"Repent, and let every one of you be baptized"* (Acts 2:38). In this case water baptism must follow our repentance—no child can repent or believe. In the revival under Philip in Acts 8 it is recorded that those who were baptized in Samaria were *"men and women"* (verse 12). It is sometimes argued that when the jailer and his entire household were baptized in Acts 16:33, there must have been babies there; but this is disproved because those who were baptized in the bathing facilities of the prison came to a meal afterward and all rejoiced, believing in God. No baby can qualify! There are many other Scriptures, but we feel that the case is clearly demonstrated against infant baptism or sprinkling of any kind. Baptism is for those who believe and repent, and signifies burial.

Paul the apostle gave us some graphic teaching in the sixth chapter of Romans, and described water baptism as a death union with Christ. Thus, *"do you not know that as many of us as were baptized into Christ Jesus were baptized into His death?"* (verse 3). Some believe that this verse teaches that they do not actually enter into the body of Christ until they have been immersed in water, but we believe the mind of the Spirit is that water baptism symbolizes death and burial. This goes much farther than the washings of the Old Testament, which had to be repeated, or the interim baptism of John for the remission of sins. This takes the forgiven penitent sinner and buries him right out of sight. There can be no more ceremonial washings for a corpse! To suggest that we are not true Christians until we have been baptized is to state in the simplest terms that Jesus did not finish the work of redemption on the cross. He filled up all that the prophets had spoken concerning Him; there was nothing more He could do. What He did, He did perfectly and cried out, *"It is finished"* (John 19:30) with His last breath. No, water baptism as a symbol adds nothing to our salvation, it is the first act of personal obedience after salvation. It is our ratification or agreement of what Jesus has done.

In 1776, the United States declared itself to be independent of the United Kingdom. On this date a nation was born; but it was still necessary to ratify it, which was done at the Treaty of Paris in 1782, six years later. The ratification did not make the United States of America any more an independent nation, but it established the fact in the eyes of other nations. In like manner, God did His part by sending Jesus to the cross to die for us, now we do our part in ratifying, publicly, that we are a new creature in Christ. We identify ourselves publicly with Calvary in being buried in the waters of baptism. We establish a testimony to the world that we are not only buried, but planted, for death means separation. Baptism is a seal of our separation, even as it was to Aaron and his sons long before. They were sanctified, separated, and called to the service of God. We ratify what God has already done. We publicly agree to it, and therefore enter into His death and resurrection. *"For if we have been united together in the likeness of His death, certainly we also shall be in the likeness of His resurrection"* (Romans 6:5). Jesus described Himself as a corn of wheat which had to be buried (see John 12:24) in order that it might be resurrected by springing to life. This simile was fulfilled in His death and resurrection, and will also be fulfilled in our death and resurrection. There is a great difference between a dry seed of corn and the beautiful green plant that grows from it to bear fruit. So, when we are planted it is for the express purpose that we might also spring up to newness of life, namely the very life of Jesus Christ in us. We enter into Christ, but He also enters into us. This is mutual. First God loved us and gave, so we in turn return that love and give ourselves. Fold your two hands together, and hold on the one to the other as tightly as you can and try to break them apart. This is the identification of one hand with the other. Jesus identified Himself with us in His earthly ministry, finally dying as sin for sinful man, and we identify ourselves with Him also. If He died and rose again, *"even so we also should walk in newness of life"* (Romans 6:4).

Most people who are baptized in obedience will testify that they realized the presence and reality of Jesus Christ in their lives as never before. It pays to obey God and enter into His plan for us.

Christian baptism is therefore both a funeral and a resurrection. At a funeral it is fitting that certain words be uttered over the dead person, and so the minister is required to baptize the candidate in the name of the Father and the Son and the Holy Spirit which Jesus told His disciples to do when they came to evangelize the Gentiles. (See Matthew 28:19.) It seems that the Jewish disciples baptized the Jewish converts in the name of the Lord Jesus Christ, in order that this name should be underlined to them because they had crucified and rejected Him as a race. In Acts 19:2, the Jewish converts at Ephesus said they had never heard of the Holy Spirit, and so they were baptized in the name of the Lord Jesus. We believe that it is not so important to become pedantic on the exact verbal formula as to realize that a pastor is saying words over a dead person. Some have even suggested that a person does not take the name of Jesus Christ upon themselves unless His name has been used in the verbal formula. This would unquestionably be adding to the finished work of Calvary. If we are to "make disciples" of the Gentiles today, we feel we are correct in using the words given by Jesus for this purpose in Matthew 28:19.

The whole work of regeneration and the rebirth belongs only to the Holy Spirit. Jesus made this very clear in John 16:8, "*And when He* [the Holy Spirit] *has come, He will convict* [convince] *the world of sin, and of righteousness, and of judgment.*" Again we read in John that we can only become sons (Greek, "newborn babes") of God by being born a second time, not of the flesh, nor of the will of man, *but of God.* (See John 1:12–13.) Nobody can help the Holy Spirit. We are only required to preach and testify. The Holy Spirit ministers to unbelievers to convince them they are sinners and then to lead them to repentance and to work in them a new life from God by a rebirth. As the Son of God was supernaturally conceived in the womb of Mary, so the Son of God is supernaturally created in our hearts. In both cases this is only a work of grace by the Holy Spirit. Man cannot help, he can only submit and receive.

It is important to realize this truth, because there are some today who teach that as we are baptized into His death, it is the act of water baptism which causes us to die, which would be direct contradiction of the words of Jesus. We never bury a man before he is dead. He must die first and then be certified by a medical doctor that he is indeed dead, and then we bury him. A sinner must first repent, believe and die to sin before he can be buried in baptism! We have heard of people who will gladly re-baptize a person several times to make them "lay down dead" more. This would not be burying; it would be progressive drowning! Jesus died on the cross; we die to our sins, and then we are baptized in water by total immersion, identifying ourselves with a fact already done on our behalf at Calvary. We become therefore baptized or immersed into His death by symbol. We are buried after we die!

It is not always wrong to baptize a second time. Many of us who were baptized as infants by our parents knew nothing about it, and so it is right and proper, and according to the Scriptures, to be baptized as a believer on confession of our faith when we reach years of understanding and enlightenment. Many have been baptized in past times because they were told they could not "join the church" unless they did. In so many cases there was no true work of grace in the regeneration of the heart. They went into the water a confirmed sinner and came out of it in the same state! We believe in such cases it is pleasing to God to be buried with Him with faith and understanding.

We have a classic case in Acts 19, already referred to, where Paul baptized the Jews in the name of the Lord Jesus. They confessed that they had already been baptized "*into John's baptism*" (Acts 19:3), and Paul replied that this was a baptism of repentance, and went on to explain the meaning of Christian baptism with the deeper connotation of death and resurrection. On hearing the Apostle's teachings, they gladly accepted God's truth and were baptized a second time. The result of this step of further obedience was that they soon received yet another baptism, the baptism in the Spirit, but more of this later.

Are you a candidate for a second baptism? Don't let personal or family pride prevent you from following the Lord and so fulfilling all righteousness.

5

THE BAPTISM OF SUFFERING

There is another baptism mentioned in Scripture, that of baptism of suffering. It must surely be clear that we do not identify ourselves in water baptism with His death unless we also identify ourselves with His resurrection and all that this entails. Paul rejoiced that he "*die daily*" (1 Corinthians 15:31), and again he had the sentence of death in himself, so that he did not trust in himself but in God alone and the resurrection power of Jesus. (See 2 Corinthians 1:9.) So may we. It is not only necessary to be baptized into His death, but to remain baptized in His death. This entails a continuing baptism, a daily reckoning ourselves to be dead unto sin (see Romans 6:11); but it is comforting to know that although we are dead, our lives are hid with Christ in God (see Colossians 3:3). This is a daily death union with Christ. It is a daily baptism into Christ, and only by daily reckoning ourselves to be dead will we find ourselves truly alive in Christ with His more abundant resurrection life that will keep us raised from the dead. How can Satan embarrass a dead person? It is to be feared that we allow Satan to disinter us too often, instead of remaining nicely and decently buried. "*We were buried with Him through baptism into death*" (Romans 6:4), and as Jesus was only buried once, and then was eternally resurrected, so in like manner it is only necessary for us to be buried once and then enjoy forever the fruits and power of His one resurrection! Those misguided people who allow themselves to be re-baptized for some special reason or in some special formula delude themselves, for they prove they did not understand what happened the first time they were buried. In truth, they could not have reckoned themselves to be really dead unto sin! We have found that many people who are baptized in water have little idea of the why and wherefore of what they do. Certainly a baby does not understand or reckon anything.

In Matthew 20:20–23, we read a pathetic story of a mother who desired great prominence for her sons in the kingdom of God. This is the natural woman, the daughter of Adam, using her charm, femininity, wiles, and psychology on Jesus. It didn't work; it never does. Jesus had already said, the *"first will be last"* (Matthew 19:30), but this teaching had entirely missed the mother of Zebedee's children! Oh yes, no doubt she was a good woman, a fine wife and mother, and a good neighbor and a warm-hearted helpful individual, but she understood nothing about the baptism of identification with Christ's sufferings. Jesus told her later, *"Whoever desires to be first among you, let him be your slave"* (Matthew 20:27). There are still far too many self-seekers in our churches, looking for position and power, rather than to minister to each other. Proud man hates being thought a servant, but Jesus was a Servant of all. He was willing to obey His Father and humbled Himself and was obedient unto death, even the death of the cross. (See Philippians 2:8.) We must have this spirit also. We must become a servant and stay a servant—and love it. Because Jesus did this for us, it is recorded that God *"highly exalted Him"* (Philippians 2:9). The way up is down. Peter again expressed this thought by writing, *"Therefore humble yourselves under the mighty hand of God, that He may exalt you"* (1 Peter 5:6).

If you remain dead, Jesus will look after you and manifest Himself in the power of the Spirit through your life, by operating the nine fruits and the nine gifts of the Spirit. *"If anyone thinks himself to be something, when he is nothing, he deceives himself"* (Galatians 6:3).

There is no room for personal ambition in the church.

There is a baptism of Christ's sufferings. We must be conformed to His death that we might be transformed in His resurrection. *"And [Jesus] said to her, 'What do you wish?' She said to Him, 'Grant that these two sons of mine may sit, one on Your right hand and the other on the left, in Your kingdom'"* (Matthew 20:21). Jesus then asked them, *"Are you able to drink the cup that I am about to drink, and be baptized with the baptism that I am baptized with?"* (verse 22). Their reply was immediate, "Yes"—they were ready and willing. We also must be willing.

The baptism of Christ's sufferings will be worked out in us as we daily walk the Christian walk. As we testify faithfully, and work His teachings in our life, in our bearing, in our conversations, in our dress, we shall immediately come into sharp conflict with those of the world who are walking in the diametrically opposite direction. Christians go uphill against the tide of fallen humanity. It is when many water-baptized and Spirit-baptized Christians come into this sharp conflict that they commence to compromise. They become ashamed to confess Christ in word and deed, but what did He say?

> Whoever is ashamed of Me and My words in this adulterous and sinful genera-
> tion, of him the Son of Man also will be ashamed when He comes in the glory of
> His Father with the holy angels. (Mark 8:38)

As we stay buried with Christ, we shall not be influenced by the sneering opinions of the worldly-wise sinners all around us, but rather glory in our infirmities and trials.

Jesus explained very clearly what He meant when He spoke about taking up our cross daily and following Him. (See Matthew 16:24.) This was to be a daily identification with Him and His bloody sacrifice on our behalf. We were always to be counted on the side of the cross and to be crucified with Him. This would inevitably bring persecution and suffering. Paul said, "*Yes, and all who desire to live godly in Christ Jesus will suffer persecution*" (2 Timothy 3:12). Paul knew what he was talking about and explained that none of these things moved him. How could they—he was dead! He also explained though that the Lord delivered him every time—out of them all! He had reason to believe this fact of faith, because the psalmist had already made it known to all Israel. "*Many are the afflictions of the righteous, but the LORD delivers him out of them all*" (Psalm 34:19). It is the fear of failure, the fear that God will desert us and let us down that causes so many to compromise, thereby denying Him before their fellowman.

History reveals the abundance of this truth. The Roman Empire is credited with destroying millions of Christians, and Fox in his book of Martyrs tells of the other millions destroyed by fanatics in the Roman Catholic Church. In recent times more millions have been destroyed by the communists in China, Korea and Vietnam. Paul wrote to the Hebrews and chided them that they had an easy time compared with some, for they had "*not yet resisted unto blood*" (Hebrews 12:4) thereby sealing their testimony in their own blood as others were to do. We often wonder what would happen in the free world if there was this type of persecution against the church. How many would gladly give their lives for His sake, and how many would "no longer walk with Him"? (See John 6:66.)

The baptism of Christ's sufferings includes all this. It might mean losing your job. Jesus said that two in a family would be divided against three in the same family. (See Matthew 12:51–53.) This is suffering hard to endure, even for Christ's sake, but many faithful ones have to endure this baptism today. Many have been disinherited of worldly possessions, many young people have been thrown out of their homes, especially is this so in heathen countries and Roman Catholic dominated countries. It might be easier to be shot against a wall than to endure suffering for a season.

We repeat that the "doctrine of baptisms" is a vital pillar in the doctrine of Christ, and if we are to enjoy our salvation to the fullest extent, we must understand the baptisms of the Bible. There are several—not just one! (See Hebrews 6:1–3.) So many are completely satisfied with water baptism "to join the church"; others believe they had a "package deal" when "they were saved" and so there is no need to look for other baptisms. Some revolt against the baptism in the Spirit, but few would easily take on the baptism of Christ's sufferings. It has a monastic ring about it! It seems that water baptism without the baptism of Christ's sufferings is largely without meaning. It becomes an interment of a living creature; no wonder the living one struggles to get out of the tomb again! There is a gruesome painting in the Wietz Museum in Brussels, Belgium, which shows a haunted faced man trying to struggle out of his coffin. He had been buried alive. Be careful that you know and understand that you are dead before you allow yourself to be buried!

> **Blessed** *are those who are persecuted for righteousness' sake, for theirs is the kingdom of heaven.* **Blessed** *are you when they revile and persecute you, and say all kinds of evil against you falsely for My sake. Rejoice and be exceedingly glad, for great is your reward in heaven, for so they persecuted the prophets who were before you.* (Matthew 5:10–12)

The baptism of Christ's sufferings by daily identification brings great *blessings* in this life and the life to come. (See Mark 10:30.) The persecutions and sufferings are made sweet by the hundred-fold blessings in this life and the life to come; the bitter waters of persecution and rejection by loved ones is more than compensated when the tree of life is thrown into the bitter waters of our sufferings. (See Exodus 15:23–25.) The apostle Paul knew this vital daily experience when he wrote *"For as the sufferings of Christ abound in us, so our consolation also abounds through Christ"* (2 Corinthians 1:5). These experiences were necessary so that we in turn might comfort others who are in trouble, with the comfort wherewith we also are comforted by Christ.

> "Buried with Christ," and raised with Him too;
> What is there left for me to do?
> Simply to cease from struggling and strife,
> Simply to "walk in newness of life."
> (Ryder 1875)

6

THE BAPTISM IN THE SPIRIT

It must be obvious to an honest reader of the Bible who is not blinded by theological prejudice, that there is a separate experience called the baptism in the Spirit as distinct from the experience of the rebirth or from baptism in water. We realize that some teach that God gives a "package deal" when one is "saved." This teaching is very unfortunate for it blocks the possibility of the Holy Spirit coming in any greater degree or measure upon a dedicated Christian. God only answers according to our faith.

We would cite three instances in the Bible to establish the fact that the receiving of the Holy Spirit baptism is a subsequent experience to receiving the gift of eternal life. The work of the Holy Spirit is to convict a sinner of his sin and to reveal the righteousness of Christ and make it possible for the sinner to receive forgiveness of sins and therefore the gift of eternal life. By this many mean "getting saved." This experience, however deep, joyous, or emotional it may be, must never be confused with receiving the baptism into the Holy Spirit.

When Phillip went down to Samaria a tremendous revival broke out. People were delivered from demons; they were healed of sickness; there was a great conviction of sin so that hundreds were baptized in water confessing their sins. This brought great joy in the city, but still the Holy Spirit had not descended upon any of these Samaritan converts in baptizing power. This necessitated two apostles coming from Jerusalem to pray with the converts that they might receive this baptism into the Holy Spirit, for it is recorded that they *"prayed for them that they might receive the Holy Spirit. For as yet He had fallen upon none of them. They had only been baptized in the name of the Lord Jesus. Then they laid hands on them, and they received the Holy Spirit"* (Acts 8:15-17). If all these Samaritans had received the Holy Spirit at conversion and water baptism, it would not have been necessary for the apostles to come to lay hands on them in order that they might receive Him! The startling logic of this should not escape the sincere seeker after truth. (See Acts 8:1–17.)

In the case of the disciples at Ephesus, we are left in no doubt at all, for Paul having found certain believers, who had a good pastor named Apollos who taught them that Jesus was Christ, immediately plunged in with no psychological finesse and said, *"Did you received the Holy Spirit when you believed?"* (Acts 19:2). Paul was not satisfied because they had been "saved" by believing upon Jesus as Savior. There seems no doubt that they were indeed believers on Christ, and so Paul sat down patiently and taught them not only about Christian water baptism, but also about the baptism in the Spirit. This sincere group of twelve men and their families entered into the deeper experience of the baptism in the Spirit and spoke in tongues and prophesied as the evidence of the infilling of the Spirit.

The third Scripture we have in mind is found in Ephesians 1:13 and this is very appropriate for we have just considered the coming of the Holy Spirit upon the Ephesian believers. Paul wrote, *"In [Jesus] you also trusted, after you heard the word of truth, the gospel of your salvation; in whom also, having believed, you were sealed with the Holy Spirit of promise."* Paul was reminding them that the baptism in the Spirit was a subsequent experience to salvation.

Jesus Himself demonstrated this principle. He, being the Son of God and dwelling in His body, still had to come to the personal experience of being anointed by the Spirit. This may seem strange, that Jesus the perfect Son of God needed an anointing or sealing to begin His three-and-a-half years supernatural ministry. We cannot say Jesus was not "saved" or "sanctified," because He was always the spotless Lamb of God without blemish. A marvelous manifestation of the Trinity working in unity occurred at this sealing. The Son was obedient in being baptized in water, the Holy Spirit descended, and the Father spoke.

When we are converted to Christ and ratify our rebirth by water baptism, we enter into Christ. (See Romans 6:3.) Jesus, however, still found it necessary to receive this subsequent experience of anointing and so must we. As members in Christ we must be baptized by Jesus into the Holy Spirit. It is important to remember that we are not baptized by the Holy Spirit into anything; there is an unfortunate translation in 1 Corinthians 12:13 which reads in the King James Version: *"For by one Spirit are we all baptized into one body."* This translation has been used to try to show that the Holy Spirit baptizes a person into Christ at conversion, and a whole doctrine has been built up on this one Scripture, but God's Word tells us that we cannot believe anything that is not proved by the mouth of two or more witnesses, and there is not a second witness to this teaching. We repeat, the Holy Spirit does not baptize us into anything, but Jesus baptizes us as members of Christ into the Holy Spirit. This is clear when we consider that John the Baptist himself said of Jesus, *"He will baptize you with the Holy Spirit and fire*" (Matthew 3:11). Jesus takes us when we are willing and immerses us into the fire of the Holy Spirit, which not only touches our body as does water, but the Holy Spirit saturates our entire triune being of spirit, soul and body.

Young's Literal Translation of the Bible renders 1 Corinthians 12:13 as follows: *"For by one Spirit we were all baptized into one body."* The American Revised Version and the British Revised Version gives, *"in one Spirit,"* as do many other translations. As Jesus was baptized into the power of the Spirit, so must we be. In the same way as the Spirit anointed Jesus, so will the same Spirit anoint Jesus in us and bring forth the full power of the Word of God. Jesus did not attempt to minister in the power of the Spirit until He received the empowering of the Spirit, and we believe it entirely scriptural to believe that no minister of the gospel today should expect to minister as Jesus commissioned us to minister until he has been filled to overflowing in the Spirit by being immersed into the Spirit. This experience reveals the body of Christ in all its fullness of power.

Of the five cases mentioned of individuals or companies being baptized in the Spirit, we find that tongues invariably was the initial evidence. First, on the day of Pentecost when it is clearly stated that the 120 spoke in tongues as the Spirit gave them the utterance; second, in the ministry of the two apostles who came from Jerusalem, Peter and John, who laid their hands upon all the Samaritan believers, and it is recorded in church history by Augustine writing in the fourth century, "We still do as the Apostles did when they laid hands on the Samaritans and called the Spirit on them. In the laying on of hands, it is expected that the converts should speak with new tongues." In the third case of the apostle Paul himself, he testified that he spoke in tongues more than any of the Corinthian Christians. (See 1 Corinthians 14:18.) No mention is made that he did when Ananias prayed for him (see Acts 9:17), but it is recorded that Ananias's faith was that Paul might be *"filled with the Holy Spirit"* (Acts 2:4). We believe that the initial evidence of tongues was indeed manifested by Paul on this occasion. He stated that he spoke ten thousand words in praising God and edifying himself, but would only speak in the vernacular when preaching. So may we.

The fourth case is when the Holy Spirit came upon the Gentiles as recorded in Acts 10. *"For they heard them speak with tongues and magnify God"* (Acts 10:46). If they had not spoken in tongues the Jewish church would never have accepted the fact that the Gentiles had been received into the same body of Christ as the Jews! It took a miracle to convince them. God knows there are still many people who need the same miraculous evidence before they will believe also!

The fifth case is that of a local church being baptized into the Holy Spirit. The Ephesian church had hands laid on them by Paul in Acts 19 and *"they spoke with tongues and prophesied"* (verse 6).

As we have explained in our book *What a Word Is This*, it is the *Logos*, the Living Word of God, that comes out of our innermost parts when we are baptized in the Spirit. As the Spirit immerses and saturates us through and through, He overflows through the orifice of our mouths and comes out as prophesied by Jesus as the *"rivers of living water"* (John 7:38). The difference between a born-again Christian having the Spirit of God with him, and one who has been baptized in the Spirit, is the difference between a pool and a fountain. The Word of God flows out of a person's mouth as a river of life bubbling up from the depths of God. A river is more useful coursing through a wilderness than an oasis in a desert.

The rebirth gives a filling, the baptism in the Spirit an overflow.

Let us not forget that the baptism in the Spirit was given by Jesus to empower the church for service. A church without divine power and supernatural ability to heal the sick, to cast out devils and to cleanse the lepers, is not the church of the New Testament. One has to be born again of the Spirit of God before being baptized into the Spirit. The two experiences are distinct and separate and must not be confused.

7

HOW TO RECEIVE THE BAPTISM IN THE SPIRIT

There are many ways that have been taught whereby believers might receive the baptism in the Spirit, some sensible and scriptural but others more emotional and not so scriptural!

In this chapter we want to show you how you can receive this baptism by pleading or sprinkling the blood of Jesus. We have literally seen hundreds of people quickly receive this gift by following the simple and scriptural teachings herein given.

First, we need to bear in mind that the Apostles called the baptism in the Spirit *"the gift of the Holy Spirit"* (Acts 2:38; 8:20). The Greek word *dorea* means a free gift; that is to say, it cannot be earned or merited, it can only be gladly accepted. John explained that it was Jesus alone who was deputed by the Father to give us this gift, and so we must go to Him and graciously take it out of His hand. This is where so many make a big mistake; they believe that if they act in a religious manner, or suffer some religious exercise like fasting, or begin to feel emotional, then Jesus will force this gift upon them and make them speak in tongues. Often have we heard misguided people say, "If God wants me to receive the Holy Spirit, He will give it to me." They never seem to realize that giving is a two-way experience, it is both giving and receiving. He gives—we take. If we do not take we do not receive; in other words, if we do not cooperate with Him, we receive nothing, however pious we think we are. The Holy Spirit is not given on the grounds of our worthiness, denomination, or piousness, but solely on the ground of our personal faith. (See Galatians 3:2–5.)

Some have taught that the Holy Spirit only comes into a holy vessel, which is true if we mean "imputed holiness," but certainly not if we mean "worked up holiness." These people have the idea that long waiting or tarrying is necessary to receive this gift, and they feel they earn merit marks because of the time they spend praying, begging, groaning, agonizing, and sometimes rolling. As long as we insist on trying to earn the gift of the Holy Spirit, God will let us wait! We are not beggars, but sons. All gifts of God, whether salvation, healing, or the baptism in the Spirit, may and should be received as soon as we take them in faith.

There is a divine protocol. We must appear in the presence of Jesus the Son of God to receive this gift, in the same way as a warrior would appear before a king to receive a medal. To appear before Jesus in heaven is a breathtaking awesome thought! To go into the Throne Room of glory requires that we approach Him on His throne in the right way! What is this way? It is the way of the blood. When the high priest went into the Holy of Holies in the Old Testament tabernacle, he went in with the blood of a sacrifice and sprinkled it upon the mercy seat. The Holy Place represented heaven, the dwelling place of God, and the mercy seat typified His Son, for Jesus is our resting place at the end of our journey of sin, and He sprinkled Himself in His own blood. As we come to the mercy seat, we embrace the blood shed for us.

The blood is also the price paid for our redemption, for we are bought with a price (see 1 Corinthians 6:20; 7:23), and so the blood of Jesus is the only recognized currency in heaven, the holy place of God. Remember that although the Holy Spirit is a gift to us, it had to be purchased for us at the great price of the blood of Jesus. Someone had to pay the price; therefore we approach Jesus in the throne room of heaven by first worshipping Him in our spirits, quietly and reverently. We then take His precious blood by faith and begin to sprinkle drops of it in His presence, thereby demonstrating that our entire faith is centered in the blood and not in ourselves, our self-righteousness, denomination, race, or education! Our faith is only in the blood.

Let us consider a simple analogy. We enter a store to purchase something costing, say, one dollar. We offer a dollar bill and receive the article without difficulty. If we were to offer the currency of another nation, we would receive nothing. If we were to offer cast off garments in exchange, or some article for which we had no further need, we would get nothing. Only by paying the marked up price can we get what we want; but in the language of heaven we are asking Jesus to give us the gift of the Holy Spirit that He alone purchased for us with His own blood. Therefore, we come joyfully into His presence and offer His blood as our only plea. This is called "pleading the blood." As there were many drops of blood sprinkled on the mercy seat, so we also sprinkle many drops of His blood by faith. Peter explained that all believers are "*a holy priesthood, to offer up spiritual sacrifices*" (1 Peter 2:5), and so we offer a "spiritual sacrifice."

Each time we say audibly "blood," it is like sprinkling one drop. As we say it several times by repetition, we offer several drops. Try to empty your mind of other thoughts and concentrate on the sacrifice of Calvary and the blood that was shed on the cross; offer it freely by sprinkling or repetition and Jesus will answer you and you will quickly feel the Holy Spirit immersing your whole being. At this point surrender your tongue and take words from the Holy Spirit and begin to praise God in an unknown tongue. You must be relaxed and in a spirit of worship. If you are tense— relax, sit (for they were all seated on the day of Pentecost, and Jesus is our mercy seat). In the initial experience of the 120, on the day of Pentecost, when they were all seated, it is recorded that they began to speak. So many have the entirely mistaken idea that the Holy Spirit began to speak! This was a matter of mutual cooperation. As in water baptism the candidate relaxes and trusts the minister to bury him under the water, so we must relax and trust the Holy Spirit to come into us and give us the words that we alone must speak. If we do not speak, His words cannot be heard and there can be no outflow of the Spirit. Our tongue in fact becomes a kind of faucet which we turn on to allow the river of life to flow! *"They…began to speak with other tongues, as the Spirit gave them utterance"* (Acts 2:4).

The Holy Spirit is a guest. He will not make you do anything. If you wish to speak His divine words, whether in tongues, prophecy or some other Charismatic utterance, you will use your own faith, and begin to speak, and the words of God will flow out of you, bypassing the mind, and you will hear the mind of God spoken as others will within the hearing of your voice.

The pleading of the blood accomplishes something else too. As soon as you make up your mind to approach Jesus Christ for the gift of the Holy Spirit, Satan will bring his demonic forces to bear to stop you receiving. He will try to come between you and the Giver. The audible pleading or sprinkling of the blood of Jesus by repetition drives him and his hellish hosts back and they flee in consternation, which is why many have experienced a sudden immersion into the Holy Spirit and come up praising God in a loud voice in tongues. The blood speaks toward God for mercy, pardon, and grace, but toward Satan defeat, scattering, and consternation.

We need to remember that some Christians who come to receive the baptism are still bound in certain areas of their lives by evil things from Satan. Evil habits, and thoughts, still plague many a child of God. Such usually fail to receive their personal Pentecost by some of the better known methods of "seeking the Spirit." So little has been understood about the ministry of deliverance that bound Christians have worshipped in Full Gospel churches for years and finally got discouraged and ceased seeking the gift of the Holy Spirit. This should not be. Pleading of the blood will reveal these binding spirits, and they can then be dealt with and cast out by the person praying with the seeker. Some seekers will dislike the pleading of the blood and consider it foolish or repulsive, but as they are encouraged, they may even find it very difficult, if not impossible, to repeat the word "blood." Only the prayer of faith in exorcism will deliver such a person to make them ready and open for the infilling of the Spirit of God. Fear is one of these spirits, quite apart from bad habits and thoughts.

In closing, this chapter mention should also be made of spurious baptisms in the Spirit. People can be possessed of an evil spirit for years and be bound. Such a person may seek for the infilling of the Holy Spirit but will be unable to receive, because the "other spirits" insist on taking over, especially in praise services. These are often religious spirits that simulate the things of God. Instead of the Holy Spirit coming in and giving words for the joyous candidate to praise God, the evil spirit already within will start to speak in another language, but the look on the face will usually be far from restful or peaceful and joyous, but it will be demonic and tense and the voice probably hysterical. Furthermore, the life of the person after such an experience will not show the fruits of the Spirit, which helps to explain some of the strange baptisms which we have seen and heard about in our churches. If the seeker will begin by pleading the blood of Jesus in faith in approaching the mercy seat, these alien spirits will have to declare themselves and be cast out, therefore delivering the person.

This shocking expose of the subtle workings of Satan should not alarm us for the Bible is full of cases of demons crying out and using words that were well understood such as *"Let us alone!... Did You come to destroy us? I know who You are—the Holy One of God!"* (Mark 1:24). Such happenings are all right in cases in the pages of the Bible, but when they spring out into our churches today, we get afraid. If the Holy Spirit can give us ability to speak with the tongues of men and of angels, cannot also evil spirits speak through us in known tongues as well as unknown tongues? The blood is the only safeguard we have. It is enough. Satan cannot penetrate the blood of Jesus, but he does run when we sing, shout and plead the blood!

8

THE PURPOSE OF THE BAPTISM IN THE SPIRIT

It is obvious by a first reading of Acts 1:8 that the believers and followers of Jesus would receive *power* at the time the Spirit came upon them. *"But you shall receive power when the Holy Spirit has come upon you; and you shall be witnesses."* The Greek word for *"power"* is *dunamis,* from which we get such words as *dynamic, dynamo,* and *dynamite;* in other words, previously powerless believers would thereafter work and witness with dynamic power, they would have the energy of dynamos and would have the explosive power of dynamite to blow up the defenses of Satan and blast him out of his strongholds. Before Pentecost this could not be so.

Before Pentecost, Peter was weak and denied his Lord. After Pentecost he became the bold spokesman for the apostolic band. He illustrates to us the change that a single encounter with the Holy Spirit wrought in his life.

Christians were not just supposed to "go to church on Sundays" and take part in the church service and functions, all of which is good and right, but they were supposed to be disciplined soldiers of the cross to fight the devil and his demon hosts twenty-four hours a day. It is not enough that they enjoy a bright "gospel service" and not be interested in the baptism in the Spirit; they must be empowered for battle. We are well aware that Christianity, which makes war and recognizes that there is an enemy to fight continually, is not a popular conception, but it is the only teaching that we find in Scripture. A limited John 3:16 gospel was for the Jews in the interim period between John the Baptist and Pentecost; it is good to get people converted to Christ by preaching John 3:16, but what are they converted for? Just to go to heaven? No, more than this; for Peter on the day of Pentecost added to John 3:16 in saying, *"Repent, and let every one of you be baptized in the name of Jesus Christ for the remission of sins; and you shall receive the gift of the Holy Spirit"* (Acts 2:38).

We see the divine order; first, repentance, second, water baptism and third, Spirit baptism. This is the minimum gospel that should be taught in all our churches today, and this is the gateway for a Christian as a member of an anointed powerful army for service. This is the church that the Apostles had in mind when they wrote their epistles. Their conception of the body of Christ was a body empowered as Jesus' own body was empowered, for wherever He moved He healed the sick, cast out devils, cleansed the lepers, and raised the dead. He told us to do the same! We are aware that some church leaders hide behind dispensationalism, and say this power was only for the apostles to manifest, but the present outpouring of the Spirit and renewal within the church is dispelling such ignorance.

This New Testament church was to be more than a collection of different denominational Christian societies with man-made rules, for these came hundreds of years later after the church had gone into apostasy in the middle ages. The original church was a powerful church that witnessed not only in word but also in *deed*. Jesus said, *"This gospel of the kingdom will be preached in all the world as a witness to all the nations, and then the end will come"* (Matthew 24:14). The purpose of the baptism in the Spirit was that a Christian might have power to witness, but what kind of witness is indicated here? Some are satisfied with basic teaching and handing out books and tracts, all of which is good, but more is intended in the context we are considering. The gospel of the kingdom had to be preached with *signs following*. This was to be the witness from heaven! Jesus told His disciples that *"these signs will follow those who believe"* (Mark 16:17)—casting out demons, speaking in tongues, healing the sick. Nothing less than this would suffice, otherwise why come to Pentecost? Why not remain like the Ephesians under Brother Apollos, saved but without the *dunamis*?

The teaching of Jesus is startling in its clarity; how can we avoid it by hiding ourselves under the respectable skirts of a denomination? *"And as you go, preach....* **Heal** *the sick, cleanse the lepers, raise the dead, cast out demons. Freely you have received, freely give"* (Matthew 10:7–8). This is the witness that the world is waiting for, and we might add, the church also. What is more thrilling than to take sufferers into our special prayer room in our church in Scarborough (Toronto), Canada and begin to deliver them in the name of Jesus? What is more thrilling and rewarding than to see terrible bondages that bind Christians' lives give way and come out of them, sometimes with violent reactions, and then to see them filled with the Holy Spirit and join the ranks of the warriors? This is the purpose of Pentecost.

The church is called the body of Christ. Jesus in heaven is the Head and that which joins us together is the Holy Spirit! When Jesus was on earth He met Satan head-on, in the wilderness, in His ministry of compassion and healing and finally on the cross. He was never defeated and, though weary at times, never sick! Then He told us to go out and do the same things, in the same way, as He had demonstrated it was possible to do them in His body. They crucified that body, but Jesus rose again and went back to His Father in heaven, and God gave Him another body, much larger this time, and we are members of His body! Our mind is His mind, our hands His hands, our feet His feet, our purpose His purpose, and our ministry His ministry—empowered to do the same works that He did. There is no theologian that can disprove this! The wonderful part is that more and more men and women are beginning to do these signs and wonders again all over the world and set the captives free. We are sometimes called "too extreme" in our views, but the ones who say these things are the ones who are not in the battle delivering the captives. If they could be with us when the captives are delivered and hear their glowing testimonies, they might be convinced, but sometimes we feel that ecclesiastical authority can cruelly bind the people in the denominations.

Why are not more people miraculously delivered? Because of the general unbelief of our churches, for this is the Laodicean Church age, neither hot nor cold. Paul wrote to Timothy about them, *"Having a form of godliness but denying its power [dunamis]. And **from such people turn away!**"* (2 Timothy 3:5). We find, however, that millions of Christians prefer the churches of those that deny the *dunamis!* These churches do not pray for the sick, they do not cast out devils, they do not speak in tongues, nor prophesy; in fact we find a close similarity between them and the Old Testament church in Ezekiel's time. Writing against the priesthood he said, *"The weak you have not strengthened, nor have you healed those who were sick, nor bound up the broken, nor brought back what was driven away, nor sought what was lost"* (Ezekiel 34:4). One might well ask, what then had the priests been doing? The same as today in many places—ruling the people with force and cruelty, and taking their money, and giving little in return.

The body of Christ should manifest Christ. Jesus the Head desires to work through our members to preach the glorious gospel that sets the captive free, and then to demonstrate it by healing the sick, by casting out demons, by speaking in tongues, by prophesying, by binding up broken hearts and bodies and visiting them in prison and hospital.

This is the day of renewal, restoration, and revival as God is preparing a people to do these things, and the people are getting hungry and are coming out of the powerless churches and being baptized in the Spirit and receiving the *dunamis* for a supernatural witness; they are speaking in tongues and prophesying again as in the Ephesian church; they are being delivered of satanic bondages and their sicknesses are being dealt with again by God's New Testament priests; the sick are being bound up. What wonderful results are seen when we go in with the blood of Jesus as one weapon and the name of Jesus as the other weapon and say, "Come out in Jesus' name," and these sicknesses and bondages *hear and obey* us. Remember that in Revelation 12:11 it is written of overcomers in all church ages, "*They overcame* [Satan] *by the blood of the Lamb and by the word of their testimony.*" What kind of testimony have you? Is it the type promised in Acts 1:8 so that you might be a witness to testify of His power, or is it a powerless witness largely given in fear?

God fill us with Thyself!

THE BODY IS FOR THE LORD

CONTENTS

1

THE BODY OF MAN

Perhaps one of the most astonishing omissions of the church in recent centuries has been the almost total neglect of the human body in its teachings of the gospel. It would seem by the teachings of some fundamentalists that every reference to healing in both Old and New Testaments only has application to the soul of man, in spite of the many clear references to the fact that Jesus continually healed the body of mankind during His ministry. Such Scriptures as *"I am the LORD who heals you"* (Exodus 15:26), which is one of the references that speaks of God in one of His omnipotent characteristics *Jehovah-Rapha,* "God the Healer," is ignored in any application whatsoever to the human body. The clear statement in Deuteronomy 7:15, *"The LORD will take away from you all sickness, and will afflict you with none of the terrible diseases,"* is applied only to the soul, in spite of the clear reference to *"diseases"* (in Hebrew, *choli*).

Again, in Exodus 23:25, we read, *"I will take sickness away from the midst of you"* (in Hebrew, *machalah*—disease), and it is obvious that when Israel rebelled, fiery serpents came to them and bit their bodies and injected poisonous venom so that many died. Immediately, in order to stem the plague, Moses was commissioned to fashion a fiery serpent of brass and put it on a pole, a wonderful type of Christ on the cross, and every bitten Israelite who looked — lived. The curse of poisonous death was stopped and healing took place *in their bodies.* Notice also that this was a case of substitution of a body for a body. It was the body of Jesus Christ that was crucified, not His soul or spirit. Every time we partake of the Lord's Supper in a Communion service, we partake of bread, typifying His body, and wine, typifying His blood. Both are physical material substances. Every time we put a piece of broken bread into our mouths at the communion table, we testify that we believe in a body for a body, a broken body for a whole body, a life for a life, His life for our lives. When Satan came in with his fiery serpents to bite with the sting of death, he did so by injecting his poison into their blood stream. It takes the blood of Jesus to cleanse our polluted blood streams. How very corporeal is all this:

There are two chapters in the Bible dealing with leprosy, that dread disease of the human body. (See Leviticus 13 and 14.) Leprosy is a terrible disease, and may be called the monster of them all. All who were afflicted in Old Testament times were told to go to the priests (they had no doctors as we know them), who were instructed to make an atonement for them. In our book, *The Power of the Blood*, we have explained that the only meaning in Scripture to the word *"atonement"* (in Hebrew, *kaphar*) is "to cover"; that is to say that the blood of Jesus applied to His body covered our sins and sicknesses on the cross.

In Old Testament times the blood of a typical animal, in this case, a he-lamb, was taken and applied to the body of the person who was healed of leprosy, and then followed the pouring of oil on his physical head, and thus a covering was made so that the sufferer would not only be healed, but remain healed so long as he reckoned on the covering of the priest's atonement. As leprosy may be taken as a type of all physical diseases, we are not surprised that we are instructed in the New Testament to anoint with oil and claim the Blood of Christ's atonement on the cross on behalf of the many who suffer physical diseases in the church today. (See James 5:14–15.) It is not the olive oil that heals, nor the physical blood; it is the faith in the atonement of Jesus that heals, so that those healed may remain healed. In case some may object that all these Scriptures only refer to the soul, may we remind them that James not only spoke of healing for the body, but forgiveness of sins. *"The prayer of faith will save* [in Greek, *sozo*] *the sick, and the Lord shall raise him up. And if he has committed sins, he will be forgiven"* (verse 15). When Jesus died on the cross, when they whipped His back, crowned His head with thorns, drove spikes through His hands and feet, and drove a spear in His side, then He made a total atonement or covering for the spiritual, mental, and physical needs of the whole human race—healing of the mind and body and the forgiveness of sins.

One of the most telling Scriptures in the whole Bible speaking of physical healing is found in Isaiah 53:4–5, where we are told in prophecy that Jesus would bear our griefs (in Hebrew, *cholr*—sicknesses, weaknesses, and pains) and carry away our sorrows (in Hebrew, *makob*—pains), and *"by His stripes we are healed"* (Isaiah 53:5). In spite of the very clear reference to the fact that Jesus bore in His *body* ours pains, sicknesses, and weaknesses, and carried them up the hill called Calvary in His *body*, to leave them on the cross under His blood, there are still many who apply this act as applying to the soul (in Greek, *psuche*) only. One is tempted to believe that this is deliberate unbelief in operation, for the whole context of these two verses is applied by Jesus in Matthew 8:16–17 to His ministry in reaching the suffering masses with exorcism and healing. Let us quote the Word of God:

When evening had come, they brought to Him many who were demon-possessed. And He cast out the spirits with a word, and healed all who were sick, that it might be fulfilled which was spoken by Isaiah the prophet, saying, 'He Himself took our infirmities [in Greek, *astheneia*—weaknesses] *and bore our sicknesses* [in Greek, *nosos*].

These two verses are a direct reference back to Isaiah's prophesies in the fifty-third chapter and obviously refer to the human body as well as the mind. It is interesting to notice that Isaiah made no reference to demon possession, but many who were so afflicted by demon powers were set free as Jesus cast out these malign spirits by speaking to them and commanding them orally, and they obeyed. Later in this book, we will show the difference between healing and demon possession.

Some have calculated that 80 percent of the ministry of Jesus was confined to the area of healing the human body. In fact, the Greek word *sozo*, which means "saved," is applied many times to the act of healing or delivering the human body or mind. It is used in the healing of the woman from the issue of blood, which we call today hemorrhage (see Mark 5:28), and the deliverance of the demoniac of Gadara (see Luke 8:36), showing that the "so great salvation" spoken of by the apostle Paul includes both the mind and body of all mankind. In fact, this mighty little word, *kozo*, is also used by the apostle James in his fifth chapter already quoted: "*the prayer of faith will save the sick.*" Salvation is total and includes spirit, soul and body of man.

Surely there can be no doubt that Paul had this in mind when he wrote to the Thessalonians, "*Now may the God of peace Himself sanctify you* **completely***; and may your* **whole** *spirit, soul, and body be preserved blameless*" (1 Thessalonians 5:23). The Greek word for "*blameless*" is *amemptos*, which means "without blemish or spot." How frequently do we speak today of "a spot on the lungs." We also speak of seeing a "shadow" on an X-ray, and it is interesting to note that the Greek word *daimon* means "a shadow." Satan casts a shadow between the sunlight of God's healing presence and our body, by causing one of his evil spirits to oppress us. Quite literally, a shadow appears. Malachi, prophesying the return of the power of the Holy Spirit in our day, culminating in the literal corporeal return of Jesus for His church, wrote, "*But to you who fear My name the* **Sun of Righteousness** *shall arise with healing in His wings*" (Malachi 4:2). Notice that Jesus is referred to as "*the Sun,*" and this must not be confused with the Son, for He is the light of the world. The Sun of God dispels the shadows (demons) of Satan. It is in this very hour in which we live that this charismatic renewal is now taking place in the church in the earth. Healing for the body is with us again after centuries of absence because of the monumental unbelief of a backslidden church.

2

THE BODY FOR THE LORD

In Paul's epistle to the Corinthians he makes a most interesting statement. He writes, "*The body is...for the Lord*" (1 Corinthians 6:13). This should leave us in no doubt as to the value of the human body. When we give our whole lives to Jesus Christ and make our total commitment to Him, which every Christian is supposed to do in every denomination before he can partake of the communion service, we give our bodies to Jesus Christ; thereafter they belong to Him, not to ourselves. In the same chapter, verse 20, Paul explains that we are not our own, but our bodies have been purchased with the price of the blood of Jesus—the ransom price. We have been ransomed, or bought back, from death, hell, sin, and sickness.

The church, which is *the body of Christ*, is subject to Jesus the Head, and He is likened to the Bridegroom and the church to the bride. This analogy should help every married Christian to understand the sacredness of our bodies, because Paul again explains in 1 Corinthians 7 that in the marriage relationship the body of the wife belongs to the husband and the body of the husband to the wife, and both are instructed not to defraud the other. We fear this is very unpalatable teaching to many married Christians who live far away from God's concept of marriage. Paul actually wrote that the husband has power over the body of his wife and vice versa. This word translated "*power*" means the authority of privilege, that is to say it is not a dictatorial mandatory power, but a power of mutual agreement; it does not give a husband a right to force his attentions on his wife, or to misuse her just because her body belongs to him—freely and lovingly given by mutual consent at the marriage ceremony. "With my body I thee worship [or "honor," in a more modern version]" is a spoken promise by millions of wives in church—well-meaning Christian women. The husband promises due benevolence to his wife, and she promises the same to her husband. *Benevolence* means "disposition to do good, kindness, generosity, charitable feeling and affectionate." The whole basis of marriage is founded on love, for the

Bible which ever speaks in frank straightforward language, explains that the married couple become "one flesh." Their bodies become as one. Jesus said, *"For this reason a man shall leave his father and mother and be joined to his wife, and the two shall become* **one flesh***"* (Matthew 19:5). This agrees perfectly with Genesis 2:24, as applied to our first parents, Adam and Eve.

Now how does this teaching of the Christian marriage relationship apply to our relationship with Jesus Christ? It applies wonderfully, for Paul, writing to the Ephesians, said, *"For we are members of His* **body***, of His* **flesh***, and of His* **bones***"* (Ephesians 5:30–31).

Our bodies of flesh, blood, and bones belong completely to Jesus, our divine Bridegroom, and He has the privilege of authority to use our bodies for His own purposes. If we refuse, we rebel and make our divine marriage a poor imitation of what it should be and can be. We should totally surrender our wills, and therefore our bodies, to Jesus.

In these chapters (see 1 Corinthians 6 and Ephesians 5), Paul teaches a most amazing truth, which seems rarely to be understood by so many Christians. It is that our bodies are the temple of God. As we consider the magnificence of the Old Testament temple that David purposed to build, we see that, according to 1 Chronicles 22:5, *"The house to be built for the* Lord *must be* **exceedingly magnificent***, famous and glorious throughout all countries."* This Scripture has never been abrogated and is now being fulfilled in our generation in the present charismatic renewal of the church, preparing it once again to manifest His fame and His glory.

The temple was probably one of the most amazing buildings ever constructed by man. Gold covered many parts to reveal in type the glory of God. People from many nations would travel to worship in it and see its magnificence. The temple in Jerusalem was the only place in the world in those days where God determined to reveal His glory. On the day of dedication, after the tremendous slaughter of animals and shedding of their blood, the power of God fell and the priests fell flat on their faces prostrated by God's awesome power. The power of God was so great that the ministering priests were not able even to enter the building, as the fire of God came down from heaven, igniting the animal sacrifice and consuming it. A body consumed by holy fire. (See 2 Chronicles 5 and 7).

Before the day of Pentecost, the disciples of Jesus had very limited understanding of God's plan, and it is to be feared that those who have not experienced their personal Pentecost will also have the same difficulties. In John 14, Jesus suddenly asked His disciples a difficult question. They had seen the miracles that He did and the supernatural power of God manifested in His life, and suddenly He put them on the spot. He asked, *"Do you not believe that I am in the Father, and the Father in Me?"*

(verses 10–11). They had no understanding, no answer, and felt acutely embarrassed, and He, realizing their lack of comprehension, said, *"Believe Me for the sake of the works themselves"* (verse 11).

Oh, how we need to see the greater works of Jesus in our churches today before the coming of Jesus back to this distracted planet! Jesus first revealed the power and the glory of God His Father before He expected them also to reveal this same power—*"The works that I do he will do also"* (verse 12). Jesus does not ask us to do the impossible. We must be anointed with the same Holy Spirit anointing that He experienced in the River Jordan. We must be baptized into the Spirit of God; a total immersion of ourselves; a complete abandonment of trust. Jesus said to His faithful but uncomprehending disciples, *"At that day **you will know** that I am **in** My Father, and you in Me, and I in you"* (John 14:20). Now though they were completely unable to understand what He meant when He tried to explain to them that He was *in* the Father and that the Father was *in* Him, He spoke of a day to come when they would not only understand this riddle, but a more intimate one also. Jesus would be *in them*, yes, right inside their bodies! Do we really understand the significance of this? It may not be too hard theologically to understand that God the Father was totally occupying the body of Jesus His Son, and the Son was totally abiding in the Father, a mutual integrated juxtaposition; but is it too hard, too embarrassing, too intimate, too personal to believe that Jesus desires to live *in* our bodies, dwell *in* us, and manifest Himself *through* us, our eyes, hands, feet, mouth, legs, and arms?

To what day does Jesus refer in verse 20? This must be a day of great illumination and tremendous importance! Of course, this was the day of Pentecost, when the Holy Spirit came upon the church of loosely-knit disciples and baptized them with fire, even as the fire came down upon the Old Testament temple. Their lives and understanding were completely revolutionized, and from the cringing position behind locked doors for *"fear of the Jews"* (John 20:19), they emerged as flaming evangelists, set on fire of God, and thus was the glory of God revealed through their lives, so that it is recorded in Acts 5:11–13 that great fear came upon the people because of the signs and wonders wrought by the laying on of their hands, members of their physical bodies, and many dared not join themselves to them, for to approach the bodies of these men of God might cause them to be burned spiritually, so great was the power of God manifest after Pentecost! Oh, for a church of members who are so "hot" that the carnal Christians and sinners will not dare to come near us, unless they want to be saved, healed, and also filled with the Holy Spirit. Nothing less will do in this wicked and adulterous generation.

Will you notice that Jesus told us to lay our hands on the sick *"and they will recover"* (Mark 16:18)? Why our hands? Are not these members of our bodies, flesh, blood, and bones? What have our hands got to do with healing the sick? Have we not got the medical profession to deal with bodily sicknesses? Why the hands of believers, who know nothing much in England, is in reality a most useful and well-made receptacle. Although actually created to be filled with dust and filth, it can also be used for most useful and clean purposes such as storing milk or grains, and in fact it is so used in some farms. Just because the garbage container is created for garbage does not mean that when it leaves the factory it is dirty. Even so, when we are born into this world made of human flesh and bone; we come out of our mother's womb empty of good or evil, but with a potential for both.

A baby knows nothing, for everything it will ever know will be received by teaching and observation. A baby is born with a mind, but the mind has to be instructed, the vessel has to be filled! This is why some churches teach that if you give them your baby for seven years, he will not depart from their church afterwards because he is brainwashed. Protestants, Catholics, and Jews all believe in God, but they believe doctrinally what has been put into their minds in their bodies. Truly the Scripture teaches that we bring nothing into this world! (See 1 Timothy 6:7.) Unfortunately, the human body, like any container made for garbage, is usually fed on garbage from the moment a child begins to open its ears and eyes. It receives the filth of this world. Among the mass of humanity television is more to be desired than the Word of God or church worship. Because Eve chose to eat of the tree of the knowledge of good and evil and later tempted Adam to eat also, they had need of a covering and an atonement to keep their minds disinfected from the filth of the world under the curse. It takes a renewed mind cleansed in Jesus' blood to cleanse the whole triune man that he might again reveal God's glory

God did not create the human body to be a receptacle for filth, so in this the analogy of the garbage can breaks down. God created your body to be filled with Himself, His Spirit, His love, His purity, His power and glory, His gifts and fruits. Those who have been so steeped in sin, and those who have been mixed up in the occult religions, often find that a tremendous work of cleansing must take place to clear out all the spiritual filth which clings so tenaciously. A stain or an ink mark on a white shirt will sometimes take the life of the shirt to wash out gradually. Many find that as they come to Jesus and ask His forgiveness for their sins and cleansing from the filth thereof, it seems to take some quite a time for the progressive work of sanctification to take its effect in cleansing the vessel.

The analogy of the garbage container is not too far off the track, however, because the Bible actually speaks of our bodies being "vessels" (in Greek, *skeuos*—utensil). Paul, writing to Timothy, tells him that it is possible to cleanse this utensil. *"Therefore if anyone **cleanses** himself from the latter, he will be a vessel for honor, sanctified and useful for the Master"* (2 Timothy 2:21). God actually takes a dirty stinking garbage container of a human body, purges it, cleanses it, and then fills it with His Holy Spirit. By so doing He buys back that which He originally created to reveal His glory!

Obviously if a body is filled with an evil mind for years, it will gradually deteriorate and break down. Hatred will produce ulcers and arthritis. Fear will produce a large assortment of psychosomatic diseases. A dirty mind will produce a dirty body by filling it with tobacco and drugs so that it smells! Hippies and tramps do not seem to wash very often. The very bodies created by God to contain everything that is pure and lovely actually reveal the filth that is in the mind; and so a renewing of the mind must take place by regeneration. Nothing less than a total cleansing of the mind will produce a clean body, and this is the purpose of Calvary! A clean mind in a clean body; not a clean mind in a sick body, or a sick mind in a clean body, but clean minds in clean bodies. We are given a body to reveal Him who said He came to give us life more abundantly. How can pulsating, vigorous, abundant life be revealed in a sick body?

Yes, we have to grow old, but was it not Caleb at eighty-four, who said, *"Give me this mountain"* (Joshua 14:12)? Where was his arthritis and where were his stomach ulcers? You see, he had another spirit; he never grumbled or complained and pitied himself—he had another spirit. His human spirit, which God breathed into him, was harnessed to God's Spirit, and being filled with God, he could see no earthly reason why he could not drive the enemies out and take the mountain. He did just that, for He was filled with a God who works wonders.

Quite apart from the odors emanating from the body due to tobacco and drugs, we have often found that halitosis, or bad breath, is often caused by internal spirits of infirmity which can be cast out in Jesus' name. Where total healing for spirit, soul and body is received fully in faith, we find that internal poisons give way to prayer, and offensive odors vanish, and the breath becomes pure and inoffensive. God wants the body to be completely fit and well, and sweet and clean.

We do not for one moment suggest that the human body carrying the life of the Son of God in resurrection power will always be as it was at twenty-one, but we do believe the body will always be equal to the tasks that are required of us until the day we lay down our old tabernacles and immediately take up our spiritual bodies, which are eternal. (See 2 Corinthians 5:1–5.) We do not see that the Bible teaches that a child of God is intended to be laid aside as useless for the last years of his life. Again, this will largely depend on the attitude of mind of the believer. If the mind is full of doubts, then the body will simply give up, because God does not want such a Christian to misuse such a wonderful body, and so He will lay you aside. If, on the other hand, the mind is full of faith founded on the promises of God, then the spirit will be strong and the mind will take over the body, and the body will obey the mind; for the mind is reacting by faith to the unalterable promises of God. If the mind is pure, and thinks on pure things, then we obey the Word of God, as taught in Philippians 4:8:

> *Finally, brethren, whatever things are true, whatever things are noble, whatever things are just, whatever things are pure, whatever things are lovely, whatever things are of good report, if there is any virtue...**meditate on these things**.*

For, as a man *"thinks in his heart, so is he"* (Proverbs 23:7).

You can have a clean body for a clean mind.

3

THE BODY IS NOT FOR SATAN

The major purpose of this book is to demonstrate that the body is for the Lord, and thus becomes the very temple of the living God on earth, so that God may demonstrate His beloved Son Jesus, in and through our human flesh. Paul leaves us in no doubt when he writes to the Ephesian church,

> *In whom [Jesus] the whole building, being fitted together, grows into a holy temple in the Lord, in whom you also are being built together for a dwelling place of God in the Spirit.* (Ephesians 2:20–22)

God's house or dwelling place; yes, our bodies are the dwelling place of God on earth, not places or brick, stone and wood with stained glass windows, but our human bodies of flesh and blood.

The enemy knows this, so he will legally occupy the bodies of unbelievers and take over control of the human mind in order to manifest himself through his demon spirits. We have a very remarkable teaching given to us by Jesus in Matthew 12:43–45:

> *When an unclean spirit goes out of a man, he goes through dry places, seeking rest, and finds none. Then he says, "I will return to **my house** from which I came." And when he comes, he finds it empty, swept, and put in order. Then he goes and takes with him seven other spirits more wicked than himself, and they **enter** and dwell there; and the last state of that man is worse than the first.*

Jesus is here teaching that a man's body is a house. It is a vessel, a utensil, a temple, and a house. A house is a place in which people live, and we have here described the case of a man who had had his house cleaned up. It is described as garnished (i.e. decorated and repainted) and swept. The house had been made fit for Jesus to live in as the new tenant. The demon had been cast out, the blood had been applied, but the man in the house was lazy and careless; he backslid and let down his defenses and

Jesus found He no longer was a welcome guest. Jesus cannot dwell in our house when it again becomes polluted with the filth of this world, and so He departed. This is what is meant when David prayed that the Lord would not take His Holy Spirit from him. (See Psalm 51:10–12.)

It is not enough that we say we are Christians or that we have been born again. Jesus said that there is a condition: *"If you **abide** in My word, you are My disciples indeed. And you shall know the truth, and the truth shall make you free"* (John 8:31–32). Note that the conditional *"if"* qualifies the fact that in order to be His disciples, we must continue to apply ourselves to the Word of God, and we shall learn the very truths that shall set us free from demonic oppression and maintain a condition of continual cleanliness in our house. Careless Christians are in terrible danger of the enemy returning. Having returned, in many cases, he then tells them that it is impossible for the Holy Spirit and Satan to dwell together in the same house; but he forgets to tell that the Holy Spirit departed before Satan could get back in. This thought is so abhorrent to many Christians that they will not hear it. John makes it very clear when he writes, *"**We know** that whoever is born of God does not sin [i.e. not deliberately]; but he who has been born of God **keeps himself** and the wicked one does not touch him"* (1 John 5:18). A born again, regenerated child of God should not desire to do things repugnant to a holy God *after* his or her conversion, in exactly the same way as the owner of a house would not want filth and garbage and dust to collect in every room. A constant cleaning program is necessary, a daily cleansing.

In our story, the man of the house did not do this. It is recorded that the unclean spirit hovered around waiting such an opportunity, and when the defenses were let down, when the house was again filthy and the inhabitant desirous of again indulging in filthy thoughts and practices, then the evil spirit came back in, but horror of horrors, he brought seven other spirits with him. Having been cheated of his home, he was determined it would not happen again, and so now it became a crowded house with one human sharing with eight demons. No doubt many in such a case would still loudly proclaim that they were Christians! Of course, we cannot judge, and only God knows just how far down one of His children may go, like the prodigal son, who ended up eating swine's food with the pigs as companions; but the son returned ultimately and was cleansed and forgiven by his father. Peter uses the same thought and describes a backslider as a sow who returns to wallowing in the mire. (See 2 Peter 2:22.)

Now we see from this account by Jesus that the body is a house in which demons may just as easily dwell as the Holy Spirit. It seems that we have the choice of the Holy Spirit or Satan's unholy spirits. There does not appear to be neutral ground in which we can dwell safely by ourselves, without God or Satan. We well remember the case that happened in our experience of a church officer of a Toronto church coming to us who was being driven to suicide. He asked what we could do to help him. We took him into our prayer room and, in one hour and a half, cast all the suicide demons out of him. They spoke, they argued, but they all came out through the throat and were violently ejected. Following the deliverance, the Holy Spirit came back in his house and the man spoke in tongues and prophesied. For seven years, he lived for God, but then he started on the downgrade again and took up smoking, drinking, gambling, and ultimately hit the bottom of the barrel by becoming a homosexual. Having experienced what the prodigal son experienced. He repented again, came back to us for prayer, but this time in delivering him, we found that the original spirit had indeed brought back others with him. These named themselves as they were cast out and all had filthy names, which caused this poor man to do filthy things. Afterward, he lived for God and did not again backslide.

It is well to remember that a demon spirit has no body. Angels who never sinned do have spiritual bodies, but the fallen angels who became the swarms of demons, were bereft of their bodies when they were cast out of heaven. (See Revelation 12:9.) Being naked and unclothed, they must find a body to express their foul natures, and so they avidly seek the bodies of humans (their first choice), but failing this they seek to enter animals. They will even find some measure of comfort in continuing to live in houses after the death of the person in whom they dwelt, because they are at least familiar with the confines of this dwelling. This creates haunted houses, which can be delivered in the same way by exorcism in the name of Jesus, as the blood of Jesus is applied for cleansing. They then leave.

We trust that this book will be a grave warning to Christians on the dangers of backsliding, thereby giving Satan and his spirits the opportunity they seek to re-enter the house, which is our body.

Paul, writing to the Corinthian church, no doubt had this in mind.

> *Do you not know that **your bodies** are members of Christ? Shall I then take the members of Christ and make them members of a harlot? Certainly not! Or do you not know that he who is joined to a harlot is one body with her? For "the two," He says, "shall become **one flesh**."*　　　　　(1 Corinthians 6:15–16)

The taking of one's human body and deliberately giving it again over to Satan for his use, whether in adultery, thieving, lying, cheating, swearing, drunkenness, etc., means that we actually become one flesh with the demons spirits, because we give our bodies over to them for them to work out their desire for sin through our bodies. Many claim to be "filled with the Spirit," whereas in actual fact, they are filled with demonic spirits! No wonder Jesus gave us the simple rule: *"By their fruits you will know them"* (Matthew 7:20).

It is written that if we confess our sins, God is faithful and just to forgive us our sins, and to cleanse us from all unrighteousness. (See 1 John 1:9.) In many cases, this cleansing does not occur easily or automatically. Once Satan has regained an entrance, he brings other spirits with him and is determined to hang on, so he has to be dislodged by the forceful commanding prayer of faith. *"How can one enter a strong man's **house** and plunder his goods, unless he first binds the strong man? And then he will plunder his house"* (Matthew 12:29). We must force our way back into the house of our body in order to recapture it for Jesus.

We are in a spiritual warfare and this necessitates "deliverance prayer sessions," in which we take the poor, bound person, bind their demons and command them to leave, which they do, sometimes reluctantly, usually contending for every foot; but as we are determined and persistent, they all come out, and thus the person is set free from sins and filthy thoughts and habits, and once again the Holy Spirit can enter in and our works will be those of Jesus and not of Satan.

What we manifest in our lives always has a spiritual primary cause. It will be of God or Satan. Our choice is what shows in our lives. Our part is to choose this day whom we will serve, whether God or Satan. One or the other will become our master and control us. *God* means "Lord," and *Baal* means "master." If God be Lord of our lives, then the Holy Spirit will minister the life of Christ to us and through us; but if Satan be master, he will hold us in cruel bondage of sin and sickness and manifest his life through us by his demon spirits.

4

DEMON OPPRESSION OR POSSESSION?

The usual and constant question that is asked regarding this deliverance ministry is, "How can a Christian 'have' a demon?" So ignorant has the church been of the workings of Satan that the very suggestion that a demon can afflict a child of God is totally repugnant; in fact large sections of the church have been taught that God actually gives sicknesses to people. Whereas of course God does indeed *permit* misfortunes to happen to His children, and will undoubtedly use them for His glory, yet the fact remains that it is not God who gives people sicknesses—it is Satan

Two words are used in the Bible to designate the activities of Satan on the lives of Christians and non-Christians alike: *oppress* and *possess*. A right understanding of these words in their context will clear up the mystery of the whole matter of mental and physical sickness.

In Acts 10:38, these important words appear: *"God anointed Jesus of Nazareth with the Holy Spirit and with power, who went about doing good and healing all who were **oppressed** by the devil."* From this Scripture, we deduce that sickness is an oppression, and is caused by Satan. The word for *"oppressed"* in the Greek is *katadunasteuo* and means "to be overpowered." It occurs only twice in the New Testament, the other case being in James. 2:6, where the rich men are called "oppressors," that is to say they totally control the lives of the poor who work for them. By no stretch of imagination can we call oppressive rich men "things" or "its." They are living people who impose their wills upon other living humans. It is clear from Scripture that Satan also has a will, which he wishes to impose upon humans (if we permit him to do so), for in 2 Timothy. 2:26, we read of those who have been ensnared by Satan and have been taken captive at his will. Our preaching and witness is that they might be rescued or saved from such entanglement, for the word for "taken captive" in the Greek means to be taken alive. That is to say that Satan's intention with us all is to put us in a cage alive and demonstrate to God, men and angels that he is more powerful than we are. He hates us and loves to torment us in a cage. Jesus, however, said that He came to set us free from all entanglements and oppressions of Satan.

Satan, therefore, overpowers us with sickness. Now it must be obvious that Satan cannot be in two places at the same time, because he is one created creature, albeit a very powerful one. The result of being sick is felt in pain and weakness, which causes us to lie down and groan. Jesus said that He is the resurrection and the life, and it is interesting to note that the word *resurrection* in the Greek means to rise up, or stand up on one's feet. It connotes an opposite picture to a procumbent sufferer who usually is unable to "rise and walk." Thus, Satan's purpose is to knock us down, drag us out, and put us on our backs by exercising a superior authority and power over us, thereby overpowering us by *force majeure*. As he cannot be in two places at the same time he has to use his "unholy spirits," who swarm the earth. These are demons or fallen angels who are entirely subject to his autocratic discipline. It is therefore the demons, or "*spirits of infirmity*" (Luke 13:11), which visit their weaknesses upon our bodies and nervous systems; the word "*infirmity*" (in Greek, *astheneia*) means "weakness." Thus, if Satan's desire is to make you sick he sends a "spirit of weakness" to work on your body so that the end result is weakness caused by sickness and resulting in an elevated temperature.

We must not allow ourselves in our thinking to go past the limitations of Scripture. The Bible does not speak of a person "having" a demon, or (in this context) being possessed of a demon. It simply states that sickness, as we understand the word, is caused by overpowerings of a superior enemy called Satan. The fact that Satan works through underlings is proved by daily practical demonstration, as we pray for people who are sick and rebuke the spirits of infirmity, which then leave and the body temperatures return to normal. Sometimes these spirits leave quite obviously, and at other times, with no visible manifestation whatsoever.

It seems quite immaterial whether the spirits of infirmity are in or on a person's body. The fact remains that the organs of the body are inside the confines of the skin, but the Bible is quite explicit that this does not mean that the sufferer is 'possessed' but is in fact *oppressed*. Again, we repeat that the sufferer is overpowered, which cannot be denied. Of course, Christians can be overpowered by an alien force if they either let down their safeguards or, alternatively, they do not erect them as defenses against Satan and his demons. As so many children of God have been poorly taught about a Christian's defenses and armor, it is not surprising that they are sick so often, and that Christian ministers are called to visit the sick of their congregations in homes and hospitals. In most cases, we find them overpowered and lying down instead of standing up with their feet on sin and sickness and "*over all the power of the enemy"* (Luke 10:19). The victorious, overcoming Christian of Scripture will never lie down except to sleep, for it is written of him that he can and should *"withstand in the evil day, and having done all, to stand"* (Ephesians 6:13). There is no suggestion of being overcome, only of overcoming; no suggestion of lying down, only standing with our feet on the neck of the oppressor.

The other word used in this context is "possession," and it is used eleven times in the New Testament and means "to be demonized or to be as a demon." This indicates that the person so possessed will manifest all the characteristics of the demon possessing him.

In Matthew 8:16, it is stated by the apostle that the common people brought to Jesus those who were demonized, or possessed of demons. He then cast out the spirits with His word. He spoke in a voice of commanding authority and the demons left the ones who were bound. It seems that this word would indicate the control of the mind rather than an affliction of the body, and it is so used in the case of the demoniac of Gadara in Mark 5, and the legion (six thousand) that were cast out of the possessed man are called "unclean spirits," which then entered unclean animals, the swine. The effect of these insane demons was to cause the swine to rush down the hill and drown themselves. Obviously, these spirits controlled the mind. Could we say in this case that the demoniac was possessed? Yes, because the Bible teaches us this, and the man was delivered only when he came and fell at the feet of Jesus and worshipped Him.

The word is also used in Matthew 9:32, where the people brought a man to Jesus who was "possessed with a demon." When this demon was cast out, the man began to speak, for previously he had been dumb. We must not deduce from this therefore that all dumb people are possessed of an evil spirit, but undoubtedly many are. Unfortunately, many would be gravely offended if it was suggested that some loved one who could not speak was "possessed of a devil." The suggestion, though entirely scriptural, would be rejected out of hand, for it seems so many are governed by emotions rather than by Scripture, or if not by emotions, by rationalizations of the human mind.

Again in Matthew 12:22, we read of a similar case where they brought to Jesus one that was *possessed* of both a blind and a dumb spirit, and when these spirits had been exorcised, the person both saw and spoke. Thus we see that some in Bible times who were dumb or blind were "demonized," for the demon actually so possessed their speech and sight faculties that they were unable to use them. We have a right to ask why the church does not openly rebuke deaf, dumb, and blind spirits today, to see what would happen. If they did it this way in the New Testament church, why do we fail to do it this way today? It must be due to our unbelief!

On one occasion, Jesus was asked, *"Why could we not cast it* [a demon] *out?"* (Matthew 17:19). Jesus replied, *"Because of your unbelief"'* (verse 20). Here was a case of a man who had brought Jesus his son, who suffered from epilepsy. Surely a clear case of possession? How refreshingly frank are the words of Jesus: *"Because of your unbelief."* Here is no room to hide behind any defensive excuses. We are exposed in our weaknesses. We have failed to do it the way Jesus told us to. We have not obtained New Testament results!

Insanity in any form, even if we call it schizophrenia, would appear to be a simple case of demon possession, and should be dealt with as such. Jesus rebuked the devil, and from that time onward, the restoration processes of healing began to take shape, because the primary cause had been removed. If we have a thorn in the hand, it begins to heal from the moment the thorn is removed. The healing process may take time, especially when a deaf person has to learn to understand speech, and thus to talk. Deaf mutes who are healed by exorcism find that this is so.

Again, referring to Matthew 8:16–17, the two categories of oppression and possession are clearly mentioned. *"He cast out the spirits with a word, and healed all who were sick"* (verse 16). He did it this way because Isaiah had long ago prophesied that the death of Jesus on the cross would be the central fact that caused dealing to come to those who were in need of it, for *"by His stripes we are healed"* (Isaiah 53:5). No limitation must be put upon this statement by applying the healing only to the soul, for in the context, it is obviously applied to both those who were possessed in their minds and were oppressed in their bodies. Isaiah makes no mention anywhere that sickness was caused by demons; he does not mention the word. Jesus, however, knew that for this prophecy to be fulfilled it was necessary to make a frontal verbal attack on the demons and cast them out of mind and body.

Whether we argue about *oppression* or *possession*, let us be careful to note that it comes from the same source—Satan. It seems that these words merely designate the type of satanic visitation. If Satan overpowers the body, he makes it weak; but if he possesses the mind, he takes a total control over the person. It seems that the differentiation is simply a matter of degree.

In what category do we put epilepsy for instance? Oppression or possession? The visible evidence of epilepsy certainly seems to be demonic in character, and while under such a spell the poor individual is not in control of his actions, and yet thousands of born-again Christians are epileptics and are treated by drugs, but how many ministers would dare to try casting the spirits out of them? For those who have tried—it works!

In finalizing this chapter, it seems vitally necessary for us to understand that the primary cause of mental or physical sickness is demonic, and therefore, spiritual and personal. We do not remove spirits by drugs; we merely drug the nervous system so that it does not readily respond to the oppression of demons. We treat the symptom, but not the cause.

5

A DEFILED BODY

No one with any normal sense of cleanliness would dwell in a house which was dirty; a good Christian would keep the home swept, cleaned, scrubbed, and polished. This would be considered normal and desirable behavior. Defilement of the home of any sort would not be tolerated. We must bear constantly in mind that the teachings of Scripture always elevate our human bodies to the status of being temples of God. Paul, in his writing to the Corinthians, says,

> *Do you not know that you are the temple of God and that the Spirit of God dwells in you? If anyone defiles the temple of God, God will **destroy** him. For the temple of God is holy, which temple you are.* (1 Corinthians 3:16–17)

It must, therefore, be obvious that Christians have a great responsibility to see that nothing is brought into the human body that will defile or make it impure, for it is the temple of God. For instance, we have not yet met anyone who would openly smoke a cigarette during a church service, because they would fear someone would object, quite apart from the fact that, instinctively, man knows that it is not right to smoke in the presence of God and in His house.

Paul tells us that God will destroy us if we bring in defilements, and as the word *"destroy"* (in Greek, *phthiero*) means to mar or to corrupt, we see that the end result, as a judgment of God, will be that our human bodies will be marred by sickness and corrupted by poisons and germs. The simple analogy of tobacco smoking, considered so harmless by multitudes of Christians, will be seen in this context as a proven cause of lung cancer, respiratory troubles, emphysema, and heart troubles, plus many other corruptions of the body. If one deliberately uses the human body as a smoking machine, the body will soon be marred and corrupted. The same can, of course, be said of overindulgence in alcohol and food.

According to Dr. Schofield, in his Schofield Bible, we are informed of the following:

> In 170 BC, Antiochus Epiphancs, after repeated interferences with the temple and priesthood, plundered Jerusalem, profaned the temple, and enslaved great numbers of the inhabitants. On December 25, 168 BC, Antiochus offered a sow upon the great altar and erected an altar to Jupiter.

No greater insult or defiling of the temple could be imagined than this. A sow is an unclean animal, both spiritually and physically, and it was offered upon the great altar on which clean meats were always offered—sheep, lamb, goat, and bullocks. These all typified Jesus Christ the spotless Lamb of God. Obviously, a sow does not, and cannot, and will never, typify the Son of God, and so Antiochus showed his satanic spirit by defiling the temple of God and defying almighty God to His face. Such an act, of course, always brought ultimate retribution, and always will. History records that no one who ever defied God got away with it.

James the apostle tells us that the tongue can defile the whole body (see James 3:6), for Jesus explained that what came out of a man's mouth defiled the man (see Matthew 15:11). If dirt is in a man's heart, it will come out as dirt from his mouth, thereby defiling the whole man, and we know that those who use their tongues for criticism, slander, idle gossip and plain dirt will reap to themselves sickness in mind and body. The tongue, therefore, can destroy our bodies by defilement.

Immoral and unnatural sexual conduct certainly defiles the body. Those in Sodom and Gomorrah are described as filthy dreamers who defiled the flesh. (See Jude 8.) For excellent reasons, God has warned us against adultery, fornication, sodomy, and bestiality, and has said that every man should have one wife only to himself. Modern society openly defies these God-given laws, given to us in love, and so reaps in mankind's body diseases, politely known as "social diseases," as well as many other types of mental and physical diseases. The body becomes defiled by sexual immorality or sexual perversions. We may treat the symptoms, but a cleansing of the heart is what is really needed, and only God can do this as we apply the blood of Jesus to our hearts.

A root of bitterness springing up in our lives will also cause great physical distress, as we read in Hebrews 12:14–15:

> Pursue peace with all people, and holiness, without which no one will see the Lord: looking carefully lest anyone fall short of the grace of God; lest any root of bitterness springing up cause trouble, and by this many become defiled.

This is a very clear warning that we can fail to receive the benefits of the grace of God by permitting ourselves to get bitter and complaining, and not only shall we be defiled, but others taking part in our bitterness will also suffer defilement. A bitter tongue produces a sick mind and body.

Under the old Jewish law, great care was taken to teach the difference between clean and unclean. For instance, if one touched a dead carcass of an unclean animal, that person was to be considered unclean. (See Leviticus 11:31.) This was a simple hygienic rule, for obviously, if one had handled any dead corpse, human or animal, it would be recognized practice to wash one's hands to remove the bacteria rapidly spreading on a dead body. To eat a meal and partake of some of the bacteria through one's unwashed hands would be to invite disease. In only relatively recent times it was discovered that the great incidence of puerperal (childbirth) fever among women, followed by death, was caused by the doctor not washing his hands when treating another mother. Such teaching of recognized hygiene was, at that time, greatly resisted by the medical profession! The washing of one's hands before eating a meal was recognized in Jewish law, but was purely ceremonial; but it also had a hygienic reason behind the law, as so many of the Old Testament laws have. Similarly in Leviticus 15, we read of certain laws governing the washing and changing of bed linen and night attire after it had been soiled by human blood or seed, or by waste products of the body. How horrible it is to go into a home where the bedding smells! The aroma fills the whole house, and this is extremely dangerous to the health of the body. Even an animal will not soil its own bed, and yet humans will! To sleep in a dirty bed or to wear dirty clothes will certainly defile the human body and bring on skin diseases.

Such rules of hygiene are accepted in all civilized countries today, but it was not always so, even in relatively recent times. These rules have to be taught to primitive tribes by missionaries before it is possible to remove such bodily sickness from among them. We recently heard a missionary to New Guinea tell us that the natives of this beautiful country only eat pork for their meat, and as a result their bodies are infested with trichina worms. Another missionary who ministered among primitive tribes in the Philippines told us how he was offered a sumptuous dish of monkey. Courtesy demanded that he partook of the kind hospitality of his primitive friends, and he was violently sick all night, vomiting back the monkey! During World War I, British troops in Egypt were fed horse meat because they ran out of beef. Most of the army went down with sickness, and the order had to be countermanded from the War Office in London. During World War II, the author served in the Royal Air Force in England, and was present at a conference before the Air Officer Commanding. The medical doctor reported that some of the men were stricken with trichinosis, a horrible infestation of the muscles with trichina worm, and when asked what this disease was caused by, replied, "Eating pork!"

These are isolated instances, given to show that if these people had not eaten these unclean animals, forbidden in Scripture, they would not have become sick. In Leviticus 11 and Deuteronomy 14, we have twice repeated for our learning that certain unclean animals are called "abominable," which means "exciting disgust, offensive, odious," and we are expressly forbidden to eat them, because if we do, we shall reap sickness in the human body—the temple of the Holy Spirit. Some of the more common unclean meats that are consumed by humans in our modern society are pork, bacon, shellfish, duck, and rabbit; also fish having neither fins nor scales, such as eels, shrimp, dogfish, lobster, crab, oyster, etc. These creatures have their place in the world to help to keep it clean, but we insult our bodies if we eat the filth in their flesh that they have consumed. A pig scavenges the farm, a crab or lobster eats the droppings of clean fish that swim above. A horse and camel are beasts of burden, but were not created for human consumption. God knows best, and to say we "like" some of these delicacies is to ignore the fundamental law of God!

We think that we have an application which many may not have seen when we suggest that as the bringing in of the sow to sacrifice on a Jewish altar by Antiochus defiled and desecrated the holy sanctuary, so in like manner, we defile our bodies by introducing unclean meats into our stomachs! It may be argued that Jesus said it was not what entered into a man that defiled him, but what came out of his mouth. (See Mark 7:19–23.) Jesus was teaching that the heart produced the filth of man's conversation and behavior, such as evil thoughts, adulteries, fornications, murders, thefts, covetousness, wickedness, deceit, lasciviousness, an evil eye, blasphemy, pride, and foolishness. These were what defiled a man, and He explained that foods and dirty things taken into the body would pass from the body by the normal elimination processes; and this is true, for the human body has great resistance to disease. However, if one persists in disobeying any law of God *continually*, whether by intention or ignorance, the body will finally break down because of the defilement. We recommend a close study of the foods of the Bible to find out those that are forbidden by an all-knowing and all-loving heavenly Father. It is better to obey than to sacrifice our health, especially if we know our bodies are temples of God.

In the days of the early church, many Christians were offended by being offered meat previously offered to idols by the heathen priests, and although this meat was clean meat within the definitions of the Bible, it was made ceremonially unclean by spiritual pollution by being offered on heathen altars. Paul's reply to their dilemma is found in 1 Timothy 4:4–5:

> For every creature of God is good, and nothing is to be refused if it is received with thanksgiving; for it is **sanctified by the word of God** and prayer.

In other words, if beef or mutton offered to idols is prayed over, it is fit for human consumption, for it is sanctified by the Word of God. The Bible sanctions it to be eaten in the first place. Pork, or any unclean meats, are never sanctified by the Word of God, so it is useless praying over them!

Would you eat rats and mice fried in lard? Would you eat a dog, even if your pastor prayed over it? In heathen lands, they do eat these things, but they are unenlightened until missionaries reach them.

Such teaching as this comes as a shock for many Christians, because of the assumption held that one can eat whatever one's palate prefers. This is due to the almost total ignoring of the human body in its relationship to God its Creator. The church has been taken up with the soul and has left the body to the devil!

Almost at once, the reader will ask the question, "What about the sheet that was let down from heaven and shown to Peter?" (See Acts 10:9–28). Peter's quick response to the command to rise, kill, and eat was simple: *"Not so, Lord! For I have never eaten anything common or unclean"* (verse 14). The vision was given to Peter to impress upon him that the Gentiles were about to come into the church—the body of Christ—something that would have been quite unthinkable to Peter, a strict Jew. He would never have spoken to Gentiles about membership of Christ's body, for the Jews were quite persuaded that all Gentiles were unclean animals—dogs to wit! In verse 28, the interpretation of this vision is given to Peter:

> *You know how unlawful it is for a Jewish man to keep company with or go to one of another nation. But God has shown me that I should not call **any man** common or unclean.*

Peter not only never ate unclean meats by his own testimony, but he also adhered strictly to the Jewish law and had nothing whatsoever to do with Gentiles of any nation under the sun. It was forbidden to talk to them, let alone eat with them, and the law was revoked by a single, miraculous act of God by giving a vision. This vision does not permit us to eat unclean meats, but it gives us permission to preach the gospel to people of all nations, and to welcome them into the family of God as brothers and sisters. In the past, black people from many lands were considered to be on the level of animals, and not of human beings. In 1949, the author visited the island of Jamaica to preach deliverance to the captives, and one white Canadian lady expressed astonishment to me, saying, "Don't you know the gospel is only for white people?"

I think the vision of the unclean animals is still needed in the church today.

Let us call no man common or unclean if God is willing to cleanse him. God will never cleanse a dog or a sow! They will always remain unclean.

6

THE BODY FOR SACRIFICE

It is written in Hebrews 10:15 that God prepared, or fitted, His Son with a body. The reason given in Psalm 40:6–8 is that Israel would have nothing to do with the type of sacrifices that God required of them, so He prepared a body to be sacrificed for His people Israel. If Israel would not sacrifice, then God would send His Son, the Lamb of God, to be the sacrifice.

As we look into the Old Testament, we find that animals were sacrificed in the temple daily. The animals were killed, their bodies burnt on the altar, and their blood sprinkled. By this, Israel was supposed to realize that their sins were atoned for, and the sacrifice of the body was that they might be forgiven. Every time we take Communion we partake of a piece of broken bread, which speaks to us of the sacrifice of the body of Jesus, who described Himself as *"the bread which comes down from heaven"* (John 6:50), and He said that if anyone ate this bread, they would live forever, because the bread which He gave was His flesh. The bread that we take in Communion represents the flesh of His body sacrificed for us. We take a piece of His flesh by faith, and feed on Him, and remind ourselves of His sacrifices, which is why He said, *"Unless you eat the flesh of the Son of Man and drink His blood, you have no life in you"* (verse 53). This Scripture has led to endless arguments and bitter recriminations in history, but basically, it means that those who partake of Communion in humility and faith receive His life. The flesh of the animals that were sacrificed on the Jewish altar were eaten by the priests and their bodies received life and strength from the proteins of the meats. In like manner, we, as priests of the New Testament, receive our eternal life by feasting on the Son of God. Obviously, this is an act of faith, and if we do this without faith or without confessing our sins and shortcomings, it profits us nothing at all. This is not cannibalism!

Again, we remind ourselves that it was the body that was nailed to the cross, not the soul, but at death, the spirit was released (see Luke 23:46), and after His resurrection, when He appeared to His disciples, He said, "*Behold My hands and My feet, that it is I Myself. Handle Me and see, for a spirit does not have **flesh and bones** as you see I have*" (Luke 24:36-39). We notice the easy tendency of many today to confuse the spirit and soul with the body, and finally to forget the body and seemingly leave it out as something unimportant.

Paul teaches us that the body is for the Lord.

Now, whether we like it or not, God also prepared a body for each one of us. It is the only one we have got and we must do with it what He commands. The body, with its five senses, is not primarily for carnal gratification, although God gives us legal outlets for our appetites of exercise, hunger, love, and sex. The body is for the Lord. It was created for the Lord. It is a sacred trust for the Lord, and as soon as we get understanding of this fact, then we must give our body to the Lord. This is our sacrifice. Jesus sacrificed His body for us, and now we sacrifice our body for Him. How simple!

In 1 Corinthians 6:20, Paul writes, "For you were bought at a price; therefore glorify God in your **body** and in your spirit, which are God's." So, our bodies were actually purchased by God for His own peculiar possession, and we are not our own. Not even a finger nail or a strand of hair belongs to us at all! This is why Paul teaches,

> I beseech you therefore, brethren, by the mercies of God, that you present **your bodies a living sacrifice**, holy, acceptable to God, which is your reasonable service. (Romans 12:1)

This is identification. Jesus went to the cross for us and so we take up *our cross* (see Mark 8:34), not His cross. We also must put ourselves on our cross and follow Him. Our body, therefore, becomes crucified with His! As He was raised from the death of the cross, so also are we raised from our death on our cross, and we then enjoy eternal life here and now in our body, which is given back to us as a sacred trust. It is when we understand this fundamental fact, then we can enter into the life of health, for Paul wrote that as we yield ourselves to God, we are as those that are *alive from the dead* (see Romans 6:13); but there can be no resurrection experience without the initial experience of voluntary death to self.

Let us see how practical it all is!

> Do not let sin reign in **your mortal body**.... And do not present your **members** as instruments of unrighteousness to sin, but present yourselves to God as being alive from the dead, and your members as instruments of righteousness to God. (Romans 6:12–13)

What are members? Are they not our hands, feet, eyes, ears, legs, and arms? Do we not sin with our tongue? Do we not take cigarettes or hard liquor with our hands? Do we not feast our eyes on filth? Do we not listen to gossip with our ears? Are not these physical members of our bodies? This is what Paul meant when he said that a fornicator or an adulterer becomes one flesh with a harlot. (See 1 Corinthians 6:15–16.) If the body has been intelligently and willingly given back to God who gave it to us, then it becomes holy, and it must only be used to glorify God. As the body contains the spirit and the soul, it follows that if the body has been given to God, the spirit and soul belong to Him also. The church at large has neglected to teach this, and has so concentrated its message and ministry to the soul that the body has been forgotten. So many look to the medical profession for help for the body, but the church for the soul! To say that this is a contradiction is to make an understatement!

A careful study of the miracles of Jesus show that He ministered healing in 80 percent of recorded cases in the Bible to the human body! Blind Bartimaeus, the woman with the issue of blood, Jairus's daughter, and Lazarus immediately come to mind. Jesus summed up His ministry in these words—speaking of believers: "*They will lay hands on the sick, and they **will** recover*" (Mark 16:18). Physical hands laid on physical heads bring healing to human bodies by His Spirit. God wants fit bodies through which He can manifest His resurrection life. A sick body *cannot* truly manifest His resurrection life, for the very word "*resurrection*" (in Greek, *anastasis*) means "a standing or rising up." How else do we rise and stand unless it is upon the physical feet of our physical bodies! Obviously the spirit must first desire to stand, and then the body will follow suit. Yielded members of a dedicated body will find it easy to stand erect. When God created Adam from the dust of the earth and breathed His Spirit into him, Adam at once rose to his feet! When Jesus, the second Adam, was resurrected by God the Father after His crucifixion, He also rose to His feet. When you or I surrender our bodies as a willing *living* sacrifice, we also walk upright on our feet!

You see, we are not a dead sacrifice. This is what people are afraid of. They think there is a catch in this "cross identification" business, and so they do not fully surrender every member, every part of their body. They hold back parts, reserved to do their own wills. This is disastrous! God does not take our bodies and keep some parts only to Himself and give back the other parts! He takes us all and then sanctifies and uses our hands, feet, tongues, and brain for His glory. Our hands become an extension of His pierced hands as they are laid on the sick; our feet become extensions of His pierced feet to carry the gospel into a thousand homes and hospitals. Is it not written, "*How beautiful are the feet of those who preach the gospel of peace, who bring glad tidings of good things!*" (Romans 10:15). Beautiful feet—are these not members of our bodies? Ugly feet would be those that would go into houses of ill repute. The same body but a different motivation, a different spirit!

I am convinced, after thirty years of ministry, that if we dedicate and use our bodies for the glory of God, and look after them according to His holy laws, we can expect Him to look after our bodies while we live here on earth. As soon as this time is up, and we believe that our times are in His hands, then we are instantly given a spiritual body, which is eternal.

The body manifests the spirit and soul! It is the living envelope of our real selves. If our minds are not at rest, it will show through our bodies. If we give way to an unclean spirit from Satan, this evil spirit will manifest itself through our bodies. Jesus called sickness being *"oppressed by the devil"* (Acts. 10:38). If our bodies are truly surrendered to Jesus, and the Spirit of God fills this body continually, day and night, then our bodies will reveal and manifest His life, His nature, His fruits, His gifts, and so our bodies become, in very truth, the temples of the living God! As we talk, people hear Jesus; our facial expression reveals Jesus; our hands minister healing, our tongue the balm of Gilead; our lives reveal His health, both mental and physical; we do not argue about philosophy, we do not give opinion, we reveal the Word of God, who is Jesus the Logos! The Spirit of God has precedence over our human spirits, which is what Paul meant when he wrote that *"the spirits of the prophets are subject to the prophets"* (1 Corinthians 14:32). We desire to reveal Jesus and not ourselves, for we are dead and yet alive unto God. How tremendous to think that God takes our human bodies and reveals His Son Jesus through them in our day!

7

LIGHTHOUSES

Most people are familiar with lighthouses and their purpose of shining forth over the angry waves to bring warning to mariners in trouble and distress. A lighthouse is a physical structure built solely for the purpose of projecting a powerful light over the angry sea. The building is that which contains and manifests the light. There could be no light without a house.

Our bodies are lighthouses! They have been given to us for exactly the same purpose as a man builds a lighthouse on a rock, to show forth the Light of the world.

In Isaiah 9, we read the prophecies concerning the birth of Jesus Christ, and it is written concerning this event: *"The people who walked in darkness have seen a great light; those who dwelt in the land of the shadow of death, upon them a light has shined"* (verse 2). In Luke 2:32, Jesus is described as *"a light to bring revelation to the Gentiles, and the glory of Your people Israel,"* and in Matthew 4:16–17, the prophecy of Isaiah is quoted at the beginning of the ministry of Jesus: *"From that time Jesus began to preach and to say, 'Repent, for the kingdom of heaven is at hand."* Jesus revealed the light that He received from His Father in heaven, and was actually God's lighthouse on earth. Many hated this, for Jesus Himself said,

> *And this is the condemnation, that the light has come into the world, and men loved darkness rather than light, because their deeds were evil. For everyone practicing evil hates the light and does not come to the light, lest his deeds should be exposed. But he who does the truth comes to the light, that his deeds may be clearly seen, that they have been done in God.* (John 3:19–21)

This same lighthouse work was passed on to the church—His body, after His resurrection and the coming of the Holy Spirit on the day of Pentecost. His church is supposed to shine like a lighthouse with cleansed lenses, but it has to be confessed by all honest Christians that the degree of light that shines forth from the church is often dimmed by doubt, unbelief, and theological hair-splitting. Above all, the church that is afraid of being baptized in the Spirit and manifesting His power in the gifts of the Spirit (see 1 Corinthians 12:8–10) and His beauty in the fruits of the Spirit (see Galatians 5:22) is not measuring up to New Testament standards!

A shining, burning Christian will terrify a timid child of God, and politically, it does not represent a good program to help "build a church" if the gifts of tongues, prophecy, healing, and miracles are manifest in the services. Theology tells us that these things are "divisive." They certainly are! They flush out the flesh and the carnality and cause an uproar. They separate the carnal from the spiritual. Actually, of course, the gifts of the Spirit are supposed to unify the church, and sometimes lack of wisdom in the use of these gifts is what divides, not the gifts!

Jesus made this abundantly clear when He taught that a man does not put a candle under a bushel basket or in a secret place where no one can find it or see it, but he puts it on a candlestick that all may benefit therefrom. (See Luke 11:33–36.) Jesus said, "*The **lamp of the body** is the eye. If therefore your eye is good, your whole body will be **full of light**"* (Matthew 6:22). Our eye is the lens which reveals the light of the world as the powerful lens of the lighthouse shines forth over waves. People and nations in Scripture are often referred to as "waters," which is why Jesus used the analogy of the sea and the waves roaring as applied to the distress of nations with perplexity that is occurring in these closing days of this dispensation. (See Luke 21:25.) Never in the history of man is it necessary for the church corporately to shine with the intense light from heaven upon the poor people bound by Satan in all nations. Truly the United Nations organization knows no way out, because it has rejected Jesus, the *only way.*

It is for this reason that the Holy Spirit is now being outpoured in an unprecedented way upon the whole church. The Roman Catholic monolithic system is cracking wide open so that the members of this organization may be set free from ecclesiastical bondage and into the glorious liberty and *light* of the Son of God, who is described as the *Sun* of Righteousness in Malachi 4:3. The Protestant section, which has for so long ceased to protest very much against sin or corruption or any evil thing, is now also receiving a Pentecostal experience, and what a tremendous difference this makes to those who receive! They begin to shine, which has always been God's purpose! The ultimate purpose of God for His church can be summed up in the words of Isaiah:

> *Arise, **shine**; for your **light** has come! And the glory of the* LORD *is risen upon you. For behold, the darkness shall cover the earth, and deep darkness the people; but the* LORD ***will arise*** *over you, and His glory will be seen upon you.*
>
> (Isaiah 60:1–2)

Not only are we told here that Jesus is to *arise* with healing in His wings, but that we too in our turn must *rise* and reveal His light and glory.

In 1968, a pastor approached a professor of mathematics in an American university with the following facts and asked him to put them into a computer. In 1910, there were approximately five thousand people baptized in the Holy Spirit, as evidenced with the Pentecostal sign of speaking in tongues, but by 1968, there were fifteen million. The answer came back from the computer that within twenty years, every Christian alive would have received the baptism in the Spirit!

Now we believe the Bible speaks quite clearly of end time restoration, by a renewal of the Holy Spirit, not according to our theology, but according to His Word. The church cannot be raptured in its present feeble darkened state. It must be revitalized. It must be reignited. It must be re-lit.

Jesus summed up His parable by teaching, *"If then your **whole body** is full of **light**, having no part dark, the whole body will be full of **light**, as when the bright shining of a lamp gives you **light**"* (Luke 11:36).

The body is for the Lord! It has been given back to us as a sacred trust to be filled *full of light*, even as He was *full of light*, for of Him it is written, *"In Him was **life**; and the **life** was the **light** of men, and the **light** shines in darkness, and the darkness did not comprehend it"* (John 1:4-5). The responsibility is ours; the ball has been passed to us by Jesus. His body must manifest Jesus, the Head of the body, in our bodies! *"You are the **light** of the world.... Let your **light** so shine before men, that they may see your good works and glorify your Father in heaven"* (Matthew 5:14-16).

Lighthouses for the Lord! What a privilege; what a challenge! God will have a remnant who will shine for Him today in the full power of His Spirit. All you have to do to be a candidate of glory and to get ready for His coming is to submit your whole *body* as a living sacrifice, and He will take care of the rest by filling you with His Spirit and His glory, and then you can walk before men as shining ones. It all started this way. Adam and Eve in the garden of Eden were shining ones. They were clothed with *light* and *glory*. It was not until they rebelled and disobeyed God and His holy commands that they fell from grace and suddenly found themselves naked! How did they know? Had they not freely been man and wife? How tragic! The *light* went out because of disobedience; but today, God is reversing this process and the *light* is reappearing again as men and women are having their spiritual nakedness removed, and being clothed as new creatures of light and love. This is the meaning of redemption in its fullest sense. The curse is removed, the darkness obliterated by the shining of *light*, and the Laodicean church of Revelation 3, which was naked, now receives God's last-day outpouring of His Spirit, and once again, it goes forth to shine in God's last-day visitation to the earth before He comes in judgment.

Let us *rise* and *shine*.

CHARISMATIC GIFTS

CONTENTS

FOREWORD

You may be sure you have reached the godly spiritual land of Canaan when you come across a book with a title like this, *Charismatic Gifts*. The author, H. A. Maxwell Whyte, is very well known to me. We have fellowshipped most happily together over the years on both sides of the Atlantic. I know him as a man of keen Pentecostal vision, who habitually translates his vision into actual New Testament living and ministry. He is much used in ministering the Baptism of the Holy Spirit to seekers, and he has an outstanding ministry in the "casting out of evil spirits." This special work of exorcism he graphically describes in his book on the subject, and he devotes to it a set time every week in his assembly in Toronto. In this present book on the operation of the gifts, he writes about the things he knows by experience and practice. I have real pleasure in taking this small part in the launching of his book on its adventurous voyage through the expansive waters of Christendom.

The subject of the book is dear to my heart. This timely study will be full of interest to many who are seeking further depths and distances in the heavenly life in the Spirit.

Maxwell Whyte takes it for granted (as no doubt the reader does) that a deeper life in the Spirit begins with a supernatural Acts 2:4 baptism in the Holy Spirit. This baptism in the Spirit is the essential source of the supernatural, which is set in motion by the dynamic of the baptism. A genuine New Testament salvation must be expressed in these charismatic gifts to reveal Jesus in the power of the Spirit in our lives. As by new birth the Christian becomes possessor of the spiritual nature of God His Father, so by the baptism in the Spirit (and by that only) he becomes partaker of an essential measure of the supernatural nature of God, accustoming him to the miraculous.

In his book Brother Whyte takes his side by Paul—and indeed by the Lord Jesus Himself in His Word—encouraging all believers to claim their blood-bought heritage, and instructs them in the operation of the gifts when they receive them. The anointed reader will especially rejoice in such chapters as "The body of Christ Ministry" and "Rivers of the Word."

As in all books of this sort, there will be details of interpretation, of course, upon which there may be differences of opinion. The author takes time to correct certain temporary or local misuses of the gifts, at the same time emphasizing that the most serious "misuse" of the gifts is the absence or neglect of them, through ignorance, fear, or unbelief.

I pray that the book may arouse a new and widespread interest in the "gifts," and I heartily endorse Brother Whyte's warm exhortation to every reader to "desire spiritual gifts" to "covet them earnestly" and to place inestimable value on such treasures as Jesus Himself purchased for us in agony and death on the cruel cross of Calvary.

—Harold Horton
Bournemouth, England
April, 1960

1

THE NINE GIFTS FOR TODAY

No serious Bible student would question that the apostle Paul wrote about the nine gifts of the Spirit as being in use in the early Apostolic Church. These nine gifts are as follows:

1. The Word of Wisdom

2. The Word of Knowledge

3. Faith

4. Gifts of Healing

5. Working of Miracles

6. Prophecy

7. Discerning of Spirits

8. Speaking in Other Tongues

9. Interpretation of Tongues

Unfortunately, so much of our evangelical fundamental theology is "dispensational," that is to say, it teaches that these spiritual gifts were only for the early church and they are not necessary today. It is difficult to understand how the mind of man can devise such a cover for their lack in many places, unless we understand that even Adam and Eve sewed fig leaves together to hide their nakedness. Why could they not find something more enduring than fig leaves? It is quite surprising what man will devise when he is trying to excuse the word of God! It is a fact that many people have amazing faith for what happened in the past, and great faith for future events, but little or no faith for the present!

It is usually argued that the early church was like a frail craft on an angry sea, and it needed every divine attribute to launch it on a hostile world, but surely today conditions are worse than in those days, for we understand that "[the devil] *knows that he has a short time*" (Revelation 12:12), and we believe that the mystery of iniquity is filling up in our day, and can only be compensated by a great outpouring of the Holy Spirit which will exceed that of the early church in power and magnitude. We are always encouraged when we think of the prophecy of Isaiah, "*When the enemy comes in like a flood, the Spirit of the* LORD *will lift up a standard against him*" (Isaiah 59:19).

There never was such a day as this when the devil is coming in like a flood. None surely can deny that evil is on the increase. Wars have fostered racial hatred and taken restraints off many, and "*evil men and impostors will grow worse and worse, deceiving and being deceived*" (2 Timothy 3:13). This is the time for God to take a hand, as He always will when there is a praying remnant, and it is significant that the present outpouring of the Spirit of God occurred at the beginning of this century, before the two world wars broke upon an unsuspecting world, and before the unhappy rise of godless communism, which has claimed one third of the world. This is preeminently God's time.

This Pentecostal outpouring of the Spirit was preceded by preparatory moves of God, like the Welsh Revival of 1904 and 1906. As God prepared a people immediately before the original outpouring of the Spirit at Pentecost, through the ministry of John the Baptist, and later Jesus and His disciples, so also God prepared a remnant who was crying out to God to do something. God moved on their behalf and sent the Pentecostal outpouring of the Spirit between 1906 and 1908, and this outpouring of the Spirit was so called because thousands received the baptism of the Spirit accompanied by the speaking in other tongues as on the day of Pentecost. We must be careful today not to confuse the denominational term "Pentecost" with the experiences of the early church. The two uses of the word are not necessarily synonymous!

This outpouring of the Spirit beginning in 1906 brought exactly the same manifestations of the gifts of the Spirit as occurred in the early Apostolic Church. It was not necessary to tell the happy recipients of this blessing that they were in serious error, or that the devil had given them this supernatural experience. At least the scoffers acknowledged that the experience was at least supernatural! Very quickly it was shown by the inner working of the Holy Spirit that tongues alone, though an initial sign and evidence of the baptism of the Spirit, was not sufficient. This was the beginning, the down payment, the earnest (see Ephesians 1:14), the "grapes of Eschol," which many brought back to testify of the goodness of this new land of power and delight and joy! Of course, most of the church lived up to its past history and pointed out that there were giants in the land, and many were so untutored in their Bible that they sullenly said that "tongues" was of the devil!

The bolder ones, filled to overflowing with the Holy Spirit, started to use tongues as a gift. It came originally as a sign, but God was trying to teach His church to develop these gifts in the assembly, and use them for His glory, and by their use to lift up a standard of the Holy Spirit in the church which is His body! The venturesome used the gift of tongues in the assembly and lo, God gave others the interpretation of those tongues into the common language. Quite naturally this very quickly led to the operation of the prophetical gift, and it was amazing what the Spirit of God would bring forth in new revelation of old Scriptures by these three oral gifts. God actually began to teach His people by the Holy Spirit *in them*. The outward manifestation of the gifts of the Spirit was to produce the word, "the logos," so that all might hear and understand and be enlightened by the great Teacher, the Holy Spirit. Jesus said, *"However, when He, the Spirit of truth, has come, He will guide you into all truth; for He will not speak on His own authority, but whatever He hears He **will speak**"* (John 16:13).

The Holy Spirit came to fulfill these words of Jesus on the Day of Pentecost, which was the birthday of the church which Paul calls "The body of Christ." When the Holy Spirit came, He came to *guide* and to *speak*. In John 14:26 Jesus said, *"But the Helper, the Holy Spirit, whom the Father will send in My name, He will teach you all things, and bring to your remembrance all things that I said to you."* It is as well to remember that the ministry of the Holy Spirit in *guiding, speaking,* and *teaching* was reserved for the Christian dispensation *after* the initial outpouring of the Spirit at Pentecost. (See Acts 1:8.) We begin to understand, therefore, that the gifts of the Spirit in the church are an expression of the divine mind through human channels of the indwelling Holy Spirit. When He came He announced His coming by causing those who were filled to speak in other tongues. As soon as He filled them, they overflowed with the *Word of God*, the very *Logos* Himself.

Quite naturally, therefore, the use of the gifts, however imperfectly they were used, brought a flood of divine revelation to the original intrepid Pentecostal believers that was so great and marvelous that many were stunned and shocked because the Scriptures became alive, and the *Word* was a living Word, instead of a dead theological letter. We need to be very careful today to be sure that we are being led of the Spirit of God and not by man through the dead theological letter.

Once the Holy Spirit had gained entrance, and made human beings His temples, He proceeded to teach new depths of revelation and understanding by the gifts of the Spirit. This was the beginning of the prophecy that God would lift up a standard against the flood tide of evil, for how else can the Spirit work than through man? This is God's perfect plan that the church, which is the body of Christ, shall be His divine instrument to cry "halt" to the devil and his works. An anointed Word is therefore vitally necessary, and we believe that this is only given today to those who have truly been baptized in the Holy Spirit as on the day of Pentecost, and who continue to be filled with the Spirit daily. (See Ephesians 5:18.) Jesus said, *"Out of [your] heart will flow rivers of living water"* (John 7:38). He was referring to the coming of the Spirit on the Day of Pentecost. It was on this day that rivers of water began to flow out of the very innermost parts of the first 120, and this river of life was manifest as the Logos, the living word of God, powerful and quick and two-edged, flowing ever-increasingly into a needy world.

No wonder the sleeping church cried out in alarm when God's sword started to prick them and wake them out of their spiritual torpor! No one likes to waken up suddenly, and no one likes to be shown up in his or her sloth by a bright light shining through people of little or no theological education!

Tongues, interpretation of tongues, and prophecy were not the only gifts to be manifest! These might be called the vanguard of triune oratory. It was found that people started to exercise the kind of faith not previously known, and this in turn brought the gifts of healing into operation and the gift of miracles. Soon demons were cast out, and people became the possessors of supernaturally imparted knowledge and wisdom. God wanted to teach His people that the body of Christ was for the revelation of Christ today. Jesus had said, *"The works that I do he will do also; and greater works than these he will do, because I go to My Father"* (John 14:12). It was, and is, God's determined will that the members of the church which is the body of Christ, shall do the same works that Jesus did in His own body, and that toward the end of this age these works shall be greater, which we believe means greater in number, spreading all over the world before Jesus returns to the earth. The word "Christ" is not a name, but means in Hebrew "The Messiah," or in English "The Anointed One." History records that Jesus received this anointing after He was baptized in water by the coming of the Spirit in the shape of a dove, lighting on Him, and immediately a voice was *heard*. A voice will always be heard when the Holy Spirit comes to anoint a member of the body of Christ for this last-day service of power and authority. If we are, therefore, to take our places in this body of the Anointed One, surely we need to have the same anointing!

2

THE GIFTS ARE IN THE HOLY SPIRIT

In the last chapter we discussed the truth that the Holy Spirit is given to individuals to enable them to manifest the nature of God in the operation of the gifts of the Spirit. The body of Christ is for the revelation of Jesus Christ to an unbelieving world, and we may add, to an unbelieving church also!

As there are seven compounded colors in white light, with infra-red on one side and ultra violet on the other, so also are there nine gifts *in* the Holy Spirit. These nine gifts are the very essence of the Holy Spirit and do not exist apart from Him. In the light spectrum we have violet, indigo, blue, green, yellow, orange, and red. Just out of range of violet is ultra violet, and just out of range on the other end of the spectrum is infra-red. Thus the nine colors which together make up white light that we get from the sun, may be used as an analogy of the nine gifts of the Holy Spirit which are all in the Holy Spirit. When a person receives the incoming of the Spirit in Pentecostal fullness, he also receives potentially nine gifts, but it seems that the Lord in His knowledge and providence stirs us up to desire certain gifts, and as we exercise the necessary faith, the particular gift, or gifts, will begin to operate through our lives, not automatically but only through our personal faith. We would emphasize that as the nine colors are in the spectrum of light, so also are the nine gifts resident in the Holy Spirit at all times.

These nine gifts are divided into three groups of three. First we have the oral gifts of tongues, interpretation of tongues, and prophecy. Second we have the revelation gifts of the word of knowledge, the word of wisdom, and discerning of spirits. Third there are the three power gifts, faith, healings, and miracles. Though all the nine gifts are inexorably interrelated, and in complete union with the Godhead, yet it seems that these three groups of three work as close teams to bring the desired manifestation of Jesus, the Head, through His body, the church. The gift of tongues plus interpretation is equal in every sense to the gift of prophecy. It may be reasoned, "Why then use tongues followed by interpretation if prophecy is sufficient for the revelation of the divine mind in human speech?" We feel the answer lies in the fact that Paul taught that *"tongues are for a sign, not for those who believe but to unbelievers"* (1 Corinthians 14:22). The balanced use of the gift of tongues in an assembly, followed by a balanced and well-delivered interpretation has a devastating effect on unbelief. We have seen unbelievers, or unbelieving believers, literally run out of an assembly where tongues were used. We have tried to explain that any manifestation of a gift orally is the Sword of the Spirit in operation revealing Christ—the *Logos*, or Living Word. It is not surprising, therefore, that unbelief has to give way, and repent! It runs before the Word!

Another reason, too, is that almost all Christians newly baptized in the Spirit must learn how to handle this initial gift before they can be trusted to use other gifts. In this connection we would emphasize most strongly that any unnecessary fleshly demonstration will seriously detract from the Word. Some untaught Pentecostal people have continually fouled the stream of divine truth and revelation by insisting that as they "felt" the Holy Spirit they had to act as they "felt." Nothing could be further from the truth! God is primarily interested in people hearing His Word, whether in tongues, interpretation, or prophecy. We are so frail that we believe that we must have our part, and so some will shout, others will wave their arms, others will jump up and down, some will even fall to the ground, and again others seem to speak in falsetto and unnatural voices. By practice, the Word in tongues may be brought forth with divine unction, and yet in a controlled manner, bringing edification to all, especially to the unbelievers present. The Corinthian church was most remiss in this respect and had to be taught to use self-control and to do everything *"decently and in order"* (1 Corinthians 14:40). So excited did they get, that they all spoke in tongues at once, and Paul, who was most concerned for the unbelievers (as we should be) pointed out to them that unbelievers coming in to the assembly would say they were mad, and it is to be regretted that some Full Gospel believers have found it very hard to learn this lesson today and have brought legitimate criticism upon the work of God by their unsanctified behavior, and their immature use of the gifts. We must learn to subject the human will to the divine will before even attempting to use holy gifts of the Spirit.

We sing in an old hymn "Channels Only, Blessed Master," and this is exactly what Holy Spirit filled believers really are—channels only. A pipe carrying water is a channel; a piece of wire carrying electricity is a channel. In most churches today we have a public address system, and this consists of a microphone, which converts our voices into electrical current, which is then amplified through an amplifier, and then converted back into a voice again in the loud speakers. If the loud speaker was to "take off" and dance round the church, it would cause great consternation, and we are sure that the majority of people would be more interested in the dancing loud speaker than in the message it was bringing forth. Similarly the microphone cable might suddenly start to oscillate and vibrate violently, but even so the electrical impulses passing through it would not be affected, but somehow we feel the congregation's attention would be on the swinging wire rather than on the message being preached through it God is interested in His Word being heard and understood, and we are "channels only" and the less the channel is seen, the more will the Word be understood.

The purpose of steam in a boiler is to produce power. If one kept on pressing the safety valve and making the boiler "let off steam" we would not have an atmosphere conducive to balanced motivation of the steam engine. The power would be lost, and it has to be admitted with sadness that so much Pentecostal power is lost in this manner and by demonstrations of false fire. We are filled with the Spirit, not to blow off emotional steam, but to produce the Word of God with dignity for edification, for guidance and comfort, and to cause demons to be cast out, the sick to be healed, and the secrets of men's hearts to be revealed and the needs of humanity understood. We have been in some so-called "Pentecostal" meetings where none of these attributes of the divine nature could have been manifest because of the confusion.

We do not go to church to "feel good." We should feel good before we get there, for in reality we are the church wherever we go. Our bodies are the temple of the Holy Spirit whether we are in the house of God or in the street or store. God gives us the ability to be filled with the Spirit all the time, anywhere and everywhere, whether we "feel" anything or not. Beware of feelings!

Similarly, the revelation gifts of discerning of spirits, knowledge and wisdom will operate best in an atmosphere of quiet strong faith. In fact, Scripture gives us to believe that these gifts are *"the best gifts"* (1 Corinthians. 12:31) for they are of a higher plane of faith. In these gifts the Holy Spirit, who is *"a still small voice"* (1 Kings 19:12), makes Himself known in divinely imparted knowledge and wisdom and in knowing whether we are dealing with evil spirits, human spirits, the divine Spirit. We have rarely seen these gifts operate in a Pentecostal church where emotion was given priority over the exercise of faith.

In the case of the three power gifts of healing, miracles, and faith, it is difficult to imagine that their exercise is helped by pandemonium or confusion. Speaking personally, when we pray for sick people we like to have quietness so that we can discern the spirits operating in the cases, and this is difficult where fleshly exuberance is unchecked. It is expected that a great shout of praise may be heard when a miracle has manifestly taken place. We have noticed that in evangelistic meetings where God is moving strongly by His Spirit, people are so fascinated that they concentrate very hard and do not make an unnecessary noise. They show rapt attention instead.

People speak of separate gifts of the Spirit, rather as they talk about separate Christmas gifts, but we have tried to show that these three groups of three usually operate as a team in those who understand. How can we separate the word of knowledge from the word of wisdom? If we receive a word of knowledge about a certain matter, as Samuel did in the case of the lost asses, then it seems we will need a word of wisdom to go with it, so that we may know how to act following the revelation of divinely imparted knowledge. Then too, when dealing with people, we must have the discerning of spirits, for many that come for special help are actually motivated by wrong spirits, and they sometimes come to deceive. Sometimes they are full of religious spirits that will deceive the unwary. Again, how can we divide the working of miracles from the gifts of healing? Is not one merely a greater dimension of the other? And these will not operate without the gift of faith in the one who ministers. These three must operate as a team.

Sometimes we have met people who say, "I am seeking God for the gift of discernment." Often the true gift of discernment will show they have a wrong spirit and therefore a wrong motive in asking for this gift. They probably are nosey people who want to pry into other people's lives. God will not grant their request. If God can trust us with the revelation gifts, they will all operate, not one apart from the other! Of course, many people with wrong spirits have attempted to produce counterfeits of these beautiful gifts, and deceived the unwary, but this is a matter we can deal with in another chapter.

3

THE GIFTS FLOW THROUGH US
SUPERNATURALLY

When Jesus promised to His disciples that they would receive the gift of the Holy Spirit in Acts 2:39, the Greek word *dorea* is used. The meaning of this word, which is used many times in the New Testament, is of an outright free gift. It is used to speak of the gift of God's Son who died for our sins. No merit that we can offer, no work that we can do, will add anything to what God did on Calvary in sending His only begotten Son to die for us as a free unmerited gift. This is the meaning of the word "grace."

However, when we begin to read about the use of the gifts of the Spirit in 1 Corinthians chapter 14, another word is used, although it is still translated "gift" in our Bible. This word is used five times in this chapter and in each of these five cases it refers to the gifts of the Spirit that are resident in the gift of the Holy Spirit. This word is "charisma," which gives us the thought of a loving kindness, or favor, bestowed upon the believer. When one has received the "*dorea*" (gift) of the Holy Spirit, one has these "charisma" (marvelous spiritual graces, favors or kindnesses) bestowed. We have heard them described as "spiritual enablements," or manifestations of the Spirit: "*The manifestation of the Spirit is given to every one for the profit of all*" (1 Corinthians 12:7). In 1 Corinthians 12:1, the apostle Paul said, "*Concerning spiritual gifts, brethren, I do not want you to be ignorant.*" In this Scripture, the word "gifts" is not in the original Greek, but the word used is *pneumatikos*, which means "things of the Spirit", or "pertaining to the Spirit." Obviously, if the gifts are *in* the Holy Spirit they must be spiritual gifts, and the thought we wish to bring out is that by using the word *pneumatikos*, the apostle shows that these nine gifts are in the gift of the Holy Spirit and not separate therefrom. Thus it is not possible to receive the gifts of the Spirit apart from receiving the gift of the Holy Spirit. This is important, for some people have claimed to have spiritual gifts apart from the indwelling of the Spirit.

When Paul urged Timothy to stir up the *"gift that* [was] *in* [him], *which was given…by prophecy with the laying on of the hands"* (1 Timothy 4:14), the word used is *charisma*, and from this, we think it is reasonable to believe that the apostle Paul was urging young Timothy to call upon the latent gifts of the Spirit within him and use them for the benefit of the ministry, and the body of Christ. What excellent advice this is today to those who have received the baptism of the Spirit, to bestir themselves and to *"stir up the gift"* (2 Timothy 1:6) and bring forth one or more of the nine gifts in the assembly. We know that Timothy was probably of a nervous disposition, because Paul advised him to take a little wine for his stomach's sake. Those who have tense stomach nerves will understand. It was not uncommon for young Timothy to have "butterflies."

The gifts of the Spirit, being of the Spirit and in the Spirit, are not subject to anything we can do, apart from yielding our whole wills to the Spirit. Man is triune, spirit, soul and body. The human spirit is that part of man that is given to him to communicate with the supernatural world. What we obtain from the Holy Spirit is not received by our mind or soul, but by our spirit. To use a simple analogy which we think will help, a television installation is in three parts: the antenna, the chassis and the picture tube. The antenna, like the human spirit, receives and picks up signals from outside; the chassis, with its tubes and coils, receives these signals which are then made visible on the screen, which corresponds to the human mind. So when we press on in faith, or "stir up the gift," we actually project our human spirit into the Holy Spirit and receive some of the mind of God, but this message or revelation must be conveyed through our body (our chassis) and put upon the screen of our mind so that we then understand what we are saying, though we did not think it before we spoke it. This is especially true in the case of the revelation gifts of wisdom, knowledge, and discernment. Before we speak, we know, for as we receive the message from God's Spirit through our human spirit, it is seen line upon line on the screen of our mind. It will readily be seen that this is an act of faith, for we begin to speak forth what we receive, and as we speak more follows. This is a good lesson for fearful beginners to learn who desire to bring forth tongues or interpretation. You do not know what you are going to say, either in tongues or interpretation (or even prophecy) until you begin in faith to say it. Often people that we endeavor to encourage to bring forth tongues will say, "I don't know what to say." Exactly. You are not supposed to know what to say. As you speak it in faith you will know and understand as well as those who hear, except in the case of tongues when the understanding is by the interpretation which should follow. And remember too, we are told that another should judge what we bring forth. We are not responsible for what we bring forth. Young Samuel was most loath to tell old Eli what God brought forth from him, but Samuel insisted and it came to pass. Eli judged it, but Samuel spoke it. (See 1 Samuel 3.)

If you watch those who are using the gift of the word of knowledge today you will observe that one thought follows another thought. God gradually builds up a picture, and some even see it on the screen of their minds while it is being received from the Spirit of God and given verbally. We repeat that no true spiritual gift will ever come by the intelligence of man; it is an act of faith receiving from a willing Father by His Spirit.

We well remember a case given in most unpropitious circumstances. Three of us were seated in a restaurant, with jukebox music playing and much tobacco smoke in the place. The conversation turned to the fact that God does reveal causes of troubles through His servants. We were at once given a case by a lady of an apartment that had been empty for eleven months, and the owner was quite naturally distressed. A word of knowledge was given, followed by a word of wisdom. Prayer was made in the apartment in two days' time, the devil was rebuked for binding the place, the blood of Jesus was pleaded out loud in every room and cupboard, and then a word of prophecy was given saying that the apartment would be rented that week, which literally took place. The person concerned was even told the paper in which to advertise the apartment. Here a combination of three gifts took place to effect one blessing. The word of knowledge (the reason for the blockage) was given, the word of wisdom (to know what to do to expel the blockage), and a word of prophecy to foretell that all was well and that the apartment would be rented. All these were gifts brought forth orally, proving them to be the Word of God through a human channel. It was not in a church, nor had a season of special prayer preceded the operation of the gifts, but God moved by His Spirit in a prepared sanctified vessel, at the appointed time. Neither was it necessary to get excited, or to jump up and down in the restaurant, or to shout and wave arms. The only thing felt was the baneful effects of the tobacco smoke! God wanted His mind brought forth as a word from Him.

When we remember that the whole purpose of the gifts of the Spirit is to edify (to build up) the church, we can readily see that we must take great care how to use such holy "charisma" in order that they do their work of building up the church, and not causing confusion in the church by unseemly behavior. We are never impressed if someone says, "I could not help it." In that case, such a person is not a suitable person to bring forth the word, and should be commanded by the overseer in charge of the assembly to keep quiet. Which brings me to my next chapter!

This chapter cannot be completed without reference to the charismatic gifts mentioned in Romans 12:6–8 and 1 Peter 4:10–11. The word "charisma" is used as in 1 Corinthians 12:4–10 and therefore refers to a grace gift. As we have shown in the nine *pneumaticos*, or manifestations, of the Spirit, that these nine gifts manifest Jesus the Head of the church, so also the *charisma* in Romans and Peter represent different aspect of the ministry of Jesus through certain members of His body.

In Romans 12:6–8, we read,

Having then gifts differing according to the grace that is given to us, let us use them: if prophecy, let us prophesy in proportion to our faith; or ministry, let us use it in our ministering; he who teaches, in teaching; he who exhorts, in exhortation; he who gives, with liberality; he who leads, with diligence; he who shows mercy, with cheerfulness.

These charismatic grace gifts may be summarized as follows:

1. Prophesying

2. Serving

3. Teaching

4. Exhorting

5. Giving

6. Ruling or taking charge

7. Showing mercy and helping

In 1 Peter 4:10–11, these same charismatic gifts are summarized again for us in the following words: "*As each one has received a gift, minister it to one another, as good stewards of the manifold grace of God. If anyone **speaks**, let him speak as the oracles of God. If anyone **ministers**, let him do it as with the ability which God supplies.*"

The gifts of speaking for prophecy, teaching, and exhorting, and of ministering for serving, giving, ruling, and helping are therefore included.

We have already mentioned that there are five ministry gifts to the church of apostles, prophets, evangelists, pastors, and teachers, and these are counseled to rule well (see 1 Timothy 5:17) and these offices are those of Christ. They are not voted by a board or congregation. The Bible allows no voting, but only acceptance of the gifts of God which He gives to the church without repentance.

Thus the grace of God is revealed through grace gifts (charisma) in preaching, ministering, healing, prophesying, working of miracles, giving of time, money and talents, and serving in every capacity in the church. Some are Sunday school teachers, organ or piano players, some carpenters, builders, bricklayers; some servers at church functions, some visitors to the sick and aged. Some painters and gardeners. The ability in all cases is supernatural and a revelation of Christ the Head or Governor. Each has his office or setting, and thus the body fully reveals Christ the Head.

No individual gets any glory, only Jesus for He will not give His glory or credit to another. This is the New Testament church full of charismata or grace gifts.

4

GOD IS NOT THE AUTHOR
OF CONFUSION

We must keep well in mind that the one who uses the God-given gift of the Holy Spirit is a human being. *"The gifts and the calling of God are irrevocable"* (Romans 11:29), and when God entrusts any of us with a holy "charisma" to demonstrate His love and compassion, He wants them to be used as befits a member of His body, called in the New Testament an "ambassador." There is never anything wrong with a gift of the Spirit—the whole nine gifts are absolutely perfect—but in entrusting their use and operation to us humans, God takes the risk of educating us while we learn how to use them. If we may use an analogy of a bicycle. A father gives a new bicycle to his son. It is the finest he can buy, it works perfectly—in the hands of an expert—but in the hands of the boy it will get misused. He will fall off, the pedals will get bent, the handlebars will go awry, and he may burst the tires against the curb of the road. A sensible person would not, therefore, assume the bicycle to be a bad one, rather would they encourage the boy to learn to ride it as an expert. So with the gifts and callings of God. We have to learn how to use them and to speak them forth, clearly and distinctly without mumbling or shouting!

We sincerely believe that anything that is introduced in an assembly that causes confusion must not be of God, for He is never the author of confusion (see 1 Corinthians 14:33), and the apostle Paul urged us all to see that everything is done decently and in order. Incidentally, the word *confusion* is the meaning of *"Babylon"* in Scripture. The city and empire of Babylon was the empire of confusion. Surely the body of Christ must be the temple of divine order!

The question is, of course, who is going to see that everything *is* done decently and in order? This presupposes that some man is going to act as a supervisor! As soon as this thought is introduced to many lawless Pentecostal people, they run in the opposite direction, like Jonah, and form a little house group where they can do exactly as they want, without coming into the "bondage" of any man or group.

Many lawless people strongly resent the "interference" of the police when they presume to do what they want. The Bible has something to say about these kind of people who *"reject authority, and speak evil of dignitaries"* (Jude 8); and again,

> Let every soul be subject to the governing authorities. For there is no authority except from God, and the authorities that exist are appointed by God. Therefore whoever resists the authority resists the ordinance of God, and those who resist will bring judgment on themselves.   (Romans 13:1–2)

The apostle Paul here told us that all authorities, whether king, president, chief of police, or our employer, are *"appointed by God."* This is a hard teaching for many people today as we well realize, but it is a very prominent part of God's Word. We are not only subject to higher powers, but we are also subject to one another! This is true humility!

If the gifts of the Spirit are misused in an assembly, who is to correct the misuse? We have so often heard people say, "God told me to do this, or to say that," when it is obvious to most spiritual people in the church that God never told them to do it at all They were actuated by a wrong spirit, a spirit of rebellion! And in case anyone should misunderstand, a spirit of rebellion is an evil spirit!

We would be the first to agree that a person who has not received the baptism of the Spirit, and knows nothing about the operation of the gifts of the Spirit, would hardly be a suitable supervisor or overseer in an assembly where the gifts of the Spirit are used. Because of this condition existing in some places, the use of the gifts, whether the use has been wise or not, have been strongly suppressed, so that one can go into such an assembly and not realize that one is in a full gospel church at all! It seems very reasonable to understand that God would hardly entrust frail humanity with divine gifts, and allow them to be used to bring confusion to the church, without equally supplying the body of Christ with divinely appointed and divinely equipped overseers! The apostle Paul therefore taught quite clearly that *"God has appointed these in the church: [1] first apostles, [2] second prophets, [3] third teachers, [4] after that miracles, [5] then gifts of healings, [6] helps, [7] administrations, [8] varieties of tongues"* (1 Corinthians 12:28). Again, in Ephesians 4:11–15, we read that God has given certain gift ministries to the church, these in order being, (1) apostles, (2) prophets, (3) evangelists, (4) pastors, and (5) teachers. These ministries, operating in mortal man, are for the perfecting of the members of the church, described as saints or sanctified ones, for the building of the church which is the body of Christ, and for the general work of the ministry. These offices are set by God to teach, guide, instruct, encourage, advise, rebuke in love, and generally see that everything is done decently and in order.

If any member despises a word of correction from any of these offices, he resists the ordinance of God. A serious thing indeed in the light of eternity!

Notice that the apostleship comes first. We have not got time in this book to deal with the office of an apostle today, but it should be sufficient to say it is God's first setting in the church, and will be seen in manifestation in teaching and overseeing the building of true New Testament Apostolic churches, teaching true apostolic doctrine (see Acts 2:42) and seeing God confirm such ministry with signs, wonders and miracles of the Holy Spirit (see Acts 15:12). Of course, the other ministries will also have their Word confirmed by signs and wonders, but they will have their part in the overall picture of teaching, pastoring, and guiding the church aright, out of confusion and babyhood into the stature of the fully grown Christ! We believe that the apostleship is a ministry of love, set of God to oversee the whole work of God like a captain of a ship. It will not be a ministry of law, but of love, but we need to remember that when Ananias and Sapphira lied to the Holy Spirit, they fell dead at the feet of God's apostle. God has respect for His servants, even if rebellious people do not!

A prophet will usually work in conjunction with the other ministries, and his ministry will be a confirmatory one to the apostle. That is to say, the prophet will hardly prophesy something which goes counter to the teachings of the apostle, but his ministry must confirm that of an apostle, because the law of God insists that "*By the mouth of two or three witnesses every word shall be established*" (2 Corinthians 13:1; see also Deuteronomy 17:6). In Ephesians 3:3–5, Paul explained that the apostolic revelation that he received by revelation of the Spirit was revealed in his day through these twin ministries of apostles and prophets. We are never required to believe a "special revelation" unless it is confirmed through a known godly man with a divine ministry. Many men have established their own assemblies with their own special revelations, and gathered deluded disciples after themselves. The gift of prophecy in the church has also a similar function. The gift of prophecy is put in the church with a restricted purpose, for (1) edification, (2) exhortation and (3) comfort. In New Testament assemblies, we recommend that the gifts of tongues, interpretation, and prophecy be used *before* the preaching, as they will so frequently confirm the message through the God-ordained pastor whose message follows. Thus everyone in the assembly will know that it is God indeed who has spoken and that the revelation and doctrine was of Him! God gives us safeguards.

A pastor will have the ministry of overseeing a particular assembly as its elder. He is responsible before God to see that everything is done decently and in order. In case of confusion, he must act in love to help the person creating the confusion. If unnecessary fleshly exuberance is being manifest, he must patiently teach the person to bring forth the word in a gift in an orderly manner. If offense is caused, it will not be the pastor's fault, but the rebellious member. The pastor should always endeavor to correct in love, rather than suppress, but if abuse is continued, then there is only one recourse and that is to forbid the person to utter a gift until he learns to do so in an orderly manner. This is for the protection of the unlearned.

The Corinthian church was a very enthusiastic church, but one in which there was much disorder and wildfire. They had the gift of tongues, but they insisted in using this gift by speaking all at the same time. The bedlam resulting can be imagined, and obviously this would scare away sincere inquirers of the true New Testament way. Paul told them quite clearly that they were at fault, and the unbeliever would have good reason for calling them all mad. There was nothing wrong with the gift of tongues—it was a divine gift. It was in the misuse that trouble started, and so Paul patiently instructed the Corinthians that *"the spirits of the prophets are subject to the prophets"* (1 Corinthians 14:32). This, of course, has to do with their human spirits, and it means that we can control ourselves even as possessors of divine gifts. We use the gifts—they do not use us!

Some people who have a deep ministry of prophecy have been known to have a strong burden of a message to give the church. This burden has been heavy upon them, but they have controlled it until an opportune time in the service. It is not necessary to burst forth in the midst of the ministry of the pastor in preaching, or the teacher in teaching. So many have done this and said, "I couldn't help it." They could, for their spirits are subject to them, and we must learn to have disciplined spirits. Many an altar call has been ruined by some undisciplined person bringing forth a message in tongues or prophecy at a wrong time, although we do not rule out that it might be God's will to bring forth a supernatural message at such a time. Great wisdom and sensitiveness in the Spirit is needed to know the appropriate time.

It is good to remember also that the five ministry gifts are held by fallible man. No modern apostle, prophet, pastor or teacher will be a pope in a dictatorial sense, he will be a loving father to the church, correcting, guiding and counseling with wisdom gained from the Holy Spirit and from experience, which is why Paul counseled that bishops (overseers or elders) must not be set apart being novices (see 1 Timothy 3:6), but must be chosen as spiritual men of experience. We believe that every one of the five ministry gifts will be apparent in a man before he is actually set apart in his office by the laying on of hands and prayer. Man will merely ratify what the Holy Spirit has given and set. If this is so, then the spiritual members of the body will have no difficulty whatsoever in recognizing true ministries set of God, nor will they have any difficulty in coming "under" them in spiritual discipline.

5

BODY MINISTRY

But now indeed there are many members, yet one body" (1 Corinthians 12:20). "We, being many, are one body" (Romans 12:5). God has set in the body of His Son all the members by His Spirit, for we read that "by one Spirit we were all baptized into one body" (1 Corinthians 12:13). As the human body has many members, actuated by one mind, so also is the body of Christ actuated and controlled by the Holy Spirit through the Head, Jesus, in heaven. Each member is set in this mystical body by God through the Holy Spirit, and it is safe to say that no two members have an identical ministry, which is why we never try to copy another's ministry, each is separate but all must work in harmony and concert.

Dr. William Smith, in his famous Bible Dictionary, has this to say regarding the church, which is the body of Christ:

> The day of Pentecost is the birth day of the Christian church. The Holy Spirit, who was then sent by the Son from the Father and rested on each of the disciples, combined them once more into a whole—combined them as they had **never before** been combined, by an internal and spiritual bond of cohesion. Before Pentecost they had been individual followers of Jesus (disciples), **now** they became **His mystical body**, animated by His Spirit.

When Jesus was crucified, the High Priest waved a sheaf of newly ripening wheat before the Lord in the temple as a first fruit offering. This typified the disciples of Jesus before Pentecost, each an individual follower as brought out by Dr. Smith. Fifty days later, on the day of Pentecost the same High Priest would wave two baked loaves before the Lord, to signify a tremendous change that had taken place. Now the disciples were no longer individual followers of Jesus, they had been baptized in One Spirit in one body on the birthday of the Christian church—they were now made one loaf, one bread, even as Jesus is the bread of life. This offering of two loaves would signify the presenting to the world of the bread of life manifest in one homogeneous whole loaf, one for the Jews and one for the Gentiles.

We mention all this to show that the church which is Christ's body is *one*—or at least it was created one on the day of Pentecost. Afterward it became torn up into many segments, but we are living in the day of the building again of the church, back into its original power, pattern, performance, and practice. Jesus said that He would return for a church wherein no spot or wrinkle existed. (See Ephesians 5:27.) On every hand we are seeing pastors and members of the more formal denominations receiving the baptism of the Spirit and coming into the knowledge of the power of God and the gifts of the Spirit. The flour is in the oven and the bread is being baked.

When sections of this body come together for worship in assemblies, they are supposed to manifest the one Christ by a supernatural demonstration. This supernatural manifestation of a supernatural Head will owe nothing to the flesh. Jesus being the Logos, the Word of God, desires that He shall be manifest through humans as the *word*. The word of knowledge, the word of wisdom, the word of faith, the word in tongues, the word of interpretation of tongues, the word of prophecy, the word that heals, the word that creates miracles, the word in spiritual song, the word in spiritual prayer, and the word in spiritual praise. Such manifestations as these are even unknown in many so-called "Pentecostal" churches. Instead we find a program. Special choirs, special singers, and special films, with the emphasis on man or the creations of man. This is not the type of meeting that is envisaged in the Bible! One is of God; the other is of man.

Paul wrote, *"How is it then, brethren? Whenever you come together, each of you has a psalm, has a teaching, has a tongue, has a revelation, has an interpretation. Let all things be done for edification"* (1 Corinthians 14:26). We see here that one member has a psalm, which means a "spiritual song." We are not to assume that such a member desires to sing Psalm 23, although such a song sung with the understanding is necessary in our worship. We believe that this means that one will literally have a song in him learned entirely from the Holy Spirit; it will almost certainly not only have words, but also the melody. Paul writes about singing with the understanding and singing with the spirit. We both sing known hymns and those given by the Spirit. Singing in the Spirit among members of the body of Christ is a most beautiful thing. The story is told by Pastor James Brooke, one time Pastor of the Assembly at Tower Hall, London, England, where freedom is given for the operation of the gifts of the Spirit. The choirmaster of a local church was on his way home on a Sunday when he heard the most beautiful and heavenly music coming from the church. He went in, and after the service was over, inquired of the pastor as to who he had to train his "choir" in such marvelous and polished singing. The explanation was a simple one, the choirmaster was Jesus, and the choir was the body of Christ. This man was amazed, for he could not understand that neither the words nor the music had previously been learned. They were not singing with the understanding, they were singing with the Spirit. (See 1 Corinthians 14:13.) Each was singing in perfect harmony as given by the Spirit.

The apostle also wrote about the difference between praying with the Spirit and praying with the understanding. He also mentions praying in an unknown tongue. We certainly know what is meant by praying with the understanding, but do we understand what is meant by praying in tongues and praying with the spirit? This is, of course, another manifestation of the Spirit for the one who prays will not know what he is going to pray until he starts out in faith to pray in the anointing of the Spirit. This manifestation of the Spirit is entirely of the Spirit. As in the beginning of the church *"they...began to speak with other tongues, as the Spirit gave them utterance"* (Acts 2:4), so as an act of faith, they will pray as the Spirit *gives* the utterance. This kind of prayer is quite different and brings greater blessing to those who hear. Many people hearing such prayers for the first time are at a loss to know how such beautiful words can be uttered without actually reading them or learning them off by heart!

Then we read that another coming into this type of assembly will have a doctrine. There is need for teaching in the Spirit, for Jesus said that when the Spirit was come, as He did on the day of Pentecost, He would teach us and guide us into *all truth*. This is a process, and as the assembly is able to bear it, the Holy Spirit desires to teach the members of the body true doctrine—progressively, and so teachers are set in the body for this purpose. Unfortunately so many, even in full gospel churches, are ignorant of doctrine and have little desire to learn, preferring emotionalism to faith, which comes by hearing the Word of God.

Then we see that room must be made for those who come in with a tongue. This does not speak of the physical member of our bodies, but of the gift of tongues. The first gift in the body is the gift of tongues, and when used in the assembly is like a spiritual trigger; it can trigger off a real move of the Spirit in other gifts. The instruction is clear; we are not to use this gift in an assembly where there is no interpreter; however, we may use it quietly to ourselves and to God, so as not to disturb the meeting, but to edify ourselves. Where it is known, however, that there is a reliable interpreter present who is respected in his or her ministry, then the gift of tongues may be used, and in turn the one with the gift of interpretation will bring forth the interpretation of the message just given in tongues. One may ask in amazement, "Why?" The answer is that this is the way that God has decreed for His body to act when they come together! How different from "organized worship" with which most of us are all too familiar! How hard it is for so many to break away from the traditions of men and move into the supernatural realm of the moving of the Spirit of God! We would emphasize that the word "interpretation" does not mean "transliteration." The message in tongues may be short and to the point, containing in itself all the points that God wants understood, but the one who interprets may bring forth this message in a volume of words, even with repetitions, and an unbeliever will pour scorn on the operation of the gifts of the Spirit. This only goes to prove that the spirits of the prophets are subject to the prophets, and the gifts of the Spirit are used by the human instrument. God wants to get the message through! Some use words such as "yea" and "even" many times as padding!

The late British evangelist Smith Wigglesworth was once asked, "Do you wait for the Spirit to move you?" His reply was typical of the man of faith he was. He replied, "If the Spirit does not move me, I move the Spirit." What did he mean? He was trying to teach that we do not wait for a special visitation of the Holy Spirit, for that is unnecessary, since when we were baptized in the Spirit He came right inside us. Before we use a gift, we must be satisfied that we are in the Spirit as well as the Spirit in us, and then we may draw upon the Word in us and bring it forth as an act of faith, not as an act of feelings! Those who walk in the Spirit may speak in tongues at any time, to edify themselves, and to bring forth a message in the church. It is argued by some that we can speak in tongues in the flesh. We must remind these dear people that we have to use our flesh to speak in tongues, for it is we who speak, and the Holy Spirit gives the words. Our physical tongues are of flesh, but we should not use the gift unless we are sure we are walking in the Spirit! If we have known sin in our lives we should keep silent.

Once when preaching we spoke in tongues, which horrified the wife of the pastor, for she said that we had spoken in the flesh because it was done so naturally, so unaffectedly, without emotion while preaching. My wife tried to explain that when I was preaching I was strongly anointed of the Spirit and the tongues was of the Spirit, but the sounds were made by the flesh! Some dear people have the idea that we must wait until a bolt out of heaven strikes us and *makes* us use a gift of the Holy Spirit, or makes us feel excited! This is not so. God gives them and we use them in faith. No hot flush or cold chill is necessary to faith.

Then we read of one coming in who has a revelation. We have already explained that there are three revelation gifts; discerning of spirits, the word of knowledge, and the word of wisdom. These may be brought out in the open assembly, and sometimes the thoughts and intents of the heart will be made manifest and an unbeliever coming into the assembly will fall down and acknowledge that God is in the place. What a wonderful method God gives the church for the salvation of souls! Some say they will not have the gifts of the Spirit on Sunday evening, which traditionally is an "evangelical service," because unbelievers may be seared and driven out. The opposite is true. Tongues are for a sign to unbelievers, as well as the other gifts, to cause conversion and conviction of sin (see 1 Corinthians 14:22), and to cause souls to depart from sin.

Sometimes a member may have a revelation of something that another member, or the pastor, may need to know, and to bring it forth publicly might be unkind or embarrassing. In such a case we believe the revelation should be brought to the individual privately, either in writing or spoken. God never wants to embarrass one of His children, for the gifts of the Spirit are for the edifying of the body of Christ, not for private use or private "fortune telling."

We repeat, the body of Christ is for the revelation of Christ.

6

RIVERS OF THE WORD

The word *"prophecy,"* in the original Hebrew, means "to bubble up," as from a spring. This truth is born out by the words: *"'Out of his heart will flow rivers of living water.' But this [Jesus] spoke concerning the Spirit"* (John 7:38–39). The bubbling up of the living water of the Word of God will come forth as a stream of life to invigorate everything that it touches. Everyone within ear of the gifts of the Spirit will be reinvigorated, as a thirsty man in an oasis. The living Word creates life. The word "prophecy," therefore, has a larger connotation than just the gift of prophecy, which carries the restricted use for *"edification and exhortation and comfort"* (1 Corinthians 14:3). Joel prophesied that God would pour out His Spirit on all flesh, and sons and daughters would prophesy, etc. (see Joel 2:28–29) and this was fulfilled in an initial measure on the day of Pentecost, for Peter quoted freely from this prophecy to justify the speaking in tongues (see Acts 2:17–18). No mention was made in the original prophecy about speaking in other tongues, but this effusion was quoted as a proof of the words of God through Joel, *"your sons and daughters shall prophesy"* (Joel 2:28), because speaking in tongues is a prophetic utterance which needs an interpretation. Similarly the two gifts of tongues and interpretation are together equal to prophesy, because in both cases the church hears the Word of God.

Prophecy can be the Word of God foretelling future events, or it can be foretelling for guidance, instruction, comfort, edification, and exhortation. It is God who gives the message, but the human brings forth the mind of God.

All the nine gifts of the Spirit come from the mind of God as part of His eternal word. *"In the beginning was the Word, and the Word was with God, and the Word was God.... And the Word became flesh and dwelt among us"* (John 1:1, 14). As God spoke in the beginning and all that exists was created by His Word (see Hebrews 1:2, Hebrews 11:3 and Genesis 1) so also that same creative word is *in* every Holy Spirit baptized believer. It is for such a person to believe that this creative Word is in them, and to use it in faith. The Word of faith can cast out devils, heal the sick and raise the dead, for Jesus said in Mark 11:23–24:

> For assuredly, I say to you, whoever **says** to this mountain, "Be removed and be cast into the sea," and does not doubt in his heart, but believes that those things he **says** will be done, he will have whatever he says. Therefore I say to you, whatever things you ask when you pray, believe that you receive them, and you will have them.

Jesus sent His Word to heal. This is an entirely different picture of prayer than is given to us in some places. One Bible college we know prayed much for revival, and suddenly some of the students started to receive the baptism of the Spirit and speak in tongues, and the Bible College was greatly concerned, and tried to forbid it, but the students read in the Bible *"Do not forbid to speak with tongues"* (1 Corinthians 14:39).

God has given us the creative Word which dwells in us, after faith has opened the river of life from our innermost parts. In actual fact, those who receive the baptism of the Spirit usually feel the movings of the Spirit in this exact part of their anatomy! We have seen miracles occur, demons cast out, the rain stopped, and a storm split in two, when the Word of faith has been spoken, nothing doubting. Elijah shut up heaven by a Word. Jeremiah was commissioned *"to root out and to pull down, to destroy and to throw down, to build and to plant"* (Jeremiah 1:10). This was done by the prophet speaking with God's authority, and giving commands that God would honor. So today in the church, there is much to pull down, to destroy, and to throw down, before we can see Jesus again building and planting, but it will be members of His body that will give commands in His name! In Isaiah we read that when the enemy shall come in like a flood, the Spirit of the Lord shall lift up a standard against him. The Spirit of the Lord today must move in and through His body, the church, and lift up a standard of the Word of God through which Satan cannot penetrate, and which will stop him in his tracks! This is why God wants His church to be built again so that it might force back Satan and bring back the Son of God to a war-torn earth, to catch away His church, and to return with it to rule and reign over His kingdom forever.

There is all the difference between "going to church" and acting as an ambassador of God in His body!

If Jesus sent the Word that healed, so can we. (See Psalm 107:20.) It He cast out devils, so can we. If He healed the sick, so can we. If He worked a miracle, so can we—in His name and with His authority! How? By sending the anointed Word of God, which will proceed over lips and tongues and cause sickness to go, devils to flee and the oppressed to be set free. No, we do not ask God to do this, for He sent His Son to do it perfectly on Calvary. We act as law enforcement officers, and speak the

Word, and it will be so. We enforce the victory of Calvary over the world, the flesh and the devil. No wonder Jesus said, *"And nothing shall by any means hurt you"* (Luke 10:19).

Thus the gifts of the Spirit are not just to give a nice feeling when they are used in the assembly, but they carry God's creative power in them, according to the faith with which we speak them. Success came again to the church in the healing ministry when pastors and evangelists started to command the sickness to go, and demons to leave. Many cried out, "What presumption." Rather should we say, "What faith, what authority"—never man spake like this man!

It is very exhilarating to do this. It is wonderful to see demons come out of poor bound people crying with a loud voice, often tearing them on their way out. It is very wonderful to hear evil spirits speak and argue and tell you that they are not going to obey you, but then see them leave in quiet obedience, all because they must obey the Word of faith. This is the gift of faith in operation. In Buenos Aires, Argentina, the writer actually spoke in English to a demon in a Spanish speaking lady, who could not speak a word of English herself. At first the demon refused to obey the Word of faith, but finally said, rather meekly, "Yes," and came out.

We do not begin to see true New Testament Christianity in operation until we begin to see the Word through the gifts of the Spirit pulling down, destroying, building, and planting. Dull religious formality must fly before the demonstration of power of the Spirit. There were Pharisees in Jesus' day. They were the fundamentalists. They knew the Bible perfectly, and also a few traditions they had added for themselves. They knew the Bible spoke of divine healing, the casting out of devils and miracles, but they were powerless in their unbelief to do these things, and when Jesus came and demonstrated what His Word spoken in power could do, they hated Him without a cause. Are we going to find any more appreciation from the dead religious formalists and fundamentalists today? No! Their reaction is the same. The Bible says that we are to turn away from them.

The gospel is the power of God unto salvation to everyone that believeth (see Romans 1:16). The word *"salvation,"* coming from the Greek root *sozo*, means to heal, to liberate, to save, to set free, to make whole. The salvation of Jesus is for the whole man, spirit, soul, and body. This salvation is visited to men through men, through apostles, prophets, pastors, evangelists, and teachers. It comes because the Word of God is spoken through anointed lips. That is why Jesus said, *"If you forgive the sins of any, they are forgiven them"* (John 20:23), for He gave to them the ministry of reconciliation, which rested in the speaking of His Word in saving and delivering power. How shall they hear without a preacher? (See Romans 10:14.) It is most noticeable in Scripture that Jesus told us to remit sins (see John 20:23), heal the sick, cast out devils, and raise the dead, because He had freely given to us, and therefore we were freely to give (see Matthew 10:8). What a different concept from traditional Christianity which is always praying for God to heal the sick if it be His will! We are to heal in His name! We are not to pray for God to do it, so much as go out and *do* it in the name of Jesus, Who gives us *carte blanche* authority to do these things by speaking His Word. This is why we need to be filled with His Word in receiving the baptism of the Spirit, accompanied by the speaking in other tongues, for this is a miraculous manifestation of the Word of God coming forth as the Sword of the Spirit from our own mouths. No wonder the devil will do all he can to stop and shut the mouths of Full Gospel Christians, so that there are no gifts, and no anointed Word heard in the midst of assemblies. Satan hates tongues like a wild beast hates fire. Therefore John the Baptist prophesied of Jesus that He would baptize us with the Holy Spirit and fire. Fire burns, but it purifies also!

The nine gifts manifest part of the logos, the eternal Word of God, to us today.

7

THE MINISTRY OF THE PROPHETICAL WORD

The question is asked many times by those who are new to the operation of the gifts of the Spirit, "Is prophecy in our churches today equal to the prophecies of Isaiah or Jeremiah?" The very misunderstanding of this fact has caused many people to be greatly disappointed in the gifts of the Spirit and the deep things of God.

Prophecy in its broadest sense, is the operation of the oral gifts for forth-telling or foretelling. So many people believe that prophecy is only for foretelling future events, but this is not supported from Scripture. In 1 Corinthians 14:3 the territory of prophecy in the church is confined to edification, exhortation, and comfort, none of which is foretelling the future. In Romans 12:6, we read a most enlightening Scripture. *"Having then gifts differing according to the grace that is given to us, let us use them: if prophecy, let us prophesy in proportion to our faith."* If one has little faith, the Word brought forth in the gifts will be very limited in depth and scope. If one has more faith, similarly the Word brought forth will be correspondingly deeper. If one has great faith, then one can expect to hear a beautiful deep searching Word of prophecy, and listeners in the assembly will know and have confidence in the Word brought forth through such a person. Realizing this truth will avoid the foolish mistakes that have happened, when a carnal person brings forth a prophetical "word" which may even contradict Scripture, and those who were equally unlearned glibly believed this word as of God, whereas it might have been of the person's human spirit, or even of a deluding evil spirit! People who are not walking in the light as Jesus is in the light should never be listened to, and certainly a pastor would be correct in forbidding such a person to speak, even if offense was caused—as it certainly would be if the person was carnal! Fear of man has played havoc in churches. We need to fear God, not Satan. (See Matthew 10:28.) A true New Testament pastor, set of God, must never try to please man, but must always be willing to see that everything is done decently and in order in the church, according to Scripture.

It will soon be evident in an assembly that certain consecrated people bring forth the prophetical word regularly, and the word they bring forth can be relied upon; but here again we must remember that all prophets and prophetical gifts must be subject to the word of God, and agree thereto.

> *If there arises among you a prophet or a dreamer of dreams, and he gives you a sign or a wonder, and the sign or the wonder comes to pass, of which he spoke to you, saying, "Let us go after other gods"—which you have not known—"and let us serve them," you shall not listen to the words of that prophet or that dreamer of dreams, for the LORD your God is **testing you** to know whether you love the LORD your God with all your heart and with all your soul.*
>
> (Deuteronomy 13:1–3)

From this we understand that it is possible for a person to prophesy or to dream dreams, and even to produce signs and wonders, and yet their prophesying was contrary to the Word of God, and God in His wisdom actually permitted such a false prophet to speak *to test* the hearers. We have seen some types of evangelism today which leave much to be desired in the practices and teaching of the evangelist, which bear no relation to clear scriptural teaching. Some incredible prophecies have proceeded from persons not living a consecrated life of obedience to the Word of God, and these have been believed, and thus the lives of some have been adversely affected, and some have lost out in their Christian life, because God was supposed to have said something, whereas He did not! God likes to prove us!

Again, there is another aspect we must remember. It is found in Deuteronomy 18:22:

> *When a prophet speaks in the name of the LORD, if the thing does not happen or come to pass, that is the thing which the LORD has not spoken; the prophet has spoken it presumptuously; you shall not be afraid of him.*

We must confess that in many meetings words of prophecy have been spoken *"in the name of the LORD"* when the Lord never said them at all. We remember a sad case that happened in Oklahoma. The pastor's wife got up in the pulpit one night, with tears running down her face, and told the people that if she did not preach, God would kill her! Apparently a so-called prophet had prophesied this rubbish, and she was gullible enough to believe it. She said to the people that she was a wife and mother and felt no desire or call whatsoever to preach, but she was afraid that if she did not obey the word of this "prophet" God would kill her. This was manifestly a prophecy of a demon, for God does not threaten to kill His children in prophecy.

The gift is for edification, exhortation, and comfort, given in love. We wrote a letter of explanation to the pastor trying to correct this flagrant happening, but he never replied! We have known cases in the past where so-called "prophetesses" have prophesied that certain people should marry certain others, when later it transpired that some of the parties concerned were already married.

Some marital disasters have happened in such cases, and we need, therefore, to remember that all prophecies must be judged and not acted on hastily. *"Let two or three prophets speak, and let the others judge"* (1 Corinthians 14:29). If this Scripture had been obeyed more, then we would not have had to suffer cases where carnal prophets and prophetesses have held a church in bondage by their false utterances. In Deuteronomy we read that we need not be afraid of their utterances!

The prophet is supposed to speak the word and the other person is to do the judging whether they will act on the word spoken or not. It is no one else's business. A prophet is not above an apostle, neither is the prophetical word above the office of a pastor. There are types of people who, if given a chance, will try to run an assembly through their prophetical gift and expect the pastor and the people to be obedient to them! This is far from the truth. The prophets who prophesied that bonds and trouble awaited Paul gave their prophecies (which came to pass), but Paul ignored their pleas to bypass Rome. Although the troubles came upon him, yet he knew the will of God for himself, and he went to Rome. Many no doubt would say that Paul had been disobedient to "their prophecies." No prophecy is of any private interpretation (see 2 Peter 1:20), and prophecies must be given in faith and received in faith. Just because a Word has been spoken does not mean that it will come to pass in all cases, unless it is received in faith by a person and made to come to pass by their faith. God may speak a word to the effect that a certain person is destined for the mission field, but if that person in judging the word decides not to go, then the word is not fulfilled, although it may be of God.

Some prophecies are hard to be understood until the time of their fulfillment. The prophecies concerning Jesus said that He would come out of (1) Bethlehem, (2) Nazareth, and (3) Egypt. How could those who searched the Scriptures know how these prophecies could ever be fulfilled, seeing they seemed to contradict each other? We must be careful not to judge a prophecy too soon; we might have to wait years for its fulfillment—but we are so impatient, we want everything to be fulfilled in a few days!

In Ezekiel 13, the prophet was told to prophesy to the false prophets of Israel and tell them that their prophecies were wrong, and that they prophesied out of their own heart. They spoke what they wanted to speak, with no regard to God. They said it "in the name of the Lord," but it was from their own unregenerate heart. When King Jehoshaphat joined with King Ahab in war, he got the national prophets to prophesy. They had a nice living, so they prophesied out of their hearts a prophecy that would be pleasing to the King, but King Jehoshaphat was not satisfied with this unanimity and asked whether perhaps there might not be another prophet. King Ahab, a very wicked king, said that Micaiah was a prophet in Israel but he only said bad things about the bad king, proving he was an honest man. He came and prophesied that King Ahab would be slain, and it came to pass. The false prophets, all four hundred of them, though they spoke in the name of the Lord, in reality spoke out of their own hearts. Four hundred to one! (See 2 Chronicles 18.) We have many false prophets today but, thank God, we have many good ones too!

King Saul was once numbered among the prophets, and this fact became a byword in Israel, but later, due to disobedience to the Word of God through Samuel, God permitted an evil spirit to come upon him (see 1 Samuel 16) and this spirit gave him the prophecies that he uttered. In both cases Saul prophesied, but in the former times God gave him the messages, but after backsliding Satan gave him his messages. It is well to remember that no backslider should ever be permitted to speak forth in an assembly, for it will not be a pure word of prophecy by any means, and may well be of an evil spirit. Sometimes it will be a mixture, part divine and part human.

We prophesy according to the proportion of our faith. Doubtless if there are prophets today with the same faith as Isaiah or Jeremiah, we would have the same depth of prophecy. Let us not forget that the prophecies contained in the Bible are selected proven prophecies. No doubt Isaiah and other prophets spoke many more words than are contained in the Bible. He had to go deeper. He was an established prophet, but still a coal from off the altar had to be put on his lips. (See Isaiah 6.) We are unwise if we accept every prophetical word as being equal with Scripture, for we must prove all things, and hold fast to that which is good (see 1 Thessalonians 5:21), and this recommendation by the apostle Paul follows the words *Do not despise prophecies*" (1 Thessalonians 5:20). The mistake made by many timid Full Gospel pastors has been to suppress all utterances because of a few false ones! Satan gains his objective by this, but we again refer to Deuteronomy 13 where we read that God wants to prove us! Proving strengthens us. Have the gifts proved you, or have they destroyed you?

We should encourage each other to use the gift that God desires us to have, for God divides the gifts to us. (See 1 Corinthians 12:11.) He will begin to make us hungry, and we will covet to prophecy (see 1 Corinthians 14:39) and then we will covet the best gifts (see 1 Corinthians 12:31), but only that we may be used as channels to edify the church. In this connection we would always most strongly recommend that gifts of the Spirit should never be used except under the proper oversight of offices set by God in the church. The use of gifts of the Spirit in private homes or cottage meetings will usually end in something going wrong, for the false will not be recognizable from the true, and confusion results from this practice. If people are undisciplined and will not come under a God-given pastor, then any word that comes forth from them should be ignored completely, especially if it is given in a "hole-in-the-corner" meeting.

"You will know them by their fruits" (Matthew 7:16). These words of Jesus should be applied to those who dare to use prophetical gifts. Holy men of God spoke as they were moved by the Spirit, not unholy people! Let us prove all prophecies, but let us not despise prophecies. Let us encourage people to use the gifts and make way for them in our assemblies.

Jesus said, *"And now I have told you before it comes, that when it does come to pass, you **may believe**"* (John 14:29). From this we see that the purpose of prophecy is that God's omnipotence may be proved in the outworking of future events spoken through man, but not aided by man in the fulfillment. God is able to cause to come to pass His Word, and we are not assumed to know exactly how it is fulfilled, but when it is, our faith will be strengthened in His Word both written and spoken.

8

THE BODY OF CHRIST MUST
BE ANOINTED

Much of the Christian church knows nothing of the operation of the gifts of the Spirit, for they have not received the baptism of the Spirit with the sign of tongues. When the Holy Spirit comes into a person the Word of God is manifest in power, for Jesus said that we should receive power after that the Holy Spirit comes upon us. This power (Greek, *dunamis*) is the same as the virtue that went out of Him in Luke 8:46. The virtue, or *dunamis*, went out of Him, but went into the woman with the issue of blood and healed her. Her faith drew out the *dunamis*, though many others touched him. This incoming of *dunamis* comes out of us as the *logos*, the living Word of God, in tongues to prove to us and everyone else that we have received a supernatural baptism of the Spirit.

It is not sufficient to receive the anointing of the Spirit, as many sincere Christians do. At conversion we receive the Spirit of Christ. (See Romans 8:9.) We must receive the overflowing baptism, which pours out of our innermost parts as a river of living water. (See John 7:38.) The continual outpouring of the Spirit from us will be in the form of the nine gifts of the Spirit.

Though we may pray for the sick before being baptized in the Spirit, as the disciples did in Jesus' day, yet no one can receive the gifts of healing without the baptism of the Spirit. We repeat, the gifts are in the Holy Spirit. If we do not have the Spirit of God in us, we cannot have His gifts.

This factor has led many "dispensationalists" to speak disparagingly of these priceless gifts, for 1 Corinthians chapters 12 and 14 means very little to them! We are told by these people that Paul would rather speak in five words of a known tongue in the church than in ten thousand words of an unknown tongue. (See 1 Corinthians 14:19.) They justify themselves by saying that Paul would rather speak five words *in the church* with his understanding, and not speak in tongues at all. Paul did speak in tongues, for he said, *"Do not forbid to speak with tongues"* (1 Corinthians 14:39), and many do forbid it in their assemblies! He also said, *"I thank God I speak with tongues more than you all"* (verse 18), and again, *"I wish that you all spoke with tongues"* (verse 5). Obviously the apostle did not mean what some "unbelieving believers" say he meant!

The context of this portion of 1 Corinthians 14 deals with the use that the Corinthians made of the gift of tongues. They used the gift unwisely, and no one was profited, because they did not allow the gift of interpretation to follow, and unbelievers coming in would think them mad! In the teaching ministry, in opening in prayer, or in preaching, it is necessary to use the *known* tongue. So Paul would rather use five words of a known tongue so that all might understand the message than ten thousand words of an unknown tongue that no one would understand. He did not forbid the use of tongues, but counseled the Corinthians to use the gift of tongues when there was one with the gift of interpretation in the assembly, otherwise to speak to themselves and to God, but not to cease from speaking in tongues! Instead of telling them to stop using tongues, he told them to use the gift quietly so as not to be heard, but to praise God in worship in tongues quietly in the assembly. We are to control ourselves in the use of these gifts.

We are absolutely convinced that the apostle Paul never visualized any other type of church than a full gospel church when he wrote his epistles. He only had in mind full gospel churches with the nine gifts of the Spirit in each assembly! I wonder what type of church Paul would choose if he could come back today? The church which is called the body of Christ commenced at Pentecost with tongues. It will be caught up speaking in tongues. The Corinthian church had much speaking in tongues. The Ephesian church started with tongues and prophecies (see Acts 19:1–6), and we are sure that all the other New Testament churches were after the same pattern! After the initial 120 charter members spoke in tongues at Pentecost, it is recorded that three thousand were added and continued with the disciples steadfastly in the **apostles' doctrine** (see Acts 2:41–42). If three thousand new-born babes in Christ came into the presence of 120 red-hot tongue talking and prophesying Christians today, we fear many of them would be most uncomfortable! They would not doubt decide to have no part with them and their tongues! The new disciples on the day of Pentecost would soon tumble into the blessing of the baptism of the Spirit and the gifts of the Spirit in such pristine glory and power of the early church.

The whole Pauline teaching regarding the New Testament church was that it should be built on the foundation of the apostles and prophets, with teachers, evangelists, pastors, gifts of healings, miracles, helps, governments, and tongues! (See 1 Corinthians 12:28.) Anything less than this would have caused the apostle to say, *"Did you receive the Holy Spirit when you believed?"* (Acts 19:2). He would then have explained, and laid his hands on the new converts of those days that they might receive the Holy Spirit as at Pentecost. The same thing happened at Samaria, where there was a great revival under the evangelist Philip; the sick were healed, demons cast out, thousands saved, a great baptismal service help, and yet the Holy Spirit had fallen upon none of them (see Acts 8:16) but God lost no time, for He at once sent two apostles, Peter and John, who laid their hands upon them, and they all received the Holy Spirit. Augustine, writing in the fourth century, said, "We still do as the apostles did when they laid their hands on the Samaritans and called the Spirit on them. In the laying on of hands, it is expected that the converts should speak with new tongues." The quotation seems to indicate that Augustine believed that the Samaritans really did speak in tongues when Peter and John laid hands upon them, and that tongues was the sign of the baptism of the Spirit in AD 400. We still do the same today, and the Holy Spirit still comes in, causing people to speak in tongues. God has not changed. Why should we?

We realize that the difficulty of many Christians is to reconcile being saved without having the Holy Spirit, but we must never confuse the gift of eternal life with the gift of the Holy Spirit. One is born again *by* the Spirit, but later one is baptized *in* the Spirit. It is a question of degree. At conversion one has the Spirit or nature of Christ implanted by the Holy Spirit. (See Romans 8:9.) The incoming of the Third Person is an entirely different experience and a greater degree. In John 20:22, it is recorded that Jesus breathed on His dispirited disciples and said, *"Receive the Holy Spirit,"* but in breathing the Holy Spirit upon them He gave them a strong reinvigorating anointing of the Spirit, which many godly people receive from time to time, but we must not confuse this pre-Pentecostal experience of the disciples with what they had later on the day of Pentecost. There was no body of Christ before Pentecost! The Holy Spirit was not given before Pentecost! The only body exited was the physical body of our Lord, which was later crucified! He had the Spirit, for He was anointed immediately after being baptized in water by John, and this fulfilled the prophecies of Daniel 9:24 and Isaiah 61:1. In fact, Jesus said, *"Today this Scripture is fulfilled in your hearing"* (Luke 4:21).

Jesus did not begin His ministry until He became Jesus the Christ, by the anointed of the Spirit at Jordan at the age of thirty. We have sadly slipped when we attempt to do His work today without the same endowment of power from on high. We must be baptized in the Spirit to manifest Jesus Christ fully in our bodies, which are the temples of the Spirit, by a demonstration of the nine gifts of the Spirit.

How blind is unbelief!

At the time this book is being written, we have had the privilege of praying through several students and ex-students of a Bible college, which is interdenominational in outlook, and also a very fine man of God who is serving a well-known evangelical body. He told us he was convinced by his reading of the Scriptures that he lacked the necessary power for the ministry that the early disciples had, and so he help up his hands, pleading the blood of Jesus, and began to speak in tongues. This is happening throughout the church today.

What a difference the glorious baptism of the Spirit makes to those who hunger and thirst after God. So simple. It is a gift!

9

SATAN'S GIFTS

It comes as a matter of great astonishment for people to learn that the devil can counterfeit all the nine gifts. We cannot deal in any detail on this interesting subject, but we would recommend to our readers *The Challenging Counterfeit* by Raphael Gasson, who was at one time a "Christian medium" in the devilish cult of "Christian spiritualism." He became converted to Christ and filled with the Spirit in Pentecostal fullness, and he has opened the lid on all the horrors of what Satan is counterfeiting in spiritualistic séances.

We have experienced hearing a demon spirit speaking in English through the lips of a person who could not speak a word of English, when it was being commanded to come out of her in Jesus' name. This is speaking in tongues! We have heard demons prophesying when casting them out. They often speak back in English. (See Mark 1:24.) Healings and miracles take place in spiritualistic séances by the power of Satan, but we are not to believe in this case that Satan casts out Satan, for he does not, for this would be a house divided against itself. Satan merely orders a spirit of infirmity to leave a body, therefore, bringing healing, in order to deceive the gullible person who goes to a spiritualistic séance right against the commands of God. If the devil can cause the healing of the body or do a miracle, then he can damn that person's soul. Satan does not come as Satan, he comes as an angel of light. (See 2 Corinthians 11:13–14.) Spiritism with its tongues, prophecies, healings, and miracles is forbidden. (See Leviticus 19:31, Isaiah 8:19.)

Spiritist mediums, filled with loathsome evil spirits, produce signs, wonders, miracles, and gifts of Satan's spirit to deceive, if it were possible, the very elect. How near we need to keep to the Word of God! How much we need to believe in the power of the blood and the name of Jesus today. We need to be filled, possessed, saturated, and baptized in the Holy Spirit.

Instead of being afraid, we should determine to be so filled with the Holy Spirit that we shall shine with the glory of God and bring the power of God against Satan and his demon spirits. We should covet the gifts of the Holy Spirit, and be able to discern the wrong spirits, which counterfeit! How sadly lacking is the church today in these wonderful gifts of the Holy Spirit, which God meant every local assembly to have and use!

We do not want anyone to be scared by the contents of this last short chapter. We are to be as wise as serpents (demons) and harmless as doves (the Holy Spirit), we are not to be tricked by Satan, but to know and recognize the true from the false. Both exist. Thank God, He has fully provided for His children, at the tremendous cost of the sacred blood of Christ, a *power* infinitely greater and superior to anything that the devil can counterfeit, and that true believers in all circumstances may fearlessly stand on His specific promise, "*Behold, I give unto you the **authority**...over **all** the power of the enemy, and nothing shall by any means hurt you.*" (Luke 10:19). Remember Satan and his demons are still absolutely subject to almighty God, and are not free agents to do what they want, but only what God permits. God delights to prove us to see whether we will search the Scripture or be deceived through ignorance.

Covet earnestly the *best gifts*.

DIVINE HEALTH

CONTENTS

1

IS THERE NO PHYSICIAN?

Many of the inspired writers of Holy Scripture ask questions. This is first to draw our attention to a fact and to make us think. The questions are not irrelevant, neither are they empty, but are asked with the one intention that a positive answer might be given. Some of these questions are very challenging, and we do well to ponder them if we are to find solutions to life's many problems.

Perhaps the greatest problem of the human race is the search for health. Millions and millions of dollars are spent annually building more modern hospitals, installing more modern equipment with up-to-date techniques of medicine. After all this tremendous effort of time and money, there is always a waiting list for those who seek hospital beds. It is true to say that many people amass a fortune and then fail to enjoy it because sickness takes its ultimate toll. Scientists are ever seeking the elixir of life; they search the jungles, the riverbeds, and the deserts for new and powerful drugs to kill unwanted bacteria. *Health* is an important word in modern civilization, but is as elusive as a will-o-the-wisp.

Almighty God, inspiring His prophet Jeremiah, spoke to His ancient people in Israel. He asked a question. We do well to ponder this question in our modern space age. *"Is there no balm in Gilead, is there no physician there? Why then is there no recovery for the health of the daughter of my people?"* (Jeremiah 8:22).

Many questions arise out of this leading question:

1. Why are people sick?

2. Why are they not healed?

3. Is there no medicine that will heal them all?

4. Have they not got a reliable physician who never loses a case?

We are told by modernistic apologetic church leaders that God heals today through medicine and doctors; in other words, the medical profession seems to have been deified by many and represents the only hope in a so-called modern world. If the medical profession fails, we have no hope, for they have become as God, Yet in spite of this attitude, sickness would appear to be on the increase, and when one powerful "miracle" drug stamps out one particular strain of germ, another drug resistant genus arises that defies medical science; in addition on to this, many horrible side effects are now being noticed and the whole balance of nature in man is being upset, and various other ailments and allergies become manifest and so a new search is made for new types of drugs to cure the new set of conditions.

Perhaps the most tragic case in recent drug history was that of thalidomide, which caused the malformation of thousands of children throughout the world, for expectant mothers were not prepared to put up with nausea and discomfort for a short period to ensure the entrance into this world of fit children. No sooner is a child born in a modern hospital than it is taken from a mother who is already supplied by God with all the necessary food, aperients, and vitamins in breast milk, and put on to a "formula," which can never equal what God has already created and supplied. No wonder many grow up subject to attacks on the body in later years.

Man is always trying to beat God and will never succeed!

Showing with what grief and compassion the Lord looks upon a disobedient people, we refer to another question asked through His prophet Isaiah,

> *Why should you be stricken again? You will revolt more and more. The whole head is sick, and the whole heart faints. From the sole of the foot even to the head, there is no soundness in it, but wounds and bruises and putrefying sores; they have not been closed or bound up, or soothed with ointment.* (Isaiah 1:5–6)

The cause of total national sickness is given in one word, "rebellion." God's remedies, potions, promises, laws, and statutes must be improved upon by man; no wonder the apostle Paul in the New Testament gave us a jolt when he writes, *"But the natural man does not receive the things of the Spirit of God, for they are foolishness to him; nor can he know them, because they are spiritually discerned"* (1 Corinthians 2:14). Paul, a possessor of the ancient equivalent of a Doctor of Philosophy degree, said, *"the wisdom of this world is foolishness with God"* (1 Corinthians 3:19).

Jesus said we must become as little children if we are to enjoy the blessings of the kingdom of God. If we insist on being "grown up" and wise in our own conceits, therefore wiser than God, we can only expect to sow the wind and reap a whirlwind of increasing sickness, suffering, and misery. We only become truly wise as we seek His wisdom, which as we shall see in another chapter, actually gives us *health*.

In this cameo picture of sick mankind given in Isaiah, we find that man is sick in his head—his whole head is sick. Today our mental hospitals are being increased in size because of emotional troubles, because mental illness is increasing, and apart from terrible electric shock treatments and powerful drugs with their serious side effects, medical science is unable to do too much to help those whose heads are sick. When we realize that we are taught that man believeth unto righteousness with his heart, we realize that there is something amiss when he tries to use his head instead. An "intelligent" man finds it impossible to believe with his heart, for this is plain foolishness to him; but the man who falls in love with Jesus Christ finds the key to the kingdom that unlocks all the treasures of the kingdom, and one of the greatest of all treasures is *health!* God so loved the world that He gave. And He has been giving ever since to those who believe. His Son Jesus purchased health for mankind.

Second on the list of God's medical indictment of the human race divorced from His love, is the heart. The whole heart is faint. There is no real bravery, and the peace of God does not find residence in faint hearts. The medical profession informs us statistically that over 80 percent of physical sicknesses known to man today are psychosomatic, that is they are caused by fear, worry, tension, uncertainty, unhappiness, and a soul in turbulence. This is the exact opposite of what the Bible teaches is possible for a believer in Christ. So here we have God's diagnosis for 80 percent of man's physical symptoms, which man treats with drugs. If Jesus Christ was preached in all His fullness and believed upon, these 80 percent of maladies would clear up, because the heart would cease to be faint, and would become strong. King Solomon wrote, *"The wicked [the unbeliever] flee when no one pursues, but the righteous are bold as a lion"* (Proverbs 28:1).

After God's diagnosis of the head and heart, we now come to the effects in the body, and every organic sickness is included in the expression "from head to foot—no soundness." Wounds, bruises, and sores, and what a lot of long technical names are included in this simple statement of truth—bruises and sores. Any sickness that causes the skin tissue to break open internally or externally is a wound. Bruises can be caused by other causes than physical blows, for the nervous system can play havoc with a body that is not at rest and at peace with God. Sores or wounds that refuse to heal are far too common an affliction for us to comment further.

Mankind, on reading such a challenging question as Jeremiah asked—*"Is there no balm in Gilead, is there no physician there?"*—might answer, "Yes, we have thousands of physicians and multitudes of medicines." But the question comes insistently, "Why then are my people sick?" Man would quickly answer that he is making rapid strides in the right direction, and that given time he will come up with all the answers, and not only kill all known sicknesses, but lengthen life far beyond the three score years and ten. Man is slow to learn.

In Deuteronomy 28, sickness is called a curse. Curses come from Satan and blessing (including healing) comes from God. A long list of these sicknesses is given and most of these we are quite familiar with today *in spite* of man's advance in medical knowledge. In verses 58–61 we read of a dire warning to those who refuse to obey God:

> *If you do not carefully observe all the words of this law that are written in this book, that you may fear this glorious and awesome name, the* Lord *your God, then the* Lord *will bring upon you and your descendants extraordinary plagues—great and prolonged plagues—and serious and prolonged sicknesses. Moreover He will bring back on you all the diseases of Egypt, of which you were afraid, and they shall cling to you. Also every sickness and every plague, which is not written in this Book of the Law, will the* Lord *bring upon you until you are destroyed.*

Sin or disobedience to God and His Word will produce the causes that precipitate sickness of long continuance, which will ultimately destroy you. There is no cure known to man for these sicknesses. Is this not true of cancer and leukemia, although a cure is constantly sought.

We can tell you of a cure. It is Jesus Christ!

Again in verse 27, "*The* Lord *will strike you with the boils of Egypt, with tumors, with the scab, and with the itch, from which you cannot be healed.*"

Here is divine healing in reverse. Satan, the cause and giver of sickness, will be permitted by an omnipotent God to kill us, for there will be no healing!

No wonder Samuel said *"to obey is better than sacrifice"* (1 Samuel 15:22). What a sacrifice the human race makes in sickness, suffering, and death, because of rebellion against God and His Word.

"Happy are the people whose God is the Lord*!"* (Psalm 144:15).

2

HEALTH FOR THE ENTIRE MAN

In considering the subject of divine health, we must be careful that we do not give the impression that this gift from God only applies to the physical body. The body is the vehicle of the mind which, together with the spirit, forms the entire man. Man cannot be subdivided into three separate "pieces" any more than the Trinity can be mutilated. Eternal God is unity in trinity, and man likewise is a triune being, yet one person. Jesus was a triune man who knew no sickness. He proved that it was possible to live in this evil world without sin or sickness. Sin did not affect His spirit and soul and so there was no outworking of a spiritual malaise in physical manifestations called sickness or illness. He died as a triune Man in a triune God who, by the processes of resurrection brought Him again from the dead, always a triune Man. As a triune Man, He died for all other triune men of spirit, soul, and body. The salvation that He purchased, therefore, is for the whole man, not the soul only. In considering divine health, therefore, we must realize that this is for spirit, soul, and body of man, and when the spirit of man is at rest and in continual spiritual union with the Trinity, then also the mind will be clean and pure and full of God's thoughts and the body will not manifest sickness at all.

The will of God is given in 1 Timothy 2:4: "[God] *desires all men to be saved and to come to the knowledge of the truth.*" Jesus further told us that His truth would set us free, i.e. save us. The word "save" used so frequently in Scripture comes from the Greek word *sozo*, and is translated in several ways. In Mark 5:23, Jairus requested Jesus to lay hands on his daughter who was dying that she might be healed—the word *sozo* is used. In the same chapter verse 28, the little woman with the issue of blood knew if she could but touch the hem of Jesus' garment she would be made whole—the word *sozo* is used. In neither case was the soul of these two intended in the context; both were physical healing. In Luke 8:35, we read the story of the man in the tombs at Gadara who was possessed of a maximum of six thousand demons. He fell at the feet of Jesus and was delivered, the word *healed* is used, but the Greek word is *sozo*.

In the account of the man with palsy let down through the roof at the feet of Jesus, we read of the astonishment of the scribes when Jesus not only healed him of his physical "Parkinson's disease," but also forgave him his sins at the same time; thus sin and sickness were dealt with in one sacrifice. *"Which is easier, to say to the paralytic, 'Your sins are forgiven you,' or to say, 'Arise, take up your bed and walk'?"* (Mark 2:9).

In Isaiah 53, which proves conclusively that salvation is for the entire man, we find that in verse 4 it was prophesied that Jesus was to die for our griefs, and the Hebrew word *choli* is used, which includes in its meaning weakness, pain, and sickness. Obviously all these cause grief to the conscious mind or soul of man. Again, in the same verse we are told that Jesus would carry away our sorrows, and the Hebrew word here is *makob*, which means simply "pains." We can have pains in the head, heart, mind, spirit, and body. Pain is integral; if one part suffers pain, the whole body reacts to that pain. Therefore in this prophetical Scripture we understand that Jesus carried away, by bearing in His body to Calvary, our pains, sorrows, griefs, sicknesses, weaknesses, transgressions, and iniquities, and *"by His stripes we are healed* [in Hebrew, *rapha*]" (Isaiah 53:5). Jesus quoted liberally from this portion in Matthew 8:17 when He delivered those possessed of demons and healed those with sicknesses: *"that it might be fulfilled which was spoken by Isaiah."* Jesus not only made the way for the forgiveness of all sins, but for the healing of all sicknesses, by the one atonement.

David knew this and praised God in Psalm 103, because Jesus *"forgives all your iniquities…heals all your diseases"* (verse 3). How can we possibly refuse to believe that God's will is the entire salvation of the spirit, soul, and body of man? The apostle Paul wrote to the Thessalonians in the same vein, *"Now may the God of peace Himself sanctify you completely; and may your whole spirit, soul, and body be preserved blameless* [without blemish]" (1 Thessalonians 5:23).

We have proved that God's will is our health, but Satan's will is our destruction by disease, misery, sin, and early death. Paul informed Timothy of this spiritual principle *"that they may come to their senses and escape the snare of the devil, having been taken captive by him to do his will"* (2 Timothy 2:26). The Greek word for *"captive"* means "to catch alive." It is to be regretted that too many who make a profession of faith in Christ in our churches may indeed have been "taken alive" like a captured animal and then tormented with fears, frustrations, and finally beaten down into a state of physical sickness and nervous prostration. This is Satan's will, but God's will is our entire sanctification (see 1 Thessalonians 4:3) in spirit, soul, and body, already proved by his later statement in 1 Thessalonians 5:23. Remember that sanctification means the setting apart of our entire being, by translation out of the kingdom of darkness into the kingdom of God. This is salvation in simple terms.

Once the loving arms of Jesus are around us, and our arms are around Him, (love is mutual), He snatches us clean out of the arms of Satan who took us captive alive!

This is that we may now enjoy Him, who is the resurrection and the life. In John 10:10, the contrast is made between Satan who is a thief, killer, and destroyer, and Jesus who came to give us abundant life, resurrection life, which life raised up Jesus from the dead! (See Romans 8:11.) The word *resurrection* means to stand erect, not to lie down as in sickness, but to be on our feet and enjoy life and health. This is the result of resurrection life. Natural biological life (in Greek, *bios*) is the gift to all mankind, but the new life which is infused into us at conversion to Christ (in Greek, *zoe*), is an entirely different form of life. This "*zoe* life" quickens every part of our spirit, soul, and body until we are literally able to be vibrant with continual health. This is the heritage of a child of God, but Satan immediately goes to work with his lies and asks, "*Has God indeed said…?*" (Genesis 3:1). This is how he broke down Adam and Eve and then bound them. He uses the same tricks today if we will permit him.

Having this truth in mind the apostle Paul instructed the warrior Christian, clothed in the gospel armor, that after he has put on this armor, and taken the sword (the Word of God) and the shield of faith, that he is to *stand* and having done all to *go on standing*. (See Philippians 6:13.) As soon as Satan comes with his fiery darts and shoots them through the chinks in our armor, we fall down. Paul said, "stand in resurrection life." We say, "No I don't feel like standing, I want to lie down." Are we surprised, therefore, that Satan takes us captive at his will and binds us alive?

Thus, when we take Jesus as our resurrection and our life, His life quickens every part of our entire being as we go on feeding on His Word, praising Him in church and at work, and looking only to Him and not at Satan's continual attacks.

God gave all mankind divine health at Calvary. Satan spends his time cheating us by telling us this is a lie, and unfortunately we more often believe Satan's lies than God's truth.

In this present day revival and the outpouring of the Holy Spirit, much has been heard of divine healing. To some this gift of God in the gospel is likened to "treatment," so that every time a Christian gets sick, he knows he has recourse to the anointing with oil and the laying on of hands which save (*sozo*) the sick. (See James 5:14–15.) This must never be considered as a treatment. It is a way to permanent cure. Divine healing is the way to divine health. The first of the seven cardinal principles of Christ is that we shall not lay again the foundation of repentance from dead works. (See Hebrews 6:1.) We do not keep getting saved, so that one day we have it, next day we have lost it; we never again renew our repentance. The gift of eternal life is to be treasured and used. It is to be regretted that some people's conception of the love of God seems to be that He cannot keep us and so we are afraid of losing it! We should enjoy our salvation to the full! Once we receive God's offer of salvation we can hold on to it forever. Jesus said that if we follow Him as sheep and abide in Him, no one can pluck us out of His hand. (See John 10:28.) It is a sorrowful fact that too many jump out of His hand, and therefore out of the secret place of God, and so Satan attacks. He has a right to. Then sickness, sorrow, and suffering come upon us, and we weep and groan instead of rejoicing. God's will is our health. Satan's will is our destruction. What is our will? We must will to do the will of God without argument. Health is determined by faith and loving obedience.

3

DIVINE MEDICINE

Billy Graham has said that he reads a chapter of the book of Proverbs every day, for it is full of the wisdom of the Lord given as a special gift to King Solomon. In fact the whole tenor of the book is around "getting wisdom" as the principle thing in life, for those who get it, also get long life, pleasantness, peace, health, absence of fear, and vigorous life. This wisdom is available to those who come in complete childlike simplicity and accept God's way of salvation given through the sacrifice of His Son on Calvary. The blessings of God's covenants are so astonishing that the worldly wise are unable to believe they really can be true. There is indeed an elixir of life, though unobtainable to science yet available for the humblest child of God. This elixir, this water of life, this divine medication, is called the Word of God.

In Proverbs 4:20–22, we read, "*My son, give attention to my **words**; incline your ear to my **sayings**. Do not let them depart from your eyes; keep them in the midst of your heart; for they are **life** to those who find them, and **health** to all their flesh.*" In the margin of the King James Version is the alternate word for "*health*"—medicine. The words, the sayings of God, actually become spiritual medicine for all our flesh. This obviously is intended to cover the whole human body, with its bones, brain, nerves, and blood cells. Every single individual cell, which carries biological life in it, will become further charged with *zoe* life as we allow the word of God to affect our behavior, and as we become humbly obedient to His commands.

We once read of a lady who was so anxious that she should really take the Word of God into her being, that she used to write down appropriate promises of God on tissue paper and then eat them! Some might shudder at such an unscientific approach, for after all both the paper and the ink might contain poison! She was not concerned about this, for she was determined to get the medicine of the Word of God into her blood stream, and this helped her faith. It should not be necessary for us to go to this extreme, but we can take, eat, assimilate, and digest such portions as are necessary for our healing. This analogy is quite scriptural for Jeremiah ate up the words of God and the effect on him was to produce joy in his heart. (See Jeremiah 15:16.) Ezekiel was commanded to open his mouth and eat the words that God would give him (see Ezekiel 3:8), which was confirmed in Ezekiel 3:1 again to him, *"Eat this scroll"* was the peremptory command. In Revelation, John was commanded to take "the little book," typical of the Word of God that was printed into the common tongue in the time of the Reformation, and eat it up. He obeyed, but afterward this same Word rolled out of him like a scroll in the form of prophecy before the nations. In other words, what you eat you become! If we want health we must eat health, and this is obtained by taking into our beings the Word of Life, the elixir from God.

In the Ronald Knox translation of the Bible, recognized by the Roman Catholic Church, the wording of Proverbs 4:22 is very encouraging: *"They will bring life and healing to his whole being."*

In Proverbs 3:8, Solomon wrote again on this subject and we quote, *"It shall be health to thy navel, and marrow to thy bones"* (KJV). Again the alternate word for *"health"* is *medicine*, and this time this medicine is associated with our navel. We believe the reason for this is that the navel is that part of the body which was at one time connected by the umbilical cord to the mother. The navel is the place where life and nourishment enters the body before birth, and it is interesting that this thought is amplified in Psalm 119:130: *"The entrance of Your words gives light."* We are the children of God by faith in Jesus Christ, and the church is our womb, or place of safety, but we have to be fed constantly, and so we have an umbilical cord of the Holy Spirit which connects us to the source of life—God in heaven. If the navel had been diseased before birth, it would not have been able to pass into the bloodstream the good food from the mother, and the baby would have died. As children of God, we must be fed first on the milk of the word (see 1 Corinthians 3:2) and then grow to be able to eat the meat of the Word (see Hebrews 5:14) and so we will develop into strong vigorous Christians. Truly the Word of God is health to our navel.

Then we find that this Word is health to the marrow of our bones. This is very interesting, for after birth, and after we have ceased to draw life through the umbilical cord, the life process continues in the marrow of the bones. Marrow is the substance in which both the red and white blood corpuscles are manufactured, and a balance is maintained in their percentage depending on our health. As soon as poison invades our body, the number of white corpuscles is greatly increased and these rush away to the infected part and rally round, keeping the poison from further advance into the body. In Leviticus 17:11, we are given to understand that the life of the body is in the blood, and so the biological life of each of us is contained in strong vigorous tiny blood cells. No wonder David said that we are fearfully and wonderfully made—man, God's greatest triumph of creation. Satan can invade these blood cells, and the dread disease of leukemia will take away a life in a few months, but those who take the Word into their beings each day, will find that this word acts as a guard and preventative medicine for these life maintaining cells, and thus the very genesis of life in our bones is maintained at 100 percent fitness and efficiency. Clean blood then flows round our body, through a clean heart. The apostle Paul actually used this metaphor concerning the church and God's purpose, "*That He sanctify and cleanse her with the washing of water by the word*" (Ephesians 5:26).

We see here then, a principle. Not that we should keep on asking for the prayer of faith, although this is good and efficacious, but that there is a deeper way, the stand of faith, wherein we do stand against all the wiles of the devil and all his fiery darts. So many of his fiery darts are sicknesses. It is possible to take a stand. The writer of this book testifies that he has stood for twenty-five years by faith in the Word of God for divine health and has found that it works. Healing has been received from varicose veins, tobacco, sinus, liver troubles, and the strengthening of the right arm when the bicep muscle broke, so that the arm is now as strong as ever, in spite of the fact that medical opinion was given at the time that at least 25 percent use was lost in that arm. We believe God is trying to show us today that we can stand *in health*. Each time Satan tries to attack you in any part of your body, immediately claim the appropriate promise, eat it up, make it substance in your blood stream and in your heart, and being the incorruptible seed of God, it will spring up and produce of its kind. If you swallow "by His stripes I am healed" (see Isaiah 53:5), you will find the seed will produce this in your life, and healing brings health. If you swallow someone's opinion expressed in doubt, and probably telling you of some loved one who died with the same symptoms, then doubt has been sown, and this is not the incorruptible seed of the Word of God, and so the seed of doubt will produce its inevitable plant of sickness and death. What you sow you reap!

Keep eating the promises of God. Keep sowing seeds of God, for "*as [a man] thinks in his heart, so is he*" (Proverbs 23:7). The heart pumps the life giving blood to every part of the flesh of man. If the blood is pure, every other tissue will be pure; if we fill our minds with filth by reading salacious literature, by attending pornographic plays, and listening to filthy stories, then inevitably we shall produce the fruits of this sowing,

> For from within, out of the heart of men, proceed evil thoughts, adulteries, fornications, murders, thefts, covetousness, wickedness, deceit, lewdness, an evil eye, blasphemy, pride, foolishness. All these evil things come from within and defile a man. (Mark 7:21–23).

If any of these things trouble you in your life, you have not been fully cleansed within, and so your mind and body will show the effects of this internal filth. Once the mind has been cleansed (and our true mind is in our heart, for with the heart man believeth unto righteousness) then it can be said of us, *"We have the mind of Christ"* (1 Corinthians 2:16; see also Philippians 2:5). His mind was pure and He was never sick, He did not suffer because of His own sicknesses, He suffered for our sicknesses, that through His death we might be healed and find life and health.

Divine health for spirit, soul, and body.

4

THE TONGUE AND HEALTH

It has been said of overeaters that they dig their own graves with their teeth, and this is supremely true and will be dealt with in another chapter, but we wish to deal now with the tongue.

The tongue can dig a grave more quickly than the teeth; the tongue is untamable, it is set on fire from the very fires of hell, and is a world of iniquity according to James 3:8: "[The tongue] *is an unruly evil, full of deadly poison*."

It is described as a fountain, capable of spraying dirty water or clean water. It is like the faucet of a wash basin, it will produce hot or cold water at the will of the one who turns it on. The words that we speak come from inside of our beings. Jesus said,

> For *from within*, out of the heart of men, proceed evil thoughts, adulteries, for-nications, murders, thefts, covetousness, wickedness, deceit, lewdness, an evil eye, blasphemy, pride, foolishness. All these evil things come from within and defile a man.   (Mark 7:21–23)

A simple definition of the word *"defile"* is "to make unclean." An unclean mind produces an unclean body, and uncleanness, both spiritual and physical, produces disease.

Wise King Solomon wrote, "*There is one who speaks like the piercings of a sword, but the tongue of the wise promotes health*" (Proverbs 12:18). The words that proceed from our tongues will give clear evidence of the state of our health. Dr. William Standish Reed, MD, of the Christian Medical Foundation, Medford, Oregon, informed us that such terribly destructive things as criticism, grumbling, self-pity, hatred, curs-ing, and bearing grudges, are the cause of much physical sickness, and all these things are manifest through the tongue. Solomon again wrote, "*You are snared with the words of your mouth, you are taken by the words of thy mouth*" (Proverbs 6:2). It is we ourselves who destroy ourselves. Satan puts into our heart all these evil thoughts that find their inevitable expression as words in our mouth, and as we speak them we ensnare ourselves so that Satan will then come along and tell us there is no hope for us, for He is the angel of death, and the wages of sin is death.

No wonder Solomon warned that these words of hate, envy, and criticism are as "piercings of a sword." (See Proverbs 12:18.) There is always a positive for a negative, a day for a night, light for darkness, and thank God, there is another sword than that of Satan—the sword of the Spirit, which is the Word of God. The same tongue that spewed out vile evil things, which corrupted and destroyed us, can be tamed, but not by ourselves, only by a true work of God by the rebirth by the Spirit of God, so that our whole nature is changed, and now the heart which was the cesspool of every foul thought becomes cleansed by the blood of Jesus, and instead of unclean water spilling out of the orifice of our lives, now the Holy Spirit will give us words of truth, of life, and of health. *"The tongue of the wise promotes **health**"* (Proverbs 12:18).

It should not surprise anyone that the first manifestation of the baptism in the Spirit as recorded in Acts 2:4 is a torrent of "glossolalia," or words of another tongue being transmitted from heaven by the power of the Holy Spirit, and coming right into our innermost beings, and flowing out of our tongues as the Word of God, the verbal manifestation of the Logos of God. He who was made flesh now appearing in our flesh. His flesh was never sick, He had divine health, and so may we. *"He who believes in me...out of his heart will flow rivers of living water. But this He spoke concerning the Spirit"* (John 7:38–39).

We can slash ourselves to an early death with the sword of our tongues, or we can pour life giving words, not only to ourselves, but to those who are fortunate enough to be within hearing of the gracious words that flow out of our mouths. By being filled with the Spirit and continually allowing Him to have His way, we can become fountains of life, spraying out life-giving water in the foul desert which we are pleased to call "modern civilization."

It is useless to come for the prayer of faith by any man of God who has a healing ministry today, unless we first examine our hearts to see whether there is any wicked way in us. It is not enough to have entered into the covenant of salvation, and to agree that Jesus is the Great Physician, unless we first examine ourselves, and this we are supposed to do every time we approach the communion table. We can always appropriate divine health afresh around the communion table. It is the table of the Lord spread before us in the presence of our enemies. It is loaded down with good things. (See Psalm 23.) The apostle Paul was insistent when he wrote, *"Let a man examine himself, and so let him eat of the bread and drink of the cup"* (1 Corinthians 11:28). As we partake of the bread we are actually partaking by faith of the very health that was in the body of Jesus, which was broken for us. As we drink the wine, we are receiving by faith the very life that was in Jesus, for the life—His life—is in His blood. (See Leviticus 17:11.) The apostle John made it equally clear that we are only cleansed from *all* sin by the blood of Jesus as we continue to walk in the light of His Word and obey it. (See 1 John 1:7.) If we grumble, criticize, or bear grudges with an unforgiving spirit, we put ourselves *outside* the terms of the new covenant in Christ's blood, and it matters not how many pray for us, or how many times we are prayed for, we shall not receive our healing, until the sin of these things is confessed and put under the blood! Once these terrible destroying sins are confessed and forsaken, it must be a permanent act of forsaking, and we must always be on guard against the subtle temptations of Satan to cause us again to use our tongues in this soul destroying manner. We must work out our salvation with fear and trembling, not treat it as some light thing. (See Philippians 2:2.)

Much of the work of psychiatrists is to probe deep into our subconscious minds to find these hidden resentments which tear our minds and bodies in pieces. In most cases the causes of distresses are unknown to the sufferer until such probings bare them to view, and thus many healings are produced by this psychiatry. How much better for the individual to ask God to shine the light of His Holy Spirit into the depths of our minds and bring to light the very causes of our mental and physical sicknesses! He will do it every time if we are sincere, and then we can confess it to Him, forsake it, and then receive not only healing, but continuing health. "*Create in me a clean heart, O God, and renew a steadfast spirit within me*" (Psalm 51:10).

It has been our experience in this ministry that when questioning people who are terribly bound or sick, the Holy Spirit has frequently revealed the hidden cause, and when this has been told the person, confession has been made and quite frequently strong demons have been cast out that have taken possession of the life. Sometimes, however, the person has not been willing to confess what the Holy Spirit has revealed, and so no healing occurred, for Satan has a legal right to occupy such a person, and to visit sickness upon them, and we cannot pray against the immutable laws of God. God is using many men of God in various denominations to pray the prayer of faith and bring healing to many people, but until and unless these people confess hidden resentment, jealousy, or criticism, they can be prayed for by many of these men, and will not be healed, and it must be sadly admitted that many seek healing today in churches, tents, and public halls, who are not willing to examine themselves and confess their faults. James said, "*Confess your trespasses to one another, and pray for one another, that you may be healed*" (James 5:16). We would hasten to say that such healing as a gift from God can be maintained providing we maintain our position in confession and forsaking. God heals to give us health.

No wonder Jesus said, "*Sin no more, lest a worse thing come upon you*" (John 5:14). This man had been impotent in a bed for thirty-six years. Sin had caused his paralysis; who knows if it may not have been bitterness or inability to forgive?

In our own ministry we have found that many painful maladies, such as arthritis, bursitis, and ulcers have been caused by bitterness, criticism, and an unforgiving spirit. The speed of healing from these things after confession has sometimes been amazing. It can even be instantaneous! Only God knows how many other terrible killing sicknesses may not be caused by these mental sins, and again we repeat that probably over 80 percent of all physical sicknesses are the result of the thoughts that find expression in our tongues.

"Oh, that men would give thanks to the Lord for His goodness, and for His wonderful works to the children of men!" (Psalm 107:8). There is health in praise. We know one child of God who warned his workmates that he would audibly praise God every time they blasphemed His name. It is impossible to grumble and praise at the same time; it is impossible to criticize and speak in tongues at the same time. We are the ones who decide what we are going to do. Health is in our hands to hold and maintain. *"Does a spring send forth fresh water and bitter from the same opening* [orifice]?" (James 3:11). *"The tongue...defiles the whole body"* (verse 6).

What comes out of your mouth? The answer will determine your state of health.

5

GOD'S WILL—HEALTH

The laws of God are perfect and immutable. They cannot be changed by altered circumstances or centuries. God establishes a principle in the law and it is outworked in our day with grace. Grace does not cancel the law as some have taught; it establishes it, it confirms it, it interprets it. The writer to the Hebrews informs us that the new covenant is a better one than the old, because the old establishes the unalterable law of God and the terms of a better covenant bring us all its blessings instead of its cursings. We need to remember that a major section of the Old Testament law concerns the inevitable judgments of a wholly righteous God. If we disobey the law we reap the judgments, for "what we sow we reap." (See Galatians 6:7.) If we obey the law *in the spirit* we reap the blessings which include health.

We find then a law pertaining to health in the old covenant. This law establishes the divine principle that health is a rightful legal possession of every child of God. Health is written in the divine statute book as our inalienable right by law. *"Do we then make void the law through faith? Certainly not! On the contrary, we establish the law"* (Romans 3:31). This very exercise of faith confirms and establishes the unalterable fact that God has, provided *health* in His law. Satan knows this and goes around repeating his age-old phrase that destroys us, *"Has God indeed said…?"* (Genesis 3:1). Satan is a liar and the father of lies; his ministry is to cast doubt continually on God's established law. If he cannot keep us in ignorance of the law of God, then he will cast doubt on it by causing ecclesiastical leaders to tell us that these laws are contained in fables, and ancient traditional mythology!

What does the perfect law tell us?

If you diligently heed the voice of the LORD your God and do what is right in His sight, give ear to His commandments and keep all His statutes, I will put none of the diseases on you which I have brought on the Egyptians. FOR I am the LORD who heals you.　　　　　　　　　　　　　　　　　　　　　　(Exodus 15:26)

In this law, we have revealed one of the seven compound names of JehovahGod, *Jehovahrapha*. The word *rapha* means to heal or repair. This reveals one of the many sides of God's nature, *health*. We are not healed to get sick repeatedly, but as we learn to abide in Him, and His Words in us, then we can ask anything in His name and He will give it to us. (See John 15:7.) Some are content to ask for eternal life after the death of the body, and He gives it to them; others ask for an occasional "touch," and He gives it to them; why not ask for *health* and He will give it to us!

We have already seen that His Words give us *health*, and if these abide in us, we actually partake health through the divine promise, for it is written, "…*by which have been given to us exceedingly great and precious promises, that through these you may be partakers of the divine nature, having escaped the corruption that is in the world through lust*" (2 Peter 1:4).

The divine nature is offered to us! We can partake of it by faith and obedience. Divine nature has no sickness in it. Jesus was tempted, tried, beaten, and crucified, but He was never sick in the sense of having corrupting disease. He was tired, weak with overwork, and often hungry, but never sick. The apostle Paul told us the amazing fact that we are members of His body on earth. This is a physical body of flesh, bone, sinews, nerves, and blood. It is a mystical body because the world does not see it, but it is a real body as far as a Spirit filled Christian is concerned! "*For we are members of His body, of His flesh and of His bones*" (Ephesians 5:30). Our flesh, bones, tissue, and nervous system become the vehicle through which we manifest Jesus in the Godhead. As the Word was made flesh and dwelt among us (see John 1:14), so today this same Word desires to use our bodies—our flesh, and this flesh will be quickened by His Spirit, as we find in Romans 8:11; it is our "mortal bodies" that are quickened, not only at the resurrection, which is the final consummation, but right here and now, for Jesus does not want to dwell in a diseased body *now*. Put briefly, the divine nature can be manifest through our mortal bodies, and this surely includes *health!*

All law brings its blessings through obedience. Ignorance of the law is no excuse if later we find trouble in our lives. This law of health informs us that the way to God's health is by…

1. Hearkening

2. Doing

3. Giving ear

4. Keeping

We must…

1. Hearken to God's voice

2. Do what is right

3.   Give ear to His commandments

4.   Keep all His statutes

And then He will be our health. Can we do this? Only through Christ.

We realize that the natural man cannot do this. In him are the seeds of his own destruction, and it is easier for the carnal unregenerate man to disobey than to obey; his self-conceit will not permit him to bow the heart and knee to a higher authority. He preaches freedom and practices license that destroys him. Man will go to greater trouble to find a way around the law, than to obey it and reap the blessings. An example of this is found in modern day driving. Few would dispute that the speed laws are reasonable, and these are designed to give maximum safety to both motorist and pedestrian, but the self-will, pride, and egoism of the average driver causes him to disobey these laws, which are known and written for his own well-being. Most accidents are caused by the "human factor," and if everyone kept the traffic laws in the spirit, our accident rate would be reduced almost to nil. The law might say "thirty miles an hour" in many city side streets, but grace would interpret this as twenty miles per hour if children were playing. Only regeneration by Christ can do this for us.

We can obey God's laws, commandments, and statutes in the spirit. No man can be expected to obey every jot and tittle of the law legally, for the law of God is perfect and man is imperfect, but by God's grace we can, and we reap the benefits of a perfect law because of the perfect work of grace. In another chapter we will show how we can use the law today to produce health. There has been far too much teaching that because we are "under grace" we are "not under law"; which is true, but not the interpretation of some who therefore teach that we can disobey the law with impunity, for grace covers our sin—and disobedience of law is sin! Jesus did not cancel the Ten Commandments. He added a new law of love to them!

How much more therefore should we expect divine health in grace if we can obtain it under law! Satan, the author of sin, rebellion, pride, sickness, and sorrow, was defeated at Calvary and we are on the right side of Calvary today. No wonder it is a "better covenant." John the apostle tells us that he that is begotten of God does not sin (see 1 John 5:18), which does not mean he is perfect, but that he does not deliberately sin, and sin is transgression of the law. It is therefore necessary to know the law that we might obtain the blessings of grace.

The truths contained in this book were obviously known to the Apostles, and John the Beloved, when writing to Gaius, a pastor of the Apostolic Church, says, *"Beloved, I pray that you may prosper in all things and be in **health**, just as your soul prospers"* (3 John 1:2). If the pastor is sick, then what expectation can we have for the flock? Jesus set the example by never being sick, and He offers to His pastors health, that they may in turn minister health to the flock, for Jesus gave a commission to all pastors and elders, "*Heal the sick.... Freely you have received, freely give*" (Matthew 10:8). If the pastors are sick, how can they give to the flock what they do not possess experimentally? Let us hasten to assure all sick pastors that they can take health from the willing hands of a risen Savior, and then dispense it through their hands to needy congregations.

The pastors are called on to give health by the laying on of healthy hands in healthy bodies controlled by healthy minds, motivated by healthy spirits. Flesh of His flesh.

Health like sickness is contagious and infectious!

6

THE BATTLE FOR HEALTH

In reaching out for the goal of divine health, we could truly say that "It is easier preached than reached," yet it is within the reach of every child of God who is willing to endure the battles, and hardships, to attain the victory.

Let it be said as plainly as possible that the moment a child of God starts to claim divine health and to testify that health is his by the grace of God; he will find that Satan will counterattack with great ferocity to prove him wrong, and to rob him of his testimony. This is why so many do not attain. There is a faith barrier through which we must go. A few years ago it was considered impossible for an airplane to go through the sound barrier, that is, to fly faster than sound. On the other side of this barrier was the unknown; many thought the plane would disintegrate, and so there was much wagging of wise heads saying it was not possible, but some dared to try, and found it possible, which revolutionized flying and permitted jet passenger air liners, and the public will soon be traveling at more than two thousand miles per hour in aircraft carrying hundreds of passengers. Once through the barrier, the horizon of speed is greatly advanced. Once through the faith barrier, we enter the world of divine health.

The story of Job is our classic to show how we may obtain this redemptive blessing. Job was a good man, in fact there was none more righteous a man of his generation, and because of this Satan wanted to smite him, and God wanted to bless him and lead him through the faith barrier. Satan meant the sufferings of Job to destroy him, but God meant them to refine him. Satan meant it for his harm, but God meant it for his good. Which way are you looking in the midst of your sufferings? Will they break you, or will you break through?

Let us keep in mind that God's will is not for us to continually seek prayer for healing, but that we might come to a place where we know we are healed! We do not keep coming to receive Christ as Savior to ensure that our soul is saved; this is done once and for all, and this is borne out in Hebrews 6:1 where we are warned about *"not laying again the foundation of repentance from dead works."* In like manner, we are not to keep on trying to lay again the foundation of health. James wrote in chapter 5:11 *"Indeed we count them blessed who endure. You have heard of the perseverance of Job and seen the end intended by the Lord—that the Lord is very compassionate and merciful."* In Young's Literal Translation, the words *"perseverance of Job"* are given as the more literal translation from the Greek. He was both patient and enduring. Job endured; he did not give in; he refused to be bowed down; he refused to die; he refused to take barbiturates and psychiatric treatment, he endured and came right through the faith barrier and for 140 years knew no sickness and God added twice to him what Satan had taken away. This is divine health.

The story of Job makes it quite clear that Satan was the instrument of suffering, but that God not only permitted this hard test, but actually ordered it. We remember that Jesus, when confronted by Pontius Pilate and all the power of Imperial Rome, replied *"You could have no power at all against Me unless it had been given you from above"* (John 19:11). Satan can do nothing to us unless the Lord agrees to it for our good. Satan will mean it for our harm, but God will use it for our good.

God permitted Satan to destroy his home utterly, to take his children, and kill all his cattle and beasts of burden, and then as a final gesture of hatred, he filled his body with a terrible infection which came out in sore boils all over his body. If ever a man had reason to lose his reason it was Job; he could so easily have given up and died insane, but he refused to do so. His wife although a believer, albeit a fair weather one, offered the "comforting" suggestion that he should "curse God and die," to which he correctly replied, *"You speak as one of the foolish women speaks. Shall we indeed accept good from God, and shall we not accept adversity?"* (Job 2:10). A foolish person is one who does not understand, and we are surrounded by them in our churches today. When they visit a sick Christian, they show lots of loving sympathy, give flowers and get-well cards, but fail to explain that God is in the suffering and sickness and desires their healing and health if they will but believe. Jesus said that we should believe to receive. To doubt is to die. To believe is to live, for James tells us *"But let him ask in faith, with no doubting, for he who doubts is like a wave of the sea driven and tossed by the wind. For let not that man suppose that he will receive anything from the Lord"* (James 1:6–7). It is a matter of everything or nothing, sickness or health. The choice is ours. Most Christians today suffer some form of sickness, but it is God's will for them to be in health, if they will determine to break through the test of sickness and suffering into the clear air of health.

Job showed great wisdom when he said, *"The LORD gave, and the LORD has taken away; blessed be the name of the LORD"* (Job 1:21). We are told that thereby he did not sin, in other words, if we grumble, complain, and refuse to believe the promises of the Word of God concerning healing and health—we sin! No wonder Christians are sick!

Job did not know that God has forbidden Satan to take his life. *"And the LORD said to Satan, 'Behold, he is in your hand, but spare his life.' So Satan went out from the presence of the LORD, and struck Job with painful boils from the sole of his foot to the crown of his head"* (Job 2:6–7). Job was terribly sick, but he refused to give in, but nevertheless was prepared to die if this was God's will for him. He came to a place of complete resignation and rest; he said *"Though He slay me, yet will I trust Him"* (Job 13:15). It was at this point that he broke through the faith barrier into a higher realm of spiritual experience. Later he was able to forgive all his well-meaning friends who tried to comfort him, but only made his plight worse, and God *"restored Job's losses when he prayed for his friends. Indeed the LORD gave Job twice as much as he had before"* (Job 42:10).

It is our considered opinion, based on experience, that when we are able to come to the place of trusting God utterly, we win the battle and break through the barrier. It is then that Satan leaves us because he realizes he can no longer torment us as before.

Permit a personal testimony. At the beginning of 1948, God brought my wife and me into the greater understanding of healing and deliverance. The story is told in our book *Dominion over Demons*, and when we began to rebuke sicknesses and demons in Jesus' name and people recovered miraculously and many demons came out crying with loud voice, Satan realized that he had to stop us before we went too far! He therefore counterattacked us both, our children, the finances of the church, and everything that we had. We refused to quit, and a slugging match took place. Finally my wife picked up a virulent germ that attacked her heart and my body became so weak that I could hardly stand to minister, but we went on preaching and praying for the sick and casting out demons. We refused to give in. We refused to consult man, but trusted God only. In every case, God brought complete victory, complete healing, and full restoration, and we entered into a broader place of personal health, and also of greater usefulness in the Lord's work in bringing deliverance to others. We sometimes had to battle our four sons through from their temptations and trials; they were not aware why they were attacked by Satan, but God made us understand. Space does not permit us to give the many details.

One day the battle became very severe. Not only was my body weakened with unknown sicknesses, but terrible "nameless" fears began to grip my inward parts. Satan tried to kill us in our sleep. I was tormented and could not sleep, but the Lord showed me the cause. In despair I said to my wife that I would have to cease rebuking Satan and his sicknesses and casting out his demons from lives, for the battle was going hard against me. My wife was not a "foolish woman." She encouraged me not to give up but to trust God completely to see us through to full victory. I then went away alone with God and prayed. I said,

> Lord, You know that when I entered the ministry in 1947, I promised that I would serve You anywhere and in any circumstances, and I meant what I promised. Now Lord, if this ministry into which You have brought us means that I have to die, that Satan will kill me, I am willing to die, but I will not give in.

The Lord heard this humble prayer and I found I had broken through the barrier of faith into a realm I had not previously known—the realm of divine health. This was in 1951!

Sometimes Satan will attack a second and third time with severe illness, but again we press the battle to the gate and come through to a greater place of health and strength. Satan cannot kill us if God does not permit him to do so. Let us trust God completely in sickness or in health, and so break through into the higher realm of divine health.

7

THE LAW AND HEALTH

It will already be noted that the covenant of health given in Exodus 15:26 promises health on the basis of obedience to the law of God. Let us never forget that *"the law of the LORD is perfect"* (Psalm 19:7); and again in Deuteronomy 28:1 we learn that health is promised to those who *"diligently obey the voice of the LORD your God, to observe carefully all His commandments"* (Deuteronomy 28:1). It is only as we read on from verse 15 of this chapter that we find the long list of diseases that will come upon those who refuse to obey God's commandments. It seems that no sickness known to man is left out!

It cannot be too strongly emphasized that in no sense of the word are we justified before a holy God by keeping the law. We are made just solely on the grounds of the sacrifice of Jesus Christ in our behalf, for in Romans we find we are justified by grace (see Romans 3:24), by blood (see Romans 5:9), and by faith (see Romans 3:28), but never by works—*"knowing that a man is not justified by the works of the law but by faith in Jesus Christ"* (Galatians 2:16). However, the doctrine of justification must not be confused with the benefits that are obtained for a child of God who is elect unto obedience *after* we are justified by faith. We do not make the law void through faith, we establish it. (See Romans 3:4.) The law then works to our good and not to our condemnation.

The natural man is not able to obey these laws. Because he is rebellious and of Adamic stock, he finds that the law of disobedience in him is greater than the law of obedience! As Paul said, *"I see another law in my members, warring against the law of my mind, and bringing me into captivity to the law of sin which is in my members. O wretched man that I am! Who will deliver me from this body of death?"* (Romans 7:23–24). It is Jesus alone who is able to deliver us from the captivity of this law of death and sin working in our mortal bodies. No wonder we are sick!

When we accept Jesus as our Savior and Deliverer, He delivers us from the inability of obeying the laws of God. He puts a new spirit—His Spirit—within us, and He always kept the law perfectly. No sin was found in Him, and "sin is disobedience of the law." Jesus therefore saves us to obey God, not to rebel any longer. It is to be feared that the interpretation of the word "grace" by many children of God would be better called "disgrace," because they consider that they can do what they like with impunity, for grace has done away with the law. Paul did not teach this. He said, *"Do we then make void the law through faith? Certainly not! On the contrary, we establish the law"* (Romans 3:31). As the Ten Commandments were written by the finger of God upon two tablets of stone in Old Testament times, *this same law* is now written on the fleshly tablets of our hearts under the new covenant. (See 2 Corinthians 3:3.)

The impelling motivation for obedience—a new law—comes from the indwelling Christ who is the *Word* of God—the *Logos*. If He dwells in our hearts, then His law also dwells there. Now instead of being unable to obey the law of God, we gladly find ourselves desiring to do so, for we now *"show the work of the law written in* [our] *hearts"* (Romans 2:15). There is a showing forth, or manifestation, of obedience to the law flowing out of our lives. If we find the contrary in experience, then a true work of grace has not been understood or fully established in our lives. There is no room for rebellion!

There are many laws that have a most profound effect on total health in spirit, soul, and body. If we disobey these God-given laws, we do so at our own peril, for "ignorance of the law is no excuse." Perhaps we could refer to the "commandment with promise," which states that we shall have long life if we obey our father and mother and honor them (see Exodus 20:12, Ephesians 6:2). Long life in the kingdom of God is not possible without the good health that Solomon said we should have (see Proverbs 3:16) if we follow wisdom. Health prolongs life.

The law of the Sabbath gives us needed health. In the Second World War, munitions factories tried working seven days a week in England, but inevitably production quotas dropped off, and sickness increased. The human body was not designed by an all wise God to work seven days a week; it was designed to rest one day in seven. We are well aware that a Christian enters into the rest of the kingdom of God seven days a week, for Christ within is our peace, but the principle of one days rest in seven stands. This is cyclic and is a continuing law of God; cattle, machinery, and servants (employees) must be permitted to rest one day in seven, if they are to be in health. One who is "under grace" who deliberately disobeys this law will have a mental and physical breakdown, and it has to be confessed that many Christians do have breakdowns!

Farmers who leave a field to lie fallow every seventh year find that this field will go on producing, but if we try to get a crop every year without resting the land, it will become barren! There is even a law governing fruit trees. After planting, we must allow all fruit to fall to the ground and not eat it, and on the fourth year the crop is to be given to the Lord as an offering, and after that, from the fifth year onwards, God guarantees continuing good crops. Perhaps the failure to keep this law is a cause of much disease in fruit, which we counter by spraying with poisonous insecticides! We then eat poisoned fruit instead of good healthy fruit. This will contribute to a breakdown of health. (See Leviticus 19:23–25.) It seems that if a fruit tree fertilizes itself, it has strength to counter disease.

It is so often argued that the law was done away in Christ, by which many mean, it has no value today. The law is divided into four sections. First, the Decalogue, or Ten Commandments, which is the absolute basis of all law toward God and man. Second, the statutes, which are the minor laws, which arise out of the major ten. Third, the ordinances, which were done away in Christ (see Ephesians 2:15), that is the laws of the ceremonies such as circumcision, the altars of incense and sacrifice, the shedding of the blood of animals, the vestments, etc.; although all these have the spiritual counterparts under grace. Fourth, the judgments. The judgments for the impenitent sinner or nation have never been repealed, and even in the New Testament we read *"If anyone defiles the temple of God, God will destroy him. For the temple of God is holy, which temple you are"* (1 Corinthians 3:17). The apostle was teaching that the body of a believer is the temple of the Holy Spirit, and if these bodies are abused in any way, God's immutable laws would cause them to be destroyed in sickness, and breakdown.

Obviously, if a Christian insists on indulging in the deleterious habit of tobacco smoking or chewing, he will destroy his body, and the medical profession leaves us in no doubt about this! Similarly, if a Christian partakes of alcoholic beverages in excess he will bring on ill health. Overeating is just as much a body destroyer as starvation, and a Christian can claim to be under grace and yet dig his own grave with his teeth while going regularly to church, and heaven in the end! Paul said some strong words about this, *"But I discipline my body and bring it into subjection, lest, when I have preached to others, I myself should become disqualified* [in Greek, *adokimos*—not approved]*"* (1 Corinthians 9:27).

Why are Christians so stubborn?

There is a law in Leviticus 15 which deals with the cleanliness of bed linen and night attire. This is not ceremonial but practical! Disease will come to those who fail to wash bed linen, and underclothes. We can be under grace but get infections of the skin if we fail to obey the hygiene laws of this chapter. It is true that these laws do carry a ceremonial teaching, but they are also practical, and we are convinced that many of God's laws carry a very practical teaching, which will bring benefits of obedience.

How often we have heard that these laws were for the Jews. Let me remind you that Paul said, *"But he is a Jew who is one inwardly; and circumcision is that of the heart, in the Spirit, not in the letter"* (Romans 2:29). The child of God of whatever race has the laws of God written on a circumcised heart, and therefore is able to keep these laws in the spirit and not in the letter, for we are justified by grace and not the keeping of the law. Thus the argument or excuse that we are not Jews by race, holds no worth when we become Jews in grace!

We stress that we must not become legal in our approach to the law, for it ceases to be a stern schoolmaster when we accept Christ, and thereafter becomes our friend! As we keep the law in the spirit, we shall reap spiritual blessings that will bring health.

Before we close this challenging chapter, let us remind ourselves that the God who made us, has, supplied us with a list of foods suitable for human consumption and those which are not. Those who claim we can eat anything under grace (including rats and mice), do so on the ground that all the food laws of Leviticus 11 and Deuteronomy 14 were entirely ceremonial. It is true that they were ceremonial, and no Israelite would ever have offered a sow on the altar as Antiochus Epiphanes did in 20 BC, as an insult to the Jews.

But we believe they also have a very definite effect on our health; a very adverse one if we eat the unclean animals, birds, and fishes.

During the first World War, supplies of meat for British troops in Egypt was cut off due to German submarine warfare cutting off supplies of Argentine beef. An order was issued from the War Office in London that horses were to be slaughtered and the meat given to the troops. After a few weeks of this diet, an outbreak of disease occurred, and the health of the British troops was gravely affected, and so the order was countermanded, and the troops recovered.

The many references in the New Testament concerning meats were caused by the custom in those days of clean meats being offered to idols in heathen temples. The priests took their portion and the rest was sold in the open market. These clean meats therefore became ceremonially unclean and so Paul advised that they would become ceremonially clean when prayed over, but he was very quick to say, *"for it is sanctified **by the word of God** and prayer"* (1 Timothy 4:5). No amount of prayer over a rat will make it clean and fit for human consumption, for a rat is full of disease, as also is a pig! In the *Detroit Daily News* some years ago an article appeared in which it was stated by the US Health authorities that at least twenty-five million Americans suffered from the disease known as trichinosis, whereby the trichina worm ingested goes into the muscles of the body, and never comes out! This is due to eating pig!

In this much misunderstood passage in 1 Timothy 4:3–5 a reference is made to those in religious orders who would preach asceticism and the denying of the right to eat meats, and we have a carryover of this today in that many religions will not permit the eating of meats on Fridays, but fish only! This does not refer to the Bible teaching that certain animals are unclean. Even in the ark the unclean and clean animals were mentioned. If we are going to take this passage as meaning we can eat any animal we want, then let such as believe this fry some rats and mice, and pray over them and eat them! I would prefer to refrain! Some animals were created for scavenging, such as the pig, some for burden, such as horses and camels, and some are verminous, and some were created for human consumption such as beef, mutton, venison, etc. We must not conclude that this is "a doctrine of demons" to help someone to health! If pig has a trichina worm that gets into the human muscles and gives one a lifelong disease known as trichinosis, then we would suggest that it would be nearer the truth to say that it was a "doctrine of a demon" to eat pork!

Some argue that the sheet let down from heaven that was seen by Peter in vision, containing unclean animals which he was told to take and eat, now gives us authority to eat what we like. The interpretation of this vision is quite clear. "*God has shown me that I should not call **any man** common or unclean*" (Acts 10:28). Peter refused to "kill and eat," even in vision, and this was to show him that the Gentile dogs were about to be admitted into the kingdom of God, an impossible thought for a Jew!

In the first Council at Jerusalem in Acts 15, the findings of the Christian Council were that Christian Gentiles were to abstain from eating meats offered to idols, birds that had been strangled, and from eating blood (this has no connection with blood transfusions). The apostle James, the president of this council, stated that Moses (the Law) was preached in every city, and it was therefore not necessary to teach the law to the Gentiles, but rather to underline certain legal aspects for the benefit of Gentiles. (See Acts 15:20–21.) Paul later countered this rule by telling Christians that ceremonially unclean meat that had been offered to idols could be made clean if prayer was made over it, but it has to be first authorized or sanctified by the Word of God; unclean meats are not sanctified, they are forbidden! A rat and a pig are just as unclean in the New Testament as in the Old, and no amount of prayer will change the poisons in their carcasses one bit! Would you eat a rat or a dog if I prayed over it?

We realize that Jesus said that "*if they drink anything deadly, it will by no means hurt them*" (Mark 16:18), but He did not therefore mean that we could go ahead and tempt God by drinking poison, or handling snakes as some misguided people have done—and died of the snake venom! If perchance we partake of anything poisonous, whether liquid or solid accidentally, it will do us no harm, but we must not seek to tempt God by eating what we like. Many state that some of these forbidden animals taste nice. This has nothing to do with the matter. Many cheat, lie, and commit adultery because they enjoy it, but the wages of sin is death! Sin is transgression of the law.

We were once asked the question, "Can a Christian smoke tobacco and go to heaven"? The answer is yes, but he will probably get there before his allotted time! A

Christian can disobey God's holy laws in ignorance and incur disease, but still go to heaven—before his time, and with ultimate sickness of the body.

Surely obedience is better than sacrifice! (See 1 Samuel 15:22.) *"Why should you be stricken again?"* (Isaiah 1:5). It is not hard to read the law with love in one's heart and a great desire to obey God and His Word. Why should we rebel? Health is so important, that we will sell houses and lands to achieve it, after we have destroyed the body! Is it not better to obey and have health? This will not cost us much except our pride!

We cannot deal exhaustively in this short chapter with this tremendous subject of the law and health. We are convinced, however, that the truly dedicated child of God who applies himself to obey and keep the laws in the spirit, and not in the letter, will reap rich dividends in health.

CONCLUSION

When the thought of health for a Christian was first presented to us, it seemed an impossible utopian dream of a fanatic. Since hearing the truth, however, we have been set free from prejudices and have met men of God who have proved the truths of Scripture for over fifty years.

For our part, we have only known Jesus as Physician for twenty-five years since we first received the baptism in the Spirit in 1939. Nothing that has happened to us in that time has been too hard for the Lord, and the idea of calling any other than Jesus for our needs and the needs of a family does not occur to us. It is not wrong to call in the medical profession, who do a great work for suffering humanity, but we have proved that Jesus always heals perfectly and keeps us in health. To be *maintained in health* is better than to be healed.

The root word for *health* comes from the old Saxon word *hal*. This root also gives us the words wholeness and holiness. Most of us are familiar with the truth that the righteousness of Jesus is imputed to us by His sacrifice on Calvary, but we do not always realize that *righteousness* means *right living*, and it is we who have to outwork His righteousness, so freely imputed to us at no cost to ourselves. As we obey His Word, and this book has endeavored to explain some of the requirements, we walk in righteousness, which includes *holiness*, *wholeness*, and *health*. Jesus told us to *seek first* His righteousness, and all the needful things of life would be added. Who could doubt that health is a necessary requirement of a full and useful Christian life of witness and testimony?

We believe that if we can be humble enough in our approach to this tremendous but simple truth, we can walk each day fully trusting in the perfect work of Christ on Calvary on our behalf and *walk in health*, not being disturbed by sickness, sin and suffering all around us, but rather going to those who suffer with the complete answer to all their needs, with the compassion of Christ. If the law of the Spirit of Life in

Christ Jesus has indeed made us free from the law of sin and death, then we can walk through life as those who know they walk with Jesus Christ in His kingdom now. We are not waiting to get to heaven to enjoy health. By His stripes we are already healed forever!

> *Then your light shall break forth like the morning, your **healing** shall spring forth speedily.* (Isaiah 58:8)

THE EMERGING CHURCH

CONTENTS

FOREWORD

I am grateful for the opportunity to write a brief introduction to this book by Pastor H. A. Maxwell Whyte. I believe him to be a man of God well qualified to speak on the subject of "the emerging church." A leader in the charismatic movement for over twenty years, his is a rare combination of ministries, both traveling apostle and resident pastor; and God has generously confirmed both ministries with "signs following."

Those of us working in the charismatic movement in Christianity are keenly aware that the outpouring of the Holy Spirit is bringing some profound changes to the body of Christ. God is bringing us out of one thing into something else. The church is in the throes of a vast and profound transition. Therefore we need the setting forth of principles and trends this book affords. Such writing helps us along the way. Based on clear New Testament teaching, it lays before us principles of restoration while neither drawing hasty conclusions nor attempting to provide finished blueprints for the "emerging church" which God Himself is bringing forth.

I find the final chapter warning against false doctrines especially timely, for we live in an age when Satan is working overtime to deceive and confuse the people of God. Sound teaching based on the clear revelation of the Word of God such as this book contains is to be warmly welcomed. It should prove a real help to all who are currently interested or involved in the move of the Holy Spirit to bring the body of Christ into the full manifestation of New Testament gifts and ministries and Tinto the unity for which our Lord so fervently prayed.

—*Don Basham*
January, 1971

1

THE THIRD FORCE

In the early sixties, Dr. John MacKay of Union Seminary, the principal man in the World Council of Churches, wrote an article in *Life* magazine which received very wide publicity, in which he stated that a third force was arising in Christendom. Reckoning that the Protestant and the Catholic forces were the two main established manifestations of the church, Dr. MacKay wrote that this third force was neither Protestant nor Catholic, but seemed to be emerging from among them to represent a vital force which was growing quite rapidly; in fact, as some Protestant congregations seemed to be decreasing, many of the congregations of this third force were increasing steadily. He basically delineated this third force as composing Pentecostal and neo-Pentecostal groups such as Holiness groups that believed in a "second experience" following true commitment to Jesus Christ. The Pentecostal groups basically believed in the manifestations of the Holy Spirit as described by the apostle Paul in 1 Corinthians 12:8–10, including "glossolalia," or speaking in tongues, prophecy, healing of the sick and divine revelation.

This third force seemed to arise at the end of the nineteenth century when the Holiness groups began to appear, probably as a result of a revolt from the liberal teachings that began creeping in at the same time, destroying faith in the Bible as the Word of God. These groups referred to themselves as "Pentecostal churches," believing that they represented a true Pentecostal outpouring of the Holy Spirit to bring them back more into conformity with the Apostolic Church. Their insistence on a "second work of grace," which they called "sanctification," gave many of their members true supernatural experiences of the Holy Spirit, including visions, dreams and a deeper walk with God. This renewal seemed to be a precursor of a still greater work of the Holy Spirit that was to start at the beginning of the twentieth century.

The Welsh revival of 1904–1906, under Evan Roberts, was again a powerful manifestation of a new work of the Holy Spirit. In this short but world-shaking revival, people would fall prostrate under the power of God after having had tremendous conversions from their sinful natures and practices. It seems that in every new work of the Holy Spirit these manifestations occur. In John Wesley's day from 1735 onwards in the eighteenth century, people would fall prostrate, many trembling violently, and then after a period of time they would arise to their feet saying they felt cleansed inside, and often praising God with a loud voice singing the new hymns of the Wesley revival and experiencing a deep conversion experience which none could deny. These people were, of course, basic members of the established churches, particularly the Episcopal Church in Wales and from among the Congregational churches. However, many of those so affected were from no church affiliation. So great was the effect on the masses in South Wales that for a while coal miners could not work and public houses closed their doors, for there were no customers for beer or whiskey. Even worldly places of entertainment such as cinemas closed their doors for lack of patrons.

This manifestation of the "third force" in Wales spent itself after about two years and then there appeared a greater outpouring when the world was alerted to the strange stories of Pentecostal outpourings in Los Angeles, California. Unlike previous preparatory works of the Holy Spirit, this new one was accompanied by "speaking in tongues." Again, lives were changed radically, but a second work of grace became very apparent when these people began to speak in strange languages they had never learned. Whereas this phenomena had occurred in isolated pockets throughout the world when spiritual renewal took place, yet no publicity had ever been given, and it seems that there was no understanding of the significance of this phenomenon. One of the preachers named Walsh, working with John Wesley, is recorded as having awakened one morning praising God in a language lie did not understand, but he felt his spirit extremely edified. Charles Finney, famous for his revivals in New England, one hundred years after John Wesley, began his ministry by praising God in a heavenly language which brought great ecstasy to his soul while praying and seeking God in a wood. It was after this that his extraordinary ministry began. Again, in his ministry, people would be prostrated by the power of God, even when he walked past them.

It is interesting to note that the initial recorded instance of tongues re-appearing in the church occurred in Topeka, Kansas, in January 1900 among a group of Free Methodists belonging to the Holiness groups. This was in a Bible school whose principal was Charles Parham. This teaching spread to Galena, Kansas, and thence to San Antonio, Texas, from whence it was taken to Los Angeles by a black preacher named Seymour. The group who invited him did not receive his testimony, but others did. This always seemed to be the pattern of the "third force."

With the coming of tongues, the Holiness groups dropped the word *Pentecostal*, and this was taken up by these new groups which believed that speaking in tongues was a true sign of a Pentecostal manifestation. (See Acts 2:4.) In actual fact the word *Apostolic* came to great prominence at this time and was used in Los Angeles, where people would gather from all over the world in an upper room with a company calling themselves "Apostolic Faith." Similarly, at Topeka, Kansas, there arose an Apostolic Faith Church, and this name was also used in the early outpouring of the Holy Spirit in Great Britain. Eventually, two groups were established there, one being centered on Wales where the previous revival had taken place, and the other in England and Scotland. Later, Pentecostal churches arose in many parts of the world all claiming the speaking in tongues as either an initial or one of the supernatural manifestations of the Holy Spirit among them. These were independent assemblies which later began to come together for fellowship and which still later became denominations.

It is interesting to note that the prophet Joel spoke very clearly of these happenings when he wrote about the Holy Spirit being out-poured "upon all flesh" at a time of "blood and fire and pillars of smoke." With the increase of worldwide wars and rumors of wars, there would be an increase in spiritual renewal to counteract the flood tide of evil that would sweep the earth at the end of this Christian era.

In studying the development of this third force, we find that man made a mistake in putting denominational fences around a greater work of the Spirit, in many cases thereby preventing the Holy Spirit from giving an even greater unfolding of the plan of God. This had been done with Methodism, and later the Holiness church made the same mistake, thereby effectively preventing God from giving them any more understanding or deeper experience of His Spirit.

Then, in the sixties, we suddenly heard of Episcopalians in California speaking in tongues. Hard on this news, we began to hear of Baptists, Methodists, and other Protestant people receiving this tremendous Pentecostal experience; but this time it seemed there was a steadying hand of God on the whole happening in that these newly Spirit-baptized people tried to remain in their own historic denominations. They refused to join existing "third force" denominations, preferring to meet in study and prayer groups in their homes, while worshipping in their more formal churches. Billy Graham has recognized the fact that there are now thousands of prayer groups, composed of people from every denomination, praying and studying the Bible with a fresh anointing, totally ignoring the importance of denominationalism, which has been such a stultifying force in the past.

The writer has been privileged to speak to many of these prayer groups on this present charismatic outpouring and has invariably been asked the question, "Where do we go from here? We cannot study the Bible and use the gifts of the Spirit in our historic churches, and yet we feel we must stay in our denomination because we have

nowhere else to worship." We believe this is the restraining hand of God governing the work of the Spirit to bring the whole church back into conformity with His
plan and pattern. We are reminded that the early Christian church was composed
of Jews from among the Jewish state denominations of the Pharisees (fundamentalists) and the Sadducees (liberals), who commenced to worship in private homes after
their baptism in the Spirit as evidenced by the appearance of the charismatic gifts.
Obviously their form of worship was totally unacceptable to the state synagogue.

We do not for one minute believe that this present position is a final one, but rather
a fluid position as the Spirit of God breathes more heavily upon all Christendom, in
both Protestant and Catholic circles. The true New Testament church would seem to
be embryonic and soon to emerge upon a needy world.

The purpose of this book is to answer the insistent question: "What is God
doing?" Many have suggested that this speaking in tongues is very dangerous and
divisive; others believe that it is the one great unifier of the church to bring a final
answer to the prayer of Jesus that we 'may all be one'. Unfortunately we are basically creatures of habit. To an Anglican the Anglican Church represents the *summum
bonum* (highest good) of Christianity, whereas the Presbyterian or Lutheran is quite
satisfied with his form of worship, and the Roman Catholic, by virtue of his teaching
from childhood, is quite convinced that he is alone a member of the true church.
A discerning person, however, notices that these patterns are changing—and quite
rapidly, too. God's purpose is not to split the church, but to breathe on it to awaken it
to its full responsibilities in these days of great evil in the earth. We are reminded of
the time when Jesus breathed on His dispirited disciples, and said, *"Receive the Holy
Spirit"* (John 20:22). If ever there was a time in the history of the world that the whole
church needed a fresh anointing, or breathing upon, it is now.

2

THE ROMAN CATHOLICS

To understand what God is doing today, we need to go back into history, as far as the time of the Acts of the Apostles. If any Jew had told another Jew, by a prophetic utterance, that Gentiles would one day be members of the body of Christ, his testimony would have been rejected and he himself might have been ostracized. We have to remember that a Gentile was nothing less than a dog to a Jew. He was on the level of an unclean animal, and therefore, despised in a haughty, imperious, cruel manner. The teaching given to Jews from their earliest childhoods was that they were God's chosen people—and the only ones chosen. This teaching clung just as tenaciously to them after many had received the baptism in the Spirit in Acts 2:4. It was completely inconceivable to any of them that God could be interested in Gentile dogs. The Jews had their own form of "apostolic succession," from Abraham, Isaac, and Jacob, right through the prophets, up to John the Baptist. *"Salvation is of the Jews"* (John 4:22) was a favorite text.

How could God break through this inbred teaching? First, the apostle Peter was given a vision of unclean animals being let down in a sheet from heaven. The interpretation was given that henceforth he was to call no man common nor unclean. In the sheet enclosing many unclean animals, there was symbolized the many groups of gentile nations that would yet accept the gospel of the kingdom of God in its fullness! (See Acts 10:9–28.)

Again, by supernatural visitation of the Holy Spirit, Peter was told to go and find three men who sought him. They are all gentile dogs! God said, *"Arise therefore, go down and go with them, **doubting nothing**; for I have sent them"* (Acts 10:20). The result of this supernaturally commanded ministry was that when Peter spoke to them about Jesus who was anointed with the Holy Spirit and with power, the same Holy Spirit fell upon the first Gentiles in history, and Cornelius and his friends, about twenty in all, began to speak in tongues and magnify God. (See Acts 10:44–46). The apostle Peter was now in a very alarming predicament. How could he possibly explain this to the other ecclesiastically minded apostles? It could almost be said that nothing would ever convince them that Gentiles had been received into the same kingdom as them—almost. There was just one thing, and only one thing—the speaking in tongues. When Peter began to recount to the horrified apostles what had happened, he said,

> "And as I began to speak, the Holy Spirit fell upon them, as upon us at the beginning. Then I remembered the word of the Lord, how He said, 'John indeed baptized with water, but you shall be baptized with the Holy Spirit.' If therefore God gave them the same gift as He gave us when we believed on the Lord Jesus Christ, who was I that I could withstand God?" When they heard these things they became silent; and they glorified God, saying, "Then God has also granted to the Gentiles repentance to life." (Acts 11:15–18)

The very fact that the Gentile church has grown to such proportions throughout the world is a proof that God accepted Gentiles only through the evidence of speaking in tongues. This is so obvious that it cannot be denied. You and I can rejoice in being possessors of life eternal because Jesus baptized these Gentiles in the Holy Spirit and they began to magnify God in other tongues!

We are all familiar with the unbridgeable gulf that has separated Protestants from Catholics since Luther's day (AD 1517). Many have been appalled at the recent troubles in Northern Ireland, where one force battles another force with carnal weapons, degenerating Christianity into a dirty political brawl. The same mistake was made in history when the Swiss reformer Zwingli battled the Catholics, entering their churches and destroying their statues and high altars. This finally ended in a real war, which the Protestants lost because they forgot that our warfare is not carnal but spiritual. Zwingli lost his life. Luther never stooped to this error, and so lived to alert the world to the beginnings of a reformation that will see its last chapter written in our lifetime.

The first to receive the renewal of the Spirit in recent times were Holiness people, who had moved out from the historic Protestant denominations. Ultimately, large Pentecostal denominations were formed, which finally combined into a Worldwide Fellowship of Pentecostal churches and people who meet triennially for a worldwide witness of the miracle of speaking in tongues. It is estimated that in 1969 there were over fifteen million Christians who spoke in tongues.

Human nature being what it is, these people had no idea that God would ever visit the Roman Catholics with the same experience as on the Jews "in the beginning." We do not think we exaggerate the point by suggesting that the average Pentecostal believer would never have imagined it possible for God to give Catholics a Pentecostal experience. Every Protestant was aware of the errors of Rome, sometimes called "pretensions." The Catholic mass was considered to be blasphemous, and so it would have to take a peculiar miracle of God if He was to bring the Roman Catholics into this final third force. God did not change His pattern at all. He did it the same way as He brought in the "Gentile dogs."

Of course, recent history shows that many Pentecostal people were alarmed when God began to baptize the Episcopalians in the Spirit: The whole method of worship, the Sacerdotalism (the belief that propitiatory sacrifices require the intervention of a priest), the teaching of apostolic succession, regenerative baptism for infants, etc., made it quite impossible for God to choose many Episcopalians for this blessing. Later, when God poured out His Spirit on so many Episcopalians, they suggested that they really had not had the same kind of baptism in the Spirit as the Pentecostals had. A note of offense was seen. It takes us a little time to adjust to these hidden moves of God. But God did not wait too long until He started giving the same blessing to the Roman Catholics, beginning significantly at Notre Dame University in the United States. Was not Mary the mother of Jesus in the upper room on the day of Pentecost?

Protestants were not the only ones to get alarmed. The Roman Catholics from their side also began to be alarmed, because this Pentecostal experience had previously been peculiar to Protestants, who were therefore right outside of the blessings of the "true church." Edward D. O'Connor, CSC, of Notre Dame University, writing in *Testimony* magazine in September 1969, reminds us of the words of the late Pope John, who prayed, "May the divine Spirit deign to answer in a most comforting manner the prayer that rises daily to Him from every corner of the earth: 'Renew Your wonders in our time, as though for a *new Pentecost*.'" It was Pope John who informed all Catholics that members of Protestant churches were also Christians and had access to the grace of God, for he said that non-Catholic Christians are "in some real way, joined with us in the Holy Spirit, for to them also He gives His gifts and graces, and is thereby operative among them with His sanctifying power."

Rev. O'Connor admitted that he had been perplexed by this charismatic effusion and said that it is the view of many religious historians that Pentecostalism is by no means a branch of Protestantism, but is rather a "third force" in the Christian world. Rev. O'Connor gives it as his personal opinion that this outpouring of the Spirit upon all flesh (both Protestant and Catholic) is to prepare for Jesus a perfect people. He is right. He did say though that he had no idea by what steps this people will ultimately attain the unity that Christ intended for His church. This book is written to try to examine the whole spiritual renewal of the church and see what God has in mind. It seems quite clear that this present baptism in the Spirit is not to make Protestants better Protestants or Catholics better Catholics. It is much deeper than that. In the ultimate, we do not visualize either a Protestant or a Catholic church as such, we only see One True Church, restored as the final manifestation of the Son of God.

The present outpouring of the Holy Spirit has been quite extensive among Roman Catholics, and there are groups of priests and nuns and lay people meeting regularly to reexamine the Bible and to pray. The gifts of the Spirit are reappearing among them—tongues, interpretation, prophesy, and praying for the sick. Groups of Pentecostal Catholics are regularly meeting at Duquesne University and Notre Dame University, as well as in Boston, Rochester, Pittsburgh, Grand Rapids, Lansing, Chicago, and Ames. In every case, God has chosen speaking in tongues as the sign of unity, just as He did with Cornelius and his two friends.

What is happening? By this baptism in the Spirit, God is releasing His people from the unhealthy grip of ecclesiasticism, Sacerdotalism and priestcraft. He is breaking through hard, thick denominational walls by His Spirit. We observe two miracles in the world today. The breaking of imperialism in the control of certain nations over millions in other lands; the collapse of empire and the subsequent release of peoples to form their own governments, and the breaking up of ecclesiastical control, as evidenced in the present increasing revolt within the Roman Catholic Church, as thousands of priests seek more liberty of conscience—and the Pope is hard put to control the revolution. We do not think he can control it, for God is at work by His Holy Spirit to release the half-billion Catholics in the world from priestly control into the glorious liberty of the sons of God.

To those who are astonished at God's present dealings with the Catholics, let them remember that the Protestant church came out of the Catholic Church. Luther was a monk; he married a nun, and he remained a man of God. Let us remember such men as St. Francis of Assisi and Savonarola of Florence, Italy, who in their day were more interested in God than in the church. They may not always have been appreciated, especially Savonarola, who tried to reform the church in Florence, but they were members of the Catholic Church and God had respect for them. He is having respect for thousands today who are emerging slowly from the traditions of Rome into the truth of God's scriptural plan. It will take a little time, but first there must be the divine illumination, which alone comes by the baptism in the Spirit.

3

JERUSALEM RESTORED

Paul wrote to the Thessalonians, *"But concerning the times and the seasons, brethren, you have no need that I should write to you"* (1 Thessalonians 5:1). Christians are supposed to be aware of important events in the unfolding of God's plan of the ages. Paul explained to them that they were not in darkness, but were children of light. It cannot be denied that the conditions described by Isaiah the prophet are in the earth—*"For behold, the darkness shall cover the earth, and deep darkness the people"* (Isaiah 60:2)—but this is the very time that His command to the church is to "arise and shine." Being children of light, we receive understanding of world events from Him who is the light of the world. He sheds light on the sacred Scriptures and we become wise in understanding. This is why there are milestones in Bible prophecy.

Simeon was waiting and prepared to see the Lord's Christ before his death, and when he saw Him, even as a babe, he at once recognized that this was the expected deliverer of Israel and the world. His spiritual eyes were full of light. God wants His church—the body of Christ—to be illuminated as Simeon was, ready for every indication of His near return. We believe we have been privileged to see one of the most outstanding signposts of Bible prophecy in recent times. We speak of the Six-Day War in June 1967, when Israel won a war against the Egyptians as miraculous as anything described in the Old Testament. We are beginning to understand the tremendous importance of this event in retrospect as events further unfold. Let us remember that Jesus said, *"Jerusalem will be trampled by Gentiles until the times of the Gentiles are fulfilled"* (Luke 21:24). This event was the *great marker* for the restoration of God's Israel people after nearly two thousand years of terrible sufferings among the Gentiles. The very people who were given rule over them from AD 70, when Titus, the Roman general, destroyed Jerusalem, until 1967, were now to have this power and dominion taken away. The word *"Gentiles"* in this passage is translated from the Greek *ethnos*, which basically means a nation, and agrees with the Hebrew word *goi*, which is translated "nation."

The organization called the United Nations is, in effect, a full manifestation of the Gentile world powers, and is made up of the nations that Jesus had in mind. His words are of so great importance that they cannot be overstressed. He meant, quite literally, that the power of the United Nations organization was taken away the moment that Jerusalem was restored to the Jews. During the course of history, many efforts were made at the times of the Crusades to deliver Jerusalem, and all failed. Even in 1917, and we shall say more about this date later in this chapter, the British, under General Allenby, delivered Jerusalem from the Turks, and many become very excited about this prophetical happening, but still, Jerusalem had not been returned to its rightful owners. The British finally gave up their mandate and handed it back to the United Nations—it was too hot to handle, for Jerusalem is described as *a cup of drunkenness*" (Zechariah 12:2) to all who try to hold it other than the Jews.

In 1945, Israel became a nation, but it was not until 1967 that Jerusalem was handed back by almighty God to its rightful owners. Then we began to see the final chapter of the unfolding of God's restoration program—restoration for natural and spiritual Israel. No longer can any nation, or company of nations within the UN framework, have any further effect whatsoever on the destiny of the Jews in the Holy Land, or of the ownership of Jerusalem. Egypt may try to roar like a lion; the Arab nations may re-echo this roar, but the only thing likely to happen if the Arabs attack Israel again is that God will deliver more of the Promised Land into the hands of Israel.

This bears out what Paul wrote to the Romans 11:25: *"Blindness in part has happened to Israel until the fullness of the Gentiles has come in."* Again the word for "Gentiles" is *ethnos*— nations. The Gentile world powers have come to their termination date; the end of the Gentile image of Daniel has occurred. It is now simply a matter of realizing that Jesus also said, *"Assuredly, I say to you, **this generation** will by no means pass away till all things take place"* (Luke 21:32).

Many earnest efforts have been made by Bible students to date the beginning of this generation, especially from 1917, but it does seem that the generation referred to by Jesus is the one living now, at the time of the restoration of Jerusalem to the Jews in 1967. If this is a correct understanding, and we sincerely believe it is, then we are in that generation *now*, the generation alive to see the whole program fulfilled. A tremendous thought indeed!

We referred to the year 1917. This was a very important year in God's time-table, for it saw the capture of Jerusalem from the Turks, the year of the Balfour Declaration, giving the Jews the right under British mandate to return to Palestine, and the year of the beginnings of Communism, the devil's challenge to the kingdom of God on earth. It will readily be seen that from 1917 to 1967 is exactly *fifty years*, and this period of fifty years is God's jubilee of release. In Leviticus, we read, *"You *shall cause the trumpet of the Jubilee to sound…. And you shall consecrate the fiftieth year, and proclaim* **liberty** *throughout all the land…. It shall be a Jubilee for you; and each of* **you shall return**" (Leviticus. 25:9–10). The Six-Day War was a clarion trumpet call by God for the Jews to return to their possessions. It was also a trumpet call for the body of Christ to return to its full power and glory—to be the new emerging *third force* in the world. This force is the one that will take over the reins from the Gentile forces as represented by the United Nations!

Satan, knowing that his time was short, came down with great wrath (see Revelation 12:12) and created godless totalitarian communism, the red beast of Revelation 17. His idea was to take over the world through this system and subjugate all nations under communist rule. This red beast was to carry the scarlet-colored woman, that many identify as the Roman Catholic Church system, centered on the seven hills of Rome. This also is totalitarian and monolithic in structure and government. The purpose of this system has always been to take over the rule of the world, but their time is up. This generation will see the destruction of both systems; one will destroy the other, and finally the last power—Red Russia—will be destroyed by God at the battle of Armageddon. Fifty years of this system have passed into history, but already cracks are appearing throughout the communist world, with Russia now at daggers drawn with China.

Cracks are also appearing in the Roman Catholic system, as we see a worldwide revolt of priests and people against this dictatorial control taken in the name of a gentle fisherman called Peter, who, the best authorities say, was never in Rome, certainly never wore a papal crown, and never sat on a throne! We need to differentiate between the ecclesiastical system and the people. God is releasing millions of worshippers in this system from its intolerable bondages, so that they may have an opportunity of coming into the third force. We need also to keep well in mind that God has promised, through His servant Joel, to pour out His Spirit upon all flesh—and this promise surely includes Russian and Chinese flesh! They must first be rescued from bondage, even as whole nations have been released in recent years from imperialistic bondage. The day of the Jubilee has begun.

The word *fifty* is *pentecost* in the Greek. The day of Pentecost occurred fifty days after the feast of the Passover, when Jesus shed His blood on the cross for our redemption and emancipation. He died to make us free—free to enjoy His jubilee. There was a period of fifty days from the cross to the outpouring of the Holy Spirit upon the disciples. Truly their generation did not pass away until all these promises were fulfilled. What a tremendous time in Bible prophetical history, from the anointing of Jesus in the River Jordan to the first few years of the Jewish Spirit-filled body of Christ. The time we have come to now is just as amazing and important.

Taking a year for a day, which is a recognized measurement in Bible chronological prophecy, we would expect that as 1967 was fifty years from 1917, it would indeed be a day of Pentecostal outpouring upon the whole of spiritual Israel. This is, of course, exactly what is happening and it is apparent that all previous outpourings of the Spirit in this present century now seem to be focusing on today, when both Protestants and Roman Catholics are being released from their particular forms of ecclesiastical bondage into the glorious liberty of Spirit-filled Christians. The third force is emerging for all to see.

This is the time of the outpouring of the Holy Spirit upon all flesh, and this will increase rapidly from this time forward throughout Christendom, and is the only answer to the rise of godlessness and immorality. When the enemy shall come in like a flood, the Spirit of the Lord shall lift up a standard against him. (See Isaiah 59:19.) We are not surprised at Satan's great wrath, but we must certainly not be surprised at the restoration of God's great power to the church to save millions of souls, to heal them, and to set them free from Satan's demonic powers. Arise, shine for thy light is come!

> If I forget you, O Jerusalem, let my right hand forget its skill! If I do not remember you, let my tongue cling to the roof of my mouth—if I do not exalt Jerusalem above my chief joy.　　　　　　　　　　　　　　　　　　　　　(Psalm 137:5–6)

4

UNITY OF THE BODY
OF CHRIST

One of the sublime prayers of Jesus in the Bible is the one in which He prayed that His disciples might all be one:

> [I pray] *that they all may be one, as You, Father, are in Me, and I in You; that they also may be one in Us, that the world may believe that You sent Me. And the glory which You gave Me I have given them, that they may be one just as We are one.* (John 17:21–22)

Now if Jesus prayed such a prayer in complete faith, it is inconceivable that it would never be answered! There was a time when the church was in unity, on the day of Pentecost, for it is recorded, *"When the Day of Pentecost had fully come, they were all with one accord in one place"* (Acts 2:1). The result of this wonderful spiritual unity was that the Holy Spirit descended and the church was empowered even as Jesus received His anointing in the River Jordan before He began His supernatural miraculous ministry. (See Matthew 3:16–17.) If there had been no unity between the first 120 Spirit-filled believers, they would not have been baptized in the Spirit!

The type is given to us in Psalm 133, where the anointing oil was poured over Aaron's head and beard and flooded right down to the bottom of the skirts of his priestly garments. Aaron is a type of Christ, and therefore, of His church. The oil is a type of the Holy Spirit and the garments a type of the righteousness which all Christians have given to them after the cleansing of regeneration. In verse one of this three-verse psalm, the emphasis is on unity: *"Behold, how good and how pleasant it is for brethren to dwell together in unity!"* Only by agreeing to come together in unity of the Spirit are we going to experience the flow of the Holy Spirit in baptizing power. This unity is that the whole wide world might believe. It is not a theological intellectual unity.

Already there is considerable evidence all over the world that thousands are being baptized in the Spirit from all denominations. In every major move of God, whether in Indonesia, South America, or Africa, the same supernatural manifestations are occurring; the gifts of the Spirit are reappearing and miracles of all kinds are taking place. This is in order that the world might believe. There seems to be such a short time left to evangelize the world that without this extraordinary endowment of power from on high we cannot expect the job to be done. A third force must emerge from the scattered, warring denominations if the gospel of the kingdom of God is to be preached in all nations, with evidence, before Jesus comes. That this must happen is obvious to all who read the words of Jesus: *"This gospel of the kingdom will be preached in all the world as a witness to all the nations, and then the end will come"* (Matthew 24:14). Weymouth uses the word *"evidence"* for *"witness."* The witness of the church must be a practical demonstration of the power of God in evidence in saving of lives from sin, healing of minds and bodies by the working of miracles, as was done in the early church, as recorded by the writer to the Hebrews: *"God also bearing witness both with signs and wonders, with various miracles, and gifts of the Holy Spirit"* (Hebrews 2:4). Once the church is brought into the required unity for which Jesus prayed, the glory will be revealed, which He has with the Father, and this glory will be revealed through the church, which is His body, and once again, His ministers will go forth into every nation to preach, to heal, to cleanse and to cast out demons. (See Matthew 10:8.)

The third force that is at present emerging from the whole church is being brought to birth as a new creation. The Holy Spirit, in His sovereign power, is visiting individuals in every Christian community in every land. God is not honoring denominations. Men may try to cling on to them, but denominational walls separate Christians. When the oil of the Spirit flows, it flows over all equally, right down to their feet, with a total Spirit baptism. As soon as this happens, the happy recipients of God's power are no longer interested in denominational names, although some have tried to hang on to these names by calling themselves "Pentecostal Catholics" or "Pentecostal Episcopalians," or even "Double Baptists" or "Bapticostals," but this is a passing phase. God is pouring out His Spirit on all flesh, and no denominational priest or pastor can stop Him, for He said He would do it! There is a time for this to happen. There was a time for Jesus to be born and for Him to be anointed with the Holy Spirit and to be crucified. All these times were in the Father's hand, even as ours are in His hand. (See Psalm 31:15.) This is the time for the outpouring of the Spirit to bring the church back into the one unity for which Jesus prayed.

One can hardly even suggest that the Protestant church and the Roman Catholic Church are in unity! In fact, it is easy to say that they never will be in unity! The break in 1517 was but a break from doctrine. History recalls that the newly-formed

Lutheran church was not deeply spiritual. The Church of England, likewise, which broke with Rome to accommodate Henry VIII, became no more spiritual because of the break, but certain doctrines were reformed. Henry VIII had been made "Defender of the Faith" by Pope Leo X and carried this title still after breaking with Rome. Every crowned head of England has been a "Defender of the Faith" ever since. Looking away from the continual inability of Rome to agree with anyone else, we see Protestantism fragmented in many pieces. Obviously, broken pieces represent the opposite of unity, and, like Humpty Dumpty, there will be no mending or bringing together of these fragments, even if councils are called and great efforts are made by sincere (but sincerely wrong) men to patch the church up in order to help Jesus fulfill His prayer!

We suggest that no denomination, as such, is a perfect representation of the body of Christ that began at Pentecost! This is called "ecumenicity," but there is a true ecumenicity when God pours out His Spirit upon all flesh in this world. This is the true meaning of the word. The great efforts being made by man to bring the church into a corporate unity express a wrong motivation. There is no doubt that many of the sincere men are thinking of the shameful divisions in Christendom, and we believe are being alerted by the Holy Spirit to this fact, but councils and committees will not accomplish what God has promised to do when He said, "*I will pour out My Spirit on all flesh*" (Joel 2:28).

A reexamination of our position as Christians is necessary. A new appraisal of our understanding of the very words *church* and *Christian* must be undertaken, and all over the world today, people are gathering again to re-examine their Bibles. In the book of Revelation, the apostle John was told to measure (1) the temple of God, (2) the altar, and (3) the worshippers. It is not difficult to see the great differences that exist today. Anyone who has seen a high altar in a Roman Catholic Church in Mexico, or a simple Communion table in many Protestant churches, will realize that a reexamination of the altar is mandatory today. The ornateness and garish decorations and imagery of many temples is at sharp variance to the simple place of worship of many Pentecostal people. The worldliness of many who worship in these churches is at sharp variance with the teachings of all the early church fathers of the Apostolic Age. No wonder the call goes out to reexamine the whole system of worship in both Protestantism and Catholicism.

However, it is not until the Holy Spirit comes in baptizing power, as He did on the day of Pentecost, that we can know and understand. We believe that this is made clear in John 14:20 when Jesus clearly stated that it would not be until "*that day*" that His disciples would know and understand some of the deeper things that He was trying to teach them. He said, "*At that day you will know.*" On the day of Pentecost, they *knew*. Once a person receives this glorious anointing, he begins to emerge as a third force in Christendom, and this force knows no barriers; it is wide open to the power and love of God as represented by the gifts and fruits of the Spirit.

This emergence of the third force would seem to be indicated in Revelation 12, where the woman (representing the church at large) brings to birth a Man-child, who was to rule the nations. As Mary brought to birth Jesus the first-begotten of God, so likewise the church of today is bringing to birth a third force of spiritual power that will emerge as the full-grown Man-child, the body of Christ, the Son of God. As Mary was moved upon by the Holy Spirit, and the Child was conceived in her womb and subsequently was born into this sin-darkened world and then grew up in grace and was finally anointed of the Spirit, so likewise, the church is bringing to birth many today who are growing up into the fullness of Christ. There are some groups that have been teaching that they are mature "sons of God." We believe this is a very dangerous emphasis. Obviously, everyone born again into the kingdom of God is a newborn son (see John 1:12) and is an inheritor of all the promises of God, but he has to grow up into a fullness of responsibility, and this is emphasized in Romans 8:14–19, where the Greek word *teknon* is used in verse 16, meaning "a baby," but in verse 19 the Greek word *huios* is used, meaning "a mature, grown son." It is in this context that many go overboard in their "sons of God" teaching.

Obviously the world is waiting for a manifestation of the sons of God, but this will not be confined to a few small groups here and there, but instead will be a blazing, worldwide manifestation of Jesus Christ in His true restored church—the third force, fully developed. It will be no small thing. It will be the final manifestation of the Man-child Jesus in His body before this body is caught up to heaven to meet Him.

5

THE BODY OF CHRIST

The fourth chapter of Ephesians gives us the details of this restored church, and as we examine the simple teachings of the great apostle Paul, we must surely be made aware that God is now restoring His church. This is not revival, but restoration. It is renewal. Paul begins by teaching the "seven ones" of the unity of the body of Christ.

ONE BODY

As Jesus is the Living Head, so is the body composed of living human beings all filled with the Holy Spirit, controlled by the charismatic gifts of the Spirit, motivated by the Head. There is only one body, not fragmented into Catholic or Protestant sections which in turn are further fragmented into Jesuits and Franciscans or Anglicans and Pentecostals, but one body speaking the same thing! (See 1 Corinthians 1:10.) Now the fact that the church has been so fragmented since the Reformation is no reason to assume it will always be fragmented. Perhaps one great reason why the mass of people will not accept the Bible today is because of these shameful man-made divisions in Christendom. The Bible states emphatically that there is one body. In this final emergence of the third force, we shall see and recognize this one body. Although Jesus said He would build His church, man has been trying to do it for Him since AD 100.

ONE SPIRIT

Obviously, there is only one Holy Spirit, but there are many spirits. The British spiritist healer Harry Edwards openly admits that he heals people by the help of the spirits, but these are not the one Holy Spirit of God, which alone controls and motivates the one church. The apostle Paul speaks of *"deceiving spirits and doctrines of demons"* (1 Timothy 4:1), and it is these divisive demonic doctrines given by spirits that have so grievously divided the denominations, one against the other, because the very doctrines that divide them are satanically inspired! This is why Paul warns of *"false apostles, deceitful workers, transforming themselves into apostles of Christ"* (2 Corinthians 11:13). When individuals in the church finally decide that the Holy Spirit alone is going to teach them afresh from the Bible, then, and then only, will they be rescued from the astonishing bondage of traditionalism and false doctrine. This is happening today as members of the formal Christian churches are being baptized in the Holy Spirit. The resulting saturation of their minds re-orientates their entire ways of thinking and understanding.

ONE HOPE

The definition of faith is found in Hebrews 11:1. It is the solid ground that is produced by the exercise of our faith after we first hoped for something. Thus, before faith (which is spiritual) is exercised, it is necessary first to have hope, which is mental. All sick people hope they will get better; all bound people hope they will be released; and without this hope, we cannot begin to exercise faith. We must have the will to get better. The helmet worn by the warrior Christian of 1 Thessalonians 5:8 is called *"the hope of salvation."* This is because we cannot receive the benefits of salvation until our mind and will desire these benefits. If we have no will to be blessed, then we cannot release faith. We can only remain lost and bound in sin and sickness. This "one hope," therefore, would seem to refer to our earnest desire to partake of all that Jesus Christ freely purchased for us on Calvary, and to accept it gladly and enjoy it by our faith. As faith is a gift of God, He will give us the faith to receive the promise.

ONE LORD

The Greek word *kurios* is used here and is the title given to Jesus Christ. There is only one Son of God, and He becomes Lord to all who believe on Him and accept Him as their Savior and Lord. He alone governs their thinking and decisions. He operates in and through us by the infilling of the Holy Spirit—the One Spirit. The Bible teaches us that there is no other name under heaven whereby men can be saved. There is only one Savior. His name is Jesus. The Lord Jesus is the Head of the true church.

ONE FAITH

This is a very important "one." Today, we use the word indiscriminately. We speak of Roman Catholic faith, Protestant faith, and Jewish faith. A member of one group will say, "Oh, I am not a member of your faith." The usage of the word in the Ephesian context is the same as used by Jude when he wrote that we should *"contend earnestly for the faith which was once for all delivered to the saints"* (Jude 3). This is apostolic faith; the type of teaching that Paul gives us in this fourth chapter of Ephesians that we are considering. True apostolic faith may vary greatly from denominational faiths; in fact, it may be almost unrecognizable to denominational people, but it is true Bible faith that God is restoring today in this great emergence of the third force. As we have already stated, faith is a gift of God, and to enter into the great and wonderful promises of the New Testament, we must exercise this faith apostolic faith.

ONE BAPTISM

It would seem to some that there is a contradiction here in view of the doctrines of Christ found in Hebrews 6:2, where we are told that there is a plurality of baptisms; but this apparent contradiction actually bears out the fact that there is only one baptism related to church unity, and that is the baptism in the Holy Spirit. Water baptism is a symbol of death, burial, and resurrection, and is administered to those who repent and believe. It does not create unity in the body of Christ. It was the baptism in the Spirit that created the original unity of the hundred and twenty. They had already been baptized in water. And so it is a wonderful truth that as there is one body, so also there is one baptism.

ONE GOD

Even the spiritists and the Mohammedans believe in one God. The demons also believe and tremble. (See James 2:19.) It is not enough that all agree that there is one God. The Bible says that if man says there is no God, he is a fool. In fact, the definition of a fool is one who claims to know more than God. We must accept the revelation that the One God is only revealed through the life and death of the One Lord, Jesus Christ. Jesus said, *"He who has seen Me has seen the Father"* (John 14:9). To say that one believes the Christian faith without accepting the offer of free salvation given by the One God through His only-begotten Son, Jesus, is to be outside of this new thrust of the Spirit today.

Following these seven ones, which are a manifestation of spiritual unity, there is an eighth "one." This is called, in Ephesians 4:7, *"each one of us."* Youth today have coined a phrase to excuse their individual Adamic selfishness; it is "doing your own thing." This philosophy postulates that each person may do exactly as he desires, without permission from any human, government, or even God. God is interested in men and women coming to a point of complete acceptance of His way, for He is *the way*. One becomes a willing bond slave to Jesus. We have a Bible, a guide book, a textbook, which shows us the way to go and teaches us what to do while we go. We do not rebel or go our own way, for immediately, the bond of willing service would be broken.

It was John, in his first epistle, who spoke of having fellowship with one another, but this was not a carnal, organized fellowship, it was a fellowship in the Spirit of people who have repented of their sins, having them consciously cleansed away in the blood of Jesus, and then having been filled with the Holy Spirit. The condition of this fellowship was that each member of the one body would walk in the light as Jesus is in the Light and is the Light. But this verse 7 is further qualified by verse 3, in which John says that his fellowship, which he shares with other members of the body, was with the Father and the Son. Each member of the body of Christ must not only be in unity with each other in faith, doctrine, and practice, but also with the Father and the Son. No organized denominational religious body has succeeded so far in creating this unity! This is what Jesus had in mind when He explained to His disciples in disunity, that on the great day of Pentecost they would *know*! (See John 14:20.) Nothing less than the baptism in the Spirit as experienced on the day of Pentecost can start to create this unity of the body. It is from the position of a personal Pentecostal experience that we begin to move forward into the unity of the church visualized by the apostle Paul.

Again, referring to the teachings of Jesus in John 14:20, we see how this fits so perfectly with what John teaches us in his epistle, *"At that day you will know that I am in My Father, and you in Me, and I in you."* Before their personal Pentecost, it was quite obviously impossible to understand from the heart the meaning of total unity with Jesus Christ. We *in* Him, and He *in* us, so if we are in Jesus, and Jesus is in the Father, then we know and understand experimentally what it means to be one with the Father and the Son, and so have sweet fellowship with the Trinity, in unity with each member of the Spirit-filled church in its final form. Head theology would rebut this, but heart experience knows it is the *truth*.

6

THE FORMAT OF THE CHURCH

Unless we go back to the Bible and reexamine it in the light of the Holy Spirit, we shall never understand what God is building today. It is perhaps hard enough to suggest to people bound by their denomination that their sacerdotal framework is not the real thing. If we take away a pope, or prelates, we knock the very spiritual crutches of many away from them and they collapse in horror. If we dare to suggest that the first Communion was conducted by Jesus with His disciples sitting (not kneeling) around a common table, and that any addition to the simplicity of this is a redundancy, they will no longer hear the truth that sets them free. There was no screen between Jesus and His disciples. They ate Jewish unleavened bread and drank Jewish wine, and when He took a piece of this bread, He broke it and said, "*This is my body.*" He did not break His finger or a leg, He broke a piece of unleavened bread that was obviously typical of the breaking of His body at Calvary—a broken body that we might have a whole body, not only individually but also corporately in the church. The church was never supposed to be broken into small pieces. It was supposed to be *one* in unity. The very fact of the different teachings of the Communion service with altar rails, screens, priestcraft, and mysticism has kept the denominations apart. The baptism in the Spirit breaks this down.

A Roman Catholic Mother Superior recently came to my home and expressed a desire to study the subject of believer's baptism, for since she had been baptized in the Spirit and spoken in tongues, she saw things in an entirely new light. Papal teachings were giving way to the teachings of Jesus. I have had the great privilege of baptizing quite a few denominational ministers in water—the Bible way. As soon as we start examining the scriptural framework of the body of Christ in the first one hundred years of its existence, we do not find popes or prelates, but we find Jesus, the Head of the church, after His ascension, gave to the church *five* ministry gifts.

The five ministry gifts did not depend on the man, but were a manifestation of the Head—Jesus, who is the Chief Apostle. (See Hebrews 3:1.) Each was a Spirit-filled gift. The man was not the gift, the gift was a manifestation of the Spirit, and was given that each member of the body might profit. (See 1 Corinthians 12:7.) The word *charismata* is used, and is the same word used for the nine gifts of the Spirit enumerated in 1 Corinthians 12:8–10. Thus, the five ministry gifts and the nine charismatic gifts are to manifest Jesus in His various attributes. He governs, teaches, and empowers His body through using men to manifest Himself.

It is very hard for people to get their eyes off of man and onto Jesus. Most Christians admit that Peter and Paul were apostles, but they do not listen to their teachings! If it was suggested that God desires to raise up apostles today, most Christians would refuse to listen, and yet Paul teaches that the primary gift to the church is that of an *apostle*! The word need not trouble us, because it means a messenger, or "one sent."

In this present renewal of the church we should expect to see a brand new breed of minister traveling from place to place, teaching true New Testament renewal to groups in every city. Is not this happening? These "sent ones" will not teach or practice man-made theology, be it modernism or fundamentalism. They will teach about the restoration of the unified body of Christ. It is doubtful that they will claim to be apostles, for they may not yet realize their high calling! In fact, it is safe to say that all the five ministry gifts are emerging at this present time. The body of Christ is emerging as the new force in Christendom. It is being born into this world from the mass of born-again Christians throughout the world. The woman of Revelation 12 is indeed bringing to birth this great Man-child to reveal Jesus to an astonished world. Yes, *"God has appointed these in the church: first apostles, second prophets..."* (1 Corinthians 12:28).

There is a law in the Bible that cannot be broken. It concerns the giving of witness or evidence. *"By the mouth of two or three witnesses every word shall be established"* (2 Corinthians 13:1). A secular court will receive evidence against another party through two or more witnesses, which will establish the truth. The Jews tried hard to get two witnesses to agree to convict Jesus, but found it difficult! Similarly, the church. Such a tremendous revelation cannot be established by God unless He has on earth a twin supernatural ministry of apostle and prophet. The word of an apostle, without the supernatural help of the gifts of the Spirit through a God-ordained prophet, could not be accepted. For this purpose, He has given us the twin ministry of apostle and prophet, and then all mouths must be shut. It seems clear that in recent years this twin ministry has in very truth been emerging. Never have we heard of an "outbreak" of so much of the supernatural of God as in these days.

Men are using the Word of Knowledge with the Word of Wisdom on a scale previously unknown. Even a woman such as Kathryn Kuhlman has astonished many, and offended many, by her obvious manifestation of a prophetical ministry. She has caused offence even as Jesus caused offence, because as she ministers, thousands are healed by the supernatural manifestation of the Holy Spirit. A Word of Knowledge is given her when Jesus touches and heals. In Old Testament times, the nation of Israel was shaken by such women as Deborah and Huldah. Were these not prophetesses? Did they not confirm the Word preached by the patriarchs of Israel? Thank God, in the body of Christ there is neither male nor female, because the body reveals not a man or a woman; it reveals Jesus the Head. Again, it is not usual for these whom God is using to designate their office as a prophet. There are those, however, who go their rounds prophesying personal messages over eager people. We would warn that this can degenerate into personal fortune telling, the work of other spirits. We do not feel that a true prophet or prophetess of God would descend to this. Their ministry is a confirmatory one, to confirm the Word revealed by the apostleship. Their ministry is to reveal Jesus the Great Prophet to edify the church.

The third ministry gift mentioned in Ephesians 4:11 is that of an *evangelist*. This word is not much used in the Bible; in fact, we only have one recorded account of the actual ministry of an evangelist, but that is enough; for according to the law of first mention, it gives us a complete blueprint of how this ministry should function. In Acts 8, Philip went down to the Gentile city of Samaria and preached Christ to them. How simple! He didn't try to create another denominational group attached to "his church," he just preached the fullness of Jesus Christ—and the result was staggering! The people gave him close attention and they heard and saw the miracles that he did in Jesus's name. The preaching brought forth the signs following as was promised by Jesus (see Mark 16:17–20), and should always happen where true New Testament evangelism is practiced *the Bible way*.

The first sign that occurred confirming the preaching was that demons reacted most violently against this incursion into their realm and the city of Samaria, which they had controlled; they cried with a loud voice and then came out of many after their futile protestations. We have heard this thousands of times, and it still shocks people so that they will not invite into their churches any man of God who causes demons to react so violently, and so out of context with their normal practices! "Why can't this be done in private?" they ask. It can, but what happens if it occurs in an evangelistic campaign in public? I have been rebuked for causing these things to happen in public meetings, and some have turned away from the evidenced power of God in operation. Should we not rejoice when we see evidence of God's ministry gifts operating again in our day?

Not only was demon possession dealt with by the Holy Spirit, but also many began to be healed in their bodies, for many who were palsied and lame were healed. After this, it is recorded that those who believed the gospel preached by Philip were baptized in water—both men and women. No babies are mentioned, because, obviously, they could not believe. This is how God wants souls to be saved in His New Testament evangelism—by preaching and signs following!

The result of such activity by the Holy Spirit through the charismatic offices of Christ will be that New Testament assemblies will be created, and these will need proper oversight. Only a gift of a *pastor* can supply this local need. This pastor may or may not have natural degrees, but he will certainly have the spiritual enablement, he will be baptized in the Spirit, and he will be exercising the gifts of the Spirit. He will be laying hands on the sick and rebuking evil spirits and he will be overseeing the assembly so that everything is done decently and in order according to the scriptural pattern, and the people will rejoice every Sunday and they will come expectantly to church, wondering what is going to happen next and who will be healed and filled with the Spirit. His weekly teaching will agree perfectly with the apostle and prophet, who may visit his assembly from time to time to confirm it.

The fifth ministry gift is that of *teacher*, and this of course is not a person who of necessity holds theological degrees, but one who is energized and activated in his mind by the indwelling Spirit, so that he finds that he has an innate ability both to understand and to impart doctrinal teaching to local churches. It must be emphasized that this gift is entirely supernatural. In many cases, it operates like the gift of prophecy and the answer to a difficult theological question often flows through the lips of a Bible teacher by inspiration, he himself probably having little or no understanding of the desired answer. In the present outpouring of the Spirit, and the unification of the church by the baptism in the Spirit, probably one of the greatest needs is for God-anointed teachers to be communicating to the churches and in seminars verbally, their teachings multiplied by tape recordings and other such means as are available today. Unless good, sound Bible teaching is given at this stage, many will be led into the specious errors that are so abundant by false teachers today.

It is not enough that a person is saved from sin, or filled with the Holy Spirit as at Pentecost. After such wonderful experiences the New Testament believer must be taught progressively the doctrines of Christ. (See Hebrews 6:1–3.) He must be encouraged to use the gifts of the Spirit in the assembly for the edifying of the church. He must be taught how to use these gifts in the Spirit and to differentiate between "flesh" and Spirit. He must understand that the spirits of the prophets are subject to the prophets, which means basically that all Spirit-filled believers can exercise the fruit of temperance or self-control, and that the Holy Spirit never "makes" anyone do anything. We use the gifts and the offices for the glory of God, by the power of the indwelling spirit. He must be made to understand that, with every new awakening of the Holy Spirit, there is a Simon the sorcerer who will come and manifest his occult gifts to confuse the unwary.

Never before has there been such a day as this, when there has been such a tremendous rise of occultism with all Satan's demons on the rampage. When there is a heaven-sent revival, Satan also gives his counterfeit revival, and unless we are well-taught and come under the five ministry gifts of Christ, we may well be sucked into the false supernatural of Satan and be bewitched by seducing spirits and doctrines of demons, believe that it is all of God. Not everything supernatural is of the Spirit of God. Every one of the charismatic gifts can be, and is, counterfeited by Satan and his demons. There is One God and His Son Jesus Christ, and One Holy Spirit to manifest the Son. There is one evil genius, Satan, but he has millions of unholy spirits. These reveal Satan, but the Holy Spirit reveals Jesus, the Head of the body.

We believe that anyone who refuses to recognize the hand of God through the five ministry gifts is likely to come under the baneful influence of these other spirits today. No little groups or private interpretations will avail or prosper. This is the day of the revelation of Jesus Christ, and He will be revealed by the Holy Spirit according to the pattern already laid down for the rebuilding of God's temple.

7

THE BUILDING OF THE BODY
OF CHRIST

Following hard after Paul's teaching concerning the restoration of the fivefold charismatic ministry, we find a seven-point restoration program. It is not chance that there is a sevenfold program, because the number seven speaks to us of perfection. These fivefold ministry gifts do not replace popes, prelates, and councils just to make a change. These ministries are to achieve a definite purpose in the final restoration of the true church.

We read that the church is built upon the foundation of the apostles, who, in turn, are under the chief cornerstone, Jesus; but it is generally assumed that these were the apostles of the early church, and that as the early church gave way, first to the Roman Catholic system and then in turn to fragmented Protestantism, these represent the terminal condition of the church to which Jesus returns. Nothing could be farther from the truth of Scripture. Neither Roman Catholicism nor fragmented Protestantism will appear in the final building, because it is now that the third force is appearing. This emerging church will grow into the completed body of Christ.

This sevenfold program is as found in Ephesians 4:12–13:

> ...for the equipping of the saints for the work of ministry, for the edifying of the body of Christ, till we all come to the unity of the faith and of the knowledge of the Son of God, to a perfect man, to the measure of the stature of the fullness of Christ.

1. THE EQUIPPING OF THE SAINTS

The word here for "equipping" means maturing. It must be compared with the words used in verse 14, which follows, "that we should no longer be children." Most

Christians in our churches today are infants, still desiring the milk of the Word, but unable to digest the meat. They still want entertainment in many churches, music and social events instead of the Word of God. It is God's determined purpose to cause many of these to begin to grow and develop toward a more mature stage, through adolescence and into maturity. A study of a New Testament Christian, as revealed in Paul's teachings in Ephesians 6, shows he is a mature warrior, wearing his gospel armor intelligently, and battling continually against Satan and his demonic powers. We can pay lip service to this Scripture in our evangelistic churches, and ignore the reality, but the clear meaning is that members of the church must war against Satan, cast him out, heal the sick, and demonstrate the power of Jesus. *"the works that I do* [you] *will do also"* (John 14:12). Nothing more and nothing less. Only mature Spirit-filled Christians can qualify. How many are there? Their number is multiplying.

2. THE WORK OF THE MINISTRY

We have already referred to the ministry gifts to the church, which are, at all times, integrally one with the body of Christ. They work as a team and yet with different ministries. This is the ministry that God will use. It is inconceivable that any of the fivefold gifts will be of men who have not been immersed into the Holy Spirit and come up speaking in tongues as a beginning of their ministry. Philip started as a deacon and was promoted to the ministry of an evangelist. We would emphasize that in this study a careful examination be made of the details of Philip's ministry in Acts 8:5–25. Let this account be compared very carefully with modern evangelism as it is practiced today! All false ministries will be swept away by the Holy Spirit, to be replaced by His ministry, which will reveal Jesus as the Apostle, Prophet, Teacher, Pastor, and Evangelist.

3. THE EDIFYING OF THE BODY OF CHRIST

To *edify* means to build up. Peter gives us the thought of each member being a lively or living stone (see 1 Peter 2:5), which is used by the Holy Spirit and placed in its correct position in the body as it pleases the Father. Each stone is a replica of *The Stone*, Jesus, for he reveals Jesus and not himself with vain philosophy or vain deceit. He works in and with the body of Christ composed of many members. Obviously, before the church can be fully built up, the exact number will have to be put in place, and we believe the symbolic number of 144,000 in Revelation 14:1 indicates this, because this number is twelve times twelve thousand, and the number twelve is the number of perfect completion. Of course there will be many more than a mere 144,000 in the completed body, but they are lively, that is, all Spirit-filled.

The apostle Paul goes into considerable detail in describing this body in 1 Corinthians 12, immediately following the list of charismatic gifts that must be in this body. He mentions the eye, the head, the foot, the ear—some will have deep spiritual vision and understand the deep mysteries of God and will be able to impart these revelations to every member of the body. Some will hear marvelous words of prophetical utterance and hear deeper words of knowledge and wisdom for the blessing and benefit of the body. Others will have special gifts of healing and deliverance for the oppressed. Others will speak as the very oracles of God. Yet there are many members but one body. (See 1 Corinthians 12:10–27.)

4. THE UNITY OF THE FAITH

The result of the first three points will be a progressive moving of the living stones toward a unity of the faith. There were 120 on the day of Pentecost, and look what happened! They were all in complete unity and in one physical place. What will happen again when the Holy Spirit brings tens of thousands into this unity? It will be a worldwide explosive Pentecost that will shake the very foundations of hell—and it is coming!

In Psalm 133, we read of all this in type. It is like the oil that flowed over Aaron's beard and clothing, right down to his feet. His whole body was running with anointing oil, typical of the Holy Spirit. The 120 on the day of Pentecost were the first company to be brought into this New Testament unity, and the pattern has not changed since. Man has wrought the changes from the pattern in the church, not God. It will take God to get the church back to Pentecost again. As we shall see in the next point in this program, faith must come before knowledge. We have put the cart before the horse and insisted that the more degrees a man has, the more he is in unity with the Trinity! His church must be right—all right and nothing more to be added! Even now great efforts are being made in ecumenical circles to bring the church together. It is impossible. Their doctrines and practices are too far apart and cannot be reconciled. God must start again, from the ground up; but actually this stone kingdom of Daniel 4 is a pyramid structure, as we see on the back of an American dollar bill (which is no coincidence). The church cornerstone is at the top, and the five ministry gifts come under Him, right down to the base of ordinary members. The church is built from heaven by the Holy Spirit, not by man and his architectural designs, and it is only one body in perfect unity of faith.

5. UNITY OF KNOWLEDGE OF THE SON OF GOD

Not until the whole church arrives at the unity of faith, and comes together on this basis, will there be any new revelation of doctrine. There is a doctrine of Christ found in Hebrews 6:1–3, but these doctrines, including plurality of baptisms, are the foundation to go on into a maturity. Many of our churches, in their various forms, have not even understood all these doctrines, and so obviously cannot possibly go on unto perfection. "*Therefore, leaving the discussion of the elementary principles* [or doctrines] *of Christ, let us go on to perfection* [or maturity]" (Hebrews 6:1). Correct doctrine revealed to the heart is vitally necessary, and this will immediately show up the false doctrines held by millions in the bloodless cults that deny the divinity of Christ, the saving power of His blood, the reality of endless torment for the unrepentant and the nonsense of the soul-sleeping theory! True Bible knowledge is power. We know who we are and what we can do in Christ. We become conscious of the fact that we are indeed *mighty* to the pulling down of strongholds of Satan. Without the essential revealed knowledge we are largely impotent in the face of the enemy, whom many in our churches pretend does not exist!

It is one thing to have theoretical, theologically taught knowledge about the Son of God and be pat with our pulpit phraseology, but it is quite another thing to *know Him* and the power of His resurrection, as Paul prayed. To know Jesus, to be so vitally part of Him, flesh of His flesh and bone of His bones, is to know the power of His resurrection. This Holy Spirit infilling gives us a foretaste of this power, for Jesus said that we should receive *power* (*dunamis*) when the Holy Spirit comes upon (and into) us. (See Acts 1:8). It is this baptism into the Spirit of God that gives us practical understanding of what it means to be in Christ, He in us as prophesied by Jesus in John 14:20: *"At that day you will **know** that I am in My Father, and you in Me, and I in you."* Before this vital Pentecostal experience, it is not possible to know this fully, and therefore, not possible to know Jesus in the deep way He desires. Our knowledge of Him must not be superficial or hearsay; it must be experimental realization, with His life thrilling and flowing through every pore of our being, our human spirit being saturated by His Spirit. This is what is meant by *"the knowledge of the Son of God."*

6. A PERFECT MAN

Obviously, this refers to Jesus in His perfected maturity, after His baptism in water and anointing of the Spirit. The body of Christ in its maturity must reveal the Head—Jesus—even as He revealed the Father when on earth. It is staggering to every child of God to understand that the church will yet be brought into this amazing maturity. Jesus was only able to travel on foot and by donkey to cover a relatively small area of this earth. Now, tens of thousands of Spirit-filled ministers will cover the whole earth and preach the gospel of the kingdom, with signs following in a last-day visitation of God's power to this distracted planet. Radio and television will be used to cover every nation. Multitudes will be healed as they hear the Word of God preached in the power of the Spirit and then will be instantly converted, convicted of sin and filled with the Spirit and made whole in mind and body. Tape recorders will play the tapes of these men of God and video recordings will be seen in thousands of homes. The Word will go around the world and enter into millions of small transistor sets now owned by the multitudes in every land. Why did God give these to the masses? Obviously not for the devil's foolishness, but for His Word and His glory.

One Spirit-filled apostle will soon be able to stand before a TV camera and speak to billions of people all over the earth.

7. THE MEASURE OF THE STATURE OF THE FULLNESS OF CHRIST

What holy awe will come upon the masses in that day, when Jesus will be revealed through His body of flesh (our flesh) to the world! It will be the death blow to communism, which will have accomplished the work for which God prepared it. It will have destroyed the last vestige of the world image of Daniel 4, and then, in turn, will be destroyed by Jesus in *"the brightness of His coming"* (2 Thessalonians 2:8). We must remember that *"the brightness of His coming"* would appear to be the events that occur immediately before He actually steps down from heaven. He will reveal Himself to the world through His anointed body before He returns as the anointed Head. When we see the terrible rebellion of our young people and our working people to all authority, it must surely make us realize that God will reveal His final authority in His Son. Then every knee will bow! The measure of the stature of the fullness. Can we begin to imagine this? The measure of fullness of God's Son revealed in His body. We have to allow our minds to think over this tremendous statement! God's fullness revealed through you and through me! Can our mortal flesh stand this tremendous anointing? Jesus said so. He said as He was in this world, so are we.

This is God's final answer to this world. He will demonstrate His full salvation to the whole world as a witness and then shall the end come.

8

FALSE DOCTRINES—
A WARNING

The result of this great church renewal will be to restore thousands of people and show them new light and life, and it will show up and expose all the many false doctrines that abound today, many of them camouflaging themselves in a Christian guise—for instance, "Christian spiritualists." What a contradiction!

When Paul went down to Samaria, there was a true New Testament awakening, and this stirred up Simon the sorcerer so that he might be exposed. He called himself a great man of God, and the people agreed that his sorcery was indeed motivated by God's power. This was Samaria's delusion. Thousands followed him and were no doubt healed in their bodies, for "spiritual healing" is part of spiritism. With the revival in Samaria came the challenge of the revival of Satan's occultism. It was finally overthrown, and God's man, Peter, told Simon frankly that he had no part in God's work, and commanded him to go and perish with his ill-gotten money, gained from the exercise of occultic, demon-inspired gifts.

We remember a lady from Bermuda coming to see us. She desired healing in her body. I had already been informed that she was a spiritist, and so spiritual healing would not be new to her. I was quite honest with her, and said that I had been told that she was a spiritist and that she attended séances. "Oh, yes," she replied, "and it has made me a much better woman." It was then that I told her that the whole practice of occultism was strictly forbidden in the Bible. She expressed great astonishment and asked me where it was forbidden. I then read her the following: "*Give no regard to mediums and familiar spirits; do not seek after them, to be defiled by them*" (Leviticus 19:31). And again, "*The person who turns to mediums and familiar spirits, to prostitute himself with them, I will set My face against that person and cut him off from his people*" (Leviticus 20:6). Other relevant passages were read and she was immediately convicted of her sin, and she openly confessed it and received God's pardon and vowed that she would turn away from such things. I prayed for her and God healed her, and afterward, she was baptized in the Holy Spirit and spoke in tongues with rejoicing. She only entered into this renewal by forsaking her error.

There are multiplied thousands seated in our churches taking part in Communion services who are openly going to séances, having hands laid on them by demon-possessed witches and wizards, and those who have familiar spirits, and their clergy do nothing, for they see no harm in this. They are blind leading the blind. The sale of Ouija boards is increasing rapidly, and our young people are giving over their minds and hands to the actual work of demons. Horoscopes are read by millions as they feast their eyes and minds on the inventions of demons, and so receive their just reward in sickness and troubled minds. Even presidents and men in high political office have sought the "advice" of such spiritist mediums as Jean Dixon and others. Hitler regularly sought the advice of demons through his pet spiritist medium. The Witchcraft Act has been repealed in the United Kingdom and open witches' covens are now quite common, and the United States even has "black mass" churches in which the devil is openly and unashamedly worshipped with a nude woman on the "altar." Our universities have classes to study extrasensory perception and spirit writing. Articles have recently appeared in the Toronto press advocating experimentation with occult practices.

Tea cup reading, fortunetelling by cards, and palm readings are increasing as the spiritual vacuum in millions of people is being filled up by the devil. If man will not serve God, he will serve Satan. Paul makes this quite clear in Romans 6:16. He said that we are servants to whom we yield ourselves and obey, either God or Satan. There is no middle position!

In Ephesians 4:14, the purpose of the church renewal is summed up as follows,

That we should no longer be children, tossed to and fro and carried about with every wind of doctrine, by the trickery of men, in the cunning craftiness of deceitful plotting.

Our churches are filled up with those who are children, always seeking some new religious stunt or some questionable doctrine, and they are so easily deceived to their eternal hurt. Only God can change :his situation, and as He confounded Simon, so today, He will confound the occultists by true signs and wonders and gifts of the Holy Spirit through the hands of God's true charismatic ministers. (See Hebrews 2:4.)

Would to God that all who are warned today would so easily and beautifully depart from these practices as this lady from Bermuda, and their hunger for spiritual reality would be met by God, who would forgive them, heal them, and fill them with His Holy Spirit. The danger of these occult practices is that the followers will ultimately become demon-possessed, and on the way to this terrible state, they will suffer many oppressions from these evil spirits trying to gain their entrance. Stubborn sicknesses of mind and body can often be traced to the time that the sufferer first tampered with forbidden demonic practices. Did not Paul write, "*Some will depart from the faith, giving heed to deceiving spirits and doctrines of demons*" (1 Timothy 4:1)? Of whom was he speaking? Surely the Spirit-filled apostolic Christians of the early church! How much more do we need to warn all in Protestantism and Catholicism to "*come out from among them and be separate*" (2 Corinthians 6:17).

Remember that the true meaning of the word *antichrist* is not one opposed to God but one coming in the name of Jesus Christ and claiming to be a minister of His to deceive the people with seducing spirits or demons. No wonder John wrote that there were many antichrists in his day. (See 1 John 4.) How much more today when the church has covered the world. Paul said of them, "For such *are* false apostles, deceitful workers, transforming themselves into apostles of Christ" (2 Corinthians 11:13). Obviously, if there are false apostles, there are true apostles. The negative demonstrates the positive. Before the rise of the true ministry, we have seen a dreadful manifestation of evil through the false ministry. God works through His Holy Spirit; Satan works through his unholy spirits. Both produce supernatural signs, but God's signs show up the wrong signs. The serpent in the hand of Moses eats up the little serpents in Pharaoh's court. (See Exodus 7:12.)

If you are fascinated by the supernatural (and we should be), seek it among holy men of God who are manifesting Jesus as Healer and Deliverer, where demons are being cast out, not worshipped in many guises; where the gifts of the word of knowledge and wisdom are exposing sin through those ministry gifts to the church.

One of the most common demonic spirits afflicting Christians today is a spirit of fear, which Paul says God has not given us. This foul spirit has so bound many that they are afraid when they come in contact with God's supernatural power. When they hear of "the tongues people," they run away in terror as from something foul, whereas the glorious experience of the baptism or infilling of the Holy Spirit according to the pattern on the day of Pentecost (see Acts 2:4) is that which can flush out every wrong foul spirit collected by playing with demonic occult powers. This is why I always teach people to plead the blood of Jesus out loud when seeking the Holy Spirit. It cleanses their minds and sets them free.

Finally, may we lovingly warn all who have read this book to depart from these evil practices, to seek God's forgiveness, and to seek to have the application of the blood of Jesus to wash them clean, ready for the baptism in the Spirit and the resultant gifts of the Holy Spirit.

The issue is clear today—which shall it be? The teachings of Simon the spiritist or of Philip the evangelist? Both had signs and wonders, both proved the power of the supernatural, both claimed to be men of God; one was and the other was not. It is time for so-called Christianity in many of our historical churches to stand up and be counted; the day is past for mealy mouthings and sentimental soliloquies.

> *And they went out and preached everywhere, the Lord working with them and confirming the word through the accompanying signs.*   (Mark 16:20)

FEAR DESTROYS

CONTENTS

1

FEAR THE DESTROYER

F*ear* is probably the greatest destructive force known to humanity.

Fear breaks down, destroys, and paralyzes the human mind and body. Fear can so paralyze a person that they will be unable to jump from a burning house, even though there are firemen with nets below to catch them. In an instant the whole body becomes rigid with fear, incapable of moving. Fear is the root cause of what are called "psychosomatic" diseases by the medical profession. Continuing fear can induce almost any physical sickness, especially is this true with such diseases as ulcers, heart failures, digestive disorders, colitis, diabetes, and arthritis. These names we give to these diseases are but the physical symptoms and evidence of inward torment, and unless we treat the primary cause, the only remedy is to cut out by surgical operations such sections of the body as have become hopelessly affected.

Fear will so bind the human mind that a person becomes incapable of making decisions, and loses all initiative and creativeness. In the end fear can drive such a person to become a schizophrenic, who will sit for hours looking into space and nothingness, a living cabbage. Fear will cause a person to rob, murder, lie, and cheat. Fear causes international wars because of lack of trust and suspicion between nations.

Fear is negative faith. That is to say that with the degree we fear we bring troubles on ourselves, and with the same degree of faith we reverse the whole process and bring blessings upon ourselves. Faith only comes by reading, hearing, and believing the Word of God, and as the Word of God takes root in our thinking and thence in our actions, we begin to appropriate blessings from God that agree with His Word. If we do not read the Bible, and do not know of the promises of God which speak of quietness of mind, health of body, and peace of spirit, then we are an easy prey for the roaring voices of Satan and his demon spirits who drive us into a frenzy of fear—and then we are in trouble—we are on the skids.

It is not surprising, therefore, that with the increasingly strong attacks against the Bible both within and without the church, philosophy, psychology, and psychiatry have failed to stem the terrible increase of fear in the world. Unless people turn to the Bible for faith and consolation, they can only expect the best that the medical profession can offer: drugs, surgery, shock treatments, and therapy. Again, this is only trying to treat the symptoms and does not get to the root of the trouble, which is primarily spiritual. As Jesus said, *"An enemy hath done this"* (Matthew 13:28).

You will either have faith or fear. There is no neutral ground between. God wants to occupy our lives with His Holy Spirit so that our minds may be impregnated with His Word, but if we turn from Him and His love and protection, then we will immediately become an easy prey to Satan and his demons. The decisions you will make will not be your own, they will be demonic decisions followed by demonic actions; actions over which you will have no control. When Satan starts to drive a person to death, he never ceases until he kills them. Most people smoke tobacco to "help their nerves," and according to statistics they thereby deprive themselves on an average of nine years of useful life and die before their time. An equal number of years before early death will be spent in a sick worn out body, because the lungs, heart, and other organs will be greatly weakened. Appeals in good faith for such a person to quit smoking usually fall on deaf ears, because Satan has them trapped. Dying early holds no more fears for them. They are driven to death and settle for such a "bargain." No wonder the Word of God says, *"The wages of sin is death"* (Romans 6:23). Satan always pays in full.

Fear drives others to alcohol and they become stupid alcoholics. Satan drives them from their loved ones, breaks up homes, and finally destroys them on skid row.

Fear of people, fear of your job, fear of the unknown, fear of responsibility, fear of leadership, and no confidence in your own ability to do anything, ends in spiritual paralysis.

Faith was the dynamic force that caused God to create the heavens and the earth. Faith creates where there is nothing. Faith creates substantial ground to walk on where previously we had no ground. (See Hebrews 11:1.) Faith creates, fear destroys, with the same degree of faith that can heal, the same degree of fear will destroy to the same intensity. It is impossible to maintain health in spirit, soul, and body if fear is continually present. Fear is a negative bias that cuts off a positive current. In electronics it is possible to increase the bias in the circuit until there is no positive current at all. The circuit just clamps up. It is like turning off a water faucet; as the negative voltage is reduced, so will the positive flow of current increase. So with fear. It cuts off positive thinking, positive action, and positive living. Fear is negative, but faith is positive.

Job of old was the most righteous man of his generation. He was an example of moral rectitude for all to follow, but he allowed fear to take possession of his thinking. Instead of praising God daily for His benefits; instead of joining with the psalmist and saying *"Blessed be the Lord, who daily **loadeth** us with benefits"* (Psalm 68:19), he began to allow Satan to say, *"Yea, hath God said"* (Genesis 3:1) and so he began to doubt that God not only loads us with blessings, but continues to load us with blessings. He does not give with one hand take away with the other. God has not got a distorted sense of humor. He adds. He does not subtract, for it is written, *"The blessing of the LORD it **maketh rich**, and He addeth no sorrow with it"* (Proverbs 10:22.) When God greatly blessed His servant Job, He gave him a mansion, a huge farm, multitudes of horses, camels and cattle, a wife, and children. Truly it was fulfilled that God had made him rich. In spite of all these blessings, Job began to fear, and this fear steadily increased (it always does) and finally Satan struck, taking away home, horses, cattle, children, and leaving him terribly sick in body—dying in fact. He explained the reason, *"For the thing which I **greatly feared** is come upon me, and that which I was **afraid of** is come unto me. I was not in safety, neither had I rest, neither was I quiet; **yet trouble came**"* (Job 3:25–26). In the margin of the Bible we read an alternative rendering, "I *feared* a *fear* and it came upon me." God had put Job in a position of safety, security, and prosperity. He had encompassed him roundabout with an impenetrable hedge and Satan knew this, for he said to God, *"Hast not Thou made an hedge about him, and about his house, and about all that he had on every side? Thou hast blessed the work of his hands, and his substance is increased in the land"* (Job 1:10). But when Satan began his work of defeat, despair, and destruction, he made Job doubt the truth, and so was able to break down the hedge and crawl through. Instead of Job being full of faith and praise, he became full of fear and despair. He said (1) I am not in safety, (2) I have no rest, and (3) I am not quiet. Only Satan could have breathed these lies into his mind, and because he believed the lies of Satan instead of the promises of God, the Lord *permitted* Satan to take away the blessing that had been bountifully given him. The introduction of fear created loss and havoc and nearly cost Job his life. If he had maintained continuing daily faith, mentioned in Hebrews 6:1 as an absolute fundamental of the doctrine of Christ, he would not only have maintained his health, possessions, happiness, security, and prosperity, but God would have daily added to them. Finally, when Job learned his lesson and forgave his tormenters, God did indeed give him back *double*.

How much is fear destroying in you? God wants you to enter into a life of fearless prosperity, by switching the lever from fear to faith.

2

THE LAW AGAINST FEAR

God knows that the natural tendency of man, when alerted to imminent danger, is to be afraid. Adamic sinful man, born after the fall of man, is not by nature a brave person; at base he is a coward. It takes a strong man to admit this and so call upon God to be a Helper in time of trouble and danger, but proud man will not do this, and so he suffers chronic fear and reaps its terrible consequences. Even those who put up a brave front and battle against fear by self-control cannot withstand the onslaughts of fear. Fear will always reap its reward in nervous tension and the resultant physical sicknesses that follow. Bravado is not enough.

God therefore made a law in Israel that would take care of fear. In time of national emergency, He commanded the priest to go before the children of Israel and tell them not to be afraid, for it was God who would go before them and fight their battles. This was supposed to be accepted in faith, and to make the Israelites brave and bold when meeting danger. Here is the law found in Deuteronomy 20.

> *When thou goest out to battle against thine enemies, and seest horses, and chariots, and a people more than you, **be not afraid of them**: for the LORD thy God is **with thee**...and it shall be, when ye are come nigh unto the battle, that the priest shall approach and speak unto the people, and shall say unto them, Hear, O Israel, ye approach this day unto battle against your enemies: let not your hearts faint. **Fear not**, and **do not tremble**, neither be ye **terrified** because of them; for the LORD your God is He that goeth with you, **to fight for you** against your enemies **to save you**.* (verses 1–4)

God had no intention of protecting them by not allowing them to fight, but like the three Hebrew youths, they proved God far more in the fire than outside of it: In life we must always come up against our enemy Satan and his cohorts. We cannot avoid conflict, however distasteful it may be to us. Those who run when Satan roars disgrace the name of their Lord. The New Testament teachings of Paul, Peter, and James are very clear. They are that we must resist Satan, giving no ground at all. As in Israel, so today, it is our God that will fight for us, if we do what David did when on a collision course with Goliath. He said,

> *Thou comest to me with a sword, and with a spear, but I come to thee **in the name of the LORD of hosts**, the God of the armies of Israel, whom thou hast defied. This day the LORD **will deliver** thee into **my hand**...for the battle is the LORD's and He will give you into my hands.* (1 Samuel 17:45–47)

God honored His law against fear. David, being a man of God, was *not afraid* of Goliath. Everyone else was, but David's faith was in God's Word, for He cannot lie and we can rest our whole life on the Word of God.

If you are suffering grievous torment, if you are in the midst of battle while you read this book, if your heart is filled with tormenting fear, then let Jesus our High Priest whisper those words again into your heart, *"Let not your hearts faint, fear not, and do not tremble, neither be ye terrified because of them; for the LORD your God... [will] fight for you against your enemies to save you"* (Deuteronomy 20:3–4)

This is why God has restored to us again the Bible deliverance ministry today. This is the day of deliverance for spirit, soul, and body.

Fear is contagious. Avoid people who are negative and are continually filled with fear, unless you can get them to believe the Bible. Even after such wonderful encouragement and counsel the Lord realized there would still be chronic worriers, and so He gave further commandment in these words, *"And the officers shall speak further unto the people, and they shall say, What man is there that is fearful and fainthearted? Let him go and return unto his house, lest his brethren's heart faint as well as his heart"* (Deuteronomy 20:8). What sound advice: All the fearful, the peaceniks and the draft dodgers were told to go home and stay there until the brave had won the battle. What a merciful God: He thinks of everything.

This law is taken into the New Testament and appears in Romans 8:2. *"For the law of the Spirit of life in Christ Jesus hath made me free from the law of sin and death."* This simply means that a man filled with the Holy Spirit is living under a new law of life (in Greek, *zoe*—that is, the life that only comes from God); that makes him impervious to the onslaughts of Satan and his demons, providing he continues to walk in the Spirit. This law of life (eternal life), means that the tremendous creative life of God is actually flowing in our members; the very power of the Spirit surges in our minds and bodies so that when faced with the enemy, we have only scorn for a defeated foe, and we are not afraid and will resist him until Satan flees as we read in James 4:7, *"Resist the devil, and he will flee **from you**."* Where is room for fear when you know Satan *was* defeated by Jesus on the cross of Calvary? If we command him to leave a situation, he has to obey if we do so in the name of Jesus. Like Gideon of old we use the sword of the Lord, which is the Word of God. If we could realize it, Satan is always *afraid* of a son of God who knows his privileges and the Word of God. It is not we who are supposed to tremble when Satan comes around, it is he who will see our stand, know our faith and flee in fear from us. This is not for "supermen" only, it is *for all Christians.*

Notice that this *law of life* makes us *free* from Satan's law of sin and death. If he can he will cause you to sin, which will lead to fear and sickness and ultimately early death. His law is to destroy and break down; God's law is quite opposite, it is to make alive with His life, and give us freedom against further attacks of Satan.

No wonder Jesus said, *"If you continue in my word...ye shall know the truth, and the truth shall make you free"* (John 8:31–32). Again, the apostle John who had so much to say against fear, wrote, *"We know that whosoever is born of God sinneth not; but he that is begotten of God **keepeth himself**, and that **wicked one** toucheth him not"* (1 John 5:18). Does not the wicked one, the author of sin and death, wish to touch you? Does he not desire to torment you, and drive you out of your mind, or into a hospital and an early grave? Certainly. Why then does he not touch a born-again child of God? Because the born-again Christian keeps himself in the Word of God; he keeps himself under the blood of Jesus; he wears the gospel armor of Ephesians 6, and keeps the enemy at bay with the Sword of the Spirit which is the Word of God, and with the shield of faith. He keeps himself. This is where fearful Christians fail. They do not keep themselves. Instead of keeping the door shut against Satan, they are careless and leave the door open. Of course, he comes in. He is not interested in your denominational affiliation, but he fears a real Christian who knows his power and position in Christ.

> *Ye are of God, little children, and have overcome them: because greater is* [Jesus] *that is in you, than* [Satan] *that is in the world.*　　　　　(1 John 4:4)

In concluding this chapter, God's Word has made a way for you so that you never need to have fear of anybody, any demon, any circumstance, or any sickness. The death of Jesus on the cross has already delivered us from fear, and its terrible consequences. It was Jesus who said *fear not.*

3

LOVE CASTETH OUT FEAR

Israel failed to obey the perfect law of God, and so it was necessary for Jesus to come and die and to introduce a new law—the law of love. By this new law it would be possible to obey the Old Testament law in the spirit, and so obtain all the blessings that come from obedience. The Old Testament law was not done away, but fulfilled in Christ, and so we are able to fulfill (or fill up) the law in our own Christian lives by obeying it in the spirit. This enables us to receive all the blessings of the law against fear discussed in the last chapter. In fact, without faith in Christ we could not obey this law—we would always be full of fear.

Paul the Apostle told us that *"Love worketh no ill to his neighbor; therefore love is the fulfilling of the law"* (Romans 13:10). It has truly been said that you cannot be afraid of someone you love. Jesus loved the entire world, and puts this love in us, so that we may minister to a dying world in His stead, with His love. If our hearts are full and overflowing with divine love, our position is one of strength, but one who comes against us threateningly as an enemy is in a position of weakness. The story is told of the little lady who had a candy store in Hamilton, Ontario, and a man entered with an imitation gun and demanded the money in her till. Her reply was immediate, "Oh, you poor man, you are in need. Come into my back room and I will try to help you, for I am a Christian, so you cannot harm me." The man became so unnerved that he fled from the store to the police station and gave himself up. This is a true story that was published in the Ontario Press a few years ago. It shows the power of love.

The apostle John therefore wrote, *"There is no fear in love, but perfect love casteth out fear: because fear hath torment. He that feareth is not made perfect in love"* (1 John 4:18). This Scripture means that where a person has a mature experience of the love of God in God in their lives, they are not at the mercy of fears, for fear cannot dwell in the same vessel where love is perfected, i.e. matured or fully developed. Our troubles usually stem from the fact that the love of God has not matured fully and so fear gains an entrance and we become tormented, for *"fear hath torment."*

A life above fear is possible for all Christians, in fact the purpose of this book is to expose the subtle workings of Satan with fears, for most fears are caused by ignorance. If we do not know the mind or will of God for Christians, then Satan will keep us in ignorance and torment us. The church remained in darkness, superstition, and fear during the long dark ages, until Martin Luther began to open the Scriptures to the people, then fear and superstition gradually were swept away. Finally, the people no longer feared the priests and their anathemas, for the common people had more knowledge of the Word of God than the priests. Martin Luther gave them the Bible in the common tongue. Similarly in England, our King James Version of the Bible was given to the English speaking world in 1616 and was declared to strike a mortal blow at that "Man of Sin" who had kept the whole church in darkness and ignorance. A person with knowledge of the Word of God is not at the mercy of the fear that ignorance and superstition brings. We become wise. (See 2 Timothy 3:15.)

John elaborates his theme of love in this fourth chapter. He propounds the truth that God is love, and that our love, given to us by God, is made perfect, mature or fully developed, and when we are in this happy state, we become *bold* in the day of judgment, trial, temptation, or attack. It is always disturbing to see Christians running away, when it is Satan who in reality should be fleeing! This is a question of understanding the Bible! Solomon of old knew this truth, for he wrote, *"The wicked flee when no man pursueth; but the righteous are as bold as a lion"* (Proverbs 28:1). Why are righteous people so bold? It is because they are in the Lion of Judah and He is in them. How can you be afraid when you have the *Lion* in you? *"Greater is He who is in you than he that is in the world"* (1 John 4:4). Even though Satan is the prince, or ruler, of this present evil world, even though he has enormous power for evil, yet he is not stronger than the One who is in us! What cause then is there to be afraid of him? It is a question of knowing our authority in Christ, and knowing how God looks upon us. Please note that Peter tells us that Satan goes about as a roaring lion. (See 2 Peter 5:8.) He does not tell us that he is a roaring lion, for only Jesus has the title of Lion in the Bible—Satan just imitates Jesus by trying to roar like Him. He is really a low down wolf in sheep's clothing. If we will just give our roar back, it will sound just like Jesus if we are in Him and He in us, and Satan will flee.

Martin Luther, when still resting in Wartburg Castle, was greatly troubled by the Anabaptists, who acted with great lack of wisdom, stirring up the people and tearing out their images and altars from the churches, using force instead of love. He met their leaders in Wittenberg, and when they haughtily opposed Luther he said, "I smite your spirit on the snout." This created a tremendous uproar and Satan was stirred up by such an attack, and all the leaders of this movement rose and fled the city, giving no more trouble; He roars like a lion, but really is a wolf afraid of *the Lion of Judah.* It is only in this century that the ministry of exorcism has begun to be understood in a greater measure, because of the approaching end of the age. This is especially so in the last twenty years. The words of Jesus, *"In My name shall ye cast out devils* [in Greek, *Daimonion*]" (Mark 16:17) are being fulfilled throughout the world as never before, and it is being found by thousands of humble people, both preachers and laymen alike, men and women, that demons exist, are real and are absolutely subject to a child of God in Jesus' name. An experience of exorcism gives a tremendous realization of our power over all the power of Satan.

When discussing the whole subject of fear, we must be very careful to explain that there is *a spirit* of fear. To explain further, this means there is a demon of fear, for the word "Spirit" (Greek: *pneuma*) always refers to an animate intelligent being, viz. Holy Spirit, human spirit, or demon spirit. In 2 Timothy 1:7, Paul taught us that God has not given us the *"spirit of fear; but of power, and of love, and of a sound mind"* (2 Timothy 1:7). This is a contrasting Scripture. The *spirit* of fear, means Satan's spirit of fear, and is used by contrast with the Holy Spirit, whose characteristics are (1) *power*, (2) *love*, and (3) a *sound mind.* The Holy Spirit gives to us the nine fruits of the Spirit, for love includes the other eight; the nine gifts of the Spirit, for Jesus said, *"Ye shall receive power after that the Holy Spirit is come upon you"* (Acts 1:8). The power of the Spirit is manifest in the gifts of the Spirit, and the mind of man becomes the man of Christ (see 1 Corinthians 2:16) by the indwelling Spirit.

It is not surprising, therefore, that *fear* in this context is referred to as *the spirit,* for it comes direct from Satan and is a living, intelligent, malign personality that actually enters our beings and takes over control. The only thing we then manifest is a total bondage to fear, which makes no sense, defies logic, and binds us; our thinking and actions are paralyzed, and we become mentally and physically impotent. Quite the opposite to having power, love, and a sound mind! In such cases as these, it is frequently necessary to use exorcism and for one or more to gather round the distracted person and attack the spirit of fear in Jesus' name, speak to it and command it to come out with strong coughing, choking, and screaming.

Fear is a very common spirit binding people in the church today. It robs them of usefulness, it prevents them praying, testifying, teaching Sunday school, etc. No wonder Paul wrote, *"For ye have not received the spirit of bondage again to fear; but ye have received the Holy Spirit"* (Romans 8:15). Here Satan's spirit, or demon, is called "bondage," but its effect is caused by fear. Satan uses fear to bind. The inference of this Scripture is that the Roman Christians had been delivered from fear, but had returned to it. It is as we continue in the Spirit, walk in the Spirit, and are led of the Spirit that we manifest our maturity of sonship (in Greek, *huios*—mature sons). It is this maturity that John spoke of in 1 John 4 when he speaks of *"perfect love"* casting out fear. A mature son with mature love will not only have had the demon of fear cast out of himself, but will in turn pray for, and cast out the spirit of fear from other bound Christians. This is revival!

Remember—God has not given us the spirit of bondage again to fear. If you have a spirit of bondage binding you with fear, may we ask, "Where did you get it from"?

4

FEAR AND DISEASE

In recent years the medical profession has discovered that nervous tensions cause physical sicknesses. These physical sicknesses are called psychosomatic, from the Greek words *psuche*, the mind or soul and *soma*, the body. This means in simple terms that the mind affects the body, and so books have been written in the psychological field of the power of positive thinking. This is quite scriptural, because we read in the Bible of a man, *"For as he thinketh in his heart, so is he"* (Proverbs 23:7). This is understood in its operation when a person is hungry and sees or smells an appetizing meal, his mouth begins to water. The mind produces the physical manifestation. Similarly erotic or pornographic literature will produce corresponding appetites for sex. The mind, therefore, controls the body.

As we understand this principle, we know that a sudden alert of the mind to danger causes the adrenal gland to pump adrenaline into the system, and this tiny shot of this powerful chemical gives one temporary superhuman strength and mental agility to be wide awake to cope with an emergency. However, if this condition is continued over a length of time, as in the case of highly emotional or neurotic people, the whole chemical balance of the highly complex human system is thrown right off balance, and so those who are in a state of nervous tension usually get to a point of extreme weakness and continual tiredness, and all the blood tonics in the world will not help because the trouble basically is fear.

Fear can cause the whole digestive system to operate poorly, too much acid is produced which in turn produces other chemical reactions which affect the whole body. The blood, instead of being clean, is now overloaded. Acids settle in joints to give arthritis and rheumatic pains; the kidneys are put under a great strain, and the liver is likewise heavily overburdened. The pancreas is affected, giving rise to diabetic troubles. Such a condition would probably soon be corrected by the marvelous recuperative powers of the human body, and the excess poisons would soon be passed out of the body, but if a state of fear and tension is maintained day in and day out, then there is going to be a breakdown of some tissue somewhere.

The only answer is that fear must be cast out and substituted by faith in Jesus and His Word. There is no other answer.

Fear of childbirth will often cause miscarriages, because the human mind will cause the body to reject what it cannot face up to. These are called psychogenic disorders. Similarly a woman can reject conception by fear, even though there may be nothing wrong with her or her husband physically. It has been known for years that frigidity can be caused in a woman by fears induced in her early life, and no amount of psychiatric treatment will help in bad cases. The only answer is that the spirit of fear shall be confessed, forsaken, and cast out.

Fear can cause blackouts, fainting spells, and falls, due to temporary weakness in the legs. Physically there is absolutely nothing wrong with the heart or the legs. Fear literally binds human arteries and muscles and temporarily paralyzes them. In such a case, the person is probably quite sure that he has developed a weak heart, and fear then increases, and so a vicious circle commences with fear causing an increasing number of physical ailments, which in turn spawn greater fear. The end of such a sorry cycle often leads to insanity or early death.

Let us remind ourselves again of the words of Scripture, "*For ye have not received the **spirit of bondage** again to fear*" (Romans 8:15). We can now see how Satan applies his bondages, bindings, and pressures on heart muscles, leg muscles, arteries, and stomach muscles. What a lot of physical symptoms will appear and continue to appear as long as we let Satan apply his paralyzing tension to our body. Truly John wrote, "*Fear hath torment*" (1 John 4:18). We fear instead of praising God in faith for the victory that Jesus purchased for us all on Calvary. We stay awake all night, we start to vomit, sleep and hunger flee from us. Why? Does this agree with God's Word? On the contrary, we read, "*It is vain for you to rise up early, to sit up late, to eat the bread of sorrows: for so he giveth his beloved sleep*" (Psalm 127:2). It is a vain, or empty, or needless thing to stay up late or get up early because Satan has induced you to believe you can't sleep. This is a lie, for God gives sleep. Again, it is a question of repudiating this spirit of fear and having special prayer for it to be cast out.

Modern medicine will give tranquilizers while explaining the cause of the fear. Once knowledge has replaced ignorance, the psychological trouble will frequently clear up, and sedation can be dropped. How much better for the sufferer to consult a minister of the gospel who knows the Word of God, and for the original cause to be understood and then the Word of God to be put into the person's mind. In cases of fear, the Holy Spirit so often impresses upon us, by the gifts of discerning of spirits and the word of knowledge, that a particular spirit of fear came into a person when they were children. This, of course, frequently happens because parents are ignorant, and so instead of encouraging a child, they continually shout, "Be careful!" Their whole teaching is negative (the Bible is positive). Then dire punishments are threatened for the slightest misdemeanor. No child will ever be afraid of the dark unless a well-meaning parent suggests that there is cause of fear. I have raised a family of four boys, but not one of them was ever afraid of the dark. In fact, when one of them said, "I feel afraid," we asked them of what were they afraid seeing that Jesus was greater than their fear. This quickly vaporized fear in a child's mind. They saw their parents were not afraid. Panic produces panic, and we have already seen this emphasized in the law of God where those who were genuinely afraid were told to go home before the battle, lest they contaminate the whole army.

Now fear might be called the primary devilish agent of our trouble, but we must not forget that fear is frequently induced by suspicion, jealousy, and hatred. Without Christ within us, our natural Adamic natures tend to be suspicious of other people, and to imagine they are thinking all kinds of critical thoughts about us, which may or may not be true. So we start to show off, or indulge in "keeping up with the Joneses." We spend large sums of money to produce parties to entertain our friends, of whom we are mutually suspicious. We have to have a bigger car, a bigger home, and so we put ourselves into a hopeless financial position, and fear comes in like a lion. The answer is to cut our garment according to our cloth, but can we do it? No! Fear, pride, and suspicion have done their terrible work of destruction; so then we begin to hate people and refuse to forgive them of real or imaginary slights. The whole of our metabolism is thrown hopelessly out of gear, and so recourse to drugs is the only answer that we know, and as we take drugs regularly they build up other body poisons and then we get to the point where we have to take drugs to combat the side effects of drugs. Did Jesus create us for this? Certainly not; for it is written *"Perfect love casteth out fear"* (1 John 4:18), and as we come to Jesus Christ and lay our poor broken spirit, soul, and body at His feet, asking forgiveness for our ignorance, stupidity, and sins, He comes in, forgives us and cleanses us; and then, wonder of wonders, our bodily functions quickly begin to get back to normal. The headaches go, the heart beats decrease, the poisons filter out, the kidneys and liver get healed, and healing of the soul brings healing of the body, because the soul, or mind, caused all the original troubles; but now that we have brought it to the feet of Jesus we find that our mind becomes sound (see 1 Timothy 1:7) and so our body is made whole. It is impossible to divorce the mind from the body. If the mind is disturbed the body will carry a hundred disturbances. No wonder Jesus spoke of the peace that passes all understanding. Only He can give you this; the medical profession and the psychiatrists do their best in their limited way, but it is only Jesus who can give you a sound mind in a sound body. There is no other name whereby men can be saved (made whole) than the name of Jesus.

5

INTERNATIONAL FEAR

This book is being written at the beginning of 1968. It has been very alarming to see the rapid degeneration of morality, crime, and violence within recent months. It seems that a great acceleration is taking place, proclaiming for all who understand that the end of the age must surely be at hand. Monetary inflation is increasing and governments cannot control it. Labor unions now determine when their members will work and how hard they will work. Governments have no more control over labor. The modernistic churches bend over backward to preach a Marxist philosophy and deny the supernatural of the Bible and the ministry of Christ. The taking of terrible drugs is rapidly increasing among our young people, and venereal disease is rampant. No wonder Jesus said, *"These are the beginning of sorrows"* (Matthew 24:8). No one knows when Jesus will return as Judge to wind up a totally corrupt civilization and to destroy the godless inhabitants of the earth. There can be no mistaking the certainty of these events, for Jesus said, *"As the days of Noah were, so shall also the coming of the Son of man be…. The flood came, and took them away, so shall also the coming of the Son of man be"* (Matthew 24:37, 39). Similarly, in the case of the wicked cities of Sodom and Gomorrah, *"It rained fire and brimstone from heaven, and destroyed them all. Even thus shall it be when the Son of man is revealed"* (Luke 17:29–30).

Homosexuality and fornication have been recommended by some of the leaders of our churches! Such defiance of a Holy God can only reap judgment and destruction. Such a civilization must be destroyed along with its anti-Christian churches, and the events that lead to the final holocaust of destruction by fire (see 2 Peter 3:7) will be progressively more frightening to an unbelieving and rebellious world whose philosophy seems to be *"Let us eat and drink for tomorrow we die"* (1 Corinthians 15:32, Isaiah 22:13).

The world, having rejected God and His Son Jesus Christ, has substituted the United Nations organization as its "Prince of Peace." It did this in desperation because after the First World War—the war to end all war—the world set up the League of Nations and blamed the United States for its failure. We wonder who will be blamed because of the ultimate failure of the United Nations. Steadily but surely the U.N. will no longer be able to stop wars between nations. Steadily but increasingly anarchy will engulf the world. Laws will be ignored. Each government will become a law unto itself, and so Jesus said. *"Upon the earth, **distress of nations**, with perplexity* (in Greek, *aporia*—meaning "without a passage out")" (Luke 21:25). It is interesting that this verse 25 immediately follows verse 24, in which Jesus said that Jerusalem would be trodden down of the Gentiles until the times of the Gentiles would be fulfilled. The incredible six-day war between the Jews and Arabs in July 1967 returned to the Jews the old city of Jerusalem. It seemed the stage was then set for a great breaking down within the other nations.

This moral and religious collapse would be the time for *great fear* to be released in the earth, and of course we know that Satan is behind all this, for we read, *"Woe to the inhibitors of the earth and of the sea! For the devil is come down unto you, having great wrath, because he knoweth that he hath but a short time"* (Revelation 12:12). In the permissive will of God, (for the Lord uses Satan as His agent of destruction), a great plague of spirits of fear will be released upon the earth and Jesus said, *"Men's hearts **failing them for fear**, for looking after those things coming on the earth: for the powers of heaven shall be shaken"* (Luke 21:26). Here is a clear statement that fear causes heart failure, and it seems that the most common physical weakness that will be experienced by millions of people all over the earth will be *heart failure*. Death due to a psychosomatic attack! Is there a cure for a terrible plague? Yes, it is that the nations accept Jesus as the Prince of Peace and confess their sins to Him to escape the judgments. *"The wicked shall be turned into hell, and all the nations that forget God"* (Psalm 9:17); but conversely we read, *"Blessed is the nation whose God is the LORD"* (Psalm 33:12). How sad that great nations like Great Britain and the United States could have almost forgotten the Lord within two generations!

The twenty-fourth chapter of Isaiah gives in graphic detail the terrible judgments of God that wind up this present dispensation. In verses 17–18 it is written,

> **Fear** *and the pit, and the snare, are upon thee, O inhabitant of the earth, and it shall come to pass that he who fleeth from the noise of the **fear** shall fall into the pit; and he that cometh up out of the pit shall be taken in the snare.*

As the judgments increase, and as heart failure increases, men will run hither and thither and find no way out. Every door, except the door of salvation, *Jesus*, will be closed. In increasing distraction, man will run from fear into the pit and from the pit into the snare, until he goes insane and dies of a heart attack. But still the door of salvation is open, the *only way* out. Imagine the heart failures of our government leaders! In a measure we have seen this hopeless chase after an escape way-out in the actions of the godless leaders in the British government. The British government sought every way to avoid devaluing the pound in 1967, but found no way out. Who knows how soon it will be before the pound is devalued still further, followed by inflation and devaluation of other currencies, including the "almighty dollar." God said He would have no other gods before Him. He meant it!

We have already stated that there is a *way out*. Many in their distractions will come to us. No doubt the gospel of the kingdom of God will receive greater publicity than at any previous time in history; it should be easier to witness to the full truth of God's Word than ever before. Churchianity will not have the answer. The anti-Christian religions will be impotent. It will only be the "army of the Lord" which is described by Joel as being very great (see Joel 2:11) that will have the answer. It is Joel who foretells the outpouring of the Spirit upon all flesh, and this coincides with the terrible destructions of the day of the Lord. The Lord is going to make it very easy to witness in these closing days of grace, which is why He is now preparing this remnant army with the Holy Spirit baptism, and it is only in very recent times that members of historic churches, together with a remnant of Roman Catholics, are being baptized in the Spirit as evidenced by speaking in tongues and a return of other charismatic gifts, including healing and exorcism.

It is the same old story. Before He destroyed Sodom and Gomorrah the Lord rescued Lot and his family; before He destroyed the world in Noah's day He rescued Noah's family, and before the final destruction of Jerusalem by Titus in AD 70, He enabled every Christian to escape into the hills of Moab. So today, before the destruction of our great religious systems along with the godless politics, He will rescue many out of these anti-Christian systems before their destruction. We must remember that the scarlet-colored woman sitting upon seven hills, easily recognized as the Roman Catholic system and called Babylon the Great, is to be destroyed by a red beast system, which we recognize as communism. Let us not forget also that this mother of harlots has many daughters, for she is described as the "*mother of harlots*" (Revelation 17:5). These prophecies will certainly be fulfilled very shortly before the astonished eyes of the world that set up these harlot religious systems and worshipped them. History reveals this, and even today multitudes would rather go to a church that denies the miracles than one that teaches the whole Bible. What a difference between the bride who makes herself ready for the coming of the bridegroom Jesus, and the harlot woman who is drunken with the blood of the saints and with the blood of the martyrs of Jesus!

Truly we wait to see these abominations destroyed, but what fear and consternation will be upon the earth when the very religious systems that multitudes looked to for salvation by prayers for the dead, by masses and indulgences and penances, are all destroyed before their eyes.

Jesus comes back to rapture the church, to restore Israel, to destroy the wicked, and to set up His kingdom with the righteous remnant. Let us be sure that we are found as part of that remnant.

6

I WILL NOT FEAR

Until there is a positive affirmation of faith, there will be no deliverance from fear, or from anything else that Satan might try to fasten on us.

In Psalm 56, we have a most revealing Scripture as to the processes of thought and action that must take place in each of us, if we are to avoid the paralyzing effects of fear. In other words, God has set down in His Word *exactly* what we must do, and the course of action to follow when we become afraid. As we have explained in another part of this book, fear is a natural reaction, permitted by God as a warning of impending danger, when adrenaline is pumped into our blood stream from the adrenal gland. This gives us sudden and super mental and physical energy to combat and face the danger. However, if such a condition of alertness is maintained, great danger to the physical system will result.

Let us look into Psalm 56. In verse 3, David declared, *"What time I am afraid, I will trust in thee."* There is no doubt here that David knew that he would be afraid many times. The very life he lived wandering around the mountains of Israel with his worthy men, ever facing imminent death at the hands of King Saul who was hunting him like an animal, would provide many moments of extreme peril. There was always the instant possibility of an alert to danger with its corresponding fear. David's instant reaction, however, was that when fear registered in his breast, he would immediately put his whole trust in God. This is where the godless man, or the carnal Christian, fails. They do not immediately put their trust in God, but they begin to run away from the source of danger with increasing fear, which can develop into total, blind insensate panic.

This is like changing gear! It is a deliberate act of faith. *"I will trust."* The will comes into focus and is put into action. As creatures made to use our free will, we must will to trust God whatever the circumstances that may surround us; in fact perhaps it could be said, the worse the circumstances, the better to trust God, for we shall find no way out. From putting the will in the gear called trust, we must shift to the next gear called praise. Trust must find an outlet in praising God for His protection, deliverance, and power. Trust is not passive, it must be active; it must start "doing something about it." There is nothing like a good burst of praise to improve one's spirit, and to put the devil on the defensive. You see, Satan does not understand praising God, for he never does it, nor does he desire to do it. It is foreign and therefore mysterious to him, it confuses him, it confuses him completely. David started to praise God *for His Word* for he said, *"I have put my trust in God"* (Psalm 56:11). This was the reason for his praise. He knew the promises of the Word of God concerning deliverance. He had experienced so many times wonderful deliverances from the enemy, and he based his trust solely on God's Word, not on sentiment or emotion or soulish feelings. Some people are always looking for feelings when they go to church. We do not need to look for feelings in church. Satan gives us so many real feelings outside the church! It is then that we trust God's Word and not our circumstances or feelings! David began to shout God's praises because he knew that God would once again deliver him.

Consider this. *"Call upon me in the day of trouble: I will deliver thee, and thou shalt glorify me"* (Psalm 50:15), so David started to glorify the Lord when surrounded by fear. It was only then that David was in a spiritual position to take the next step and to change into the high gear of affirmation. He said, *"I will not fear"* (Psalm 56:11). He believed it, so he declared it, which reminds us of the Scripture, *"If thou shalt confess with thy mouth."* (Romans 10:9). This is a very important part of the ministry of deliverance, to say out loud what you believe will happen; to let Satan hear that you are not going to be afraid even though your enemies would daily swallow you up. (See Psalm 56:2.) With some people, fear is a daily experience that cripples them mentally and physically. Again we read that Solomon said, *"Thou art snared with the words of thy mouth, thou art taken with the words of thy mouth"* (Proverbs 6:2). If you confess defeat, Satan hears you and gives you defeat. If you confess victory and stand on the fact that Satan is a defeated foe, he must flee from you and leave you alone, for he knows he is a defeated being: He lost the fight at Calvary.

Until you can get into the high gear of confession, you will be defeated but if you go through these steps of faith, you will be the victor over fear. Let us consider them again. (1) fear, (2) trust, (3) praise, and (4) confession.

The word for confession in the Greek is *homologia*, which literally means "saying the same thing." It could be explained as the mixing of the word of God with the person, so that the person thinks and speaks as the Word declares, from two Greek words: *homo*, meaning "same"; and *logia*, meaning "saying or speaking." So when we confess as David did, *"I will not fear,"* we say the same thing as the Bible says, so we agree with God; and if we agree with God we agree with His Son Jesus Christ who completely defeated Satan and all his hosts of spirits of fear on the cross of Calvary. We then demonstrate that we are on the Lord's side and shall not fear any man or demon spirit. As Jesus is Victor, so do we become *"more than conquerors through him who loved us"* (Romans 8:37). How Satan hates a confession of the Word of God!

This word *homologia* is used in Hebrews 4:14: *"Seeing then that we have a great high priest, that is passed into the heavens, Jesus the Son of God, let us **hold fast** our profession"* (*homologia*—confession). This means that because Jesus Christ is alive, and is our Savior, Friend, and Deliverer, let us be sure that we hold fast and refuse to panic, and confess as David did when he said, *"Though an host should encamp against me, my heart **shall not fear**"* (Psalm 27:3). Immediately, as we say this, our Great High Priest in heaven confesses the same thing to His Father on our behalf. Jesus is delighted when we agree with Him.

Again, in Hebrews 10:23 we read the same wholesome remedy, *"Let us hold fast the profession [homologia] of our faith without wavering."* It is good to ask ourselves from time to time, "What is our faith?" Is it in man, or the remedies of man, or is it in God and His Word alone? Our faith will only stand and produce results if it is mixed with the Word of God as explained in Hebrews 4:2, *"For unto us was the gospel preached, as well as unto them: but the word preached did not profit them, not being **mixed with faith** in them that heard it."* Here a contrast is made between those who failed to enter the Promised Land, and those that did enter. The difference was not of race, but of faith. The new generation believed Moses and Joshua. The old generation did not believe the Word and so perished. Was this favoritism? It helps to explain why some continue to suffer and others are healed and set free. Just your own personal faith mixed with the Word of God: this is the broad meaning of the Greek word *homologia*.

When you are a *homologia* Christian, you can face fear and win. You must continue to affirm a positive statement of faith which will cancel out the negative threat of Satan. Let *"I can"* be heard instead of *"I can't."* Let *"I will not"* be heard instead of a weak submissive *"I will"* to Satan. It is the Word of God that gives us this inner fortitude, which is manifest in outer boldness. Affirm the truth daily. *"I can do all things through Christ who strengthens me"* (Philippians 4:13).

7

FAILING HEARTS

It is abundantly clear from the Scriptures that the present Christian dispensation comes to an end. The vials of judgment in the book of Revelation are finally full to overflowing with man's rebellion against God, and they are outpoured upon a defiant world which has consistently refused God's holy laws and His offer of pardon through His Son Jesus Christ. God is not mocked, and although He may bear with such evil for hundreds of years in this dispensation of grace, He does not bear with it forever. He must judge it and remove from the earthly scene all people and their governments who oppose Him.

It is not that mankind has not had previous evidences of His wrath poured forth. We remember the flood in Noah's day, when only eight souls were saved alive from the holocaust. (See 1 Peter 3:20.) We remember that the hideous sins of homosexuality in Sodom and Gomorrah finally brought on God's judgments in utter destruction of property and life. (See Jude 7.) The story of the destruction of Jericho shows that all were killed by the wrath of God excepting Rahab and her family who repented. Even the angels in heaven were judged and cast out to the earth to become the demons that torment us, because they rebelled. (See Jude 6.) Even in later times we have seen that the Jews have been a persecuted people with their wars of the Maccabees and destruction in AD 70 by Titus, and the culmination of the death and terror camps under Nazi Germany when six million of them were murdered. How could these things be? Because they had avowed publicly that they accepted the responsibility of the crucifixion of Jesus the Son of God in these terrible words. *"Then answered all the people, and said, His blood be on us, and on our children"* (Matthew 27:25). It is a terrifying thing to trample underfoot the blood of God's son, for Paul, a Jew, wrote a general letter to his Hebrew brethren in strong terms, *"Of how much sorer punishment, suppose ye, shall he be thought worthy, who hath trodden underfoot the Son of God, and hath counted the blood of the covenant, wherewith he was sanctified, an unholy thing, and hath done despite unto the Spirit of grace?"* (Hebrews 10:29). One day the Jews will understand these words, for Zechariah tells us that their families mourn apart because the One they rejected returns to them. (See Zechariah 12:10.)

Mankind is incredibly rebellious. He never learns by his mistakes and laughs at preachers who warn him of judgment to come, and in every generation says, "*Where is the promise of his coming? for since the fathers fell asleep all things continue as they were from the beginning of creation*" (2 Peter 3:4). This statement, like so many others made by "responsible" church leaders, is not true, neither does it have any proof from Holy Writ; but on the contrary, the Bible record tells us quite the opposite. When God made the world in Genesis 1:1, He made it a veritable paradise, but because of Satan's rebellion already referred to in this chapter, the devil was cast out of heaven with his angelic army onto the earth. Such a judgment destroyed this planet as God had made it, and it became inundated with water. "*The earth was without form and void; and darkness was upon the face of the deep. And the Spirit of God moved upon the face of the waters*" (Genesis 1:2). The first of the creative acts was for the Holy Spirit to breathe upon the results of the previous judgment and to start another creation. This creation came to an end in like manner, by the flood, but God had prepared an ark this time and eight faithful ones were saved, while the rest perished. Again, these were to be used to begin a new creation. Things did not continue undisturbed from the creation: This creation from Noah continues until this day in spite of the First and Second World Wars which were warnings; but it is now up for judgment and destruction, not by water but by fire. "*Therefore hath the curse devoured the earth, and they that dwell therein are* **burned**, *and few men left*" (Isaiah 24:6).

Jesus reminds us that,

*As in the days that were before the flood they were eating and drinking, marrying and giving in marriage until the day that Noah entered into the ark, and knew not until the flood came, and took them all away, **so shall also the coming of the Son of man be.*** (Matthew 24:38–39)

And again,

Likewise as it was in the days of Lot; they did eat, they drank, they bought, they sold, they planted, they builded; but the same day that Lot went out of Sodom it rained fire and brimstone from heaven and destroyed them all. Even thus shall it be in the day when the Son of man is revealed. (Luke 17:28–30)

It seems to us that there has been a very sharp falling away from all previous moral standards during 1967, so that the governments of the world "united" in the so-called United Nations, are powerless to deal with the problem. Satan is riding rampant for he knows his time is short. The future can only hold out increasing disasters, wars and rumors of wars, and worldwide rebellion against all authority on the rapid increase. These terrible happenings, such as the destruction in Detroit, USA, and other cities will cause tremendous alarm, and so great will this alarm be that Jesus graphically wrote these words, *"And there shall be signs in the sun, and in the moon, and in the stars, and upon the earth distress of nations, with perplexity; the sea and the waves roaring; men's **hearts failing them for fear,** and for looking after those things which are coming on the earth"* (Luke 21:25–26). In spite of the fact that these judgments are clearly prophesied, yet the people will not believe, but they will suffer the consequences of their unbelief; they will die like flies all over the world with *fear*. They will not have faith in Jesus the Savior, so they will die of *fear*. What kills thousands today will kill millions tomorrow—*fear* the great destroyer. Fear hath torment indeed.

However, there is another side to the coin, for God's Word says, *"I will seek thee early: for when thy judgments are in the earth, the in habitants of the world will learn righteousness"* (Isaiah 26:9). When God's judgments are clearly apparent, then there will be a great inquiring, and this will precipitate revival to restore the church back to its original apostolic power and pattern. In chapter 24 of Isaiah already referred to, there is mention of revival in verse 14: *"They shall lift up their voice, they shall sing for the majesty of the LORD…wherefore glorify ye the LORD **in the fire**."* The prophet Joel who told us so graphically both of terrible destruction and marvelous New Testament revival in his second chapter, shows how in the midst of *"blood, and fire, and pillars of smoke"* (Joel 2:30), and *"those that call on the name of the LORD shall be delivered"* (verse 32).

Jesus told us to look up, or look away from these terrible earthly happenings, and to wait expectantly for His return. King David long ago foresaw this time; but in his day he was confident of the protection of God in any circumstance. He wrote, "God is our refuge and strength a very present help in trouble. *"Therefore **will not we fear**, though the earth be removed, and though the mountains be carried into the midst of the sea: though the waters thereof roar and be troubled, though the mountains shake with the swelling thereof"* (Psalm 46:2–3). It is necessary to emphasize that the troubles and judgments coming upon this wicked world could terrify Christians if they do not understand, and the resultant terror would cause all the mental and physical distresses already referred to in this book; but not so—we are told not to fear, and we must encourage and teach all these new ones who will come in during the last day revival and believe upon the Lord Jesus Christ, that they also shall not fear, because they will be delivered from fear and understand that the coming of Jesus is drawing nigh; He will come to catch them away (as in Noah's ark) but the sinner will be destroyed.

Let us end this chapter with a thought of the invincible faith of King David.

*The LORD is my light and my salvation: **whom shall I fear?** The LORD is the strength of my life: **of whom shall I fear?** The LORD is the strength of my life: **of whom shall I be afraid?**...Though an host [army] should encamp against me, in this will I be confident.* (Psalm 27:1–3)

No heart failure for David or any in our day who believe as he did.

There is never any need to fear.

Never.

8

TESTIMONY OF A PASTOR'S WIFE
BY MRS. H. A. MAXWELL WHYTE

I f anyone had ever told me that I would one day come under the bondage of a spirit of fear, I would never have believed them.

I had a very deep conversion to Jesus Christ, and two days later I was filled with the Spirit. It was a glorious baptism and I spoke freely in tongues, and that same night the Lord began to give me the gift of interpretation. I immediately experienced a consuming hunger for the word of God, and in three months I had read completely through the Bible, marking each chapter as I read. I also studied books on the Bible as I went along, and so at the end of the three months, I had a good foundation on which the Lord could begin to build faith.

When the call of the Lord came on our lives, we went out into a new country, Canada, leaving family, friends, and security behind us and trusting completely in the Lord. There were many difficult days ahead, but the Lord took us triumphantly through and in the process we certainly learned to trust the Lord for all our needs.

In 1948, we began to move into the deeper teaching of deliverance and faith, and as I worked with my husband and saw many delivered from the grip of satanic bondage, my faith grew and became, as I thought, soundly established. I sat week by week under strong faith building teaching, both from my husband and from many other fine men of God whom the Lord saw fit to send our way. I also had the privilege of attending conventions and seminars that were encouraging and faith-building. You would have thought that such training would have left little ground for Satan to work on. Also, I would point out that I am not by nature a timorous or fearful person. I am not a worrier, and I usually tend to be optimistic rather than pessimistic.

At the beginning of 1965, we were attend a Ministers' Seminar at Oral Roberts University in Tulsa, Oklahoma, and were in an atmosphere pulsating with the move of the Spirit of God, where faith was built up and encouraged. In this atmosphere, we received news of negotiations being undertaken for the sale of our church, and the purchase of a much more modern one in the suburbs. We sought the Lord for His guidance, and we both felt sure that this move was of God, and with our faith mounting high, we felt we should encourage the friends in the church to go ahead with the transaction. I had a moment of doubt, wondering if this really was the will of the Lord for us, but the Lord moved in such a way that I was convinced that this move was really ordered of the Lord.

At first, all seemed to be going well, but then Satan began to attack: First one and then another of our tried and trusted friends felt that they would not be able to support us in the new location. Of course, it was always those who had been faithful and generous in their financial support. In the course of the next few weeks the income of the church began to fall, even before we had actually made the move. I realize now that for several years, although we had never been a wealthy church, we had known a measure of financial security. We had always had sufficient funds to meet all our needs, with enough left over to pay off all our mortgages (until we took out a new one in order to help build a sister church further north), and to make considerable improvements to the old property. For years, it had not really been necessary to exercise very much faith for finances—they had just always been there when we needed them. Now, suddenly, I had to begin to walk by faith again, as in the early days after we had first come to Canada, and like a soldier who has lived away from the fighting for years and become soft, I was out of condition.

Day after day, the devil tormented me with fears. He showed me all that we had built up under God in the years we had labored in Toronto was about to fall to pieces. If people were leaving us now, how many more would leave when we actually made the move? How could we contemplate losing everything, and perhaps having to start all over again, now that we were no longer so young? What would happen to our two youngest boys who still had to be educated? On and on went the tormenting jibes of Satan. All the time, the Lord was moving in a marvelous way to encourage us. Whenever the finances seemed at their lowest ebb, someone quite unexpected would come along and give us a gift that was just what we needed to see us through. Other difficulties that occurred in the course of the move were marvelously smoothed out, in such a way that we know that the blessing of the Lord was certainly with us. In spite of all this, night after night I tossed and turned in my bed, sleepless, with terrible visions of the future filling my mind, and my whole body literally shaking with fear.

I realized that this was an all-out attack of Satan. I realized that I had to fight back with the word of God. This I did to the best of my ability. All the faith-building Scriptures that were necessary the Holy Spirit brought to my remembrance, and

I honestly did my best to stand upon them. I rebuked Satan, I pleaded the blood against him, and I would get temporary relief. In fact many times I really thought I had come through to complete victory, only to go down again as another vicious blow was dealt by the enemy.

Gradually, the fear and the constant warring of faith and doubt in my mind, began to affect my whole personality. I became very defeated in my outlook, and very irritable with my family. My husband tells me that I even began to look "haunted." However, the Lord is always at hand to deliver those who trust in Him, even though they may at times go through deep water of unbelief and fear. Two things happened which finally broke the grip of Satan on my life. One day while my husband was preaching he mentioned the Scripture found in Romans 14:23, which states that everything which is not of faith is sin. This struck right to my heart and I realized that in my failure to believe the promises of the Lord that I knew so well, I was actually sinning.

Now, I love the Lord with all my heart, and I want above all things to be found pleasing to Him. I first came to the Lord on the grounds of obedience, a strong conviction that although I did not fully understand what "salvation" was, yet I must obey the call of the Lord to follow Him. Ever since, I have never consciously done anything that I knew would grieve Him, although I am sure that many times I have unconsciously done so. Here I was face to face with the realization that I was sinning against my Lord by doubting that He was able to take us through this time of trial and testing. I began to battle Satan more strongly than ever with the word of God, but still could not quite break the grip of fear on my life. Finally, my husband insisted that we go away alone for a few hours. He had realized my plight, and he was determined to pray for me. However, at this stage, I also was very rebellious and was not really willing that he should do so. Finally, my husband just had to brush aside all my protests and come over and lay his hands on my head and rebuke the spirit of fear and cast it from me in Jesus' name. Nothing apparently happened, but from that moment the power of Satan was broken, and victory was experienced more and more each day, until I was once more walking in faith and rejoicing in the marvelous provision of the Lord.

Looking back now, I can see that I really needed this wilderness experience. I had been walking too much by sight and budgets, and I needed to learn afresh that if the Lord has called you to perform a task, He will always provide all that is needed to complete that task. Some people say that a Christian, particularly a Spirit-filled Christian, cannot be bound by Satan. I can only say that from my personal experience a Spirit-filled Christian certainly can come under satanic bondage, and it is often necessary that someone else should pray the strong prayer of faith, rebuking the binding spirit, before victory is finally won. Of course, we must battle ourselves with the word of God, but sometimes we need reinforcements to push the battle to the gates. *"Confess your faults one to another, and* **pray one for another** *that ye may be healed"* (James 5:16).

> *Now thanks be unto God, which always causeth us to triumph in Christ.*
>
> (2 Corinthians 2:14)

HIDDEN SPIRITS

CONTENTS

FOREWORD

Every great revelation of God's Word, every move of God, has had its pioneers.

There was a Martin Luther for the Reformation, an Evan Roberts for the great Welsh outpouring, a John Wesley for Great Britain and America, and so on to the present day. These men were misunderstood and in their day, the doctrines they preached were rejected by many. Nevertheless they were true and were finally accepted.

So it is with the message contained in this book *Hidden Spirits*. Although not a new doctrine, for it is as old as Scripture, few have practiced it since the Reformation, and it has been sadly neglected. This is sad too since, due to this neglect, strange and unscriptural doctrines have taken its place. One teaching prevalent today is that if a person is a Christian he cannot be touched by Satan. To preach contrary to this commonly accepted plea is considered heresy. Many refuse to accept it or even listen to the truth.

In this book, H. A. Maxwell Whyte has conclusively proved that many Christians can be, and are, controlled by evil spirits. In some parts this message has not been well received, but Pastor Whyte has time after time proved his message by casting spirits out of many Christians in many cities of the world. He could be considered a pioneer in this field.

I have stood with Pastor Whyte when the command of authority was given and have watched the amazing results—the glorious glow of God's presence on the countenance that a short time before plainly showed the stress of inner spiritual conflict and bondage. In my own experience I have proved this truth in practical operation.

Therefore it gives me great pleasure to present a book with a message designed to deliver you.

—*Evangelist G. M. Farley*
Williamsport, Maryland
October 1962

INTRODUCTION

One cannot read the Gospels and the Acts of the Apostles without becoming aware of the fact that Jesus taught, and the disciples and apostles acted, in accordance with Christ's teachings that there are satanic entities in this world that are capable of causing serious problems in man. Jesus stated that in His name we should cast out devils. This has been interpreted by modern psychologists and psychiatrists to mean that we should have dominion over the realms of mental illness. This has been accepted in a pragmatic sense and we have assumed that all mental illness is a direct result of developmental or environmental processes. Consequently psychiatrists have encouraged man to delve back into his past and find out when times of conflict, anxiety, and fear arose in his life so that he can deal with the mental problems that he has by ascertaining the reason for their development. There are, of course, mental diseases that arise as a result of toxic and hereditary factors.

As a physician goes along in his medical practice he begins to be aware that there may be an area of his practice that is comprised of patients who do not apparently fit into the categories set forth by the psychiatrists. In this regard it is most difficult for us to explain duality of the personality. How can it be, for example, that a young man who has been active in his church and religious activities suddenly turns about and commits a murder? This may be explained on the basis of conflicts arising in his early childhood, but as we read the Scriptures we find that there is such a thing as sin, and sin entering into the lives of men. This comes about by the individual turning his back upon God and going toward the realms of darkness, and when this occurs certainly evil forces can take possession of his soul. If we are to presume that man has a soul, it is oriented either in the direction of God or the direction of Satan. There appears to be no area of neutrality even though the large percentage of modern men would prefer to remain on completely neutral ground. If one is going toward God and is completely committed to Jesus Christ, he is doubtless in an area of protection against evil. However, if he decides to sin and go toward the realms of evil he then loses protection and may be subject to his soul being captivated by the forces of evil.

The most common way for a person to have his soul captivated by evil is to leave the house of worship and to enter the realms of darkness represented by the halls of drunkenness and debauchery so common on every side these days, even though they be dressed up in rather glamorous attire. Once a person has allowed his soul to become captivated by the forces of evil, it is not going to benefit his psychological or spiritual situation to be treated in the usual ways of reassurance, tranquilization, or even shock therapy. What the person in this instance needs is to be dealt with by a physician or minister who has read the Gospels and believes that Jesus was right in saying that evil forces must be cast out in the name of Jesus Christ. Anyone who has ever attempted this has been amazed to see how people can be delivered from terrible spiritual and psychological oppression through the use of exorcism. Therefore, since I have been asked to write a short introduction to Maxwell Whyte's booklet on *Hidden Spirits*, it is my feeling that his is a very useful contribution in this area and may serve as a guide to those who are seeking more knowledge in these realms. Mr. Whyte has had a very wide experience in the realm of casting out of evil entities from oppressed people, and I feel that his experience as indicated in these writings merits careful consideration.

It certainly behooves the church seriously to look into Christ's commandment to heal the sick, and this certainly includes the casting out of evil. I should also like to suggest to the church and to Christian psychiatrists that while we are trying all other means to make people mentally well we should seriously investigate on a clinical basis the role of exorcism in making people mentally well. This cannot be undertaken by anyone who is not deeply committed to Jesus Christ and thoroughly convinced that the gospel writings are true. It might prove disastrous for anyone to attempt to investigate exorcism on any other basis. Investigations are under way in Geneva by the Rev. Bernard Martin in this regard and I should certainly feel that we in the Western Hemisphere should also look into this Christian ministry.

As medicine and psychiatry become more and more scientific and less and less spiritual, it is indeed enlightening and spiritually invigorating to see members of the church, such as Maxwell Whyte, come to the fore again pointing us to scriptural truths in an effort to help modem man in all of his dilemmas back toward wholeness, body, mind, soul, and spirit.

—*William S. Reed, MD*
Diplomate American Board of Surgery
October 1962

1

REVELATION IS PROGRESSIVE

It is interesting to note how the Holy Spirit has progressively increased His illuminating power as Guide and Teacher upon the church. In the eighteenth century He broke through superstition and showed Martin Luther that those who are justified before God must be made just alone by believing on the finished work of Calvary. It took another two hundred years for the Holy Spirit to break through afresh and teach that salvation without holiness produces little evidence of the finished work of Calvary in a human life. John Wesley was the instrument chosen for this fresh illumination, and it took another two hundred years for the Holy Spirit to reveal that salvation with holiness was not enough—the power was still lacking in the church, and so at the turn of the twentieth century the Holy Spirit was outpoured by Jesus Christ, and this began the "Pentecostal Revival" of this century. *"Ye shall receive power after that the Holy Spirit is come upon you"* (Acts 1:8).

In each of these three phases, many were quite satisfied with the revelation given; and even today we have Reformed churches, Evangelical and Holiness churches, and Pentecostal churches, but we would be quite wrong to assume that the Holy Spirit has finished His revelation to the church, or that there is no more to be revealed.

In 1948, it seemed that God sent a refreshing to the Pentecostal groups in an endeavor to teach them concerning the gifts of the Holy Spirit. Little was being made among Pentecostal groups at this time of these gifts, supernaturally given, and there was mistrust and opposition to their use in many assemblies, for Satan by counterfeits and fleshly manifestations had brought confusion. As always happens in a revival, some went on with God and the gifts of the Spirit began to appear in many places, with particular emphasis on the three oral gifts of tongues, interpretation, and prophecy, and on divine healing. In addition, the revelation gifts of the word of knowledge and wisdom were heard to a degree previously unknown. These gifts were sometimes wrongly called "the gift of discernment," because the true gift of discerning of spirits began to be manifest also. Of course, wherever a new move of God is seen Satan will do his best to interfere, disrupt, divide, and imitate, and he caused a lot of confusion in this true move of God, but the Lord also caused many of these people to learn by their mistakes, and many realized that the five ministry gifts of apostles, prophets, pastors, evangelists, and teachers were again necessary in the church to control and guide the operation of these gifts, for we believe that gifts of the Spirit are subject to God's settings in the church. (See 1 Corinthians 12:28.)

The next move of God was to bring to the attention of the denominational churches the glorious truths of the Holy Spirit, and this can be dated from about 1959, and we believe that under God the chosen vessel was David DuPlessis, a South African who found residence in the United States. He was able to take the full Pentecostal message to leaders of these formal churches, which many received eagerly, and these leaders of reformed and modernistic churches have been falling into the blessing of Pentecost, but they have not been content with the limited interpretation put upon the work of the Holy Spirit by so many Pentecostal groups, but have desired to see the nine gifts in operation whenever the Holy Spirit baptism is given. Their faith is being rewarded! It should be mentioned that the Full Gospel Businessmen's Fellowship International have been used in a singular manner to encourage these denominational pastors and to give them opportunity of public witness to their full gospel experience.

To illustrate the importance of this new move of God, we were privileged to witness in the closing weeks of 1961 an Episcopalian surgeon of repute laying hands on an Anglican lady in Toronto, Canada, urging her to "let go and let God" fill her, and she sweetly began to speak in tongues as the Holy Spirit came in. Nothing less than this would suffice, then to our astonishment, he *immediately* urged her to seek God for the gift of interpretation!

This move of God is taking place among many of the leaders of the reformed churches, and Episcopalian rectors are praying their congregations through to the Pentecostal experience, and in their prayer meetings it is reported that all nine gifts of the Spirit are in frequent operation and manifestation. This is true also of Methodist, Baptist, and Mennonite churches! All this is happening outside of the well-fenced walls of the Pentecostal groups.

What is God doing? Are we to assume that He has finished with His revelations? Is there anything more to be revealed? Is the church to be restored without spot or wrinkle as is indicated in Ephesians 5:27? Have we a right to assume that the future holds more glory than the past? We believe it does—much more. The glory of this latter house shall be greater than of the former. (See Haggai 2:9.)

We believe that the five ministry gifts, the nine gifts in the Holy Spirit, and the nine fruits of the Spirit will all be seen in perfection before Jesus comes to catch away

His church. It will be completed, both in number and in quality! This church—the true body of Christ—will reveal the Christ (the Anointed One) on earth before the Head—Jesus—returns to claim it as His own and to take it away to heaven. We believe it would be wrong to assume that the church is now ready for the immediate return of Jesus. We may be disappointed if we hold this view. The Lord said He would make a quick work on the earth. We believe we are living in the day of a great quickening in the body of Christ—a quickening in the womb of the church that will reveal Jesus rather than so many of our pet theological ideas, and this will sweep away traditions fondly held, and much "religion" will give way to the pure work of the Holy Spirit.

We believe also that where men and women are filled with the Spirit as in Acts 2:4, this is God's true way to bring together the body of Christ and is the *fulfillment* of Christ's prayer that they all might be one. What love and unity are suddenly created when Christians of various communions come together with this glorious experience of speaking in tongues! They do not talk about "their church," they talk about Jesus and His power! *"For ye shall receive power after* [or at the same time] *as the Holy Spirit comes upon you"* (Acts 1:8). The indwelling Holy Spirit sheds light from the Bible on the errors of denominationalism.

We also believe that the day of denominations has ended. There will be no more within the true church. It seems as if the angels are now being sent by God to sever the just from the unjust, to separate the sheep from the goats, to divide the unclean fish from the clean in the drag net. It is good also to remember that an angel is not necessarily a good spirit—can also mean a good servant of God! It seems that as the anointed servants of God, whom He is raising up for the blessing of the church, preach the fullness of the gospel message, a dividing is bound to occur. Those who truly love God in the formal churches will flow to the blessings of God, and the false who resist the moving of God's Spirit.

In his footnotes on the parable of the children of the kingdom and the children of the evil one, Dr. C. I. Schofield makes the comment that many who fondly believe with all their hearts that they are in very truth children of God are in reality children of the devil, and yet they are in our churches—not only in the World Council of Churches, but in every group. At the end of the age there comes a dividing. This time is *now*. Sheep follow the Shepherd when He leads into pastures new of the Holy Spirit, and His gifts. Goats jump and skip from one place to another.

2

DEMONS AND CHRISTIANS

The parables of the drag net, the wheat and tares, and the good seed and bad seed show that there is much evil in the church. Pastors who have a heart of love for their flocks will know the shocking cases that come to light. Adultery, lying, cheating, stealing, pride, and pettymindedness are all too common in all our denominations. Whispering and backbiting seem almost to be more common these days than the fruits of love and gentleness.

It is too easy to say that only non-Christians would evidence such carnal fruits and manifestations of the devil; for we find many Holy Spirit baptized Christians in our Pentecostal churches doing the same things! Leaders of churches seem more interested in politics, power, and money than in the moving of the Spirit and in humility! In fact it seems almost impossible to imagine that God can break through some church groups with their bazaars, bingos, and bake sales!

The church for centuries has taught that once a person has accepted Jesus as Savior, then Satan goes out and Jesus comes in and both cannot dwell in the same vessel at the same time; and this "doctrine" has completely blinded the minds of multitudes to the origin of the fruits and works of Satan in the church!

In *Christian Life* magazine (December 1961), read by thousands of Christians, there is a question and answer column ably answered by Dr. V. Raymond Edman, the principal of Wheaton College, Illinois. One of the questions asked in this column was, "Can Christians be demon possessed?" His reply was a classic:

> Theory says, No, but facts say, Yes. It is theoretical that a demon cannot possess a body in which the Holy Spirit dwells. However, I have known true Christians who were truly demon possessed, and who were delivered in answer to prayer given in the name of the Lord Jesus.

Again, in another issue of the same magazine, an interview with a Christian psychiatrist was given by the editor, Bob Walker. Here is a verbatim quotation:

My psychiatrist friend explained that he had been a psychiatrist before he became a Christian. He had moved into psychiatry from medicine in order to be of greater help to his patients. Here, however, he discovered that there were areas of spiritual experience which he did not understand. Finally he determined to find out about this. Purchasing a Bible he began a tour of the churches in his city. At length the Holy Spirit caught up to him and he accepted Christ as Savior and Lord.

After his conversion it appeared as though the whole mystery of the spiritual life opened like a flower. He explained that ultimately, there appear to be only two forces in the world, God and Satan. Everything else in life as we know it today can be reduced to these two basic factors. Because man is born with the tendency to sin, God has provided a plan of redemption by which men may become members of the family of God. Meanwhile, those who reject God and His Son, Jesus Christ, automatically become members of the family of Satan. There is no middle ground: man must become a member of one family or the other.

The psychiatrist explained that the man who becomes a member of the family of Satan is easy to understand; he is nothing more than a tool in the hand of Satan, and he has only one objective, to discredit God and His Son. Satan may drag some men to the gutter. In doing so he says in effect, "Man is simply an animal, so how can there be a God?" To other men Satan will give wealth and power and then say, "Why submit yourself to God? I will give you everything you want."

With these traps men are inveigled to believe that they can find the solution to their problems within themselves and apart from God. Nothing could be further from the truth. History as well as sociology and psychiatry provide plenty of evidence to the contrary.

The psychiatrist continued by saying that the Christian, on the other hand, is more difficult to understand. When he becomes a member of the family of God, God dwells in him. As a man surrenders to the Holy Spirit, allowing Him to take control of the various areas of his life, he is able to live a normal, balanced and successful mental, physical and spiritual life; but when he is unwilling to turn over certain areas of his life to the Lord, then Satan attacks. Because Satan is stronger than the man in the flesh, he submits to the temptations of Satan and sins. If this man is spiritually alert, he knows he has immediate recourse to God on the basis of 1 John 1:19, "If we confess our sins, he is faithful and just to forgive us our sins, and to cleanse us from all unrighteousness."

If a man does not confess his sin, Satan or one of his fellow demon spirits is in control of the phase of the Christian's life. He may enlarge his hold by inviting other stronger and bolder demon spirits to join him. Soon the Christian becomes so confused and defeated that he must seek mental or physical help. (See Matthew 12:43–45.)

The psychiatrist concluded by saying that he was convinced that except in the cases of physical injury or deterioration of brain cells, that all cases of mental sickness can be traced to demon power.

Such statements in a reputable Christian magazine would have been impossible a few short years, or even months ago. God has a time for a deeper revelation of old truths. Did not Jesus say, *"In my name shall* [ye] *cast out devils"* (Mark 16:17)? How many church groups have even tried to do it? How many Christians would even recognize the presence of a demon in a Christian by the operation of the gift of discerning of spirits? Up till recently very few, but God is moving by His Spirit so that those in the church who desire deliverance may receive it, for God is equipping men and women today with the power, authority, and ability to cast out demons in Jesus' name—and they are doing it!

In our own experiences which date back to the beginning of 1948, we have only prayed for and delivered Christians. In fact, experience shows that it is necessary for a sufferer to turn to Jesus before he can be delivered. It is not often realized that the demoniac of Gadara fell at the feet of Jesus and worshipped Him before the legion were cast out into the swine. Jesus did not go around indiscriminately casting out devils. When He went to the pool of Bethesda, He only healed one man whose faith was turning from means (the pool) to God. Jesus met him at the exact moment of faith. He always will!

One of the reasons for this book is to teach that Christians can be oppressed, depressed, possessed, and obsessed by demon spirits, and equally that they can be set free by concentrated, commanding prayer in Jesus' name, if they first confess their need and exercise their own faith. Jesus on one occasion said to a motley company of seventy disciples, *"Behold, I give unto you* **power** *to tread on serpents and scorpions, and over all the power of the enemy"* (Luke 10:19). This authority has never been cancelled. Are we any different today from those seventy disciples?

It has not been realized until recently that Satan, being an independent created being of great power, has to employ his demon spirits to do his work of destruction. God moves upon all flesh by His Holy Spirit who is omnipotent and omnipresent, but Satan is not omnipresent, neither is he omnipotent! He has limited power and authority, but this power and authority is absolutely subject to Jesus the Son of God. Neither Satan nor his demon spirits can do anything unless our heavenly Father permits them to do so. (See the story of Job.)

When Satan sees a Christian letting down his standard and exposing areas of his life to Satan, he at once jumps in with a demon spirit into that exposed area and begins to take possession of it, for it is not under the blood; and then when the first evil spirit (possibly criticism, jealousy, or lust) has established a good reliable beachhead, he holds it in order to make the way for other different types, who will also enter and start to establish their characteristics in the Christian's life, until the end of that Christian may be worse than before he was converted. Why do some Christians commit suicide?

As growth in grace is always forward for a true child of God, so a backsliding Christian grows backward into disgrace. We believe that as a Christian grows, the Holy Spirit takes increasingly greater control of his life. We often hear the theoretical statement made that so-and-so is "filled with the Spirit." There might have been an experience of the Holy Spirit in that person's life, but to say that he therefore was completely filled would seem to be contradicted by the obvious evidences all around us. We would suggest that when the Holy Spirit came upon that person certain areas of his life were taken over by the Holy Spirit—in fact as many as were surrendered—but what of those areas that *never were surrendered?* Experience shows that there are many Christians in our churches today who made a partial surrender, but hold on to certain other areas. Can we say that the Holy Spirit possesses the unsurrendered areas? We would hardly think so!

3

OPPRESSION

The title of this book, *Hidden Spirits*, was given of God through Evangelist G. M. Farley, of Williamsport, Maryland, who has designed the covers of our books. We have ministered together in prayer for Christians who have been cruelly bound by "hidden spirits." These tormenting spirits deliberately hide themselves so that the church as a whole has been unaware of their existence. The fact that so many Christians need to recognize their needs of deliverance is known to God and He is bringing these secrets out into the open as Jesus promised. At the same time the Lord is now increasing the number of His ministers who are having their eyes opened to the reality of evil spirits hidden in Christians. It is true that the opposition to this tremendous truth has been great by unthinking ministers, but there is a time for each new progressive revelation of the Holy Spirit.

Here is a story to illustrate how the Holy Spirit works today. A lady in Toronto invited us to her home and told us that she had internal pains and digestive troubles. As we began to pray, the Lord revealed through the gifts of the Spirit that her trouble was an inflamed gall bladder, from which she had had trouble for years, but it sometimes seemed to be healed and would then flare up again. She agreed that this was a true revelation of the Spirit, for she was familiar with the medical diagnosis, details of which she had not disclosed. As commanding prayer in the name of Jesus continued, the lady began to feel uncomfortable pressure internally in the region of her gall bladder, and then these wicked evil spirits of infirmity began to come out of her, being coughed out from her. The pain and pressure left and next day poison in her swollen ankle which had troubled her greatly left, and the swelling went down. This case is mentioned, for continuing gall bladder trouble in a Christian would not be associated with demons! They were hidden until the Spirit of the Lord revealed them and then the authority in the name of Jesus was used, and the power in the Holy Spirit, to exorcise them and cause healing to return to the lady. The only alternative that medical science can offer is to cut out the inflamed gall bladder, which is a very expensive operation, and why should a child of God have to have a piece of her body cut out when the Bible says that our bodies are the temples of the Spirit of God? Does God honestly want our bodies to be dismembered when He offers divine healing and deliverance?

Some of the evil spirits enumerated in the Bible are called deaf, dumb, and blind. What has not been recognized by the church when reading the relevant passages of Scripture is that a "blind spirit" means exactly what it says: an evil spirit or demon which is lodged in the human body of the person to cause deafness, dumbness, or blindness. If the "doctrine" was true that when the Spirit of Christ came in at conversion Satan went out, we are then forced to the repulsive idea that God wills the person to remain deaf, dumb, or blind! The Word of God does not agree with this apologetic theology! It is written that *"God anointed Jesus of Nazareth with the Holy Ghost and with power: who went about doing good, and healing all that were oppressed of the devil; for God was with Him"* (Acts 10:38). *"**All** that were **oppressed** of the devil."* Sickness is an oppression of the devil! It is not a gift of God—oppression means "to tyrannize." To illustrate by a simple analogy the meaning of the word "oppression," let us refer our readers to the story of Sinbad the Sailor, a classic of our childhood! On one occasion he landed on an island, and an old man jumped on his back and wherever Sinbad went the little old man refused to leave him and he was therefore compelled to have this wretched creature clinging around his neck, night and day. The little old man that sorely oppressed Sinbad the Sailor could be seen as well as felt, but demon spirits, though living creatures of malign intelligence and intention, cannot be seen, but they can be felt, and the feelings in the body are given medical names by the medical profession. In cases of sickness of the body, it seems that the evil spirits that oppress parts of the body are called by the generic name of "spirits of infirmity."

People get terrified at the thought of another living creature actually being *inside their body*, and flee to the comfortable thought that when they turned to Christ all these hidden spirits left their bodies. It is a sad commentary to have to acknowledge that there seems to be more sickness of the body in the church today, in spite of the increased knowledge of the medical profession, who do their best and deal with the symptoms. The servant of God gets at the cause—a spirit of infirmity, and casts it out of the area of the body that it is occupying. So many people who have been prayed for with cancers in their body have later submitted to a surgical operation only to be informed that the growth is no longer malignant. If the sufferer had waited patiently in faith for the Lord to complete the work of restoration, the benign growth would have dissolved away. It is the life of Satan in it that causes a cancer to grow, the evil spirit seeks to destroy once it has gained a bridgehead. It is the work of God to create, but the work of Satan to destroy. God made the human body after His own image, but Satan ever seeks to wreck the human cells, and cancer is one of his means.

This book is not written because of preconceived theories, nor is any attempt being made to disrupt existing theories held in unbelief. We are writing with a full knowledge of what is being done today in Jesus' name by men and women praying the commanding prayer of faith in Jesus' name with the power that comes alone by the baptism of the Spirit. Our "experiments" began at the beginning of 1948, when a congenital asthmatic case was completely healed and delivered in one-and-a-half hours of commanding prayer. We were frankly carrying out a spiritual experiment. This man, aged forty, had received the normal anointing with oil and the prayer of faith with the laying on of hands, but he did not recover! Something stronger—more violent—was needed; we decided to challenge the devil in Jesus' name. First we knowingly covered ourselves in the precious blood of Jesus by faith, then we attacked and commanded the evil spirits to come out—we did not know their name, we just decided we would find out the hard experimental way, and anyone who does so today will produce astonishing results! The man was completely delivered after being bound by spirits of infirmity in his breathing tubes, and was set permanently free—in one year he put on fifty pounds in weight, and his heart which had been weak was made strong. He had been "oppressed of the devil" and these evil spirits were inside him—naturally they had to be. They coughed and vomited out of him in a one-and-a-half-hour prayer session. This man had previously been gloriously saved and delivered from the Roman Catholic Church, and baptized in the Spirit as evidenced by speaking in tongues. When Jesus and the Holy Spirit came in, did the spirits or demons of infirmity go out? No! They had to be cast out violently later! If we had not prayed that prayer of faith for him, he might have been sick today, and possibly in his grave!

One lady, suffering from extreme weakness and nervous exhaustion, was prayed for in 1948 as one of our early experiments, and she was never expected to get out of bed again. We spent a few hours in special prayer with her and these spirits of weakness (infirmity) coughed out of her as we prayed, and today (1966) she is still alive and walking about enjoying herself—well past seventy!

It would be impossible to catalogue all the cases of all the hundreds that have received healing by the prayer of faith practiced in this forceful manner. It is a question of recognizing that it is a demon or demons, and then learning to attack and wrestle with them, for they are entirely subject unto us in Jesus' name. It is not safe to attack unless we have faith in the protection of the blood of Jesus applied by our own faith. As the children of Israel used it on the doors of their homes, so we sprinkle it on our lives, so that the destroyer shall not harm us. (See Exodus 12:23.) In many cases, no immediate evidence is noticed, but this should not discourage us. We should press the battle in full assurance of the victory of Calvary in each case. Simply command the evil spirits to come out of the bodies in Jesus' name, and go on commanding until they do. There is not always a manifestation. Sometimes it is quite violent, and they come out through the throat as the person is in great discomfort and coughs convulsively as evil spirits leave the body! This is sometimes evidenced by milder coughing of a constant nature, and in lesser cases occasional coughs. Sometimes the sufferer yawns or sighs, and sometimes a feeling of great release is felt. Weeping as an evidence of release is quite common, as the demon seems to express his crocodile tears at leaving!

Do we say, therefore, that these Christians were possessed of a devil? The Bible says they were oppressed by the devil! Jesus spoke of those who were vexed of a devil. If we use Bible expressions we shall not be misunderstood. Whether oppressed, possessed, vexed, or obsessed, the same prayer of faith will avail!

4

PARTIAL POSSESSION

In the last chapter, we endeavored to demonstrate and prove that Christians can suffer chronic sicknesses due to being indwelt by evil spirits of infirmity lodging in areas of the physical body. It is obvious that non-Christians are similarly affected, but it would be unrealistic to try to continue to take the foolish theological position that sickness is sent of God to Christians when Jesus healed people oppressed of the devil. We do not by any means suggest that all sickness is caused by an indwelling demon in the body. Some troubles are caused by accidents and actual destruction of physical parts of the body. Even in these cases evil spirits will often hinder healing, or take advantage of a physical weakness of the body.

However, the body is not the only part of man to be attacked by Satan. Man is triune—spirit, soul, and body. He also has a will, which is related to his mind. Satan will send his demons to attack the mind of the believer; he will implant thoughts such as murder, suicide, theft, adultery, filthiness, etc. It is an interesting thought for us to consider. From whence do thoughts originate? There are possibly three answers to this complex question. The first is, from the Holy Spirit of God who gives us thoughts of purity and nobleness. Conversely, Satan and his cohorts give us thoughts of impurity, wickedness, licentiousness, and lust. In the middle is our subconscious mind, about which we do not understand very much, but it seems to be a kind of reservoir or tape recorder of thoughts and impressions of forgotten things that happened, even in impressionable childhood. From these three sources we suggest all our thoughts and dreams materialize. "First the thought and then the deed" is a true saying, and Jesus told us that the evil thoughts that proceed from the human mind defile the man, and God would never give us a thought to defile us. It must be Satan who gives it to us. In John 13:2, Satan first put the evil thought into the heart (mind) of Judas Iscariot, and then when Judas agreed to the thought it is recorded in verse 27 that *"Satan entered into him."* From a thought to possession and death. Satan used the channel of a human life, through his mind, to sell Jesus for thirty pieces of silver. We are sure that Judas could have resisted, for he also had free will. He loved money more than God—have we met any professing Christians today like this? What about those who are convinced about tithing and do not tithe?

One of the first cases with which we had to deal in 1948 was a deacon in a church who intended suicide. We had enough discernment of spirits in those days to tell him over the telephone that he was possessed in his mind of a demon of suicide. He came for deliverance, and in one-and-a-half hours he was gloriously delivered as these strong killing demons, which spoke to us, were coughed violently out of him. To say that the poor man was not a child of God would have been cruel. He needed deliverance and came to Jesus like the demoniac of Gadara. The destroying spirit had taken possession of him, though he had made a profession of faith in Jesus Christ and had been baptized in the Spirit.

A few years ago we prayed for a man in Chicago, Illinois, who had a sweet and lovable spirit and was always at every service of his church and helped where possible. He truly loved the Lord and freely worshipped Him. This man was terribly bound in his mind and was unable to remember either the text or the message preached by the pastor. For over forty years he had been bound in his mind. As a young man in the army of the First World War, he had committed sins common to young soldiers, though he was a professing Christian, and this backsliding from the path of moral rectitude, due to the pressures of war, had caused a binding spirit to come into his mind. In a half hour these spirits were coughed out of him and he expressed overwhelming joy later that his mind was now fresh and he could remember both the text and the context of the sermon preached by his pastor, who is also regularly casting out demons in Jesus' name today! It is highly probable that this man would have gone to his grave, a believing Christian, with these binding spirits in his mind unless God in His great mercy had brought to light this tremendous truth of new spiritual dimension. *"In my name shall ye cast out devils"* (Mark 16:17).

Is it not true today that in our churches there are people who have unforgiving spirits, lustful spirits, unclean spirits, thieving spirits, and suchlike? To those whose ministry it is to pray for those so oppressed we record with sorrow that these people are in our churches, and many of them have had the baptism in the Spirit, and when we have prayed for them the evil spirits have named themselves, and told us when they entered; sometimes when the person was a child. Coming to Christ and receiving the baptism of the Spirit had not cast out the evil tormenting spirits. Later prayer was necessary for that, and then and then only did these evil characteristics leave and they lost the desire to steal, commit adultery, and to lie. We must not assume that some of these poor people want to continue living this type of life, for they do not! They are seeking those who will pray them through to deliverance! Some of them have waged unsuccessful war for years against these horrible traits in their natures, but have failed. Yes, we know of others whom God cleaned up when they came to Christ, but it does not seem to happen in all cases—by any means. We have to deal with facts as God presents them to us, not fanciful theories of apologetic theology!

Why do we have so many denominations and sects today? Is this God's perfect will for His children? Why are some sects obviously so far off the truths of pure Bible doctrine and obstinately stick to their errors? Paul left us in no doubt. He said they are led away by doctrines of demons and seducing spirits. (See 1 Timothy 4:1.) These demons are deliberately sent to seduce a child of God away from the love of Jesus, and then when they have enticed him, as we read in James 1:12–15, they lead him to his spiritual death, and sometimes suicide. This Scripture states quite clearly that God does not tempt a man. It is Satan that does this dirty work, and entices the child of God; then he implants his own erroneous doctrines, and the evil spirits will continue to teach and enlarge these false doctrines in the poor deluded person's mind, while they carry on their false cult with all the zeal of the prophets of Baal, who were so in earnest that they cut themselves with knives. (see 1 Kings 18:28.) We can be earnestly wrong—away by a seducing spirit and fed by doctrines of demons! There never was a day of so many false doctrines and false cults, even denying the blood of Jesus and His divinity. Let us be sure that we do not entertain these demons in our minds that they might so easily seduce us from the truth of God's Holy Word, which alone is able to save us from Satan and his enormous power.

Once a child of God has opened the door of his mind to the Holy Spirit, this same door is also open to other spirits. Let us not be deceived. It is only as we *walk in the light* as Jesus is in the Light, that the blood of Jesus is able to keep our minds clean and clear. (See 1 John 1:7.) When a Christian backslides in any particular he is wide open for the oppression of demons, which leads ultimately to possession.

Attacks upon the minds of Christians is one of Satan's most popular and common devices. If Satan went out when Jesus came in, we would have perfect churches!

We cannot close this chapter without referring to the tragic tricks of Satan that he plays on sensitive Christians by obsessing their minds with a lie. Spiritual obsession is very common and may actually lead a person into a mental home where the medical profession will administer electric and insulin shock treatments in an attempt to smash this tormenting obsession in the brain. An obsession of Satan is a lie that is first whispered into the mind by a demon, then it causes consternation or alarm, and eventually brings in reinforcements which then take over more and more of the mind with the one thought, until it is difficult for this person, now known as a neurotic, to think of anything else. Appeals to reason fail because the lie is now believed as truth, and this is a most difficult sickness with which to deal. Two things seem to be necessary, the first of course is believing prayer, and many sessions may have to be undertaken in such a case, until the mind begins to clear, and then it must at once be fed on the truth of God's Word. The opposite truth to Satan's lie must be continually implanted by the Christian friend or minister. It may be a case of insomnia, and so we must continually remind the sufferer that it is written, *"He giveth his beloved sleep"* (Psalm 127:2), and by this means the poor obsessed mind will be led into the light of God's truth, which alone sets men free. No wonder James wrote, *"Confess your faults one to another, and pray one for another, that ye may be healed"* (James 5:16).

In connection with this Scripture it must be emphasized that no person can be delivered if they are not willing to confess their need and their great desire to be delivered. We will save ourselves a lot of time, energy, and trouble if we make quite sure that the person really does want to be free. Strange as it may seem, some people will come for the prayer of deliverance, but deep down in their hearts they still have some love left for their sin. Practical experience has taught us that alcoholics and moral perverts find it very hard to "come clean." They still love their sin from which they ask to be set free. Moral perverts will go to any length to hide their sin under a cloak of religion, and will actually ask for prayer to pretend that they have been delivered in the eyes of the church, so that they can continue their terrible sin under the cloak of deceit.

Unless a person desires Jesus Christ above all else, it may be dangerous to pray the prayer of deliverance, for if the demon is cast out at the time of prayer, he will not only seek reentrance, but will bring seven others worse than himself and the last state of the person is worse than before we prayed. Backsliders caught in Satan's grip must be certain they really mean business with God before we pray. Jesus must be their heart's desire, not just deliverance.

5

ATTACKS ON THE
HUMAN SPIRIT

The body and the mind are not the only parts of man that Satan seeks to occupy and destroy. If he can attack the human spirit he wins a tremendous victory. Who has not despaired in trying to help a person suffering from spiritual depression and melancholia? Although this may sometimes be called mental depression, yet we believe that its primary cause lies in the human spirit. A deep shock, or the loss of a near relative, or the loss of a business or prestige can induce a condition of spiritual hopelessness, when the individual gives up all hope and loses all initiative. Arguments and reason fail to reach such a case, and many end their days in a mental hospital.

Mrs. Agnes Sanford, well known in the Episcopal church of the United States, a lady filled with the Holy Spirit, has had some invaluable experience in such cases, as she herself at one time knew the hopeless depths of a crushed human spirit. She advocates that the first step is to enter into the sufferings of the individual as far as is possible by compassionate understanding—in other words to get down into the pit with them, to weep with them, and to identify oneself with their pitiful state, and then to pray a positive prayer of faith on their behalf, to break the hold that Satan has on the crushed human spirit. From this point it should be possible gradually to encourage the sufferer and get him back on the Word of God. Such people will endeavor to cling like ivy to the one who enters into their sufferings, and great patience and understanding will be necessary, but every effort should be made to get the suffering one out of this depression and to stand on their own feet and to occupy their minds by doing something of interest, as this mental therapy will help greatly to get the mind to function in a positive manner. As the mind begins to work, so will the human will begin to take over, and instead of willingness to be negative, positive desires will once again be found in the human mind, and then as the mind begins to operate afresh it can be fed progressively on the Word of God. Negative thoughts must never be entertained or discussed. By showing sympathy and compassion, we do not mean that we have to be negative and listen to their negatives for too long. If we do they will not progress, but desire only to dwell in their shadows. We must lead them out into light by feeding them afresh on the pure Word of life.

It seems that Christians are in many cases victims of spiritual depression, even those filled with the Spirit. Even though Christ may have come in, Satan seeks to overthrow His rule by taking advantage in times of shock. We do well to remember the words of Scripture found in 1 Corinthians 10:13, "*There has no temptation* [trial] *taken you but such as is common to man: but God is faithful, who will not suffer you to be tempted above that ye are able: but will with the temptation* [trial] *also make a way to escape, that ye may be able to bear it.*" It is clear from this Scripture that all who suffer by Satan's attacks as he seeks to "take" them, must ultimately enter into the way of escape for themselves, although we may pull on the rope. The only sure way of healing in spirit, soul, or body lies in the individual being willing to believe God's Word for themselves and act as though they believed.

Our prayers break Satan's strong grip, leaving the individual unchained, though weak, to walk out of the enemy's strong prison. In Bunyan's *The Pilgrim's Progress*, the hero, Christian, got off the straight and narrow path and was captured by Giant Despair and locked up in his foul dungeon of Doubting Castle. There, poor Christian lay for days waiting death at the giant's hands, and he was in a most miserable and hopeless state, though a bright Christian a few hours before! His spirit was crushed and his mind filled with fear and forebodings at what Satan's emissaries would do. After being in acute misery and depression for days, he put his hand into his bosom and pulled out some promises of God, which acted as keys to all the locks of the prison and castle, and even though Giant Despair saw him leave he was powerless to stop his escape to freedom, because he had the promises of God. Jesus said the truth would set us free.

In Isaiah 61:1 we read that Jesus was anointed of the Holy Spirit to "*bind up the brokenhearted, to proclaim liberty to the captives, and the opening of the prison to them that are bound.*" He comes again today through his anointed servants to bind up our wounds of spirit, to preach the glorious truth that He has set us free—emancipated us from the hands of the lying deceiving devil, and then He throws the door of our prison wide open and says, "You are free." It still remains for the poor bound captive to get up and walk out. This is his part. He may elect to remain in prison and we must then pray that Satan's power shall be broken over his spirit that his will may begin to operate.

There can be no failures in the ministry of deliverance from the cruel bondage of the devil if we can get the cooperation of the sufferer.

A young man came to us for help. He had been in touch with Dr. Oswald Smith of The People's Church, Toronto, who very graciously advised him to visit us, for Dr. Smith believed we had the experience to help. This man had been in a hospital for psychiatric help. He had had many shock treatments and was on strong drugs. He was so bound that he could not leave home, and was so filled with fear that he broke out in a sweat at the very mention of doing anything. It was explained to him that Jesus would heal him if he made the first effort. The prodigal son took the first step and God the second. We believe this is a pattern of all restoration. This man came to a church service and immediately felt the different spirit in the church—different from his home or the hospital. Compassion was shown—we endeavored to enter into his torments of spirit and mind as far as possible, and then prayed for him. This began a chain reaction, although he had downs as well as ups for a few weeks. We prayed several times, and each time he improved, finally we prayed for him and he received a most powerful baptism of the Spirit, speaking forth in unknown tongues as the Holy Spirit came in and possessed him. He attended the services regularly and then was baptized in water, understanding that this signified death to the old life of torment. He grasped this truth and continued to walk in newness of resurrection life purchased for him by Jesus. His doctor was astonished at his progress, but he freely told him how Jesus had healed him. We venture to say that his progress will continue and be permanent as he applies himself to learn about Jesus and His Word, and attends the services of the church as often as humanly possible.

The reason that people backslide is because they begin to grow cold in their love for God and His Word and let other things draw them away from the house of God. This is Satan's opportunity and he pounces and then the backslider is in trouble, which may lead to physical sickness, mental disturbance, or a spiritual depression, or all three. Let us never forget that the gift of God is eternal life, but the wages of sin is *death*. (See Romans 6:23.)

6

SECRETS REVEALED

In spite of the clear statement of Scripture that sickness is an oppression (tyranny) of Satan (see Acts 10:38), most Christians have been very slow to understand this simple fact. If Satan is the author of sickness and disease as seems clear, then it must be understood that he is not omnipresent as is the Holy Spirit, but he must use his underlings, cohorts, devils, demons, or evil spirits (call them by what name you prefer!). These wicked spirits do their work as invisible beings, and are therefore hidden from view, but their baneful effects are all too obvious in sickness, suffering, and disease.

Smith Wigglesworth has been one of the greatest men of faith in this twentieth century, but like many such men he had to go down to the depths of near death to bring the message of deliverance to the captives. As a pastor of a mission in the north of England, he held the traditional view that sickness had to be endured if it could not be healed, and if it was permitted of God to work out a deeper Christian walk, it might be better to keep the sickness rather than lose it! This illogical approach is still held by multitudes who go to a doctor and yet secretly believe they are suffering for the glory of God.

Mr. Wigglesworth went down to death's door with chronic appendicitis. His wife did not expect him to live and was preparing for his death. For six months, he had been going downhill, and one night rolled on the floor of his mission in agony, for as yet he only had a very faint vision of Jesus as the Healer of the body! They brought him home and put him to bed in his agony, and all night he prayed and pleaded with God for healing and deliverance, but none came! The family doctor was called in that night and he said there was no possible hope, for his body was too weak to stand an operation. The doctor left the house and Mrs. Wigglesworth was heartbroken, expecting the angel of death to visit the home that night.

Just after the doctor left, God began to undertake, no doubt in answer to importunate prayers. A young man and an old lady visited the home, the latter being known as a woman of prayer. They entered into the sick room, and without any preliminary discussion, the young man jumped onto the bed and commanded the *evil spirit* to come out of him! He shouted, "Come out you devil; I command you to come out in the name of Jesus." Smith Wigglesworth explained that there was no chance for argument or opportunity given to tell the young man that there was no demon inside him, for he would never have believed it. What Christian would have believed such "heresy" in 1900? Naturally the demon had to go, and *it went*, and he was instantly healed.

He arose and dressed and went downstairs, and as he was a plumber he asked his astonished wife if there were any jobs to be done. Yes, there was one, so he took his tools and went off to do it. Just after he left the doctor returned and walked upstairs to the bedroom. To his astonishment he found the dying patient had gone. On inquiring what had happened, Mrs. Wigglesworth said, "He has gone to work." "In that case," said the doctor, "you will never see him alive again; they will bring him back a corpse." Mr. Wigglesworth lived to be a ripe eighty-seven years young and prayed for the sick until he went to be with the Lord after a service in God's house. He never needed another doctor, for he had found the power that there is in the name of Jesus to cast out demons of infirmity that cause such mundane sicknesses as appendicitis.

Dr. Alexander Dowie, who founded Zion City, Illinois, and who had such a marvelous deliverance church in Chicago whose walls were covered with crutches, braces, and other evidences of the divine healing power of God, came into his ministry by realizing also that it is necessary to take dominion over the devil and his demons. In 1904, he was a pastor of a Congregational church in Australia, and the area was hit by a terrible plague, which caused the death of many of his congregation. He was hard put in his house visitation work to explain how this could be, especially to faithful Christian people. He saw their agony and writhing, but was impotent to stop the plague. He visited one home in which a young girl and her brother were in their death throes; the girl was foaming at the mouth, her face turning black, and the death rattle in her throat. With the desperation of despair, and with a righteous holy indignation arising in his breast, he openly faced the demon of death, Satan (see Hebrews 2:14), and commanded him to come out of the girl in Jesus' name. Instantly, the blackness in the face began to disappear, and the frothing at the mouth stopped, and the breathing became normal. He then went into her brother's room and again faced the devil and rebuked him in Jesus' name, commanding him to come out of the boy. The same glorious result was seen. Satan, the angel of death, left that home and it is recorded that from that moment there were no more deaths in Dowie's church. He arrested the plague by using the name of Jesus as his authority to rebuke the devil—and the devil went!

A pastor's wife once told us of a very remarkable experience in her life. Having been brought up to believe that Jesus is the divine physician, she refused to consult a physician when she developed gangrene of the leg. This wound grew in size, until she was no longer able to walk or stand. With dogged spirit she continued to attend to her needs by dragging herself about on the floor of her kitchen. One day she looked at the terrible open wound and she said, "I saw the face of the devil in it." This realization, which apparently was made clear to her by the Holy Spirit, caused her at once to shout, "Satan, I rebuke you in Jesus' name and command you to come out of my leg." From that moment onwards, the wound began to heal, and later when she was examined by a doctor, he refused to believe she could have had such a terrible wound healed without the help of medical science. Her name was Mrs. Daisy Horton, late beloved wife of Harold Horton, the author of the classic *The Gifts of the Spirit*.

Again referring to the late Smith Wigglesworth, he used to say that there are times when you pray for the sick and appear to get rough; here we are not dealing with a person, we are dealing with the satanic forces that are binding and oppressing the person. Our hearts are full of love and compassion for the sufferer, but we are moved to holy anger as we see the place that Satan has taken *in the body of* the sick one, and we deal with his entrenched position with power, authority, and force vested in us as Holy Spirit filled believers. He said that we are *always right* when we dare to deal with sickness as a devil. Much sickness is caused by some misconduct, mistake, or neglect, but this has given Satan an opportunity to get in by his evil spirits of sickness. He then says that the person may need to repent and confess where the door had been opened for Satan to come in, and then the prayer of faith and the rebuke in the name of Jesus can be given to the spirit of sickness or infirmity, and the person healed.

In the case of cancer, a far too prevalent killing disease, Wigglesworth tells us to recognize that there is a living evil spirit in the cancer that is destroying the body. He used to curse the evil life in the cancers and command it to come out in Jesus' name. He often saw the dead tissues of cancer leave the body after such prayers.

In our own ministry, we commenced delivering people in the name of Jesus by the same methods. We attacked the devilish power behind the sicknesses in Jesus' name, and in twenty years to the time of writing we have seen some amazing healings and deliverances in spirit, soul, and body. It was after these initial experiences that the Holy Spirit began to teach us from the Scriptures that this would seem to be the accepted method of approaching sickness in Apostolic days. Did not the seventy elders return from their healing mission with a shout of triumph saying, *"Lord even the **devils** are subject unto us in thy name"*? (Luke 10:17). It was then that Jesus assured them they had *power* to tread on serpents and scorpions, and to take authority over all the *power* of Satan. The last part of this promise has often fortified us in our battle against demons powers, *"And nothing shall by any means hurt you"* (verse 19).

(For more information on this subject, read *Demons & Deliverance* by the author).

7

GIVE ME THIS MOUNTAIN

When an understanding person comes to Jesus Christ and accepts Him as Savior, he enters into a legal agreement with Him. This document is known as the New Testament and is the last will and testament of our heavenly Father. It is recorded that God in Christ died reconciling the world unto Himself, but though the whole world is reconciled, yet this contract and the terms of it have to be accepted by the individual. Most Christians only accept portions of the terms of this will, and so do not receive very much. This is a document of love, founded on love, but all the promises of it must be received only on the grounds of our personal faith. It is here that most Christians fail. They are satisfied to settle for small blessings in this life so long as they can be assured of eternal life in heaven after death.

This conception is a far cry from the truth. This new covenant carries promises of *divine health* for spirit, soul, and body. It carries promises of prosperity in the sense that God will supply all our needs according to His riches in glory. It carries promises of joy, rest, peace, and happiness in the midst of turmoil and trials that destroy our neighbors. Too frequently our eyes are on the circumstances around us, and not on the Word of God. We compare ourselves with others, which is not wise, instead of with Jesus who loves us. It must be confessed, if we are honest, that too many of us are poor representations of the more abundant life that He promises to give to all who will believe *and accept*. We are more often sick than well; we are more often complaining than full of praise; we are more often scraping for existence than relaxing in abundance; we are too often critical and do not enjoy the success of others. In fact it seems we are one great contradiction. We say we are Christians, but where is the evidence? God wants everyone to know that we are Christians by the more abundant life that we radiate in health, wealth, happiness, and love. Too many Christians try to live the Christian life and do the works of the Spirit without the baptism of the Spirit, and yet this great blessing is free for the taking—it is ours—but unbelief, fear, jealousy, pride, and ignorance keep us from entering in. One of the greatest of the spirits that Satan sends is the spirit of bondage. What a contrast, for we read, *"For ye have not received the spirit of bondage again to fear; but ye have received the Spirit of adoption"* (Romans 8:15). The Holy Spirit adopts us into the family of God and Jesus our Savior and Deliverer becomes our elder Brother. He is the only begotten Son of God, but we become sons of God by adoption. Surely our elder Brother does not want us to live at such a low level of Christian experience. Is it not His will that we should live like the royalty we are in Christ? We are sons and daughters of the King!

If it is true that when Jesus Christ comes into our hearts and lives Satan immediately goes out, then where does the spirit of bondage that grips us in vicelike fear come from? We are told God does not give it to us! Where do the spirits of pride, jealousy, greed, deceit, lying, cheating, and lust come from, for God does not put them upon us. King Saul was among the prophets of Israel, but because of disobedience God sent a lying spirit who prophesied through him after the Holy Spirit had departed.

It seems to us that when a person dedicates his life to the service of Jesus Christ he has entered into the contract, but there is still a long and serious battle ahead to clear out the giants who have occupied the territory of our lives. The type is found in the story of Caleb, who requested that the mountain of the Anakims should be his, as was promised by God to Moses forty years before. He exclaimed, with a heart full of faith and a body full of health and strength at eighty-five years of age,

> Now therefore give me this mountain, whereof the LORD spake in that day for... the Anakims were there and the cities were great and fenced: if so be the LORD will be with me, then I shall be able to **drive them out**, as the LORD said.
>
> (Joshua 14:12)

The mountain belonged to Caleb as a sacred trust from God, but before he could enjoy his inheritance he had to make war and drive out the giants from the mountain. He had to go up and attack, but having God's Word behind him and the certainty of God's help, he knew before he started that he could possess fully the inheritance by making progressive war against the enemy entrenched in strongly fortified cities.

When we give our lives to God, He gives them back to us as a sacred trust. Our lives belong to God, but the outworking of His promises rest in our hands as we exercise our own faith, and remember, where fear is present faith cannot operate. Fear paralyzes our actions and makes our inheritance to be immobilized. We must be full of faith and have a different spirit to some, and wholly follow the Lord. (See Joshua 14:14.)

Our lives are sometimes most complex, due to early environmental upbringing, prenatal care, heredity, illnesses, and shocks in early impressionable childhood.

Psychologists are beginning to try to probe some of these problems, but those who regularly pray for Christians who are sick, bound, and oppressed, are finding out some very interesting answers. If Satan went out when Jesus came in, then it seems obvious he would be perfect at the rebirth! Experience shows that this is not so—far from it! It is only as the Holy Spirit comes to our help, and shines into the inner recesses of our complex lives that we begin to see ourselves as God sees us, at least in a measure, and the results are not very flattering to those who rely on self-righteousness to see them through life. It is the continuing revelation of our imperfections that drives us to seek God afresh to deliver us from these traits, or areas in our lives that Satan has never vacated. Why should he vacate them? The Anakims would have gone on living on the mountain belonging to Caleb unless he boldly drove them out, and this did not happen in one day or one week. Even after every Anakim was dead, or had fled, there was still the need to consolidate, and to cultivate the newly acquired territory. The vineyards had to be pruned, dug, and manured to bring forth their fruits.

There is nothing automatic about salvation. The connotation of the word "salvation" does not only indicate the right of entry into heaven at death, but carries the thought of full deliverance for the whole man, spirit, soul, and body in this life. The word *sozo*, which is Greek for salvation, is translated as "healed, made whole, delivered, set free," and means complete emancipation. When the slaves of the South were emancipated by proclamation of Abraham Lincoln, many of them preferred to remain tied to their old masters. They did not lay hold fully of their legal rights.

We are convinced that most Christians need to recognize that they can get rid of chronic bondages and fears in their lives, they can get rid of those stubborn sicknesses which have plagued them all their lives, and without the help of the strong prayers of deliverance, rebuking the sicknesses as of Satan, they will probably go to an early grave with their sicknesses, in spite of being "good church members." Jesus never meant for this to happen, for the terms of the New Testament give us freedom and more abundant life. If we remain satisfied to permit the demons of pride, anger, avarice, fear, bondage, and false doctrines to remain in their fenced cities in our lives, then God can do nothing to help us until we recognize these truths and go to work to cast them out. Satan lulls many into the sleep of hopelessness if they say that Jesus drove them all out for them when He came in. The truth is that Jesus only occupies the areas of our lives into which we invite Him. It is true that our lives belong to Him and He returns them to us to take care of, as stewards of the mysteries of God, but we must clean up every area governed by Satan and his evil spirits.

Once confession of a need is made, we can then pray objectively for the Christian, and it is marvelous how these evil spirits then come out of them in a most spectacular way, and the relief and release is sweet indeed as Jesus comes in and takes over that area in the mountain of our lives as one more giant has been cast out. The price of freedom is eternal vigilance, and we need thereafter to keep that area under the blood of Jesus so that the destroyer does not seek to reoccupy the area. (See Exodus 12:23.)

Remember, we receive Jesus as Savior and the Holy Spirit as Baptizer entirely on the grounds of our personal faith. He takes us as we are, not as we think we are, and comes into us in the measure that He is able. Our lives are like a one-hundred-room hotel, and we must surrender all these rooms to Jesus and the Holy Spirit, and sometimes Satan will strongly resist, especially in the smoking or drinking room! Rooms of lust are very prevalent in Christians today and some have fought losing battles in their own strength against these demons. A life of victory is possible for all Christians, but we must learn to humble ourselves under the mighty hand of God, not to excuse ourselves and talk about heredity or subconscious influences from childhood. If we can indeed do all things through Christ who strengthens us, then we can take the mountain and drive out the giants for God is with us.

Lord, give me this mountain!

HOW TO RECEIVE THE BAPTISM OF THE HOLY SPIRIT

CONTENTS

1

OBJECTIONS EXAMINED

Many books have been written on the experience known in the Bible as "the baptism in the Holy Spirit." One would have thought that enough had already been written on this subject without me adding another small book about this blessing, but as I travel in many places I pray for hundreds from all denominations to receive this baptism, and they almost invariably receive the ability to speak clearly in other tongues.

I find much ignorance among Christians, largely due to wrong teaching, fear, and lack of hunger. My purpose is to try and remove the effects of wrong teaching and to show how beautifully easy it is to submit oneself fully to the Holy Spirit and allow Him to take over and saturate our whole being.

One large denomination in Canada has written through its council of bishops that there is only one baptism, which is the sprinkling of babies. Later, they say, this visitation of the Holy Spirit is confirmed at a service called "confirmation," and this solemn service is equated with the happenings on the day of Pentecost (see Acts 2:4), and one may or may not subsequently "speak in tongues." If one does not, it does not mean that the person has not received the Holy Spirit, for there is no "baptism in the Spirit" as such, only a development of receiving the Spirit which begins at infant baptism and continues at confirmation; later tongues may or may not occur. It is all one baptism they teach, administered by "the church." This is, of course, far from what the Bible teaches! Unfortunately it sticks in the minds of those who are so taught and becomes a stumbling block when praying for the baptism in the Spirit.

In past history, there were a very few isolated cases of individuals who spoke in tongues as the Holy Spirit gave them the utterance. The leaders of the historic churches knew nothing of the experience themselves, and therefore were hard put to explain what had happened to those who did receive. It was normal theology to teach that their members or communicants had received the Holy Spirit at the confirmation service, and so any suggestion that they had not received the baptism of the Spirit was loftily rejected as the teaching of the ignorant. Others taught that one received the Holy Spirit at conversion, which was usually equated with a crisis experience.

These strong teachings had the effect of short-circuiting the power of the Holy Spirit in people's lives, for they were not willing to seek what they supposed they already had. I remember sharing my personal experience of the receiving the baptism of the Spirit with a minister of a historic denomination, for I had once belonged to his denomination; when I spoke of the glory of God that suddenly flooded my whole being, as on the day of Pentecost, and of this glory flowing out of me as rivers of living water in tongues, he not only rejected my testimony but accused me of being a very arrogant man. I was very surprised and asked him why. He replied that I had said that I entered a new spiritual dimension. This he could not accept, for it assumed he had not entered this dimension. Human pride is a terribly strong thing. It is what caused Satan to fall from heaven onto this earth, and Adam and Eve to be rejected by God from their Edenic existence. Beware of this sin of pride.

There are those who teach that we receive "everything" at conversion. As soon as a new convert becomes a newborn babe in Christ and has become a member of the kingdom of God, then there is nothing more to seek. Their names are written in the Lamb's Book of Life, they are adopted sons of God, and they are taught to stay with this experience and be faithful in church, and especially to witness about their rebirth. It comes as a great shock to them and to others to realize that Jesus never expected us to be witnesses unto Him until we also had received our Pentecostal experience! (See Acts 1:8.) There is such a thing as witnessing in the power of the mind and intellect and not in the power of the Spirit. We admire the sincerity of these fundamental Christians who produce various helps and methodologies to win souls for Jesus, but they forget the one absolute ingredient: the baptism in the Spirit! We have to remember that Jesus never began to minister until He also had His personal experience of the Spirit coming upon Him. We will deal with this in a later chapter.

Another loophole for some is the fact that John the Baptist was filled with the Holy Spirit from his mother's womb. (See Luke 1:15.) It therefore becomes easier to equate oneself with the greatest prophet of the Old Testament than to seek the baptism in the Spirit. Let it be remembered that if John the Baptist had been permitted by God to live until the outpouring of the Spirit on the day of Pentecost, he would have been one of the first up the steps to the upper room, because he prophesied by the Holy Spirit that Jesus would baptize all the converts under his ministry with the Holy Spirit and fire. (See Matthew 3:11.) He deliberately compared the baptism in water which he administered with another baptism which Jesus would administer. To suggest that there are not two separate baptisms here is to destroy the clearly intended meaning of the words of John. He compares Spirit baptism with water baptism.

The whole of the ministry of John the Baptist was in the closing days of the old covenant. The New Testament had not yet been sealed with the blood of Jesus. Another who was filled with the Spirit under the old covenant was Zacharias, who prophesied about the coming of Jesus into the world as a babe. (See Luke 1:67.) Elizabeth likewise was filled with the Holy Spirit when she prophesied over Mary the mother of Jesus. (See Luke 1:41.) Are we to assume that because these three were filled with the Holy Spirit they were also baptized in the Spirit? Obviously not, because Mary later received this baptism in the upper room.

The ministry of John was one which called to repentance thousands of Jews in a great national awakening. This "revival" was a precursor of the outpouring on the day of Pentecost. John's preaching was focused on repentance and confession of sins. The baptism that followed was understood by the Jews as being a symbolic washing away of those sins already confessed. (See Matthew 3:6; Mark 1:4–5.) They understood that this baptism or washing ceremony assured them that their sins had been remitted. It was not the water but God's forgiveness that remitted their sins, because Jesus was slain before the foundation of the world in the mind of the Father. The whole of the ministry of John the Baptist was therefore emphasizing the need of (a) repentance, (b) confession, (c) baptism, and (d) knowledge that sins had been remitted. This is shown in strong relief when the Pharisees and Sadducees came to John and asked him what they should do! His reply was neither tactful nor diplomatic: *"O generation of vipers, who hath warned you to flee from the wrath to come?"* (Matthew 3:7). Obviously the baptism of John was only for those who had a repentant heart and wanted to live right before a Holy God, and John knew that many of the religious people and their leaders were hypocrites—going to the synagogue and going through the motions of religion with no change of heart. There can be little doubt that the penitents under John were truly born again of the Spirit of God and knew it. From among their number, no doubt, Jesus later found His disciples, and these went forth healing the sick and casting out demons years before the birth of the Christian church—the body of Christ!

Are not the evangelicals of our day in the same position spiritually as the converts in John's day? They confess their sins, forsake their sins, accept the Lamb of God as Savior, and are baptized in water, but usually they do not then heal the sick and cast out demons! In other words, the early disciples of Jesus under the old covenant did more than many who today claim to be filled with the Spirit (but have never spoken in tongues), and yet none of the disciples had come to their personal Pentecostal experience! It comes as a shock to many to realize that the famous text of John 3:16 was spoken by Jesus to Nicodemus in the closing days of the old covenant.

It is an Old Testament text, not a New Testament Scripture. The rebirth by the Spirit of God was offered to Nicodemus under the terms of the old covenant. The new covenant was not made until Jesus sealed it with His own blood on the cross. Calvary is the dividing line between the old and the new. This confusion comes from the fact that our Bible carries the gospel accounts of Matthew, Mark, Luke, and John under the heading "The New Testament."

It must be obvious that the disciples of Jesus who healed the sick and cast out demons (see Luke 10:17–19) were saved, baptized in water, and had allied themselves to Jesus. Their names were written in heaven. (See Luke 10:20.) There was no corporate body of Christ in these days, because Jesus, after He was anointed of the Holy Spirit, was Himself the body of Christ. This is why He said that the temple of His body had to be destroyed: if it had not been, it would have been impossible for us to be made members of His body after the cross. These early disciples had the same experiences as most of our fundamentalists have today, without the baptism of the Spirit. They were "saved."

If we look for John 3:16 in the New Testament we find it is contained in Acts 2:38 where Peter, after the 120 had been *"filled with the Spirit"* (Ephesians 5:18), said, *"Repent, and be baptized every one of you in the name of Jesus Christ for the remission of sins, and ye shall receive the gift of the Holy Ghost."* Here we find the same sequence as in the preaching by John: (a) repentance, (b) confession, (c) baptism, and (d) knowledge that sins had been remitted—but now we have an addition, (e) the receiving of the gift of the Holy Spirit. What is this gift? As salvation was a gift of the Holy Spirit, so also is the baptism of the Spirit a gift of the Holy Spirit! Some teach that this means that we receive the Holy Spirit as a gift, but the text does not show this. The reference is to the gift of the Holy Spirit that Jesus imparts to the believer. All true believers have in themselves the *"Spirit of Christ"* (Romans 8:9), and, likewise, the Spirit of Christ or the nature and life of Christ is imparted by the Holy Spirit into the believer's heart. God's nature comes right into the very center of the human—his heart—and this life infuses the whole body as the heart pumps life-giving blood round the body. How easy it is to confuse simple Bible statements! We must be very careful to understand Scripture as the Holy Spirit wrote it, not as some theologians interpret it for our impoverishment.

Other gifts of the Holy Spirit are found in 1 Corinthians 12. We doubt that we could enumerate all the blessed gifts that the Holy Spirit desires to bestow upon us, but one of the greatest—after we receive the gift of eternal life—is the gift of the Holy Spirit when Jesus baptizes us in the Spirit!

Our fundamentalist friends have been taught that they receive the gift of the Holy Spirit at conversion and use Acts 2:38 to prove it! If this were so, then they would also have received water baptism at the exact instant they received Jesus as their Savior, but we know that water baptism was a subsequent experience, and in like manner the baptism or gift of the Holy Spirit is a subsequent experience (although salvation, baptism and the gift of the Holy Spirit may be received within very short order on the same day!). They are not synonymous. If we receive the gift of the Holy Spirit at conversion, then what would Mary, Elizabeth, Zacharias, or John the Baptist have received in the upper room? John never got there, but he was filled with the Holy Spirit. One cannot imagine Mary the mother of Jesus as not being filled with the Holy Spirit before the cross, but, later, she entered the upper room and received the gift of the Holy Spirit! How we confuse ourselves!

2

MARY—A TYPE OF
THE CHURCH

To understand the difference between the work of the Holy Spirit in conversion, and the baptism of the Holy Spirit, we must consider the life of the Virgin Mary.

I believe that Mary was a type of the pure virgin church, described as a chaste woman in Scripture. There is an opposite in the book of Revelation called the scarlet woman, or the harlot church. The harlot sells herself for money, but the virgin gives herself in love. These two have been in the world since the days of the early church, and both call themselves "Christian." Another type is Judas Iscariot, who sold his Lord for money; he is a type of the antichrist for Jesus described him as *"the son of perdition,"* the exact words used by Paul to describe the man of sin, or the antichrist of 2 Thessalonians 2:3. The *antichrist* (which means false Christ) sells salvation for money, while claiming to be the very representative of Christ on earth. The English word "vicar" from the Latin *vicarius* is one who stands in the place of, or instead of, Christ. He is a vicarious Christ, but if he does not offer the salvation of Jesus as a free gift to all people, then he becomes per se an antichrist. The Scriptures teach that an antichrist is not primarily a political person, but a religious person. The reformers between 1517 and 1800 recognized this fact.

Mary the mother of Jesus was probably the purest young woman who ever lived. We give her honor as the blessed mother of Jesus. She was a virgin and conceived. The story is told for us in Luke chapter 1; the angel Gabriel prophesied that the Holy Spirit would *overshadow* her, and *"that Holy thing which shall be born of thee shall be called the Son of God"* (Luke 1:35). Had we been present at the time of the conception we would have watched as Mary became lost to view in a cloud of *shekinah* glory, as the Holy Spirit enshrouded her, saturating her whole being, reaching right into her innermost parts, until the body of Christ was formed in her womb. It would be fruitless to suggest that Mary had not been filled with the Spirit at this point in time, but the gift that she received was the creation of the Christ Child. The work of the Spirit was the creation of the body for Jesus—the logos—to dwell in. It was in this body that the Word was made flesh and dwelt among us. (See John 1:14.) This is still the purpose of the body of Christ: that the Word (the Logos) might dwell in the body of Christ today, that all might behold Jesus veiled in human flesh.

Much later, Mary was commanded by Jesus to *"tarry...in the city of Jerusalem"* (Luke 24:49), until she was endued with power from on high. When teaching on this subject in a seminar, I was asked the question, "Where does the Bible teach that Mary was in the upper room in Jerusalem?" I was quite surprised at the question, but it shows that many people who are moving into the charismatic dimension of the Spirit today are still ignorant of the Bible. In Acts 1:14, we read, *"These all continued with one accord in prayer and supplication, with the women, and Mary the mother of Jesus."* There was no hesitation in obeying the command of her Son. Much earlier she had said at the wedding in Cana, *"Whatsoever he saith unto you, do it"* (John 2:5), and this excellent advice to both Catholics and Protestants today exhorts us to obey instantly the command to be filled with the Spirit as on the day of Pentecost. "Tarry...until" has never been abrogated. Mary obeyed these words and went into the upper room. Had she not *received* the Holy Spirit already at the time of the conception? Had she not watched over the tender early life of her Son? Had she not fed Him, prayed over Him, and educated Him in the ways of His Father? Certainly. In every point, she was probably faultless. Why then move on to another experience of the Holy Spirit? This seems to be the stumbling block of so many church-indoctrinated people. They have no desire for a deeper relationship with Jesus. They make excuses and want to have no part in any upper room experience. Remember, Mary had brought to birth the Son of God in humble circumstances in a stable. No wonder Elizabeth prophesied by the Holy Spirit that Mary was blessed because she *believed.* (See Luke 1:45.) Thank God, many are beginning to believe again today. Mary was in the upper room and so were Peter, James, John, and the brothers of Jesus. Mary had her family as well!

What happened to Mary? After ten days of prayer and supplication, the Holy Spirit came down a *second time* on her as her Son in heaven shed forth the *shekinah* glory of God upon these 120 men and women. The second time, Mary was filled and impregnated with the Spirit, but the manifestation that occurred was different. The first time she brought forth the Son of God in human form, but this time she brought forth the Son of God in Word form. The very *logos*, the living Word, began to flow from her lips, coming again from her inward parts, magnifying the name of the Father and the Son. Jesus was speaking through His mother's mouth. The first time, Jesus was manifest in physical form. The second time, He came forth in spiritual manifestation—the creative, life-giving Word of God. No wonder Satan hates "tongues"!

Let us consider these two visitations of the Spirit upon Mary, a beautiful type of the virgin church. Are we not made virgins? Incredible though it may seem to a carnal mind, the very power of God in conversion and the cleansing blood of Jesus make us virgins! In Revelation 14:4 we read, *"These are they which were not defiled with women; for they are **virgins**."* The inference is clear that the blood-washed children of God were not contaminated by the harlot church (see Revelation 17), but were mystically adopted as sons of God into the very virgin bride of Christ—His body; and from His body on earth other virgin children are continually being born. We may view the life of the Virgin Mary with some measure of awe, but when it comes home to us by the Spirit that we also are virgins, it should help us to live holier lives!

As the Virgin Mary brought forth the Son of God from her womb in her inner-most parts (see Psalm 22:10), so also do we bring forth the Son of God today, not from our womb but from our heart. Both men and women who turn to Christ whole-heartedly find that the Father implants the Spirit of Christ, the nature of Christ, when we are born again from above by the Holy Spirit (see John 1:13). The very life of Jesus fills our hearts and is then carried round our bodies by our blood, which has been cleansed at conversion as we read, *"For I will cleanse their blood, that I have not cleansed"* (Joel 3:21). Though we receive the Holy Spirit into our innermost beings, the end result is that Jesus is born in us. He then begins to manifest Himself in us as our lives are progressively changed from glory to glory; for even as Jesus had to grow and develop in His body, so does He also have to mature in our bodies. He manifests His fruit—love—by changing our old carnal nature into His nature. This is why Jesus said, *"Ye shall know them by their fruits"* (Matthew 7:16). We can't fool God or man. We are known by the fruits of Galatians 5:22.

The fruit of love, joy, peace, long-suffering, gentleness, goodness, faithfulness, meekness, and self-control are the manifestation of Jesus implanted into the very center of our life by the Holy Spirit. This is the first work of the Spirit in a believer's life.

Like Mary we then mount the steps into the upper room. You see, we have no power yet, for Jesus told Mary (and the other disciples) that they would receive power (*dunamis*) when the Holy Spirit came *upon* them. (See Acts 1:8.) We enter into a higher dimension, indicated by the ascent into the room. It means we take intelligent action. We do not say that "God can give me the baptism of the Spirit if He wants to!" He not only wants to, but He commands us to tarry until we mount the steps and put ourselves in a position spiritually of receiving this "coming upon" of the Spirit. We will probably be prayed for in public by other Spirit-filled Christians, and then we shall manifest the Son of God as we begin to speak, and as we do so, the Holy Spirit saturating us will give us words of an unknown language and these words (*glossolalia*) will be the very voice of Jesus speaking through us supernaturally, miraculously, as a sign to the unbeliever.

Maybe we have missed this way of winning souls for Jesus! We have so concentrated on our methodology, with our spiritual laws and workshops, that we have forgotten that Paul wrote, "*Wherefore tongues are for a sign, not to them that believe, but to them that believe not*" (1 Corinthians 14:22). The very first time that a stubborn unbeliever hears tongues of the Spirit, he will have to make up his mind about the matter. He cannot remain unmoved. When Mary spoke in tongues the religious leaders said she was drunk. When the Corinthians spoke in tongues the public said they were mad. (See 1 Corinthians 12:13.) In the beginning of the century the evangelicals said it was of the devil. Some still do! The speaking in tongues by a believer, whether in church or in the home, will cause an instant reaction. Thank God, that some will fall down and say, "It is God!" This is a good way to win souls for Jesus! Probably the best!

Do we speak gibberish or monkey chatter as some ignorant people have said? The very word *glossolalia* used in the Greek in Acts 2:4 tells us that they spoke words of distinct meaning. Gibberish does not contain words. It is composed of meaningless noises; but the Greek word *glossa* means an intelligent language.

That which came pouring out of the mouths of the 120 was a torrent of words, described as "*the logos.*" *Logos* is a Greek word meaning the very nature of God in spoken word. John helps us by speaking of Jesus as the Word (logos) that was with God and was God, and was then "made flesh" so that every word that Jesus spoke was not an idle word but a direct manifestation of His Father in heaven. His hearers said, "*Never man spake like this man*" (John 7:46). True, but the difference was that gracious words proceeded out of His mouth from His innermost parts, and these words, this flow of language, was Jesus, the living Word, flowing out of 120 mouths of the newly formed body of Christ on earth. Jesus had one mouth in His one body, which was crucified, but now He created a body with initially one hundred and twenty mouths, and the same day there were added another three thousand. Today the number of these divine utterance orifices has grown to millions. Satan is about to be routed and blasted out of his kingdom by the power of the Spirit in Holy Spirit baptized Christians. We are just beginning to learn the power of the spoken Word, the manifestation of Jesus in power.

The fruit and the gifts must be manifest so that the world may see a full-orbed Christ. This is why Paul, writing to Timothy, penned, "*For God…given us…power… love*" (2 Timothy 1:7). We receive love at conversion and power when the Holy Spirit comes upon us a second time and Jesus baptizes us into the Holy Spirit.

After the gift of salvation, we receive the gift of the Holy Spirit, and then we are candidates for all the charismatic gifts of the Spirit. We can receive gift upon gift, all from the same Giver. God so loved the world that *He gave*. We are so slow to receive!

3

JESUS OUR EXAMPLE

We will now consider the life of Jesus Christ, who said that His sheep would follow Him. He is a perfect example for us, and we must follow Him, for He said that we must manifest Him in the world. How can we manifest Him if we do not have the power? We do not receive this power (*dunamis*) until we receive the baptism in the Holy Spirit. (See Acts 1:8.) We must never confuse the work of the Spirit in the rebirth and in the baptism in the Spirit.

Jesus was born the Son of God. He was the Word made flesh. God dwelt in His human body fully. He was truly filled with the Spirit in a degree greater than any man before or since. *Emmanuel* means simply "God with us." God dwelt in Him and He was God. It is most illuminating to realize that Jesus did not commence His public ministry of healing and deliverance until the Holy Spirit anointed Him to do so. Why did not Jesus immediately plunge into the ministry at a much earlier age than thirty? Surely He could have done so! A study of the Bible shows that the law of God in Numbers 4:3 only permitted a priest to minister from the age of thirty. At his ordination service, he was first washed with water, then he put on his priestly robes, and then the anointing oil was poured on his head and flowed down to the hem of his garments. Here we see in type: (1) water baptism, (2) the imputed righteousness of Christ to all believers, and (3) the baptism in the Spirit. No Levite could commence his ministry before the age of thirty, and then he had to submit to God's consecration. (See Leviticus 8.)

In Psalm 133, the anointing oil flowed right down to the skirts of Aaron's priestly garments, and as Jesus was the fulfillment of Aaron and all of Israel's high priests, He had to conform to His own laws! Jesus was always obedient to the law of His Father; and so at the age of thirty He submitted Himself to John the Baptist in his great revival in Israel, as we read in Matthew 3:13–17. John was astonished that Jesus desired water baptism, for John had already had the revelation from heaven that Jesus was the Lamb of God; and how could such a Man desire water baptism from John? John was of the Adamic creation, but Jesus was a new creation, the last Adam. Jesus had to press His case, telling John that this obedience would fulfill all righteousness; and here we see the robe of righteousness being prepared for Jesus to wear! The Savior went down into the Jordan River and was baptized in water. Young translated "*baptism*" here as "by pouring out on, or putting into" water. Either way, Jesus was thoroughly washed from head to foot, which fulfilled the requirements of washing all over in the law. In fact, this was the basic meaning of baptism to Israel at the time of John. A few drops of water on the head may be a symbol, but it is not a washing. The early churches in Bethlehem and Jerusalem still have the baptismal tanks cut out of the ground, with steps down, where the candidates for Christian baptism in the early church went down into the water for their ceremonial washing!

Jesus was washed all over by John, and then, wearing the spiritual robe of righteousness, He experienced a great miracle. A dove seemed to descend. The Third Person of the Trinity took on visible form (a dove speaks of peace) and at the exact time when the Third Person touched the Second Person, the First Person spoke! How beautiful. Jesus did not begin to speak about the kingdom of God until His Father spoke, and He said, "*This is my beloved Son, in whom I am well pleased*" (Matthew 3:17). The Father announced to the world by a supernatural voice that Jesus was about to begin His high priestly ministry to Israel and the world. No voice—no ministry! Can't you see?

What happens to us who believe on the Son of God as our Savior? First, we are born again by the operation of the Spirit of God who penetrates right into our heart and implants the Spirit or nature of Christ. Our whole nature becomes changed from the Adamic rebellion to obedience to Christ and His Word. Then we are equipped with the robe of righteousness given us freely by Jesus as a gift. It fits us perfectly, but remember the very word "righteousness" means "right conduct" or, basically, obedience to the Word of God. There can be no variation from the law. We must be baptized in water following heart acceptance of Christ, and, thus, we too fulfill all righteousness, as did Jesus. A Christian confession without obedience in water baptism is an incomplete confession, which is why Peter commanded the first Gentile converts to be baptized in the name of the Lord. (See Acts 10:48.) Baptism was not an option, it is a command to us. "*Repent, and be baptized **every one of you**"* (Acts 2:38) was how Peter expressed it on the day of Pentecost. Let us also note, without desiring to be controversial, that baptism was always following repentance and belief. Ceremonial washing before conversion makes no sense, for there must be cleansing of the heart *first*. Water does not cleanse us. It takes the blood of Jesus to cleanse us from all sin (see 1 John 1: 7), but water is both a symbol of cleansing and burial to a Christian.

Now what is *supposed* to happen after water baptism? Obviously, to complete the ordination of a Christian priest (and we are all priests) we must have the anointing oil flowing right down to the hem of our robe of righteousness, to the very skirts! Our robe must be saturated in anointing oil! Is this not what happens when Jesus the High Priest takes us and immerses us in the Holy Spirit? Our whole beings become impregnated with the life-giving power of God! Such an infilling could not possibly be contained in a human vessel without some overflow! How could God flowing in and running down into our very innermost parts have no noticeable effect? Do we receive the Holy Spirit in faith? Certainly, but there is a manifestation of this faith in the pouring forth of the Logos—the Word of God in spoken form!

Let us remember that when Jesus was baptized the Holy Spirit descended and the Father *spoke*. There was an instant manifestation of the Word of God. It was not a negative experience, it was positive. There were results for the blessing of all who heard.

As we refer to Acts 2:4 and penetrate the upper room in Jerusalem, we witness an amazing sight. The Holy Spirit descends as a rushing wind (in Jesus' case, He came as a dove) and tongues of fire are seen, for fire is a symbol of the Spirit and John the Baptist prophesied that Jesus would baptize all in the Holy Spirit and fire. The tongues of fire and then the power of the wind came down and the fire was transformed into them as spoken tongues. They began to speak in other tongues as the Holy Spirit gave them the utterance. They uttered; the Spirit gave. Mutual cooperation between the 120 humans and the Spirit of God. In Jesus' baptism there was mutual cooperation between God and man. So again, in the upper room, God came down to man, who cooperated with God, and the result of this spiritual conjugation was the birth of the Christian church!

Every baby born into this world alive must utter a cry. If he does not he is pronounced dead. Honest people must admit that some sections of the Christian church today are dead. There is no life of the Spirit in them at all. There is a hollow shell of higher criticism of the Scriptures or philosophy, and the preachers bring forth their sophistries and apologetics. They have their forms and ceremonies, their robes and their crosses, but no power. It takes the baptism in the Spirit to give us the power! No wonder the apostle Paul wrote in 2 Timothy 3:5 that some have a form of godliness but they deny the power (*dunamis*), and he tells us to turn away from them. I wonder why? Perhaps it is because they will contaminate us!

What kind of cry did this infant church utter? What was the evidence of life that came forth? The very Logos Himself, speaking from heaven. As the Father spoke through His Son announcing the beginning of His ministry, now the Son speaks through His body, the church, announcing the beginning of His ministry. The Holy Spirit will only reveal the Son, for in John 16:16 we read that Jesus said that when the Holy Spirit came, which He did on the day of Pentecost, He would: (1) guide us, (2) speak to us, (3) hear from God, (4) show us, (5) glorify the Father, and (6) receive from the Father for us. He will not speak about Himself, but only reveal the Son—the living *Logos*. As soon as the hundred and twenty in the upper room began to speak in other languages, the Holy Spirit began to speak about Jesus through their mouths. He heard the Word from the Father and spoke it through the disciples. This *glossolalia* Word was to glorify God, and as we shall see later in this book, to bring forth the life-giving power of God in prophecy (He will show you things to come), in healing the sick, in raising the dead and in casting out demons.

The church on the day of Pentecost was supernaturally created and supernaturally alive. The first great miracle was the healing of the lame man who was born deformed. This was caused by Peter speaking creative words in the power of the Spirit. He said, *"In the name of Jesus Christ of Nazareth rise up and walk"* (Acts 3:6). Christ-denying Peter could not have said this before his personal Pentecost, and the lame man would not have been healed without the experiences of Pentecost. The church is not a natural creation by the will and intellect of man. It does not rely upon philosophy and psychiatry. It operates solely by the power of God as revealed through the anointing of the Spirit.

As Jesus was ordained for the ministry by water baptism and Spirit anointing, so likewise do we have to travel the same route. It was *before* Pentecost that Jesus promised His disciples they would be witnesses to Him, but not before they met the Holy Spirit in the upper room. Now, many try to witness in the energy of their minds and human spirits, lacking the power (*dunamis*) of the Spirit in their lives. We were never supposed to be just "born again," but, as the Holy Spirit anointed Jesus, so today the same Holy Spirit must anoint Jesus *already in our hearts* and release Him through ourselves in power; and let us not forget that that power is manifested in the charismatic gifts of the Spirit. This is what the charismatic move of God is all about.

Many today are satisfied and say, "I am born again and am a member of the church, His body." They like the program of their local church and find their friends within the church and are quite unable to understand that they have not fulfilled the requirements of New Testament Christianity to be filled with the Spirit. Paul tells us in Ephesians 5:18 to be filled with the Spirit, and the Greek tense here means to go on being filled every day—an infilling and an outflowing. In other words, a fountain. Again in Ephesians 3:19, Paul wrote, *"And to know the love of Christ, which passeth knowledge, that ye might be filled with **all the fullness of God**."* How can this be, unless we receive our personal Pentecost evidenced by the outflowing of the Word of God in tongues?

4

RIVERS OF WATER

We have already found that the Holy Spirit is likened to fire and wind, and this is in order that we might understand the mysterious workings and properties of God's Spirit as His power is released to us. Now we consider the Holy Spirit as flowing like water. Water flows, it cleanses, it refreshes, it sustains life, and it should be pure. These are all attributes of the Spirit that He brings into our lives. Without water nothing would live, and our planet contains an abundance of it. It is just a combination of two basic elements, hydrogen and oxygen—H_2O. Two gases make a liquid. Have you ever thought what a great miracle this is? Only God could have thought of that!

Water can be contaminated and the pollution can kill us. In like manner our own human spirits can be contaminated with Satan's evil spirits, and these evil spirits will destroy us mentally and physically. We are warned to have nothing to do with the occult and only to serve the living God. As we apply ourselves to obey the simplicity of the commandment, *"Thou shalt have no other gods before me"* (Exodus 20:3), and only seek after God as revealed by His life-giving Holy Spirit, our spirits and minds will be refreshed, our thoughts cleansed and our bodies restored to health.

Jesus used this analogy of water in His discourse to the Jews on the Feast of Tabernacles, the last of the seven Jewish feasts. In His audience there were both believers and unbelievers, because both were given an opportunity to be candidates for this baptism of the Spirit. Today we have believers and unbelievers who need to hear the message of this book.

There would have been no original Pentecostal outpouring on the world if Dr. Charles Parham of the Bible School in Topeka, Kansas, had not instructed his students to search the Scriptures on this subject in 1900. It was when they found there was scriptural substance for this baptism accompanied by speaking in tongues, that they began to pray for a like experience, and the Holy Spirit, agreeing with the Word of God, came upon them and over twenty were baptized in the Spirit, demonstrating *glossolalia*. This was back in the beginning of 1901, so the whole church has had a long time to consider this miracle without trying to argue it away by vain philosophizing! In 1907 the Church of England at Monkswearsmouth, near Sunderland, England, experienced similar blessings under their Pastor Canon, Alexander A. Body, but, in general, they ignored this visitation of the Spirit until the same things happened again at Van Nuys, California, with Rev. Dennis Bennett in 1964. The Roman Catholic Church had no experience of this baptism until 1968, when the Spirit was outpoured upon some in Pennsylvania. It took Rome sixty-seven years to heed what had happened in a Methodist Holiness Bible School in 1901. How slow is the church to see the signs of the times! Why is she so blinded?

We must go to the Word! Jesus said,

If any man thirst, let him come unto me, and drink. He that believeth on me, as the scripture hath said, out of his belly shall flow rivers of living water. (But this spake he of the Spirit, which they that believe on him should receive: for the Holy Ghost was not yet given; because that Jesus was not yet glorified).

(John 737–39)

We asked the question, "Why is the church so blinded?" I think the answer is given in the words of Jesus. It is because they are not thirsty. They are self-satisfied and in many cases self-righteous. They like their church the way it is, and are so stuck in the mud that they have no desire for change, which they will strongly resist. Once we are dissatisfied and want more of God, He will meet us at the fountain. We have to do something about it. We have to come to Jesus where He is. I have often heard it said, "Oh, well, if God wants me to have this baptism, He will give it to me!" Yes, He wants you to have it, but on His terms. You go to Him and ask Him, then you will receive. As long as you wait for Him to come to you, you will wait in vain. Did He not say, "**Come unto me**, all ye that labor and are heavy laden" (Matthew 11:28)? We must go to Him.

Jesus said that the baptism of the Spirit was only for those who believed on Him. It is necessary first to accept Jesus as your own personal Savior, to have been born again of the Spirit, and then if you are thirsty you may receive *at once*. No tarrying is necessary in the New Testament! These living waters will flow from heaven into your belly, or innermost parts, and out from the orifice of your mouth will flow living waters to a weary generation! Turn on the faucet of your tongue!

Permit me to have a discussion on biology. In the middle of your belly is your navel, a reminder that at one time in your life you owed your very life to another— your mother. It was through the umbilical cord that food and aperients were transmitted into your body. Your life was sustained by another life. It was only after you were born into this world that this lifeline was cut and you began a new life cycle of breathing in oxygen for yourself. Help from mother was rudely cut off.

When we enter into this new life cycle of the Holy Spirit, we must become joined up to God in heaven; an entrance of living water must be given for it to enter into our innermost parts. This will mean a long umbilical cord, because a search in the Bible shows us that this living water is found in heaven. In Revelation 22:1, we read, *"And he shewed me a pure river of water of life, clear as crystal, proceeding out of the throne of God and of the Lamb."* The marvelous umbilical cord of the Holy Spirit will stretch right down from the throne of God, and Jesus alone will couple us up right into our navels! There is still something missing, however, for it is our responsibility alone to open the valve of our mouths and to release the flow of living water. In the original happening in the upper room it is recorded that *they* began to speak. It does not say the Holy Spirit began to speak; they did the speaking and Jesus did the giving of words.

Let us use a down-to-earth simile. If we have a new house built, and shiny new plumbing fixtures installed, and the water department connects us with the main water supply of the city, all this becomes useless until we turn on the faucets for washing, showers, bathtubs, toilets, washing machines, and laundry tubs. It is the responsibility of Jesus Christ to connect us with the heavenly water supply, but He will not turn the faucets, valves, taps, or spigots for us. We alone have to do that. So it is with living water. If our innermost parts are full of the Holy Spirit, we must release the living water by opening our mouths, using our tongues, and speaking forth the flowing Logos. This is entirely controlled by our own volition. God does not "blow the washer" and force us to speak in tongues. We turn it on and turn it off. Paul told us that the spirits of the prophets are subject to the prophets (see 1 Corinthians 14:32), and we have complete control over the operation of this gift of the Spirit. Any one of us can use or misuse a gift. The gifts and callings of God are without repentance and Jesus never regrets giving us the ability to pour out, from our innermost beings, rivers of living water. Most of us bring forth too little; God wants rivers, not streams or trickles or occasional squirts. They call them gully washers in Texas.

I well remember praying for a Baptist brother who came to our church one Sunday evening for the express purpose of receiving the baptism of the Holy Spirit. Being a Baptist, I assured him that I did not doubt he was already filled with the Spirit, and I just urged him to release the Spirit already in him; immediately he began to speak in tongues and praise God. Some may question this theology, but I applied Baptist teaching to this case and God rewarded him!

I cannot overemphasize the importance today of all Christians receiving this baptism in the Holy Spirit. In Psalm 68:9, we read the prophecy, *"Thou O God, didst send a plentiful rain, whereby thou didst confirm thine inheritance, when it was weary."*

Surely it must be admitted by all that the institutional church is weary today. All kinds of gimmicks and stunts have been tried to get people back to church, but what God's people of all denominations need today is a fresh, divine outpouring of the Holy Spirit as on the day of Pentecost! Only rain brings life back to dying plants, and the Holy Spirit is likened not only to rain but to rivers, which are formed by deluges of rain. First the rains, then the deluge, then the rivers overflowing their banks. In a matter of an hour a dry riverbed can overflow its banks, and as God's rain is poured out upon all flesh, both Christian and non-Christian, the banks of the denominations, so closely fortified for so long, will be submerged and we shall merge together—a weary inheritance brought to spiritual life and power. Just rain.

Today there are many who oppose this visitation of God, for they are dry. Such expressions as "Praise God," "Hallelujah," and "Thank You, Jesus" cause shivers to go down their chilled spines! What else shall we say when we are filled to overflowing with God's Spirit? So many of these chilly people will be caught up in the deluge, because God loves His inheritance when it is weary, and He must permit us to get weary with all our humanism and worldly activities, so that He might refresh us in the end; and this is the end time!

The church began in a deluge and consequent rivers of living water. We are told it will not happen again, but already we have Pentecostals, Baptists, Episcopalians, Lutherans, Presbyterians, Methodists, Mennonites, Roman Catholics, and many others speaking in tongues and beginning to flow together again into one true church. What the Lord has started, He will finish. It is written that the earth shall be filled with the knowledge of the glory of God as the waters cover the sea. (See Habakkuk 2:14.) The whole earth will be covered with God's rains. It will be an outpouring that will be as universal as the flood in Noah's day. It is promised upon all flesh, and everyone will see the glory of God before Jesus comes back in judgment.

Just imagine what happened when 120 mouths were opened in the upper room. Rivers of living water flowing out of each of the assembled believers and all these 120 streams merging into one river of life. Then, on the same day, three thousand more mouths were opened and the river grew in strength and depth. By the end of the first week 8,120 mouths had been opened, and this caused a great stir in the city. The day before Pentecost had been as dry as dust in Jerusalem, spiritually speaking, but the next day a cloudburst occurred and a great river of life coming from heaven above started to flow in the City of Peace. Today, there are millions of mouths pouring forth the Word of God in the gifts of the Spirit, and these are being multiplied daily. The whole earth is yet to be filled with the knowledge of the glory of God as the church rises to its full stature as the very body of Christ.

The future is as bright as the promises of God.

5

THE SPIRIT OF TRUTH

In John 14:16–18, Jesus gave a very clear prophecy and promise of the coming of the Comforter. This Comforter was described as being the *"Spirit of truth"* (verse 17); in other words, there was yet to come a manifestation of the Spirit of God which would make real to us Him who is *Truth*. Obviously, at the time that Jesus made this promise to His disciples, the second Comforter had not come. His arrival was yet future. This is a very important thing to remember, for all the disciples of Jesus were saved men, capable of casting out demons and healing the sick and, as we shall show in the next chapter, they had had the Holy Spirit breathed into them.

Obviously, the world could not receive the Spirit because, as Jesus explained, it could not see or understand Him with the material mind. If scientists cannot see the Spirit of God, some state that therefore they cannot believe there is a God. Thank God, we cannot put God in a test tube. The surprising fact, however, is not so much that the world cannot believe and receive, but that the church at large, especially the evangelicals, cannot receive! I do not think I overstate the case in believing that the disciples of Jesus were the evangelicals of the old covenant.

The wording used is so clear, *"But ye know him, for he dwelleth **with** you and shall be **in** you"* (John 14:17). Nothing could be clearer than that. The disciples were told that this Spirit of truth was already dwelling among them, but that at some subsequent time the same Spirit would dwell *in* them. By inference, this Spirit of truth was not yet *in* them, yet they were believers! Furthermore, Jesus told them that they already knew this Spirit and therefore recognized Him. What is the key to the "mystery"?

When Jesus was anointed of the Holy Spirit in the Jordan River (see Matthew 3:16), the Spirit of truth was released through His ministry. Remember that the title "Spirit of truth" would indicate that Jesus, who is personified *Truth* when manifested in public ministry, would bring His ministry into full focus and blazing light by healing the sick, casting out demons and raising the dead. The scribes did not do this in their ministry. It took the Spirit of truth to reveal and manifest truth to the people. This is why the Jewish clergy were so jealous and enraged. It was religion versus the Spirit of truth.

So today, the issue is the same: denominational religion versus the Spirit of truth! Jesus the Son of God in His body contained all truth. Please note that Jesus also promised His disciples that the coming of this Comforter would lead them into *all truth*—a mindshattering promise. Just imagine us all having the capability of being led into all truth! And yet this is what the Spirit of truth will do for us. Jesus stood in the midst of them, full of this Spirit and revealing the potential of this indwelling Comforter. As they looked upon Him and watched His ministry, they saw the Spirit of truth revealed. Thus, He was with them. He was not in them, for this Spirit was *in* Jesus; only after the shattering and destruction of His body could this Spirit be released to fill the church. This began on the day of Pentecost. (See Acts 2:4.)

No doubt the disciples had to think a little to understand what Jesus meant when He said, "*Ye know Him.*" They knew Jesus, but what about the motivating Spirit within Him? This helps us to understand the words of Paul when he said that he knew no man after the flesh, for whereas the disciples had known Jesus after the flesh, from henceforth they would not because they would only know Him, or recognize Him, after the Spirit. (See 2 Corinthians 5:16.) The late Smith Wigglesworth used this Scripture because he refused to recognize any importance in man, however much God had used him; he only looked to the Spirit of Truth revealed through any man.

The body of Christ could do nothing without the indwelling Spirit and so they were not to look at Jesus but at the Spirit motivating Jesus. If we all had this spiritual insight, what a difference it would make to the church! Even in modern evangelism we have the personality cult, and the magazines published by some evangelists have photographs of them on nearly every page, including postures of kneeling evangelists praying for people's needs! I believe it would be best if we gave no recognition to man and only looked through him to the Spirit of truth operating through him. Let us give all glory to God.

Now, in exactly the same manner in which the Spirit of truth was *in* Jesus after His anointing in Jordan, so this same Comforter was promised to be in all His disciples. No difference, and for the same purpose: that they might do the works of Jesus. He had promised them that they would do the same works as He had done by this Comforter. (See John 14:12.) The majority of Christians in our denominations today make no attempt to do the works of Jesus. When people are sick they go to the doctor. If they are mentally disturbed they go to a psychiatrist, and if death should come they go to an undertaker. Why? Because the Spirit of truth is not in most believers today! When asked why they do not at least attempt to do the works of Jesus, they say that these miracles were for the early church and we must not expect them today. But let us realize that the early church had the Comforter and used His powers. Why should the latter day church be any different from the former church? The Bible hasn't changed. Is it that we have changed?

Jesus said, "*Heal the sick, cleanse the lepers, raise the dead, cast out devils*" (Matthew 10:8). To whom did He speak these words? To twelve ordinary disciples that He designated apostles, that is, "sent ones." I believe that today most Christians do not believe in apostles because they do not see the works of apostles. Think of the titles used in our churches today—Pope, Prelate, Archbishop, Cardinal, General Superintendent, President; but the Bible term for a father of the church is Apostle—a sent one to establish New Testament churches with the gifts of the Spirit, the offices of the Spirit and the fruit of the Spirit. I often wonder what would happen if the apostle Paul were to try to teach some of our churches today about New Testament Christianity and how to establish it. I think there would be great opposition just as there was in the days of the scribes and Pharisees. It was Paul who proudly boasted that he spoke in tongues more than anybody! (See 1 Corinthians 14:18.)

In our day there is a charismatic renewal that has affected all denominations. By this I mean that within these denominations there are thousands who have received this baptism in the Spirit as evidenced by glossolalia. The charismatic renewal, as it is sometimes called, brought together these rejoicing people. Catholics freely worshipped with Protestants of every kind. They had a wonderful time praising God and great love flowed from one to another through denominational barriers. This was great until the first flush of praise was over and they got down to serious Bible study. Then what happened? The denominational differences became very patent. Most of the charismatics were in favor of no-holds-barred Bible study, but the leaders of the denominations became distressed. A council of Roman Catholic Bishops in Canada published a pamphlet warning Catholics not to take the Bible literally, as some Protestants did. Some of the historic reformed churches became alarmed at the free discussion of the meaning of the Greek word *baptizo*, which means to dip. Discussions took place very freely about whether we should only baptize believers, because it was difficult to see how a baby could believe. The subject of the Lord's Supper was approached cautiously, because it was a very big issue at the time of the reformation under Martin Luther in 1517, and of course, prayer to the saints became an issue.

The leaders of the denominations formed denominational charismatic groups who disassociated themselves from other groups. This, in turn, led some charismatic leaders to become impatient, so efforts were made to force or frighten some to follow their teaching and become "discipled" to them, even at distances of thousands of miles.

Now what does the Word of God say about all this? What does the Spirit of truth teach about it? I refer to Ephesians chapter 4, the "Body of Christ" chapter of the Bible. In verse 13, we have four definite steps of the Holy Spirit. Let us quote it in full: "*Till we all come in the unity of the faith, and of the knowledge of the Son of God, unto a perfect man, unto the measure of the stature of the fullness of Christ.*"

The first point is unity of the faith. This, I believe, is brought about by the baptism of the Spirit which causes tongues to be manifest. This baptism is, I believe, the one referred to in verse 5 as "one baptism." Obviously, water baptism has never brought unity of the faith. The purpose of water baptism, whether of babies or adult, is interpreted differently by different church groups. This first step brought Catholics and Protestants together for the first time in history—together in worship and praise, but not in doctrine. The second step is "*knowledge of the Son of God.*" This can only be achieved by sincere, in-depth Bible study by those who have already come in faith unity by the one baptism of the Spirit. The indwelling Spirit of Truth is the one which begins to lead charismatics into all *truth*; if only they will listen to the voice of the Spirit and forget their man-made church traditions! This second stage is now beginning, and it will cause a spiritual revolution within the denominations! With Spirit-baptized Christians growing in grace and knowledge of the Word of God as they are today, the next step will yet be reached; it is yet future. "*Unto a perfect man.*" Obviously Jesus was the perfect Man, but the church must manifest Him today and so must be built up to a much greater state of maturity. The Greek word for "perfect" here indicates a state of completeness, and so the true body of Christ must come together completely and both speak and believe the same things! Did not Paul write, "*That ye all speak the same thing, and that there be no divisions among you; but that ye be* **perfectly joined together** *in the same mind and in the same judgment*" (1 Corinthians 1:10)? Paul would not have written this, *and* prayed about it, unless it were to be fulfilled. I believe it is about to be fulfilled in the charismatic move of God.

The fourth and final step in the move of the Spirit is to bring the church "*unto the measure of the stature of the* **fullness of Christ**." What a day this will be—Jesus Christ seen in all His fullness, on the earth, astounding the intellectuals by His miracles and great works. Remember, Paul believed that Jesus (by the Spirit) would present to Himself "*a glorious church, not having spot, or wrinkle, or any such thing; but that it should be holy and without blemish*" (Ephesians 5:27). This restored church will be full of God's glory. There will be no blemishes, which includes all sicknesses, and it will be holy! Let us admit that this is a far cry from denominationalism, and no leader will be able to stop it, for God is now rebuilding His true church with living stones, which He is taking from among all denominations as well as outside of them! It doesn't take too much imagination to see that the day is coming when denominations will no longer be necessary. They will have outlived their past usefulness.

In charge of this one church will be apostles, prophets, evangelists, pastors and teachers who will be used by the Comforter to perfect the saints and to build up the body of Christ! (See Ephesians 4:12.) We pray that some holding high office within the denominations will submit to the Spirit of Truth and allow Jesus to guide them into all truth so that they might then aspire to one of the five ministry gifts!

When Jesus started to build and form His church He did not go to the established clergy; He chose fishermen, tax gatherers, and others instead. His church is built upon the foundation of these apostles and prophets! It will likewise be built today.

6

HE BREATHED ON THEM

After the crucifixion of Jesus, the disciples became greatly dispirited and afraid. They dejectedly went into a room and locked the door *"for fear of the Jews"* (John 20:19). If their Master Jesus had been crucified, no doubt the same Roman soldiers would come and get them and crucify them also. Peter had demonstrated a real spirit of fear and of lying when he denied his Lord three times. Real panic entered into the apostolic band.

It was in this very understandable situation that Jesus appeared to them, after having neatly passed through a solid door. To say that they were amazed would be an understatement. They had supposed Him dead in the tomb, and to make matters even more miraculous, He had just entered a closed door! How dramatic! He showed them His hands and His side and they were astonished and delighted to see Him alive. It was then that He offered His peace to them and breathed on them all saying, *"Receive ye the Holy Ghost"* (John 20:22).

Now, obviously, by the very wording, they *did* receive the Holy Spirit. To deny this would be foolish. This took place before the day of Pentecost and before His ascension. I have never had any difficulty with this verse, as seems to be the case with so many. In 1939 when I was introduced to a group in England who spoke in tongues, my Presbyterian heart became strangely warmed because of this miraculous truth. There were a lot of adjustments to be made in my life; for one thing I smoked heavily and I became very convicted that this must go. I became very conscious of my sinful state in many areas. It takes a little of the supernatural to do this! During the period of preparation for this marvelous experience, which I understood they called the baptism of the Holy Spirit, there was quite a cleanup program in my life, and during these months of spiritual readjustment Jesus would breathe upon me in all sorts of unexpected places. I would be walking along a street in London, England, and suddenly He would breathe upon on me and I would feel as light as a feather and clean as a flake of snow. He did the same when I was driving my car on London streets and I felt I would float right through the roof of the car. So unusual and astonishing were these new experiences to me that I sought information from my newfound friends, and they enthusiastically informed me that I was receiving "anointings of the Spirit." This was a correct definition of what was happening to me; they did not confuse me by suggesting I had already received the baptism of the Spirit, or as some call it, the baptism of love, for Jesus was breathing upon me, not once but many times, to encourage me to go deeper with Him and receive the genuine baptism of the Spirit. He was making me very hungry. I had no theologian to discourage me or to turn me out of the way. I did receive this wonderful experience on July 19, 1939.

Some have suggested that the disciples were born again into the kingdom of God when He breathed upon them, but we know they were already disciples of His before He was crucified. They knew they had their names written in heaven. (See Luke 10:20.) They had healed the sick and cast out demons in His lifetime, so I cannot see that it makes any sense to suggest that they did all these things before being born again! Nonbelievers are not called disciples in the Bible. Others, of course, have taught that these disciples received the baptism in the Spirit at this time; but this again cannot be true, because Jesus commanded them to go into Jerusalem to receive this promise. (See Luke 24:49.) In case some believe that people cannot be born again of the Spirit before the cross, let us remember that the words of Jesus to Nicodemus in John 3 were spoken before the cross in the closing days of the old covenant. The rebirth was offered in Old Testament times!

The disciples were so dejected and terrified that they needed a "shot in the arm," and Jesus gave them more than this; He filled them with the Holy Spirit. Let us remember that others were filled with the Spirit before Pentecost—namely Mary the mother of Jesus, John the Baptist, Elizabeth and Zacharias—but none of these was baptized in the Spirit. In Old Testament times the Spirit would come upon a person and enter into him for a specific purpose, mostly to prophesy to the House of Israel. When the Spirit had finished His work in the person, He would depart until the next visitation. We must remember that being filled with the Spirit under the old covenant is not synonymous with the baptism in the Spirit, which occurred on the day the church was born into this world. Because of the absence of the supernatural in the churches today, it has been considered sufficient to have a service in which hands are laid upon the believer so that he may receive the Holy Spirit. This is often called a confirmation service as the individual confirms the vows made at the time of his christening (which means anointing). It was not expected or taught by these denominations that tongues should follow as an outflow from their innermost parts, although we have actually heard of cases where this did happen—in one case the bishop could not understand what was happening and said so.

We are told in Hebrews 8:6 that Jesus made a *better* covenant established on *better* promises. I might add that this covenant was for better people also. God expects a great deal more from New Testament Christians than He did from Old Testament believers. This is why He had said that the least in the kingdom of God would be greater than John the Baptist, who was filled with the Spirit from his mother's womb. (See Matthew 11:11.) The baptism of the Spirit of Acts 2:4 is a far greater and deeper experience of the Holy Spirit than ever occurred before the cross. We must not minimize this glorious blessing of releasing the very power of the spoken word of God in *Logos* manifestation. Satan will do his best to stop this teaching and discourage those who seek it; even those who do have a glorious baptism in the Spirit are often discouraged within a few days as Satan comes and tells them that they "made it up" and that it was not the Holy Spirit but *they* who were speaking. In this case, Satan is right, for "they" began to speak on the day of Pentecost, not the Holy Spirit; but that which they spoke was of the Holy Spirit for He gave them the words to utter. This is beautiful cooperation between God and man. God gave, and man used. Jesus said of the gifts of the Spirit, *"Freely ye have received, freely give"* (Matthew 10:8). God gives us freely of His Holy Spirit and all the gifts and abilities of the Spirit, including healing of the sick, casting out of demons, and speaking in tongues. Our trouble has been that we have not received, so we have not given. The church and the world have therefore been impoverished; but God is changing that today. He is pouring out His Spirit upon all flesh just as He promised. He is giving (He always does) so that we might give in return. The pipeline from heaven will never dry up. The river of life flows on forever and as long as we remain connected up we may overflow all the time and refresh all with whom we come in contact. This is what the world needs—refreshing.

Let us get back to the dispirited and fearful disciples hiding in that room. As I have said, they did receive the Holy Spirit, but not in the deeper way that the same disciples received on the day of Pentecost. In John 20, they received a refreshing and an infilling to invigorate them. It should be called an anointing or even a christening. It should never be called the baptism of the Spirit. I am trying in this book to show the difference between receiving the Holy Spirit at conversion and again in new anointings, and the climactic experience that brings forth tongues. Let us not limit God's workings in our lives because our minds are bound by theological excuses; but again, we must hunger and thirst if we are to be filled. The tragedy is that so many are so satisfied with so little while God is waiting with His hands dripping with blessings—they *are* not hungry or thirsty.

In the *Amplified Version* of the King James Bible, in Acts 19:2, Paul asks the Ephesian disciples, *"Did you receive the Holy Spirit when you believed (on Jesus as the Christ)? They said NO, we have not even heard that there is a Holy Spirit."* In the *New Living Translation* it is also quite clear. *"Did you receive the Holy Spirit when you believed? 'No,' they replied, 'We don't know what you mean, what is the Holy Spirit?'"* There can be no doubt that the Ephesians to whom he addressed this question were already believers, because they believed that Jesus was the Christ; yet Apollos had given them no teaching on receiving the baptism of the Spirit because he knew nothing of this experience himself. He had gotten the disciples at Ephesus to be "born again of the Spirit," but not to be baptized in the Spirit. They were quite honest and said, "We don't know what you are talking about!" I wish that people were as honest today! If their denominations do not teach this experience, why teach against it? It is much more honest to admit your ignorance; after all, how many of us know "all about" God and His Word? None of us. Because Apollos was a humble, honest man, he later did receive the baptism of the Spirit and was ultimately elevated to the apostleship. (See 1 Corinthians 4:6, 9.) This is possible for some of the leaders of our denominations today. God is looking for humble ecclesiastical men to be filled to overflowing with the Spirit today!

We must also refer to the great salvation/healing campaign of Philip the Evangelist at Samaria. (See Acts 8.) Thousands were brought to a saving knowledge of Jesus Christ. They were healed of sicknesses and delivered of demons and baptized in water on confession of their faith, but the Holy Spirit had fallen upon none of the converts. (See Acts 8:16.) *"For He (the Spirit) had not yet fallen upon any of them, but they had only been baptized into the name of the Lord Jesus"* (Acts 8:16 AMP). Were they believers? Obviously. The wording is quite clear believers upon whom the Holy Spirit had not yet fallen! Are we told what happened when the Holy Spirit did fall on them? Yes, Peter and John laid their hands on the new converts and they received the Holy Spirit. We can safely state that they also spoke in tongues, since Simon the sorcerer was so impressed with what he saw and heard that he offered Peter and John money for a like experience!

In the early days of the outpouring of the Holy Spirit at the beginning of the century, those who became hungry began to "seek" the Holy Spirit, based on the promise made by Jesus: *"I send the promise of My Father upon you: but **tarry** ye in the city of Jerusalem, until ye be endued with power from on high"* (Luke 24:49). This very important Scripture, which looked ahead to the coming of the Spirit on the church in the upper room, was used by early Pentecostal pioneers as if it still looked forward, but the upper room is past history and the baptism of the Spirit present experience whenever we choose to ask for it. Jesus clearly told us that if we ask Him for this gift He will freely give it to us, for He said, *"How much more shall your heavenly Father give the Holy Spirit to them that **ask him**?"* (Luke 11:13).

Tarrying used to be the "in thing," and this produced a real tradition. It was explained that the Holy Spirit only comes into a holy vessel and, in order to prepare for His coming, the human vessel had to be made ready, or sanctified; and so "tarrying" for years produced progressive sanctification, until, at long last, after many exhausting years of agonizing prayer, the person was blessed and filled! This presented a real problem to some of these sincere old-timers, because when some of the younger generation began to receive, almost immediately they were told they had a spurious baptism because they had not tarried!

I remember holding a combined meeting with a Pentecostal pastor in Toronto some years ago. I had taken about six of his members and prayed them all through to the baptism by the pleading of the blood of Jesus, and their pastor stated they had had a forced baptism, and that if they did speak in tongues they perforce had done so "in the flesh." This became another cliché: that one could speak in tongues in the flesh as well as in the Spirit, and that it was necessary to wait for the coming or anointing of the Spirit to "make" a person speak in tongues. This, of course, ignored the obvious Scripture in 1 John 2:27, which spoke of the anointing of the Spirit being within, and said that the Holy Spirit would teach us all things. Obviously, if the Holy Spirit dwells within as a welcome visitor, we do not have to wait for Him to come when He is inside! Thus, a Spirit-filled person may at any time start praising in tongues, which is a most edifying experience strongly recommended by Paul.

Today, there is no purpose in tarrying after Pentecost. All we have to do is reach out in our human spirit and receive His Spirit, and as soon as we cooperate with Him and speak the words He gives us, we shall experience the outflowing of the *glossolalia*. If we refuse to speak forth and tarry for years, it will be our fault and not God's. Far from producing progressive sanctification, the longterm tarrying in some cases used to produce defeat and despair so that many gave up seeking any longer because they were waiting for God to do everything as they kept their mouths shut tight!

We repeat that this matter of God filling man to overflowing is mutual cooperation between man and God. Do we not find this same excuse in many who desire healing? They say, "If God wants me to be healed He will heal me." Not so—we must reach out in faith and receive His healing and join it to ourselves. Those who seek with hunger to be baptized in the Spirit must take and receive Him, and the power will only be manifested through us as we turn on the faucet of our tongues and speak. This principle applies also to the gifts of interpretation or prophecy.

Fortunately, in this present charismatic effusion, the doctrine of tarrying is unknown, and thousands are receiving the moment hands are laid upon them and they use their flesh of lips and tongues to speak forth the praises of God. If you just start pleading the precious blood of Jesus as your prayer, as you read this book, you may begin speaking in tongues as the Spirit will give you the utterance. Many have done so.

7

HOW TO RECEIVE THE BAPTISM OF THE SPIRIT

Whe the outpouring of the Spirit occurred at the beginning of this century, especially in the British Isles, a new revelation of the blood of Jesus was given to many. It was quickly realized by these early Pentecostal pioneers that God honored the prayer of the blood. The practice of the "pleading of the blood" came into sharp focus, and those who sought the Holy Spirit baptism by the pleading or honoring of the blood of Jesus quickly received deeper dimensional baptisms. Some actually saw rivers of blood in vision as they used this word in prayer. Visions were given and prophecies heard which magnified the blood of Jesus.

What did this revelation mean? We know that Scripture teaches that we are *"bought with a price"* (1 Corinthians 6:20), and this means that we are no longer our own. We belong to Jesus and the purchase price of our redemption was paid in the blood of Jesus which contained His life. A simple analogy will help us to understand. If we go into a store to buy an article costing one dollar and we tender that dollar to the cashier, we will be given the article without question. We will not try to convince the store manager of our worthiness to have the article, or to impress him by our well-articulated "long prayers." We simply show the price and we get the article we desire. Now what is the price paid for every redemptive blessing? Obviously, the blood of Jesus; so it is not necessary to make long prayers or to beat the pews, or to shout to heaven or to roll on the floor to attract the One who gives us the gift of the Holy Spirit. Note, it is a gift and therefore free to us because He purchased this gift for us with His own blood.

The analogy breaks down here, because we do not offer anything for this gift, but we honor the price that Jesus paid. Remember there was still a price that was paid for our free and glorious gift of the Holy Spirit. All we have to do is to go into the presence of Jesus in heaven, being on earth in our bodies, and just say, "Lord, we plead, or honor, your blood." God knows that there is no other One that can give us this gift but His Son, and He knows that He has to give it to those who seek Him in faith honoring the price. He has absolutely no other option than to give us this remarkable gift. As soon as we receive it, we shall use it and manifest tongues!

There is a most wonderful equation in 1 John 5:7–8. In fact, there are two equations, one dealing with God's operations in heaven and the second with His workings on earth.

Equation 1: *"There are three that bear record in heaven, the Father, the Word, the Holy Ghost"* (1 John 5:7).

Now it is not difficult for us to understand this. The Father is over all, the Son (Word) sits on His right hand, and the Holy Spirit agrees with all that is done and is the One who visits earth continually to bless God's creation. The Holy Spirit is omnipresent, in earth and heaven at the same time. There is complete agreement between the three Persons of the Trinity.

Equation 2: *"And there are three that bear witness in earth, the Spirit, and the water, and the blood"* (1 John 5:8).

This is a most remarkable triad, and we notice that, whereas the Father was first in heaven, now He is replaced on earth by the Holy Spirit, who becomes number one, and the One with whom we all must deal. In heaven, the second place was given to the Second Person of the Trinity, Jesus, described as the Logos or the Word of God. (See John 1:1.) The Word in heaven becomes the water on earth in second place, because water is the symbol of the Holy Spirit and water flows. I refer you again to the words of Jesus who said, *"Out of his belly shall flow rivers of living water"* (John 7:38), and the Word in heaven flows down to earth by the Holy Spirit as living water from the River of God. When this water comes into us, as we have read in a previous chapter, it must flow out of us, for we are only channels and the vessels of the Old Testament sanctuary were for pouring out blessings, not just for containing blessings.

The Word, therefore, must flow, and it begins in heaven and is poured out of our mouths in the form of the living, flowing Word of God. The speaking in tongues is always God's Word flowing, and this may come forth, according to our faith, as tongues, interpretation of tongues, or prophecy, but it is always the *Logos* Word flowing to people to bring them refreshment and blessing. A Christian who claims to be filled with the Spirit and who does not pour forth the Word of God supernaturally is not measuring up to the record of the Bible that the Spirit and the Water agree perfectly. A Christian who does not pour forth is a dry one—his vessel has dried up. He is saved but not doing what he is supposed to do—to witness in the power of the

Spirit. He is without power (*dunamis*) for Jesus said we would have His *dunamis* when the Holy Spirit comes upon us in Pentecostal fashion.

Now notice that both the Holy Spirit and the flowing Word agree absolutely in their witness with the blood of Jesus. How can this be? The blood is living blood. It is on the mercy seat in heaven, sprinkled by the hand of Jesus when He ascended, because in the antitype in the Old Testament the High Priest sprinkled the blood of the sacrifice once a year on the gold-covered mercy seat of the ark behind the veil of the temple. The mercy seat means the place of propitiation or mercy, where God meets with us on the common ground of the shed blood of the Lamb.

The very moment we start honoring and pleading the blood, there is an instant reaction in heaven. God is honor-bound to give us the blessing, because we are once again taking His precious blood in faith and honoring or sprinkling it, as the priests did in Old Testament times; but now, as New Testament priests, we are offering to God the spiritual sacrifice of the blood. (See 1 Peter 2:5.) We cannot offer literal blood as the priests did in Old Testament times, but we now offer or sprinkle the blood of Jesus spiritually.

In the early days of the outpouring of the Spirit, the earnest and hungry people simply went before the Lord seeking His gift. They relaxed and many cupped their hands as if they were making an offering, which they were, but it was a spiritual offering. As the priests of old sprinkled many drops of blood, so can we as New Testament priests sprinkle many drops of blood spiritually. Each time we repeat the word *"blood"* with our lips, it is a prayer and an act of faith. We are only offering His precious blood, the price paid for this redemptive blessing. The effect of this prayer approach is astonishing. The Holy Spirit descends upon us almost at once, and then we will find it difficult to say the word "blood" any more. Something strange will begin to happen to our jaws and to our tongue and at this point we give place to the Spirit and take the words that He gives us, and they start to flow through us as we deliberately stop saying the word "blood" and just speak forth the words of the Spirit. As we start, it is like opening a water valve or faucet, and then the living water begins to flow forth from our lips and tongue. We are now speaking in other tongues as the Spirit gives us utterance.

It is very important that we understand that it is we who do the speaking. Let us refer to Acts 2:4 where we read that it was the disciples who *began* to speak. If they had refused to cooperate and turn on the valve, there would have been no flow of living water! Some wait for God to start speaking and so they refuse to pray and they keep their mouths shut! Others go on beseeching in English (or whatever their native tongue may be). They beg for what rightly belongs to them. It is the gift of the Holy Spirit. Some old-fashioned seeking meetings were painful and many prayed and prayed for years and never received. Had they known how to honor the blood of Jesus they would have received.

The late Smith Wigglesworth used to say that in prophesying or interpreting, the first few words were from our own mind and then, as we begin to speak, the Spirit takes over and the flow is of God. Our initial approach to God, therefore, must be to open our mouths and speak; but it is sufficient that we just honor the blood and as the Spirit begins to give us the supernatural words, we keep on speaking—we must not stop—and we will hear ourselves speaking in other tongues as the Spirit gives us the utterance.

Many make the mistake of thinking that they are going to hear the words in their minds before they speak them forth. This is not so, for the Holy Spirit only flows through our human spirits, never our minds; it actually bypasses our minds. When we begin to speak in new tongues we will hear ourselves and the strange words in the same manner as others will hear them. It is the same with prophecy. We do not know what we are going to speak forth and we will hear as others will and we all get blessed.

I well remember a lady who came to our church in about 1950. She was sent to me by a relative who had told her that Pastor Whyte would pray for her to receive the Holy Spirit. She was told absolutely nothing about what would happen. All that had been explained to her was that this was a great experience to have; so the lady came before me. I just asked her to plead or repeat the word "blood," which she did quite obediently. Almost immediately, she burst forth, praising God in a new language, and then she stopped and looked at me with astonishment and said, "What was that?" It was a little amusing, but I encouraged her to continue, which she immediately did with tears of joy running down her face. Later, explanations from the Bible were given to her.

Wherever I have been privileged to minister, in many countries of the world, I have taught this method of seeking God's gift of the baptism of the Holy Spirit. Almost 100 percent of those who have come have begun to speak in tongues as they were encouraged. Some who come are full of discouragement and doubts, for they have approached God with lack of understanding. They have prayed in English. They have gotten tense and shouted. They have begged and implored and besought Jesus— and nothing has happened. They did not understand that it is impossible to speak in English with the mind and speak in tongues at the same time by the Spirit. The mind must get out of the way and give precedence to our human spirit. Like goes with like—the Spirit of God merges into our human spirits.

Others come to us who are not completely dedicated to the Lord. They are following from afar, but they want the blessings. They are probably bound by some habit, or they have an unforgiving spirit or a critical attitude toward people. They may have been immersed in some form of the occult, such as horoscopes, spiritism, or Ouija boards, and they have attracted to themselves unclean spirits. These will react quickly to the pleading of the blood, which will cleanse them out of their hiding places. Often, deliverances begin to take place among these people when they plead the blood of Jesus, and they will start choking or coughing as the spirits are ejected because of the cry of the blood. As they press on, the deliverance takes place and then the coughing is replaced by halting tongues, which gradually increase in volume and clarity. Sometimes, the person being delivered will speak in tongues, then cough, then speak in tongues, until the channel is clear and the tongues are clear. It is obvious that in such cases the seeker actually helps to clean himself up by using the blood as a purifier.

Many, in times past, have never been able to receive the baptism of the Spirit because they have been bound and have not known the way to get free, and their pastors have not known either! It has been strictly a "hit and miss" affair, and despondency descends upon those who are bound; but the use of the blood will disclose lurking spirits which Satan had put there to resist the incoming of the Spirit! I have helped so many of these chronic seekers, for they first needed a measure of deliverance before the Spirit could enter them.

Many reading about this method have applied the instructions. I received a letter from a man conducting a Bible class in Nigeria, West Africa. His students were all evangelical and none had received the baptism of the Spirit. He instructed them to start pleading the blood, and within a very short time twenty Nigerians were praising God in tongues. All he had done was to read my book *The Power of the Blood*. I have amplified this theme in this book, and I pray that thousands will seek God's blessing of the baptism of the Holy Spirit by approaching the mercy seat in heaven (where Jesus is) and He will respond and fill you quickly with the Spirit.

This glorious experience can only be appreciated *after* you receive. The gift brings you into an entirely new dimension of power with God. It does not alter your status as a son of God, for Jesus was still the Son of God before He was anointed of the Spirit in the Jordan River. We waste our time with those who oppose us if we try to argue them into this blessing, for they must thirst first. If our friends are not thirsty, the baptism is not for them. It is beautiful to see many today as they first begin to speak in tongues. Their faces light up, a new look of glory appears on them, they walk with a lighter step and praises begin to be heard from their lips. "Hallelujah" and "Praise the Lord" become the norm, much to the embarrassment of some of their dry Christian friends! Oh, yes, there is a price to pay. You may be asked to leave "your church." It is worth it!

8

THE MANIFESTATIONS OF
THE SPIRIT

We have already seen that people were filled with the Holy Spirit in Old Testament times. All the gifts of the Spirit were manifest before Pentecost, except the gift of tongues. There was one possible exception when an ass spoke words of God to Balaam; but this was not a human speaking, although he spoke more wisdom than many humans. The initial manifestation of speaking in unknown tongues was the peculiar way chosen by God to announce that His church—the body of Christ—had taken material form by being born into this wicked world in the upper room. In Old Testament times the Holy Spirit would move upon and enter into a person to do a particular work, and after this He would withdraw His anointing until the next occasion. In the New Testament, the gift of the Holy Spirit is given to manifest all the gifts of the Spirit as occasion may demand; in fact, the gift of the Holy Spirit by itself as a onetime experience is not what God intends. It is not His purpose for His church that a member should have only initially spoken in tongues as a sign of having been filled with the Holy Spirit. The intention is that this power be projected in the church to manifest more than tongues, which includes the whole range of deliverance and healing gifts.

The apostle Paul told us that we should be filled with the Spirit, using the Greek progressive tense (see Ephesians 5:18), meaning that we should go on being filled, like a fountain which never dries up. We should overflow every day with living water as manifested in the gifts of the Spirit. In the Old Testament, God turned on the faucet and turned it off again, but in the New Testament we are permanently connected up to the River of Life and it should flow every day without cessation. God never turns it off, but the devil sometimes tries to, and he succeeds too! We prove that we are connected up, even if depressed in spirit, by turning on our faucet and praising God in tongues, thereby edifying ourselves. (See 1 Corinthians 14:4.) Thus assured that the flow of heavenly water is always available, we may manifest the other gifts of the Spirit, which are compounded parts of the whole—the gift of the Spirit—and edify first ourselves and then the church. The edifying of the church is the reason God baptizes us with the Holy Spirit.

To illustrate the need of constant infillings of the Spirit in a progressive sense, let us consider the story of the disciples who gathered together after the initial persecutions following the healing of the lame man. They prayed,

> *And now, Lord, behold their threatenings: and grant unto thy servants, that with all boldness they may speak the word, by stretching forth thine hand to heal; and that signs and wonders may be done by the name of thy holy child Jesus. And when they had prayed, the place was shaken where they were assembled together: and they were all filled with the Holy Ghost, and they spake the word of God with boldness.*
> (Acts 4:29–31)

These early disciples were under pressure, but they were determined not to cave in to the threats of the ignorant Jews and so they held a prayer meeting. They were not praying against the Jews, they were praying a positive petition for healings, miracles, signs, and wonders that would be done when they laid hands on needy people. They wanted the Jews to be confounded by a demonstration of God's power through the operation of the gifts of the Spirit within them.

Every time we have a need, or are under pressure or opposition, we should hold a prayer meeting and ask God again to fill us afresh in a progressive sense with the Holy Spirit, that we might go out again from our place of prayer to work miracles in His name. This alone will close the mouths of the ignorant. The gift of the Holy Spirit is given to confound the mighty.

Jesus is the light of the world (see John 1:4) and the Holy Spirit is sent by the Father to shed forth this light in a darkened world. This is the supreme task of the Holy Spirit—to reveal Jesus. In the light of the sun there are nine compounded colors, each having its own frequency and manifestation and yet collectively making up white light. The colors are ultraviolet, violet, indigo, blue, green, yellow, orange, red, and infrared. In like manner there are nine compounded charismatic gifts of the Spirit, which collectively manifest Jesus, the light of the world. They are wisdom, knowledge, faith, healings, miracles, prophecy, discerning of spirits, interpretation of tongues and tongues, and they all work in complete unity to edify the church, but they all operate through humans. This is why we must at all times realize that once we have been filled with the Spirit we must go on being filled with the Spirit, never drying up. Those who do dry up, or find their pressure going down, or find a leak somewhere, are those who collapse under outside pressure from Satan. We are more than conquerors through Him who loved us. We are always conquerors. We give the commands and Satan obeys.

Some have limited the gift of the Holy Spirit to the use of a "prayer language." This is true, but it is only a part of the whole truth. We are not only to edify ourselves, but our primary aim must be to edify the church, to help to build it back to its original power and format. To pray and intercede in tongues is a wonderful ministry, but to heal the sick and cast out demons is also wonderful.

It will readily be seen that the church that Jesus said He would build must operate in the power of the Spirit. In Romans 8:14, it is written that, *"As many as are led by the Spirit of God, they are the sons of God."* The Greek word for sons here is *huios*, which means a mature developed son of God, not a baby wanting spoon feeding by the pastor all the time. After receiving the guide—the Holy Spirit—we must be prepared for Him to guide us into all truth and to cease from relying on our own intelligence. We must listen carefully for the gifts of the word of wisdom and the word of knowledge to operate in the deep quiet recesses of our minds. He will speak to us by His Spirit. We must have our senses exercised to *discern* both good and evil. (See Hebrews 5:14.) This privilege is given to those who are of mature age; and as we look and listen in the Spirit, the gift of discerning of spirits will quietly operate.

Because the church in history has not had the baptism of the Spirit with the charismatic gifts, it has not been equipped to discern the true from the false, so many wrong spirits lurking in the dark corners of people's lives have not been discerned (see 1 John 4:1–2), and many times they have caused sicknesses, family strife and church splits. The apostle John warned us not to believe *every spirit*, because some spirits are not of God (occult spirits). The Church of England recently did a lengthy research on the supernatural in the psychic world of these spirits. There is one Holy Spirit and many other evil spirits, but these often come in disguised as angels of light. Unless we have our spiritual radar working, we will be taken in by their deceptions.

It was never God's intention that we should be just born again into His kingdom, but that we should possess these divine attributes in order to help, teach, heal and deliver the church from the powers of darkness that have so easily gripped it since before the reformation. This is why the Lord is now pouring out His Spirit afresh upon us all: to bring the church back to function as He always meant it to do, to heal the sick, cast out demons and cleanse the lepers, both spiritual and physical. We cannot fulfill this ministry unless and until we have been baptized with the Spirit and fire.

For at least twenty-five years we have had hundreds of people coming to our church in Toronto seeking healing and deliverance. Many have telephoned me long distance for help, and when I suggest they call their own pastor their reply is that he does not pray for people in the New Testament way. Some have traveled right across the continent seeking help, and many have been miraculously healed and many delivered of demon powers afflicting their minds and bodies. It is my prayer that many of these impotent pastors will submit themselves under God's hand and receive His anointing of power. So many churches only preach a social gospel, and others preach John 3:16 and are quite satisfied when men and women receive Jesus into their lives as Savior.

The word *charismatic* is a relatively new word, and was originally applied to those groups from among the historic churches who were receiving the baptism of the Spirit, as evidenced with glossolalia or tongues. This word had never been applied to the various classic Pentecostal groups, but as the word came into popular usage, the Pentecostals also "borrowed" it, and now also claim to be charismatics together with those groups from the historic churches.

The evangelicals have now adopted the word, and claim that all born-again Christians are also charismatic, based on the Scripture in Romans 6:23, "*For the wages of sin is death, but the free **gift** of God is eternal life through our Lord Jesus Christ.*" Here the Greek word for "*gift*" is *charisma*, which means "grace, favor, or kindness"; and so the original gift of God, administered by the Holy Spirit, is an unmerited favor or kindness bestowed upon the penitent sinner. The evangelicals therefore claim that, as they have received this charisma, they have a right to be considered as charismatic!

Theologically, they have a point which is difficult to argue; but the gift of eternal life, though basic to becoming a Christian, does not in itself produce the other charismata of the Spirit which manifest Jesus Christ through His body in the power and energy of the Holy Spirit. The original gift of eternal life transplants us into the kingdom of God, but after that transplantation we need power from on high to release His presence in us. Jesus was born the Son of God, but it was still necessary for Him to receive the anointing that came when the Holy Spirit descended as a dove before He could release the full power of God in healing the sick, casting out demons and raising the dead. So it is with us—we may be charismatic Christians to begin with, but the power of Jesus in us must be released by the oncoming of the Holy Spirit upon us in our baptism. The release is tongues.

As born-again members of the body of Christ we must become Holy Spirit-anointed members, then the full manifestation of the charismata in 1 Corinthians 12:8–10 can be, and should be released.

Are you a true charismatic?

9

TONGUES EXAMINED

There are some who say that the speaking in tongues that occurred at Pentecost was not identical with that which occurred when the Gentiles first received in Acts 10, and again when the Ephesians were filled with the Spirit in Acts 19.

We have tried to explain that when the Holy Spirit came upon and filled the initial 120 members of the body of Christ in the upper room, the Word of God (the *Logos*) was spoken forth from each of their mouths. Thus was the Spirit-filled church born with its initial birth cry of divine life. Could it be that the manifestation of tongues in Acts 10 was a different happening? I would suggest it was the same, and the context bears this out.

Peter, an orthodox Jew, was sent to the home of Cornelius, a Roman captain, by a vision. Peter saw a large sheet let down from heaven containing all manner of unclean beasts (see Leviticus 11), and he was commanded to eat. Being entirely orthodox he refused to disobey the known law of God for he said, *"Not so, Lord; for I have never eaten anything common or unclean"* (Acts 10:14). The purpose of the vision given three times to Peter was made clear in verse 28, where he explained to Cornelius that God had shown him that it was wrong to call *any man* common or unclean. The Jews looked upon the Gentiles as unclean animals—dogs and pigs and skunks. The Lord was about to bring the Gentiles into the kingdom of God, so He had to remove prejudices from Peter's theological mind by showing him that he was about to cleanse these unclean Gentiles. Peter was to look upon them as clean, not common or unclean.

In obedience to the heavenly vision, Peter started to preach to Cornelius and his friends. He began by declaring that he perceived that God was no respecter of persons, Jew or Gentile, but that people from every nation who feared God and worked righteousness would be accepted into His Kingdom. He told how Jesus healed people and said that if anyone believed in Him, he would receive remission of sins. As soon as Peter finished his message, the Holy Spirit suddenly and unexpectedly descended upon these Gentiles and Peter and his Jewish friends were *astonished, "For they heard them speak with tongues, and magnify God"* (Acts 10:46).

The Greek words used are the same as in Acts 2:4—*glossa-laleo. Glossa-* means a tongue or language and -*laleo* means to speak. The one hundred and twenty in the upper room spoke new languages and so did the Gentiles. This is quite clear when Peter, in his defense before the Jewish apostles, said, *"And as I began to speak, the Holy Ghost fell on them, as on us at the beginning"* (Acts 11:15). Nothing could be clearer. The experiences were identical.

Because of this supernatural miracle, the Jewish leaders at Jerusalem unanimously concluded that God had also granted to the Gentiles repentance unto life (see verse 18). Peter had preached that the Gentiles could be saved, and God confirmed His Word with signs following—just exactly as we read in Mark 16:17, *"These signs shall follow them that believe; in My name shall they...speak with new tongues."* Again the words *glossa-* and -*laleo* are used and that which was prophesied in Mark 16 was also fulfilled among the first Gentiles. I think the marvelous thing about this miracle is that the Jews concluded that God had *saved* the Gentiles. If there had not been an effusion of tongues, no Jew would have believed it. Contrast this method used by God with the methods used by man today (appeals for salvation), and follow up with tracts and simple Bible teaching of the way of salvation. Peter gave the Gentiles some simple teaching, but God had to confirm it by *glossa laleo*. So, today, the simple teaching of the gospel should always be confirmed by the coming of the Spirit with signs following the new believer.

It is awesome to think that we Gentiles today would never have been admitted into the family of God unless God had poured out His Spirit in this manner. If Cornelius had just said, "All right, Peter, I accept your Jesus as my personal Savior," and if his friends had said, "Amen, we do, too," no Jew would have ever believed them! It took a miracle of tongues and a vision of unclean beasts to convince first Peter, and then the other Jewish leaders. I think we should see a pattern today in the charismatic renewal—that God is willing to baptize all new converts with the Holy Spirit—because the early disciples prayed that He would stretch forth His hand to heal and that signs and wonders might be done in Jesus' name. (See Acts 4:29–30.) This was for the very simple reason that men and women might be born again and won into the kingdom of God by a supernatural visitation, not by intellectual reasoning or persuasion.

I am sure that this is still God's way. He does not change.

The next case is when for the first time God poured out His Spirit upon a local evangelical assembly at Ephesus. It is a classic story of what should happen to every congregation of believers today. First, we read in Acts 18 that Aquilla and Priscilla,

Spirit-baptized Christians, witnessed to Apollos, a Jew of Alexandria, who was renowned as an eloquent preacher and who was mighty in the Scriptures. He was a fervent man desiring to know the truth that sets us free, and when this husband and wife team told him about Jesus the Christ, he readily believed upon Him as Savior and then taught about Him and the spiritual rebirth with conviction and eloquence; yet, he had not yet received the baptism in the Spirit!

In Acts 19, Paul is sent of God to visit Ephesus (where Diana was queen of the city), and although Apollos was away preaching in another part, his assembly was ready to hear what Paul had to say and the twelve male members were quickly obedient to Paul's admonition to be baptized in water in the name of Jesus; and then Paul laid his hands upon these twelve men and *"The Holy Ghost came on them; and they spake with tongues and prophesied"* (Acts 19:6). Again, the same two Greek words are used—*glossa* and *laleo*—so that it is quite obvious that these Jewish evangelicals all received the baptism in the same manner as the Jews in the upper room, and the Gentiles in Caesarea. I have been privileged to stand in these two places and praise God in tongues myself for these ancient miracles!

Apollos was later elevated to the apostleship (see 1 Corinthians 4:6, 9), but not before he had also received this experience, for the whole local church was set on fire of the Holy Spirit. There are so many cases of this happening across the world in 1976, as evangelical and historic churches come into this Ephesian experience by the initial evidence of speaking in tongues. We see little bonfires being ignited by the Holy Spirit in every city of North America and in other countries. These fires will spread until they join, assembly with assembly, denomination with denomination, until the one true church is burning fiercely with the love and power of God. This is happening!

We need to remember that one of the analogies of the Holy Spirit is fire. Others are water and wind. God in His love is setting His church on fire, and the result is tongues of fire being seen spiritually upon whole groups of believers. This actually happened in 1917 in the little Methodist church on Collier Street, Barrie, Ontario, Canada, where tongues of fire burst through the roof as early Pentecostals were praying for the Holy Spirit baptism. One of my elders in my church in Toronto was present, and he told me the story. He rushed to the door of the building and saw many people shouting and pointing to the roof, which was on fire. The fire engine and pumpers arrived to put the fire out, but it was the supernatural fire of the Holy Spirit. Elder Cecil Arnold told me this story, and his widow, still living in 1976, confirmed it. I think this will happen again! The church needs some shaking!

We have sometimes been asked a question about the promise made by John the Baptist that Jesus would baptize believers with the Holy Spirit *and fire.* (See Matthew 3:11.) Was the fire separate from the experience referred to by Jesus in Luke 24:49

and Acts 1:5? No; because Jesus referred to John's ministry, and therefore his teaching, and that which occurred in the upper room was that which John had promised. Jesus baptized the disciples with the Holy Spirit and fire; and in the initial experience, tongues of fire were actually seen on each one of them.

Some argue that those who claim to receive the baptism of the Spirit today should also have tongues appear on them when they speak in tongues. If we get too didactically exact we may have to insist that all go into the upper room in Jerusalem as well to receive! In the Old Testament type (and there is one) we find Elijah in a cave and God appears to him because he is dejected and cast down. It is at such a time that we need a supernatural visitation from on high! Let us read in 1 Kings 19:11–12.

> And, behold, the LORD passed by, and a great and strong wind rent the mountains, and brake in pieces the rocks before the LORD; but the LORD was not in the wind; and after the wind an earthquake; but the LORD was not in the earthquake; and after the earthquake a fire; but the LORD was not in the fire: and after the fire a still small voice.

Before the voice of God was heard, there first of all occurred visitations of awesome divine power. A wind, then an earthquake, then fire, and then God spoke. In the upper room we find first the wind, then the fire, and then God spoke, and later in Acts 4:31, when they were again assembled together and prayed, the place was shaken, but after the shaking, *they spoke* the Word with boldness. If fire, wind, or earthquake occur, they are merely evidences of God's divine power, but the end result must always be the manifestation of the Word of God, the *Logos*, Jesus speaking Himself.

I believe we are going to see these three signs in our day, and probably many more unexpected ones, so that God can break through the stony heart of unbelief in so many Christians today. Many rocky hearts will be broken by the wind. The wood, hay, and stubble on which many have built will be burnt up by fire (1 Corinthians 3:13), and denominational earthquakes are scheduled! Everything is being shaken today as it has never previously been shaken—governments, churches and nations. The wind and the fire are doing this, for we read, *"And this word, yet once more, signifieth the removing of those things that are shaken, as of things that are made, that those things which cannot be shaken may remain"* (Hebrews 12:27). After the Lord has finished blowing and shaking and setting things on fire, the only thing that will be left is the church built of precious stones, gold, and silver; the wood, the hay, the flimsy carnalities will be burnt up. The philosophies and conceits of man will give place to the Word of God appearing again in power, and the gifts of the Spirit will confirm His power in a true Spirit-filled church; but it will all begin with tongues!

In conclusion, let us quote from Paul. *"I would that ye all spake with tongues [glossalaleo]"* (1 Corinthians 14:5), and, *"Forbid not to speak with tongues"* (1 Corinthians 14:39).

IS MARK 16 TRUE?

CONTENTS

1

THE ANCIENT MANUSCRIPTS

History has shown that where a portion of the Bible sharply contradicts doctrines fondly held by denominational leaders, a great effort is made by them to discredit the clear statements of Scripture.

The church, which is called the body of Christ, was born on the day of Pentecost in a blaze of glory. Wind, tongues of fire, and speaking in tongues came upon the 120 people gathered in the upper room. The effect of this effusion of the Holy Spirit was not understood at all by the religious Jews who observed it. The best explanation they could offer was that Mary, the mother of Jesus, and the other disciples were drunk! Their reaction was one of amazement and astonishment. They could offer no logical or coherent explanation for such an act of God. Let us remember that these religious Jews were present in the delivery ward of the greatest creation that God ever made— He prepared a body for His Son in which He would dwell and manifest Himself on earth *after* His resurrection. As the body of the Son of God had been prepared in the womb of the Virgin Mary, so also had His body—the church—been prepared in the womb of Israel, whom Mary represented in type. It was a sudden, supernatural creation. Nothing like it had ever been created or seen before by man. There was no scientific or rational explanation for wind, fire, and glossolalia. What attitude, therefore, should the Jewish church take? Acceptance or rejection?

If these same signs happen today as promised in Mark 16:9–20, then what are the established and historic church groups to say? The fundamentalists have taken the position that whereas these supernatural happenings of tongues, healings, and exorcisms really took place in the early church, they do not and cannot happen today because their denominations decree it that way! The fact that millions of Protestants and Catholics are indeed speaking in tongues moves them not at all. It is simply stated that it is impossible for today, and if pressed they will say that it is probably of the devil, thereby acknowledging that Satan has more power and ability than the Holy Spirit, which is, in simple terms, blasphemy against the Holy Spirit.

The more pseudointellectual sections of the church dig into their records and find that two ancient manuscripts did not include these verses. This is just what they are looking for. Here is their answer—the casting out of demons, the healing of the sick, the speaking in tongues, etc., are a monkish annotation. They owe nothing to the Holy Spirit speaking through Jesus, they are not authentic—they are false. It is the age-old strategy of Satan in the garden of Eden, to cast doubt on the Word of God. *"And the serpent was more subtle than any beast of the field…and he said unto the woman,* *'Yea, God hath said…?'"* (Genesis 3:1). In this case Eve was a type of the righteous line, the church, the bride of Christ, and Satan was quick off the mark right at the beginning to cast doubt on (not to contradict) the plain statements of the Word of God. This is all that thousands desire, an excuse to avoid the obvious inference.

They tell us, "Don't you know that all those verses are not in the original manuscripts?" They fail to add that these signs are not in their dead churches either. As their particular denomination *must* be right, and all others wrong, then it follows the Bible must be wrong also. This is human conceit. The apostle Paul described this as being *"vainly puffed up by his fleshly mind"* (Colossians 2:18). The Greek word *phusioo* means that the person is inflated with wind, like a bullfrog—just breathing forth a lot of hot air with no substance in it. When the true wind or breath of the Holy Spirit saturates a person, then these signs shall follow them that believe! They are the evidences of the indwelling Spirit who manifests Christ the miracle worker.

Paul even had this trouble in the early church where they had the gifts of the Spirit. Pseudointellectualism was creeping in, for he wrote to the Corinthians, *"But I will come to you shortly, if the Lord will, and will know, not the speech of them which are puffed up, **but the power**"* (1 Corinthians 4:19). Paul sought for the evidence of the power of God as manifest in exorcism, healing the sick and the gifts of the Spirit, not apologetic theology.

A few years ago, the largest Protestant church in Canada introduced a new curriculum that stated that the first eleven chapters of the book of Genesis were just folklore. The content of these chapters was not the literal mind of God, and in spite of the fact that Jesus referred to statements in these chapters, they were not to be accepted as authentic. Doubt was cast on them. Following this "puffed up" diatribe, the membership of this denomination began to dwindle; some lost out altogether and others went to other denominations. I understand that it is probable that this statement of unbelief will shortly be removed from their curriculum. If Genesis states that God created man after His own image and likeness, and this denomination states that man evolved from a protoplasm born in primordial oceans, then these chapters must either be removed from the Bible or discredited by doubt. The average churchgoer has little knowledge of the Bible and looks to his leaders for guidance. What did Jesus say of the religious leaders in His day? *"They be blind leaders of the blind, and if the blind lead the blind, both shall fall into the ditch"* (Matthew 15:14).

Is it true that these marvelous verses are not in two of the original manuscripts? Yes. In the two oldest Greek manuscripts, the Siniatic and the Vatican, verses 9–20 are omitted, but the latter leaves a blank space, indicating that the chapter is incomplete. It must be recognized that it was not until the fourth century that anyone questioned the authenticity of these verses. It was at this time that general unbelief in the supernatural was coming upon the church like an icy cloud.

Monsignor Ronald Knox made an excellent translation from the Latin Vulgate as authorized by the hierarchy of the Roman Catholic Church in Great Britain. This is accepted as a standard work in the Catholic Church which is now experiencing such a wonderful renewal of the Spirit in so many ways. Monsignor Knox writes of Mark 16:9–20 as follows:

> It seems that the manuscripts of St. Mark were mutilated at the end of very early times; the whole of this chapter being sometimes omitted (St. Jerome Ad Hedy b.q. 3). And in a few remaining manuscripts these last twelve verses are wanting, which fact (together with the abruptness of their style) has made some critics think that they were added from another source. But they are evidently a primitive account, and there is no reason why we should not ascribe their inclusion here in St. Mark.

This scholar sees *no reason* why we should not accept them as the Word of God.

In actual fact there are over 4,200 Greek manuscripts of the New Testament, of which 618 contain the record of the Gospels, and only two do not contain these verses. Of those, 616 manuscripts record verses 9–20 and two do not. Is this sufficient evidence on which to base the statement, "These verses are not in the originals?"

The New Testament was first translated into Syriac, and two existing manuscripts (the Peshito—AD 150, and the Curetonian—third century) both record these verses. Thus the earliest records known to man teach that the church was commissioned to work the supernatural works of God, including speaking in tongues and the expelling of demons. The two manuscripts that omit these verses were scribed several centuries later.

There are eight thousand known Latin versions, all copied from Jerome's Vulgate of AD 382. Jerome used the existing Greek manuscripts of his day. His Latin translation contained these verses, to which Monsignor Knox agrees. He largely worked on a previous second century translation known as *Vetus Itala*, which also contained these verses.

As we look back into antiquity, we find that not only the Latin and Greek versions contained these disputed verses, but also the Gothic version of AD 350, the Egyptian versions of the third and fourth centuries (Memphidic and Thebaic versions); the Armenian, the Ethiopic, and the Georgian versions all contain these verses; and so our researches show us that only two Greek versions left the verses out, because of their unbelief!

One of the manucripts already referred to is the Codex Vaticanus, that omits Mark 16:9–20, but if we are going to use this fact as a proof that these promises of Jesus cannot be accepted today, then we must also remember that other very important (and accepted) portions of Scripture are also left out in this manuscript. For example, it also leaves out the first forty-six chapters of Genesis! Psalms 105–137 are not recorded. From Hebrews 9:14 to Hebrews 13:25 is omitted, as well as both epistles to Timothy, all of Titus, Philemon and the whole of the book of Revelation. These books may well have been lost to make a complete Codex Vaticanus, but how can we prove that Mark 16:9–20 was not also lost along with the Book of Revelation? It is certainly no proof! There is not one early manuscript that does not leave out some portions that we have in our Bible today.

These verses are in perfect harmony with other parts of the Bible and also with events that are occurring in the present-day outpouring of the Holy Spirit. The day of unbelief is giving way to a renewal of faith and power. The Holy Spirit is proving to us that Mark 16:9–20 is indeed in the original!

2

CASTING OUT DEMONS

The first of these five controversial signs that should follow every believer who is saved and baptized in water is the ability to cast out demons. The word in the Greek is *daimonion*, which means an intelligent spiritual being who casts a shadow between a believer and Jesus. The word can correctly be translated "shade" or "shadow" because its work is to cut out the sunlight of the presence of Jesus. All demons are liars and visit "lying vanities" upon the human race and deceive believers. The origin of demons is adequately explained in my book, *Dominion Over Demons*. They are fallen angels of various degrees of power and rank. The word *daimon* expresses the thought of a higher-ranking evil spirit that would seek to be deified. There are principalities, powers, rulers of the darkness of this world, and myriads of wicked spirits (*daimonion*) in elevated places. (See Ephesians 6:12.) As there are descending ranks in the army from general downward to private, so also Satan, the devil (*diabolos*), is the high-ranking demon who controls and governs completely all who voluntarily joined with him in their original rebellion against Jesus Christ. (See Revelation 12:7–9.) Day and night Satan and his cohorts are making war with the saints, determined to destroy them. The battle is unceasing and the ignorant Christian lies down and suffers continuing abuse, instead of rising in the name of Jesus and casting them out! He has not been taught, and this first sign undoubtedly is one of the main reasons for the church in the past trying its best to cast doubt on this passage as "not in the originals," so that a weak and disobedient church is no longer required to obey the words of Jesus and attack and rout the devil and all his forces.

In the historical account of the first exodus under Moses, the *first* sign that was given to him was the ability to handle serpents. The second was physical healing. (See Exodus 4:1–7.) It was therefore taught to Moses that he had complete authority over the devil and his demons, which was demonstrated in the rout of the serpents in Pharaoh's court. (See Exodus 7:12.) The same order of primacy of signs follows throughout Scripture. In Luke 9:1, Jesus gave the twelve Apostles His power and authority over *all demons* as well as to cure diseases. In Luke 10:1, this same ability was transmitted to the seventy elders who made it work. (See Luke 10:17–19.) In the five signs that we are considering, the ability to cast out demons is put in number one place, and it is interesting to record that when Philip went down to Samaria the very first supernatural happening was that the demons in the people started to come out crying with a loud voice. We are sure that the people were startled and many were afraid (see Acts 8:5–7), and yet there was great joy!

All over the world this first sign is the last to reappear! The fifth sign of healing, which will be considered later in this book, was the first to reappear at the end of the last century. It was not until the last half of this century that the sign of the casting out of demons was restored, and today all over the world reports are coming in of great miracles and deliverances happening as Christians once again rise to their high calling in Christ and attack demonic strongholds and expel the intruders in their lives. It is aggressive, objective prayer. Most prayer in the past has been passive, subjective prayer.

It was this very verse that the Holy Spirit gave us when faced with our first encounter with spirits of infirmity in 1948. We had had no theological training concerning this ministry, and therefore our approach to the unknown had to be one of faith in the Scriptures! What should we do? The Spirit said, "*In my name shall ye cast out demons*" (Mark 16:17). It was enough—we commanded and the demons commenced to obey. Twenty-five years later, they are still obeying, but with this amount of experience behind us they are obeying more submissively and quickly as we bind them and rob them of their spoil (the bound sufferer). (See Matthew 12:29.) We thus bind, tie, or fasten the offending demons and rob them of their power. They then come out quite easily with the minimum fuss. We rob them by *force majeure* of their victims. This should be the ministry of every child of God. No wonder Satan has bound our minds to understand this during the ages! "*These signs shall follow them that believe*" (Mark 16:17).

We have known cases where a person has started rebuking demons in themselves and commanded them to come out, and sometimes to their astonishment the demons started to leave, often choking out of the throat and bringing with them poisons and putrefactive material from the inside of the body. Thus miracles of healing take place. We knew a lawyer who heard about this teaching and who gave us his testimony in Birmingham, Michigan. His legal mind just could not easily accept the account he had just heard of the existence of demons today, but on the way home he thought he would just try the experiment to see if there were any demons in him. He did so, and immediately felt deathly sick and barely managed to drive his car to his own garage. He struggled out of the car and then vomited them forth from his person. Was he surprised! We do not recommend this solo method, because James tells us to pray one for another that we may be healed, and both Jesus and the disciples prayed for the sufferers. We have found in our own ministry, when we have seen thousands of miracles of every sort, that people seem to react best when we lay hands on them and rebuke their sicknesses. It is also true that where hundreds of people are present and personal ministry becomes impossible, multiple deliverances happen when we stand and rebuke the spirits in Jesus' name and command them to leave. People immediately start coughing, choking, crying with loud voices, and sometimes collapsing. This is not said to alarm people, but to give them factual information on what the Spirit of God is doing today through consecrated men and women (there is no difference). (See Galatians 3:28.) As we may have been instrumental under God in helping to pioneer this ministry in our generation, we have up-to-date information from many sources of people all over the world who write to us, many with questions, telling of how the same things are happening in their fields of service. Missionaries especially are finding this ministry to be scriptural and the final answer to many previously not understood problems. Once the demons are cast out the problem clears up, even if it be deep-seated and of long duration.

This ultimate ministry in the body of Christ has undoubtedly been restored to deal with the baneful effects caused by the drug subculture. Although our young (and older) people may be coming off of drugs and accepting Jesus as Savior, and even in many cases being baptized in the Holy Spirit as evidenced by glossolalia, it seems there are still areas in the mind that need this strong ministry. One of the fruits of "being stoned" on drugs is that the mind becomes grievously bound, both from the point of view of spiritual appreciation, but also of natural learning abilities which are gravely marred. The mind becomes dulled because it is bound by demons. The demons gained entrance when the experimenter with drugs (or alcohol) was temporarily out of normal control of his mind. Not without cause did Peter tell us to resist the devil! How can any drug taker resist anything? The prayer of faith casts out these demon spirits and thus makes way for a greater moving of the Holy Spirit through their minds. The spirits usually come out manifestly choking or crying.

If we do not exercise the first sign, then we are selling our newfound friends short. We are asking them to accept Jesus as their Savior without helping them by forcing out demons which have gained access. Why, since Jesus told us that we should cast out demons, are we so often unable or unwilling to do it?

The ministry of casting out of demons is equated with the gift of miracles, one of the nine charismatic gifts of the Holy Spirit mentioned by Paul in 1 Corinthians 12:10, as separate from, but closely related to, the gifts of healing, which is why the two manifestations of the power of God always go together. *"Then he called his twelve disciples together, and **gave them** power and authority over all demons, and to cure* *diseases"* (Luke 9:1). In the story of the enthusiastic but ignorant disciples in Mark 9:38–39, they said,

> *Master, we saw one casting out devils in thy name, and he followeth not us: and we forbad him, because he followeth not us. But Jesus said, Forbid him not; for there is no man which shall do a miracle in my name, that can lightly speak evil of me.*

Here is the cure for the sectarian spirit across the land. Get into the gospel team and start casting out a few demons in His name! You then become a worker of miracles!

Whereas this ministry is now at long last coming into prominence, in this last-day ultimate restoration, Martin Luther believed it and practiced it. He said, "How often has it happened, and still does, that devils have been driven out in the name of Christ; by calling on His name and prayer, that the sick have been healed."

Because of fear, tradition, and uncertainty, the church has been very slow to measure up to the commands of Jesus. It has preached almost every other doctrine but the casting out of demons! And yet we see in this ministry the very heart of the gospel; the very epicenter of the workings of the Holy Spirit. As quoted from Isaiah by Dr. Luke we read that Jesus was anointed of the Spirit to *"preach deliverance to the captives"* (Luke 4:18). Who had bound the captives? Who should set them free? None other than you and I *in Jesus's mighty name.*

3

THEY SHALL SPEAK IN TONGUES

This sign has caused more contention than any other. It is strange that those who object do not usually speak in other tongues. It seems they are trying to find an excuse for their lack. It is "reasoned" by some that if there are five signs then "tongues" does not have to be accepted as the only evidence of the baptism in the Holy Spirit. The fact that the other signs do not seem to be in evidence in their Christian experience either troubles them not. They are born again of the Spirit of God and they do not want their Christianity marred by things that are beyond them. Is this not again a case of, *"Yea, hath God said…?"* (Genesis 3:1).

Of course, it is readily agreed that there are five signs that should follow all believers, but the casting out of demons and the healing of the sick occurred before Pentecost, and handling of snakes was done by Moses, but no human ever spoke in tongues until the birthday of the church on the Day of Pentecost. It is a peculiar sign and a very important one. Even if we sympathize with those who claim to have been baptized in the Spirit with no evidence of glossolalia, we must remind them that they could speak in tongues if they tried! All they would do would be to speak forth words that the Spirit of God *in them* would give them. We must remember that on the Day of Pentecost as recorded in Acts, chapter 2, it was a case of mutual cooperation between 120 humans and the Spirit of God. The Spirit does not force anyone to do anything. He does not take over by *force majeure* the human faculties and break through their wills to speak in tongues. We speak—He gives. If we decide not to speak, then there is no oracular flow of words, we simply dry up. The words are always there flowing from heaven, but we control the faucet, or valve, which stops or starts the flow. The result is that the church hears His words spoken by us.

Whereas it is expected of all believers that they shall manifest the five signs promised, yet we find that at the time of the coming of the Holy Spirit upon the church at the moment of its birth, apart from rushing wind and cloven tongues of fire, which are not mentioned among the five signs, the end result was "speaking in tongues" or "glossolalia," which means speaking in clear enunciation of words of known languages. This is explained to us as we refer back to the happening in the time of Elijah as recorded in 1 Kings 19:11–13. Here we find (1) a strong wind, (2) rocks broken by earthquake, (3) fire, but the Lord was not in any of these three. They only occurred because He came down to Elijah. It was in the *still small voice* that God revealed Himself, for the Father reveals Himself by the Word—the *Logos*. It was when Elijah heard the Word that he was roused to action, and then the *voice* spoke again.

In the first chapter of John, the Logos is explained to us in these words, *"In the beginning was the Word, and the Word was with God, and the Word was God.... And the Word was made flesh"* (John 1:1, 14). The Greek word *logos* is used in a personal sense. Jesus was the living Logos or Word. Out of His mouth came the Word of God without measure; thus it was said of Him, *"Never man spake like this man"* (John 7:46). It was the Father speaking through the mouth of the Son. The Logos flowed through Him in the form of human speech. It was "in the beginning" that we find how the Father created the earth and all things therein by *speaking* and the Word that proceeded from the Father was the Logos—the Son. This is why John in his epistle refers to the Word as "water" (see 1 John 5:8), because water flows; that which flows out of the innermost parts of a believer at the time he receives the baptism of the Spirit is *Living Water*, a verbal flowing manifestation of the Logos.

In John 7:37–39, Jesus promised that the tangible manifestation of the coming of the Holy Spirit on the day of Pentecost would be that the Spirit would flow into their inward parts and then out of them as rivers of *Living Water*. Though the Holy Spirit has always been in the world, yet in this sense He would flow through them, and the day was yet future, but to us it is in the historical past and present reality. This is the day of the outpouring of the Spirit. The baptism in the Spirit takes us into a new life cycle, previously we experienced wells of salvation as in the case of the woman at the well (see John 4:14), but now instead of drawing *Living Water* out of a well as in the gift of salvation, we have this *water* connected into us by the umbilical cord of the Holy Spirit, drawing this water from the River of Life, which is clear as crystal and which flows through the Paradise of God. (See Revelation 22:1.) This Living Water flows out of our mouths as the *Logos*, the Word of God. This is why it is so necessary to speak in tongues, for thereby we release the Water of Life to the members of the church, who become refreshed when God's inheritance is weary, and it is weary today! *"Thou, O God, didst send a plentiful rain whereby thou didst confirm thine inheritance when it was weary"* (Psalm 68:9). This is God's confirmation service to all baptized believers, which confirmed the church on the day of Pentecost and confirms us when He comes upon us in the same manner. If there is an infilling, there must be an outflowing of the same pressure, and as this flow starts in heaven with the River of Life it is not unreasonable that the resultant outflowing should be in the form of *rivers*, and not wells, streams or trickles! It was the speaking in tongues that entranced and shocked and amazed the marveling Jews, not the wind or the tongues or fire. Wind and fire are natural things. They can be explained away by rationalization; but speaking in foreign languages cannot be explained away, and so these Jews actually called the disciples and the Virgin Mary drunk! It is probable that the apostle Paul had this in mind when he wrote, *"Be not drunk with wine...but be filled with the Spirit"* (Ephesians 5:18). There is a correlation. Wine will cause a person to shout and to act in an exuberant manner, and become verbose. The Spirit will cause us to glorify God in tongues.

We suggest that there would have been no opposition on the day of Pentecost if it had not been for the outflowing of the Word (*Logos*) of God. Jesus came forth from the 120 in the upper room as manifested by speaking through them; not only in tongues, for it is quite obvious that this began a spiritual chain reaction which produced interpretation of tongues, prophecy, the word of knowledge, the word of wisdom, the word of faith, and other charismatic gifts to bring healing and salvation to a lost generation. It was when Jesus *spoke* that miracles took place. It is the same word that precipitates miracles by the Word of command that casts out demons today.

Remember that if the city water supply is connected to your home and comes in under pressure, this pressure is manifest through the faucets in your home as you exercise your free will by turning them on. All the prayer in the world will never make water flow if you won't turn on the tap! So the Word of God is waiting to flow through *every baptized believer* (see Mark 16:16) the moment you cooperate with God and allow the living water of the Spirit to flow into you and out of you by turning on the faucet of your tongue as your own act of free will. Every believer has the Spirit with him. He could not become a child of God without a supernatural visitation of the Spirit, but Jesus told His disciples that the Spirit was with them but would be in them on the day of Pentecost. (See John 14:17.) Once you open your mouth, the Word which is near to thee *"even in thy mouth"* (Romans 10:8) will come forth in another language, and this is so obviously a miracle that it takes away from the possibility that man spoke it out of his mind; for this obviously must be a manifestation of God without the help of man's mind. So much religion comes from the human mind and is called "metaphysics," but this Word comes into man's spirit—his heart, his innermost parts—and circumvents his mind, so the rational man does not understand and is at a loss for an explanation. It is a miracle that manifests Jesus the spoken living Word of God.

When the Spirit came in the great evangelical revival in Samaria (see Acts 8), many things happened before the baptism in the Spirit was given. After Philip opened his mouth and manifested Christ (he preached Christ the *Logos*), then demons started to scream and come out, the sick were healed, there was great joy and then a mass baptismal service. It is recorded in verse 13 that Simon the magician, the warlock, beheld the *miracles* and *signs* which were done. Some of these signs are mentioned in the five signs promised by Jesus in Mark chapter 16, but none of these signs moved Simon to try to buy the gift of the Holy Spirit. This only happened after Peter and John came down to Samaria from Jerusalem. Schaff, in his church history, tells us that the Samaritans spoke in tongues also as the Jews did on the day of Pentecost. It was the coming of the Holy Spirit that caused Simon to realize that a greater power was being manifested than his strong demon power. It was the outflowing of the logos that convinced him, and this seems to be made clear in verses 20 and 21 of Acts, in which Peter said, "*Thy money perish with thee, because thou hast thought that **the gift of God** may be purchased with money. Thou has neither part nor lot in this matter.*" The Greek word for "matter" is *Logos*! This literally could be translated, "Thou has neither part nor lot in this spoken utterance."

There is no doubt that tongues spoken in proper order in a prayer meeting has a devastating effect upon carnality or theoretical theology. It comes against the mind of intellectual man with shattering effect. It also breaks down stubborn unbelief and melts hearts to believe upon the Son of God manifest in tongues, the *Logos*.

Perhaps one of the most convincing arguments for "tongues" is found in the case of the Virgin Mary. None will question the purity of the "mother of My Lord." It was upon her, a chosen vessel, that the Holy Spirit came. The Scripture records that the Holy Spirit overshadowed Mary (see Luke 1:35), and the result of this unusual visitation was that a creative act was performed by God by the power of the Spirit in that the body of Jesus was created and conceived in the womb of Mary. In other words, by the overshadowing of the Third Person, the Second Person was manifest. It is important to remember this differentiation. Mary brought to birth the Son of God, Jesus, the eternal Second Person of the Trinity. The Holy Spirit did not overshadow her to bring forth a manifestation of the Holy Spirit. He is not sent for that. Jesus commanded His mother, along with the other disciples, to go into the upper room and wait there until they received the promise of the Father. It is clear from the account in Matthew 3:11 that the promise was the coming of the Holy Spirit, referred to by Jesus in Acts 1:4–5. Mary is specifically mentioned in Acts 1:14 as being among the disciples. She then received the Third Person, the Holy Spirit, as evidenced by speaking in tongues. At this point the Son spoke through His mother by the coming of the Spirit. Previous to this upper room experience she was a disciple, a believer who had had marvelous anointings of the Spirit, but she had not received the Spirit as on the Day of Pentecost.

Similarly with a born-again believer. At conversion he receives and manifests Jesus the Son of God in the fruits of the Spirit, but when he receives the Holy Spirit, the Son is revealed in power in the gifts of the Spirit. From the time of John the Baptist and his evangelical ministry, the church was in the formation or gestation period in the womb of Israel, but on the day of Pentecost the church was born into this world by the coming of the Spirit, Who announced this birth by speaking, even as a newborn babe utters a cry of life. Mary is a type of the church; first the generation of the Son of God at the rebirth, then the anointing with the Holy Spirit at Pentecost.

4

HANDLING SERPENTS

The first Exodus of Israel from Egypt was occasioned by one man, Moses, being obedient to God and practicing two major signs before Pharaoh and the elders of Israel. These two major signs were the handling of serpents and the healing of the sick, as shown in Exodus 4. First, Moses took hold of the serpent and it became harmless in his hand; second, with the same hand becoming leprous, he saw a miracle of healing from the worst form of physical sickness. The very hand that was to be used to deliver Israel became diseased. Moses was a type of Christ, who is the Arm and Hand of the Lord (see Psalm 98:1) reaching down from heaven for humanity today. Jesus became diseased for us; He became a curse for our sins and sicknesses. As leprosy is a type of all sin, Jesus became sin that we might have life.

These same two signs have now been restored to the church so that spiritual Israel—the church—can be set free from satanic bondages and healed of every sickness, mental and physical, in our day. In addition to these two major signs, mentioned in Mark 16:17–18, we have the addition of speaking in tongues, dealt with in the last chapter, and then two additional ones, the handling of serpents and the drinking of poisons. These are signs that increase our depth of understanding of our authority in Christ for the deliverance of spiritual Israel. Most people who are faced with the realization that they are to be instruments in healing the sick and casting out of demons become afraid, and run away as Moses did from the serpent. Frankly, due to the unknown, they are afraid of Satan and demons, although we are told repeatedly in Scripture that Christ *in us* is greater than Satan in the world! (See 1 John 4:4.) Moses was a type of Christ, for God is not calling another Moses today for Jesus fulfilled that call of God. He is calling for men and women who will arise and exercise their full authority as sons and daughters of God to deliver the afflicted. We do not pray and ask Jesus to deliver humanity—He has done that on the cross—we now enforce the law of love on Calvary by healing the sick, by casting out demons and generally handling serpents in His name! (See Matthew 10:7–8.)

Signs three and four are therefore signs of authority to encourage the believer. Three is the outward sign, whereby we use the power of the Holy Spirit and the authority of Jesus to take complete control of Satan and all his demons. We actually *handle* him by the tail—he is in our complete control if we go about it the right way. Four deals with the *inward*. Anything that Satan can try to poison us with, either natural or spiritual poison, is nullified by the inward power of the Holy Spirit. We deal with this in the next chapter.

Notice that when Moses was commanded by God to throw down his rod, a dead stick typical of his authority, immediately it turned into a serpent, to his astonishment. So shocked was he that he ran away. (See Exodus 4:3.) As soon as we start to teach and practice the whole area of the deliverance ministry today, many people are appalled and run away. We cast the rod of God's divine authority to the ground by quoting from God's yard stick, the Bible, and immediately we become confronted by Satan, just as Jesus found in the synagogue at Capernaum, when He read the Word of God and unclean spirits cried out against Him and were suitably dealt with on the spot. Jesus took hold of Satan's tail, twisted it and cast out the demons, and later we read of Philip doing the same in Samaria. (See Mark 1:23–26; Acts 8:6–7.) Satan hides until we start to expose him, and pretends he is not there, and millions of Christians agree with him and would much prefer to believe that Satan was not hiding in our churches. However, God is raising up men and women today who are daring to go in and flush out the demons, catch them by the tail and cast them out, thus bringing healing and deliverance to thousands *in the church*!

In Psalm 91:13, a believer is told that he can trample on an adder, a very poisonous serpent. However, this is not usually what Christians do. They run away from the uncomfortable satanically inspired situation, but no victory can be obtained until we return and take hold of Satan by his tail and then trample on him!

We do not do this in our own puny strength, we do it in His Omnipotent power and authority. Jesus gave all of us His authority in these words, *"Behold, I give unto you power* (in Greek, *exousia*—authority) *to tread on serpents and scorpions, and over all the power of the enemy"* (Luke 10:19). This commission to the twelve apostles and the seventy disciples was again emphasized to us in Mark 16. This power and authority has never been abrogated. It stands today for us to use, and thus we shall see the same deliverances today.

At the time of writing this chapter, I was ministering in the State Convention of the Full Gospel Businessmen's Fellowship, in Birmingham, Alabama, in November, 1971. A lady came for prayer, stating that she was strongly tempted to destroy herself. My wife and I prayed and took dominion over this destroying suicide demon, but immediately it reacted, but being so strongly entrenched it took over control and she shook her head vigorously, saying, "I want to die!" In spite of all appeals the demon kept crying out of her, "I want to die!" She was merely expressing the desire that the demon had put into her, so for the moment we left her alone—we could do no more. Next day she came again for prayer, but I explained that our prayers were useless if she had made up her mind that she wanted to die! This time she got control and confessed that she wanted to live. Before praying we told her that she must confess Psalm 118:17 out loud. Faltering she said, "I shall not die, but live." Again she said it with more confidence and power, then immediately the stick of confession turned into a serpent! Without our giving any command the demon reacted strongly, threw over a large table, and with flaying arms she fell to the ground and the demon choked out of her throat. This was done in public in the Thomas Jefferson Hotel, Birmingham, Alabama. Within two minutes she was made whole, the meaning of the word *sozo*, which is "to be made whole, or saved." She was saved from the power of the serpent which we trampled underfoot, just as Jesus told us to do!

We have found in this deliverance ministry that it is usually impossible to bring lasting deliverance to anyone who will not openly confess that they are finished with the devil's bondages. *"For with the mouth confession is made unto salvation* (in Greek, *soteria*—safety or soundness)" (Romans 10:10). Confession must first be made with repentance for allowing ourselves to get into such a mess; and so many churchgoers are in a real mess today and need this ministry. Satan has coiled his serpents round their minds and bodies and robbed them of health. We must go in and set them free!

It is interesting that when Paul visited the island of Malta, the inhabitants gathered a bundle of sticks and made a fire, and from among these dead sticks came a viper. The viper fastened on Paul's hand and bit him, but the poison was nullified by the power of the Spirit—we discuss this in the next chapter. As soon as fire commenced among the dead sticks, a serpent appeared. This is a parallel of the dead members of the church being ignited today by the coming again of the Holy Spirit in charismatic power, setting them on fire (see Matthew 3:11) and flushing out all serpentine evil. As soon as a dead church gets stirred by some of its members receiving the baptism of the Holy Spirit *and fire*, all the other dead members get stirred up, and many cases have occurred where they have cast out of their midst the pastor and some of the Spirit-filled members! What a travesty! It should be the Spirit-filled pastor and people who should cast the devil out of the dead sticks! Paul shook the viper into the flames and it perished in the fire in the midst of the sticks among whom it used to hide. The fire of the Holy Spirit cannot live alongside demon influences in the church. The coming of the Holy Spirit today is dividing the wheat from the chaff—the sheep from the goats. The goats were always there, but when the Holy Spirit came in power He revealed them for what they were. Many were wolves in sheep's clothing *in the church*!

An innocuous church member can become a serpent when the fire starts burning. When the serpent is handled, the church member becomes a Spirit-filled Christian!

Without the fire we have dead formality, but with the fire we have a New Testament church! What a lot of carnal rubbish has to be burnt up today in our churches!

The church must make up her mind in our generation that it is going to arise and take up serpents. We must handle satanic evils in the church. This is close proximity, isn't it? It is getting down to the business of the church to bring cleansing and healing to a dying world in confusion. All the prayer meetings in the world will not avail very much until we begin to stop running and meet Satan head-on and take him firmly by the tail and twist it.

Anything else is but an apology for New Testament Christianity.

5

DRINKING DEADLY THINGS

There is no actual biblical record of anyone actually drinking deadly liquid poisons with no resultant harmful effect. However, in contemporary Christianity there are many such cases recorded, especially on the mission field where hostile tribes resented the intrusion of missionaries. In the town of Kupang on the island of Timor, Indonesia, in about 1968, a party of Christians paid a visit to evangelize the people, who were steeped in witchcraft and sin. One of their specialties was the making of strong poisonous potions. The Christians were warned not to go near the place, but claiming the Lord had sent them, they went. The party was greeted hospitably and food was given them. The food was poisoned and the natives expected the party to die. After two hours one of the people came up to inquire what had happened, for none of the Christians seemed troubled at all. They should have died within three minutes! The man was converted and threw all his witchcraft impedimenta into the fire.

This is the *inward sign* for believers. Handling serpents is the *outward sign*. It includes within its scope every evil thing that is taken within the spirit, soul, or body, for man is indivisibly triune. Drinking deadly things does not only refer to liquids, but also spiritual things. The connotation of this sign has far greater fulfillment in the deadly spiritual influences which are all around us than the less common ingestion of physical poisons. It applies to both.

In 1 Corinthians 12:13, the reference is made to drinking into One Spirit, the application being the receiving of the baptism or fullness of the Holy Spirit, which totally saturates a person, in the same way a dry sponge becomes "baptized" by immersion into water and overflows through every pore.

Again a direct prophecy of the coming of the Holy Spirit on the day of Pentecost is given by Jesus in John 7:37: "*If any man thirst, let him come unto me and **drink**.*" By drinking in the Holy Spirit, he becomes full. In like manner, those whose thirst is for evil things develop an increasing appetite for filth which is ministered to them by Satan through his evil spirits, who progressively fill the person in answer to his perverted thirst and appetite. According to the measure of the fullness of evil spirits, so will the actions of the person correspond in the same measure.

As water is a fluid, so also is spirit—it flows. The River of Life in heaven flows through the midst thereof, and flows down the "pipeline" of the Holy spirit into, and out of, our innermost parts, refreshing everyone with whom we come in contact. In like manner, those who are oppressed or possessed of evil spirits have a deadly effect by poisoning the very people with whom they come in contact. They pollute their dwellings and places of work. Their language is filthy, their thoughts are vile, their actions depraved, and their imaginations continually evil.

We are surrounded by deadly poisons. The growth of pornographic literature is one case in point. Our young people can so easily obtain stories and descriptions of sexual perversions for which cause Sodom and Gomorrah were destroyed. Even in our newspapers, stories of occultism are carried and regular horoscopes are printed to poison the spirit. We were recently in the city of Binghamton, New York (November 1971), and learned of an open line radio program that had carried two hours of instruction by a medium on how to do spirit writing and consult with the spirits, and people listening were encouraged to conduct these deadly experiments.

Many of our television plays are full of evil practices and suggestions glorifying unlawful sex and perversions. One Roman Catholic priest recently wrote in the *Toronto Globe and Mail* that in his church were large numbers of young girls who would be embarrassed if they were called virgins!

What has gone wrong? It is simple. People, often unknowingly, are drinking deadly things through their eyes and ears, as well as their mouths. In fact it seems that it is absolutely impossible to avoid these poisonous influences all around us today, and at times it seems that those who wish to *"live godly in Christ Jesus"* (2 Timothy 3:12) are suffocated by the sulfurous smells of hell that greet us at every turn.

It is for this reason that the inward sign for all Christians is the impervious power of the blood of Jesus that has cleansed us, and will continually cleanse us, from all sin and temptations to sin. Under the law of God a symbol was given all who were ordained into the Levitical priesthood. Blood of the sacrifice was put upon the tip of Aaron's right ear (see Leviticus 8:23–24) and then on the tips of the ears of his sons. When Jesus shed His blood on Calvary, His own blood poured over His ears and fell to the ground, and all who come to the cross may also have His blood applied to their ears by faith. The continual presence of this blood today upon our ears will actually destroy all poison afflicting our ears, and nullify it completely, neutralizing its deadly effects upon our spirits and minds, so that our minds remain uncontaminated. This is built-in cleansing which operates continually providing we daily confess our sins and depart from them as something loathsome. The power of the blood of Jesus is ineffective if we tempt God by deliberately listening to gossip or filth or go to places where evil things take place to be entertained by them. *"Let no man say when he is tempted, I am tempted of God…but every man is tempted when he is drawn away of his own lust and enticed"* (James 1:13–14). We cannot blame God for our backslidings, but only ourselves, for it is then that Satan takes advantage through his demon spirits to inject spiritual poison into us. It will then be necessary for complete repentance and turning away in horror, that the blood of Jesus will neutralize this deadly poison.

The Old Testament application of this principle occurred when the three Hebrew youths were cast into the fiery furnace and not burned, and when Daniel was cast into the den of lions and not harmed. In both cases the power of the Spirit was stronger than the power of Satan. This is why John equated the blood of Jesus with the Spirit of God. (See John 5:8.) Wherever the blood of Jesus is *used* in application to the ears, heart, thumb, or toe, we are assured of the protection of the omnipresent Spirit of God, for the "Spirit answers to the blood" (Wesley 1742) and, in Leviticus 8:30, it will be noted that the blood was applied as well as the oil: *"And Moses took of the anointing oil* [typifying the Holy Spirit] *and of the blood* [typifying the blood of Jesus] *which was upon the altar* [typifying the cross] *and sprinkled it upon Aaron and his sons."* Jesus did the sprinkling upon the cross and we may avail ourselves of that sprinkled blood today by applying it to our persons, as Paul put it, *"Having our hearts sprinkled from an evil conscience"* (Hebrews 10:22). When we plead the blood of Jesus we attract the power of the Holy Spirit.

As the heart is the center of operations of our spiritual life, which likewise affects our whole triune person, we find that an inbuilt spiritual cleansing is continually in operation, even when we sleep. What comes into our ears or eyes or mouth is killed, rather as certain powders sprinkled on the doorsteps of our homes destroy roaches and ants before they penetrate our dwellings.

There is no place where a Christian cannot go, for if he goes to witness to the power of Jesus, he is safe. The Salvation Army officers go into drinking dens and many unsavory places to rescue the perishing. Jesus ate with harlots and risked the evil accusations of the religious clergy without suffering harm. The "Jesus people" freely mix among those being destroyed by the drug craze, and go into rock sessions, to win their own for Christ. The church must reach out with the outward sign and grab the devil by his tail, and we are protected in doing so by the inward sign because we shall suffer no harm. How else are we to reach those who are lost and perishing if we do not go where they are? We must go into the fire of hell and the dens of lions with our armor on!

Satan's great demon, *fear* comes upon many when confronted with evil in form. Jesus gave His disciples *"carte blanche"* protection in Luke 10:19, *"I give unto you **power** to tread...over all the power of the enemy, and **nothing** shall by any means **hurt you**."* Similarly in this fourth sign, *"If you drink any deadly thing, **it shall not hurt you**"* (Mark 16:18). Here is a two-witness Scripture to cause us to rise and advance on the enemy, and ignore his threats and conquer over his evil.

Obviously, we do not deliberately handle snakes as some misguided people have done, or experiment by drinking poisons, for in both cases we would die. We must not tempt God.

6

THE SIGN OF HEALING

In the first translation of the Bible into English, by John Wycliffe in 1380, he always used the word "*health*" for "salvation." Thus, in the context of Mark 16:16, he wrote, "*He that believeth and is baptized shall have health.*" The Greek word *sozo* is used in this verse and means basically "to be made whole." Thus when a convert to Christ is baptized, he receives potentially *health* for spirit, soul, and body, seeing that man is an indivisible triunity.

The sign of healing, therefore, should follow progressively everyone who accepts Jesus Christ as Savior from sin and its consequences, which include every conceivable malady known to mankind. We believe that this sign must be understood in its progressive nature. The working of miracles may often be more sudden and spectacular, but the sign of healing will work silently in the person of a believer as he continues to hold his faith steadfast and not waver from the written promises of God.

The statement of Jesus is simple and to the point. The believer lays hands on sick people and they recover. There are no "if and but" clauses in this New Testament contract. In the case of cold weather when a car battery freezes and refuses to give power to the motor, it is necessary to bring into action a live battery, which will have two long arms with two claw hands on the ends. These are clipped on to the poles of the dead battery and immediately strong current flows into the weak battery through the imposition of positive and negative wire arms and hands! When a fully charged believer lays his hands on a weak believer, he discharges divine power from the Holy Spirit into the sick person's mind and body, and the process of the sickness is arrested. This rule must include the willingness of the sick person, who can reject the flow by unbelief, and the faith of the Spirit-filled believer who must have faith that there will be a healing flow of divine energy.

It seems that this flow is precipitated by a command of faith, releasing the powerful Word of God by saying, "In Jesus' name, let this sickness depart." This spoken

Logos triggers off the flow and the evil spirit behind the sickness will depart, sometimes slowly, but progressively, providing the sick person continues to believe and not to doubt. The symptoms, which the Bible calls "lying vanities," may not instantly clear up and it is here that many say, "I am not healed," thus confessing a negative confession. Personally I have found that the command of faith does in fact usually start a healing, and often the manifestation of the sickness leaving is quite obvious to all. Sometimes the person will fall to the ground under the impact of the power of God and the spirit of infirmity leaving. At other times, there will be a shaking, coughing, or weeping. Obviously some of the strong sicknesses that bind the human race make their exit known as they depart. These are not "little" things but strong spirits that bring sick people into subjection in mind and body. From this point on, it will be necessary for the healed person to live much closer to the Lord than previously, and we believe it is clearly in God's plan to win souls to Himself by this laying on of hands and the imparting of a gift of healing, which broadly speaking is a gift of *sozo*, or total health.

To try to separate healing of the soul from the healing of the body is plainly impossible. The medical profession openly speaks of psychosomatic sicknesses today, showing that they believe the cause of the physical breakdown has a beginning in the mind. If the mind can be healed then it follows that the physical manifestation will progressively disappear. This is why Jesus said to the Pharisees, "*Whether is easier to say, Thy sins be forgiven thee; or to say, Rise up and walk*" (Luke 5:23). Obviously the same Gospel includes both. What a wonderful example King David set to the nation when he sang, "*Bless the LORD, O my soul…who forgiveth all thine iniquities; who healeth all thy diseases*" (Psalm 103:2–3).

It is only unbelief that has tried to separate and dissect the blessings of the gospel. There are no exceptions. "He that believeth" includes every believer of every denomination. In the same way, every believer may cast out demons; may tackle serpentine evil; may partake inadvertently of poisonous things, and may speak in tongues. It has been said by some Bible students that these signs are only given to certain believers, but this is not true. All believers should expect these signs to follow them. Mothers and fathers should pray for their children by the laying on of hands; in fact, I have seen little children lay hands on their parents and healings take place! John the Baptist had no doubt during his preparation ministry when he pointed to Jesus as the One Who would baptize every convert in the Holy Spirit. (See Mark 1:8.) He had not brought them to the rebirth to stay on that level, but to go forward to Pentecost when these five signs would become fully operative, in every believer. After Pentecost there were no "fundamentalist-evangelical" churches as we know them today. There were all Spirit-filled churches manifesting the gifts of the Spirit, of which tongues would be the outward sign and healing would be the normal expectation. Thank God we are living in the day when the Holy Spirit once again is being poured out on every denomination and the five signs are reappearing.

Of course, the sign of healing is not new to the New Testament church. It was known to the Old Testament church and practiced. It was Solomon with his many wives who brought in physicians to attend these wives. God expected the Israelites to trust Him, and this is made clear when a person healed of leprosy was supposed to show himself to the priests, not to the medical profession! (See Leviticus 13; Luke 17:14.) Notice also that the ten lepers received their healing as they acted their faith in obedience to the command of Jesus—*"as they went, they were cleansed"* (Luke 17:14). If they had not obeyed they would not have been cleansed. The healing started only as they obeyed the Word of God.

The church has strayed a long way from this simple sign of healing! It was toward the end of the last century that divine healing began to be practiced. A. J. Gordon, F. F. Bosworth, A. B. Simpson, and others brought back the simple teaching and by the laying on of hands brought miracles of healing to thousands. It was a sad story to note that most of the denominational leaders of their group have not followed their godly example; and when tongues broke out among them circa 1910, all who had received this experience were ejected from their midst. From this point onward the practice of divine healing largely disappeared among them denominationally, and was taken up and practiced by the early Pentecostals who largely sprang from their ranks, such as Smith Wigglesworth and Dr. Charles Price, not forgetting Aimee McPherson.

The first of the five signs to reappear is the last one mentioned in Mark 16:18. Tongues followed and this introduced the Pentecostal movement, which tended to build denominations around tongues rather than around all the Word of God. Now today the first of the five signs is reappearing everywhere—the casting out of demons. The fundamentalist churches have been forced to the realization of demonic power because of the revival of witchcraft, spiritism, and astrology. Billy Graham has openly exposed demonic power behind these practices and other practices, such as nudity, pornography, and drugs, on his national television hookup. Now that these things are being named and exposed, it remains for the Spirit-filled church to arise and cast them out, and to recognize that sickness has a demonic cause, even if the sufferer himself was not to blame. It may go back several generations, but it is still demonic in origin.

The manifestation of the five signs presents a full-orbed presentation of Jesus in His church, the body of Christ. These five signs are given so that Jesus may be presented to a unbelieving world (and church) in a balanced way to deal with every besetting visitation of Satan's power. If we leave out one sign, we present an incomplete Christ, an unbalanced revelation of His omnipotence. Without these five signs, we are unlikely to see Christians who are really Spirit filled in fact; for many who claim to be filled are in fact still in need of further deliverance from Satan's oppressing powers in their lives. Many young people who have been on drugs come to Christ and accept Him as Savior, but this act of faith in itself does not automatically mean that they have been healed of the terrible effects of the drugs. This part comes by the laying on of hands and the command of faith. In actual fact, I have found that numbers of young people who have been experimenting with drugs have dulled their minds—there is a spiritual bondage to be removed by the prayer of faith. If we do not do this by the laying on of hands, they may not get fully delivered, though possessing the gift of eternal life. To say they are "saved" may be potentially correct, but remembering that this word means "health," we may have to liberate them by the prayer of faith!

"These signs shall follow them that believe" (Mark 16:17). Let us look for and expect them. This is the reason why God is pouring out His Spirit upon all flesh today. In the revival in Timor, Indonesia, in 1965, suddenly the Spirit came upon a group of staid Presbyterians. One by one they started to speak in tongues, which astonished many of those who were looking on. It was a sovereign act of God. Following this baptism in the Spirit, the other four signs quickly began to operate through this and other assemblies. Demons were cast out, sickness of every type was healed, and the dead were raised in at least twelve known cases. Serpents wriggled away when parties of the Spirit-filled Christians marched through the jungles, and poisoned food failed to poison them. These things would never have happened by theology alone. It took an outpouring of the Holy Spirit to bring back a balance of all five signs.

7

GIFTS AND SIGNS

Some have suggested there is a difference between the sign of tongues and the gift of tongues. It is as well to remember that the words in the Greek are different. For *"sign"* the Greek word is *semeion*, and is always used to indicate a sign of the supernatural from God. In the *Amplified Version* of the New Testament, the word *"attesting"* has been added to the sense—*"attesting signs"* that follow. We have already shown that Moses was commissioned by God to liberate Israel in the first Exodus by the use of two attesting signs (see Exodus 4:8–9), the handling of serpents and the healing of sicknesses. These two signs were again introduced by Jesus when commissioning His disciples in Luke 9:1. He gave them power and authority over *all demons* and to cure diseases. Just two signs, which were again given to the seventy in Luke 10; but when we come to the final commission of the church in Mark 16, we find these two signs encompass three others.

When we come into the operation of the power of God in the New Testament, after Pentecost, the Greek word *charismata* comes to the fore and is not well translated as *"gifts,"* for some get the impression that they are the possessors of certain gifts and make claims that cannot be substantiated. In actual fact, the gift in the New Testament is the gift (in Greek, *dorea*) of the Holy Spirit, and in the Holy Spirit are the *charismata* that God operates through us as He wills. (See 1 Corinthians 12:11.) They are all potentially in the Holy Spirit, but when there is a special need of faith or a word of knowledge or wisdom, it is God alone who operates the gift through us for His glory for the liberation of the captives.

The five encompassing signs of Mark 16 receive their full realization and fulfillment in 1 Corinthians, chapters 12, 13, and 14. The *charismata* are the outworking of the signs. Instruction is given how to use tongues, interpretation, and prophecy in the assembly. Obviously, we may all speak in tongues for personal edification (see 1 Corinthians 14:4), but in the assembly we need instruction on how to release a full-orbed Christ as Prophet, Healer, Miracle-Worker, and the Giver of Divine Revelation. We cannot have one spiritual manifestation without all of them as the need arises. A church that only permits tongues is very immature. The needy should be able to come into our services and receive the gift of eternal life, a gift of healing and the gift of the Holy Spirit, all transmitted by our ministry. They should then stay in such a New Testament assembly and grow in grace and strength. If they wander back into areas where these *charismata* are not known or permitted, they may well grow cold and get sick again and backslide.

There is a distinct operation of tongues in an assembly to bring forth an interpretation for the edification of all present as in the case of prophecy. These three oral gifts arise from the sign of tongues. The gifts of healings arise from the sign of laying on of hands, and the gift of miracles from the handling of serpents and the casting out of demons. John's teaching, that we should prosper and be in health even as our souls prosper, arises from the built-in immunization given against the effects of poisoning. There is a sign of tongues for the believer and there is a charisma of tongues to be used in the assembly, but the latter is the outworking of the former. We must remember that all these *charismata* are for one purpose, not to magnify men but to reveal Jesus Christ. The body of Christ, being full of the Holy Spirit, draws from the *charismata* in the Spirit and presents different facets of Jesus. He is like a magnificent gem sparkling with divine rays in every direction, and each ray represents a penetrating charisma for the salvation, healing, and deliverance of all who will come to the light. (See John 3:19–21.)

It is a strange fact that most people do not want these divine shafts of healing light. They run away from God's beneficent power into churches where these rays do not shine. Thus the church remains sick and powerless. To say proudly (as some do) that they are members of the body of Christ and fail to reflect these charismata for the blessing of humanity, should cause them to reexamine their spiritual position in the light of the Word of God. This is what Jesus meant when He told us to let our lights shine before men that they may see our good works. (See Matthew 5:16.) What are these "good works" other than the manifestation of Christ through the operation of His charismatic gifts? They are not so interested in your own shining health if we let them remain in their sin and sickness. We have to shine with the many facets of Jesus in the midst of their prevailing darkness, and how dark is the world today! Jesus is beginning to arise with healing in His wings. (See Malachi 4:2.) The darkness is dispersing.

In the Freer manuscript, there are some additional verses that are not carried in other manuscripts. It might be of interest to quote this addition, which follows on from Mark 16:14 and is inserted between verses 14 and 15. Quote,

And they excused themselves, saying that this age of lawlessness and unbelief is under Satan who, through the agency of unclean spirits, suffers not the true power of God to be apprehended. For this cause, said they unto Christ, reveal now at once thy righteousness. And Christ said unto them, the limit of the years of the power of Satan is not (yet) fulfilled, but it draweth near; for the sake of those that have sinned was I given up unto death, that they may inherit the spiritual and incorruptible glory of righteousness in heaven.

If these missing verses were indeed in some original, they are of interest. So, not only are we defending the normal translation in our Bibles for Mark 16:9–20, and showing that these verses are the veritable Word of God, but we are daring to add a few! Jesus taught that the age of lawlessness and unbelief was controlled by Satan through his demon spirits who blocked the revelation of the righteousness of Christ in full manifestation, but the time was coming when Satan and his cohorts would be put down, which agrees with the Book of Revelation. (See Revelation 20:10.) Because of His death on the cross, He was able to release the full power of the Holy Spirit to the church so that it would indeed make war against Satan and his demons and win. We believe we are in the very generation that will see the full power of the risen Christ revealed as all the signs and spiritual gifts are seen in operation for the release of humanity from its appalling darkness and captivity.

This is why God is pouring out His Holy Spirit upon us all and bringing us into this thrilling unity of the Spirit. Once the church is in one accord in one place, as it was on its birthday, we shall see the full power of God released to the astonishment of the governments of the world.

These signs shall follow them that believe. Do you believe? Are you looking for the signs? They are following the church today.

THE PROPHETIC WORD

CONTENTS

FOREWORD

It has been my privilege to have read this book before publication. My strong impression is that it will become a valuable addition to the available literature on the subject with which it deals—the last day outpouring of the Spirit and the manifestation of the gifts, or *charismata*.

The author possesses certain unique advantages in preparing a volume of this nature. Some ministers have exceptional talent to put their knowledge into print. On the other hand, there are gifted writers who have attempted to deal with this subject, but who have had little practical experience in the manifestation of the gifts. In the case of Rev. Whyte, however, he not only has had the benefit of long experience as a pastor in which he has had an unusual ministry in the operation of the gifts, but he is articulate with the pen and able to express himself in clear and lucid language. It is one thing to manifest a gift of the Spirit, and it is another thing to thoroughly understand the special problems involved in the local church where such gifts are operative.

In perusing the manuscript, I have noted that Rev. Whyte has given some excellent instructions on the working of the revelation gifts. There is unfortunately much misunderstanding and misinformation on this subject. The writer has given us some very wise and illuminating counsel concerning the operation of this important group of related gifts.

There is a special reason why I believe that the appearance of the book *The Prophetic Word* at this date is timely. As most people know, there has of late been a remarkable acceptance of the charismatic gifts in the historic denominations—a fact that has been widely publicized in national periodicals. Thousands of people who in years past have thought of Pentecost as something beneath their dignity to consider have suddenly discovered that these manifestations of the Spirit are altogether real and genuine, and for them. For indeed Pentecost is not the monopoly of any group, but it is a blessing which God has promised would be poured out on all flesh.

We are certain that this book will find a wide field of usefulness throughout the whole church of Jesus Christ.

—*Gordon Lindsay*
August 1964

1

I WILL POUR OUT MY SPIRIT

It has been said that if the apostle Paul came to one of our modem cities he would be most perplexed if he entered into some of our churches. The mode of worship, the forms and ceremonies, the robes, the unabashed entertainment, and the absence of the gifts of the Spirit would cause him astonishment, and if he was ever invited to preach in these churches, (which is most improbable) he would preach such truths as would shock the worshippers, and it is doubtful if many would shake his hand as he left the church—not having received a love offering!

Christian magazines have carried articles on the present outpouring of the Spirit in the historic churches, which have apparently upset some who have been taught "dispensational truths," that charismatic gifts were only for the early church, but certainly not for the sophisticated church of today. A certain pastor of a dispensational church wrote a letter to one magazine stating that these reports of a renewed outpouring of tongues, interpretation, and prophecy could not possibly be true, because they were not for today, but even if they were, God would not give these gifts to Episcopalians, for of all Christian communions, they were the most carnal! What a Christlike spirit indeed!

In spite of man's monumental unbelief, God is, nevertheless, pouring out again His Spirit upon all flesh, in exactly the same manner as He did in the early church, with the same purpose in mind—that we may all be one *in spirit*. There is no denominational favoritism, no hit-and-miss watering—for this revival is coming down on all flesh. Roman Catholics are being filled with the Spirit, even Jews are being converted to Christ and filled with the Spirit, and in each case the manifestation is the same—glossolalia.

We repeat—the manifestation is invariably the same—each one filled overflows like a fountain and out of his or her mouth comes the Word of God in the form of *glossolalia*, or "other tongues."

This single fact has produced the continual question "Why tongues?" The purpose of this book is to answer that question, and to show the purpose of God in this final outpouring of the Spirit upon all flesh, with the accompanying signs and gifts of the Spirit.

It was Joel who prophesied this outpouring. The emphasis was that our sons and daughters would prophesy, which was again reemphasized in the account in Acts chapter two where we are told that "my servants" and "my handmaidens" would prophesy. (See Acts 2:16–18, 28–32.) From this, we conclude that it is God's unchanging purpose in this dispensation and generation that "His servants," i.e. His ministering servants, pastors, elders, deacons, etc. should "prophesy" and that the lady workers, i.e. pastor's wives, deaconesses, Sunday school teachers, etc. should also prophesy. As our sons and daughters are also included, we understand also that it is God's will for our children growing up in our churches to be so affected by this last day outpouring of the Spirit that they also shall prophesy! This surely adds up to the fact that all our churches should be composed of members most of whom should prophesy. What tremendous churches—churches in which the apostle Paul would feel quite at home, and in which his ministry would be received with gladness and praise to God. He would be free to teach on 1 Corinthians 12, 13, and 14, without embarrassment!

On the day of Pentecost, the birthday of the Christian church, this prophecy received its initial fulfillment. This fulfillment was only partial, and we believe it receives its fullest consummation in our day. When the Holy Spirit was outpoured on the 120, without exception, they commenced to speak in other languages, sixteen of which were understood by Jews coming from surrounding nations in which they had been born, and which languages they spoke in addition to Hebrew and Aramaic. Out from the mouths of 120 disciples came the Word of God—the *Logos*—in unknown tongues. This was the pattern, and this pattern is being faithfully reproduced in our day all over the world.

Peter quoted freely from Joel to show that this supernatural demonstration was *a fulfillment* of prophesying. It has been common theology to teach that prophesying carries the restricted meaning of "preaching," and whereas we believe that Holy Spirit anointed preaching should always be inspired utterance, yet we believe the words "to prophesy" carry a far deeper connotation.

The initial evidence of speaking in tongues at Pentecost was put under the heading "prophecy," for it was God forth-telling through his 120 disciples and they heard *"them speak in our tongues the wonderful works of God"* (Acts 2:11). This was a manifestation of pure prophecy. We wish to try and demonstrate that *glossolalia*, is one of the forms of prophecy referred to by Joel, and that without this initial prophetical utterance, it is doubtful that the other forms of inspired utterance can be brought forth. The initial evidence of tongues is the beginning of a supernatural outflow of the Word of God by His Spirit that will finally put Satan out of business. It is the Sword of the Spirit, which is the Word of God unleashed from heaven against Satan's kingdom on earth.

There is much more in "tongues" than meets the eye—or the ear! *"If any man speak, let him speak as the oracles of God"* (1 Peter 4:11). Broadly speaking, "prophecy" is the speaking forth of the Word of God—under the inspiration of the Holy Spirit. When Jesus was here on earth in His own personal body—the body of Christ—it was said of Him, *"Never man spake like this man"* (John 7:46). He Himself said that "of Himself He could do nothing." (See John 5:19.) The words He spoke were not His words, but were received from His Father. Every word spoken by Jesus came direct from heaven; He did nothing, He said nothing, He thought nothing, apart from what He received from His Father. He had no original philosophical thought, He had no personal opinion, He did what He saw the Father do and spoke what He heard the Father speak. He was the verbal expression of the Father—the *Logos* of God.

In Hebrews 11:3, we read that *"through faith, we understand that the worlds were framed by the word of God, so that things which are seen were not made of things which do appear."* God did not create something out of nothing, as some have taught, He created matter out of "things which do not appear," in other words matter is a physical expression of spiritual forces already in existence and which belong alone to God, who is *Life* and *Creation* Himself. It was the speaking Logos that created substance out of spiritual forces. How near is the physical realm to the spiritual! This same creative word that was in Jesus now comes into all the members of the body of Christ when they receive the baptism in the Spirit and speak in other tongues. In the beginning at creation, the Father spoke, the Word proceeded and the Holy Spirit moved upon His creation. God *said*…and it was so. He created light, firmament, waters, grass, herbs, stars, fish, animals, birds, and finally the Trinity created man, the highest created being of God, His masterpiece, after His own image. Can we not see that if God created matter from His own spiritual but invisible forces, and then breathed His own life into bodies composed of matter, then when Satan invades such delicate creations it is necessary to speak the Word in faith, and we in Christ are able to reverse the processes of destruction, because the words that we speak are Spirit and life to those who receive? The evil spiritual invasion by Satan and his emissaries is forced to give way before the power and authority of the *Logos* which created matter!

The centurion understood this principle. His servant was lying shaking with palsy, and the centurion said that it was necessary to *"speak **the word** only, and my servant shall be healed"* (Matthew 8:8). When Jesus spoke and said, "Be healed," it was so and his servant was healed in the selfsame hour. (See verse 13.) When Jesus opened His mouth, the Word proceeded from the Father and created life, for Jesus had said,

"It is the Spirit that quickeneth…the words that I speak unto you, they are Spirit and they are life" (John 6:63). He said, *"I do nothing of myself; but as my Father hath taught me, I speak these things"* (John 8:28), and again, *"For I have not spoken of myself; but the Father which sent me, he gave me a commandment, what I should say and what I should speak"* (John 12:49). No wonder that those who heard Him were astonished, for His Word was with power (see Luke 4:32) and He taught as One who had authority (see Mark 1:22). He manifested the authority of the almighty Creator, for he was the *Logos*—the manifested Word of God.

This *same Word* is that which God puts into the mouths of every Holy Spirit baptized believer, and when we speak it is a manifestation of glossolalia—the *Logos*.

No wonder Satan fights tongues!

Jesus demonstrated this new dimension of divine authority and power, but He desired that His body, the church, should also have and use this power and authority, and so He promised to send *"another Comforter"* (John 14:16) that would be *in us* (see verse 17) and He would guide us into *"all truth, for he [the Holy Spirit] shall not speak of himself; but whatsoever he shall hear, that shall he speak"* (John 16:13). Here is an amazing truth: when the Comforter, the Holy Spirit, comes into us, He receives the word—the *Logos*—from Jesus and speaks it through us! As the Holy Spirit spoke through Jesus, so after the resurrection it is God's plan that this same Spirit shall now speak His word through our lips of clay, to bring to fruition the same life-giving plan as was ministered by Jesus in His earthly body. Our bodies become His body! His words are spoken by us and through us. Oracles of God!

When we speak in tongues, interpret, or prophesy, we do so with words that come from heaven. They are not our words, but we speak them. They are not our thoughts, they proceed from the Father to accomplish the purpose for which they were sent. We are channels only.

A good analogy is that of a telephone radio repeater station. These have been installed in remote areas in Canada by the Bell Telephone Company to receive and retransmit telephone conversations. On one side of the high tower is a receiver that picks up the voice transmitted from a transmitter situated on a tower many miles away. This is then amplified, or boosted, and passed into the transmitter on the same tower, and retransmitted to another receiver on another high tower many miles further on. In no case does any operator interpose his thoughts or words into the telephone conversation. The repeater station only speaks what it hears.

We are God's repeater stations on earth to relay the good news of the gospel of the kingdom heard from heaven, and spoken in the power of the Spirit on earth.

2

TONGUES

When Jesus was obedient to His Father and associated Himself with sinful mankind at His baptism, He chose a son of Adam, John the Baptist, to baptize Him, the Son of God. Thus did He show that sinful man can identify himself with God in this form of burial and resurrection enacted in water baptism. When Jesus came up out of the water, the Spirit of God descended upon Him; the *third* Person descended upon the *second* Person, being sent of the *first* Person, and the result of this anointing by the Spirit was that the Word was heard from heaven, *"This is my beloved Son, in whom I am well pleased"* (Matthew 3:17). Immediately the spoken word was sent forth from heaven to glorify the Son, which is the ministry of the Holy Spirit. It was a supernatural Word. It came in the power of the Spirit, and immediately Jesus—the incarnate Word of God—His amazing three-and-a-half years of supernatural ministry. It was then said of Him, *"Never man spake like this man...for he taught them as one having authority, and not as the scribes"* (John 7:46; Matthew 7:29). This was the Word that was released from heaven by the coming of the Holy Spirit on that eventful day. Man, in the person of John, had his part and Jesus the Son of God had His part. So today, God calls man to cooperate in the amazing experience that is called "the baptism in the Spirit," when the Word of God is heard as tongues or languages (*glossolalia*).

To help to overcome our unbelief, God seems to have ordered it that we should speak in other tongues or languages. This is not ecstatic gibberish as some unbelieving people have suggested, but tongues of men or angels. If we were immediately to commence to prophesy in our known tongues, Satan would immediately counter by telling us that were speaking out of our mind; but when we speak in unlearned tongues, we must be speaking by the Holy Spirit. This is received via our spirit and so bypasses our mind. In our book *Dominion over Demons*, we have explained that demons may also speak in tongues through people in spiritist séances, but this is outside of the scope of this book. By the pleading or honoring of the blood of Jesus in our prayer for the Holy Spirit baptism, we shall begin to speak in tongues as the Holy Spirit gives us utterance as He did on the day of Pentecost.

Speaking in tongues supernaturally given is a prophetical oracular utterance from heaven. It is not of man, nor of the wisdom of men, but of God who knows all the languages, past, present, and angelic. He can give any language to His servants if they open their spirits to Him.

Objection is frequently made that many members of the historic or fundamental churches are already "filled with the Spirit" and they have no need of receiving this "embarrassing" tongues experience. It is true that John the Baptist was full of the Spirit from his mother's womb. It is also true that Anna the prophetess was full of the Spirit. Simeon and Zacharias were likewise filled, and it seems quite clear that Elizabeth and Mary the mother of Jesus were filled "right up to the top." All this was *before Pentecost.* At Pentecost they were not only filled, but they overflowed. Jesus has said, *"Out of [your] belly shall flow rivers of living water"* (John 7:38). He was not think-ing of a pool, however refreshing, but of springs of water, rivers of water, fountains springing up in the desert all around us.

A good analogy is that of a sponge. A dry sponge is useless, and many church going people are dry sponges today. A little of the Holy Spirit in their lives and these people can become damp—some damper than others, and some even become sat-urated, i.e. filled so full that no more water can be absorbed. Take this saturated sponge and plunge (baptize, in Greek, *baptizo*—immerse) into water and the satu-rated sponge becomes supersaturated and overflows from every hole and pore. It is this overflowing of the Spirit that produces the *Logos*, the Word, flowing in the power of the Spirit. This is analogous to the baptism in the Spirit. When, as an act of free will, we turn on the faucet or tap of our human tongues, the flow of living water from the illimitable reservoir flows out of our mouths as the life-giving Word of God. Jesus said, *"The words that I speak unto you, they are spirit, and they are life"* (John 6:63). These words can create life, destroy death and sickness, and cast the devil out of lives and situations. Jesus cast out demons with the Word of God. (See Matthew 8:16.) We also cast out demons and heal the sick today by the same Word.

There are seven major usages of tongues:

1. FOR PERSONAL EDIFICATION

"He that speaketh in an unknown tongue edifieth himself" (1 Corinthians 14:4). We must always remember that in the Spirit he will be speaking mysteries. Man has invented many palliatives—pills, potions, drugs, heating pads, drink, cigarettes, pep pills, etc., ad infinitum. But when a Holy Spirit-baptized believer turns on the valve that brings forth the water of life from heaven, he refreshes himself so intensely, and

washes away the cobwebs and the blues and the pains, that recourse to the means of man becomes unnecessary, and the resultant joy and ecstasy must be experienced to be understood. One with the experience is not at the mercy of one with an argument against it.

2. FOR PRAISE

Praising God in tongues will cause depression, despondency, and despair—the three Ds of the devil—to disappear. Praise is natural to a person released from Satanic bondages, and Paul told us that it is possible (and desirable) to praise *"with the Spirit"* as well as *"with the understanding"* (1 Corinthians 14:14–15). A burst of tongues of praise to God will bring one up from the depths to the heights, always remembering that the Word of God teaches us that we are in heavenly places in Christ. This is the Christian's position. When we join our tongues with the tongues of heaven and angels in praise, we find that this statement is true. *We are* in heavenly places in Christ. The expressions "Hallelujah" and "Glory to God" become natural expressions.

3. FOR SINGING

We have often heard people baptized in the Spirit begin by speaking in tongues, and then proceed into spiritual song, with tunes and words received direct from heaven. On one occasion we were staying in the home of a Lutheran Pastor in Colombia, South America, and it was arranged that we should pray for his wife to receive her personal Pentecost, he having already received. Very soon, she was in "heavenly places" and speaking in tongues, and then, after a few minutes, she went from speaking to singing, and four of us present all joined in—and a heavenly choir was heard on the earth. We believe it is in God's plan in His church that both singing with the understanding and singing in the Spirit should take place in all local assemblies.

4. FOR PRAYER

Oh, how many have agonized in prayer without this blessed baptism in the Spirit! In Romans 8:26, it is written, *"Likewise the Spirit also helpeth our infirmities: for we know not what we should pray for as we ought: but the Spirit himself maketh intercession for us with groanings which cannot be uttered."* It is when we have a deep need in prayer that the Spirit of God helps us in our human weaknesses. We know not how to frame our thoughts into words, we only groan with groanings that are uttered, but turn on that valve and the Spirit will begin to pray for us, and our prayers will be answered. We shall feel the burden lift and peace will reign in our hearts. For intercessory prayer, "praying in the Spirit" is a necessity, and God has provided us with this weapon in the power of the Spirit. By this means we can also obey God's Word and *"pray without ceasing"* (1 Thessalonians 5:17), we can pray as we work!

5. FOR REBUKING EVIL SPIRITS

The ministry of casting out of demons, and the strong prayer of faith that liberates the oppressed in mind and body, is now returning to the church. A most cogent method of attacking demon's powers is to rebuke them in tongues. Evil spirits cannot stand this frontal attack, and will be glad to be cast out of a person rather than listen to a heavenly language spoken by a believer in the power of the Spirit. It stirs them up, and if used in conjunction with pleading the blood of Jesus out loud, lays an artillery barrage that weakens the demon's powers. Remember always that the manifestation of tongues is the manifestation of the living Word, Jesus Himself, proceeding out of our mouths like a two-edged sword. (See Revelation 19:15.) The more faith we put into the utterance, the more Satan will crumble up in his defenses and flee.

6. FOR SPEAKING IN THE TONGUE OF ONE WHO UNDERSTANDS

The experience on the Day of Pentecost is frequently duplicated in our day, when Jews from sixteen surrounding nations understood the tongues spoken by the 120. (See Acts 2:4.) They understood in the tongues wherein they were born. To quote a case in recent times, we heard Rev. Harald Bredesen, a Reformed Church Minister from Mount Vernon, New York, testify that he spoke in tongues in the lobby of a New York City hotel and was understood by an Egyptian lady sitting nearby. Harald Bredesen did not know this lady, but he was impelled to speak as prompted by the Holy Spirit. This lady explained that he had spoken in high archaic Egyptian only possible in certain Egyptian universities. She was most intrigued to know how he could have told her of her past history in this language. He at once opened his Bible and showed her the relevant passages, and it is believed that she was greatly moved to accept Christ as her Savior by this act of the Holy Spirit through human lips. Cases of this type can be multiplied where languages unknown to the speaker have been understood by another listener, who has often been won to Christ, for the Holy Spirit always glorifies the Christ.

7. FOR USE IN THE CHURCH

The time for personal prayer and edification must come to an end when we enter the church. Now we are members of one body coming together to manifest Jesus the Word corporately. The gifts of the Spirit are to be used in the church for the edification of the church members. The time of personal edification should have taken place at home before coming to church, so that we are prayed up and full of the joy of the Lord. We should not go to church to "get a lift," but rather to "give a lift." The church is the place where we give forth in the power of the Spirit. Thus we are instructed not to speak in tongues out loud unless we know there is a person with the second gift of interpretation present. If we know or believe there is no such gift in a particular assembly, then Paul instructed us to speak to ourselves and to God (see 1 Corinthians

14:28), quietly and reverently, for the Holy Spirit is gentle and will never startle or cause confusion in a worship service. Such disturbing occurrences must be influenced by other spirits.

A person able to speak in tongues for private use should wait on the Lord to be enabled to exercise a tongue for the purpose of bringing forth an interpretation for the edification of the whole church, for we must be zealous of these charismata that we may excel to the edifying of the church. (See 1 Corinthians 14:12.) When one possesses a clear tongue, it should be spoken out clearly, distinctly, reverently, without shouting, gesticulating, or using a high pitched or hysterical voice. Such a tongue must not be mumbled. If it is not possible for a person to bring forth the gift of tongues in the church in this clear convincing manner, then it would be better to keep silence and continue to wait on God until it becomes possible. If the church is to be edified, unbelievers must be convinced by the very way this gift is used. They will then be in awe of Him. (See 1 Corinthians 14:25.)

This is what was meant by Paul when he wrote, *"Have all the gifts of healing? Do all speak with tongues? Do all interpret?"* (1 Corinthians 12:30). This is the ministration of a particular charismatic gift for the edification of the church. It is quite obvious that although all may speak in tongues for personal edification, yet all do not speak in tongues to edify the church, nor do they all interpret or pray for the sick. Satan has prevented thousands from receiving the gift of tongues from a wrong twisted interpretation of this Scripture. May he suffer in eternity for this grievous misrepresentation!

3

THE PROPHETICAL WORD

In the last chapter we discussed the purpose of glossolalia, the initial manifestation of "prophecy." God greatly desires that the church which is His body should be fed by the living Word, bread from heaven, which the manna typified in the Old Testament. Not only do we have the written canon of Scripture, but in the plan of God He desires to confirm this Word by speaking audibly to His people, thereby the Holy Spirit becomes a Guide and Teacher.

By the three oral gifts of tongues, interpretation, and prophecy, God's *voice* is heard in our day. It seems that the single charismatic gift of prophecy is confined to *edification, exhortation*, and *comfort*. (See 1 Corinthians 14:3.) In every worship service in church, the voice of God should be heard in this gift edifying the body, exhorting to holier living, deeper consecration, and stirring it up to bring others under the sound of the gospel. There will always be those who are sorrowing or grieving, and God will speak directly to them in their sorrows with words of comfort. How necessary is this gift in the church!

Where the gift of tongues is used in the assembly to bring forth the Word in interpretation, the manifestation of this twin gift is equivalent to the single utterance of prophecy. Where a prayer meeting is held of believers only, it would seem that the use of tongues was in some measure unnecessary, for the gift of prophecy may be used by several members. *"Let the prophets speak two or three, and let the other judge"* (1 Corinthians 14:29). Where unbelievers are present, or those who have not come under the teaching of the need of the baptism of the Spirit and the gifts, then the use of tongues plus interpretation is most desirable, and it would appear that this method has divine approval for it is written, *"Wherefore tongues are for a sign, not to them that believe, but to them that believe not"* (1 Corinthians 14:22). It is not possible to overestimate the tremendous impact that speaking in tongues has upon an unbelieving ear. We have seen people rush out of church when a well-modulated tongue has been used!

Interpretation of tongues, which is the twin of the gift of tongues, is only used following the manifestation of glossolalia in the church, where such a tongue has been used for this purpose. Interpretation is not transliteration, but rather giving forth the message that has already been spoken in an unknown tongue. The person giving forth the tongue may have spoken few words, but the interpretation may be many words, but the sense will be received by the listening members of the church. Practice makes perfect in the use of these gifts, as in other things of life; they are not automatically spoken, but the human vessel cooperates with the divine Word to bring it forth under a strong anointing of the Spirit. Some have not become expert, and so do not know when the meaning of the message has ceased, and will sometimes repeat themselves in slightly different ways, like a phonograph record repeating itself. God never takes away the human responsibility, for *the spirits of the prophets are subject to the prophets*" (1 Corinthians 14:32), which means that we use our free will, and stop and start at will, which disposes of the ridiculous claim made by many untutored people that "the Holy Spirit made them" speak, usually out of place. The Holy Spirit does not force us to do anything.

We prophesy according to the proportion of our faith. (See Romans 12:6.) Some have more faith than others in this gift, and will usually bring forth a deeper word. If faith is weak, or the anointing not strong, it is possible for the human mind to intrude some of its own thoughts, and so the prophetical utterance will be partly of the Holy Spirit, and partly of the mind of man, even if that mind is a sanctified mind. In fact some "prophecies" are simply a sanctified mind giving forth a truth already learned. What is said may be true, and possibly edify, but great care has to be taken that personal opinions or instructions are avoided. It is good to remember the confines of this particular gift—edification, exhortation, and comfort—not fortune telling or instruction given to any member of the church! Practice makes perfect!

When it is realized that mistakes can be made in the prophetical gift, some get greatly discouraged, and therefore have no confidence in the Word spoken; but this is a great mistake, for the apostle Paul clearly taught us that we must not despise prophesyings, nor quench the Spirit, but we must encourage the use of these gifts, and then deliberately *prove* the Word spoken, and apply it, if we can, to ourselves, but never to another! Some assemblies have thrown out all the gifts of the Spirit, because some unruly members, who were unteachable, have misused these gifts. We must never quench the Spirit, or the utterances of the Spirit, but must teach our assemblies how to use them, for the Bible teaching is quite clear. Pastors must be bold and instruct and correct misuse where necessary.

Not all prophetic words spoken are of necessity "interpretation" when following a tongue. Sometimes, members of the church may not have a ministry of tongues to the church, but may burst forth in ecstatic praise and worship, which may well be followed by a prophetical utterance. At other times, tongues are sometimes used to trigger off a prophetical utterance, because the speaker desires to be in the Spirit as much as possible, and to keep the human mind silent. A "burst of tongues" followed by a prophetical utterance will not be "tongues plus interpretation," but prophecy launched by tongues! It seems clear from Paul's teachings that it is unwise to speak in tongues and then endeavor immediately afterward to interpret one's own tongue. "*If any man speak in an unknown tongue...let one interpret*" (1 Corinthians 14:27). The context would seem to indicate that if there be no interpreter present one should speak in tongues quietly to God, but conversely if one has a gift of tongues then prayer should be made that the second gift of interpretation be given so that the church might be edified.

God might overrule, however, in all these instances.

In all utterance gifts we need to remember that all things must be done decently and in order. (See 1 Corinthians 14:40.) Confusion, disorder, and interruptions must be avoided if the unbelieving are to be convinced. Unruly members will sometimes interpret the sermon, and say "God told them to do so!" These people must be taught and disciplined if necessary. Similarly when a call is made to the unsaved, great care must be taken if it is felt to be God's will to bring forth an encouraging Word to the unsaved.

In the Old Testament, schools of prophets were held, which would seem to be the ancient counterpart of Bible Schools or theological seminaries. Here young men were trained in giving forth the supernatural word, and we believe our churches should similarly be places where members are trained in the voice gifts. Obadiah took a hundred prophets and hid them, fifty in a cave, and fed them during the persecutions in the time of Jezebel and Ahab. (See 1 Kings 18:4.) Before his translation, Elijah visited schools in Gilgal, Bethel, and Jericho. It was during the building of a new school residence that the axe head was made to swim. (See 2 Kings 4:40–41.)

Great skill has to be used by prophets in the church, and it seems there are three degrees of this utterance gift. First the ministry of a prophet to the church. This ministry gift is usually associated with the apostolic ministry, for these two offices seemed to work as a two-witness ministry to the early church. It would therefore be expected that when an apostle and prophet visited an assembly the Word would be brought forth richly and in great power. In local assemblies prophetesses were frequently great assets to the church, for Philip had four daughters who prophesied at Caesarea. (See Acts 21:9.) In this case a local church can have a local prophetical ministry, and the members of this church will develop confidence in the prophetical utterances spoken by these chosen vessels, male or female. As the testimony of Jesus is the spirit of prophecy (see Revelation 19:10), it is not surprising that any member who is baptized in the Spirit may be moved upon under special circumstances to prophesy in the church. If these utterances are brought forth in the assembly, we must encourage the users to go on with God, so that the supply of prophets or prophetesses shall increase and not dry up!

If a prophecy is heard that condemns certain members (or the pastor) they must not be accepted as of the Spirit of God, but must be suppressed, for *"there is therefore now no condemnation to them which are in Christ Jesus"* (Romans 8:1). It is certain that the person concerned has a wrong spirit, and if necessary must confess it and deliverance must be prayed for before any further utterance can be trusted. Jesus gave us His yardstick—*"By their fruits ye shall know them"* (Matthew 7:16). Anyone not manifesting the fruits of the spirit, or living in some sinful state, should under no circumstances be permitted to speak in the church.

When King Saul backslid, God permitted a lying spirit to come upon him, and he prophesied by the lying spirit, although previously he had prophesied by the Holy Spirit. Later the Spirit of God came upon Saul again when he repented, but again he backslid and finally became possessed of the lying spirit, which finally drove him to the witch of Endor, and then to his destruction. Great care must be taken that we do not permit evil spirits to utter their prophecies out of the unsanctified minds of backsliding Christians.

It will be obvious that the gift of the discerning of spirits must be in every church, especially in the pastor.

One of the ascension gifts of Christ to the church is a pastor. The ideal of a New Testament pastor is one who has a great knowledge of the Bible and is filled with the Spirit and possesses the charismatic gifts of the Spirit. By the gifts of discerning of spirits and the word of knowledge, he will be able to know what he is dealing with, and in the love of Christ, but in the power of the Spirit, he must discipline and teach those over whom the Lord has made him the overseer! (See Acts 20:28). The conception that an assembly may hire or fire a pastor is alien to Scripture and the Spirit of God. In fact we are instructed to give the pastor double honor. The body of Christ is not a democracy but a theocracy, ruled by Jesus through the Holy Spirit through His fivefold ministry of apostles, prophets, pastors, evangelists, and teachers. These are God's gifts to the church for the blessing of the body of Christ.

4

THE WORD OF POWER

Immediately following the anointing of the Holy Spirit upon Jesus at His baptism, as described in Luke 4, we read that *"Jesus returned **in the power of the Spirit**"* (verse 14). Like an arrow from the bow of God, He returned right to the very place, Nazareth, where He had been brought up, where He was well known and where He had always worshipped as a young man. No one knew who He really was before His anointing with the Spirit, and likewise no one knew who He was that day when He entered His own synagogue. He was just a local man, a son of Joseph the carpenter. In like manner, those who are beginning to manifest the *Logos* of power are not recognized today by the church leaders or congregations of our cities. There was a difference this day, however, for the *Logos* of God had been anointed by the coming of the Spirit, and when Jesus entered the synagogue He was granted permission to read from their sacred scrolls, and quoted from the very Scriptures that spoke of Himself, and the reason for His anointing: to preach, to heal, to open, to deliver, to set at liberty, and to give sight to the blind. This needed a power that the Jewish clergy did not possess. He preached to them a little sermon, and told them that *"no prophet [was] accepted in his own country"* (Luke 4:24), and true to form they manhandled Him, leading Him out of the city, and tried to throw Him over a cliff—all because He came to deliver them in spirit, soul, and body. They did not want deliverance, or to be shown a better way; they wanted no competition from an ignorant carpenter's son; He was not of their priestly class or training.

He then entered into Capernaum and they were astonished at His doctrine, *"for his Word was with power"* (verse 32). As no one knew Him in Nazareth, so in Capernaum; He was just a Jew, a carpenter, certainly not a priest! How wrong could they be? He was the High Priest from heaven! He was the King of Kings. He was the chief Apostle and Prophet. He was all these offices, rolled into one. He was the living

Logos, the Word made flesh. (See John 1:14.) When He opened His mouth that His Father had filled, they were amazed, for His Word was *power*.

The only living creatures that recognized Him were demons! Demons in the synagogue; unclean spirits recognized Him as Jesus of Nazareth, the Holy One of God. (See Luke 4:34.) They were afraid of His Word, and immediately they spoke, Jesus spoke and manifest the Logos and they fled from His Word of power. This manifestation of God's living Word produced such consternation in Satan's kingdom that the demons were unable to hold their peace and kept crying out through the mouths of people as they came out, "*Thou art the Christ, the Son of God*" (John 11:27). The Word manifest in the flesh only had to appear and to speak, and demons came out crying with loud voices, naming themselves and acknowledging His Messiahship. The same happens today!

No wonder they said, "*What a word is this!*" (Luke 4:36).

There are three *power* gifts of the Spirit that are given to the body of Christ to manifest the Word of power to do the same work as Jesus did in healing the sick, casting out demons, and cleansing the lepers. These words of power must be "prophesied," that is, spoken forth by human lips in the power of the Spirit as divine oracular utterances, against Satan and his cohorts. If this is done in faith, then we shall see the same results today as they saw in the synagogue at Capernaum!

The apostle Paul told us to seek the "best gifts." We believe that the power gifts are certainly in this category, for whereas the three oral gifts are given to edify, to comfort, and to stir us up, the power gifts are what we use after we have been so edified and prepared. We go into battle encouraged from the exhortations and briefings given by the Holy Spirit. We start to preach and proclaim the meaning of Calvary and the complete defeat of Satan; we show forth the Word of power which brings us head-on into conflict with demon powers.

We heard one Anglican pastor testify that he had known nothing about demons, and certainly did not realize their presence, until *after* he received the baptism in the Spirit and spoke in tongues. This began the flowing forth from him of the river of life, the *Logos* of God, and Satan will cry out against such ministry, sometimes with a loud voice! There is only one thing to do, to rebuke with this Word of power and cast him out and tread him under foot. This will certainly astonish, and will bring considerable opposition as well as joy, but this is what God is bringing us into today in this last day revelation of the *Logos* of God.

In Joel 2:11, it is written, "*The* LORD *shall* **utter his voice** *before his army…for he is* **strong** *that executeth* **his word**." Before the army of the Lord, the Holy Spirit anointed church—His true body—is prepared to go into the final battle of the ages against sin, sickness, suffering, and sorrow, it will be necessary for the *voice* gifts to be restored and used in the power of the Spirit. Thus today we are seeing a restoration of the power charismatic gifts, which are healing people of all known diseases, driving out demons, and delivering people from the cruel bondages of Satan. Jesus used this Word of power at the tomb of Lazarus. Just three words were necessary and life came back into a corrupting human body.

What a word is this!

Jesus showed us how to pray for the sick. He stood *over* Peter's wife's mother, who had a high fever, and rebuked it and it left her, showing a fever has intelligence! He told His disciples to cast mountains into the seas, providing they did not doubt in their hearts. This could only be done by the Word of faith which He told them to have, and which is always given to heal a sick person or do a miraculous work. (See Luke 11:22–24.) He taught His disciples to take dominion over the circumstance and cast it away violently with the faith of God! The apostle James instructed the elders of the church to pray over the sick, not to pray a pious hopeful prayer for them, but to take the initiative and dominion and to cast out the sickness and cast away the mountain! Cancers are indeed mountains to those who have them. We need to speak as those with authority.

These three *power* gifts of *faith, miracles,* and *healings* manifest the Word of power in action: *Jesus* in action through the members of His body. This mouth of ours was not given for cursing, grumbling, or confessing failure, but to be used as an orifice through which God's power could flow to cause devilish things to disintegrate and disappear. Thus, we address ourselves to sicknesses, to demons, and to circumstances: "In the name of Jesus I *command* thee to go." Remember Jesus said, "*If* [you] *doubt not in* [your] *heart,* [you] *will have whatsoever* **[you]** *saith*" (Mark 11:23).

This is the prayer of faith. It is a saying prayer. The saying with "no doubt in our hearts" is the manifestation of prophecy in the form of *powerful words* against which Satan cannot stand.

When these words are spoken by more and more anointed men and women today, Satan's kingdom will be invaded by the army of the Lord, and His army is very great. Satan may scheme and plan for the overthrow of the kingdom of God; he may plot to take over the world by communism, and to kill Christians with sicknesses or drive them into mental hospitals, but his day is ending. The Lord's army is very great and very terrible; the *Logos* of God is proceeding out of thousands of mouths as this army enters Satan's territory with banners flying. Consternation will be seen on the faces of Satan's army of demon spirits. They will flee in every direction in confusion, vacating lives that they have held in captivity for centuries. Jesus the living Word of God was manifest that He might open prison doors and set the captives free. This is the day of the church. This is why it was created at Pentecost by the coming of the Holy Spirit. This is the "*acceptable year of the Lord*" (Luke 4:19).

5

THE WORD OF REVELATION

As we have already explained, the original coming of the Holy Spirit in power upon the church on the day of Pentecost was accompanied by an effusion of tongues, which Peter likened to "prophecy." This effusion is not confined to glossolalia, but to nine particular manifestations of the prophetical utterance called "spirituals" (in Greek, *pneumatikos*) or gifts (in Greek, *charismata*). In both these words we have the thought conveyed that these gifts are for the purpose of showing forth the love of Jesus in the power of the Spirit; in fact they are the many facets of the ministry of Jesus shining forth from His anointed body.

The three revelation gifts of the word of knowledge, the word of wisdom, and the discerning of spirits are to enable the warrior Christian in the army of the Lord, to have revealed to him secrets by a word from *the Logos* of God. Thus, the Holy Spirit is able to make known things that are unknown to unanointed men and women. These three gifts should only be used by Christians who are very experienced in the ministry of the gifts of the Spirit, for they are so high and heady, as the best of the best gifts, that Satan can easily attack in this area. The word of knowledge will reveal the secrets of men's hearts (see 1 Corinthians 14:25) including their intentions, their thoughts, their sicknesses, and the causes of these things. Such knowledge is not for broadcasting, but in order that we might know how to help such people. This gift also includes foretelling things to come, which is sometimes called the gift of prophecy, but as we have shown, this gift is deeper than the prophetical gift in the church. This is a ministry that is more likely to be used by a prophet in the church. Again we repeat that these gifts in the hands, or mouths, of an un-humble person can be spiritual dynamite to wreck a person's life! They are not fortune telling gifts. The gift of fortune telling belongs to the demon world, and we must be most careful about inquiring of demons. (See Isaiah 8:19–20.) Jesus told them to hold their peace and come out.

It is quite usual that where God permits us to have a word of knowledge on any matter whatsoever, He will at the same time give us a word of wisdom to go along with the revealed knowledge. This will enable us to give divine guidance to one in need of it, and sometimes a sufferer does not know what ails them, or the reasons for it, but the gifts reveal this and the Holy Spirit will usually confirm the revelation to the afflicted one, and so faith rises and it is possible to deliver the person.

Great care must be taken that before a word can be accepted as from the Lord Himself, the vessel through whom such a word is given is known to have such a prophetical ministry that has brought great blessing to others. Such a man or woman must be held in great love and esteem for their work in the ministry; it is not sufficient that any person claiming to be a prophet shall hand out guidance and counsel, for many false prophets have gone out into the world. We would again mention that God has a law—"*in the mouth of two or more witnesses shall every word be established*" (2 Corinthians 13:1). In matters of personal guidance, it is prudent to receive similar words of guidance and wisdom from at least two trusted servants of God, which is why the Lord caused apostles and prophets to go in pairs when establishing New Testament churches! He wants us to be as wise as serpents and harmless as doves. In the same way, as we are not to believe any doctrine of Scripture unless it is confirmed out of the mouths of two writers, so also no revelation of the spoken Logos shall be believed without confirmatory witnesses.

The responsibility of action taken after the Word of guidance is given rests with the one who receives it, not the ones who give it. Paul was warned not to go to Jerusalem because bonds awaited him, and he heard this confirmed in every city, but he decided to go in spite of the Spirit-given warning, and he was bound when he got there! The wisdom given to the apostleship overrode the warning counsel in the gifts.

Beware of freelance prophets!

One of the most common ways to test a false prophet is to check their message. If the prophesy is that you will receive a ministry of great importance, and the flesh of man loves to hear this kind of thing, then their utterance is suspect. Try the spirits and see if they are of God. If a personal prophecy unveils events of great importance which will bring glory to the Lord and His work, and cause us to cast ourselves prostrate at His feet, we can then ask God to fulfill it His way in our lives while we prepare ourselves to be so used for His glory and honor.

So many prophecies given seem contradictory. Consider the words that came saying that Jesus would be born in Bethlehem, yet He would be of Nazareth and yet come out of Egypt! How could this be from God? It is safe to let God work out His own prophecies, for Jesus said, "*I have told you before it came to pass, that, when it is come to pass ye **might believe!**"* (John 14:29). What goes for prophetical utterances in our day also goes for prophecies of the Bible yet unfulfilled. Let us not guess how God is going to do it!

Joseph in prison heard many wonderful prophecies concerning himself and his future ministry, and it is recorded that *"the word of the Lord tried him"* (Psalm 105:19). Many nights he went to sleep in bonds wondering how the impossible could become the possible. His promises were fulfilled in a far greater degree than he could ever understand or imagine. He allowed himself to be tried by the prophetical word.

Remember too that a prophetical Word will never go past the written Word of God. The two must agree. John wrote that *"the Father, the **Word**, and the Holy Spirit all agree in one"* (1 John 5:7). The written Word of God is the final authority, and the means whereby we test false utterances. If such prophecies are heard in your church, the pastor should lovingly but firmly counsel the "prophet." If they will hear, they will have a humble spirit, but if not it shows they are false, for they have a proud spirit, which God abominates. Not only should we not receive such prophecies, but the speaker also should be commanded to be silent, in the name of the Lord, for it is of another spirit.

In cases of difficulty when a word is not understood by a member of a church, he or she should take such a word to the pastor, who will seek the understanding from God by a word of wisdom, and better still, take it to several men of God who are known to be *experienced* in the use of spiritual gifts. *"Let the prophets speak **two** or **three**, and let the other judge"* (1 Corinthians 14:29). The men of God can speak wisdom, but you will have to judge! It is obvious that one who does not regularly use a prophetical gift will not be able to help in cases of difficulties or misunderstandings.

If a single individual comes to you and says, "I have a word from the Lord for you," listen to it with respect, and apply all the above tests to it. It might be of God, or it might be from a proud human spirit giving way to a lying spirit, but let us be careful we do not make the easy mistake of despising prophesyings, against which we are warned. (See 1 Thessalonians 5:20–21.) Receive everything, test and prove everything, and *hold fast* to that which is proved to be good. If it is of God, it will happen and you will be blessed. If it is not of God, it will not come to pass anyway, and the prophet will be proved a liar, which is the test of a prophet in the Bible. *"When a prophet speaketh in the name of the Lord, if the thing follow not, nor come to pass, that is the thing which the Lord hath not spoken, but the prophet hath spoken it presumptuously: thou shalt not be afraid of him"* (Deuteronomy 18:22).

Do not turn away from the greater gifts of revelation, for they are in the church for the purpose of causing it to win the great battle of the ages, the defeat of Satan's kingdom, and the bringing in of the kingdom of God's dear Son.

Many who begin to get the first manifestations of these revelation gifts, especially the gift of discerning of spirits, often get greatly troubled, because in "seeing through" a person, they think they are judging them, and of course judgment belongs to God. To know is not to judge in a condemnatory sense. We have the mind of Christ, and will realize this supernatural knowledge in a greater degree in the day in which we are living. God wishes to warn us sometimes that we are speaking to a wolf in sheep's clothing, a false prophet in the church, a deceitful worker of iniquity masquerading as a child of God. "*Of your own selves shall men arise, speaking perverse things, to draw away disciples after them*" (Acts 20:30).

God does not want us to be fooled. The commonest form of deception is from alcoholics and dope addicts who want a hand out from kind hearted Christians, not for food or bed, but for drink, cigarettes, and dope. Do not give them money, but offer food both natural and spiritual; they will almost certainly refuse both! Their stories will tear the heart out of a tender Christian, but the revelation gifts will show us they are not often genuine. Ask God to reveal to you their true state before you are unwise in helping a drunk get more drink!

6

THE RETURN OF ELIJAH

In the last chapter of the Old Testament, it is very significant that New Testament revival is prophesied by Malachi:

> Behold, I will send you Elijah the prophet **before** the coming of the great and terrible day of the LORD: and he shall turn the heart of the fathers to the children, and the heart of the children to their fathers, lest I come and smite the earth with a curse. (Malachi 4:5–6)

This "Elijah ministry" is obviously a restoration ministry to save the world from judgment. If there was ever a day that Satan under God could curse this old world, it is today, but God has prophesied that He will send *"Elijah the prophet"* to stem the tide of iniquity, to reverse it, and to bring in righteousness. Today is either a day of destruction or recreation. There is no middle ground.

The name *Eli-Jah* means "God Himself," or "The Lord is God." When the prophet Elijah came suddenly upon a backslidden Israel in the time of wicked King Ahab and his idolatrous Queen Jezebel, he was a manifestation of Jehovah in the flesh. He was a type of Emmanuel, the greater Elijah yet to come. What he prophesied came to pass; he both shut up heaven and opened it again. He turned off the rain and turned on the rain. This is a major result of the prophetical ministry today. We can bind and loose on earth and God in heaven will answer our commands! This is the power of the *spoken word* given in faith. This is the word that breaks in pieces the rock. It is a *hammer* and a *sword*.

God Himself was manifest to a completely wayward and backslidden Israel and in *one day* the people chose unanimously to serve God. The revival was rapid and caused by the prophetical words spoken by Elijah. *"When all the people saw it, they fell on their faces: and they said, the LORD, he is the God; the LORD, he is the God"* (1 Kings 18:39).

591

Elijah's prayer before the fire came down from heaven was a short prayer; he did not shout, stamp his foot, look pious, or try to be important; he prayed the prayer of faith—just sixty-three words, and asked God to send fire from heaven according to *His word*. (See 1 Kings 18:36–37.) Without any hesitation, we read, *"Then the fire of the* LORD *fell"* (1 Kings 18:38).

The Spirit of Jehovah that was in Jesus Christ was in Elijah, for the testimony of Jesus is the spirit of prophecy. As God was in Christ manifesting Himself to a dead Jewry, so also was God in Elijah to win back Israel to Himself. This is the Elijah ministry. It is a ministry of the prophetical Word to offer reconciliation and to give restoration.

In like manner, God sent John the Baptist in the power and spirit of Elijah to prepare the way for the greater Elijah, Jesus Himself. John was a prophet full of the Holy Spirit from his mother's womb. He spoke the Words of God that prepared the way for the ministry of Jesus. The same spirit that was in Elijah was in John for the same purpose.

> *But what went ye out to see?... A prophet? yea, I say unto you, and more than a prophet. For this is he of whom it is written, Behold, I send my messenger before thy face, which shall prepare thy way before thee.... And if ye will receive it,* **this is** [Elijah], *which was for to come. He that hath ears to hear, let him hear.*
>
> (Matthew 11:8–10, 14–15)

John demonstrated the Elijah ministry in his day.

Obviously John did not fully fulfill the prophesies of Malachi concerning the coming of Elijah, because all things were not restored by John, but Jesus again reiterated that Elijah would indeed come to restore all things, *"Why then say the scribes that* [Elijah] *must first come?"* (Matthew 17:10). Jesus answered them, *"*[Elijah] *truly shall first come, and* **restore all things**" (verse 11). This same Spirit that was in Elijah and John the Baptist is yet to restore all things back to God's paradise.

Jesus was a personal fulfillment of all the kings and prophets before Him. He was a greater than Solomon, a greater than Elijah, to *"turn the heart of the fathers to the children, and the heart of the children to their fathers"* (Malachi 4:6). Jesus is *God Himself*, the Word made flesh. However, Jesus came and ministered in the power of the Spirit for only three-and-a-half years. The ministry of Elijah did not finish at the cross, but commenced to increase at Pentecost when the *Logos* came into 120 empty vessels, forming the true body of Christ on earth. Now there were 120 mouths to sound forth the *Logos* instead of one. When Satan silenced the mouth of Jesus, he caused 120 other mouths to be opened; Satan always defeats himself by his actions. These 120 mouths were not a final count, because this great blessing of Pentecost was to go to the uttermost part of the earth. (See Acts 1:8.) In our day, we can expect millions of mouths to be anointed by the Holy Spirit to sound forth Word hammer blows to Satan's kingdom. *"Behold, I have put my words in thy mouth"* (Jeremiah 1:9). The same words that were in the mouth of Jesus are now found in the mouths of the members of His Holy Spirit filled body. These words manifest Elijah—God Himself.

The Elijah ministry that God is raising up in our day will include again the restoration of the apostleship and the prophetical ministry in the power of the Spirit, for the revelation of the restoration of the New Testament church can only come through the twin ministries of the apostle and prophet. *"How that by revelation He made known unto me the mystery…which in other ages was not made known unto the sons of men, as it is **now** revealed unto his holy apostles and prophets by the Spirit"* (Ephesians 3:3, 5). This revealed mystery was that the Gentiles were to be made fellow heirs, and of the same body of Christ, and truly when the Gentiles were received by God through the Holy Spirit's visitation upon them, they also "spoke with tongues, and magnified God." (See Acts 10:46.) By this manifestation of the Logos God showed the Jews that "repentance unto life was also granted to the Gentiles." (See Acts 11:18.)

The manifestation of the spoken prophetical word brought life to the Gentiles!

As God continues to pour out His Spirit upon all flesh today and our sons and daughters, and servants and handmaidens begin to prophesy, i.e. manifest the gifts of the Spirit through their lives, so will the Word of God be brought in the power of the Spirit to break down the strongholds of Satan, to open the prison house of those that are bound, to set the captives free, and to build up again the temple of the Holy Spirit, built without hands of living stones of human beings on fire for God. As in Elijah's day so in ours, "And then the fire fell," for he who came in the Spirit of Elijah prophesied " [Jesus] *shall baptize you with the Holy Ghost, and **with fire***" (Matthew 3:11).

The *Logos* is not only a hammer, but it is also burning fire. His ministers shall be a flame of fire. As the members of the historic churches receive this glorious baptism in the Spirit, He will be a Guide and Teacher to them and will lead them into all truth. He will teach them that the purpose of this baptism in the Spirit, accompanied by the effusion of the *Logos*, is not to make them better denominational members, but to bring them into the true temple of the Spirit to reveal Christ the living Word. The leadership will be of the Spirit, it will not be political or repressive; it will not be carnal according to the cunning devices of men's hearts. It will be open and honest for all to see the wonderful works of God. Apostles, prophets, pastors, evangelists and teachers will again be set in this body, and will minister the things of God to the hungry. Thus will Elijah return to restore all things—the church, the nation of Israel and then the world. The alternative is that the earth shall be smitten with a curse.

Shall we pray that we shall not hinder Elijah—God Himself—in this restoration work? Shall we lend our talents to cooperate and be filled with the Spirit? Thus shall we anticipate and precipitate the return of Jesus in power, the final manifestation of Elijah. When Jesus returns He does so with the Sword of the Spirit, which is the Word of God, coming out of His mouth as a sword of fire, a flaming sword. *"And out of his mouth goeth a sharp sword, that with it he should smite the nations"* (Revelation 19:15). When He comes, our ministry in the power and Spirit of Elijah will bring in the kingdom of God on earth which Jesus will establish in righteousness. As Elijah brought revival to Israel, and John the Baptist brought back Jewry to prepare them for the New Testament age, so we are being used of God to restore all things ready for His coming.

Even so come, Lord Jesus.

7

THE LATTER RAIN

As rain is poured out in the spring to help germination of the seed, so also does God pour out a harvest rain to bring the crop to a final harvest. These rains are described as former and latter rains in the Bible. Both are necessary for the successful harvest, and as we are now in the harvest time of this age, it is to be expected that we should be in the time of latter rain to swell the grain and prepare it for the great harvest when the angels shall gather it into God's barns. This is why we are instructed by God through His prophet Zechariah to ask for rain in the time of latter rain (see Zechariah 10:1), and this prayer was necessary because there was a great harvest of souls in his day which came about by the spoken Word in the prophecies of both Haggai and Zechariah. In fact, the temple would not have been rebuilt without their prophecies, because the latter rain was sent to confirm God's inheritance when it was weary. (See Psalm 68:9.) They did not just come to preach, but to speak as the oracles of God and give God's children encouragement, exhortation, counsel, and comfort, so that they went right through all the Satanic opposition and built the temple again.

As the true temple was rebuilt in the day of Ezra and Nehemiah, with Haggai and Zechariah prophesying the Word of God, so today, the Elijah ministry with the prophetical Word is being sent again to confirm His weary church, to refresh it, to set it on fire with a renewed outpouring of the Logos. This temple is not built with wood and stone, but with living stones, not made with hands, and this temple composed of Holy Spirit filled men and women, utterly dedicated to the task on hand, will be for an habitation of God through the Spirit. (See Ephesians 2:20–21.)

It is to be regretted that in past times when there has been a renewed outpouring of the Spirit, instead of this power being canalized and harnessed to bring forth the Word of God, it has frequently degenerated into fleshly excitement and emotion, and so the whole purpose for which the outpouring was sent was lost. It is obvious that when the weary church is refreshed (see Psalm 68:9) it will feel good, but the feelings are not the primary purpose; it is rather that the vessels shall bring forth gifts and fruits in the power of the Spirit.

In Deuteronomy 32, the real purpose of the latter rain is made clear:

> *Give ear, O ye heavens, and **I will speak**; and hear, O earth, the **words of My mouth**. My **doctrine** shall drop as the rain, my **speech** shall distil as the dew, as the small rain upon the tender herb, and as the showers upon the grass.*
>
> (verses 1–2)

There comes a time when God wishes once again to speak. Most of the time the church has been doing all the speaking, and much that it spoke was inconsequential, without power or authority and its doctrines have so often been wrong, or at least limited. Truly, as Israel of old, the New Testament Israel has limited God. (See Psalm 78:41.) The shameless divisions in Christendom caused by man's ignorance of his Maker and Savior; the lack of the Holy Spirit in the lives of both clergy and congregations, has created a church that is unaware of the voice of God, but this condition is now changing. God is causing His voice to be heard through the charismatic gifts to refresh the members, and to enable them to bring forth the harvest, that this great church—the body of Christ—shall be full of the Word of God.

To most people, doctrine is a boring subject to be avoided. Bible study is the least well attended service of the church, and in many churches there is no Bible study at all, and in others even the morning and evening lessons are not read. The Word of God, which teaches us sound doctrine, is hardly used in the services of some denominations, and so the people are in complete ignorance of the wonderful doctrines that set us free. The very churches hold their flocks in bondage and darkness as bad almost as if they lived without Christ.

The Word of God is coming again to set the people free.

Possibly the greatest result of this folly is that Satan, knowing that his time is short, is going around with false cults to confuse and interfere with God's true revival (see Revelation 12:12). It has been truly said that, together with God's true revival, Satan is having his revival too, and his revival is based on false doctrine with false prophets at work. God's revival is centered on true doctrine, with true prophets. *"Now I beseech you, brethren, mark them which cause divisions and offences contrary to the **doctrine** which ye have learned; and avoid them"* (Romans 16:17). *"If there come any unto you, and bring not this **doctrine** [the doctrine of Christ], receive him not into your house"* (2 John 1:10). Due to the great ignorance of the Word of God with Christians of most denominations, these false prophets have gained entrance not only into houses, but into churches and split them. With the renewed outpouring of the latter rain, the Holy Spirit baptized Christians will be filled with the *Logos* of God. A great hunger will arise, and is arising, for the Word of God. In our service in Toronto, Canada, the Bible study night is now one of the most popular when every doctrine of Scripture is carefully examined and taught to Holy Spirit filled children of God. When God's inheritance ceases to be weary, they become hungry and keen, and therefore easy to teach, and they in turn easily assimilate the Word into their beings.

In Hosea, there is a remarkable prophecy about this latter rain,

> Come and let us return unto the LORD: for he hath torn, and he will heal us; he hath smitten, and he will bind us up. After **two days** will He **revive us**: in the **third day** he will raise us up, and **we shall live** in his sight. Then shall we know, if we follow on to know the LORD: his going forth is prepared as the morning; and he shall come unto us as the rain, as the **latter and former rain** unto the earth. (Hosea 6:1–3)

Reckoning on the basis of one day for a thousand years (see 2 Peter 3:8), and beginning at the dates when Israel was cast off for her rebellion between 740–720 BC, and given a bill of divorcement (see Isaiah 50:1), and coming through to the third day, we are brought to AD 1517, which commenced the Protestant revival under Martin Luther, a beginning and a partial reformation of the church; and then we come through the evangelical awakenings of the eighteenth century with the Wesleys, on to the twentieth century with the outpouring of the Spirit in Pentecostal fullness, which brought back the supernatural *Logos* to the church, but much had to be learned. With the renewed outpouring upon all the churches in 1961, we are now witnessing the final stages of the reformation, which will bring a remnant into the fullness of the Spirit and finally unify the church without spot or wrinkle. Thus will the prayer of Jesus be answered, "that we all may be one." (See John 17:21.) This will not be a work of ecumenical councils, but entirely a work of the Spirit as He is outpoured as the former and latter rain. The whole of the outpouring occurs within the period of the third day of Hosea's prophecy and let us note the things that occur.

God will heal us. This means complete healing for spirit, soul and body—a return of divine healing. He will bind us up, divine love and compassion comes with the return of the Holy Spirit's outpouring. The story of the Good Samaritan has an echo of this. In the *third day*, or the period covered by the Reformation (1517 to the end), He will raise us up, and we shall live in His sight. As the manna came down each day from heaven like dew and soft rain, so also does the manna—the bread of life (see John 6:51)—come down from heaven in the form of the life-giving latter rain. During the time that Israel fed on manna, they had no single sick or feeble persons among their tribes (see Psalm 105:37), because the manna was such a perfect food. It sustained them in perfect health. The Word of God—the *Logos*—is our perfect food, and as we allow ourselves to receive the refreshing of the latter rain today, and take down the umbrellas of our traditions and unbelief, we shall find that God will begin healing us, binding us up, and causing us to live in perfect health. Amazing but true! What a far cry from our traditional forms of Christianity, but this is the end result of the present outpouring of the Holy Spirit.

In the wonderful second chapter of Joel, wherein he tells us that *"the LORD shall utter his voice before his army; for his camp is very great"* (verse 11), he goes on and enlarges the vision and tells New Testament Zion to *"rejoice in the LORD your God: for he hath given us the former rain moderately, and he will cause to come down for you the rain, the former rain, and the latter rain in the first month"* (verse 23). As the former rain came moderately on the day of Pentecost to create the body of Christ, so in exactly the same manner, will the latter rain come as at first (the word *"month"* is not in the original), without moderation. It is prophesied to be on all flesh (see verses 28–29) and *"unto the uttermost parts of the earth"* (Acts 1:8). As Elijah saw the cloud the size of a man's hand, which he interpreted as a token of the deluge to come, he started to outrun the chariot of wicked Ahab, for it is written *"It came to pass in the meanwhile that the heaven was black with clouds and wind, and there was a great rain"* (1 Kings 18:45).

The sign of the coming of the Holy Spirit on the day of Pentecost was a rushing wind, and the heavens discharged the latter rain moderately, and the first 120 members of the body of Christ started speaking in other languages as the Holy Spirit gave them the Words. The *Logos* had returned in the power of the Spirit. It is always a source of great blessing to read that Mary the mother of Jesus was among the charter members. This should encourage our Catholic friends, who are now receiving the Holy Spirit. The Holy Spirit is becoming a person to many instead of a doctrine!

We cannot end this chapter on the latter rain without reference to the writings of the apostle James.

> Be patient therefore, brethren, unto the coming of the Lord. Behold the husband-man waiteth for the precious fruit of the earth, and hath long patience for it, until he receive the **early** and **latter rain**…. For the coming of the Lord draweth nigh.　　　　　　　　　　　　　　　　　　　　　　(James 5:7–8)

The greatest sign of the near return of Jesus Christ to this earth to fulfill the many prophecies (see Acts 1:11) is the coming of the Holy Spirit to reveal Jesus in His body the church before His literal descent with clouds (see Revelation 1:7). The latter rain is preparing the precious fruit for the return of Christ. The gifts of the Spirit, when used through oracles of God, are continually reminding us of the return of Jesus to this earth to rule and reign over His kingdom in equity and justice. (See Isaiah 9:6–7.) It is an amazing fact that as soon as a person receives the wonderful baptism of the Spirit and speaks in tongues, the result is that they get right back to the Bible and the Holy Spirit begins to teach them! Thus we can look forward to the time when the counsel of Paul will be realized, *"Now I beseech you, brethren, by the name of our Lord Jesus Christ, that ye all* **speak the same thing***, and that there be no divisions among you; but that ye be perfectly joined together in the same mind"* (1 Corinthians 1:10). Only the baptism in the Spirit can accomplish such a miracle, and this miracle is taking place today. If we have all received the same Word we must all speak the same thing. Do you see?

"Ask ye of the LẁRD *rain in the time of* **latter rain***"* (Zechariah 10:1). This is the time to pray for the heavens to become black with clouds, and for there to be a cloudburst upon us all. Amen.

8

THE BODY OF CHRIST

It is generally accepted that an individual is made a member of Christ by the rebirth at conversion, but we must remember that Jesus, although He became the Word made flesh at His birth (see John 1:14), when an earthly body was created for Him in which He was to dwell among us, He did not commence to manifest the power of God in His body until He received the anointing of the Holy Spirit at the age of thirty. Apart from one reference to His astonishing knowledge when He was twelve, no further reference is made of His supernatural abilities until He became the Anointed One (in Greek, *Christos*) by the coming of the Holy Spirit following His obedience in water baptism. (See Daniel 9:24.) It was after this anointing that He returned in the *power* of the Spirit (see Luke 4:14) and entered in synagogues, and cast out demons, and healed the sick. It was after this anointing that the people said *"Never man spake like this man"* (John 7:46), and it is recorded that they were astonished at His doctrine, for His Word was with *power.*

The apostle Paul wrote to us today in this twentieth century:

*And are built upon the foundation of the apostles and prophets, Jesus Christ himself being the chief corner stone; in whom all the building fitly framed together groweth unto an **holy temple** in the Lord: in whom ye also are builded together for an habitation of God through the Spirit.* (Ephesians 2:20–22)

It is clear that we become living, or lively stones, framed together by the Holy Spirit in the body of Christ which is *"an habitation of God."* It is the temple of God. It is that through which God wishes to manifest Himself, and none other. In 1 Corinthians 12:7, the *charismata* are referred to as manifestations of the Spirit. These nine manifestations of tongues, interpretation of tongues, prophecy, faith, gifts of healing, working of miracles, discerning of spirits, the word of knowledge and wisdom, are *manifestations* of the chief Cornerstone, who said He, and He alone, would build this church—*His own body.*

The church, which is built on the ministry of the apostles and prophets, is not an organization, it is not a denomination, it is not a society, it is not a collection of disciples (there were disciples before Pentecost). It is built of willing men and women, utterly dedicated to the task of revealing Jesus, and this can only be done by the Spirit of God, dwelling in each member who thereby become fitly framed together.

As we look at our powerful denominations, our theological colleges and seminaries, our Christian organizations, we see man determining what he is going to do for God, rather than to allow himself to be a channel through whom God may manifest Himself in the person of the Logos through our flesh—His body! God has today prepared a body for His Son, even as He did for His Son when He ministered on earth. Satan caused the crucifixion of that body—that Holy Spirit anointed body—but God brought good out of evil and Satan was defeated by this act, and now the body has become so enlarged that it covers the whole earth and there are Holy Spirit filled members in every country of the world. Each assembly of these Holy Spirit anointed saints should manifest Jesus in the power of His Spirit, through the nine manifestations already referred to. Jesus said of His disciples *before* Pentecost that they had their names written in heaven (see Luke 10:21), and the sick were manifestly healed and demons cast out *before* Pentecost. Why then bother to bring these men and women to a personal Pentecost with the "embarrassment" of tongues? Why not leave them in their own groups rejoicing in their salvation and healing? God wanted to use them, as one body—anointed and charged to overflowing with the Holy Spirit—so that His Word could be manifest through them corporately in the power of the Spirit; the Word that would edify, bless, encourage, comfort, strengthen, heal, deliver, and cast the devil out of lives. The body of Christ was to be a vehicle of the flowing Word of God. This is why He said that rivers would flow out of their innermost parts—but not before the baptism in the Spirit was experienced by each individual stone, fitly framing them together as one composite temple—the body of Christ with Jesus as the chief cornerstone. He determines the angles of the building, and our angles must be His angles.

Each member of this temple does not carry a denominational tag. He is filled with Father, Son, and Holy Spirit, and this is what was meant by Jesus in John 14:20, when He referred to the outpouring of the Holy Spirit on the day of Pentecost in these words, *"At that day ye shall **know** that I am in my Father, and ye in me, and I in you."* Up to this time they were unable even to comprehend that Jesus was in His Father, and that His Father was in Jesus. (See John 14:10–11.) In their unanointed carnality, they could not understand how God could actually indwell His Son, and how the Son could indwell the Father. This was a mystery far too deep for the finite mind of man, and Jesus knew this and told them that on the Day of Pentecost they would know and understand. It was necessary for them to be baptized in the Spirit. It takes the indwelling of the Third Person in baptizing power to give us supernatural understanding of the mysteries of God. This is why so much theology makes no sense to the Holy Spirit, because it comes from the wisdom of man, which God tells us is foolishness with Him. (See 1 Corinthians 2:14.)

Many ministers have testified that after Jesus baptized them in the Holy Spirit, they realized how much nonsense bad been taught them by the mind of men. Before their personal Pentecost, they taught man-made doctrines from their minds, but after their Pentecost they became channels for the flow of the supernatural Word of God in wisdom and understanding. Truly it is the same today, *"In that day ye shall know"* (John 14:20). You must come to that day—your personal day of Pentecost. If you do not, you will not be able to understand the purposes of God in creating the church which is the body of Christ.

If Jesus did not attempt to manifest the power of God before He was anointed to begin the work of the Christ, how much more we, who claim to be members of Christ, should not attempt to minister, either as laymen, or ordained ministers, until we have been anointed with that anointing which Jesus called the baptism in the Spirit. He baptizes us into the Holy Spirit, and then we overflow with supernatural manifestations of the Holy Spirit, beginning with tongues! This initial manifestation is only the beginning of the outflow of the *Logos*—the Word of God.

We were talking to a minister of the Southern Baptist denomination who received his personal Pentecost while praying in his study, because he was dissatisfied with programs, committees, people, carnality, and entertainment in the church. These did not satisfy. No one had told him about a personal Pentecost—he had avoided those who claimed to speak in tongues, believing them to belong to the fanatical fringe of the church. He knew nothing about the baptism in the Spirit doctrinally—why should he? No one had ever taught him in his seminary. God met his earnest cry to heaven for power to minister as he believed they did in the early church. Suddenly, and without outward emotion, he began to speak words of another language. His whole being was supernaturally charged—he had never had an experience like this before; something unusual had happened! He went into his home and met his wife, who saw his face was aglow with a divine radiance. She knelt with him and soon she also was manifesting glossolalia. This faithful pastor began to minister in the power of the Spirit. Others in the church also received their personal Pentecost, including his deacons. People were healed, programs disappeared, head counting stopped, some left but more came in, because the gifts of the Spirit, the manifestations of the Logos began to appear. The deacons of the church were filled to overflowing, and now this same denominational church has become a New Testament Assembly to manifest Jesus, the Word of Life! No more straining in the energy of the flesh to do God's work man's way—now just resting in the Lord and permitting God by the Spirit to manifest Jesus in their midst! What a contrast! What a blessing!

This church—the body of Christ—is God's secret weapon which will yet upset the counsels of man whether in government or church. Let Satan have his servants and schemers, but God has His Spirit, which He is now pouring out upon His church. This is not a denominational organization, it is composed of men and women of every race, all baptized in one Spirit in one body. Incidentally, this is the literal meaning of 1 Corinthians 12:13, all have been made to drink *into* one Spirit.

In this present outpouring of the Spirit upon the church as promised in the Word of God, denominational walls come crumbling down, for this glorious baptism in the Spirit truly makes them all one in Christ, as never before. If He of Himself could do nothing, unless the Father did it through Him, how much more we members of His body should not be anything or try to do anything, without the baptism in the Spirit to manifest Jesus in and through us!

One of the purposes of this book is to teach those who have already received this glorious personal Pentecost why they did receive, for many are worshipping in churches where the gifts or manifestations of the Spirit are never heard. They worship in man-made program churches. Surely this must quench the power of the Word resident in them by the indwelling Spirit! If you cannot find a true New Testament church in your area in which all nine gifts are regularly manifest, then gather in groups of those of like mind and experience and ask Jesus to manifest Himself through you in times of prayer, and this will bring new meaning to His Word, *"Where two or three are gathered together in my name, there am I in the midst"* (Matthew 18:20). Pray also that God will supply the necessary anointed oversight. Thus will New Testament Spirit-filled Christians be edified, and be able to teach and encourage others in our churches for this glorious end-time visitation of the Spirit of God upon hungry lives. Do not disassociate yourself from a local church completely, but help it.

This revival or charismatic renewal has only begun. It will sweep through like a deluge, breaking down man-made barriers of spiritual intercourse, and produce a church—His body—which will be so invincible in a compromising world that Satan will tremble and have to acknowledge his defeat at Calvary. Jesus said of His church that the gates of hell would not prevail against it. Sin, sickness, error, carnality, and demons will be swept away before the mighty torrent of living waters flowing out of the innermost parts of millions of living stones, fitly framed together by the Holy Spirit. As Jesus, the *Stone*, was smitten at Calvary and living waters flowed out of Him at Pentecost, so we today, as stones made after the likeness of *The Stone*, will find waters gushing out of ourselves in desert places, because the Headstone was smitten of God! The miracle of waters gushing out of the smitten stone in the desert will be repeated in millions of stones today, for the same purpose, *"to make a way in the wilderness, and rivers in the desert"* (Isaiah 43:19) so that His people may drink. This is called "doing a new thing"!

The disorganized churches and the overorganized churches will be given an opportunity to come and drink at the fountain of waters in the desert of ecclesiasticism, sacerdotalism, and entertainment.

The *living Word—the Christ*—has come down to deliver.

PULLING DOWN STRONGHOLDS

CONTENTS

INTRODUCTION

P*ulling Down Strongholds* is a book that every present-day Christian should read.

Too long have the churches of our Lord and Savior Jesus Christ preached an almost powerless gospel. Much of today's teaching and preaching in our churches of the twentieth century is so lacking in the fundamental biblical truths, that one is prone to wonder how people can trust Jesus Christ with the mighty matter of their eternal salvation when they have not as yet been taught to trust Him in the everyday affairs of this present life.

The Bible promises us, *"But my God shall supply all your need according to his riches in glory by Christ Jesus"* (Philippians 4:19). Yet all about us we see defeated, discouraged, ailing, and needy Christians. It is tragic to see God's people so completely fettered by Satan and his demons. Safe to say, the Lord God never intended for His people to live in such bondage and subjection.

Jesus declared, *"And ye shall know the truth, and the truth shall make you free"* (John 8:32). *Pulling Down Strongholds*, a book replete with scriptural truth, will be an eye opener to any believing Christian who is willing to lay aside old misconceptions and to permit the Lord to speak to his heart concerning our true heritage in Jesus Christ.

When one considers that the prophecies of the Bible are largely fulfilled, and that, therefore, we are living in the last days, be this period longer or shorter than we might suppose, one begins to ask himself what else must be accomplished before our Lord returns? The answer to this question seems obvious to me. The church, that body of true believers, must take her rightful place in God's plan. The Lord Jesus Christ awaits our awakening from the sleep of spiritual lethargy. How the heart of God must agonize over our failure to utilize what He has purchased for us in Christ's own precious blood.

The Word of our Lord calls to us through His servant Paul:

Awake thou that sleepest, and arise from the dead, and Christ shall give thee light. See that ye walk circumspectly, not as fools, but as wise, redeeming the time, because the days are evil. Wherefore be ye not unwise, but understanding what the will of the Lord is. And be not drunk with wine, wherein is excess; but be filled with the Spirit.
(Ephesians 5:14–18)

For said Jesus, "*Ye shall receive power after that the Holy Ghost is come upon you*" (Acts 1:8). Personally, I must agree with Brother Whyte; I believe that this power is even unto *Pulling Down Strongholds*.

—*Pastor Frank A. Downing*
Baltimore, Maryland
February 1964

1

WHAT IS MAN?

In Psalm 8, we find this pertinent question, *"What is man?"* Surely we see him as the most contradictory, irrational, irresponsible creature in God's universe. He does things that animals would not do; he feeds on things animals would ignore; he lies, he cheats, he steals, and he kills. He is capable of creating great masterpieces of music and art; he can find medicines to heal himself, and at the same time invent means of destroying himself. Try as one might, it is difficult to see anything that makes very much sense about so-called "homo sapiens."

Did God create man that he should behave like this? It may be supposed that his incredible behavior is a reason why some do not believe that God made him, for would God make anything so vile? And yet he is capable of such rich and fine things.

The apostle Paul gave us an answer. He was not impressed with man and he wrote a most unpleasant story about him; he painted a picture that is repulsive, knowing that the prophet Jeremiah had said long before that man's heart was desperately wicked, so wicked that he is unable to understand why he acts as he does.

Paul wrote that there was not one righteous man. Did he exaggerate? As we look around our big cities, in our business houses, our factories, and our farms, is there not one righteous man? "No, not one" is the verdict of the Holy Bible. No wonder it makes unpopular reading! Here is a list of the shortcomings of man as Paul saw him:

- None understands.
- None seeks God.
- All have gone out of the way.
- All are unprofitable.
- None does good.
- Their throats are open sepulchers.

- They use their tongues for deceit.
- Under their lips is the poison of asps.
- They curse with bitterness.
- They shed blood.
- They destroy and are miserable.
- They know no peace.
- They do not fear God.

These thirteen condemnatory characteristics describe mankind without God in his thoughts. This is the natural man in our streets and cities. Man without God—the unbeliever. He may go to church, he may be agnostic, and he may even say he is atheistic, but these thirteen points describe him perfectly.

"What is man?" asked the psalmist. "A strange creature indeed," we would reply.

Did God create man to behave in this irresponsible and illogical way? Was man as we see him today the pattern of mankind that God created? No, a thousand times no—man is far removed from the picture that God had (and has) in mind when He created him. Something must have happened between the creation of man and the present-day caricature. This happening was the fall of man from his high estate in the garden of Eden.

In Psalm 8, David explained what God had in mind in the beginning. Even now God is still mindful of man; that is to say, God cares and God loves him, even if he is a fallen creature, and did indeed visit him in the Person of the Lord Jesus Christ.

In verse 5 we read that God created man a little lower than the angels; not a great deal lower, but "a little lower." Before He created mankind God created the angelic realm of thousands upon thousands of glorious spiritual beings, who are called angels or messengers of God. They are wonderful and powerful, but even among this great creation, one-third fell also from their first high estate and were cast into the earth as "fallen angels"; and as they fell with Satan, they became his angels, or messengers. This we read, *"And the great dragon was cast out, that old serpent, called the devil and Satan, which deceiveth the whole world; he was cast out into the earth, and his angels were cast out with him"* (Revelation 12:9). Man would have remained the wonderful creation that he was in Eden if Satan and his angels had not preceded him there. Satan tempted Adam and Eve and they both fell, and in turn they also were cast out of Eden, the earthly paradise.

God cannot have either sin or sinners in His presence, either in heaven or on earth. Fallen man cannot dwell in the presence of God. It is only as God visited man in the person of Jesus Christ that the way back to His presence, His glory, His blessings, and His kingdom was made. Although man was cast out of Eden, a way is made for him to return and recapture all his past glory (and more). Jesus, *"I am the way, the truth and the life"* (John 14:6).

In the beginning, man was created to have *dominion* over all the works of God's hands. Nothing on this earth was to have dominion over man. Man was to be stronger than circumstances. Man was made to go over, not go under. He was to have dominion over all animals; sheep and powerful oxen, lions and tigers, rhinoceros and elephants, rats and mice—germs! He was to have the rule over everything that flies, including the eagle; no fish was to be too great for him, even whales would be subject to him. The trees and vegetation, the minerals would all be ruled over by God's man—not Satan's man! It is Satan's fear that causes man not to believe this and run from beasts. *"For ye have not received the spirit of bondage again to fear; but ye have received the Spirit"* (Romans 8:15). God does not intend man to be afraid of anybody or anything!

In Genesis 1, we have the sacred record of man's creation. *"So God created man in his own image, in the image of God created he him; male and female created he them"* (verse 27). No half men and half women, but either man or woman. Manly men and womanly women. Not perverted, effeminate men or masculine women; these are perversions of the devil, for the sins that these persons produce are grimly described in Romans 1:21–32 as the ultimate sins of fallen mankind.

This man, having God's image and likeness, was to multiply himself on the earth with similar sons of God, made in God's likeness. God's original purpose (which has not changed) was that this earth was to be filled with men and women created in the image of God. God-men and God-women all over this planet. What a paradise—and it will yet be so; God's purpose will triumph in the end, and this world will yet be filled with the glory of God. God has made a way, mankind must enter into that way, and he will become a son of God, a God-man again, with all his previous dominion given back *in Christ*.

The earth was to be replenished by these lovely God-men and God-women, not the vain strutting fashion models, or conceited educated man, but by humble, powerful, gracious humans; and they were to subdue the world and have it under their control, not under any other power. God-men were to rule the world, not dictators or imperialists. No fear, no wars, no famines, no want, but plenty for everyone. This was God's original intention, and He has not forsaken His throne or His purposes for puny rebellious man. *"He that sitteth in the heavens shall laugh: the Lord shall have them in derision"* (Psalm 2:4).

God's men were to have *dominion* over animals, fishes, and birds. Nothing that moves on the earth was to have dominion over man. (See Genesis 1:26–28.)

So when David asked that question "What is man?" in Psalm 8, he was looking at God's promises, and not at the travesty that walks our streets today. Even so, we should always see, or try to see, as God sees things, by believing His Word and all His wonderful promises. As we continue in this little study of man's authority in Christ, we shall marvel that such provision has already been made for sinful man to rise higher even than the angelic realm, *on earth*. Let us look through the window of God's Word and not at the changing circumstances all around us. Man will let you down, but Jesus will lift you up!

2

JESUS—THE WAY UP

Jesus told us that *"I am the way, the truth, and the life"* (John 14:6). In this triad we have the recipe for a life of dominion over the world, the flesh, and the devil. There is not a created being, be it an elephant or a germ, that can harm a son of God, *unless we permit it to harm us by fear!* Once we have fully understood our authority vested in us by God through Christ, we can progressively and experimentally take our place as invincible creatures of faith, and not conquerable captives of fear. Paul wrote, *"We are more than conquerors...through [Christ]"* (Romans 8:37). Not just conquerors, but *more than* conquerors. When Satan and his cohorts view us in this light, it is not surprising that the Bible teaches that *"the wicked one touches him not"* (1 John 5:18)!

Jesus is *the way* out of our captivity, our bondage, our sorrows, and our feebleness. He blazed a trail clean out of captivity. He was manifest and anointed with the Holy Spirit at Jordan that He might bind up the brokenhearted, proclaim liberty to the captives, open the prison doors to those who were bound in chains, and to set them free. This fullness of salvation is not necessary to be repeated. We are saved, and set free once and for all, that we might enjoy a fullness of blessing in this kingdom of God on earth—restored Paradise indeed. The salvation of the soul is the way into the new life, with healing of the mind and body, so that we might enjoy divine health and strength. The prison door is not opened that we might come out one day and go back in a week's time because we got so used to "being cared for by the devil." It was said that many slaves who were emancipated in the days of Abraham Lincoln continued to work for their old masters, rather than venture forth into an unknown world. Truly the kingdom of God is an unknown world to most people, and unfortunately so few Christians today have much idea of the blessing given by Jesus to us on the cross. They would rather live like other churchgoing people, than begin to act as sons of God—royalty indeed. Being of the royal family of God sets them too far apart from even members of their own families, who remain in sin and ignorance. They dare not be different. However, the Bible teaches us that we are different—completely different and separate from the world. It is as we learn to live and act differently that we begin to have experiences of divine power, authority, and blessing that amaze us, and demonstrate God's glory.

Jesus said, "I am...the **truth**." Once we have accepted the way, we must walk in the light as He is in the light. (See 1 John 1:7.) We no longer walk by traditions taught to us by others, even if these traditions sounded so sensible, and were taught by church leaders. In Jesus' day, there were many rabbis, and a powerful church, but He said they had made the Word of God of none effect by their traditions. This means in plain language, they had thrown the Book out of the window. They had church, ceremonies, religion, priests, and services, but *no truth*. Once a son of God enters the kingdom of God, he must adjust his life, his thinking, his speech, and his bearing, and realize that *"perfect love casteth out all fear"* (1 John 4:18). What a challenge. The more our lives become readjusted to His truth, the more authority we will exercise over Satan. Though all men may laugh at you, it is better to obey God than man.

Jesus said, "I am...the **life**." Christianity is not an imitation of the life of Christ (even if that were possible). It is not obeying "your church." It is not a monastic life suppressing natural desires and appetites. It is a life of abundance for spirit, soul, and body. Jesus said that He came to give *life* and to give it more abundantly. He came to take that tired, bound, captive life and fill it with His overwhelming abundance. Can we imagine Adam being sick, depressed, miserable, weak, and fearful in the garden? Jesus came to give us back everything that Adam lost, and as we shall see, even more under the new covenant in His blood. *Abundant life* means just what it says for every child of God, everyone who approaches the mercy seat will have made available immediately every blessing in the Bible, and there are thousands. Abundant life, including joy, peace, strength, health, and prosperity is laid to your account in heaven by Jesus Christ. *"My God shall supply all your need according to his riches in glory by Christ Jesus"* (Philippians 4:19). Unfortunately, when a child of God does venture into the bank of heaven, after knocking timorously, instead of walking in boldly as if he owned the place (and he does!), he usually cautiously and apologetically approaches one of the tellers, and proffers a check with a small amount and frankly wonders whether it will be honored! This is not an exaggeration concerning the approach in prayer of the average child of God. We might just as well write "million" as "two" because it belongs to an heir of God anyway. Let us therefore go *boldly* into the holiest place by a new and living way, and plead the blood of Jesus as our reason for expecting fantastic blessings. The world uses the word "pay off." Our "pay off" includes everything the moment we dare to enjoy it by faith. The blood of Jesus purchased every redemptive blessing for us.

"But I am not worthy of His blessings." Who said so? The opposite is the truth; this is a lie of Satan. *"Thou hast a few names...which have not defiled their garments and they shall walk with me in white, **for they are worthy**"* (Revelation 3:4). Jesus makes us worthy in Him. As long as we abide in Him, and permit His Words to abide in us, then we will continue to walk worthy of all His abundant blessings. Though these wonderful blessings have been made available to us at the cross, yet each promise must be appropriated by our own personal faith, and not that of another; no promise of God is automatically bestowed on us. It must be appropriated by faith.

The story is told of a soldier son who faithfully sent his uneducated mother a monthly check, enough to keep her in comfort, health, and happiness. The mother could not read, and so she received her son's letters, but did not understand what the check was, and so over a period of years she used to stuff the money under her mattress. She died in abject poverty, bringing early death upon herself because of lack of proper food. Had she not the means? Were not the checks good? Was not the son faithful in all that he did? Had she understood the ways of the bank and of her son, she need not have died in misery. She was worthy for she was his mother. We are worthy of these blessings because we are sons. Ignorance is robbing Christians of their blessings, because we do not know our throne rights. This book is helping to expose the cruel bondage of Satan, and to open the windows of heaven that such a blessing will be poured out that we shall not be able to contain! (See Malachi 3:10.)

You must walk in the *way*; you must feed upon His *truth*; and you must live the more abundant *life*. God will not make us do anything. He offers, we receive, and we use. Jesus did His part on Calvary, and it was perfectly done. There is nothing for us to do except gratefully take and use.

3

A KINGDOM OF POWER

Jesus said, "*If I with the finger of God cast out devils, no doubt the kingdom of God is come upon you*" (Luke 11:20). The proof of the restored kingdom of God among men was the tremendous demonstration of the power of God over every other power. This power and authority becomes ours as we enter into this kingdom by faith in Jesus as Savior. Not only are we saved from the power and penalty of sin, but we are delivered to a position of authority whereby we can now exercise God's divine power over all other powers, secular, ecclesiastical, or demonic. Jesus ushered in a new dispensation which was so vastly different from that exercised by the priesthood that they failed to see His kingdom at all. Are there not many in our churches like this today?

"*Never man spake like this man*" (John 7:46). "*He taught them as one that having authority, and not as the scribes*" (Matthew 7:29). "*Even the winds and the sea obey him!*" (Matthew 8:27). These were some of the many statements made by those who saw Him minister. They were both astonished and offended. He put them to silence by deeds, not words; "*for the kingdom of God is not in word, **but in power**"* (1 Corinthians 4:20). "*The works that I do shall he do also; and greater works than these shall he do*" (John 14:12). Those who accept the Son and believe on Him are given His authority and His ability to work the works of Jesus right here on earth. This is the plain meaning of the words of Jesus and no amount of apologetics or reasoning will reduce the plain meaning of Scripture. If it is believed and acted upon, the Words become alive, and bring forth results; if they are rejected and not believed, then we continue in our unbelief and misery, even if we claim to be sons of God. James said, "*For so faith, if it hath not works, is dead.... I will shew thee my faith by my works*" (James 2:17–18).

Jesus came first to demonstrate this new kingdom. He then chose twelve others unto whom He gave His authority, and He sent them out to preach that the kingdom of God had arrived, and they were told they had His power and authority to cast out *all demons* and to cure all diseases. (See Luke 9:12). Among these men were fishermen, a tax gatherer, and a medical doctor. They were not required to bring their skills, they were only required to use His authority, and then to expect things to begin to happen. Many have supposed the first twelve apostles were super men. They were in one sense, but first they became humble men to do supernatural miracles of healing. Natural man doing supernatural things. Is this possible for us today? Certainly. Jesus has not changed, neither has His kingdom.

Thank God, this wonderful miracle working ability did not stop with the apostles, neither was it confined to them. God wants us all to exercise this authority today, both men and women, and to do the signs and wonders and miracles that He did when on earth, for today He is on earth in us, members of His body.

It is recorded of these twelve that they departed and were obedient and went into the towns, preaching the gospel and healing *everywhere!* (See Luke 9:6.) No limited gospel here; no system of apologetics; no explanation for failures; and let us note well that this occurred before the cross in time, and before the New Testament Church was born on the day of Pentecost. The cross was the dividing line between the Old and New Testaments, so if these miracles were done on the Old Testament side of the cross, how much more should we be doing these things on the New Testament side? What a challenge we have, to preach and work the works of Jesus.

Jesus was the firstfruit of a new creation. There quickly followed twelve apostles, who were equally quickly followed by seventy ordinary men. These seventy might have had a lesser rank, but they certainly did not have less power or authority! We are not to suppose that they were specially educated for this ministry, or that they were more than a cross section of society of their day. It is not known whether there were any priests or scribes among them, but there is no suggestion that there were. It is more likely that they were tradesmen, craftsmen, and businessmen. To these additional seventy Jesus gave the same authority and power as to the apostles, and they also went forth into different towns and villages. It would seem they were unfamiliar with our modern tools of evangelism, and perhaps it is just as well that they were, for we do not get the same results with these tools as they did with His authority!

"And the seventy returned again with joy, saying, Lord, even the devils [demons] *are subject unto us through thy name"* (Luke 10:17). Now how did they know there were any demons? Today in our churches the word is hardly mentioned, and our testimony would not be received well if we explained that there were billions of them! Jesus Christ healed all who were oppressed of the devil. (See Acts 10:38.) Satan can only oppress, vex, and torment by his demons, he is not omnipresent! They are his agents. The first missionary journey undertaken by this group of seventy, who went two by two into every town, was to seek out those who were sick, and to tell them the kingdom of God had come unto them. The proof of divine healing was the proof of the kingdom!

In November 1963, the writer was privileged to preach in a church seating five hundred people in Atlixco, Mexico. It was a martyr church, having lost nine members over the years who had been murdered by religious fanatics. One man heard the truth of the gospel, of how Jesus promised to heal the sick, and so he went home to his town with the love of God and the authority of Jesus. He was a very unlearned man, as the world counts education. He wanted to establish a New Testament Church (they had plenty of other types of churches) and so he wondered what he should do to make the first move to preach. He felt led of the Spirit to go to the drug store in Atlixco, and saw a man going into it. He asked him if there was sickness in his home and the man said there was. Our brother then told him he knew of a Physician who would heal him and offered to introduce him. The man made his purchase and gladly took this disciple back to his home, whereupon he explained that Jesus was the Physician and proceeded to pray for the sick people in the home, and Jesus healed them all. He then returned to the drug store and found a woman going inside, and he told her the same things and accompanied her back to her home, prayed for the sick, and Jesus healed them all. This method was used to establish a New Testament assembly just a few years ago. After they grew in numbers, the devil stirred up opposition to them, and they were all cast into prison, and then they found to their joy that Paul and Silas were also cast into prison for the same reason, and so they began singing hymns at the tops of their voices (and these people can sing!), and finally the prison authorities could stand it no longer and released them all. They even carried their faith to surprising limits. A man's horse fell sick, so they realized that a horse was also a creature of God and was a blessing to the owner, so they got an extra-large bottle of oil (because the horse was large) and poured it all over the large horse in the name of Jesus, and the horse recovered. This story was told to me by the members of the church, who now worship in a large building without opposition.

When the disciples of Jesus returned with joy, he explained to them the reason for their success. May we not hearken well to what He said? *"Behold, I give unto you **power** to tread on serpents and scorpions, and over **all the power** of the enemy* [Satan]: *and nothing shall by any means hurt you"* (Luke 10:19). *Power to tread*—He was only echoing what the psalmist had said, that which was written on the sacred scrolls of Jewry: *"Thou shalt tread upon the lion and adder: the young lion and the dragon shalt thou trample under feet"* (Psalm 91:13). This was no new doctrine. Jesus was just bringing it up to date, to demonstrate in His dispensation that God is greater than all the works of the devil. Two feet to tread on serpents and scorpions. We do not exaggerate if we suggest that our two feet may be firmly placed upon the sins and the sicknesses that assail us. Moses took the serpent by the tail and it became harmless, and the seed of the woman was to bruise the head of the serpent (see Genesis 3:15), and it is by crushing our foot upon serpents heads that we destroy them. *"Sin shall not have dominion over you"* (Romans 6:14), wrote Paul, because we should have dominion over sin. We must put our feet firmly upon both sin and sickness, the double curse, if we are to live a life of victory every day. It is possible; it is provided for; Jesus' authority is complete, for we are complete in Him. (See Colossians 2:10.)

We also have two hands to hold on to the right hand of God, the holy arm of the Lord (see Psalm 98:1), for it is this holy arm and hand that has gotten us the victory. Hold on tight to Jesus every day, and tread upon Satan every day, and we are safe for time and eternity.

4

HIS AUTHORITY IS FOR US ALL

Some have tried to hide behind the fallacy that Jesus only vested His authority in the twelve apostles. These twelve men were the foundation stones of the New Testament church, and they were built upon Jesus the *cornerstone*. They were the messengers of the new covenant, but the church—the body of Christ—is composed of many members, and these are supposed to exercise His authority each day in their own lives, so that the church shall arrive at a point of having no spot or wrinkle, no sickness nor disease, no defeat nor frustration, and no oppression of Satan. We are told to go on unto perfection!

Before Jesus left this earth, He gave a last commission to His church, which was not a limited dispensational commission, but binding for the whole Christian age or dispensation, which ceases at His second coming, and then we shall be like Him. In Matthew 28:18, Jesus told His disciples that He had been given *all power* in heaven and upon earth. He had earned this power by His death and the shedding of His blood. The whole power of the universe was vested in one Man who rose from the dead. Because of the death of the Testator, the new covenant now came into operation, and as in the case of common earthly testaments, or wills, the Father left all to His Only Son. God in Christ *died*, reconciling the world unto Himself, and in this manner was the new covenant ushered in when Jesus shed His blood and gave up the spirit on the cross, crying *"It is finished"* (John 19:30). Because God died in the person of Christ, it became legally possible for His Son to possess all things, and because He possessed them, He had a free hand to give them to whomsoever He wished. The gifts and callings of God are without repentance, and Jesus His Son was called to bring in the kingdom of God upon earth, to establish it, to order and govern it. (See Isaiah 9:6–7.)

It was this thought that was no doubt in His mind when He gave seventy men His power, for it was His to give by right of sacrifice. When they dared to us it in faith—it worked! This should not surprise any of us, for we have a demonstration of higher authority every day in the police force of any nation or city. When the policeman holds up his hand in traffic, the vehicles grind to a halt, because the authority of the head of state is vested in that policeman's hand! In the British Commonwealth, that authority belongs to the queen or king, and is known as the authority of The Crown. When we accept Jesus as Savior, we accept the authority of the *crown*, for we are a royal priesthood, we are kings and priests, we are of royal family, we enforce the law of Calvary! His crown covers our authority and when we hold up our hands before all the might of Satan, he also must grind to a complete stop. Can we give Satan a ticket? Certainly, we can give him one with these words, *"Know ye not that we shall judge angels?"* (1 Corinthians 6:3), for the day is coming when God will permit us to rule over His kingdom with Him, and to judge righteous judgment in His name. Even demons and Satan are under God's judgment through us. He knows it, but he tries to keep the truth from us and keep us in ignorance, so that we do not exercise this tremendous power. Satan is a defeated foe.

Therefore, it is in keeping with the gospel that we should all understand that we have His authority and that we can use it today. *"These signs shall follow them that believe; in my name shall **they** cast out devils; **they** shall speak with new tongues; **they** shall take up serpents; and if **they** drink any deadly thing, it shall not hurt **them**; **they** shall lay hands on the sick, and **they** shall recover"* (Mark 16:17–18). To whom does *"they"* refer? To those who believe and are baptized—every child of God born into the kingdom of God by the Holy Spirit. The same authority that was vested in the seventy is now vested in all who believe. Hallelujah! To cast out demons, to heal the sick, and to handle serpents as harmless things, just as Moses handled a serpent in Exodus 4:4. Moses' ministry was to deliver the people, and the ministry of Jesus was also to deliver the people, and He handed on His mantle to the church on the day of Pentecost, to continue the same ministry that the people might be delivered today. *"Let my people go"* (Exodus 9:1) is still God's cry to us today. Are we doing it, or making excuses? We have the authority and the power—all that is now required is that we should go forward and prove that it works.

Jesus gives us a parable in Luke 11:21–22. He speaks of a strong man being armed and keeping his palace. Satan is this strong man, and he is described as the prince, or ruler, of this present world in which we live. He certainly does a good job at keeping this world bound in sin, sickness, sorrow, and suffering. But Jesus said that when a stronger man comes, he binds the strong man and delivers him of his captives and takes his house and possessions. This Jesus did at Calvary, and He hands on the keys of the kingdom to all who will take them and go into Satan's strongholds to set the people free. Greater is He who is *in you* than he (Satan) who is in the world. (See 1 John 4:4.) Tremendous truths! We do not call on Jesus to do this for us; this is apologetic unbelief, for He is *in us*, and so we go forward in Him and do it *in His name*. Jesus did not tell His disciples to pray for Him to heal the sick or cast out devils—no—for we read, "As ye go, **preach**, saying, The kingdom of God is at hand [present with them]. **Heal the sick, cleanse** the lepers, **raise** the dead, **cast out** devils: freely ye have received, freely **give**" (Matthew 10:7–8). We are on the receiving end to give to those who are in need.

As we hold on to the right hand of the Lord who got the, victory, then we take from Him the healings, deliverances, and blessings that He commands us to *give* to the people. He broke the bread and gave it to the disciples in the account of the feeding of the five thousand, but they in turn gave to the hungry. *"Give ye them to eat"* (Mark 6:37) still echoes from heaven today. We do not try to be religious and kneel down and ask Him piously to do the giving for us; this is unbelief in action. We take and we give, and there will be many basketfuls left over after our ministry, so that we have a never decreasing supply to give to everyone who is hungry for God and His blessings. While we are busy giving bread, we can eat as much as we like ourselves, so both the giver and the receiver get blessed, healed, restored, and caused to prosper.

Don't limit God. This was why Israel failed to go into a land that flowed with milk and honey. They limited God. In Psalm 1, in simple language we are told that a child of God will prosper in everything that he does. This means material prosperity, mental and emotional prosperity, and spiritual prosperity. We shall have had supplied to us all things needful from the bank of heaven. This is a land that flows with milk and honey; so much milk and so much honey that we shall have twelve basketfuls left over; the cruse of God's blessings will never dry up, the barrel of meal will never cease to supply our needs. Whatsoever we do shall *prosper!* But we have to keep ourselves planted by the river of life that flows through the paradise of God. We must feed upon Him who died for us.

And so the disciples *"went forth, and preached every where, the Lord working with them, and confirming the word with signs following. Amen"* (Mark 16:20). Notice, the gospel ends with *"Amen,"* which means "So let it be." God desires that He should be given an opportunity to do His part by confirming His Word that is preached by us. These signs will be the casting out of demons, the healing of the sick, and the taking dominion over every evil sin and sickness and handling them as dead serpents and scorpions. We preach, and the signs will follow. Amen.

5

JOINT HEIRS

Now we consider the amazing teachings of the apostle Paul in his famous eighth chapter of Romans. If nothing that has been written so far has convinced the reader of our tremendous authority in Christ over all the works of Satan, then let us turn to Paul.

> For as many as are led by the Spirit of God, they are the sons of God (in Greek, *huios*—mature sons). For ye have not received the spirit of bondage again to fear; but ye have received the Spirit of adoption, whereby we cry, Abba, Father. The Spirit itself beareth witness with our spirit, that we are the children of God (in Greek, *teknon*—new born ones): and if children, then heirs, heirs of God, and jointheirs with Christ. (Romans 8:14–17)

Paul started by telling us that as mature sons of God we can be led of His Holy Spirit. This is quite different from being led of the wisdom of man, for being led of the Holy Spirit is the daily experience of an experienced son of God who has grown out of the milk stage to the meat stage. God expects us to be led of His Spirit, which is a continual operation of the gifts of the Spirit in our daily lives. He then proceeds by explaining that if we have fear, we did not get it from God. It is an evil spirit—a demon—sent of Satan, but not of God. What God gives us is the Holy Spirit that adopts us into His family. As a natural born child and a legally adopted child in a family would carry the same name, the same privileges, the same standards of living, the same education, and finally would share in the estate of the father, in like manner we are adopted into the family of God. Jesus becomes our Elder Brother, and He is the only begotten of the Father. He was conceived of the Holy Spirit, but born of a woman. He was the natural born. We are the supernatural born. He was (and is) the only begotten. We are adopted sons. We are born a second time into the kingdom of God, or family of God, by the Holy Spirit. But although He is the only begotten of

God, and we are adopted out of every tongue, tribe and race on earth, we still become sons of God and are reckoned to have all the privileges, all the favors, all the blessings that belong by legal right to the Son of God. He does not withhold anything from those that walk uprightly. He is more anxious to bestow His favors: upon us than we are to receive them. We cannot imagine or understand such blessings, such prosperity, and such health. We are as one in a dream, but the Word of God is true, "*if children then heirs, heirs of God*" (Romans 8:17). As Jesus became the rightful possessor of all His Father's estate, so also do we become heirs of this estate through faith in Christ. We become heirs of the same estate that was given to Jesus because He was obedient unto the death of the cross. He paid for all these blessings in His own blood. They are His and they are ours.

Does He share them with us? No! They are just as much ours as His. Now we find we have become *joint-heirs* with Christ. A jointheir is one who has as much right to the estate as the other joint heir. Now notice that it does not matter how many children apply for the blessing of this New Testament estate, for the *riches in glory* never dry up, and to borrow from John Bunyan's *The Pilgrim's Progress*, "The more we give away, the more we have." There is room at the cross for you, my friend, even though millions have already come. You will never exhaust the riches of glory. They are unlimited.

Jesus has taught us that He inherited all things in heaven and in earth. All power is His, the silver, the gold, the cattle, all are His by right of inheritance, because the Testator died, thus establishing, ratifying, and probating the New Testament. All the promises of the Old and New Testaments are ours today and forever. He does not share or give us handouts; He is the Good Shepherd of the sheep, and we can go in and out and find pasture, knowing the wolf shall not touch us. He is our Brother; we are His brethren. What is His is ours, and all we have to give is ourselves, and He multiplies our station, our prosperity and makes us into kings and priests. From commoners to royalty in one rebirth; no wonder so many find it hard to appreciate such riches and such glory. It seems to take us all so many years to begin to lay hold on this prosperity; we are so used to being stupid, and fearful, and poor, that it takes a little time to realize what the expression "Riches of Grace" really means!

Some may argue that these promises are only to make us spiritually rich, but physically poor. Let us remind you that Jesus told us He became poor to make many rich. (See 2 Corinthians 6:10.) We must be careful not to seek riches as an end, but to seek only Jesus and His righteousness, and He will become our prosperity in spirit, soul, and body. We shall lack nothing, and this is riches indeed. Let us not indulge again in apologetics, but enter into His riches in glory by Christ Jesus. John knew this when he wrote, "*Beloved, I wish above all things that thou mayest prosper and be in health, even as thy soul prospereth*" (3 John 1:2).

David, in Old Testament times, put no division between the blessings of soul and body health. We have two feet to tread upon the two curses of Satan, the scorpion of sin and the serpent of sickness. *"Bless the LORD O my soul, and forget not **all** his benefits: who forgiveth **all** thine iniquities; who healeth **all** thy diseases"* (Psalm 103:2–3). His power and authority is sufficient, for if He puts all things under His feet, then they are under ours also, if we abide in Him, for our feet become His feet on earth, our hands His hands, for our bodies are the temples of the Holy Spirit through which God wishes to manifest the Son by the Holy Spirit

Before we leave this chapter, we must refer again to the apostle Paul, but this time in Galatians 4 where he gives us a double witness to the amazing truth of our adoption into the royal family of God. He begins by reminding us that we were under bondage before we found liberty in Christ, but Jesus redeemed us, or purchased us from this bondage into the glorious liberty of the sons of God. It was as if we were a slave to Satan. Jesus came and paid the price of His own blood and we were set free from the power of Satan, for *"If the Son therefore shall make you free, ye shall be free indeed"* (John 8:36). Thus a complete freedom from want, fear, poverty, suffering, and sickness was given to us as a free gift, and is called the good news of the kingdom of God. Good news indeed. One hundred percent free.

The redemption price at Calvary introduced the law of adoption. By believing with our whole hearts that Jesus paid the penalty of our sins, we were reckoned to have been adopted by God into His family. We may not have been aware of this, nor of the amazing blessings that accrue to us, but God reckoned it nevertheless, and it is as we become aware of this truth that we progressively enter into a greater degree of blessings as we exercise our faith, and our faith only comes through reading and believing the Word of God. Paul concluded therefore, by telling us that we are no more servants, but *sons*, and if a son, then an heir of God through Christ. It is all through our Elder Brother.

Are you *free indeed?*

6

IN HEAVENLY PLACES

In chapter one, we wrote on the creation of man, how God created them, male and female in His likeness, and that they were a little lower than the angels.

Now notice the tremendous change that takes place when Jesus incorporates us into His royal family. No longer a little below the angels, but now lifted up into heavenly places in *Christ*. (See Ephesians 2:6.) It is always necessary to remember that as we abide *in Christ*, we are where He is. He is the New Creation, and we also are reckoned to be a new creation in *Him*. If He is far above all principality and power, might, and dominion, and every name that is named, not only in this world, but also that which is to come (see Ephesians 1:21), then we also are positionally the same when we learn to abide in Him. No wonder Jesus told His disciples that they had power over all the power of Satan. Only Jesus obtained that power through the cross, and now we are jointheirs with Him in His reigning position on the right hand of God, set down in heavenly places. This truth is so amazing, that it alarms the timid who think more of their unworthiness than His worthiness. *"Worthy is the Lamb"* (Revelation 5:12), the angels cried.

Paul understood this truth when he reminded us that we *"wrestle not against flesh and blood, but against principalities, against powers, against the rulers of darkness of this world, against spiritual wickedness in high places"* (Ephesians 6:12). In this verse are enumerated the various degrees of Satanic spiritual wickedness. These are not earthly powers, they are Satanic spiritual powers that control earthly kingdoms, dictatorships, political systems, and religious systems opposed to God. Every evil foul demon working for Satan is mentioned in the categories; Paul said we wrestle with them! Is this a hopeless wrestling match? Are the odds 100 to 1 against us? Do we go in the ring doomed to be pulverized by these powers? No, a thousand times no. We go in to win, to defeat the enemy by commanding, by prayer, by our very attitude of victory. The very moment Satan sees us enter the wrestling ring, he knows that he is defeated before we start. He will certainly put up stiff and stubborn opposition, but he knows he is defeated, and it is only a matter of time before he will throw in the towel, and declare that he can no longer oppress us in the way he tried so hard to do. Our faith must *never waiver*. The battle may be long and fierce, but *"I can do all things through Christ who strengtheneth me"* (Philippians 4:13). Defeat is not in the dictionary of heaven unless it speaks of Satan and his demons. For the Christian there is only victory all the time.

Why is this? It is because our lives are hid in Christ in God, and the wicked one touches us not. Resist the devil and he will flee from you.

When ministering in Uruapan, Mexico, we met a Christian man who was a cotton grower with a farm given to him by the Mexican government. The surrounding cotton farmers resented his faith, for they were fanatical religionists being stirred up by their priests. They commanded this man to leave his farm, and he refused. They came again and ordered him to run and they would shoot him. He refused to run and told them he would stay where God had put him. Then an enraged fanatic said he would shoot him where he stood, so he said, "Go ahead and shoot, but I'm not quitting," at which a strange thing happened; the man began to tremble violently and he turned and slunk away. This is a true story, for the man gave me his sombrero as a memento of a New Testament story. Resist the devil steadfastly *in the faith*. Sometimes we do not wrestle long enough. We give up and *Satan wins*, whereas he was only supposed to lose and run!

We once had an objection raised to this teaching of our authority in Christ. How could we command Satan when even the great and mighty archangel Michael dare not rebuke Satan himself, but said, *"The Lord rebuke thee"* (Jude 1:9)? This is a wonderful and marvelous revelation. Before Calvary man had been created in God's likeness, but a little lower than the angels, including Michael the archangel, but after Calvary we were elevated far above all principalities and powers. Now an angel becomes a ministering spirit to those who are heirs of this salvation. This is where our position of being jointheirs with Christ is rightly understood. Now Michael and other angels become our ministering spirits; now we are recreated *in Christ* to be above them, not a little lower, but now far above. As Michael never sinned, he was never lost, and so does not need a Savior. It was the fallen angels who sinned, and were divested of their spiritual bodies and position. They were cast out into the earth (see Revelation 12:9–10), but Michael is still an archangel and is still subject to obedience of rank. Satan was created the greatest and the most powerful of all the angels, and Michael was next in rank with others like Gabriel, therefore Michael could not rebuke his superior officer, even if his superior officer had sinned. He still carries his rank, for the callings of God are not to be repented of. He now uses this rank to break down God's heritage instead of helping to build it up by ministering to it, as Michael does.

Satan was created as the supreme commander-in-chief of all angelic forces. Before the cross he even entered heaven to give an account of himself as we read in Job 1 and 2, and he correctly reported that he was walking to and fro in the earth, for that was his domain, as prince of this world. At the cross Satan fell heavily again and lost his right of entry into heaven, but he never lost his rank. (See Luke 10:18.) Michael cannot rebuke Satan, but Jesus did, so we can do so today in His name. This is why we cast out demons in the name of Jesus; we heal the sick in the name of Jesus; we can do all things in the name of Jesus, even commanding a mountain to be cast into the sea, and if we do not doubt in our hearts, it will happen! Try it and see! We suggest we begin with mountains of difficulties, before we join forces with the earthmovers!

Thus we find in God's Word that He is imploring us to understand our high calling in Christ.

> That the God of our Lord Jesus Christ,…may give unto you the spirit of wisdom and revelation in the **knowledge of him**: the eyes of your understanding being enlightened; that ye may know what is the hope of his calling, and what the riches of the glory of his inheritance in the saints, and what is the exceeding greatness of his power to us-ward **who believe**, according to the working of his mighty power, which he wrought in Christ, when he raised him from the dead, and set him at his own right hand in the heavenly places, far above all principality…power… might…dominion…name…and hath put **all things** under his feet.
>
> (Ephesians 1:17–22)

This is the position of Jesus Christ today. God put Him there after He raised Him from the dead, and as we abide in Him, and are "*found in him*" (Philippians 3:9) we can exercise all the power and authority that He vests in us, His brethren and sisters.

In Romans 8:11, Paul recorded that "*if the Spirit of him that raised up Jesus from the dead dwell **in you**, he that raised up Jesus from the dead shall also quicken your mortal bodies by his Spirit that dwelleth in you*" (Romans 8:11). The quickening power of the Holy Spirit will be continually restoring our mortal body to health and strength for every time of need in our victorious battle against Satan. Finally, when it is God's time (and not Satan's time) for us to go to be with the Lord, He will quicken our bodies so completely that we will have a body which is from heaven. (See 2 Corinthians 5:1–2.) Every punch that Satan might put into us, in suffering, sickness, frustration, and sorrow, if resisted will be repulsed by the quickening power of the Spirit of God in our mortal bodies. Perhaps this is what Paul had in mind when he wrote that if a believer speaks in tongues he edifies himself, for in so doing he would cause the Spirit of God to move mightily in his mortal body. Paul also recommended to Timothy that he stir up the gift that was in him. Christians today have been far more prone to let the devil stir them up and kick them around, and stamp on them, rather than taking the initiative and stirring up the Holy Spirit in them, going into Satan like a quarterback and knocking him down and casting him out of the way. It may seem a crude thing to say, but either Satan is going to kick you around, or you are going to kick him around. Just choose which position you want to play on this winning team!

7

MIGHTY TO THE PULLING DOWN OF STRONGHOLDS

Not only did Paul tell us we were more than conquerors through Christ, but he also taught us that we are *mighty* to the pulling down of strongholds. (See 2 Corinthians 10:4.) This means that in Christ we are a mighty breed, mighty men and women, strong and invincible; in fact we are like David, and we can tear in pieces the lion and the bear that attack the sheep of God. How wonderful if every pastor could realize this. When the devil comes in like a roaring lion into your assembly, or comes like a strong bear, you are *mighty* to pull the lion and the bear to bits and destroy them before they destroy you or the flock over which God has made you the overseer.

Mighty to the pulling down. Every high and exalted thing that rears its ugly head against Christ and His church is your prey to pull down. It matters not how strong or tall, or how loud the roaring, you are *mighty* to tear it down. It may have taken a week, but Joshua was *mighty* to the pulling down of the stronghold of Jericho. Moses was *mighty* to divide the Red Sea; Caleb was *mighty* to take a mountain; Samson was *mighty* to pull down a house over his head. This *mighty* army of conquering heroes is mentioned in Hebrews 11, and in verses 33–34 it is recorded, "*Who **through faith** subdued kingdoms, wrought righteousness, obtained promises, stopped the mouths of lions, quenched the violence of fire, escaped the edge of the sword, out of weakness were made **strong**, waxed valiant in fight, turned to flight the armies of the aliens.*" *Mighty* men of valor.

Gideon reacted as we might when suddenly God said to him, "*The LORD is with thee, thou **mighty** man of valour*" (Judges 6:12). Gideon agreed to obey God and so was used to deliver Israel. He could have refused, but God reckoned him to be a mighty man of valor nevertheless. God looks upon each one of us as *mighty* men of valor as we abide in His Son. Every one of us is *mighty* in Christ to pull down the opposing forces of Satan arrayed against us so formidably. These forces are arrayed against the church, which is so weak and feeble, when God reckons it to be so strong and mighty. These forces are arrayed against us in our homes and private lives; they affect our spiritual and physical health; we are oppressed and give way instead of resisting and pulling down.

In every major city of the world today, there are gaps where old buildings are being pulled down to make way for new ones to be built. The machines used seem to be mighty to the pulling down of well entrenched buildings, and we are glad to see bright new buildings take their place. The pulling down has to take place before the new creation. All around us we see things that need to be pulled down before God can build a new life, a new home, or new church.

This principle is brought out in Jeremiah 1:7–9. First, God told Jeremiah to speak only what He told him, and that He would be responsible for putting words in his mouth. He was not to be afraid of anyone, however demon possessed they appeared to be, or however politically strong, for God promised to be *with him* to deliver him. God can deliver us only if we do what He commands. Let us not be like Jonah and run away! First, Jeremiah had to *root out*; second, *pull down*; third, *destroy*; fourth, *throw down*. These four necessary things were to utterly destroy and remove all the works of Satan in Israel. Even right down to the basements of Satan's works, he was to root out the last remains of evil. Then when the ground was cleared—after he had been *mighty* to pull down the strongholds—he was to *build* and to *plant*. We find that Jesus did all this perfectly. He destroyed the old order and brought in the New Testament building of God, built of lively stones, without the help of man. The Old Testament temple typified the New, but the Jews clung to their religion so God caused Titus, the Roman general, to come down in 70 A.D. and destroy the city and the temple, which fulfilled Daniel 9:26. The Jews had these prophecies in their scrolls, but failed to recognize their Savior and Messiah when He came. On the cross our Savior utterly pulled down and destroyed all the works of Satan. It is for us today to use our vested authority and do the same, remembering that God is with us, and will deliver us even as He did Jeremiah.

Friends, we *are mighty*. God only sees us as mighty men of valor. We sometimes see ourselves as craven defeated unworthy children of God. The idea seems to be "Satan, if you leave us alone, we will leave you alone." Let us make a pact of peaceful coexistence with Satan. We will give him room if he gives us room. We will compromise and learn to live together. Is this your philosophy my friend? God's Word says, "Go in, defeat him, tear him down, spoil his goods, throw him out, and then build on his territory the kingdom of God with saved lives, delivered human living stones for the New Testament temple." *"Every place that the sole of your foot shall tread upon, that have I given unto you"* (Joshua 1:3).

Not only are we *mighty* to the pulling down of strongholds of Satan, but we are *mighty* to remove the rubble of false teaching, apologetics, and weaknesses. Jesus made this clear by telling us to have the faith of God, and then with this gift of faith, we could cast the mountain into the sea if we doubted not in our hearts. Zerubbabel long ago, when building the temple under much persecution and provocation, commanded "*Who art thou O great mountain? before Zerubbabel thou shalt become a plain*" (Zechariah 4:7). Our *mightiness* is not by natural strength of armies or munitions, nor by national power, but by the *Spirit of God*. It is this anointing that *breaks* the yoke of Satan, and pulls down his strongholds. It is this great baptism of the Spirit that He gives to all who ask Him that gives us this tremendous dynamic power to attack, tear down, break, and subdue the works of Satan. The church has for so long relied on politics, doctrines, bylaws, and committees that it has forgotten to rely on the Holy Spirit alone. The church is supposed to be terrible as an army with banners, a winning army.

This state will not continue. We are now in the time of great revival, the return of the power of God to the church. Multitudes in all denominations are being baptized afresh in the Holy Spirit; a new vision is being seen; a new day is dawning. "*When the enemy shall come in like a flood, the **Spirit** of the LORD shall lift up a standard against him*" (Isaiah 59:19). We shall become a terrible army with banners, we shall hear the voice of the Lord coming to us in the gifts of the Spirit in our churches, the precious charismatic gifts which He is giving back to us, "*And the LORD shall utter his voice before his army: for his camp is very great: for he is strong that executeth his word*" (Joel 2:11).

We believe that this little book will play its part in awakening God's people to realize what giants He has made us, and that the tide of evil has reached its high water mark; it is now time for God to blow with His spiritual wind of the Spirit, through His church, to blow back this tide of evil and set the people free. All over the world nations have received their independence. Africa is wide open to Christ or chaos, which shall it be? South America is seething to bring forth a new order. What shall this new order be, Christ or communism? Asia is wrestling with destiny. Which way will she go? We have the answer. We are God's people, *mighty* to the pulling down of these ancient strongholds of Satan. Our prayers must be the strong believing prayers of faith, our praises full of faith and joy. If we doubt not in our hearts, Jesus said, we shall have whatsoever *we say* and *command*. God will not let the world go to the devil or continue to be ruled by antichrists, as long as Jesus is on the right hand of God and we are complete in Him. We must arise now, and force Satan to give ground by sending the gospel—the full gospel with signs following—to every nation, by evangelist, by literature, by radio.

Let us arise in a newness of faith, buckle on the gospel armor, take the sword of the Spirit afresh, and the shield of faith, and pull down the strongholds of Satan. This is God's hour, and our opportunity. *We are mighty in Him.*

8

WHO ARE WE?

The greatest hindrance to the realization of our tremendous power and authority as Christians is Satan's lie that "we are not worthy." This produces a powerful inferiority complex and freezes us into a state of spiritual immobility. It is the age-old stratagem of Satan to say, *"Hath God said…?"* (Genesis 3:1). Yes, He has said it! We are powerful, we are invincible, we are more than conquerors, we have all the winning weapons; if we fight according to His rules *we cannot lose. It is impossible to lose.*

Who are we? We are *sons of God*, and we are worthy in Him. We repudiate utterly the old lie heard in so many defeated churches that "we are not worthy." What does Jesus say? When He wrote to the church in Sardis, a typical Christian church that exists in our cities today, He said that there were some in Sardis *who were worthy*, and they would walk with Him in white. (See Revelation 3:4.) The reward of walking in white was given solely on the grounds that they *were worthy* because they did not defile themselves. Presumably the other Christians at Sardis would walk in gray, or some other color, and they were not worthy. It is this second class of Christian who is always in trouble and always excusing himself for his troubles, by comparing himself with other "gray Christians" and then postulating the theory that it is normal Christianity to be defeated, to be sick, to be depressed and to be on the losing side most of the time. The "white Christians" know who they are. They do not apologize for God's Word, they believe it and live it, and their lives are blessed to themselves and to all others with whom they come in contact. They do not go down in defeat, for they will not defile themselves with Satan or his works of darkness. They walk in the light as Jesus is in the light. They do not compromise, they resist the devil steadfastly in the faith, and this becomes their normal Christian experience. There is nothing abnormal about continual victory. It is the normal Christian life. Anything less is abnormal or subnormal.

They walk in white for they are worthy.

Yes, we are sons of God, coheirs of Christ, possessors of all His riches in glory as our inheritance. (See Ephesians 1:18.) All the power, strength, might, health, and prosperity sufficient for our needs, is ours now. Coheirs with our elder Brother, *the only begotten Son* of God. Let us hold our heads high. Let us know our calling and our authority and with love and determination put down the works and lies of Satan wherever we find them. This book is dedicated to that end.

Who are we? We are kings and priests. (See Revelation 1:6.) There are some who insist that this Scripture should read, "We are a kingdom of priests." We will not quarrel with this, but the literal Greek tells us we are kings as well as priests. This has a clear meaning. We therefore are divine royalty; our blood has been cleansed by His precious blood and now royal blood is in our veins, carrying the power of the Holy Spirit in every corpuscle. No need to tell Prince Charles that he is of royal blood. He knows it, for his mother is queen. Does God have to remind us that we are royal also, for our Father is God and our Brother is King of Kings and Lord of Lords? Not by right of birth, but by right of adoption, cleansing and sanctification. Notice the wording of Revelation 1:5–6: *"Jesus Christ…hath made us **kings and priests**."* He did this by washing us in His own blood! We realize that it is very hard for humble people born in humble circumstances to realize that Jesus Christ turns them into a king or a queen, but Scripture teaches it, and those who begin to ask Jesus to give them grace and ability to walk as kings and queens find that He does so. One of the fundamental teachings of royalty is that they are always gracious and never make those of lesser station in life feel uncomfortable. Queen Elizabeth's mother, herself Queen Elizabeth, is an outstanding example of royal graciousness, and she is also a Christian lady by confession.

We are also *priests*. Peter taught us that we should offer spiritual sacrifices as priests. We should pray and intercede for others, we should plead the precious blood on their behalf, for the Old Testament priest used to sprinkle blood every day, and so should we—the blood of Jesus. We should offer the sacrifice of praise continually for all His wonderful blessings, not just sometimes, but continually. We should give of our time and talents to Jesus, a tithe of our time, talents and money, and offerings afterward.

Who are we? A chosen generation—regenerated by the Holy Spirit, born again into His kingdom, born to be priests and kings. Chosen and called of God for a high office. A peculiar people; that is, unusual, out of the normal run, regenerate, different; and it must be obvious to all that we are different; not fanatically different, but radiantly different, diffusing the love and graces of God in every breath and look. Having His power and authority. A peculiar people indeed!

Never say, "I can't" again, will you? It is written, *"I can **do all things** through Christ who strengtheneth me"* (Philippians 4:13). There is not one thing you cannot do. You are "the boss." Satan is "the slave."

Satan is very subtle, and he will very easily deceive us, unless we wait on the Lord with the gift of discerning of spirits, and other charismatic gifts He gives to those who are filled with His Spirit. God will show us the stratagems of Satan, and then we can begin to take our absolute authority over him and all his works of sin and sickness, not only for ourselves but for others also.

More than conquerors and mighty to the pulling down of strongholds—is who we are!

ADDENDUM

This book is purposely written in a very positive tone, to help make people realize their tremendous power and authority as sons of God. There may be some who will say, "What about the Scripture *'If we suffer, we shall also reign with him'* (2 Timothy 2:12)"? Is not suffering in God's plan? Yes it is truly, but if you wish to identify yourself with Christ's sufferings, do not include sickness, for He was never sick. He was a Man of Sorrows, acquainted with grief; He was persecuted, spat upon, insulted, and He asked His disciples if they were willing to be baptized with the baptism of His sufferings, and they said they were; and indeed they did suffer with Him. Remember in Psalm 34:19 that though the sufferings of the Christians are many, yet the Lord *delivers* him out of them *all*! Satan will attack, and God will use his attacks to purify and make us more like Himself, but do not wallow in the suffering. Jesus died to redeem us from these things; claim the promises of God and rise out of every battle victorious.

Christianity is not a rest cure. It is not a bed of roses, but a battle to the finish against the world, the flesh and the devil, but in this protracted battle, God expects us to win every round! When we slip we rise and fight on. In the description of the warrior-Christian in Ephesians 6 we are told that having done all, we are to stand and withstand. *No* falling down or being knocked down!

*Thanks be to God, which giveth us the **victory** through our Lord Jesus Christ.*
(1 Corinthians 15:57)

RETURN TO THE PATTERN

CONTENTS

FOREWORD

By way of introduction to the present volume, I would draw the reader's attention to two statements made by the apostle Paul.

In Acts 20:26–27, Paul said to the elders of the church at Ephesus: "*I take you to record this day, that I am pure from the blood of all men. For I have not shunned to declare unto you all the counsel of God.*" These words indicate that a man called to the Christian ministry is under an obligation to declare the whole counsel of God as revealed in the New Testament. He must not permit considerations of personal expediency, or the fear of ridicule or unpopularity, to keep him from this sacred responsibility. He must not suppress, withhold, or distort any portion of the total revelation of God contained in the New Testament. Only by a faithful presentation of the whole message can he fulfill his sacred obligations both toward God and toward man.

Again, in 1 Corinthians 2:13–14, speaking of the gospel message committed to him, Paul said:

> *Which things also we speak, not in the words which man's wisdom teacheth, but which the Holy Ghost teacheth; comparing spiritual things with spiritual. But the natural* [soulish] *man receiveth not the things of the Spirit of God: for they are foolishness unto him: neither can he know them, because they are spiritually discerned.*

Paul said here that there are two different ways to approach the topics with which the gospel deals. The first way, which Paul endorsed, is the spiritual way: to acknowledge the objective reality of the spiritual world, and to be guided by the revelation of this world given through the Scriptures by the Holy Spirit. The second way is the "soulish" way, the way of "man's wisdom"—that is, the approach of what is today called "psychology"—which, literally translated, is "the study of the soul." Paul indicated that these two approaches are entirely different in methods and conclusions, and that to those who follow the "psychological" approach the conclusions drawn from the spiritual approach will appear foolish and unintelligible.

In approaching the present book, the reader will do well to bear in mind both these statements of the apostle Paul quoted above. For this there are two reasons. First, because the topics dealt with in this book have in the past been more or less universally "shunned" by preachers and theologians, and therefore they are unfamiliar to multitudes of contemporary Christians. Second, because these topics are approached in this book from the spiritual standpoint, and therefore—in confirmation of Paul's warning—they are likely to be termed "foolishness" by those whose approach has been conditioned by "man's wisdom" and contemporary psychology.

However, the reader who will approach this book with a humble spirit and an open mind will find in it the key to an effective understanding of a whole area of problems and frustrations for which neither formal Christianity nor modern psychology has any positive solution.

—*Derek Prince*
Cambridge, England

1

FIRST OCCURRENCES

In the present day outpouring of the Holy Spirit upon the church, sometimes known as the Charismatic Renewal, we are beginning to learn a very important fundamental, and yet a simple obvious truth. For want of a better name we call it "The Law of First Occurrences."

The church has tried every human approach and gimmick. Its forms and ceremonies have failed to manifest Jesus Christ in the power of the Spirit. They may have revealed Him in shadows, but not in substance as the Mighty Savior and Healer, the Emancipator of captive humanity.

The Law of First Occurrences can be interpreted to mean that if we return to the way it was done originally, we shall get New Testament results. Many church "leaders" insist that they have improved upon the original methods, but if their "improved methods" could improve greater signs and wonders and miracles of the Holy Spirit today, we would believe them; but as in Israel of old time, it seems they have only brought to birth wind! (See Isaiah 26–18.)

When Jesus, the second Adam, came into this world, He came not to improve it; not to reconstitute or strengthen the sects of the Pharisees and Sadducees, two major denominations of the Jewish church, but to build an entirely new church and new creation. He said, "I will build my church" (Matthew 16:18). He instituted new methods and approaches which were entirely foreign to the Jewish clergy, and they challenged Him, stating that He was casting out demons in the name of Beelzebub; but He simply asked them, "By whom do your children cast them out?" (Matthew 12:27). This was an embarrassing question, because they were so powerless in all their traditions and ceremonies that although they tried as did the seven sons of Sceva, they were not very successful! We think we see a parallel today.

When Jesus is *again* manifest in the power of the Spirit through His anointed body—His true church—we shall again see demons cast out, the sick healed, and great joy in each city. This is the day, therefore, of the renewed outpouring of the Spirit that the church may do what Jesus always told it to do, *"greater works than these shall he do"* (John 14:12).

We want to demonstrate in this book that the casting out of evil spirits should be the normal and expected practice today, not the exceptional. Some frightened pastors suggest unkindly that those who are getting New Testament results today are "demon hunters," implying that there are some who indulge in "spiritual McCarthyism," going around looking for demons everywhere! There are others, equally afraid, who suggest that some have this ministry and others do not, therefore excusing themselves from having any part in it, because it is "not their ministry." As one pastor once said to us, "I have not been called to preach the full gospel." Such terms as "evangelical," "full gospel," are meaningless unless we realize there is only one gospel, which is "called the gospel of the kingdom." It is the gospel in fullness. Jesus emphasized this by saying to the powerless clergy, *"If I with the finger of God cast out devils, no doubt the kingdom of God is come upon you"* (Luke 11:20). It seems from this that the very evidence of the reality of the gospel is in the demonstration of the power of Jesus in His church over the power of Satan in the world and in the worldly church!

As we return to the "first occurrences" of the introduction of the gospel, we find that demons manifested themselves with constant regularity, and were then cast out, first by Jesus and then by the disciples. It was not a question of McCarthyism, but of the inability of demons to hide themselves any longer when in the presence of Jesus. They cried out in terror. It is Christians today who cry out in terror if it is suggested that the church needs delivering from every imaginable bondage of Satan imposed by his demon spirits. In prayer meetings where the New Testament gospel is *demonstrated* as well as preached, we find a mixed reception. There are some who are delighted that such power is given to the sons of men (see Matthew 9–8); there are others who are overcome with shock that their "lovely" Christian friends put on such a demonstration of deliverance when the name of Jesus is used as a command of faith. There are others who speak against it.

Whichever way you look, God is today restoring His long lost power and authority to the church. The sick are being healed, demons are coming out crying with loud voice, and as a few short years ago many cried out against speaking in tongues as the sign of the baptism in the Spirit but later had their spiritual eyes opened, so today many are being taught of the Spirit after seeing a demonstration of the gospel of the kingdom and are rejoicing with us. The members of the true New Testament church are the fingers of God, even as Jesus is the finger of God. Jesus is the arm of God that reaches down from heaven; we are His fingers. (See Psalm 98:1.) We should cast out devils in Jesus' name and set the people free.

The writer tiptoed into a prayer meeting in Brooklyn, New York, in May 1966. There was a young lady seated in prayer, her eyes tight closed. Suddenly she felt a tightening in her throat and her body stiffened; she was entirely unaware of our entry. Several days later she came for prayer. She had a spirit of fear that caused her to be afraid of people. It was a strong spirit and as we rebuked it in Jesus' name her whole body became taut and she trembled from head to foot. After about a half an hour of commanding prayer she was delivered. She was a fine Christian girl baptized in the Spirit.

We were in another Sunday evening service in Brooklyn, about the same time, and in the time of praise a woman commenced to praise God and then her face became terribly distorted, her body was convulsed, her antics were demonic, she wailed, wept, and put on a terrible demonstration and we were able to explain to the pastor that this was a demon "taking over." The writer stepped from the platform and explained to the lady that she needed deliverance from a very strong binding spirit. She was quite cooperative and willing to be prayed for in the after deliverance service. When finally we rebuked this spirit and commanded it to come out of her, the demonstration was tremendous. She was nearly shaken off her seat and beat herself and screamed with a loud voice as the demons left her. After fifteen minutes she was at rest and at peace. She confessed to feeling terrible at times in church, and the fact of the presence of the servant of God in the church was sufficient for the demons to be unable to hold their peace, even as in the synagogue at Capernaum when Jesus preached.

The power of the risen Christ is returning!

2

THE EXAMPLE OF JESUS

After Jesus had been anointed of the Holy Spirit and baptized in water, He was driven by the Spirit into the wilderness for a forty day trial of His faith. As a man, He first had to prove God for Himself; no man can war a good warfare against Satan today unless he has proved God. After proving that He was greater than Satan in all points, He came forth to begin His ministry of preaching and demonstrating the gospel of the kingdom. After being rejected by His own hometown synagogue at Nazareth, He went to Capernaum and taught the Jews on their Sabbath days. They were astonished at His doctrine, for His Word was with power and not as the preaching of their clergy. (See Mark 1:22; Luke 4:32.)

As the second Adam preached, the inevitable happened. Demons hidden for hundreds of years began to manifest themselves and cry out, imploring Jesus to let them alone and not to press them down into the pit before their time. They testified that they knew who He was, the Holy One of God. (See Mark 1:24.)

Here is a case of the Law of First Occurrences. Neither the Jewish clergy nor the people knew who Jesus was, but the demons did! So today! The poor man bound with unclean spirits probably did not know he was vexed by them; he probably was a good member of the synagogue, looked up to in high respect by family, friends, and rabbis alike. He may have held some office in the synagogue, and would never have understood that unclean spirits dwelt inside him. The word "unclean" indicates that they are impure, unholy, and is a generic adjective describing the nature of all demons. It is not recorded what peculiar characteristic they manifested in this poor man. They may have been spirits of infirmity, causing the man to have a physical sickness, or he may have had some quirks or eccentricities in his nature that made him "a little odd" with his friends; they may have been religious spirits simulating a hypocritical spirituality or sanctimonious behavior. He may have had an uncontrollable temper, or may have had a hidden dirty mind. Whatever was their nature we may never know, but we do know they were living creatures, with unclean desires to transmit to humans who would allow them place in their lives. They spoke, they recognized, and they obeyed. An evil spirit must use a body to express his nature.

Jesus did not go into the synagogue "looking for demons." By the gifts of the Spirit He knew exactly how many demons there were in that synagogue; He knew their names, their power, and when each had invaded the lives of the Jews. He also knew that His preaching would stir them up to a fever pitch, for His words would be as smoke in a hornet's nest. Some would let the hornets alone for fear of their sting, and get on with their religious observances, but Jesus came to set people free, for He had told them, *"The Spirit of the Lord is upon me...to preach deliverance to the captives"* (Luke 4:18). The only way to get to grips with these spirits of bondage was to cause them to reveal themselves, and then to cast them out. This He did.

We read that *"Jesus rebuked him, saying, Hold thy peace, and come out of him"* (Mark 1:25.) The unclean spirit tore the man; they often come out tearing through the throat, sometimes bringing up mucous and even causing a bleeding of the throat, and cried with a loud voice in terror and came out. And that was the end of the matter. Jesus had set a man free. This was the first successful encounter between Jesus and Satan after His forty-day trial. He proved what He had come to prove over and over again, that He had not only come to preach and to heal, but to set men free. Those whom He set free were delivered from Satan, because we read, *"And that they may recover themselves out of the snare of the devil, who are taken captive by him at his will"* (2 Timothy 2:26).

There are thousands of people in our churches today who have been taken captive at the will of Satan. The poor lady who was crippled for eighteen years was bound by Satan. (See Luke 13:11–16.) In this story we are told that Satan's binding power was done through a "spirit of infirmity," which translated literally means "a demon of weakness." The cause of the crippling may have been arthritis, but it was a demon. No drugs can destroy a demon, although they may make his work more difficult by drugging sensitive cells of the human body. It is going to take the command of faith in Jesus' name to set the captives free.

Perhaps it may be as well to remember a spiritual truth, not always recognized. All good things come from God by the agency of the working of the Holy Spirit, the third person of the *Trinity*. These are called "blessings" in the Bible (see Deuteronomy 28), but all bad things are called "curses" and come from Satan. There is no third spiritual force other than ourselves, and we are between the good and the bad, between God and Satan, between Holy Spirit and demons spirits. It is only the faculty of our free will that determines which power—God or Satan—will control us! We are not free agents! We are servants to whom we obey *"whether of sin unto death, or of obedience unto righteousness*" (Romans 6:16). We are not free until Jesus sets us free from the thralldom of the devil to enjoy the glorious liberty, of the sons of God.

God works by His Holy Spirit—by Himself. Satan works through the agency of his trillions of demons for he is not omnipresent. He can only gang up with a crowd. He simulates the things of God and is the father of lies and the master counterfeiter. He deceives the Christian masses. It is only as we learn afresh to pray the way Jesus prayed, *against* these foul demon forces, that we are going to bring healing and release to those who are "*oppressed of the devil*" (Acts 10:38). This book will endeavor to show that the cause of evil is spiritual, and the agency of evil is Satan through his demons. We must not therefore be horrified if evil spirits are expelled from sick people when we pray the strong commanding prayer of faith. It may be we shall have to change our theology in the light of a new experience.

In this first case of deliverance in the synagogue at Capernaum, after the initial words of protest were forced out of the throat and tongue of the poor bound Jew, Jesus commands the demons to "hold their peace." We have often heard demons speak and name and number themselves, but we believe it unwise to continue to hold converse with them, although we have proved it is possible. They delight in this, for they can "show off" and also hold on to their bridgehead for a little while longer. Our object is to get them all out as soon as possible. There have been records made in recent years of talking and crying demons which are quite authentic, but we seriously question the wisdom of this, even if the purpose is to draw attention to this ministry of deliverance. These records have a horror fascination, rather like a horror film, and if heard by the frightened and scoffing may actually make room for demons to enter those who listen. The only safe place today is knowing that we are covered in the precious blood of Jesus.

We are warned against holding converse with demons in Isaiah 8:19. When people tempt us to listen to evil spirits in spiritist mediums, or to wizards or fortune tellers, "that whisper and mutter," we are commanded to listen only to the Word of God, not as living persons listening to the voices of "dead" persons. If we go to these séances, we are wide open to possession by demons, for we give ourselves over to them and they will quickly take advantage of this. At the time of writing we have just delivered a lady who held a spiritual office in a Christian church, from very strong demons that tormented her for years, giving her visions, delusions, and prophesies, until she came to our New Testament services in Toronto. These demons could no longer hold their peace and they began to torment the poor lady, and only after several times of forceful prayer were they cast out of her. Even after they were expelled they tried to get back and gave the poor woman a terrible time. It does not pay to disobey God; we lay ourselves wide open to the entrance of deceiving spirits and angels of light!

3

HEALING AND DEMONS

Hard on the heels of this first case of the Law of First Occurrences, we find Jesus coming out of the synagogue into the home of Peter, where the latter's mother-in-law was lying in bed with a very high temperature, probably delirious. It is highly probable that her temperature was 103°F or higher. She was dangerously ill and antibiotics had not been discovered in Jesus' day! How unfortunate! We want to emphasize that this story is told in detail by a medical doctor, Luke! This is no account of an ignorant fisherman, or a proud tax collector, but of a medical practitioner, not given to hallucinations or imaginative guesswork. He does not record that Jesus used a clinical thermometer, nor did He take her pulse. It is not even suggested that He used aspirins!

Here is a first class case of healing of a physical sickness. "A great fever" could be called by so many Greek and Latin names today, many of which seem to have frightful connotations. To see a middle aged respected mother in delirium is not a pleasant sight, and unless we have Jesus as Healer, can give cause to great apprehension. The taking of the temperature and pulse can only add to our anxiety, until we get into such a state that it seems we will call for the doctor, a nurse, and anyone we think can help. We will send round urgently to the drug store to administer drugs to combat the fever, but how many send for Jesus? Even if some remember as a kind of afterthought to call in the pastor *after* the doctor has been and the nurse is in attendance, what kind of prayer can we expect from him? Will it be the commanding prayer of faith as in this "first occurrence," or will it be a prayer for guidance for the medical profession? Will it be a prayer asking God for patience in suffering? Will flowers be sent to soften the pain and weakness and as a demonstration of our love? Will many "get well" cards be sent, some with funny cartoons? Such is the way and understanding of our modern generation—we do everything but "beseeching Jesus" for our suffering relatives! It is time we got back to the law of first occurrences! When we do, we shall get the same results, with no need for "get well" cards, no need for flowers, no need for drugs, and dare we say it—no need for a doctor when we have Doctor Jesus who has never lost a case when He was invited in with faith and love.

If Jesus had no medical means why send for Him? It would be wrong to assume Jesus knew nothing about antibiotics or medicines, for such understanding has been revealed to man by God in recent years. Jesus did not need to use natural means, for He came to use supernatural means. He wants us also to use the same supernatural means today!

Let us note what happened.

First He stood over her. Why? Because this is the correct position when dealing with all sicknesses. God has given His children dominion over all creatures (see Genesis 1:28; Psalm 8:6–8), and all germs are living creatures or organisms. They are not greater than we are in Christ; they are subject to us in Christ. It is as we fear them that we fear Satan's intention. When they attack we should counter attack as Jesus did. Paul the apostle tells us that having done all we must stand (see Ephesians 6:13), never lie down *under it*, but rise up *over* it. The absolute authority given to us all, as we shall read later, is to tread on serpents and scorpions. The position of the believer must always be on top, never underneath. "*The* LORD *shall make thee the head, and not the tail*" (Deuteronomy 28:13). The head is the overseer, the governor, or "the boss." He takes orders from no one; he gives the orders. He commands the germs to leave and die in Jesus' name. Fantastic? The Bible says so! If Satan is commanded to leave a situation as in Peter's wife's mother, and the one who commands it means it, for Jesus said that he shall have "*whatsoever he saith*" (Mark 11:23), then Satan must give way. How much saying have you been doing lately? How many authoritative commands have you been handing out to Satan and his demons in that sickness or domestic impasse? It is as we return to the Law of First Occurrences that we shall get the results of the gospel of the kingdom. God has not changed. We have.

From a standing position of power and authority, Jesus spoke. His Word was with power. He meant what He said and knew Satan would obey. This was the purpose for which He had come into the world; to heal, to set free, and to unbind. Was not this poor delirious woman in desperate need? Jesus *spoke*. He commanded the malign intelligence behind the fever to leave her body! What is this but exorcism? We are so often asked the question, "What is the difference between healing and the casting out of demons?" Frankly, we cannot see a great gulf between them. It seems they are inseparable. It is impossible to rebuke "something" that has no intelligence! We can't rebuke a chair or table; even the spiritists have to use demons for table turning and chair walking in their séances! Tables and chairs just don't walk by themselves! Sicknesses do not just leave by themselves, as doctors know. If there is a primary spiritual cause, then it makes sense that Jesus rebuked the fever! If there were germs or viruses, they could no longer exist where a physical state of health had been created by the Word from Jesus. They must die.

Let us remember that Jesus rebuked the unclean spirits, and they obeyed Him, for we read, *"And they were all amazed, insomuch that they questioned among themselves, saying, **What thing is this?** what **new doctrine** is this? for with authority commandeth he even the unclean spirits, and **they do obey Him**"* (Mark 1:27). To the Jews who went to their synagogue regularly and listened to the vaporizings of their clergy, this was a *new thing* and a *new doctrine*. Their clergy had not taught them about how to heal the sick and cast out demons. Dr. Luke in his younger days had not known either, and he did the best he could to help stricken humanity. He studied medicine, and no doubt ministered to them with compassion, but there are many things that compassion and drugs cannot heal. It was Jesus, the first fruits of a new creation, who brought this teaching of a *new thing* and a *new doctrine*. We do not labor the analogy to suggest we have an exact replica of this situation today! Jesus through His Spirit anointed church—His own body on earth—is now again demonstrating a *new thing* and teaching us a *new doctrine*. The doctrine of Divine Deliverance is being revealed to the church today. Jesus was the first to receive the D. D. of the New Testament Church, but it meant "Divine Deliverance"!

In this second case of "first occurrences," Jesus used the same method. He *rebuked*. The word "rebuke" means to "set a weight upon," and whenever Jesus opened His mouth and commanded Satan, He set a weight upon him, and crushed him out of the situation in which he was discovered. In other words, the rebuke of Jesus was crushing to Satan and his demons and they had only one recourse, to get out as quickly as possible from a place that was no longer comfortable as a resting-place, even though some had occupied the bodies for years. As soon as the spirit of fever had left Peter's wife's mother, she was instantly healed. The force, the oppression, and the tyranny of fever left her; the temperature came back to normal, the pulse steadied. Now today, after such an experience most of us would urge mother to stay in bed until she regained her strength, and many lazy people would prefer to do so. But not this lady; there was much work to do, to keep the home clean, to cook for the men including Jesus, no time for laziness. What a lesson today when many are seeking less work for more pay!

Immediately, she arose and *ministered* unto them. Here was a woman of spirit who believed that we act our faith. Why lie in bed when we are well? Is it not written, *"As thy days are so shall thy strength be"* (Deuteronomy 33:25), and again *"out of weakness were made strong"* (Hebrews 11:34)? Oh, if only we could realize that we can do all things through Christ who strengthens us, and stop whining and grumbling about our weaknesses and aches and pains! Let us rise to our high calling in Christ Jesus.

Now do we pray for the sick like this? Most of us do not pray at all, for we frankly do not think it will do any good. Others maybe do belong to a church that prays for the sick, but how do they pray? Do they pray, like Jesus did in this first recorded case of divine healing after His revealing to Israel? Do we not rather ask Jesus rather timidly to heal our friends? Should we? Should we not rather stand and rebuke the sickness in His name and expect it to leave? Why should we ask Jesus to heal when it is clear from the Bible that He did indeed heal everyone on the cross of Calvary, for *"with his stripes we are healed"* (Isaiah 53:5)—now. What is expected of us is to act as law enforcement officers of the law of love of Calvary.

4

APOSTOLIC FAITH

Following these first two recorded cases of exorcism and divine healing, the same Dr. Luke ends his chapter 4 by recounting that *"all they that had any sick with divers diseases brought them unto him, and he laid his hands on every one of them, and healed them. And devils came out of many, crying out.... And he **rebuking** them suffered them not to speak"* (Luke 4:40–41).

Jesus continued to use the same methods. As He took His dominion and authority over all diseases that were brought before Him, the demons began to manifest themselves. He did not look for them; He did not go on a demon hunt as some suggest we do; they could not bear the crushing weight He brought upon them in their hideouts, in human minds and bodies. Cruel foe indeed, but a conquered one, and Jesus makes us *more than conquerors!* As soon as we realize we are indeed more than conquerors we shall arise to our high calling and do it the way Jesus did it in these first occurrences. We shall then see the church in action as a mighty irresistible force against sin, sickness, and demons. The revival is coming. Our God is marching on today.

Jesus continued to set the captives free; He used the same new doctrinal methods, and multitudes were healed. He called twelve men; no clergy apparently, but fishermen, a tax-gatherer, businessmen, tradesmen, and carpenters like Himself, and He showed them what this new doctrine was accomplishing and they were thrilled. No wonder they left all and followed Him. This was more rewarding than catching fish or collecting taxes. Jesus said He would *make them* fishers of men; what wonder, what thrill, to be used as He was by His Father. Wouldn't you feel like leaving your nets if you could do this? But you can! Glory to God! What had they that you have not got? Had they got better education than we have? Were they PhDs or DDs? Had they better psychology or psychiatry, or were they just ordinary men like most of us? It would seem that higher or lower education really had nothing to do with this ministry.

*"Then he called his twelve disciples together, and **gave them power and authority** over **all devils**, and to cure diseases"* (Luke 9:1). This is very interesting. Even Judas was among them, and some say He was never saved! If an unsaved man could do this, then what about us who boast in being saved? Some of our theology is nonsense!

Jesus gave them all His power and all His authority. What an incredible thing to do; but He was merciful and wanted this great gospel of the kingdom to be preached all over the earth before He came back again. A policeman has the authority of the head of State, and his gun is his power. He has authority to arrest evil doers, and to use force if necessary to make the arrests. The Canadian Mounted Police have a motto; they always get their man, even though they encompass land and sea to do so. They use their authority and their weapons to accomplish it. If we always used this same power and authority, we would always get our man, for Satan and his demons are absolutely subject to us in Jesus' name.

Jesus explained clearly to this motley company that their authority and power was over *"all devils."* We are trying to imagine the reaction in the minds of many of our clergy and church officers today if they received such an authority. In a thousand theological colleges today the students—trainees for the ministry of the gospel—are taught that there is no devil, and obviously, therefore, no demons. What a pathetic and deplorable state our church is in, and no wonder it is bound by the very demons it denies—lying demons, religious demons, unclean spirits, and spirits of infirmity reign supreme because we do not believe there is a devil!

Even if it is allowed in some of the more fundamental Bible colleges and schools that there is in fact a devil, could we get these students to rebuke the devil? Some believe in a personal devil in rather an abstract sense, but they have no knowledge of demons as literal beings who cause sickness and suffering. Their paralytic condition is further aggravated by the stupid theology that a Christian cannot "have a demon." There are six churches in Toronto that pay the salary of a psychiatrist to help their members in their emotional problems! To suggest to a psychiatrist that there are active demons would be to put ourselves, in their minds, in the need of their psychiatry! This is not surprising, for we read and know that psychiatrists are going to other psychiatrists for psychiatric help today. What a mess and a mix up!

Thus our churches are being pastored by men, few of whom would even believe it necessary to rebuke a demon in cases of mental or physical disease. Even many who have received the baptism in the Spirit in recent years are still largely in ignorance about this deliverance ministry, and this book is written with the express purpose of helping all who will be helped and so speed on the way the great message of mercy, that Jesus shed His blood to set the captives free from Satan and his demons. *"If I with the finger of God cast out devils, no doubt the kingdom of God is come upon you"* (Luke 11:20). Are we not glad that Dr. Luke recorded this for us all? He writes so much about the true healing ministry. It is not psychological, it is not philosophical, it is not psychiatric, it is *Jesus!*

The power and authority was vested in the disciples that they might cure diseases! Praise God. What a shout there will be in the camp when the church believes this portion of the words of Jesus recorded by a medical man! The Greek word for "cure" is *therapeuo*, from which we get our English word *therapeutic*. God has given therapeutic ability to His church for all diseases! Of course, the Jews should have, known this for King David long ago used to sing about it, and the singers of Israel used to sing about it too on their feast days, *"Bless the LORD, O my soul, and forget not all his benefits: who forgiveth all thine iniquities; who healeth all thy diseases"* (Psalm 103:2–3). What a mutual benefit society is the church of Jesus Christ, equipped with total therapeutic qualities and the most powerful disinfectant against disease known to God and man, the blood of Jesus Christ.

We cannot separate the power and authority over all devils, from the ability to cure all diseases. They go together. It is one gospel of the kingdom; one is not exorcism and the other healing; for the root word for *"authority"* is *exousia*, to which "exorcism" bears a strange resemblance. To exorcise is to use divine authority. To use divine authority is to cure diseases. We do not pray and ask Jesus to do it, we use the power and authority and do it in His name. Yes, demons will cry out against this practice, but we will rebuke them and command them to hold their peace and put a crushing load on them!

The trouble begins when the opposition comes from one's own family or pastor or church. We are told these things are divisive. Yes they are. *"Suppose ye that I am come to give peace on the earth? I tell you Nay; but rather division: for from henceforth there shall be five in one house divided, three against two, and two against three"* (Luke 12:51–52). As soon as any of us go and exercise this power and authority over all devils, we shall be in trouble from carnal Christians and others motivated by Satan! No wonder Jesus spoke to His beloved Peter and said, *"Get thee behind me Satan"* (Matthew 16:23).

This is total opposition. It is total war. As soon as we open our broadsides against sin and sickness in our church or home, we really are going to smoke out demons in most unexpected quarters—sometimes among these nearest and dearest to us! There is only one thing to do, having done all to stand. Stand for truth, for the Word of God; stand for one's convictions in the Holy Spirit, stand up for Jesus and be counted. There is none who can harm you anyway!

Jesus gave a commission to these first twelve. It was to go from city to city and abide in the homes where the friendly lodged them, and then *to heal the sick* in these cities, and say *"The kingdom of God is come nigh unto you"* (Luke 10:9). It was the same message of Jesus; the casting out of demons proved the reality of the kingdom among them. It will prove the reality of the kingdom in your city and in your church too.

Matthew gives us a graphic account of this commission to the twelve. *"As you go, preach, saying, The kingdom of heaven is at hand.* **Heal** *the sick,* **cleanse** *the lepers,* **raise** *the dead,* **cast out** *devils"* (Matthew 10:7–8). It is not enough to preach, unless we also do the rest. We do not ask Jesus to do the preaching for us, unless we believe that we are the instruments to bring forth the inspired word of God, which we are indeed; we must believe that we are instruments in His hand, the very fingers of God, to heal the sick, to cast out devils, and to manifest the resurrection power of God.

5

CHRISTIAN EVANGELISM

We now come to the first great mass evangelistic invasion of enemy territory. Jesus was teaching and entrusting the emerging church to do the same thing that He had done at Capernaum, in the same way. As He had demonstrated the Law of First Occurrences, now He wanted men to prove to themselves that they could do it too, but only by using the same methods.

This is the First Occurrence of Christian evangelism! It will do us all good to compare our methods with theirs; to see how our evangelistic workshops, seminars, and retreats compare with the simplicity of Christ's leadership and teaching. We shall surely be amazed at the differences! It seems to us that man has tried to create a church machine, and then to use it for the purpose of saving souls; he has formed committees, boards, and rules, and the demons never came out and the sick were not healed! Let us remind ourselves again that Jesus also said He would build His church by His Spirit, by His miracles, and by His healings; He did not talk about it—He did it!

First Jesus, then the twelve, and now the seventy. This new creation church was spreading. Jesus wanted to share His blessings, and take away Satan's cursings on a worldwide scale; first in Jerusalem (our own home church), in Judaea (our home town), in Samaria (home missions), and unto the uttermost parts of the earth (foreign missions).

"The LORD appointed other seventy also, and sent them two and two before his face into every city and place, whither he himself would come" (Luke 10:1). Here were thirty-five teams; they were not equipped with modern tools of evangelism; they just had the authority and power that Jesus vested in them, and they went forth to *use it*. To use authority and power is something brand new for Christians today. It is a *new thing*, a *new doctrine*, and it produces *new results*. These seventy were not learned theologians. We really are not told anything about them—just *"other seventy."* We

can assume they were a cross section of Jewry, many trades and professions represented. Their theological knowledge was very little to nil; their medical knowledge likewise nil; their psychiatric understanding nil; their psychological approach poor; they were too blunt and direct. They went straight to the towns and villages and asked whether there were any sick and suffering people. Of course there were, there always are in every community, and our churches are full of them! It seems the people readily brought out their sick when these disciples explained they had come to heal them in Jesus' name!

Jesus gave His disciples their commission—how simple, and how easily the church has missed it in the innumerable workshops of evangelism. "**Heal the sick** *that are therein, and say unto them, The kingdom of God is come nigh unto you*" (Luke 10:9). Again we find the practical evidence of divine healing and deliverance was to be the proof and demonstration that the kingdom was in their midst. This is reiterated with a constancy that cannot be overlooked. We have preached the kingdom of God, but we have not proved it or demonstrated it. Can we imagine a seminar or workshop today where the simple commission was repeated for our evangelists today? We are not trying to be unkind in making such comparisons, but where were the decision cards, where the literature explaining the way of salvation (they demonstrated it), where the discussion of church preference? These tools, though useful can be substituted for the real thing. Heal the sick, cleanse the lepers, cast out demons. The words were echoing in the minds of the seventy and these were the only things they knew how to do, for they had watched Jesus do these things, He had been their example, their Teacher, their workshop; they must do it His way or not at all.

What a revolution this will create in the kingdom of God when we once again start doing it His way. Many are starting today, and soon the church will hear about it. In February 1966, the author was greatly privileged to speak before an assembled company at a banquet of the Full Gospel Businessmen's Fellowship in the staid city of Boston, Massachusetts. By God's arrangement we had full liberty to preach and demonstrate as we always endeavor to do, wherever God sends us. A separate room was given us in this public restaurant, to heal the sick, and to cast out demons! About twenty-five to thirty came in for prayer. Helpers were with us who knew this ministry, and explanation was given to them of what might be expected by previous results. Of course the results were the same! Commanding prayer was made as we walked through the assembled company; our workers were pleading the blood of Jesus audibly, and almost at once demons began to manifest themselves. Students were there who fell to the ground groaning "lust," as these unclean spirits were violently ejected in Jesus' name. A television announcer joined in the fray, and prayed for others. The noise was tremendous; demons screamed, talked, cried out, and fought back, but they all came out! One woman out from a mental home was there; she had been insane.

Three ladies from our Toronto church started to pray with her; the demon talked back, told how many there were in the woman; they argued and cursed and even said they would get back after being cast out. There were apparently twelve, and all these were cast out, and within a few minutes, they rushed upon her trying to get back in. The change on this woman's face when deliverance came was wonderful to see. While all this was going on, others were being baptized in the Spirit and speaking in tongues as the Holy Spirit came in. This is the order that God has shown us today, first get rid of the unclean spirits and then invite in the Holy Spirit, to fill up every area previously occupied by other spirits.

How do we do it? It is simple; gather a company of your friends who are in need of deliverance and start commanding the sickness to leave their bodies in Jesus' name and you won't have to look for demons! They will soon manifest themselves.

The thirty-five teams eventually returned and met Jesus, who was waiting for them expectantly to hear their report. It burst forth from them with uncontrolled enthusiasm, "Lord, even the devils are subject unto us through thy name" (Luke 10:17). There was great joy!

A few days before the account given in the preceding paragraph we had been ministering in a seminar at a retreat in New Hampshire, with similar results. A Spirit-filled Presbyterian minister was helping us, and so great was the power of God, and so many were getting delivered, that this staid Presbyterian started to do a holy dance in the Spirit! Joy is infectious, so it is not surprising that the seventy returned with effervescent joy!

It must surely be clear to us that Jesus had not given His followers long and detailed theological explanations of the demon world of fallen angels. Certainly He had not taught them against demons and told them to "be careful," and see that they did it the tactful, loving way, and not to expect any indecent excitement or noise, and for that matter not to expect too much. There are no inhibitions in total war. War is ugly, it is loud, it is messy, and Satan's oppositions will not be with kid gloves or good manners. The *stronger man* in each of us must first bind the *strong man* in the poor sufferer, a brother or sister human, and cast him out ruthlessly! The battle is for the strong, not the timid.

When these glowing, victorious disciples returned, Jesus underlined His previous commission. He put first things first and pointed out that their first object was to rejoice because theirs and many new names were written down in the Lamb's Book of Life in heaven. He said, "Behold, I give unto you **power** [in Greek, *exousia*] to **tread** on serpents and scorpions, and over **all the power** [in Greek, *dunamis*] of the enemy: and nothing shall by any means hurt you" (Luke 10:19). Jesus was telling them to understand that His power of exorcism was absolute and could deal with the most dynamically powerful demon out of hell. There could be no exceptions. As soon as we today try to teach this deliverance ministry we are met with frank dismay and fear; fear of the unknown; but Jesus closed His commission with the comforting words *"**nothing** shall by any means hurt you."* It is for us to believe His Words and to go out on a limb and prove them! The author has been proving it for nearly twenty years and it is getting easier all the time as more prayer ascends to God to break down the fearsome opposition of Satan. The deliverances are increasing.

6

BELIEVER'S EVANGELISM

We are all priests. There may be leaders, the apostles, prophets, evangelists, pastors, and teachers, but every believer is a priest equipped to offer spiritual sacrifices to God. (See 1 Peter 2:5.) There is neither male nor female in the body of Christ (see Galatians 3:28), and all may heal the sick and cast out demons. This truth is bitterly opposed in some theological circles, for they ignorantly hide behind the cliché that only certain people are specially anointed for this ministry; and whereas we agree that God has to raise up teachers and demonstrators, it is only that the flame may catch to the other believer-priests. How can we bring deliverance to the masses today unless God uses believer's evangelism? The principle of one, or two, for one seems to be in God's perfect pattern. We believe it best to keep these times of exorcism and violent prayer to prayer rooms in churches under the oversight of one set of God. The Bible is clear on this point, *"And God hath set some in the church"* (1 Corinthians 12:28). These are charismatic ministries for the building up of the church. Furthermore of the believer-priest, we read that Jesus Himself has washed them in His blood and *made them* priests. (See Revelation 1:5–6.)

The excuse that only certain people can cast out demons is not born out by Scripture. If we go back to the original first commission to the church at large, in contradistinction to the same commission given to the twelve and the seventy elders of the church, we find that the power and authority to cast out devils was vested in "all who believe." This is a good qualifying clause, because most Christians are fearful and do not really believe! My wife and two lady helpers were not aware of this apologetic theology when they went in as a team and brought deliverance to the insane woman at Boston. We were far too busy helping others, both to deliverance and into the baptism in the Spirit, even to notice what the ladies were doing until it was all over, and then they explained that even insane demons were subject to them in Jesus' name. Jesus was now teaching us that the commission must pass on from ministers, to elders and then to the members of the church.

In Mark 16:16–18, the first qualification was that a believer must be baptized, and that he was to be a believer in the whole gospel of the kingdom of God, not a believer in a watered-down, powerless gospel of theology. This type of believer, who is now rapidly multiplying, was to cast out devils and heal the sick. He was not to argue on finer points of theology or dispensationalism, not on whether a believer is baptized as a baby or as a believer. We feel that a *true* believer will not be in doubt on these issues for the Holy Spirit will guide him and teach him, even into all truth!

We are regularly baptizing men and women today who are receiving enlightenment and understanding on what Jesus meant when He said, *"He that believeth and is baptized shall be saved"* (Mark 16:16). What a depth is in this word *"saved"*! In the Greek it is *sozo*, which is variously translated in the Bible healed, set free, made whole, and delivered. Our theology has lost these meanings in its desperate effort to get people to heaven, even before their time, and while we must strongly underline the forgiveness of sins, without which we cannot maintain healing of other troubles, we must never overlook the usual meanings of *sozo*!

Jesus said to His assembled disciples, above five hundred in number, that He gave them unlimited authority and power to cast out devils, to speak in new tongues, and to heal the sick, and showed that in so doing close contact with evil things like poisons and serpents would do them no harm. This is only a repetition of what He had given the seventy! Jesus did not change His plan, and He has not changed it today. It is when we dare to put this plan into effect that we get the same results. Of course, we grow in knowledge and understanding by experience. Each case seems slightly different, but the principles governing divine deliverance are all the same. As we handle such tremendous authority and power, we grow in boldness, and our natural timidity vaporizes away and consequently we get better results as we force our way into the dark recesses of Satan's kingdom of darkness.

The first of the five signs or evidences that the gospel of the kingdom had come to them and to us, was the casting out of demons. It seems obvious to us that Jesus had to put this first, because it is as we drive forward against sin and sickness that we discover the underlying cause of these troubles. Many soldiers in battle have been amazed to come up to enemy trenches that they had not seen in their drive forward, and suddenly the enemy threw up their hands in surrender. Before coming upon the trench no enemy could be seen, but his bullets could be felt. The effect of his warfare was evident, even if he remained hidden, and he would remain hidden until we actually invaded his trench with our weapons blazing. What are our weapons? The name of Jesus, and the blood of Jesus, for they overcome him (Satan) with the Word and with the blood. (See Revelation 12:11.) We use the name of the living Word (the Logos) and the power in His living blood today. Thus do we overcome every entrenchment of Satan and his demons spirit soldiers.

Great emphasis today is being placed upon the second sign of speaking in tongues. More and more are understanding that every Christian may and should speak in tongues for private devotions, quite apart from other usages in the ministry. Now we encourage both men and women to receive the baptism in the Spirit with the sign of speaking in tongues, and this is happening in every denomination today in an increasing crescendo, in spite of satanic theological oppositions. No doubt there are still some who try to tell us that not all Christians have to speak in tongues. Of course we do not have to do anything; it is by grace and not by law. We can and may speak in tongues if we desire to with all our hearts. For one who speaks in tongues daily, we can thoroughly recommend that you go in under the blood and attack the devil in any entrenchment in your home or church. The author has prayed for many pastors and brought them deliverances, some spectacular! Two pastors who came to us were saved from suicide and other spirits. Satan tries to discourage pastors, who are precious men in God's sight. If we can get one pastor delivered, we can get hundreds more delivered through their ministry! Pastors are tremendously open to temptations that do not assail their flocks. Pastors can fall easily into sin, unless we pray for them. Never criticize a pastor; just pray with him and encourage him. Aquila and Priscilla did that with tremendous results to Apollos, who then became the leader of the Ephesian New Testament Apostolic church. Pastors are growing hungry today. God is making them hungry. God is moving by His Spirit with refreshing winds of new light and deliverance.

In the same manner therefore as all Christians may speak in new tongues, so also may they cast out demons and heal the sick. This is a church commission for the whole body of Christ, and the leaders in the five ministry gifts are supposed to be setting the pattern for the flocks.

The fifth sign is that of healing the sick. It seems that Jesus put this last in order, for if we do it the way He commissioned we will find indeed that we have healed the sick in His name. We tend to forget the first sign and then ask Jesus to heal, putting the responsibility on him because of our failure to accept the responsibility from Him!

They went forth and preached everywhere, the Lord working with them and confirming the Word with signs following. (See Mark 16:20.) They did the preaching, they did the rebuking, they gave the commands, and Jesus did the rest. His resurrection power flowed through their ministry bringing healing and deliverance to the captives; the normal was that signs followed in every meeting! We are convinced that as the number of ministers and laymen bring this true New Testament ministry to bear against sin and sickness, there will be a toppling over of Satan's strongholds. There are still too few of us, and each one that enters into the flight will make it easier for all the others. What we have seen is truly amazing, but we desperately need more volunteers, more recruits, and then we can expect to see greater works done in Jesus' name.

We pray this book may help to sound the clarion call.

7

NEW TESTAMENT EVANGELISM

Although the scope of this book is to demonstrate a divine principle, that if we return to the methods used by Jesus and His early disciples we shall get commensurate results, mention should be made of the Law of First Occurrences in the matter of the baptism in the Spirit, which is given by Jesus to His disciples so that they also may minister in the power of the Spirit in this day.

The original descent of the Spirit upon the waiting company of 120 in the upper room is the all-time precedent and pattern. It is the first occurrence of this miracle. We do not have to enlarge, for we know the result was that these 120 men and women, including Mary the mother of Jesus, all spoke in tongues, many of which were recognized and understood as known tongues by the Jews visiting Jerusalem for the Feast of Pentecost. Experience shows that wherever Christians today are hungry and not prejudiced by false theology, they invariably receive the baptism in the Spirit according to the Pentecostal pattern. It seems that any other experience, such as anointing or breathings of the Holy Spirit, must not be confused with this initial outpouring at Pentecost. (See Acts 2:1–4.) Any child of God may receive many prePentecostal visitations of the Spirit, but a serious mistake is made if these are called "baptisms in the Spirit." Similar experiences may also be received after a child of God has received a personal Pentecost. In John 20:22, Jesus breathed upon His dejected disciples and said, *"Receive ye the Holy Ghost,"* and thus they received an overwhelming anointing which must have felt a most invigorating experience, but these same disciples still had to come to their personal experience of the baptism in the Spirit at Pentecost.

The initial outpouring at Pentecost was confirmed to Jews only, and the first occurrence of this miracle upon the Gentiles was similar. In Acts 11:15, we find the apostle Peter explaining to his other apostolic brethren that the Holy Spirit fell on the Gentiles *"as on us* [Jews] *at the beginning."* The Scripture is quite clear as to what happened among the first Gentiles to be baptized in the Spirit, *"For they* [the Jews] *heard them* [the Gentiles] *speak with tongues"* (Acts 10:46). Peter was definite in, his reference to the *"beginning,"* showing that he tied the initial occurrence of the baptism in the Spirit upon the Jews to the initial occurrence upon the Gentiles. He did not look back before Pentecost for a *"beginning."* The Day of Pentecost was the beginning of the empowered church, even as the coming of the Spirit upon Jesus at Jordan was the beginning of His supernatural ministry. Many today begin before the beginning. This results in powerless ministry and a powerless church. All the apologetic theology of man will not produce the power that comes from a personal Pentecostal encounter with the third Person of the Trinity.

Again, according to the Law of First Occurrences, we come to the initial outpouring of the Spirit upon a local congregation. This occurred in Acts 19:1–6, when the Ephesian church was born in the midst of gross idolatry. Nothing could stand up against the goddess Diana, with all the demon power associated in her worship, but the baptism in the Spirit given by the resurrected Jesus. The reason that heathen idolatry satisfies millions today is because there is a powerful demon behind every idol, statue, and picture that is worshipped. God knew what He commanded when He forbade such practice. Satan can and does answer prayers if they are prayed to him through the idol with faith. His power is limited, but the power of the Holy Spirit is unlimited. The baptism in the Spirit makes all the difference!

The equipping and creation of this New Testament Ephesian church is described graphically. *"And when Paul had laid his hands upon them, the Holy Ghost came on them; and they spake with tongues, and prophesied"* (Acts 19:6). We believe that this is the all-time pattern for every local congregation of believers, even if it is necessary to baptize some of them in water according to the Scriptural mode, sometimes called "Believers' Baptism."

The first account we have of New Testament evangelism is found in Acts chapter 8, when Philip, created an evangelist by the Holy Spirit, went down to Samaria and preached Christ. How simple. He preached Christ, not about Him, or apologizing for the miracles that He had done, but He preached *Christ.* Such preaching soon drew fire from Satan, as had occurred when Jesus went into the synagogue at Capernaum. Christ fully manifest, through His body, will always produce a satanic manifestation. These first occurrences do not change in God's mind of purposes. It is we who change them, or think we do, and so we bring forth a powerless church.

If all evangelistic campaigns throughout the world were conducted as the Holy Spirit and Philip conducted this one at Samaria, we would have worldwide revival overnight! The people gave heed to Philip, then they heard and saw the miracles that Philip did in their sight by using the power and authority vested in him by Jesus. It was not necessary to "look for demons," they could no longer hold their peace; they started to scream, and tore the victims, and were violently expelled from their throats. Not just a few but many. It was a scene of unqualified pandemonium, and both Philip and all the people were filled with tremendous joy at such a spectacular! This is the kind of "extravaganza" that local churches need today—not gimmicks.

We are glad that this agrees with the Law of First Occurrences' The preaching of Christ by a Holy Spirit baptized evangelist, who had been a deacon a short time before, caused a multitude to *hear*, the commotion caused by demons as they were violently ejected by exorcism in the name of Jesus. If Philip could do it by simple obedience to Jesus' teaching and example, then should not we also do it the same way? We guarantee that our congregations would hear a commotion! It is sometimes reasoned that if demons are to be cast out as a kind of last resort, then this special ministry should be done in private. Now we fully agree that where individuals are to be ministered to by counseling and prayer, this would best be done in the prayer room of a church. If such a ministry is done in private homes, the resultant noise created by the demons might well be misunderstood by neighbors who might call the police. We have known of such cases. It has been found that demons do not stand on ceremony when overcome and cast out. They object very vociferously and cannot be restrained, even if we should desire to restrain them. However, in large evangelistic campaigns where Christ is preached, it will not be possible to control some of the manifestations of demon power being stirred up to be summarily dealt with. In campaigns in Sao Paulo, Brazil and Buenos Aires, Argentina, we have seen the results of the commanding prayer that rebuked sickness in the audience! Some started to scream, others fell to the ground, and the noise can be imagined! It has been found in Latin countries that when the people see and hear the real thing, they are not afraid, but they immediately gather round and start rebuking the demons in Jesus' name in their own languages. This is a wonderful sight! These people have been cruelly oppressed by religious leaders for centuries, and the time of their visitation is at hand. Let us see that we know when our day of visitation has come in the English speaking nations. We may take advantage of it, not only to deliver the people in our own churches and Christian societies, but then to take it to all the countries of the world. (See Luke 19:44; 1 Peter 2:12.) This is God's day of visitation and more and more are going forth according to the pattern in Samaria.

It is good to notice that as soon as the multitudes heard and saw the miracles that Philip did, Satan had his man there to confuse the truth. The people said of Simon the Sorcerer that he was *the great power of God* (Acts 8:10). He himself had advertised his ministry by claiming to be a "great one." He knew his power and the people also saw and recognized that he had something that neither they nor their clergy had. He had demon power. This is real. There are many who use this occult power in our churches today. We remember speaking at a retreat of the Anglican Church in Ontario on the ministry of Christ at the request of one of the Anglican clergy.

Imagine our horror when we learned that the speaker to follow us was a "Christian medium." Apparently it was necessary for this lady to have certain music played on a tape recorder before she could go into a trance, and for the familiar spirit to take control. Quite unknown to us, the preaching of Christ with emphasis on the power in His precious blood, had caused the tape recorder to fail to function. An urgent SOS produced another recorder from a visitor's car, but it also had been affected by the power of the Holy Spirit in the presentation of Christ. It refused to work and the "Christian medium" was unable to minister at all. This is a true authenticated story. The ignorance of many seeking understanding of the power that is lacking in the church is appalling. Imagine inviting demon possessed persons to demonstrate in a seminar of "spiritual healing." We agree it comes under this heading, but which spirit is being manifested? The Holy Spirit of God or an evil spirit from hell? Never forget that Paul warned us all *"And no marvel; for Satan himself is transformed into an angel of light. Therefore it is no great thing if his ministers also be transformed as the ministers of righteousness"* (2 Corinthians 11:14–15).

Yes, Simon the Sorcerer had something to offer the people and bewitched them until Philip and the Holy Spirit came and cleared up the spiritual mess in Samaria. Peter, with no diplomatic niceties of the clergy, said to him, *"Thy money perish with thee…. Thou hast neither part nor lot in this matter for thy heart is not right in the sight of God"* (Acts 8:20–21).

Today Satan is doing his best to counterfeit the true ministry of Jesus and to confuse the people. He cannot continue forever for the day will declare it. Satan's time of exposure is at hand.

8

EVEN HANDKERCHIEFS

We would not wish to give the impression that every physical infirmity is caused by an indwelling evil spirit. It is easy to gain this impression, since large numbers of sicknesses are caused by demons. Obviously where a weakness has been left in a child caused by destruction of bodily cells, or some deficiency caused before birth or at birth, it would be necessary to ask God for a creative miracle. It seems that a higher order of faith is necessary for this type of miracle, but nevertheless, with God all things are possible, and we must not limit God.

In the case of the writer however, a childhood attack of hepatitis had left a weakened liver with resultant recurring headaches and stomach upsets. This was not healed until some friends gathered round and spent about twenty minutes rebuking the spirit of infirmity that had taken occasion to lodge in the diseased liver at the time of the attack. This spirit of infirmity stayed in the liver for forty years until cast out. We need to remember also that where a spirit of infirmity is dislodged from a part of the body, healing processes must take place progressively after the spirit has been cast out. Many feel that an instantaneous miracle should always take place. The ejection of the primary cause is a miracle in itself, but it may be that certain cells have to grow again in the body to replace damage done. This may take many months or even years, and helps to keep the person from backsliding, while the Lord restores. It is a very regrettable fact that far too many people who have been healed or delivered grow careless in their allegiance to the Lord, and in such a case it is not surprising if the cause, a spirit of infirmity, or unclean spirit, comes back again with others to torment. This seems to cause grave concern and confusion in the minds of Christians, but we always remember the salutary warning given by Jesus when He said to the man whom He healed at Bethesda, *"Behold, thou art made whole; **sin no more**, lest a worse thing come unto thee"* (John 5:14). We not only have far too many carnal Christians in our churches, but also far too many careless backsliders. A definition of sin is "all unbelief," and we therefore must be very careful to continue to believe after we are healed, otherwise we might get worse. The fact of sickness coming back does not disprove the whole truth of divine healing, it merely confirms the words of Jesus that we must follow Him, for He said, *"My sheep hear my voice…and they follow me"* (John 10:27). We believe that it is incumbent upon all who receive healing from Jesus to live closer to Him than they did before.

In our experience many people who have been delivered from various types of evil spirits have later had to have another time or times of prayer to dislodge another unwelcome visitor that came upon them because of grumbling, criticizing, or just giving place to the devil.

Have you noticed the words of Acts 19:11–12? For many years their import was not seen. We read it like many other parts of the Bible, but we had never grasped its full significance. It is a very common thing to ask preachers and evangelists in the healing ministry to send a prayer cloth or handkerchief. Other tokens are sometimes used like an apron and any piece of clothing. The reason for this is, of course, that in the early church the people were so full of joy and expectancy that their faith was very high, and somebody hit on the bright idea of bringing portions of the clothing of sick persons in lieu of the person, and touching these to the body of Paul and then expecting Jesus to honor faith, which He did, and He healed their friends and relations at a distance. Some have been afraid of this because it seems to them that this can lead to idolatry, and the cloth becomes a talisman or juju. Of course, anything that is not of faith is sin (see Romans 14:23), but we believe that where this practice is carried out with the same degree of faith that was in the early church, we shall get comparable results.

If we can take this as a case of the Law of First Occurrences, we should expect the same things to happen as we do this today. What did happen? It is recorded, *"And God wrought special* [unusual] *miracles by the hands of Paul: so that from his body were brought unto the sick handkerchiefs or aprons, and the diseases departed from them, and the evil spirits went out of them"* (Acts 19:11–12). From the time that the pieces of clothing touched the sick bodies, the sicknesses departed, and the primary causes of the diseases—demons—went out. The pattern introduced by Jesus, practiced by the twelve and the seventy, and given as a Great Commission to the church, was now working through exceptional faith in Paul's ministry. Many people have testified that suddenly they began to tremble and sweat after prayer, and there was an inward struggle and then suddenly they felt better. They were not aware of what was happening, but in actual fact there seems little doubt that as the disease departed, the evil spirit went out and they felt it go. The writer was healed of the tobacco habit in 1939, and literally "felt" the habit go. There was an unclean spirit at work which departed and there was no more habit left after that. It had vanished! We did not know at that time that smoking (or any other filthy injurious habit) was connected with a demon. We were to understand this many years later when God began to open our eyes to these truths.

We would not want to frighten anyone by these disclosures, but as they have been made known to us by practical experience in the commanding prayer of faith, what can we say but that this is of God. If He is working this way, and we both hear and see the miracles that happen today, and see demons come out crying with a loud voice, even speaking and objecting, we would be remiss in our testimony if we kept silent. Wherever God enables us to bring these truths publicly, the results have always been the same.

In Dennison House, Victoria, London, England in May 1965, right in the heart of the West End of London, the capital of the British Commonwealth, the first few we prayed for fell to the ground and writhed as evil spirits came out, including epilepsy and spirits causing homosexuality. We did not instruct them to behave in this alarming manner; we just rebuked their troubles in Jesus' name and the evil spirits reacted with violence. The people were amazed and said they had never seen it like this before! Sometimes there is a delayed reaction. In prayer lines, we do not have time to stay with those for whom we pray; we can only lay on hands, take dominion over the sickness or mental affliction, and command it to come out and leave in Jesus' name. Often it will do just that, several hours later, and a fit of vomiting, or heavy coughing may come in the middle of the night as the evil spirits leave and the sickness departs. We cannot apologize for the way the Holy Spirit works, we can only cooperate with Him as co-laborers. It is not our plan; we have enough of those in our church organizations. It is God's last day plan, His *new thing*, His *new doctrine* which is getting New Testament results in our day.

To the timid we would say, "Have faith in God and nothing shall by any means hurt you! If you go in under the blood, you cannot be touched. You must be right with God. Every sin must be humbly confessed and put under the blood of Jesus. God is looking for men and women who will rise from the powerless mediocrity of our 'churchianity' to the heights of sons and daughters of God, working with Him in the one New Testament Church—His Body, bone of His bone and flesh of His flesh."

This is what is meant by "preaching Christ."

THE WORKING OF MIRACLES

But the manifestation of the Spirit is given to every man to profit withal.... To another [is given] the working of miracles. (1 Corinthians 12:7, 10)

CONTENTS

INTRODUCTION

In the last few years there has been an outpouring of the Holy Spirit unequalled since the days of the early church. This new visitation to the church, in its largest sense, has seen a return of the charismatic gifts of the Spirit enumerated in the twelfth chapter of 1 Corinthians, including the one called *"the working of miracles."* The ability to work miracles is given to some in the church. It is not hard to understand the basic meaning of the English words, for in *The Living Bible*, we read "He *gives power for doing miracles to some."*

This is a big departure from the old approach in prayer, where petitions have been made to God through Jesus Christ, for these prayers do not fulfill the primary requirements contained in 1 Corinthians 12:10. Here we understand that certain Spirit-filled persons will actually precipitate a miracle by *doing it*. Once this fact has been realized and one has developed the faith and the ability to work miracles, then these will occur, depending on the faith of the one desiring the miracle.

This book unfolds the principles involved in the working of miracles and the explanation of what a miracle really is. Some are still saying that the day of miracles is past, but they are not up to date or with the times, for the days of miracles are very much with us today.

1

EVANGELISM BY MIRACLES

Many believed in his name, when they saw the miracles which he did.

(John 2:23)

The world is beginning to witness the greatest outpouring of the Holy Spirit since the days of the apostles of the early church. The only answer to the mounting problems of the world is a fresh revelation of God and His Son, Jesus. The expression "renewal of the church" is being heard on every side today, but to some this means "renewal of my denomination," and there has been a tendency for charismatic groups to gather within the confines of their old-line denominations and try to corral the Holy Spirit in their group. God will not revive sectarianism, but will destroy it by the brightness of His effulgence. It is written in Revelation 21:5 that in the end time, *"Behold, I make all things new."* The renewal of the church by Jesus Christ through a renewal of the Holy Spirit will not only completely change the present structures of denominations, but will bring back one true church in which the working of miracles will be the norm. These abundant miracles will be recognized by denominational leaders, who win then have to make a decision, whether they will line up with Jesus or try to bolster up their collapsing walls. They will find the roof will fall in on them as the new wind of the Spirit blows.

The religious leaders of the state religion of Israel made a council to discuss the embarrassment caused by Jesus coming among them with miracles. *"Then gathered the chief priests and the Pharisees a council, and said, What do we? [or, What shall we do?] For this man doeth many miracles. If we let him thus alone, all men will believe on him"* (John 11:47). Their anxiety was not spiritual but political, for they feared that the Romans would take their authority away from them and recognize the spiritual authority of Jesus, and that they would lose many members. This is the spirit of denominationalism—and it is a spirit. They were more interested in status, properties, salaries, men's opinion, and manses than in seeing the Jewish "church" renewed.

Let us keep right in front of our understanding that the methods that Jesus used were essentially miraculous. Jesus never held a workshop on evangelism. He never taught people how to "save souls." No spiritual laws were given to His disciples. His method was simple—just do miracles! Then many believed on Him, *when* they saw the miracles that He did. The priests did not deny that a large number of unexplainable miracles had been done. They feared them. They knew that these supernatural signs would cause the people to believe that Jesus was their Messiah. This was the last thing that the church leaders wanted to happen. They knew perfectly well what Jesus thought about them—*"scribes and Pharisees, hypocrites!"* (Matthew 23:13). They not only prevented anyone going into the kingdom of God, but they did not go in themselves. It seems we would call them modernists or liberals today.

If the Jewish clergy had believed on Him and welcomed Him as the sent one of God and the deliverer of Israel, the whole of the Jewish organization could have moved forward to the next step—spiritual renewal. All the Jewish people could have moved toward the Day of Pentecost, which was a Jewish feast day; and instead of there being 120 Jews only in the Upper Room, there could have been hundreds of thousands upon whom fire would have rested. The wind of the Spirit would have blown throughout the streets of Jerusalem, and thousands upon thousands would have begun to speak in other tongues as the Spirit gave them the utterance. (See Acts 2:1–4.) This was the crucial day of church renewal, and the church that then was, failed, but a remnant succeeded. In fact, by the end of the first week the score stood at 8,120 Jews—renewed in the Holy Spirit, manifesting the charismatic gifts of the Spirit. Many of the Jewish leaders explained away this renewal by stating that these were drunk at nine o'clock in the morning!

There were no such groups as "charismatic Pharisees" or "charismatic Sadducees," for on the Day of Pentecost, there came into existence the true church, which is the body of Christ. Always remember that a Jew who accepts Jesus as the Messiah, and who is baptized in the Holy Spirit as on the Day of Pentecost, becomes a "completed Jew," ready to explore the mysteries of Jehovah's kingdom. All the original apostles of the Lamb were Jewish, and Paul was the first apostle of the church and also was a Jew. Today, we are witnessing the Holy Spirit raising up a new leadership among the Gentiles. There will be modern apostles and prophets, but the same hallmark will be upon them—they will be workers of miracles. This will be their spiritual seal of office. *"And Stephen, full of faith and power, did great wonders and miracles among the people"* (Acts 6:8). Instead of rejoicing that the power of God was revealed through a humble servant of God, they stoned him to death, as they did the Son of God.

In Acts 4:16, the Jewish church leaders did not try to hide the fact that a miracle had been done; in fact they referred to it as a "notable miracle." Peter and John were apostles of the Lord and they had been used as instruments to give healing to the lame man at the gate Beautiful.

> *And beholding the man which was healed standing with them, they could say nothing against it* [the miracle]. *But when they had commanded them to go aside out of the council, they conferred among themselves, saying, What shall we do to these men? for that indeed a notable miracle hath been done by them is manifest to all that dwell in Jerusalem; and we cannot deny it.* (Acts 4:14-16)

Their only answer was to threaten the apostles Peter and John and forbid them to speak about Jesus who was risen from the dead. (See Acts 4:2, 18.) Of course the apostles refused this ungodly council from the recognized religious rulers of the Jews. Do we not see a parallel today among some denominational leaders? Others, however, are beginning to see and believe because of the miracles.

What is a miracle? Today the word is usually applied to drugs or food stores. If a new drug cures a stubborn sickness, it is called a miracle drug! If prayer causes healing in a person with cancer it is called a recession. This is the acrobatic reaction of unbelief. The press and media will widely publish a new miracle drug but suppress true miracles of healing and deliverance.

A miracle is an act of the power of God that transcends human ability or understanding. There are two words in the Greek: one of them is *dunamis*, which simply means "power," and the other *semeion*, which means a sign given supernaturally. Thus, the charismatic gifts of 1 Corinthians 12 are often referred to as "sign gifts." The original speaking in tongues on the Day of Pentecost was a sign gift from heaven—a supernatural sign that the Jewish leaders failed to understand. Speaking in tongues is always miraculous. The healing of the sick or deliverance of those whom Satan has bound are power manifestations of *dunamis*. Jesus used this word when He promised, "But ye shall receive **power** [*dunamis*], after that [or at the same time] the Holy Ghost is come upon you" (Acts 1: 8). The word is used again when Jesus healed the little woman with hemorrhage; after she touched the hem of His garment, He felt virtue (*dunamis*) go out of Him. (See Mark 5:30.)

It can readily be seen that when we are baptized in the Holy Spirit, as at Pentecost, we receive power (*dunamis*) as the normal manifestation of the indwelling Spirit. Thus, one of the nine charismatic manifestations of the Spirit is *"the working of miracles"* (1 Corinthians 12:10). This spiritual enablement is for all believers who submit themselves to Jesus to receive the baptism in the Spirit. It is as well to remember that in the great revival under John the Baptist, he promised that all who repented of their sins and submitted themselves to water baptism would receive the baptism of the Holy Spirit and fire. (See Mark 1:8.) Thus, the Jewish church was intended to merge toward Pentecost after having seen the miracles that Jesus did while on earth.

There are two types of miracles, therefore, one a sign gift, such as speaking in tongues, interpretation of tongues, prophecy, the word of knowledge, or wisdom. Paul himself said that the speaking in tongues was a sign *(semeion)* to the unbeliever. (See 1 Corinthians 14:22.) He used the same word translated as "miracle." Thus, when we speak in tongues in the presence of an unbeliever we actually manifest a sign miracle. Tongues will not be understood by the unbeliever, but it will have a shattering effect on him, and he will have to make a decision one way or the other, either for the full gospel or for no gospel, or possibly for a limited, emasculated gospel as taught in some denominations.

The other type of miracle is the power type. Jesus used both. To the woman at the well He used a word of knowledge that caused her to say, *"Come, see a man, which told me all things that ever I did: is not this the Christ?"* (John 4:29). This was a *semeion* miracle, which caused her to recognize that He was indeed the Christ. At other times, He opened blind eyes, unstopped deaf ears, raised the dead, healed bent spines, and restored the common people to health. These were the *dunamis* miracles. The clergy resisted Him at every step, but the common people heard Him gladly. (See Mark 12:37.) They had everything to gain. The clergy could not do these things, and so they hated Jesus who did work miracles.

I want to try and show that in the great restoration of the church that is upon us, this renewing will be done solely by a mass demonstration of miracles following the preaching of the full gospel. Gimmicks, church entertainment, and way-out stunts will disappear. We shall not even need "magicians" to entertain the children. God will bare His holy arm as the word sounds forth—for it is written, *"And they went forth, and preached everywhere, the Lord working with them, and confirming the word with signs [semeion] following"* (Mark 16:20). We shall fulfill the commission as given in Matthew 10:8: *"Heal the sick, cleanse the lepers, raise the dead, cast out devils."* We shall stick to this divine commission. We shall not vary from it. We shall not substitute anything else for it. It is the heart of the gospel. We shall not quail when the angry churchgoing people tell us that Christians cannot "have demons," or when they say we need a social gospel only. We shall adhere to the divine remedy for all mankind. We shall work miracles in His wonderful, holy name, and the people will hear us gladly and multitudes will believe.

It all has to happen before Jesus comes.

2

LEG LENGTHENING

And, behold, there was a woman which had a spirit of infirmity eighteen years.
(Luke 13:11)

The progressive outpouring of the Holy Spirit on the church has been gradual since the Reformation began in 1517. A greater move occurred at the beginning of the century by a reappearance of the sign miracle of speaking in tongues. In recent times the effects of this new visitation have become very apparent in the charismatic renewal of the church. This renewal is a deeper move of the Spirit of God to bring people into a deeper knowledge of the Son of God, both experimentally and doctrinally, and also to demonstrate greater degrees of the miraculous.

An alert, praying Christian today will not be taken by surprise at greater revelations of the Spirit, but he will actually premeditate them and watch for them. We must ever keep in mind the words of Jesus: *"He that believeth on me, the works that I do shall he do also; and greater works than these shall he do"* (John 14:12). This promise has been in the Bible a long time, but it still shocks the institutionalized church and those who have taken an unrealistic dispensational stand. Greater works are for today.

It was in the late sixties that I began to hear about "leg lengthening." My good friend Rev. Richard Vineyard was in Toronto at Evangel Temple "lengthening legs." The reports were that miracles were taking place. This was a little too much for me, but I went along to see. Unfortunately, it was impossible to see among the congregation what was happening on the platform. We were informed that "legs were growing." Frankly, I was not impressed. I did not see any evidence. I largely dismissed the matter from my mind as just another gimmick.

In 1971, I visited Huntington Beach, California, and was ministering healing and deliverance to about two hundred people. I came face to face with a man who told me he had a totally locked spine, and although he could stand straight, he could not bend and had not touched his toes for twenty years. As I stood before him, the Lord brought to my remembrance the story of the woman who had double curvature of the spine. The Bible says she was bowed together and could in no wise lift up herself. I explained that this man's trouble was probably identical to this woman's in Luke 13. I said that I was going to rebuke the binding spirit of infirmity, and afterward, he would commence to bend his back. To this he readily agreed. I laid my hands on his head and roundly rebuked the spirit in Jesus's name and then commanded him to begin bending. It took eight minutes, and then he began shouting the praises of God. He could touch his toes for the first time in twenty years! This miracle did a great deal for my ministry; for one thing, it showed me that Richard Vineyard had probably been right, and I had been showing ignorant prejudice when confronted by a "greater work." How easy is this for the ministry!

The next shock came to me when visiting in Pompano Beach, Florida. I had been staying with Rev. Don Basham and we went to a local house group. After ministering healing and the gifts of the Spirit, a young man approached me saying, "The Lord has revealed to me that you have one leg shorter than the other." This was indeed news to me, for I had lived with my legs all my life and was quite unaware that there was anything wrong with them! Of course, it must be admitted that I had never measured them! We usually don't behave like that, do we? The young man almost commanded me to sit down, and so I went along with this enthusiastic fanatic and sat down. He then told me to stretch my legs out and he held the heels in his hands. Straightway he said, "Yes, your left leg is shorter than your right by a quarter of an inch!" By this time, I could do nothing. I was powerless! He was holding on to my feet! He prayed a short prayer and then exclaimed that God had done the miracle and my legs were now the same length. My reaction was of benign unbelief, for I couldn't I see a thing, and I felt nothing. I just had to thank him rather sheepishly and try to forget the whole embarrassing experience.

For as long as I can remember, whenever I had a suit made by my tailor, I had to emphasize that my right arm was half-an-inch shorter than the left. The tailor had to be careful, for on one occasion, he reversed the order; he misread the instructions on the order sheet. I had about six jackets, all of which had the right arm sleeve cut half-an-inch shorter. It was while preaching, a few weeks after this embarrassing experience, in my church in Toronto, that my right sleeve kept riding way up my arm. I kept pulling it down, and then it rode up again. Next week, I had a change of suits, but the same thing happened. By this time, I was becoming distinctly suspicious that something had happened to my arm length. I didn't say a word to anyone, not even my wife. I was beginning to wonder! I returned to my Jewish tailor and asked him to measure my arms. He reported they were exactly the same length, so I asked him to alter the sleeve length of these two suit jackets. When I called for them, I took all my others along and asked him to alter them too, which he did—without comment or question. After all, let's face it, if I could not easily accept this kind of miracle, I could hardly expect a Jew to start asking me difficult questions!

I suddenly began to realize what had happened. When this young man prayed for my leg lengthening, the hand of Jesus had actually straightened my entire spinal column, and thereby, the shoulders were adjusted and my arms came out even! I must say, I was overawed and told our congregation, who praised God and really rejoiced. It seemed they had more faith for the miraculous than their pastor!

It was a full year and a half later that I attended a conference of ministers at St. Louis, Missouri, in the summer of 1973. Among the ministers present was my friend Rev. Derek Prince. In his typical way, he nonchalantly offered to pray for anyone who might have a short leg. Several ministers volunteered for the experiment, and Derek held their ankles and prayed a simple prayer of faith. Before my eyes, I saw legs growing! Was I dreaming? I had never *seen* anything like this before. It was real! I was stunned! Richard Vineyard had been right after all, for he told me some year later in Baton Rouge, Louisiana, where we had lunch together, that the Lord had actually revealed to him that He would do this miracle on people if Richard would pray, so he began!

Naturally the ministers began asking Derek Prince about this strange happening. He stated quite simply that it came under the heading of the *"working of miracles"* (1 Corinthians 12:10).

On returning home to my church, I felt I was riding on air. I had seen a visible miracle. Could I dare try? If so, who should I ask first? Obviously, the members of my own family. I was not aware that any of them had "short legs," for none limped, but at least if I made a fool of myself before them, they would forgive me! I wasn't so sure about the church, though! I finally asked my son Stephen, who was my assistant pastor. Sure enough, one of his legs was shorter, and when I prayed, it lengthened before my eyes! Stephen's wife, Gail, then approached a lady member of the church, and to her astonishment, she saw a leg grow as she prayed and watched. So this miracle could work for anyone, providing we prayed and believed.

Anyone who has been used of God to pray for this miracle and has seen it will never be quite the same again. It opens up the tremendous possibilities for miracles in minds and bodies, just by the laying on of hands and the simple prayer of faith. Knowing nothing about the chiropractic profession, the Holy Spirit began to teach us many things by revelation. He showed us that as the central nervous system runs through the middle of the spinal column, from the brain to all parts of the body, even to the soles of the feet, then any kink in the spine caused by worn or misplaced vertebrae would bring pressure on this nervous system and produce pains in various parts of the body. Some of these pains would be constant and stubborn, in the neck, back of the head, shoulders, arms, thighs, legs, and feet. I myself found that after my own leg miracle all dull pains ceased in the right thigh, which used to be made manifest when I drove the car any distance. I even discovered that apparent allergies could be caused by this, as well as migraines and kindred distressing pains. No wonder the Word of God told us that Jesus bore our pains. In Isaiah 53:4, the word *"sorrows"* is from the Hebrew *makob*, which means pains. How many pains can be caused by a spinal column being distorted, diseased, twisted, locked, or bent! This opened up tremendous possibilities.

We were glad to meet a full gospel Christian chiropractor who later confirmed that this was a genuine miracle known to him. Of course, the legs did not increase in length, but the hipbones became readjusted, because the spinal column was made straight.

We began to ask for those who had pains in their head, neck, back, thighs, legs, and feet to receive the laying on of hands in anticipation of this miracle. I can only say that the results in the last five years have been tremendous. We hear everywhere that others are believing for the same miracles and God is working quietly and smoothly. This is a beginning of "greater works." How great they will become when we exercise more daring faith to see greater miracles. This miracle is but the beginning of greater miracles. It is hard for those who are bound in wheelchairs, for they have lost so much faith and hope, but their day is coming fast.

It was in Sydney, Australia, in November 1973, that an unusual miracle took place. A lady present had seen cases of leg lengthening and had been most impressed, for this was relatively new in Australia. Some had heard about it, but were very wary of it. This lady had a bent nose and had apparently never been able to breathe properly through either nostril. She asked me to pray for her bent nose. I laid my clumsy hands right on her nose and prayed in Jesus's name. The Lord immediately straightened the nose and she began breathing freely through both nostrils for the first time in her memory.

On the same tour, I was asked to pray for a young lady who had diseased and inflamed hips, which caused her to walk with difficulty. She called it *synovitis*. I asked my wife to lay hands on this girl's hips while I laid my hands on her head and prayed. Her hipbones began to move under my wife's hands. She said it felt uncanny! A naturopath doctor standing right behind testified that he could see the bones in the hips moving as we prayed.

Just a week before writing this chapter, in our Deeper Life Convention in Toronto, I prayed for a woman who was facing an operation for a degenerated hip. In this case, I sat her on the pew, for she was hobbling and hardly able to walk. I held her feet in my hands and one leg was "way off." I then prayed. Both legs began to move, mysteriously, and as the very hands of Jesus performed that awesome miracle, the hip joints came into place—she felt them moving. Her legs grew about one inch or more, and then she walked down the aisle and actually ran a few steps. These miracles are real.

In the next chapter, we will consider the miracle in the Bible that is our proof text—the healing of the lady with the double curvature of the spine. If it happened in Bible days, it should happen today if we will believe. All things are possible to them that believe.

3

MIRACLES AND DISEASE

And a great multitude followed him, because they saw his miracles which he did on them that were diseased. (John 6:2)

In modern evangelism, the success of the campaign is usually determined by the crowds. In fact, every effort will be made to bring on special singers or special spectaculars to attract crowds. Of course, the whole crusade has to be paid for, so the greater the crowd the greater the offering. This syndrome is according to the mind of man. It is, frankly, a psychological approach. John 3:16, with variations, will be faithfully preached, an appeal made, and decision cards filled out. Much good work has been done and genuine conversions have taken place—but did Jesus do it this way? Did He expect us to do it our way?

The reason that a *great multitude* followed Him was not caused by singers, spectacles, or gimmicks, but by miracles. The word used is *semeion*, so the healing of diseases is described as supernatural signs, which were supposed to alert people and to attract their attention. Organized religion could not do these miracles, and had no desire to do them. They offered forms and ritual instead. Jesus invited sick people to come to Him, and He healed them all. Thus, the healing of sickness is clearly defined as God's miracle-working power, and was done to bring blessing to the people, and I can think of no greater method than this to get a crowd! Free healing for great multitudes!

"And Jesus went about all Galilee, teaching in their synagogues, and preaching the gospel of the kingdom, and healing all manner of sickness and all manner of disease among the people" (Matthew 4:23). If the healing of a disease is a miracle, then we must find out what is meant by the word *disease*. It simply means to have been deprived of ease—in other words, to be unwell. From the Greek words used in the New Testament, we

get the variant meanings "want of strength, weakness, unsoundness, sickness, to feel bad, to be ill." The literal meaning of the word *sozo*, which is often translated "saved" in the Bible, is *to be made whole*. Thus, the salvation brought by Jesus to us all by His death on the cross was soundness and wholeness instead of disease, either of mind or body.

The manifestation of this salvation upon the Jews is called the working of miracles on those who were diseased.

Toward the end of 1974, I began to be made aware by the Spirit of God that we were approaching a time of a greater manifestation of God's miracle-working power throughout the church and the world. It must be appreciated that renewal of the church without miracles is a meaningless expression. Instead of a miracle only occurring very occasionally in history, more often by the sovereignty of God than the faith of man, we must expect that miracles will be the *normal* manifestation of God's glory in the church. Our big problem has been twofold. First, our clergy have not preached for miracles, neither have they expected them. Second, the evangelicals have taken a broad position called *dispensationalism*, which admits that Jesus worked miracles in His day but that they cannot and will not occur today. This is a theological cop-out. The liberals have not believed for miracles in any age. Neither did the Pharisees or the Sadducees. This is plain unbelief.

I began studying again the purpose of miracles in the church, and as I studied, I began preaching about them and expecting to see a greater manifestation of God's power. If I preached it, I had faith to expect it, and it began to open up. However, the second great obstacle was the tremendous unbelief of the people to whom I preached. They were not conditioned for miracles in their thinking. Most of them were in a denominational rut, and they did not expect to get out. The Son of God, with all His omnipotence, could do no miracles in His own hometown. *"And he did not many* **mighty works** *there because of their unbelief"* (Matthew 13:58). This means that He did a very few miracles only, because the word for "mighty works" is *dunamis*. In the very town of Nazareth, where He was known by the residents as a "hometown boy," they were offended in Him. They said He was only a carpenter's son, and His mother was well known. Jesus first went into their synagogue and *taught them*; then He performed "mighty works" or miracles. Instead of praising God for using their hometown boy in such a way, they reasoned among themselves, "Where did He get this wisdom? From the Nazareth High School? How did He heal the sick?" There was no medical school in Nazareth. He showed amazing wisdom. Could He have gotten a master's degree in philosophy? But where? Certainly not in Nazareth. His glory was veiled because of their unbelief, because they were a small-town people with small-town minds. They were circumscribed by parochialism and the teaching of their priests. I think there is a parallel in our denominational churches today—restrictive parochialism with a great bias of unbelief. Thank God, the Holy Spirit is breaking through the bonds of sectarianism and setting people free.

I started in my home church, preaching and teaching for more miracles. I had the people come to the front and believe for their miracle. The first Sunday, it seemed that all who came, about ten, received very quick healings. Legs were lengthened, minor things like pains disappeared instantly. Yes, the removal of a headache in a split second is a miracle. It takes three aspirins much longer.

One is a supernatural, mighty act of God; the other is healing by medical means. I then traveled to Port Arthur, Texas, to a charismatic group in the city. I preached for miracles. To my astonishment, a lady came for prayer with cataracts on the eyes, and two minutes later, while still praying for people, my attention was drawn to this lady who was calmly sitting in a pew reading her Bible—a thing she had been unable to do for years. Greatly encouraged, the next person prayed for was partly deaf in both ears. Instantly, she heard perfectly. Next to her was another case of deafness in one ear, and this yielded to the prayer of faith. Legs were lengthened and there was great joy in that church. One lady whose leg was lengthened was wearing a built-up shoe. After prayer, she no longer needed this. Remember that in Samaria, when Philip went there, the same thing happened and there was great joy in that city! We will soon find that miracles in the local church will spread to miracles in the market-places, or city squares, of the big cities. This is God's time to move. Are we ready to move with Him?

From Port Arthur, I traveled to Peterborough, Ontario, a city about ninety miles northeast of Toronto. Here I was to speak to the local chapter of the Full Gospel Businessmen's Fellowship. Usually I give my personal testimony of God's progressive dealings in my life, but this time I felt strongly urged to preach on miracles, and to encourage the people to believe for them. I told them of the visible miracle of spine straightening and leg adjusting that inspires such great faith. I explained that if they could *see* a miracle of this type, what were we to imagine happened inside the body among organs that we could not see? Then, realizing that there were over two hundred people present, I called for six volunteers who really believed. I got eighteen. The first lady had her leg lengthened one-half inch. She wept for joy—in fact, they all wept for joy! The next lady was paralyzed. She could not move her left arm and dragged her left foot. After praying for her, I told her to start moving her paralyzed arm, which she did, swinging it in increasing circles above her head; then she started to move her legs as in marching. Finally, she took off and walked easily round the assembled throng of praising people. This was very encouraging.

We soon came to one in the line who admitted to having a congenital diseased hip. Her left leg was *two inches* shorter, and she wore a two-inch buildup in her shoe. I frankly wondered whether a degenerated hip would react quickly to the prayer of faith. I prayed and nothing moved. I then started to explain that miracles sometimes occurred more gradually over a period of weeks or months. They were miracles nevertheless. While I was explaining, the leg grew two inches before my eyes, and before a whole lot of other people eagerly watching. I held up the shoe for all to see the two-inch built-up heel, and I told the lady she must not wear these shoes again, and by God's provision another lady present remembered she had a spare pair of shoes in her car and she went and fetched them, and they fit her exactly.

The next in line was a lady claiming to have multiple sclerosis of the spine. She was sitting, so I had no time to get her to demonstrate her weakness or disease, but after prayer and the adjustment of her spinal column to its normal position, she wept for joy believing she was healed. All eighteen received their miracle.

Two weeks later, I received a letter from a young lady stating that the people who watched were openly weeping. They had never seen anything like it, nor ever expected to. She called it "the day that miracles came to Peterborough." A Presbyterian minister from Port Hope, Ontario, was present and was going back to his church expecting miracles. Why not? I was raised a Presbyterian! God loves them. Later, this minister brought his wife to our church. She was wearing a built-up shoe and the Lord lengthened her leg also.

While on the subject of gradual miracles, I well remember the infant daughter of a gospel singer and his wife in Toronto. It happened several years ago after we had attended a gospel service in the band shell at the Toronto exhibition grounds. This little girl was born with one leg withered. It was about two to three inches shorter than the other. I felt the compassion of the Lord and offered to pray for her in the open air. Her leg was whole within six months.

Of course, I realize that in writing a book like this, many may think that the working of miracles is something that ought to happen to anyone. According to the Bible it can happen to anyone who believes. (See Mark 16:16.) Notice that the qualification is simple belief. The opposite is unbelief. If you expect a miracle, you must state you expect it. This will be your confession of faith, Let us hear from Paul:

> *The word is nigh thee, even **in thy mouth**, and in thy heart: that is, **the word of faith**, which we preach; That if thou shalt **confess with thy mouth** the Lord Jesus, and shalt believe in thine heart that God hath raised him from the dead, thou shalt be **saved**. For with the heart man believeth unto righteousness; and **with the mouth** confession is made unto salvation.* (Romans 10:8–10)

This is tremendously important Scripture. First, the word of faith comes from our heart into our mouth. If it is not spoken it produces no results. It must be spoken. It must be confessed with the mouth, and this confession produces salvation; that is, it produces the miracle that makes a person whole, from his state of disease. The confession must be a bold confession, and the word spoken is *faith speaking*. Jesus explained it this way: "*Whosoever shall say unto this mountain, Be thou removed, and be thou cast into the sea; and shall not doubt in his heart, but shall believe that those things which he saith shall come to pass; **he shall have whatsoever he saith**"* (Mark 11:23).

The receiving of your miracle not only rests upon what Jesus did in shedding His blood on Calvary, but it also rests on your personal verbal confession of what you expect will happen to you, based on the law of love of Calvary. Instead of confessing pain, disease, weakness, misery, hoping you will be healed, you must boldly come to Jesus confessing your miracle. (See Hebrews 10:19.) Our problem today is this lack of boldness, and the inarticulate confession of most churchgoing people. If you want a mountain miracle, you must make a bold confession. "Please pray for me. I believe the mountain in my life will go away—I really do, so help me, God."

4

THE MIRACLE OF THE LOGOS

And everyone present was filled with the Holy Spirit and began speaking in languages they didn't know, for the Holy Spirit gave them this ability.

(Acts 2:4 NLT)

In order to understand the miracle of the *Logos*—the spoken Word—we must consider the Virgin Mary and her two experiences of the Holy Spirit. As recorded in Luke, chapter 1, the angel Gabriel informed Mary that the Holy Spirit would overshadow her and the result of this intimate embrace would be the conception of the Son of God. This enveloping in a shroud of glory would cause a supernatural miracle to take place—the creation and placing of the very Christ in the virgin's womb. In the due course of gestation, the beautiful body of the Christ was born into this world— Jesus, the Son of God. This Man had to wait thirty years before He was anointed of the Holy Spirit as prophesied by Daniel. (See Daniel 9:24.) Then, and only then, did this miracle Man begin a demonstration of miracles. For three-and-a-half years, this miracle Man lived a miracle life and produced miracles at every turn. This is still the purpose of the anointed body of Christ today. This is why God is pouring out His Spirit upon all flesh today.

The word *logos* is used in John 1:1 and 14. *"In the beginning was the Word, and the Word was with God, and the Word was God.... And the Word was made flesh, and dwelt among us."* This describes Jesus, the Son of God, as the *Logos*, or the living, vital Word of God. This same Word that proceeded from the Father in Genesis 1 and 2, and brought forth creation, was placed into a human body, and after Jesus was anointed of the Father by the Holy Spirit in the Jordan River (see Matthew 3:16), this Word was manifest supernaturally. First, the Father *spoke* saying, *"This is my beloved Son, in whom I am well pleased"* (Matthew 3:17). Then, the Son continued to manifest the

Word, which He received from His Father, for Jesus became the Living Word veiled in His human body. Every time He opened His mouth, out came the living Word of God. It is this living Word that creates miracles. He spoke and it was done. The people's officers said, *"Never man spake like this man"* (John 7:46). These Jewish elders had never heard the Word of God proceeding out of a human. They had only heard the dead theological letter of the law. This Word spoken brought fife where death reigned. It was and is a creative Word. The people said that He taught as one who had authority, not like the religious priests. (See Mark 1:22.)

This Word of life, spoken by Jesus in the synagogue in Capernaum, challenged the demons in a man, and they started to cry out. Demons will always oppose the living Word.

The work of Mary in bringing to birth the Son of God was not finished at Bethlehem, for thirty-three-and-a-half years later, she went into the upper room in Jerusalem, for Jesus had commanded her to wait for the promise of the Father, which was the baptism with the Holy Spirit. (See Acts 1:4–5.) She had no idea what would happen when she and 119 others received this *"baptism with the Holy Ghost."* It was a mystery to her, as it is to thousands today, but she did not back off, but obediently went into the upper room, which was to become the maternity ward of the church.

After ten days of prayer, the Day of Pentecost arrived, and suddenly, the Holy Spirit descended a *second time* on the head of the Virgin Mary. As soon as this heavenly embrace was felt, she brought forth the living Word of God—the *Logos*. The first time, she had brought to birth the body of her Son. Now, she brought forth the Word of her Son. Her Son spoke! It was the same creative, healing, miracle-working Word that He had spoken while on earth. Now, His church—His body—was to continue the same ministry. By the baptism with the Holy Spirit, Mary could now do the miracles that her Son had wrought in His flesh.

Every live child born into this world must cry out to express its God-given life. The maternity wards of hospitals are full of crying infants. The infant church also cried out, expressing its newfound spiritual life. The cry that was heard was the voice of Jesus speaking supernaturally through His mother and 119 other disciples. As He waited for the anointing of the same Spirit to begin His ministry on earth, so likewise His disciples had to wait in the upper room for their anointing to do the works of Jesus. That we might be in no doubt as to what this experience meant to them, we must remember that Jesus had told them that His followers would not only do the works that He did, but that they would do greater works and miracles. (See John 14:12.) This is the day for the greater miracles to be done by the church as it is progressively restored to its former power and format. Miracles are soon to be the order of our day.

We have already referred to the operation of the Word of faith spoken from the mouth of believers. (See Romans 10:8–10.) This is a true expression of the *Logos* spoken from the heart through the mouth. It creates its own confession. As God spoke in Genesis 1, and creation took place, so also as we speak the Word of faith we may expect to see creative miracles, if we doubt not in our heart. This is the obstacle that prevents miracles—unbelief in our heart. Remember that faith is a gift of God, one of the nine charismatic gifts enumerated in 1 Corinthians 12:8–10. If faith is a supernaturally implanted gift, then it creates of its kind, that is, it creates supernaturally. The Roman centurion knew this rule, for he said to Jesus, "*Speak the word only, and my servant shall be healed*" (Matthew 8:8). Jesus opened His mouth and said, "*Go thy way; and as thou hast believed, so be it done unto thee. And his servant was healed in the selfsame hour*" (verse 13). What healed the servant? The Word of God (*Logos*) that created life, because the centurion released this Logos by his faith. His gift of faith as spoken pressed the trigger that sent the life-giving Word from heaven. It was just as easy for God to heal the servant as to swing the sun into place. All He does is speak. All we have to do is speak—in faith. It is no use at all speaking empty words. They must be supernatural words released by our gift of faith; then the word becomes the Word of faith.

It must be admitted that speaking in languages that we have not learned is a miracle. It is called a sign (*semeion*) miracle in Mark 16:17. The experience is for all believers. In fact, as I understand the Bible, all believers *must* have this evidence of the baptism with the Holy Spirit to do the works of Jesus and work miracles. This list of miracles in Mark 16 includes the casting out of demons, speaking in unknown languages, handling deadly demonic situations, absorbing evil poisonous things by natural and spiritual ingestion, and healing the sick and diseased. Every single one of the (*semeion*) signs is a supernatural miracle, and they all follow the believer; and this supernatural miracle-working ministry begins with the living Word (*Logos*) coming forth from our mouths, supernaturally speaking divine words of praise to God that we never learned naturally. Speaking in tongues is a supreme miracle, and one that begins a whole chain reaction of miracles, such as interpretation of tongues, prophecy, the word of knowledge and of wisdom, discernment of spirits and, of course, healing and the working of miracles. The life of a true Spirit-filled believer is one continuing miracle.

As in the case of Mary who brought forth the Son of God, so likewise when the Spirit of God moves upon us initially and woos us and we accept Jesus as our Savior, the Holy Spirit implants Jesus in our hearts or innermost parts. Jesus becomes the new Tenant and Controller of our lives, but in order that His power might be released, we must be saturated with the Holy Spirit, and this second work of the Holy Spirit in our lives produces the outflow of the Word—the *Logos*. This is why Jesus prophesied that rivers of living water would come out of our innermost parts. It is interesting that the Son of God is called *"the Word"* in heaven in 1 John 5:7, but called *"water"* in verse 8. The Word in heaven becomes the flowing river of life through us on earth. The Word in us must always be manifest as a flowing, life-giving verbal expression. Like Jesus, we speak and it is done. Water in a jug remaining static will get foul, but flowing water from the river of God (see Revelation 22:1) is always fresh and pure and will give life wherever it flows. This fountain of living water is desperately needed today to flow into the barren churches. This is why in Psalm 68:9 the psalmist writes, *"Thou, O God, didst send a plentiful rain, whereby thou didst confirm thine inheritance, when it was weary."* This is God's true confirmation service, when Jesus the great Bishop lays His hands on us and we manifest His life in speaking in other languages. This brings great refreshment when we are weary, so Paul admonishes us to edify or refresh ourselves by speaking in tongues. (See 1 Corinthians 14:4.)

If all believers would open their mouths each morning on awakening and praise God in their unknown tongue, we would almost have the dawn of the millennium upon us. It may well be that this will be the spiritual state of the church in our generation, when Jesus has built it back without spot or wrinkle or any such thing. (See Ephesians 5:27.) I am convinced that those who do regularly greet the Lord in tongues daily have less problems with depression, worrying, and consequent physical sicknesses. Many who have had the baptism in the Spirit and have spoken freely in tongues later have been robbed by whisperings of Satan, either saying they can no longer praise in tongues or that it is a poor quality tongue and thus it dries up with discouragement. Oh, the subtleties of Satan and our gullibility in listening to him!

I would rather be among those who overdo praise (if that is possible) than those who praise seldom but grumble much.

Isaiah knew it would happen. *"For I will pour water upon him that is thirsty, and floods upon the dry ground: I will pour my spirit upon thy seed, and my blessing upon thine offspring"* (Isaiah 44:3). Joel knew it too, for he prophesied of Christ, *"I will pour out my spirit upon all flesh; and your sons and your daughters shall prophesy"* (Joel 2:28, Acts 2:17). As Jesus pours out His living Word upon His church today, it becomes alive, and each mouth of each believer becomes an orifice out of which this living Word flows to the thirsty multitudes who have been weary too long.

It is our mouths that He uses. Our bodies are the temple of the Holy Spirit, and it is from under the altar in heaven that this water flows and from under the altar of our heart (innermost parts) to the thirsty ones. We become water fountains in the wilderness, *"For in the wilderness shall waters break out, and streams in the desert"* (Isaiah 35:6). What a favored generation we are when God makes His church into one huge, life-giving fountain all over this barren world. Are you ready to overflow?

5

CONTROLLING THE ELEMENTS

And he arose, and rebuked the wind, and said unto the sea, Peace, be still. And the wind ceased, and there was a great calm. (Mark 4:39)

This is a true story! It not only happened in those far-off days, but it also happens today! Jesus has never changed. It is the church that has changed in departing from its original power and authority. Jesus gave the twelve apostles of the Lamb miracle power (*dunamis*) and authority (*exousia*) over *all demons* and to cure diseases. (See Luke 9:1.) The same legal authority and power was given to the seventy. (See Luke 10:1.) It was later given to the whole church. (See Mark 16:16–20.) They did not endure long years at a seminary learning negatives. They were given an assignment that relied entirely upon their positive faith in Jesus. It was very simple—to oppose all demonic forces wherever found and to cure diseases. How simple! Notice that the Greek word for "*power*" is that miracle word *dunamis*. It means that Jesus handed first to the twelve apostles, then to the seventy evangelists, and lastly to the whole church the ability to work acts of power, or miracles, wherever they ministered His Word. Miracles and healings were to be the normal expectation of their ministry. First preach, then heal, then cast out demons and raise the dead. (See Matthew 10:7–8.) If you put your faith and confidence in John 3:16, or any other Scripture, by logic you must have faith in any other promise or command in the Bible, especially if Jesus spoke it.

And they went forth, and preached everywhere, the Lord working with them, and confirming the word [Logos] with signs following. (Mark 16:20)

Let me pause for a moment and tell you of two miracles that happened between the fourth and fifth chapters of this book. This chapter is being written on a Monday at the beginning of December 1974. Yesterday was Sunday, and as usual people we had not seen before came to the church for a miracle. They could not receive it in their home churches, but they exercised faith and came. A German-speaking man came forward for prayer. He had injured his back in a German coal-mine twenty years before. The pain was so bad that he frequently had to roll out of bed in the mornings; to take a bath he had somehow to roll into the bathtub. He had pain in the back in the region of the kidneys. Let us see what Jesus did to this man in five minutes. I sat him down on the front pew of the church in full view of the congregation. His left leg was half an inch shorter than the right, a frequent trouble in back injuries. While we held his feet and prayed, Jesus caused the shorter leg to grow longer than the left leg; then the left leg began to grow and both ended up equal. This meant that a miracle of spine straightening had taken place. He explained that his kidney area hurt badly, so my hand was laid on him, the pain rebuked in Jesus' name and commanded to go away. While still holding my hand on his back, I asked the congregation if they believed this pain would go—they all agreed fervently, the man agreed, and I agreed. I took my hand away and commanded him to touch his toes. He hesitated but I encouraged him, and he did so, touching the ground. He arose with a look of curious wonder on his face, for all pain had gone and the act of touching his toes was a thing he had been absolutely unable to do in twenty years. Seeing that Satan was on the run I said, "Have you received the baptism in the Holy Spirit?" He said he had not, so I again laid my hands on him and almost immediately the Holy Spirit came upon him and he began to praise God in a new language, which he called "a prayer language." He then turned to the congregation and told them in English and German (for some of our people speak German) that God had given him three miracles—all in five minutes.

After that, I faced a lady from a city in Ontario called Peterborough, where miracles had been performed a few weeks earlier. This lady had continual head pains, neck pains, and weakness. First she sat down, and again her left leg was half an inch shorter than the right, and so I held her feet and prayed, but there was only a very small movement. I had seen this before, so I asked her to stand and then placed my hands on her head and prayed against the head oppression, then on the back of the neck and commanded these pains to go in Jesus's name. At this point she sank to the floor under the incoming miracle-working power of God and lay there peacefully for a minute while Jesus did the necessary internal physical operation by His Spirit. I then asked her if she would like to receive the baptism in the Holy Spirit, and quietly she replied in the affirmative. Again, I laid hands on her head and she immediately began to speak in tongues as the Spirit gave her the utterance. Then I again examined her leg length, and now they were both absolutely equal. It had a tremendous effect on her son who accompanied her. This is why Jesus does miracles today. I asked the lady about her church affiliation, and a little to my surprise she said, "I am just about to join the Roman Catholic Church." I said, "Praise the Lord, and God bless you." She was weeping. God is moving everywhere today!

Some years ago, around 1958, Toronto was visited with a tremendous snow-storm. In a few hours, three feet of snow lay everywhere and some of the drifts were six to eight feet high. This naturally caused all traffic to come to a halt! It cost the city of Toronto one million dollars to clear up the mess. Three days later, a report came over the radio that a storm of similar intensity was approaching from Pennsylvania and it was expected to dump an equal load of snow on Toronto. This was the day of our weekly prayer meeting, so as we were worshipping the Lord, the Lord put into my heart a gift of faith. I suggested to the small congregation that we agree together in prayer to stop the expected snowstorm. We rose to our feet, and I raised my hands toward heaven and said, "I rebuke the storm in the name of Jesus and command it not to visit our city!" At the time of its expected arrival, there was a small dusting of snow, and then it stopped. An announcement came over the radio that for reasons which could not be explained, the expected storm had split into two while crossing Lake Ontario, completely missing Toronto and dumping its load on the farm lands in Ontario, where it was badly needed. One of our ladies telephoned the weather bureau at the airport and asked them if they would like to know why this happened. They said they were interested, and she proceeded to tell them the whole story! The man thanked her and suggested we might be useful on future occasions in controlling the weather! Jesus stopped a storm by rebuking the wind and the waves!

How is it that wind, waves, and snow obey a command given in Jesus' name? Is the miracle explainable? Not by natural science, of course, but when we understand the principles involved it becomes clear. I have already quoted the words of Jesus giving His commission to His disciples that they could have His miracle power over all demons. The trouble with most Christians is that they know nothing of the reality of an invisible world of malign spirits, operating under the direct command of Satan, their prince. Satan is described as: (1) the prince of the world (see John 12:31), and (2) the prince of the power of *the air* (see Ephesians 2:2). God is the author of peace and order, not confusion. A storm represents destruction and confusion, and Satan is behind a storm. This may not sound scientific, but when a believer operating the gift of faith rebukes a storm, in effect he rebukes and binds the demonic forces actually causing the wind to blow, the waters to surge and the snow to descend in volume. A Christian who does not understand this principle would not even attempt to work such a miracle!

In Mel Tari's book, *The Gentle Breeze of Jesus*, he tells of a team of Christian workers who hired a boat owned by Muslims to visit an offshore island off Timor, Indonesia. Between this island and the mainland was a dangerous whirlpool that had sucked many to their death. The journey was quite safe in calm weather, for they skirted the danger, but on this occasion a terrible storm arose and they were being inexorably drawn into the whirlpool. One of the young Christian men heard the voice of the Lord telling him that He would deliver them all safely if he would take dominion over the storm in Jesus' name. The young man was obedient to the Lord and informed the Muslim skipper that the Lord had told him to tell the skipper that he was to stop bailing and trying to save both boat and crew and give the matter to this young Christian. Of course, the captain was completely contemptuous of this young man and showed it with hostility; but after a few more minutes of hopeless struggling against the forces of nature on the rampage, he gave up, knowing that they would all drown in the whirlpool. It was then, and only then, that the young man said, "I told you to stop struggling and let me do it, as the Lord showed me." So then he stood to his feet and openly rebuked the storm in Jesus' name and commanded it to stop. *Instantly* the sea became deadly calm, and the only evidence that there had been a storm was the foam floating on top of the calm water. The wind stopped instantly and the sea was like a millpond, because a young man believed God. This miracle so shocked the Muslim crew that they all accepted Jesus Christ as their Savior that day, acknowledging that no other God could work such a miracle. It takes miracles today to change the world. Miracles will be seen on television and will be done before millions, and millions will believe on the Son of God. This is what church renewal is all about.

In 1970, my wife and I were invited to teach in the Bible School of Christ for the Nations Institute in Dallas, Texas. We had our airline tickets, but on the morning of departure a fog developed. It was a bad one. We phoned Toronto airport, but they assured us that all was "go." On arriving at the airport a half-hour later, however, the fog had worsened and we were informed at the desk of American Airlines that their plane coming in from Chicago had been diverted to Buffalo. This left a United Airlines plane still in the air en route for Toronto. They told us that if this plane could land, we would be transferred to it. I sat waiting and took my wife's hand in agreement and we commanded that United Airlines plane to land *and* take off. The next we heard was that this plane was circling the airport trying to seek a way in, but then the announcer on the PA system said that all planes were unable to land and recommended that people return to their homes or seek hotel accommodation. I looked at my wife and she said that it looked as if this miracle had failed for the first time. I refused to accept this, and again took her hand and prayed, "Lord, I have commanded this plane to land in Your name and take off again with us, and I believe it will be so according to our prayer." A few minutes later, this plane loomed up through the fog outside the window. In ten minutes we were aboard and it roared away through the fog en route to Chicago, as far as I know, the *only plane* to land and take off after the announcement in the airport building. You see, I have never missed an appointment for the Lord. He controls the elements, but we have to do the commanding!

Another incident comes to mind. I was due to speak in a conference in Champaign, Illinois, but we had had a strike of technicians at the Toronto airport and the timetables of scheduled flights had been thrown haywire. After a half hour's delay, I entered the aircraft and as soon as we were comfortably settled in, an announcement came over the intercom stating that this plane would not take off for one and a half hours. I would therefore miss the connections at Chicago and not arrive in time for the first ministry of the Word. I closed my eyes and said quietly, "Lord, in Thy name I command this plane to take off." Instantly, the same captain of the aircraft switched on the intercom again and said, "Ladies and gentlemen, we are about to take off right now." It quickly taxied to the runway and was away and I caught my connecting flight out of Chicago and arrived on time. When Satan sees we are working for the Lord, he tries to stop us, but as we oppose him in the Master's name he has to give way and let go and retreat. This is what James had in mind when he wrote, *"Resist the devil, and he will flee from you"* (James 4:7). Have you ever tried? It always works.

What wonderful days we are living in today—the times of the restoration of the true church to all its original power and beauty.

6

A CHRISTIAN'S SAFETY

Behold, I give unto you power [exousia, authority]…over all the power of the enemy: and nothing shall by any means hurt you. (Luke 10:19)

In 1948, when the Lord began to open up my eyes to see the amazing authority that He has vested in us to work miracles, the above Scripture became extremely important. I was being used as a pioneer in what is now called "the deliverance ministry." I began casting out evil spirits from people who were cruelly bound by the enemy, and I saw before my eyes tremendous miracles of healing of the body and mind taking place. The first three in order were asthma, suicide, and epilepsy. These three people are still healed today, over thirty years later. It works.

Having proved that we had the authority of Jesus to do these things, we suddenly realized that we were far out on a theological limb. No one understood. Other pastors in the city began to shun us and I was no longer acceptable on the Toronto Full Gospel ministerial. To be alone (with my wife, of course) and to be far out on this limb in 1948 seemed to be a dangerous position. This became especially obvious when Satan attacked my wife and I in the middle of the night trying to stop our hearts from beating. We were cautioned to stop this ministry. I remember telling the Lord in prayer that if this amazing, miraculous ministry meant that I would lose my life, I was willing to die for His sake. From that time onward, and by facing Satan squarely in Jesus' name and honoring His precious blood, I won through to a deliverance ministry that I am told has influenced many men of God today to do the same. What did Jesus say? *"Nothing shall by any means hurt you"*! Nothing, absolutely nothing. No disease, no problem, no storm, no marriage problem, no financial disaster—nothing. Does this really apply to us? Yes, all of us. This means to hurt, to harm or to injure and includes the whole area of accidents!

From 1948 to this year of 1979, I have found Jesus to be true to this promise. We speak the word of faith coming from our hearts through the mouth directed against Satan, and he gives place! He retreats, he runs before the blast from heaven that honors the name of Jesus, the blood of Jesus and the Word of God, for we read a most simple statement of the early Christian martyrs—"*they overcame him* [Satan] *by the blood of the Lamb, and by the word of their testimony*" (Revelation 12:11). It was the living blood of Jesus (for His life is in His blood) and the Logos Word, Jesus Himself, spoken out of their mouths that drove back Satan and his demonic cohorts. Victory after victory occurred. Jesus is Victor and so are we *in Him*. Your present life of defeat can change into a life of continual victories.

Those who overcame Satan in the early church were not always delivered from death or torture. They were promoted to a higher order of life through death, for it is written of them "*And they overcame him* [Satan] *by the blood of the Lamb, and by the word of their testimony; and they loved not their lives unto the death*" (Revelation 12:11). Losing their life in this life was the means of gaining their life in the next. If they had denied their Savior while facing persecution, they would have forfeited eternal life, for Jesus had said that if we deny Him in this life, our Father which is in heaven will deny us. (See Matthew 10:33.) In our generation, it is more likely that we shall be delivered out of our troubles in this life, if we are faced with persecution for our testimony. Either way, in life or death, we glorify God and maintain our victory in Christ. There is no sting in death or life in Christ.

If Jesus said that nothing would hurt or harm us or bring us injury, He meant it. It is true, for He is truth.

A lady (P.B.), who originally worshipped in our church before she went to work as a nurse in Chicago, was suddenly accosted one evening by two youths, one of whom was wielding a knife. The lady saw the youth approaching with the open knife pointing at her stomach. Her first reaction was to freeze, but then she remembered her authority as a child of God and she spoke the Word. She said, "I plead the blood of Jesus against you, and I rebuke you in Jesus' name." Then lunging forward she said, "Give me that knife," and the youth released it into her hand. She then moved toward him and said, "You stand right there." Then she commanded the second young man, *in the name of Jesus*, to go into an adjacent building and telephone the police to come and pick the boys up. He immediately obeyed according to her command. When the police came, the second boy ran away. The police picked up the boy who was being held up at knife-point and later picked up the other boy also. The lady was unharmed because Jesus said, "*Nothing shall by any means hurt you.*"

Just a woman? Yes, but mighty to the pulling down of strongholds. (See 2 Corinthians 10:4.)

Every air hijack attempt could be thwarted if there was just one Son of God on board who knew his authority over the demonic forces that work against humanity. If Satan can't stop an aircraft taking off, he can't bring one down either, if he is commanded not to do so. Just imagine what will happen in this world when the church—the body of Christ—is fully restored.

Faith is the opposite of fear. Where faith reigns fear cannot operate, but where fear is present with all its disastrous torments, ulcers, and nervous tensions, the devil reaps a full harvest at your expense. It is about time we learned to turn the tables on Satan, to command him *not* to do the things he does and to take his dirty hands off our minds and bodies. Peter meant exactly what he said. *"Be sober, be vigilant; because your adversary the devil, as a roaring lion, walketh about, seeking whom he may devour: Whom resist stedfast in the faith"* (1 Peter 5:8–9). How many Christians can you find doing this? How many are giving place to Satan, giving way, giving up, giving in? He knows our weaknesses and takes every advantage against us, but Jesus has made a provision for us all. He said, *"Nothing shall by any means hurt you."* Why, then, do we get hurt? Our aches, pains, problems, and troubles seem to deny the words of Jesus. We read them but they do not work. We get discouraged, maybe because our pastor doesn't teach it even though he claims to believe the entire Bible. We have doctors and psychiatrists, so why bother Jesus?

It was on the cross that Jesus purchased our entire salvation, which means soundness, from the Greek *soteria*. He purchased total soundness for spirit, soul, and body of mankind—all mankind, but only those who dare to believe may enter into the benefits of this so great salvation, otherwise *"how shall we escape?"* (Hebrews 2:3).

We can't go around demonstrating miracles "just for fun." This is a serious business. It is only when we are faced with danger and the enemy is at the gates of our lives that we use the authority Jesus has given to us. It is for emergency use only, like the emergency door in an aircraft. When danger strikes, we have the victory and immediate recourse to all the help of Father, Son, and Holy Spirit, plus uncounted angels who will leap to the defense of the man or woman who says, "I come against you, adversary, in Jesus's name." Let us remember, however, that Jesus will not act until we take the initiative in His name to precipitate the miracle. This is why He commanded His disciples to preach and then *heal...exorcise*. This is why we are told to lay our hands on the sick so that they shall recover, because our hands become the extension of His hands from heaven, we being members of the body of Christ acting with His authority and power. Through our mouth comes the word of faith, sounding like Gabriel's horn, and through our hands is transmitted the necessary power (*dunamis*, miracle power) to work the miracle.

Any pastor, worker, or believer can do these things. This book is being written to help to encourage and stir up the faith of those who read, to join together and force

Satan out of many of his strongholds. Begin in yourself. You can deliver yourself! Command Satan to get out of your mind, your body, your life. Then turn your power and authority on Satan in your family. Drive him out of your home. Give no place to him anywhere; give him no quarter, no compromise; tell him you mean business at last; you have put up with him long enough. This is the day the Lord has made and you are going to rejoice in it instead of being sad and sorrowful in it.

I was talking to a Spirit-filled mailman recently. I asked him how he got on with his workmates. He said that at first they used to use the language normal to an unbelieving working man, but as he showed his love toward them and had opportunities of witness, they stopped swearing in his presence and the whole atmosphere of that post office changed. One man against the devil. He showed them love, he prayed for them quietly, he testified of God's goodness and they thawed. This is what is needed in every home and office—one who prays, binds the power of the devil, pleads the blood of Jesus; and this will make it more uncomfortable for Satan to stick around. He will progressively leave.

Have you pastors tried this in cases of church problems and splits? The Holy Spirit brings unity always, but Satan divides. By this you will know what spirit is working in the midst of your congregation. The moment that Jesus went into the synagogue at Capernaum, demons started to cry out and oppose Him. He did not run away; He stayed to give the whole congregation a first-class demonstration of His power and authority. *"And Jesus rebuked him, saying, Hold thy peace, and come out of him"* (Mark 1:25). There was no question as to who was the Master, for it is recorded that *"when the unclean spirit had torn him, and cried with a loud voice, he came out of him"* (verse 26). What a shock this would be if it happened in some of our churches today! I can see a lot of people scurrying out of the church as fast as their legs could carry them! Then again they said, "What new doctrine is this?" You see, their pastors had not taught them to expect this! The poor suffering man who needed Jesus' love and compassion would have remained bound by demons until his dying day unless Jesus had intervened. Do you realize what this means today in the restoration of the church? It means He has chosen us to be the deliverers to the church in His name. This is not the day for buck passing or cop-outs. This is the day for positive action.

Moses long ago had to learn this lesson. No backing away, but taking hold of the serpent by the tail, twisting it and destroying it. (See Exodus 4.) The serpent is a type of Satan, and Jesus took him by the tail and twisted it at Calvary and now tells us to go and cast him out of every situation.

"Behold I give you power [authority] *to tread on...all the power of the enemy"* (Luke 10:19). How delightful to squelch the very life out of every demonic situation that we encounter, to put our feet (shod with the preparation of the gospel) on demons and sicknesses, and command the devil to surrender. David went one further long

ago—he cut off Goliath's head and then stood on him. He knew in his day that it was true, as John said later, *"Greater is he that is in you, than he* [Satan] *that is in the world"* (1 John 4:4). Even though Satan is the prince of this world, Jesus has overcome the world for us.

We have only begun to touch the beginning of this great ministry of the working of miracles. It is one of the nine charismatic gifts of the Spirit mentioned in 1 Corinthians 12. With this charismatic renewal, we must have a full operation of all the nine charismatic manifestations of Christ. Miracles is an exciting one, and it is here.

A priest in one of my recent meetings in Florida saw demons coming out when I prayed, so next day he met a lady who was sick. Remembering what I had said, and watching how I had done it, he asked her permission to try. She agreed, so he put his hands on her head and roundly rebuked the sickness. The spirits of infirmity causing the bodily weakness came out with deep coughs. Afterward she said, "Oh, I feel so much better now!" Yes, but what had he done? He had worked a miracle in bringing health to this lady by dislodging the cause of her sickness in Jesus' name. In the same meeting, I was praying for a man and rebuking the unclean spirit behind the smoking habit that bound him. It began to come out with deep coughs, and a man, an unbeliever, sitting behind suddenly began to feel terrible. His pulse rate began to increase and he started to perspire and said it felt as if his head was about to burst. Why? Because the same unclean spirit was in him also. The pastor of the assembly explained this to him and asked if he were a Christian. On finding that he was not, the pastor pointed him to Christ, whom he readily accepted. Then the pastor cast out the unclean spirits, which came out quite readily with coughings. Then, when he had been cleaned up and the vessel of his body was made ready, the pastor prayed for him and he began to speak in tongues as the Spirit came in. One miracle of deliverance precipitates another, until the domino theory goes into effect. Satan drops out of a number of situations. A miracle will always precipitate further blessings.

7

WALKING MIRACLES

Behold, I and the children whom the LORD hath given me are for signs and for wonders in Israel from the LORD of hosts. (Isaiah 8:18)

N o doubt the primary reference to this Scripture is to Isaiah's own family, for he married a prophetess (see Isaiah 8:3), but Isaiah typified the Lord Jesus Christ, as do all the Old Testament prophets, and in the larger fulfillment of this prophecy, it refers to the Son of God as Head of His church, composed of many sons and daughters, whom the Father would give Him in the New Testament age. We see the same principle operating in the understanding of Bible prophecy where Isaiah speaks of God speaking to Israel by an alien people. If Israel refused to obey God, He would send foreign armies against them, and they would be unable to understand their language. This is the primary fulfillment, but in the New Testament Paul brought out this verse which reads, *"For with stammering lips and another tongue will he speak to this people....yet they would not hear"* (Isaiah 28:11–12), and interprets its fulfillment as the ability to speak in tongues, which all Spirit-filled Christians may enjoy. (See 1 Corinthians 14:21.)

As we project Isaiah 8:18 into the New Testament, it applies to Christians who are *in* Christ. Obviously, if New Testament Christians have measured up to the minimum requirements of Acts 2:38, which is the basis for their experience, then the threefold promise will be (1) repentance, (2) water baptism, and (3) receiving the Holy Spirit—in that order. If this verse is taken by some to prove that all born-again believers received the Holy Spirit at conversion, I would ask the question as to whether they were also baptized in water at the instant of conversion. The order is obvious. The sinner received Jesus as Savior and then identified himself with Jesus in His death and resurrection by being immersed in water, and then the new believer may receive the baptism in the Spirit. In a previous chapter I mentioned this happening to a person who reacted in the Baptist church in Florida where I was ministering when an unclean spirit was rebuked in another person. This man went through the first stage of repentance, then deliverance, and within ten minutes spoke in tongues as the evidence that the Holy Spirit had come. Water baptism would follow in this case.

Anyone who speaks in tongues is a walking miracle. No wonder Satan hates this sign, for it is the outflowing of the River of Life from heaven. He will try to shut it off, dam it, and block the faucet if he possibly can. He hates tongues, for they manifest Jesus in spoken form. Our trouble in past centuries has been that many people who went to church were dead spiritually, or to be charitable, some had a spark of eternal life in them. Paul, writing about these very people, said, *"Having a form of godliness, but denying the power [dunamis—miracle power] thereof: from such turn away"* (2 Timothy 3:5). These people go to a church that has a form of godliness. It has forms, liturgy, ceremonies and communion, but the leaders of these churches deny tongues, healing, and miracles. We are commanded to keep away from them, for their errors will quench our zeal. We must remember, and remember again and again, that the church *began* with tongues. It will end with tongues at the coming of Jesus. Those who oppose the miracle-working power (*dunamis*), which is supposed to be in the body of Christ are in reality opposing Jesus. To have forms and traditions in churches and deny His glorious power to baptize in the Spirit, to heal sicknesses of members of His body, to cast out demons from these people, is like going to a food store and coming home with empty bags full of air. We would soon die of starvation. We need fullness, the fullness of the Spirit, to satisfy our deepest longings.

As we turn to our Scripture in Isaiah, we find that this was the same thought. Children of God were supposed to be miracle children. The very word used for "wonder" can be translated from the Hebrew as "miracle." All Christians are supposed to be walking miracles. One of the names of Jesus recorded by Isaiah 9:6 is Wonderful. It is because He was a miracle-working Man while on earth, and now He wants us to be miracle-working men and women while on earth. When Simeon prophesied over Mary, the mother of Jesus, he said that her Son would be for a *sign* (*semeion*—miracle) that would be spoken against. His whole life was a living miracle, and the leaders of the state religion hated Him because He did (and was) what they could not do and be. The contrast was too great. It was white light showing up black darkness.

And this is the condemnation, that light is come into the world, and men loved darkness rather than light, because their deeds were evil. For every one that doeth evil hateth the light, neither cometh to the light, lest his deeds should be reproved.

> *But he that doeth truth cometh to the light, that his deeds may be made manifest, that they are wrought in God.*
>
> (John 3:19–21)

Jesus is the Light of the world. (See John 1:4–5.) He loved mankind. He was kind to them and to their children. He healed people and blessed them, but those in darkness could not comprehend. He was a sign that was spoken against. They crucified Him. They tried to turn off the heavenly light, but after He arose from the grave it grew brighter in the upper room. This is why Jesus tells us in Matthew 13:43 that we shall *"shine forth as the sun in the kingdom of* [our] *Father."* We are supposed to be shining people, with the glory of God radiating out in every direction. Of course, those who love evil and want to dwell in darkness will hide from shining Spirit-filled Christians. We are too bright and too hot for them hiding in their denominations that deny God's miracle-working power.

While writing this chapter, one of our church elders told me that he had visited a farm recently where he found that certain cattle had mysteriously died, and a cow had given birth to a calf but the afterbirth would not come away and the cow was desperately sick. First, he rebuked the spirit of death working among the cattle in the barn; then, he laid hands on the sick cow and prayed for it. The same day, the afterbirth came away and the cow recovered and the production of milk increased one hundred pounds a day. Why did this happen? Because this elder was a walking miracle. Even the veterinary doctor could do nothing! It took a miracle to heal the cow.

If Jesus was a walking miracle, He wants us also to be the same, for He said, "As I am in the world so are you." (See 1 John 4:17.) He shone, so He gives us the Holy Spirit to radiate from us His miracle-working power. This is why God is now pouring out His Holy Spirit afresh upon all flesh (cows included) to restore His church and to bless His creation. *"Fear not, O land; be glad and rejoice: for the* LORD *will do great things. Be not afraid, ye beasts of the field"* (Joel 2:21–22).

A Christian should therefore be a sign and a wonder among the people. Today, this is so necessary because of the general degeneration of the average man. He is emotionally and physically sick. He takes alcohol in increasing quantities. He is spending more money on healing "miracle" drugs. He knows we live in a dangerous age and is therefore trying to escape from the inevitable collapse of this world system, called Babylon or confusion in Scripture. It is to be replaced by the kingdom of God on earth. If we want to help our neighbor come to the Christ of the Bible, we must be such a sign and wonder that it will be quite obvious that we are different—in every respect. We have healthy minds in healthy bodies. We do not spend large sums of money to try to buy health out of a bottle or to escape reality through a bottle. Every time Satan attacks us, we repulse him; we resist him in Jesus' name. We cast him out by force from every situation and maintain a position of strength and health. Again, let me remind you that salvation (*soteria*) means "wholeness." Dr. C. I. Schofield in his footnotes in his well-known Bible states that the word "salvation" is the most inclusive word in Scripture. It includes all the redemptive acts of the cross. It includes continuing health up to the time of death, for we read in Psalm 91:16, "*With long life will I satisfy him, and shew him my salvation.*" The Hebrew word for "*salvation*" is *yeshuah*, which is the root meaning of the Greek *Jesus*. Thus, Jesus is the one who gives us salvation—health, wealth, happiness, forgiveness, ease (in contradistinction to disease), and safety. There are many more things He gives us under the comprehensive word "salvation"! In fact, our personal manifestation of these attributes shows we are walking miracles because they are not natural to us by our biological birth. These are supernatural manifestations of a risen Savior and are outworked in and through our minds and bodies. First, He comes into our spirits; then, He occupies our minds and bodies. Instead of having psychosomatic sicknesses, we have psychosomatic health. A healthy mind outworks through a healthy body. A soul at ease dwells in a body without disease.

What should our spiritually built-in reaction be when we are attacked in sickness of mind or body? It often begins with a shock! We should immediately call for the pastor or a friend to pray with us. This casts away Satan's cohorts who would want to put a sickness upon us. If we accept the sickness we become sick. If we reject it in forceful, believing prayer, we put up the covering of the blood of Jesus so that Satan is not able to penetrate. We remain well. The problem, of course, is that sometimes Satan catches us unawares, and before we realize it he has put a sickness upon us. It is then that the battle begins. We trusted God and now we are sick, and then Satan shouts at us, "Yes, and you trusted a phony Bible." In this day of deliverance, there are uncounted thousands coming for help because their churches have not taught them. They are believers but not walking miracles, and they need the help of those who are. We pray for them, cast the sicknesses and demons out of them, pray for them to be filled with the Holy Spirit, and put them in a position so that they also can become walking miracles.

Some Bible colleges and schools actually forbid their students to speak in tongues, to pray for the sick or to cast out demons, and yet they advertise themselves as Bible colleges! When Jesus walks in their doors in miracle form, through any of their student body, they reject them, thereby rejecting Jesus. It is time for the whole church to be shaken from top to bottom by a return of miracle-working men and women in their midst. The whole creation groans and waits for the manifestation of mature, miracle-working sons of God. This is the time that a great maturing is taking place. It is the time of the outpouring of the latter rain. It is now.

As we read the psalms, we find that the word *praise* is mentioned 165 times in 150 psalms. The whole emphasis is one of praise at all times. "*I will bless the LORD at all times"* (Psalm 34:1). In the New Testament Paul had no doubt about it. Though he was stoned, shipwrecked, and starved, he always praised God and wrote in Ephesians 5:20, *"Giving thanks always for all things unto God."* Again, in 1 Thessalonians 5:18, *"In everything give thanks."* For everything, and in everything. When we get in a mess, we should start thanking God for the mess, because the mess is the way to deliverance. There can be no suffering without its corresponding healing. There can be no problem without its answer of deliverance. As soon as we go into battle, we start singing like the Israelites did of old. *"He* [Jehoshaphat] *appointed singers....they went out before the army and* [said], *Praise the* LORD; *for his mercy endureth forever"* (2 Chronicles 20:21). It was when the 120 singers praised God in the newly dedicated temple that the house was filled with the shekinah glory of God and the priests could not stand but fell to the ground and the glory of the Lord filled the house of God (see 2 Chronicles 5:12–15). Notice too that the exact number of priests is given as 120. This is the number of the miracle-working power of God, for there were 120 initial members of the body of Christ who sounded forth from their lips the praises of God in tongues. They were the fulfillment of 120 silver trumpets, for silver is the metal of redemption, and 120 trumpets represent the miracle-working power of God sounding forth out of their mouths. They became miracle workers. If 120 singers brought down the visible *shekinah* glory of God in the temple under the old covenant, what will 120 Spirit-filled people accomplish in the supernatural realm by praising God together in tongues? No wonder Satan fights tongues.

Great emphasis is being made again today in charismatic circles to praise God for everything and in every situation. It is no exaggeration to teach that this will be the beginning of your deliverance to a life of miracle health. It is your trial that forms the first part of your deliverance. Praise Him for it, for His mercy endureth forever.

8

CREATING MIRACLES

Whosoever shall say unto this mountain, Be thou removed, and be thou cast into the sea; and shall not doubt in his heart, but shall believe that those things which he saith shall come to pass; he shall have whatsoever he saith. (Mark 11:23)

Just before Christmas 1974, my wife and I went shopping in our largest shopping mall. It was a Friday night and it seemed the huge parking lot was crammed full. I circled the perimeter, but no place appeared and other cars were milling around looking for the elusive parking spot. I said to my wife, "Say, 'In the name of Jesus I create a parking spot.'" She repeated the words somewhat halfheartedly, because I told her to do so. Then, I turned into the middle of the area and every place was full. My wife said, "Let's turn down this lane." "No," I replied, "I feel a leading to go down this one." We approached the entrance to the main shopping center, and as we drove a car backed out of a parking spot nearest to the main entrance. It could not have been nearer, and we slid our car into this place with no waiting.

My wife admitted she was halfhearted in her commanding prayer and not listening too closely for guidance afterward. The point had been proved. We had created a parking spot. Isn't this typical of so many of the small details of our lives? We first give a negative confession. We say, "The parking lot is full; we shall never get in there." Or "I'm too busy today; it will be impossible to do that." "Impossible," did you say? That word is used by Jesus as referring to men. *"With men it is impossible, but not with God: for with God all things are possible"* (Mark 10:27). We try in our own strength and fail. We reason with carnal reasoning and come up with defeat, but the impossible becomes the possible by the command of faith that creates something that does not appear to be there.

Conversely, in the case of the mountain before us, we destroy it by the command of faith and it disappears. To do such a thing is ridiculous to the reasoning mind of man. I well remember a case that almost seems to be stupid. It was in England. I was doing up a parcel and needed some string. We were staying with friends, and they could find no string at all and the stores were closed. Thereupon I said, "I command a piece of string to appear." My friend looked up in surprise and said that this was fanatical, I then opened a drawer in his kitchen, and there lying on top was just the length of string for the parcel. Did I create it? I don't think so, but my commanding prayer had caused me to open the only drawer in the house where the only piece of string existed. It saved a lot of trouble.

This kind of thing would seem to be a series of coincidences, but to those who use this form of commanding faith it works too often to be coincidence. Our problem is that we think it ridiculous to talk like that who would ever think to command a mountain to disappear!

Long ago, Zerubbabel was rebuilding the foundations of the temple. This is typical of the rebuilding of the church in our day. There were (and are) many difficulties. The people living in the land opposed every move and the builders held the trowel in one hand and the sword in the other. The position grew into mountain-sized proportions until Zerubbabel started talking to the mountain—yes, right out loud. He said, "*Who art thou, O great mountain? before Zerubbabel thou shalt become a plain*" (Zechariah 4:7). As the builder began to work, the mountain slowly disappeared and became as flat ground. The building was completed, and so will it be in this last generation, as the Word of the Lord comes again through the lips of His servants, commanding all opposition of Satan to cease, so that the completed church without spot or wrinkle may grow into a holy temple. (See Ephesians 2:21.)

The church in past times has been very timid. It has not had the baptism of the Holy Spirit for power and service, but has relied upon the experience of the rebirth to be sufficient. It has not proceeded from the cross to the upper room. It has wrongly assumed it received the power of the Spirit at the cross and failed to go into the upper room at all until this generation. Now, thousands are climbing the steps and returning speaking in other tongues. The early church did not stay in the upper room, although the religious Jews rudely cried out that they were drunk at nine o'clock in the morning. The church then mingled with the people and immediately demonstrated the miracle of healing the man at the gate Beautiful. As has been said, the beggar asked for alms, but God gave him legs! Peter said, "*Such as I have give I thee: In the name of Jesus Christ of Nazareth rise up and walk*" (Acts 3:6). What did Peter have? The *dunamis* miracle of the Holy Spirit, received shortly before in the upper room. He was able to give this miracle power to the lame man, for had not Jesus said, "*Freely ye have received, freely give*" (Matthew 10:8), and Jesus was referring to healing the sick, cleansing the lepers, casting out demons, and raising the dead. It is clear that believers are supposed to give these things to people today. How? By first going into the upper room, receiving the miracle-working power of the Spirit and then going into our churches and giving it to those who thirst.

So many in our classic Pentecostal churches have not realized this tremendous truth. They have received the Spirit and spoken in tongues but have not moved out with the commission of Jesus. Denominations have been built around Acts 2:4 and the gifts of the Spirit were dropped in favor of programs. We must demonstrate these supernatural gifts of the Spirit to those who are emerging from the historical churches today. They must *see* and *hear* the miracles as the people did in Philip's visit to Samaria. (See Acts 8.)

It is for us who have received the baptism in the Spirit to start enforcing the law of love by setting people free instead of letting them remain in bondage in our churches. No, we will not be popular when we start, but a full-gospel Christian is not supposed to be popular! The law of love of Calvary is that Jesus has set the prisoners free. He forgave their sins, healed their sicknesses, and delivered them from their satanic oppressions.

I heard recently of a learned pastor of an old-line denominational church who wrote an article for publication in some erudite magazine against speaking in tongues. He mailed it to the publisher and then visited a convention that weekend, during which time he received the baptism in the Spirit, speaking in tongues. He immediately wrote another letter instructing the publisher to destroy his previous manuscript. It takes a miracle to change our theology sometimes. When this man had a miracle in his mouth, his very speech changed from negative to positive. What beautiful rectification!

To create a miracle it is better to say than to pray. Of course, in this case saying is praying, but it is creative praying. Jesus did not pray to the Father to calm the storm; He calmed it by speaking to the forces behind the wind and the waves and they obeyed Him. If He hadn't commanded, they would have sunk, and where would you and I be if Jesus had drowned? We would have been sunk too! Zerubbabel said that as he had started the building, he was going to finish the building and nothing, liter-ally nothing, was going to stop him fulfilling the command of God. Are you going to let anything stop the conversion of that son, that daughter, or the recreation of your marriage entered into by solemn covenant with God and man? Are you going to allow that church to collapse in schisms, or your neighborhood to go to the dogs? You and I have it in our power to command what is going to happen. If we are snared by the words of our mouth (see Proverbs 6:2) and bring ourselves into captivity as a frenzied, frustrated beast in a cage, we can likewise open the doors of that cage by speaking words of authority and turn a negative confession to a positive one. Look around you, and see where you have accepted defeat and bondage, and decide to change your life by doing a bit of commanding for a change. Start off by saying, "I refuse to accept this situation in the name of Jesus, and I command that it shall agree with Scripture. Sickness go and health return." Keep this up until it becomes a self-evident fact. You create your own miracle.

It is hard to find church members who will enter into such a covenant with you. Even if you get them to start praying-saying in this unfamiliar way, they will do so with little faith, rather wondering what people would say if they heard them, or wondering if anything will really happen. Jesus said, "If you doubt not in your heart." (See Mark 11:23.) This is the real crux of the matter, the touchstone that tests our faith. Can we really say it and believe it will happen? Whether we can or not does not alter the fundamental law given us by Jesus.

Our first approach to any difficulty is usually a rational one. We start thinking and scheming and we add and subtract. We measure the tons of dirt in the mountain with our puny machinery, and we give up. It isn't possible, and every reasonable person will agree with us. Maybe, but not Jesus. He will say, "Have you tried commanding?" No, we have not. "Well, will you start today?"

I am sure that the reason why few believe in miracles today is that they have not expected them. They had no idea how to create them, and so modern civilization has crawled into a rational cave called "Cave Despair." We expect to get ourselves out of every mess by self-help and psychology. Pride will not allow us to ask Jesus to help. Jesus says, "Take my name and the authority vested in you to do the same works that I did on earth and make it work." This is how the seventy acted. (See Luke 10:19.) *"Even the demons are subject unto us in thy name"* (Luke 10:17). Yes, but they had to command the demons! They had to speak out loud; then they saw the miracles.

In Luke 9:43–44, we read that the people were amazed at the mighty power of God and wondered at the miracles that Jesus did; then He said, *"Let these sayings sink down into your ears"* (verse 44). Our trouble is that we are so taken up with our problems (and other people's), with television and other mind-drugging recreations that the sayings of Jesus accompanied by His miracles fail to reach our minds at all. I think it most striking that Jesus should have used such words as "sink down." Do we give time today in our hurried world to allow His words to sink down deep into our consciousness?

The disciples failed to understand what Jesus was talking about and they were afraid to ask Him. Isn't this true of us today? It takes a marvelous miracle of speaking in tongues to pull us out of our troubles and put us on new faith ground, where we can know the will of God and we can enforce it by commanding and believing. We *shall have* whatsoever we say. Go on, I dare you to say it!

This teaching need not amaze people. The Bible clearly teaches that a fullgospel Christian is *in Christ*. We operate in Him and not outside of Him. He is our strength and intelligence and we have the mind of Christ. (See 1 Corinthians 2:16.) We may not always use His mind within us, but we have it! This has been our trouble. We have not used what He has given us—His authority, His power, and His mind. Without wishing to appear irreverent, He is the ultimate Boss. He is so great that He is the King of kings and the supreme potentate of all time. And we are *in Him*. He is *in us*. So, when we start acting as if we are the boss (in Him), then the devil must give way to the Boss's voice. We roar like the Lion of Judah. We give the commands and woe unto Satan if he obeys not our commands.

Know the Bible and your authority first. Doubt not in your heart, and start taking the position of the officer in command and not the slave under the lash.

9

FALSE MIRACLES

For they are the spirits of devils, working miracles.　　　(Revelation 16:14)

Not everything that glitters is gold; neither is every apparent miracle of God. Many get greatly perplexed when they are told that supernatural things can happen apart from God.

This Scripture above describes the conditions of the world in which we live today. The work of these demons, whom Young describes as "deified spirits," that is, evil spirits that are worshipped as gods, are sent forth into the world for one express purpose, to bring the kings of the earth down to Armageddon for judgment. Their work is to deceive by miracles. Always remembering our definition that a miracle is an act that transcends the understanding or ability of man, these powerful demons, often called familiar spirits because they are familiar to the mediums through whom they operate, work behind the scenes of all occult groups to deceive. Just before the Battle of Armageddon, it seems their activity greatly increases to the point where Satan worship, spiritism, and witchcraft become extremely common. This is certainly true in our generation.

When the Bible was taken out of American schools by a foolish Supreme Court, and prayers in the name of Jesus were forbidden, Satan immediately came in with witchcraft into every high school in the United States. The true religion of Jesus Christ, God's Son, and the Holy Spirit was replaced by the false religion of Satan and his demons. The Holy Spirit's beneficent powers were replaced by the debilitating powers of unholy spirits. If there is a spiritual vacuum, Satan will fill it with demons. They desire to be worshipped, so they get into young girls in high schools who become the oracles, or witches, of their peers. Fortune telling becomes the name of the game, and then courses are held in "parapsychology" in some of our universities to study and examine the "scientific" basis of the supernatural and the unknown. Subjects such as levitation, bending of metals, breaking of concrete slabs, and the disappearance of objects, the making of holes through walls and the catapulting of people out of bed, etc., are studied for a scientific basis. These are genuine miracles, for they transcend the understanding of man. They are false miracles, for they do not glorify God.

These are pointless miracles, unless one understands them in the entertainment sense. They do not glorify Jesus. Demons bend metals in front of television cameras. Men and objects can sail into the air as transported by invisible demons. Evil spirits can take an object and carry it out of the room so quickly that it becomes demonic sleight of hand. There is nothing new in these things, but great attention is now being drawn to them, for they are happening all over the world because of the great increase of interest in the occult.

If a heathen prays to an idol in a heathen temple, there is a demon who operates through that idol and may actually come right inside it when candles are lit and incense burned (or joss sticks). The spirit will endeavor to answer prayers, sometimes spectacularly, so that the person will believe that either God Himself or some great, powerful deity is ready to answer their prayers. This principle is known by witch doctors in Africa and Asia who have fetishes, or images of their gods in picture form or in bodily form. These are often hung round necks or put round the necks of cattle or children for protection! Each of these replicas will entice the demon who serves the idol or picture. He works through this system. Witch doctors can cause death in a person by sending an evil spirit of death to kill. They are sent after the prayers and oblations are made to the false god. Destruction of crops can occur, but the witch doctor will charge heavily for his services. How different to the prayers made in Jesus' name for healing or blessing upon an individual. No charge!

The whole business of inquiring of the dead that occurs in spiritist séances is called necromancy and is expressly forbidden in Scripture (see Deuteronomy 18:9–11); in fact, there is absolutely no statement in Holy Writ that a human living on earth may communicate by prayer or supplication with any departed person, saint or sinner, whether in heaven or hell. The only one with whom we may communicate is the Lord Jesus Christ Himself, and the means whereby we do this is the Holy Spirit. Caution must be urged about the practice of praying to dead people, so expressly forbidden, because if we do communicate with someone on the "other end" it may well be a simulating evil spirit. There is only one Mediator between God and man, and His name is Jesus. (See 1 Timothy 2:5.) Absolutely none other.

In Genesis 6:11–12, we see a description of the world in Noah's day. It is described as being corrupt and filled with violence—an apt picture of modern (socalled) civilization. God told Noah He would destroy the earth and all mankind. Who made them corrupt? None other than Beelzebub, the Lord of the flies, and of all corruption upon the earth. Satan, through his angels, will always corrupt. He will always cause men to exercise violence toward each other, individually and nationally.

Jesus told us that the world before His coming would be as in Noah's day. (See Matthew 24:37–39.) The world system is up for judgment. It is called Babylon or confusion, and its primary contents are political, financial, and ecclesiastical. The three spirits like frogs (see Revelation 16:13) are behind these systems, which are now disintegrating as we watch the hand of God at work restoring the true church. Satan and his demons are doing their best to cause as much confusion as possible today, for they know their time is short: "*Woe to the inhabitants of the earth and of the sea! for the devil is come down unto you, having great wrath, because he knoweth that he hath but a short time*" (Revelation 12:12). This time is also described by Jesus—"*Upon the earth distress of nations, with perplexity*" (Luke 21:25). There is no way out. God has trapped man in a corner, and when he sees there is no way out he will cry to God. Politics, money, and a backslidden church will be unable to help him. This is the day of the unparalleled demon activity. We should also remember that Jesus said that it would also be as in the time of Sodom and Gomorrah, which were destroyed by fire and earthquake, so that the exact location under the Dead Sea is unknown (see Luke 17:28–30). Their sin was homosexuality, for which they were utterly obliterated, and today there are homosexual churches where men are "married" to men and women to women. There is a so-called "gay world" of sin. Such days have been unknown during the entire Christian dispensation. All these things are of Satan and he knows his time is short, so he is bringing his harvest of tares to maturity while Jesus is bringing His church to maturity for His coming. Both these harvests are being prepared by miracles, the true and the false.

It is interesting to note that when Jesus told His disciples that they had power (*exousia*—authority) over all the power of the enemy (see Luke 10:19), the word used for Satan's power here is *dunamis*, which, as we have already explained, means miracle power. This verse, therefore, means that all Christians have authority over the very miracle-working power of Satan. He does work miracles!

One of the best cases that comes to mind is the British healer named Harry Edwards. He makes no apology for explaining that he heals "by the spirits," not the Holy Spirit as in the case of true divine healing and the working of miracles. He can pack the Royal Albert Hall in London with seven thousand people and they will witness miracles done by demons. Many that attend believe all this is of God.

It should be explained that, in case of healing by occult spirits, Satan does not cast out Satan, for that would mean his house would be divided against itself. (See Matthew 12:26.) If it brings glory to the devil he will temporarily take away a spirit of infirmity so that sick persons will believe they have been healed by God, while yet in an unregenerative state, and thus the apparent healing will not keep them out of hell. In many cases the spirit is actually driven deeper into the soul of the sufferer, and ultimately they may suffer some strong emotional problems. They are not delivered in the sense that the evil spirit is cast out by force in Jesus' name; they have a temporary easement as the indwelling evil spirit changes positions. To go to an occult healer is a sufficient reason to end up in a worse state than at the beginning.

I corresponded with a spiritist medium by tape some years ago, and he explained to me that he healed with the help of the angels, and he was right, but they are fallen angels. Jesus makes this clear to us in telling us why God created hell, which is a mystery to so many. Here are His words: *"Depart from me…into everlasting fire, prepared for the devil and his angels"* (Matthew 25:41). Hell was not made for man, but if man insists on doing business with Satan, he will have to accompany him there, with all his angels. Yes, Satan has angels, messengers, evil personalities who fell from heaven in their first rebellion. (See Revelation 12:7–9.) There has to be some place to dump all these terrible evil spirits that are even now trying to destroy society and everything therein. This is why the Greek work *Gehenna* is taken from the Valley of Hinnon, the old rubbish dump outside Jerusalem, where everything from rotting vegetation to dead animal carcasses was burned and the odor was terrible. Flies everywhere, and Satan was lord of them.

It is these angels that work with spiritist mediums. When the mediums go into trances, the demons take over control of the human by his desire and intention. The voices and the healing miracles that follow are done by the demons through the medium, even as healings are done by Jesus indwelling the believer when he prays. The one is the converse of the other. How nice it sounds in the ear of a gullible Christian who doesn't know his Bible, to be told that he can go to a sanctuary and receive prayer from a man (or woman) healer who will lay hands on, probably rub his hands on, the sufferer and the angels will help in the healing. Beautiful, isn't it? No, it's diabolical! Healings are not the only miracles, however. In a séance all kinds of different colored lights can appear, trumpets can sail round the room and objects move through the air. Horrible odors can be smelled and the demons will talk either through the medium or through trumpets. But why advertise the devil and his miracle-working power? Only to warn the unwary.

If only the church in past generations had worked true miracles by the power of the Holy Spirit and honoring of the blood of Jesus, Satan would have had much greater difficulty in getting his show on the road. A large section of the Christian church has denied the power of God and not expected any miracles and has taught people that the day of miracles has passed. While they are saying this, the day of miracles is rapidly reappearing for them to see. Bishop Pike tried to communicate with his son. He believed in the supernatural, but the very god he sought after destroyed him in the desert of Israel. The bishop was a member of the church, and it must be said with sorrow that some of these old-line churches that deny the reality of miracles of God today will excuse anyone seeking after the false miracles of Satan, for it is taught by them that this proves the "afterlife." It does nothing of the sort. It proves the existence of the world of spirits behind the natural sight of man. The reality of the afterlife is only to be accepted on faith by reading the Word of God. Jesus demonstrates the reality of the world beyond our world by baptizing us in the Holy Spirit, bringing us the miracle of tongues. That should prove everything for those who want proof.

In Revelation, chapter 13, reference is made to *"another beast,"* who comes up out of the earth. He does great wonders (*semeion*—miracles) and deceives mankind by the miracles (*semeion*) that he had power to do before men. The first beast in Revelation 13:2 was given power (*dunamis*—miracle) by the dragon, so these two beast systems, which many believe were the successive Babylonian empires with their false religions, right up to recent times, were actually operated by strong demon powers, and they were backed up by false miracles in their religious systems. The only trouble for the devil is that after he has exercised great power and authority among nations, God finally finishes him and locks him up, whereas Jesus is the Alpha and Omega, having neither beginning nor ending. His miracles stand for all time.

Do not go to soothsayers and astrologers to know the future.

Go to the Bible and pray for the Holy Spirit to give you understanding. If you need salvation in any aspect, go to Jesus; bare your soul and ask His forgiveness and ask Him to save you and fill you with His Spirit. You will be satisfied with His miracles after that.

Expect a miracle every day.

10

SPONTANEOUS MIRACLES

Without the shedding of blood is no remission. (Hebrews 9:22)

Perhaps some of the most spectacular and exciting miracles are those that happen when people least expect them. The medical profession refer to these cases as "remissions" and, of course, though many of the medical doctors may not realize it, the Word of God teaches us that *"without the shedding of blood is no remission"* (Hebrews 9:22). Because Jesus shed His blood for all mankind, it is possible for people to have a remission from their sickness or killing disease. There is no question that in the Western world, many will pray for someone who is grievously sick. Especially is this true among our churches. Prayer requests are sent in and congregational prayer is made, or the request is passed to groups who exist especially for this ministry. How can we understand the love of God in bringing a remission to someone who is not even aware that others far off and unknown may be praying for their healing? We cannot limit the hand of God in reaching down from heaven and "sending away" a sickness because Jesus shed His blood for all mankind. The expression "sending away" is the exact meaning of the word "remission" (in Greek, *aphesis*).

We remember the time when the well-known Congo missionary W. F. Burton, of the Congo Evangelistic Band, was dying of cancer in Congo. A lady in Melbourne, Australia, was awakened at 3 AM local time to pray for Rev. Burton, who was in dire need.

She obeyed the prompting of the Spirit and interceded for this missionary. At that exact moment of time, Willie Burton had a remission of his cancer. He published a photograph of his cancerous colon before and after this miracle. It was a spontaneous remission. It was a long time later that the truth was learned. Melbourne to the Congo jungles is a long way. Distance is nothing to God.

In our own church, we have often been amazed at the testimonies that have later been reported to us by people for whom we prayed in our regular services. We probably did not even know them, but their case was reported to us, and usually before our opening time of prayer, we ask for spoken and unspoken prayer requests. We do not do this as a form, for experience has shown us that spontaneous remissions do take place in many cases. Of course, I do not even attempt to explain why some are not healed, but I suspect it may have something to do with the attitude toward God of the unknown person prayed for. Not only are many sicknesses spontaneously healed, but it seems that a Spirit-filled Christian will "automatically" react to another person's need. The Spirit in us seems to be most anxious to rise to the help of the person who is stricken, and before we realize it we are praying for that one. Many times, when an aircraft flies over, I find myself praying for the safe journey of those in the air. Is this a kind of superstition for the ignorant, or is it a God-given attribute? I think there is a connection here in Romans 8:26: "*Likewise the Spirit also helpeth our infirmities: for we know not what we should pray for as we ought: but the Spirit itself maketh intercession for us with groanings which cannot be uttered.*" The *Amplified Bible* puts it this way: "*The Spirit Himself goes to meet our supplication and pleads in our behalf with unspeakable yearnings and groanings too deep for utterance.*" The *New Living Testament* translates this: "*The Holy Spirit prays for us with such feeling that it cannot be expressed in words.*"

Here we have a fact revealed. The Holy Spirit (not us) intercedes, prays, pleads, and goes to meet us in our desperate need. This is a spontaneous act of a loving God to start in motion a process to bring a miraculous remission to a person groaning in need. How wonderful that this ministry is inbuilt in the Spirit-filled church!

How do we know how many people may have prayed for one sufferer? How do we know how many people God may have urged to pray in distant lands? Suddenly a person is healed, and it is called a remission. Blood for blood. Jesus's pure, clean, precious blood for our sick, defiled blood. Remission.

The amazing ministry of Kathryn Kuhlman has proved this point beyond any further doubt. I was speaking to one of the leaders of the Catholic healing ministry, Father Francis McNutt, and he explains that thousands of Catholics went seeking healing and remission in her meetings, and thousands of them found health. Miss Kuhlman's large healing services were in no sense a shrine. She happened to be a woman prophetess. She did not claim to be an evangelist or a preacher. She was certainly no healer. We leave that word to the metaphysicians, but she established a ministry where Jesus was honored through the omnipresent Holy Spirit, and people from all denominations came hoping or believing they would receive healing. Doctors were present to confirm these healings.

How do spontaneous remissions occur in such services (because they do!)? The answer must be found in the fact that the whole auditorium is charged with the presence of the Holy Spirit. The service is conducted in such a way as to cause people to expect the Holy Spirit to work. These healings are the sovereign work of God. If a dead battery comes in contact with a live battery, the life in the fully charged cells goes into the dead cells. So it is in the case of the cells of the human body. The presence of disease means there are many sick cells, rundown cells, and exhausted cells. They need a new charge of divine life. By moving into an auditorium that has been prayed over, sung over, rejoiced over, and the blood of Jesus honored, tired cells in weary, sick people begin to experience a new charge of *zoe* life from God by the Holy Spirit. The presence of the Holy Spirit will send away—remit—the sickness as a new infusion of divine life flows into the body. Remember that when God created man in His own image He did so by breathing His divine breath into the lifeless body of Adam, who thereupon became a living soul . (See Genesis 2:7.) All the cells of Adam's perfectly formed body were good cells, but they were all dead cells. It took the breathing of *ruach* (Hebrew for breath) to bring full life and strength to Adam. All of us are descended lineally from Adam and Eve and so when our cells are attacked by Satan with disease, there is a force far greater than the devil and sickness which can drive out disease, namely the very breath of God, strongly present in these Kuhlman healing services.

If you put a damp, rotting object in a warm oven, the process of degeneration and decay temporarily ceases as the object is dried out. Where a sick person exposes himself to the warmth of the Holy Spirit this "drying out" process begins to take place. After the decay has been arrested in the cells of the body, the restorative processes already resident in the bodily cells begin to take over, and with a supercharged "shot" of the Holy Spirit, healing may take place very quickly. This is a spontaneous remission.

Symbols of the Holy Spirit are fire, which cauterizes; water, which cleanses away dirt; breath, which revives and resuscitates; and oil, which soothes. All these represent the work of the Holy Spirit in a public meeting hall or church where Jesus is honored as Healer and His blood honored as a life restorer. Kathryn Kuhlman often said publicly that she could not understand why miracles took place in her meetings, for not all people who went had faith. Even if a person is compelled to go by a loving wife, husband, child, or friend, the fact that they go is in itself an indication of faith, however small. The fact that the loving relatives, who almost compel the sufferer to go, are all praying, is reason for a miracle of spontaneous remission to take place. We are not always healed solely on our own faith; in fact, in deep distress and sickness it might be very difficult indeed for the sufferer to exercise faith at all. The fact that they come brings them into the power-charged presence of the Holy Spirit Himself who intercedes for us. Try to imagine a large healing service in which are many poor suffering people. Most of the people present are in an attitude of prayer, and this causes a spontaneous pleading by the Holy Spirit to the Father to release His life-giving breath to all. People in wheelchairs who have been unable to gain access into the main auditorium are healed in the outside passages, or even outside the building. It is sudden, it is spontaneous, it is a miracle, but it is Jesus who creates the remission.

As the church is increasingly restored by the Holy Spirit in the days in which we live, we shall see much more of this mass healing. In the Old Testament the priests were not able to stand to minister after the blood was offered, because the temple area was filled with a visible glory cloud. *"Then the house was filled with a cloud, even the house of the* LORD; *so that the priests could not stand to minister by reason of the cloud: for the glory of the* LORD *had filled the house of God"* (2 Chronicles 5:13–14). In Kathryn Kuhlman's meetings, many people fell to the ground, either when touched or in the presence of this lady. Many have queried this unusual manifestation, for admittedly it does not happen in many churches; but spontaneous remissions do not happen in many churches either, which is why people literally flocked to Miss Kuhlman's meetings seeking their healing. It seems that the falling to the ground may be a New Testament fulfillment of what happened in the Old Testament temple. The glory of God was present and as it is recorded in Luke 5:16–17 that Jesus withdrew into the wilderness to pray, and afterward He returned and started to teach doctors of the law who had gathered out of every town in Galilee, Judaea, and Jerusalem. It is recorded that in this unusual instruction class, the power (*dunamis*) of the Lord was present to heal. The fact that Jesus Himself was there and that He was teaching the Word of God created a situation where any one of those learned doctors could have received a spontaneous miracle from the miracle-working power of the present Spirit.

When we have the same conditions today, we get the same results. When Spirit-filled men or women dare to get up and pronounce that Jesus is present to heal, the very air becomes charged with the healing virtue of God, and going into such a building, it is not surprising that many do get healed.

I mention Kathryn Kuhlman, but there are others today with similar ministries, and these are proliferating, but the gifts of the Holy Spirit revealed to her with perfect accuracy the individuals who were at that moment being healed and the sickness from which they were receiving remissions, showing the presence of the Holy Spirit in a vital way. This happened all over the auditorium, and then with the help of ushers those healed were encouraged to come to the platform and testify. It was then that many fell to the ground under the power of God. Let it not be said they were "slain of the Lord," for this expression is reserved for the enemies of God. (See Jeremiah 25:33; Isaiah 66:16.) We sometimes get our expressions a bit mixed up! These coming into the strong presence of the Holy Spirit who is honoring the evangelist simply fall to the ground. They are not heated because they fall; they just fall! The priests in

Chronicles could not stand in the presence of the glory cloud—the *shekinah* of God. They were not slain!

We can see the day coming when people will not only fall before the glory of God, but many may fall before they get into the church or public auditorium! In 2 Chronicles 7:1–2, we read:

> Now when Solomon had made an end of praying, the fire came down from heaven, and consumed the burnt offering and the sacrifices; and the glory of the LORD filled the house. And the priests could **not enter** into the house of the LORD, because the glory of the Lord had filled the LORD's house.

In the same way as many were healed just by passing by the shadow of Peter, so likewise many will be healed in the cities where divine healing services are held. Many sick people lying in hospitals and homes in these cities will suddenly come under the beneficent power of the Holy Spirit and will receive spontaneous remissions. The power of God will so greatly increase in the great restoration and renewal of the church that a saturation point will be created inside the church auditorium, and it will be so great that people will fall before the Lord in streets and on the steps of the building. The power of the Lord will be present to heal in a citywide sense.

These will be very exciting days. Remember the Scripture I quoted: *"And a great multitude followed him, because they saw his miracles which he did on them that were diseased"* (John 6:2). Imagine what will happen in some of our modern cities when people actually fall down under the power of God and are spontaneously healed right on the sidewalks! Imagine the crowd of press reporters and TV cameramen who will quickly converge on such a scene, and afterward the publicity and the pictures, so that multitudes will see and believe on the Son of God. No wonder Kathryn Kuhlman was always saying, "I don't heal anybody"! These healings are from Jesus by the presence of the Holy Spirit saturating the auditorium. The only way to get our generation out of the impossible conditions of crime and debauchery that prevail is for signs and miracles to take place on a large scale. Then people will follow Jesus, not politicians!

11

THE NEW BIRTH

Wash thine heart from wickedness, that thou mayest be saved.

(Jeremiah 4:14)

I f there are degrees of intensity of miracles, and it seems there are, then the rebirth of a person's whole nature is a great miracle. The changing and cleansing of the human heart is a spiritual-surgical operation that would be impossible by the skill of man. As we shall see in this chapter, Jesus the Great Physician actually takes our heart out, washes it, and puts it back again an entirely new heart.

Jeremiah knew something of the essential wickedness of the human heart. He wrote, *"The heart is deceitful above all things, and desperately wicked: who can know it?"* (Jeremiah 17:9). Young's Literal Translation is interesting: *"Crooked is the heart above all things, and it is incurable—who doth know it?"* We see, therefore, that the very generator of our lives, that great pump of the heart, is a crooked, off-center thing; its nature is wickedness and there is absolutely no natural cure for its state. It can only continue to pump pollution throughout the mind and body of man unless there is a radical operation.

Jesus leaves us in no doubt as to what this pump will do to us:

But those things which proceed out of the mouth come forth from the heart; and they defile the man. For out of the heart proceed evil thoughts, murders, adulteries, fornications, thefts, false witness, blasphemies: These are the things which defile a man. (Matthew 15:18–20)

The mouth is the orifice from which the pump of the heart pressurizes all kinds of filthy talk and behavior. Man cannot help it. He has always been like that since

Adam was cast out of Eden. He is a fallen creature and a pathetic one. The very motivating power of our lives is the heart; without this life-giving organ we would be dead, and yet it goes on pumping its garbage through our bloodstream. Is there any hope for us? We can understand what Paul had in mind when he wrote, "*O wretched man that I am! who shall deliver me from the body of this death?*" (Romans 7:24). Paul knew the answer: "*I thank God through Jesus Christ our Lord*" (verse 24). He is the only answer; He must do the divine operation.

Unfortunately, so many wait so long before they apply for this radical operation, They try every means to ignore the impurity which is wrecking their marriage, their job and their life. They are indeed living in a body of death. We have no chance; the heart goes on pumping, pumping, pumping death into our bloodstream. We cannot get away from this death. We are trapped by a monster—Satan. As a male child is supposed to have its foreskin circumcised on the eighth day of its life, so we also are supposed to have our heart circumcised as soon as possible. The sooner the better, if we are to escape the dangerous actions of the heart, especially when we approach puberty.

Paul understood the mystery of this great operation. He expressed it in Colossians 2:10–12:

> And ye are complete in him [Jesus]...in whom also ye are circumcised with the circumcision made without hands, in putting off the body of the sins of the flesh by the circumcision of Christ...through the faith of the **operation of God**.

In recent years, man has been able to transplant a human heart. This is an outstanding medical technique, for the old, diseased heart is cut right out, the arteries carrying the blood are severed, and the old heart is removed and thrown away; in its place a healthy heart from a recently dead person is quickly put into place, and all the arteries are sutured and the blood is again allowed to flow. This is equivalent to the change of a motor in an automobile. Some have lived for a number of years with a new heart. To Bible students, this thought reminds us of David's cry, "*Create in me a clean heart, O God*" (Psalm 51:10). The Lord promised it to Israel and to all in New Testament Israel—"*A new heart also will I give you...and I will take away the stony heart out of your flesh, and I will give you an heart of flesh*" (Ezekiel 36:26). This radical operation of God can only be done by His Son, Jesus. First, we must place our bodies on the altar as a living sacrifice. (See Romans 12:1.) We must trust our whole lives to Him, knowing that He has the power to bring life out of death. We must be prepared to die, for obviously if we receive a true circumcision (cutting round) of our heart and then it is removed, we die. This is what Paul meant when, writing to the Colossians, he said, "*For ye are dead, and your life is hid with Christ in God*" (Colossians 3:3). Jesus takes the scalpel of the Word of God, which is sharper than any earthly instrument, and as we lie on the operating table of the altar of God, He neatly inserts His knife, the sword of the Spirit, does a quick 360degree turn, and all the vessels to our heart are severed. Then He takes our old sinful, dirty, crooked, and wicked heart and cleanses it in the most concentrated disinfectant in the universe, the blood of Christ. In Joel 3:21, the Lord promises, *"For I will cleanse their blood that I have not cleansed."*

Once the blood has been applied by sprinkling from the hand of Jesus, our evil conscience is removed (see Hebrews 10:22), and now our heart is ready to put back into our body again, for all the old filth and garbage has been destroyed. I always remember my childhood in England when the garbage man would sprinkle carbolic powder into the bottom of our garbage containers, as a service from the city! It smelled very nice and destroyed effectively the corruption in the can. A dirty garbage can smells horrible, and so does a dirty heart, for the author of all corruption is Beelzebub, the lord of the flies from the manure pile; but the author of cleansing is Jesus who sprinkles His blood on our dirty heart. Suddenly the motor is cleansed. The body of death has been delivered, for now a *new heart* is put back, miraculously sutured without a trace of surgery, and the blood of our bodies becomes cleansed by this disinfectant, and now the body of death becomes the body of life. We are now walking in *"newness of life"* (Romans 6:4). We are those who are alive from the dead. (See Romans 6:13.) We died because our old heart was taken out. We live because a new one has been put back. This is God's great operation, and now the new heart pumps cleansed, life-giving blood round our bodies, which brings spiritual and physical health. This great miracle is the root cause of our obtaining divine health.

Within a very short time after I had this radical operation, my language changed. My mouth became filled with praise instead of swearing and off-color jokes. Any desire for liquor instantly disappeared, and my binding habit of tobacco smoking was miraculously broken when I prayed by myself in all simplicity. I suddenly felt the unclean habit literally lifted off me like a smothering sack. This was a miracle. The renewed heart no longer had any evil things to pump into my brain, and so a corresponding change naturally occurred in my body, which now obeyed my new heart, and a complete transformation of character took place. The first one to notice this change was my wife, and later she also found Jesus Christ as her Savior and the One who baptized her in the Holy Spirit, and then she found herself a stranger in her church! No one ever spoke of the rebirth in most of the staid state Church of England. I was a member of a Calvinist Presbyterian Church, but I had never heard anything about a radical surgical change in the heart.

Isn't it amazing that forms of religion can be developed around the old, unclean heart in the body of death! The very deceitful heart of man devises religious systems that put the worshippers into a spiritual torpor, so that they no longer are able to comprehend the way of salvation or the need of it. They explain away their weaknesses and mistakes to the weakness inherent in all mankind; this they describe as "human nature." They are right, but human nature can be changed to the divine nature. Peter knew it and wrote, *"Whereby are given unto us exceeding great and precious promises: that by these ye might be **partakers of the divine nature**, having escaped the corruption that is in the world through lust"* (2 Peter 1:4). To partake of this divine nature, we must have a cleansed heart and a new Spirit; this Spirit is the Spirit of Christ, and now instead of our old heart pumping satanic filth, the renewed heart pumps round the very nature of Jesus Christ in our veins.

We are taught in the Bible a divine principle, that our life is in our bloodstream. (See Leviticus 17:11.) This would seem to indicate that our blood carries the inherited sin of our forefathers. We cannot help being sinners. We are born with the corruption of Adam in our blood. We realize that such Bible teaching is totally abhorrent to those who go their own way, but how else are we to explain the continual appalling behavior of our fellowman? Today, crime in America has reached an all-time high, and at the time of writing, the American Police Forces feel that crime has got on top of them. This is the only way that people in the United States and other "free" nations will be forced to cry to God for help, and His help can only come by Jesus performing the surgical operation of renewing the hearts of individuals. It is my prayer that God will change the hearts of our leaders. We are commanded to pray for them:

> I exhort therefore, that, first of all, supplications, prayers, intercessions, and giving of thanks, be made for all men; for kings and for all that are in authority…. For this is good…in the sight of God our Saviour; who will have all men to be saved. (1 Timothy 2:1–4)

If all the rulers of the free world were to have a true experience of the rebirth, it would transform nations within weeks.

In the Welsh Revival of 1904–06, sin largely disappeared. The police had nothing to do. The public houses closed down; the theaters had no patrons. This can happen again, and I believe it is beginning to happen in this great charismatic restoration of the church.

The renewal of the heart of the believer will be followed by the renewal of the body in health in this life, and in the ultimate to a *"house not made with hands, eternal in the heavens"* (2 Corinthians 5:1)—an everlasting body! One miracle follows another. There is no limit to the number or quality of miracles that will daily occur in the life of one who has received the rebirth. In fact, as we have already shown, our very lives themselves become walking miracles. What a marvelous promise in these days of inflation and depression: *"But my God shall supply all your need according to his riches in glory by Christ Jesus"* (Philippians 4:19). There is no inflation or lack in heaven—just a steady flow of blessing, healing, and daily supply from an inexhaustible storehouse.

Jesus promised the same thing. *"But seek ye first the kingdom of God, and his righteousness; and all these things shall be added unto you"* (Matthew 6:33).

In the days that are ahead of us, before the great day of the return of Jesus, we are going to experience many amazing miracles—special miracles, outstanding wonders that will confound the world. Our daily provision is in itself a daily miracle. Consider the Lord's Prayer when we pray, *"Give us this day our daily bread"* (verse 11); but this is contingent upon our being willing at all times to forgive those who trespass against us! As we seek to enjoy the Christian life to the full after our heart transformation, we enter into the life of continual miracles. This is why this book is being written.

12

SPECIAL MIRACLES

And God wrought special miracles by the hands of Paul. (Acts 19:11)

T his is a very interesting verse. It means, in effect, that there are degrees of miracles, or degrees in the intensity of the power or the signs of God. It is difficult enough to convince many people that God can do just one small miracle, but when we come to the realization that there are great or special miracles, we are entering into the area where God wants to attract attention to Himself in an unusual way today in order to break through the prevalent unbelief in a materialistic age.

The meaning in the Greek for the word *"special"* is "not ordinary," that is to say, extraordinary miracles. This is exciting, especially in our day where it is quite obvious that miracles are increasing in the church.

What was so extraordinary in this nineteenth chapter of Acts? It was a "first." There was no precedent for this action by the apostle Paul. We read, "So that *from his body* were brought unto the sick handkerchiefs or aprons, and the diseases departed from them, and the evil spirits went out from them" (verse 12). This Scripture has often been used today with great success, and it has also been abused. We remember a man in the Middle West of the United States who used to anoint pieces of cloth with oil and wine. He explained that the oil was a token of the Holy Spirit, and the wine of the blood of Jesus, and for ten cents he would send these to those who applied for them. It was recommended that the cloth be worn by the sufferer, and after a month or two, it should be sent back with another ten cents, so that it could again be anointed with oil and wine. There is no scriptural precedent for such action, but nevertheless God is able to heal by any means, as long as faith is found.

As we examine this Scripture by trying to read between the lines, we arrive at the conclusion that this was not a hasty decision by those present in Paul's healing ministry. Obviously, sick people, or the aged, could not easily travel distances to be in Paul's meetings. There were no ambulances, taxis, or private cars, but only donkeys and stretcher carriers walking on foot. Even the Virgin Mary traveled on a donkey! The Spirit of God revealed to someone that if the sufferer was agreeable, a piece of their personal clothing could be taken and put upon Paul's body, or put under the laying on of his hands. This apron or handkerchief would then be merely a token, and a point of contact, so that when the sick person received the garment, they would be in exactly the same position as if Paul laid his hands upon them personally. It was really the laying on of Paul's hands by projection over a distance, for there is no distance in the prayer of faith. If there was a precedent for this action, it would have been found among those who touched the garment that Jesus wore: *"And the whole multitude sought to touch him* [Jesus]: *for there went virtue* [*dunamis*] **out of him**, *and healed them all"* (Luke 6:19). The lady dying of hemorrhage (probably cancer), who was declared unclean by Israel's law, broke through the crowd and touched the hem of His garment and was healed, and again Jesus felt virtue (*dunamis*) go out of Him. (See Mark 5:30.) In both Scriptures, miracles went out of Him into them!

Because of the miracles that Jesus did among the sick people, *multitudes* followed Him, and Jesus had to move out into the lake because of the crowd pressing upon Him. It is recorded that *"he had healed many; insomuch that they pressed* [rushed] *upon him for to **touch him**, as many as had plagues"* (Mark 3:10). This almost developed into a mild mob scene; the people rushed upon Jesus just to touch Him, and when they did they were healed, and each time a *dunamis* miracle went out of Him, bringing health where incipient death reigned in their bodies before. What a ministry!

Some years ago in Congo, Africa, a young native evangelist who had learned his ministry from the men of the early Congo Evangelistic Band prayed for so many hundreds of people and so many miracles took place that in the end he was totally exhausted, and he sat upon a stone, but still the crowds seemed unending, pressing him for the laying on of hands. Finally, he said, "All those who sit on this stone on which I am sitting will be healed, just as if I laid my hands upon you." And so the crowd moved forward, each sitting on the stone, and each received his miracle of healing. These were special miracles. Outstanding, extraordinary evidences of God's miracle power. The young evangelist was drained of virtue and human strength. This is a very real problem, for with the increasing manifestation of the power of God today in 1979, I personally know what it is to feel all virtue leave me, and I have to stop, even if there are others to pray for! I remember ministering with Rev. Don Basham in Birmingham, Alabama, among seemingly hundreds of needy people, when suddenly, Don said, "I quit," and he walked to his bedroom. I managed to keep going for another ten minutes and then I quit and went to my bedroom! What shall we do with the multitudes who are yet to come in this great revival and restoration of the church, for the days of extraordinary miracles are upon us again!

The answer to this problem will be that we shall use established methods, such as handkerchiefs and aprons, but no doubt the Spirit of God will open up new methods that He will honor. Oral Roberts has probably prayed for more thousands than most evangelists, and in some cases was required to lay hands on over two thousand people in one service. He became so emotionally and physically exhausted that he had to walk for an hour or more because he was so strung up that he could not sleep. Today, he finds that television is a better method of reaching the masses, and there is no doubt that both television and radio will play a tremendous part in bringing healing to the masses.

In the final great outpouring of the Spirit to bring the church back into conformity with the original pattern, we are going to see extraordinary miracles wrought by extraordinary means, unknown in Jesus' day. Remember that He not only told us that we would do the works (or miracles) that He did, but that in this end time, this last generation, we would do "greater works"! What can this mean? I certainly think it refers to greater in the sense of a much larger number of people affected by the healing ministry of Jesus, but I also believe it means that a greater intensity of extraordinary or special miracles will occur. The people who flocked to Jesus in His day to touch Him will be manyfold greater today—all over the world. The gospel in His day was confined to Palestine, but today it is for the whole wide world. "*This gospel…shall be preached in all the world for a witness unto all nations*" (Matthew 24:14). Jesus used the word "witness" when telling the Jews that they would become witnesses when the Holy Spirit came upon them (see Acts 1:8), and the meaning of this word from the Greek *martus* indicates a person who has been martyred, but is risen from the dead. Thus, a true New Testament witness is in reality a walking, living miracle, showing in himself that he is as one who is alive from his old dead ways of life in trespasses and sins. He not only is a miracle, but is able to impart miracles to others. This is the gospel of the kingdom that in these last days will be presented to the world by a restored church. It is a gospel that is always confirmed by signs following. The preaching precedes the miracle.

In the Scripture, we have taken to explain special miracles, I would ask you to note that reference is made to sicknesses departing and evil spirits going out. I would suggest that the healing of the sick is often accompanied by the departure of evil spirits. We have shown that the casting out of a demon is equated by Jesus with the working of a miracle (see Mark 9:38–39), and in Matthew 8:16–17, the correlation between casting out evil spirits and the healing of the sick is very close. When Jesus sent out the seventy to heal in His name, He did not actually tell them to cast out demons. He said to them, *"Heal the sick that are therein, and say unto them, The kingdom of God is come nigh unto you"* (Luke 10:9). This was their commission, and the proof of their preaching would be the evidence or witness of healing for mind and body. As soon as they returned from this evangelistic journey, they exclaimed, *"Even the demons are subject unto us through thy name"* (Luke 10:17). Their commission was to heal the sick, but in doing so they obviously cast out demons, and this was before Pentecost. How much more today, with the power of Pentecost returning to the church, shall we heal the sick by the casting out of demons.

This method would surely seem to be in line with the original commission given by Jesus to the twelve apostles. He commanded them first to preach, and then to heal and to cast out demons. *"And as ye go, **preach**, saying, The kingdom of heaven is at hand. Heal the sick, cleanse the lepers, raise the dead, cast out devils: freely ye have received, freely give"* (Matthew 10:7–8). The twelve were not commanded to pray that Jesus would heal them, but that they, using His power and authority, should heal the people by laying on of hands and commanding the sicknesses to depart, just as they did when handkerchiefs and aprons were laid on sick people at a distance. The witness or evidence of their preaching, announcing that the kingdom of God was right there at hand, was the obvious evidence of miracles of healing that occurred before their eyes, often with the evidence of evil spirits leaving.

In my own ministry, as I often tell, it was really when I started being offensive to sickness by rebuking it in Jesus's name and commanding it to come out that I found myself in a new dimension of faith, for demons manifested themselves to our astonishment when we rebuked sickness, and we found experimentally that evil spirits were often the cause behind visible sickness.

Some astonishing miracles are taking place today. I read in the Australian magazine *The Revivalist*, published by my friend Rev. Leo Harris, of the Christian Revival Crusade, Adelaide, in whose church I have preached and prayed for the sick, that a girl who was always sick stopped growing at the age of twelve. Her health rapidly degenerated until she was confined to a wheelchair, unable to walk because of a form of arthritis in her knees. She was paralyzed in her whole body and unable to drink water except through a baby's drinking bottle. She was in a home for incurables—a sad case indeed. Some of the ministers of the Revival Crusade got interested in her case and began to pray for her and there were some evidences of beginnings of deliverance. Then, one day, she called another friend of mine, Rev. Ian Simpson, who prayed for her. She asked that the cast be taken off her leg and then asked for a glass of water. Her feet had straightened, her legs and spine had straightened, and she found herself able to drink water normally. Her health rapidly improved and she fell in love with a man in the home who had been injured, and who was recovering. They married, and this hopeless cripple with an underdeveloped body of a twelve-year-old gave birth to a perfect baby. An unusual miracle! This was published in the Victoria press.

A few years ago, another woman lying in a wicker-basket bed on wheels in South Wales was prayed for, but no immediate evidence was seen. Her body was weak, emaciated, and very small! As she was praying one day, her body began to change shape; the bones and sinews began to crack audibly; she grew in height; her legs grew, sinews began to develop, and flesh began to come upon her body. In a few minutes, a tremendous miracle had taken place. This was published in the Welsh press, with photographs before and after the miracle. It was published again in the *Voice of Healing* magazine some years ago in Dallas, Texas.

We think of the lady, Marjorie Stevens, in Bournemouth, England, who was crippled with multiple sclerosis. She was in a wheelchair and unable to move her body, but rang a little bell with her mouth if she needed attention. She also was prayed for, and no immediate result was seen. One day, the Lord spoke to her and told her the exact day and hour when the miracle would be manifest. She waited for it, and suddenly, at the time given, every joint in her body came back into place. The arthritis left her instantly and she stood and walked. Then she realized that her parents, who were looking after her, would be shocked, so she got back into her chair, rang the bell, at which they came to help her, and she told them what had happened and prepared them for the shock. Then she slowly arose, walked across the room and then walked downstairs to the piano and began playing hymns. Up to that time, both her arms and legs had been totally paralyzed. She then returned to her profession of nursing. After that she also traveled the British Isles telling of this miracle. We were privileged to hear her in Luton, Bedfordshire.

Other equally great miracles are being reported in an increasing way today, and we can certainly look forward to a proliferation of extraordinary miracles by apron, handkerchief, letter, radio broadcast, and live television, where the preacher will rebuke sicknesses and people hearing and seeing will be healed by extraordinary means.

God wrought special miracles. He is still in the same business!

13

NEGATIVE MIRACLES

And great fear came upon all the church.... And of the rest durst no man join himself to them.   (Acts 5:11, 13)

What is a negative miracle? It is an act of God that brings judgment upon the scornful to protect the church from the invasion of wrong spirits. A positive miracle is one that brings blessing to the church by removing sickness, but a negative miracle is one that causes a serious happening to come on those who willingly oppose God's power. The Bible teaches this.

A negative miracle may be spontaneous, but also it can be precipitated by the prayers or counsel of God's servants. God is determined that His settings of apostles, prophets, pastors, evangelists, and teachers are sacred, which is why we read in the Old Testament: *"He suffered no man to do them wrong...saying, Touch not mine anointed, and do my prophets no harm"* (1 Chronicles 16:21–22). As we approach the time of the full restoration of the church with the five ministry gifts, we are going to see a return of the protective confirmatory power of the Holy Spirit, which will confound the scornful, so that as we read in the early church, *"durst no man join himself to them"* (Acts 5:13), that is, the Spirit-filled, miracle-working church.

In past ages, and especially today, the church has been held in scorn by many in such areas as the medical profession, the press, and the television networks. This is because it has only a form of godliness, with forms, ceremonies, and superstitions, and we are commanded to turn away from such hypocrisy, because it lacks the dynamic miracle-working power that brings fear into the hearts of the ungodly. The church is supposed to be a giant in our society and literally to inspire holy fear into those that oppose themselves to the Spirit of God. When the church is sick, it inspires confidence in nobody.

When the early church was enjoying pristine power and zeal, there was a man and wife who did not understand that God was a holy God. They thought they could say one thing and do another, and God would not even know their thoughts! Their names were Ananias and Sapphira, and they were so touched by the moving of the Holy Spirit that they felt led to give money to the work of God, which is always a good thing. They sold a field—a piece of real estate. They had promised God and His servants that the church would receive all they obtained for their land. It is quite possible that they obtained more for it than they had anticipated, and so there was an easy temptation to give God only what they thought they would receive, and they decided to keep the rest. Many would think this a fairly harmless thing; after all, God got most of the proceeds of the sale, and He would certainly understand if they kept some for themselves; after all, it was *their land.*

The miracle-working Spirit of God came upon the apostle Peter and told him that this married couple was lying to the Holy Spirit—not to man. To say to Peter, "We will give you the proceeds of this sale and you can use it in God's work," was equivalent to promising God—not Peter. All that Peter did verbally was to remind Ananias of his promise, and he told him that he had actually lied to God! The result of this spoken rebuke and admonition was that Ananias fell down dead. Many have thought that the great apostle killed him, but not so. God took his life, because he had lied to the Holy Spirit in the midst of the beginnings of the greatest and dearest creation of God—the church, His bride. God would not allow His servants to be mocked. God was quick to bring a negative judgmental miracle. His power was revealed.

Three hours later Sapphira arrived and said, "What have you done with my husband?"

> And Peter answered unto her, Tell me whether ye sold the land for so much? And she [lying] said, Yea, for so much. Then Peter said unto her, How is it that ye have agreed together to tempt the Spirit of the Lord? behold, the feet of them which have buried thy husband are at the door, and shall carry thee out.
>
> (Acts 5:8–9)

She immediately fell dead at the apostle's feet. Did Peter kill her? No, but when he spoke with divine authority, knowing that this woman could not escape the same judgment that came on her husband, the Lord carried out the death sentence. It was these two miracles that brought such great fear upon the members of the church, in order to warn them that there could be no lying in their promises to God. As far as the rest of the Jews were concerned, they just moved out of the orbit of such tremendous people with such powerful leaders like Peter. This was a radical operation of God in the early church. We need more radical operations today to cut out the cancers of lying, stealing, and looking upon God almost with contempt. *"Be not deceived; God is not mocked"* (Galatians 6:7).

It is a serious business to become a full-gospel Christian today. Our vocation is to magnify the Lord Jesus in our lives, to exercise the gifts of the Spirit, and to bring healing and blessing upon our neighbors, even if they are scared of us! Many people have said to me, "I'm scared of you!" especially when they hear and see demons coming out crying with a loud voice!

Another case comes to mind—the story of Elymas the sorcerer. This man was a warlock, a spiritist medium, possessed of demons, and we have a proliferation of them in the world today! He was even known as "BarJesus," which means "son of a Savior." He was an impostor, but nevertheless full of demonic power, and when the deputy of Paphos enquired of Paul and Barnabas about the true Jesus, this demon-possessed man rose up and opposed their ministry and teaching, trying to turn away the deputy from the knowledge of the truth. Satan tried to interfere with God's true servants. Doesn't he try to do this today, and don't we let him get away with it?

> *Then...Paul, filled with the Holy Ghost, set his eyes on him, And said, O full of all subtlety and all mischief, thou* **child of the devil**, *thou enemy of all righteousness, wilt thou not cease to pervert the right ways of the Lord? And now, behold, the hand of the Lord is upon thee, and thou shalt be blind, not seeing the sun for a season. And* **immediately** *there fell on him a mist and a darkness; and he went about seeking some to lead him by the hand. Then the deputy, when he saw what was done, believed, being astonished at the doctrine of the Lord.*
>
> (Acts 13:9–12)

This is a good way to get souls saved!

Did Paul make him blind? No. The context shows us that Paul had a word of knowledge of God's intention and merely spoke it to the sorcerer. Then it happened, and God made him blind. This is a very illuminating story and full of warning for the rebellious Christian who dabbles in the occult. Paul was full of the Holy Spirit and Elymas was full of the devil, and because Jesus conquered Satan on the cross, it was an uneven contest for the warlock. The word that came out of Elymas's mouth was a perverted word, but that which came out of Paul was a miracle word, and God worked the miracle, not of giving him sight as He had earlier to Paul, but of taking away his sight. A miracle can work both ways! Paul was three days without sight because of his rebellion against God, but afterward when he obeyed God he received his sight back again, and was baptized. (See Acts 9:18.) Paul learned his lesson for all time, and maybe we sometimes have to learn the same lesson, the hard way! It is easy to blame the devil for our sicknesses and infirmities, but maybe it might more profitable if we examined ourselves. In Psalm 51, we read of David's searching prayer that all wickedness and uncleanness might be removed from him. David suffered many chastisements of the Lord. Before we take communion we should pause and examine ourselves. (See 1 Corinthians 11:28.) The blood of Jesus Christ received by faith in the communion cannot wash away our sins if we are opposing a husband, a wife, or children in their search for God. We are in danger. I wonder if Elymas ever got converted and received his sight back? We can only hope so.

Perhaps one of the most awe-inspiring abilities of the church is to give a rebellious person over to the devil. Some people's concept of a loving God would reject such a proposition as contrary to their understanding of God. Do we not read God is love? (See 1 John 4:8.) Yes, but we also read in the same book, *"Behold therefore the goodness and severity of God: on them which fell, severity; but toward thee, goodness"* (Romans 11:22). The word *"severity"* means "a cutting off." It checks with Jesus's teaching in John 15, that a branch in Him that did not bring forth good fruit was pruned—cut off (see John 15:6). God prunes us down to size when we get uppity and rebellious. This is a miracle.

There was a case of gross immorality in the Corinthian church. A young man was living in an incestuous relationship with his mother. The very concept of this cancer in the church makes a Christian shudder, or should do so! The members of the church did not know what to do. They didn't like the situation and had no doubt often spoken, rather cautiously, to the two church members, but they refused to alter their filthy ways. Paul told these Christians they should have removed the offenders out of the church, not allowed them to contaminate the whole body and even partake of communion! He told them what they must do: come together in the house of God, and in the name of Jesus Christ and by His power (miracle-working *dunamis* power). *"Deliver such an one* **unto Satan** *for the destruction of the flesh, that the spirit may be saved in the day of the Lord Jesus"* (1 Corinthians 5:5). The whole church was commanded by God's servant to deliver him *over to Satan*, not to pray the prayer of deliverance from Satan, because the man and his mother were not repentant, and no one can be delivered who is in rebellion to God. They can only expect His miracle judgments.

What would happen to this young man? As the reference shows that it would be his flesh or body that would be judged, we must assume that he either became very sick in body or suffered some kind of accident. The purpose of this judgment would be to bring the young man up with a spiritual jerk and give him time to consider his evil ways, and so to cry out for his healing. Later, we know he was restored to the Corinthian church. (See 2 Corinthians 2:6.) He must have learned his lesson, and so did not lose his salvation. We often wonder why some people do get so sick! Sometimes, it might be that the Lord is dealing with them.

Some years ago, my wife and I had a very ugly situation of rebellion in the church, particularly against God's servant. It was not only hurting me and making it extremely hard to minister the Word to the flock, but it also carried the possibility of splitting the church, which is a very common thing today in some churches! My heart was almost breaking, for a true pastor still loves the rebellious sheep, and after everything had been tried in love, to no avail, my wife and I decided to give the rebellious ones over to Satan. Without enlarging as to how God moved, the rebellious ones were smitten in their bodies and the whole unpleasant business was brought to an end. It makes me sad even to relate this happening, but the word of prayer from a servant of God, with others in the church, is mighty to the pulling down of strongholds. God's work—His church—must not be allowed to suffer and be prevented from manifesting the glory of God in our day and generation. *"For our God is a consuming fire"* (Hebrews 12:29).

How can we deal with those who try to infiltrate our churches with false doctrine?

> *And that because of false brethren unawares brought in, who came in privily to spy out our liberty which we have in Christ Jesus, that they might bring us into bondage: to whom we gave place by subjection, no, not for an hour; that the truth of the gospel might continue with you,* (Galatians 2:4–5)

Here is a most interesting account of true apostolic dealing with doctrinal error. Some people described as *"brethren,"* members of other assemblies possibly, came into their midst to try to bring them back into bondage of false teaching, possibly Judaic legalities of touch not, taste not, don't do it this way, etc. Did Paul give them a hearing? For, after all, philosophy tells us there are two sides to every question! Did he give them "equal time" as we are supposed to do in a democracy? Not so. He told them to get out and stay out within the hour, and used both his authority as an apostle and the power of the Holy Spirit. If they had stayed after such sharp admonition, no doubt they would have been in deep judgmental trouble. I can hear Paul saying, "Get out in Jesus' name!" Was this a "Christian" act? Should we speak to brethren like that? Was it a Christian act for Jesus deliberately to whip the moneychangers in the temple area and cast them out with divine wrath? Some would think that Jesus was hardly a Christian at all, and certainly Paul must have been a monster.

When we think of the case of the two shebears coming out of the wood to attack the forty-two young men (probably teenagers) who insulted the prophet Elijah by jeering at him and calling him "old baldhead," we realize that the anger of God is swift against unseemly behavior toward His chosen servants. I know many reject this story as showing that God must be a monster and not a God of love, but it seems that wherever rebellion is found against God and the church, we find this wrong concept of God arising. The story, though terrible, agrees with the same principles that I have discussed in the New Testament. God is a God of judgmental miracles against those who mock Him. God is not mocked. He says so. Here the teenagers were injured in their bodies, the same as Elymas.

Was God wrong in opening the earth and swallowing up 250 men who offered incense to God when in a state of rebellion? (See Numbers 16:35.) Our offerings are repugnant to God if we do not obey Him. They are hypocritical. What about the case of thousands of Israelites being bitten by serpents because they rebelled? (See Numbers 21:6–7.) It seems that God's miracle-working judgments often become a blessing in disguise to arrest us in our rebellion. While lying on our backs, we have time to reflect a little and to read our Bibles afresh.

I am sure that as the church grows to maturity in our generation, we are going to see a great return of supernatural judgments, by miracles from God, to cleanse the church of rebellion and to cause fear to come upon the church, and to keep away those who would pervert the church. She is going to be a bride without spot or wrinkle or any such thing, and to get rid of a wrinkle it becomes necessary to apply a hot iron with pressure.

14

THE CLAY AND THE WAX

What shall we do to these men? for that indeed a notable miracle hath been done by them is manifest to all them that dwell in Jerusalem; and we cannot deny it.

(Acts 4:16)

Reference to the above Scripture was made in chapter 1. The birthday of the true church occurred in Acts, chapter 2. Let us never lose sight of the fact that before Pentecost Jesus Himself was the body of Christ, and until He was crucified He could not send the Holy Spirit to cohere the initial 120 members into a corporate whole. Dr. William Smith, in his *Bible Dictionary*, writes, "The day of Pentecost is the birthday of the Christian church. Before Pentecost they had been individual followers of Jesus; now they became His mystical body, animated by His Spirit."

Many have restricted the miracle of the rebirth to the total necessary requirement for membership of the body of Christ, but we must bear in mind that the teaching of Jesus to Nicodemus in John, chapter 3, was given in the Old Testament dispensation, because the New Testament did not come into effect until after the cross. It was just as possible to be born again of the Spirit under the old covenant as under the new. The formation of the body of Christ on the Day of Pentecost was brought about by something more than the rebirth by the Spirit of God. It was the baptism of the Holy Spirit, another work of the Spirit, that created the true body of Christ, and this infilling was immediately accompanied by the miracle of speaking in tongues. The birth of the new body was evidenced by the birth cry from heaven. We emphasize this theological fact because we want to demonstrate that the true church began with a miracle and should continue with miracles. It is a miracle church. The conception of Jesus was a miracle; the resurrection was a miracle; and the subsequent outpouring of the Holy Spirit was a miracle. The forms of the old covenant gave place to the reality and substance of the new. It was a better covenant.

Following the exciting events of Acts 2 and Peter's initial sermon, a few days passed and then God dropped His spiritual bomb into the midst. He caused a notable miracle to occur at the Gate Beautiful with the healing of the crippled man. This miracle caused such a stir that everyone in Jerusalem knew about it, without the aid of radio or television. God was working to a divine principle. Peter had preached the Word of God and God Himself had confirmed it. This is all according to the pattern of Matthew 10:7–8. Let us face the facts. The Word of God teaches that we should not only expect to preach or teach the Bible, but to have it confirmed by miracles. *"And they went forth, and preached everywhere, the Lord working with them, and confirming the word with signs [miracles] following"* (Mark 16:20). Our problem in so-called Christian lands has been that the Word has been partly preached, often with mutilations, additions, and traditions, but it was never even expected that God in heaven would confirm the preaching with miracles, and so they did not happen.

With the healing of the cripple the church militant began its major offensive against sin and disease. God was determined to let the Jews in Jerusalem know that His Son, whom they crucified, had indeed risen from the dead. How better to advertise the gospel! Every time someone prays and God answers from heaven, it is proof that Jesus lives and that He arose from the dead.

The rain falls on the just and the unjust (see Matthew 5:45), and the sun shines on the evil and the good. The Holy Spirit shines upon mankind like the sun, and some react like clay and become harder and harder. Other humans react like wax and become softer and softer. God can do nothing with baked clay, but He can mold the wax to His pattern. With the increase of the present outpouring of the Spirit upon all flesh (see Joel 2:28), the same miracles that bless some will be the cause of others becoming bitter, jealous, and more condemned. This is why Jesus spoke in parables, because He said His disciples would understand, but the religious leaders would be much more condemned if they heard Jesus speak in language they could understand. He knew their hearts.

The healing of the cripple brought blessing to thousands, but the reaction of the religious leaders was quite the opposite. They recognized that a notable miracle had occurred; they said they could not deny it. They were arrested by the Spirit into a place of impotent rage. They noted also that it was Peter and John who had worked the miracle. Peter said to the man, *"Such as I have give I thee"* (Acts 3:6). The cripple received it by his faith, Peter gave it to him with his faith, and when the two came together a miracle took place. Yes, it is quite consistent that Peter and John worked the miracle, for Jesus had already commanded His disciples to heal the sick, because they had freely received from Him and were expected to give freely. What had He given them? Paul called the ability *"the gifts of healing…the working of miracles"* (1 Corinthians 12:9–10).

When the Holy Spirit came upon them in the upper room, the divine charismatic abilities were given with the Holy Spirit; they were integral in the Spirit. When they received the Holy Spirit from the risen Christ, they received His divine miracle-working attributes. These gifts (nine in number) are not given for personal use, or for personal blessing, but they are given to give, and to whom should we give them? Surely to the sick and crippled of our age. We transmit them after we receive them. We speak and He confirms our speech with a miracle; but if we never speak it, it will probably never happen.

Peter and John were all keyed up waiting for the great miracle to take place, and when they saw the cripple they received a word of knowledge that this was the one God had chosen for the miracle. They ignored the plea for silver and gold and gave him healing, worth far more. Could it be that much of the church has been more interested in receiving silver and gold than in giving miracles?

Peter and John, who had been brought up to come under the spiritual headship of the priests, now found themselves under a greater Headship, that of Jesus, the chief High Priest. This High Priest rightly interpreted the Scriptures, thereby confounding the official custodians of the divine mysteries. The priests commanded them, with threatenings, that they should no more teach the Jews about these things. They were terrified that more miracles would occur; but Peter and John answered with divine anointing, *"Whether it be right in the sight of God to hearken unto you more than unto God, judge ye. For we cannot but speak the things which we have seen and heard"* (Acts 4:19–20).

The priests let them go and they returned to the other new Jewish believers in Jerusalem, and they rejoiced together and had a prayer meeting. They reminded the Lord of the prophecies in Psalm 2 about kings and rulers rising up against the Lord and His Christ, and then they prayed, *"And now, Lord, behold their threatenings: and grant unto thy servants, that with all boldness they may speak thy word, By stretching forth thine hand to heal; and that signs and wonders may be done by the name of thy holy child Jesus"* (Acts 4:29–30). They did not pray to play it safe; they were not cowed by the self-righteous priests; their one object was to preach and expect God to do His part by baring His arm in working many miracles in the immediate future. Their understanding of the preaching of the gospel of the kingdom was to expect miracles. If they had not occurred they would have been astonished. The place shook where they prayed, and they went out and demonstrated great power (*dunamis*—miracle power), thus proving the resurrection of Jesus. Here, it is stated that the working of miracles was the indisputable evidence of the resurrection. How many church buildings shake today!

It was at this point that great fear came upon the church: *"And by the hands of the apostles were many signs and wonders wrought among the people"* (Acts 5:12). Can we imagine the utter frustration of the religious leaders? More and more, miracles were proliferating throughout Jerusalem; the whole city was full of the news and the very ones that the people had looked to as spiritual leaders now turned out to have feet of clay, baked hard by the outpouring of the Spirit. Instead of the leaders with their theological degrees doing miracles, it was now seen that the men with feet of wax, whom they called "unlearned and ignorant men," were doing the "impossible," and they were shown up in all their fancy dress and spiritual impotence. Pride was too strong among most of them to humble themselves under the hands of these apostles and to receive forgiveness of sins and healings of mind and body, particularly from the spirit of jealousy.

Today, we are seeing the same thing, but as in those days many priests did believe, *"And the word of God increased; and the number of the disciples multiplied in Jerusalem greatly; and a great company of the priests were obedient to the faith"* (Acts 6:7). In the old-line denominations, we are hearing of many priests and ministers who are being obedient to the faith and are receiving the baptism in the Spirit and entering into the life of the miraculous. The church is becoming one again, returning to preaching the Word with the Lord confirming the Word with miracles. Unfortunately, if history is our guide, many will also try to block the moving of the Spirit, for the charismatic move is challenging their formal methods of conducting religious services. This is most noticeable because of the large increase of charismatic books arising today, which is very disturbing to many of our evangelical brethren who have decreed the doctrine of dispensationalism. If they say it cannot happen today, then they have to pretend that it isn't happening all around them. Some ministers have been fired by their denominations or local church boards. The Spirit of God being breathed into their moribundity has caused the hardening of the clay in their midst, even as in Stephen's day when he spoke out boldly and denounced these men, *"Ye stiffnecked and uncircumcised in heart and ears, ye do always resist the Holy Ghost"* (Acts 7:51). As they represented the state, they brought to bear their law of stoning and the first martyr fell to the earth, the first of the martyr seeds that would bring forth a great harvest like unto Stephen. No one apart from Jesus spoke straighter to the religious leaders. Jesus said, *"Scribes and Pharisees—hypocrites"* (Matthew 23:13). Would a Christian minister utter these words today?

We are glad that the late pope, the bishop of the Church of Rome, indicated his approval and blessing upon the present outpouring of the Holy Spirit upon Roman Catholics worldwide. This augurs well for a great renewal of the church within the Roman structure, but this in turn will bring enormous changes of practice and doctrine, which are already taking place now in 1979. There is a real sense that Roman

Catholics, in spite of their traditions, will receive the baptism in the Spirit with the sign of tongues more easily than many of the Protestants in their communions. The Catholics will be greatly encouraged by the presence of Cardinal Suenens of Belgium, who has received the Holy Spirit baptism, and he will no doubt act as a great strength to them. The editor of *New Covenant* magazine, Ralph Martin, whom I know, has written that there are three distinct rivers flowing today—one, the classic Pentecostal river made up of those denominations known as Pentecostal; the second, those who are receiving the baptism in the Spirit among the Protestants and Baptists; and third, the Roman Catholic charismatics. These three rivers are flowing parallel at present, but they will shortly merge into one great, broad river, *"a river that I could not pass over: for the waters were risen, waters to swim in, a river that could not be passed over"* (Ezekiel 47:5). There will be an agreement on all essential doctrine in that day. While the three rivers are flowing separately, yet in the same direction, there is little point in raising acrimonious discussions on variant doctrinal issues. We are all aware of them, but God Himself will resolve the matter to everyone's complete satisfaction, for we shall see eye-to-eye in that day.

The Archbishop of Canterbury has also noted that there is an increase of interest in this renewed outpouring of the Spirit among Anglicans worldwide. It is recognized as a fact in many Anglican dioceses, including the one in Toronto, Canada. The outpouring of the Spirit is going to be received in our day, and multitudes of priests and ministers and their congregations will be baptized in the Holy Spirit and begin a renewed life in the Spirit, expecting and seeing miracles in their midst. Nothing can stop it today. *"This is the day which the LORD hath made; we will rejoice and be glad in it"* (Psalm 118:24).

15

HOW DO WE START?

God also bearing them witness, both with signs and wonders, and with divers miracles, and gifts of the Holy Ghost. (Hebrews 2:4)

Many who are truly children of God by faith in Jesus Christ would frankly be at a loss to know how to anticipate miracles. It is clear from our study on the subject of miracles in the New Testament that these should always occur following the faithful preaching of the gospel of the kingdom; but after we have preached the full gospel, how are we to act, or try to precipitate miracles? Is there anything we should do after preaching? We have been so used to preaching, and some have made it a regular practice to have an altar call, that our understanding of "what next" seems to stop with our methodology.

Many have asked me, "How do we cast out a demon?" The idea behind the question is often fear that one day they might be faced with the necessity to do so. There is always a first time for every new experience, and assuming a demon is present, then Jesus tells us to cast it out in His name. We may not be sure, because we have not listened to the still, small voice of the Spirit giving us either the discerning of spirits or a word of knowledge; this may be beyond our spiritual understanding, but it is clear that where a demon is present Jesus told us to cast it out! How do you cast an unwanted dog off your property? Do you pray and ask Jesus to do it for you, or do you take action by word and deed to evict the unwelcome stranger? As I have recounted in my book *Dominion Over Demons*, there was a first time in my experience in 1948. 1 had tried praying for a man with congenital asthma by the only known methods of anointing with oil and *asking* Jesus to heal, but nothing happened! I did not know that I was doing it the wrong way. After prayer and some advice that was given to me, I decided I would deal with this man's sickness in an entirely different (yet scriptural) way. I addressed myself to the demon behind the sickness and said, "You foul spirit, come out of him in Jesus' name!" The demons of sickness immediately reacted and began to cough out of him accompanied by much mucous. I had precipitated a miracle, which may not have occurred unless I had rebuked the spirit behind the asthma. He was permanently healed.

While realizing the fact that spontaneous miracles do occur in right circumstances, yet it seems that we must do our part if we expect God to do His part. In many cases, Kathryn Kuhlman actually rebuked sicknesses in people when they came to the platform and she was face to face with them.

We have the story of the healing of Peter's wife's mother as a good guide to find out how Jesus healed her. There are three accounts in the gospel of this important healing, and all three give us a different aspect of truth, and I want to tie these together. In Luke 4:38–39, we find that Jesus *rebuked* the great fever. In Matthew 8:14–16, we read that Jesus *touched* her hand and the fever left her, while in Mark 1:30–31, we find that Jesus took her by the hand and the fever left her. Let us deal with the three things that Jesus did. He did *not* ask the Father to heal her for His sake. He took definite action, and I believe we should do exactly the same.

First, He rebuked the fever. The word *rebuke* means to set a weight upon; in other words, when Jesus opened His mouth and spoke to the spirit behind the fever, He put such an intolerable weight upon this demon spirit that it could no longer remain in such an uncomfortable situation, and left rapidly to get away from the Spirit of God emanating from Jesus's presence and from His Word. It must be obvious that Jesus would not speak to an inanimate "something." He spoke to the spirit, which heard, understood, and obeyed. Only an intelligent being will do this.

Second, Jesus touched her with His hand. This is important, because He teaches us to lay hands on the sick so that they shall recover. The touch imparts the gift of healing into the sick person. Let us not forget that the charismatic manifestation of Christ called *"gifts of healing"* (1 Corinthians 12:9), which are within a Holy Spirit-filled Christian, gives all of us the ability to impart a particular gift of healing from the many gifts of healing within us. This charismatic ability has often been wrongly understood and interpreted to mean that the one who prays has "a gift of healing," rather like the healers of the occult groups. Some have a ministry of healing, and they are enabled to impart a particular healing for a particular sickness. It is the sick person who receives the gift! As we touch in faith, even a fingertip touch, the gift of healing flows into the sufferer to replace the sickness which has been rebuked, The sickness becomes paralyzed and bound. The touch imparts new health.

Third, Jesus took her by the hand and gently lifted her up, because He wanted to prove to her that to continue to lie in bed would be quite unnecessary, for she was healed! She might not have realized how wonderfully she was healed until she received practical help. Many times when I prayed for people who have been paralyzed in an arm or leg, I have said, "Now move your arm." They shake their heads, for they know that in the past they could not do so! Their minds have not understood how a miracle takes place so silently. Then it becomes necessary to take their arms and begin to motivate them in Jesus' name. At first, this can produce some pain as the stiffness or soreness leaves, but the action of faith helps it to leave, and easement begins to come. Sometimes, I have found it necessary to pray against the problem a second time, with the cooperation of the sufferer, and so often the pain and stiffness give way to such prayer and action. As a person begins to act his own faith and walk, or run, or dance, the symptoms begin to go. Faith must be accompanied by action—as the lepers went, they were healed.

I remember praying for a lady named Mrs. Woods in Toronto, some years ago. Her legs were swollen and painful with arthritis. She was sitting, so I took her hands and prayed, rebuking the sickness in Jesus' name. Then, I said, "Come on now, rise and be healed," so she acted on this instruction of faith and found that all the pain and stiffness had gone. She remained perfectly healed for years.

Jesus gives us this principle of faith in the story of the healing of the impotent man at the Pool of Bethesda. He had been lying down unable to walk for thirty-eight years—a long time—but Jesus said, *"Rise, take up thy bed, and walk"* (John 5:8). The man immediately arose, like Peter's wife's mother, and took up his bed and walked. If he had not obeyed the words of Jesus he would have remained in a procumbent position and not realized that after the command of faith he could walk. Our trouble today, especially in hospitals, is that we are called on to pray for people who have no intention of getting out of bed and walking, because they would not want to disobey their doctor's instructions! In fact, they would not expect to get out of bed and walk if a minister or a priest prayed for them. If the minister was so bold as to command them to get out of bed and start walking around the hospital ward, they would look upon him with horror and astonishment. It is this unbelief among Christians that is such a stumbling block to the working of miracles.

A few years ago, I was called into a Scarborough, Ontario, hospital to pray for a Mr. Larry Snellgrove, an international director of the Full Gospel Businessmen's Fellowship. He had been rushed to a hospital with bleeding of the bladder, a serious thing indeed, and the doctors found a growth in the bladder and said they would operate the next morning early. I prayed for him, rebuked the growth in Jesus's name, and, after a few words of encouragement, left the hospital. It was not long afterward, on the same evening, that Mr. Snellgrove telephoned to say he had signed himself out of the hospital, against the wish of the doctors, because he believed that he had indeed been healed at the time of the prayer of agreement. There was no visible evidence that healing had taken place, for he was still hemorrhaging, and this lasted for eleven days, days of testing. On the eleventh day, the bleeding stopped, and a few weeks later, he passed from his body granular matter. Some months later, he was examined by the doctors again, and they could find no trace of a tumor, for it had completely disappeared. Would this miracle have happened if he had not acted his faith, which in this case was basically, "Arise, take up your bed, and walk"? I may not know the answer, but it does seem that because he acted in accordance with Scripture he received a miracle.

It seems we must adopt this method if we are to expect to see miracles following our preaching. Let us remind ourselves of these three steps. (1) We address ourselves to the spirit behind the sickness and rebuke it. (2) We impart the necessary gift of healing by the laying on of hands. (3) We help the sick one to realize that by the stripes of Jesus they really are healed. Earlier in this book, in chapter 2, I told of the healing of the man with the totally locked spine. It was when he started to do what he had been unable to do for twenty years that he realized he had been healed and proved it by touching his toes. No doubt he could have refused to believe and so he would have stayed rigid.

I have seen cases of people in wheelchairs who have arisen and started to walk afresh. Often they will be weak, but as they continue to act their faith, the strength returns to them, given by Him who is the resurrection and the life. It is His life that quickens or brings strength back to our sick, tired bodies. It is real, but we must believe, and our belief will be shown by our actions. This is what James taught: "*What doth it profit, my brethren, though a man say he hath faith, and have not works? can faith save* [or heal] *him?... Even so faith, if it hath not works* [or action], *is dead*" (James 2:14, 17). So many will say, in desperation, "I have all the faith in the world," and after prayer get no miracle. Faith alone will not heal you or show you your miracle; you must begin to act as though you have it.

When the mother of my eldest son's wife was healed of arthritis and bursitis, she was stiff with pain in shoulders and elbows. After rebuking the sickness, I took her arms and started slowly moving them. She felt great pain and her forehead broke out in sweat drops, but I ignored her cries and continued moving her arms. They got looser and looser, and the pain began to go. Then I took her knotted fingers and started to move them, and slowly the pain and stiffness went out, and she has maintained her healing for some years at the time of writing. She goes around everywhere telling of her miracle. Without the healing power of the Lord, she would have been in a wheelchair by now.

Another daughter-in-law was able to turn hand spins after being prayed for a badly injured, bandaged ankle. She had been given cortisone by her doctor because of the severe pain. Her mother had degeneration of the spine and had been told that she would shortly be confined to a wheelchair, but after prayer she went back to the swimming pool and swam fifty lengths to prove her miracle. All these have held their healing miracle for years. In my own family alone, quite apart from the church of which I was proud to be the pastor, miracles have taken place as soon as faith action was taken.

I went to London, England, in 1974, and I met a lady who told me she was suffering so much from the bondage of arthritis, but she said, "I have never seen a miracle." Owing to the grip of the state church with its formal worship, it is not expected that worshippers will see miracles in their services, and this has bred over hundreds of years a dead unbelief for the supernatural. The whole emphasis is the worship that they give. They are not taught to expect anything in return. Sick people go to hospitals, not to churches for healing. They go to doctors, not to Jesus. They have faith in the efficacy of drugs, not of the blood of Jesus. They need encouragement and teaching. Preaching and praying for miracles in Europe is a very hard thing. They have never seen a miracle! I began to rebuke the spirit of arthritis in this lady, and slowly and stubbornly it began to respond, and finally began to cough out of her with deep coughing. After my return to Canada, this lady wrote telling of a definite improvement in her health. She was rejoicing.

We can see that the more faith that can be engendered in the one hearing about the gospel of the kingdom, the more quickly will the sicknesses leave the mind and body. This is why Jesus puts preaching first, to be followed by action on the part of the ministers and priests, who should then expect to see miracles taking place. They may happen slowly or quickly; this seems to depend on individual faith, and as we see healings taking place, our own faith grows stronger, so that we in turn may impart a miracle more easily to others. This prayer of faith that heals the sick is mutual. (See James 5:14–15.) This is why preaching must come first—because it inspires faith: "So then faith cometh by hearing, and hearing by the word of God" (Romans 10:17). It may be true that our strong faith may bring a miracle to a person who has little or no faith, but without their own faith, they will be unable to maintain their healing, and they will probably get sick again.

On the last Sunday of 1974, a lady and her husband came from Windsor, Ontario, just to see what our church was like. They had heard of us! They had no intention of asking for anything special. This lady had arthritis all over her body, but I preached on the receiving of miracles, and then some went into the prayer room to receive theirs. A Presbyterian minister's wife had a leg lengthened by one inch—she had been wearing a built-up shoe. The lady from Windsor, who was originally from the Greek Orthodox Church, asked me to pray against her arthritis; so I asked her to sit down and examined the length of her legs. Sure enough, on the side of maximum pain (the left side) her leg was one inch shorter than the right. As I prayed, it came level with the other, and all pain instantly disappeared. Next day she ran upstairs! The doctors had called it arthritis and treated it as such, without much results. Could it not have been caused by a pinched nerve in a crooked spine bringing arthritis pains throughout the nervous system?

Next day, before returning home, she brought her husband and he also had a leg one-half inch short, and it was made whole. He also had a touch of diabetes and we prayed for a miracle for this too—only time will show if he got this necessary miracle. More on this in the next chapter.

16

HOW TO KEEP YOUR MIRACLE

Behold, thou art made whole: sin no more, lest a worse thing come unto thee.
(John 5:14)

Obviously, we are not made whole to live the old life that we used to live, for it was probably this way of life that brought our trouble upon us in the first place. No one repairs a house and leaves it without a tenant. Our bodies become the very temple of the Holy Spirit, and who ever heard of a temple that was run down and dilapidated and failing to bits in ruins? Satan knows that our bodies are dwelling places, for in the story of the unclean spirit that was cast out of a man, the spirit was determined to get back and hung around waiting for a favorable opportunity and said, *"I will return into my house"* (Matthew 12:44). It is a fact that our bodies do indeed become the dwelling place for God or the devil. It seems we just cannot occupy them alone and be neutral. We must have God or the devil to dwell with us. We get lonely otherwise!

It is very dangerous to be beautifully delivered by the power of Jesus and His blood, to have our house "swept and garnished" and then have no tenant inside except ourselves. Our body or house is first swept clean of all filth of the flesh (see 1 Peter 3:21) and then garnished with beautiful fittings; the walls become decorated with the luscious fruits of the Spirit; the furniture is heavenly and the carpets lovely. The gifts of the Spirit are available in every room and the glory of God covers the place like a cloud, so that everyone who enters will be blessed and healed also.

But there are some who feel they are healed because it is their inalienable right as a Christian and that it really does not matter too much how they live, because they believe "once saved, always saved" and their names are in the Lamb's Book of Life. Whereas it is true that we do not inherit eternal life by our works, yet we do maintain our health by living close to God in this life; in fact, the very reason that we are delivered from the power of the enemy should cause us to live closer to the Lord than before we were set free. The love of God begets our love in return, and the definition of love is given by John the Beloved: *"For this is…love…that we keep his command-ments"* (1 John 5:3). Love of God is not a sentimental, mushy kind of love, but a true obedience founded on deep reverential love.

According to the teaching of Jesus, it would be better not to have been delivered than that we should afterward live a loose backsliding life, for it is exactly at such a moment that the same evil spirit that was cast out will return into *his house* with seven other spirits worse than himself. Jesus said, *"And the last state of that man is worse than the first"* (Luke 11:26). This is a terrible prospect, and a solemn warning, that being a true, happy Christian is not a state that can be lightly handled. If you want a miracle in your life to deliver you from some oppressive satanic bondage of soul or body, you must be prepared to live all out for the Lord. In the Scripture, we have quoted at the beginning of this chapter, Jesus told us about the man who had an infirmity for thirty-eight years and who, to maintain his miracle, must *never sin again*. This is a tall order, isn't it?

There are several definitions of sin. Sin is transgression of the law (see 1 John 3:4), but John shows us that a true Spirit-filled, born-again Christian does not sin! *"All unrighteousness is sin: and there is a sin not unto death. We know that whosoever is born of God* **sinneth not***; but he that is begotten of God keepeth himself, and that wicked one [Satan] toucheth him not"* (1 John 5:17–18). There are two contrasting definitions of sin in the Bible, the sin of ignorance and the sin of presumption. (See Leviticus 4; Psalm 19:13.) The sin of ignorance is one we all commit, because we are still imper-fect, but these are not sins that we willingly commit, because we love the Son of God. As soon as a sin that is caused by our imperfections becomes noticed as such, we immediately confess it, renounce it, and reckon it is under the blood of Jesus. The sin of presumption, however, is when we deliberately do something that is known by us to be contrary to God's will and Word. There is no forgiveness for such a sin until it is confessed and forsaken and put under the blood. The *"sin not unto death"* is the sin of ignorance. A Christian who really loves the Lord has no desire to sin intentionally, and so to use the simile given by John, "he keeps himself." This thought is taken from James, who wrote, *"To keep himself unspotted from the world"* (James 1:27). The Christian who does this is described again by James in these words: *"But whoso looketh into the perfect law of liberty, and continueth therein, he being not a forgetful hearer, but a* **doer***, of the work, this man shall be blessed in his deed"* (James 1:25).

So we should be able to see that the command of Jesus to sin no more, to avoid a worse condition of life (that is, by seven other spirits) is a most reasonable proposition.

I have found in years of practical experience with the life in Christ that when, in God's overruling providence, He allows me to be attacked by Satan, whether in soul or body, it is a most humbling way of attracting my attention again to His promises of deliverance. *"Many are the afflictions of the righteous: but the LORD delivereth him out of them all"* (Psalm 34:19). As soon as we get sick, Satan comes against us very strongly indeed and tries by lying and bluff to win us away from the glorious promises of the Word of God. We are tested and refined, for He deals with us as sons and not as bastards. (See Hebrews 12:8.)

Now, after experiencing deliverance of any kind, we are counseled in plain language to resist the devil for ourselves. The keeping of our house, the cleaning of the house, is our sole responsibility. We do not hire cleaning women to do these elementary chores—we do them ourselves, while others may encourage us to do a good job. Any pastor knows that it is not always easy to get some members to help in such chores as painting the church, cleaning out the washrooms, or caring for the garden, because many, unfortunately, think such work is too menial for them. In fact, I must express surprise that I have met some Christians like this. They would rather pay someone else to do it for them. This puts them in a position of superiority. The Bible teaches us that Jesus humbled Himself and became obedient. (See Philippians 2:8.) He was even born in a stable, by the will of God. Jesus started at the bottom. It seems to take some of us a little time to get there!

The greatest position of strength in the Lord is the position of true humility. Nothing is too much for us to do for God. We are so glad to have the opportunity to serve. I remember way back in 1940 in Dublin, Eire, I was first asked to administer the bread and wine in the Communion service to the people. My heart almost burst for joy at this great privilege. I, who had been a contaminated sinner, was now asked to serve the sacred elements of the body and blood of Jesus to the people. What an honor! I used to take every opportunity to serve, in big healing conventions in the United States. I loved to take up the offerings, to do anything to help. Always be prepared to take the lowest station; otherwise how can He call you up higher?

Both Peter and James tell us the way to resist the devil. It is first from the position of true *humility*. *"Yea, all of you be subject one to another, and be clothed with **humility**: for God resisteth the proud, and giveth grace to the humble...the devil...walketh about, seeking whom he may devour: whom resist stedfast in the faith"* (1 Peter 5:5–9). Note that our attitude at all times must be easily and willingly to be able to be subject to each other; as Paul puts it, *"in honor preferring one another"* (Romans 12:10), and thus wear the very mantle of humility, not a false humility which is obvious to all, but the deep outworking of the love of Christ, loving and honoring the meanest among us. If this is our state, we can easily knock the devil out of the ring every time he enters in, or knocks on the front (or back) door, of our house. James in his fourth chapter also tells us to humble ourselves and then resist the devil and he will flee.

Many, desiring to become humble, put on an act. They then pray, and say, "O Lord, keep me humble." This is not the prayer of faith, nor is it according to Scripture. Peter gave it to us straight. *"Humble yourselves therefore under the mighty hand of God"* (1 Peter 5:6). We are the ones to take the humble position without God helping us. As soon as action is required, we are the first to volunteer, because there is no menial job that is beneath our dignity, because we have already taken the lowest place. We remember the words of our Savior, who told us to say, *"We are unprofitable servants: we have done that which was our duty to do"* (Luke 17:10).

Humility is a most beautiful attribute of the Holy Spirit. By nature the Adamic man is proud, boastful, knowing nothing about God (see 1 Timothy 6:4), and we have to be most careful that these old traits of rebellion are put to death and buried in the waters of baptism. If pride rears its ugly head, we must immediately bring ourselves back into the place of humility before God, confessing it is all of Him and none of us. Let us not wait to be knocked off our horse as Paul was. (See Acts 9:4.) We should fall at His feet daily, and worship and adore Him, confessing that we know nothing apart from Him. Then our position is one of strength against the world, the flesh and the devil.

17

THE BRIDE PREPARES

And the Lord said unto Moses,...see that thou do all those wonders before Pharoah, which I have put in thine hand. (Exodus 4:21)

The great story of the Exodus of Israel from Egypt is one of a succession of miracles whereby God bared His holy arm and delivered His people. They were not delivered by preaching, but by the supernatural.

Moses was a most unwilling candidate for the high office of being Israel's leader. He tried his best to argue his way out of a difficult situation. Why should he give up his church in the wilderness where he had sheep to supply his food and raiment? He had his tentmanse and a wife and family. For forty years he had lacked nothing and had grown into a rut. Many of us have, too. We look for no changes in our religious thinking or our church orientation.

To a reluctant Moses God gave two great miraculous signs: one, the ability to deal with serpents, and the other, to cause healing to come to diseased flesh. (See Exodus 4.) After the initial shock of realizing that miracles could happen through Moses, God said that if the Israelites did not believe the first sign of handling serpents, they would believe the second sign of healing. However, the Lord warned that if anyone in Egypt refused both signs, then Moses was to continue to do miracles, which would be against Pharaoh, in order that by such pressure he would let Israel go.

Moses took his rod in his hand (verse 20), and this rod represented his Godgiven authority; today, it is represented by our Bible, God's final authority. It is with the Word of God today that we do miracles that the masses may be convinced that God *is* God. When Moses used his rod, a miracle took place.

These miracles were: (1) God's rod turned into a serpent swallowing up all the little serpents produced by the magicians; (2) rivers turned to blood; (3) plague of frogs; (4) plague of lice; (5) plague of flies; (6) destruction of cattle; (7) plague of boils; (8) plague of hail; (9) plague of locusts; and (10) plague of darkness. It was only when the blood was applied that the miraculous deliverance of the firstborn of every family and their cattle was accomplished. This represented the church of the firstborn, and today we must be born from above to be members of this New Testament church. (See Hebrews 12:23.)

It was the shedding of the blood of Christ that delivered us clean out of spiritual Egypt (see Revelation 11:8), and we are living in the days of the second Exodus, as spiritual Israel is being brought out of captivity from the world system known as Babylon or confusion, into the law and order of God's kingdom on earth.

The Lord does not have to invent new ideas to do the same job. If miracles delivered ancient Israel out of bondage into freedom, so likewise exactly the same methods will produce the same results in our generation. In the interim period between the old covenant and the new, Jesus came to deliver Israel again with miracles. The first was the casting out of demons from the man in the synagogue in Capernaum; the second, the healing of Peter's wife's mother. (See Mark 1:23–31.) Notice the same order—first handling serpents, and second dealing with disease. Jesus then handed this ability to His twelve apostles by giving them His power (*dunamis*, miracle) and authority to cast out demons and to heal diseases. (See Luke 9:1–2.) His purpose was to educate His men, the very foundations of the coming New Testament church, to deliver Israel as Moses had done. When this proved successful with the twelve, He multiplied this ability by giving the same power and authority to seventy additional men, who went out into all the towns and villages round about and made the gospel work! These men were astonished and exclaimed, *"Even the devils are subject unto us through thy name"* (Luke 10:17). They cast out demons and healed the sick after saying, *"The kingdom of God is come unto you"* (Matthew 12:28). What a simple sermon! Anyone can say that and then go ahead and prove it! Sermons without miracles may appeal to the intellect, but they will never help in casting out demons and healing sicknesses.

It may be a very bold statement to make, and I believe it is entirely prophetic in content, but the day is fast coming upon the church when she will only use those methods to deliver herself. Already today, in 1979, I am personally seeing men and women delivered, healed, and filled with the Spirit every week in our home church in Canada, quite apart from those similarly blessed in the various cities and countries which I am privileged to visit. The pattern is always the same, first to open up the Bible and show people what is meant by the kingdom of God being among them, and then to pray for them and *expect* miracles to happen, and *expect* demons to come out of many crying with loud voice!

In Revelation 19:7, the cry goes up among the righteous and angels in heaven, *"The marriage of the Lamb is come, and his wife has made herself ready."* How is the wife of Jesus to make herself ready? How does any bride make herself ready for a wedding? By working at it. Every detail must be right. The marriage garment must be without spot or wrinkle. The body must be washed and clean. Suitable perfume must be applied. Her hair must be perfectly styled. Her flowers must all express joy and beauty. It takes a lot to prepare a bride. It costs money, too! Let us take a look at the bride of Jesus today. James asks the valid question, *"Is any sick among you?"* Surely the answer must come back, "Oh yes, I am sick in my mind and body, and there is to be a wedding. What shall I do to prepare myself?" James tells us, *"Call for the elders of the church"* (James 5:14). What for? Why not call for the medical men and the psychiatrists? Are not these the ones to prepare the bride? No, the elders. Why? Because they will pray the prayer of faith, and the bridegroom Jesus in heaven will send all the miracle-working power of His Holy Spirit into the sick people and heal them and cast all the demons out of them when the elders of the church use His name and authority and exercise it. They must make the gospel work!

It seems also that the bride will carry a lamp, with a bright-burning flame, because the lamp is full of pure oil, representing the Holy Spirit. It does seem, if we can understand anything from the parable of the wise and foolish virgins of Matthew 25, that those who had lamps but no oil were not ready! How wonderful has been the teaching about the baptism of the Holy Spirit in our generation, but there are some who still resist. God gives a whole generation for the bride to prepare herself for a marriage of eternity.

As we look at the various fragmented denominations of the whole church today, we surely must cry out in alarm. She is *not* ready by a country mile! Oh yes, there are many, many signs that she is doing something about it. The whole charismatic move of God is supplying the elders to help in the preparation. The members of the bride are being convicted, and they are coming for healing and for deliverance. They are receiving the baptism in the Spirit; they are exercising the gifts of the Spirit; they are healing each other in Jesus' name. Don't let us get hung up on only using elders. There are not enough of them to do it alone. We need every laborer in the wheat field—men and women and young people, but all working under the help and discipline of the eldership. God doesn't set apostles, prophets, evangelists, pastors, and teachers just to embarrass the established denominations, but to deliver their members into the glorious liberty of the gospel. Out of darkness into light, out of bondage into freedom. No wonder Paul called it *"glorious liberty of the children of God"* (Romans 8:21), and he used the Greek word *teknon*, which means baby children, ones who have not matured. This is what is happening. God is pouring out His Holy Spirit all over the world onto babes in Christ emerging from the shadows of their denominations.

Many classic Pentecostals find it hard to believe that Roman Catholics could even be children of God, but the Lord began to baptize them in the Spirit and they began to speak in tongues, so some said that these were phony baptisms. Their idea seems to have been that God could not give His Spirit to someone who held doctrinal error. But don't Protestants hold doctrinal error also? Is God going to wait until every member of His bride believes doctrine identically the same as all other members? Not so. The baptism of the Spirit is being given in answer to personal faith and the present need to prepare the bride for the marriage.

Without the oil, there would be no healing or deliverance from binding demon powers. Jesus set the pattern in Matthew 8:16 by casting out spirits *and* healing everybody. This same pattern is going to be performed in our generation by us.

It has pained so many to realize that sick people in churches may be afflicted by evil spirits called "spirits of infirmity" or weakness. The clergy have not been prepared for such a revelation. For one thing, they were never taught anything about it in seminary, and for another thing, it never happened in their denomination; but it is happening today for all to see or read about. Is God going to be circumscribed by the limitations of our theological seminaries or Bible schools? Must He only do it our way and not His way? You remember that Amos wrote, *"Can two walk together, except they be agreed?"* (Amos 3:3). We may be quite sure that Jesus is not going to agree with us! It is we who are going to agree with Him! If we are to walk in white with Him eternally it will be on His terms and doctrine, not on ours! We may delude ourselves and say that our doctrine is the same as His, but suppose it isn't? We are then in a mess. It should be our delight to know God's ways. We should spend this whole generation seeking God's ways, and in order to do this we shall have to listen to the Holy Spirit after we have received Him in our personal Pentecost. Did not John clearly tell us, *"But the anointing which ye have received of him abideth **in you**, and ye need not that any man teach you"* (1 John 2:27).

After a Roman Catholic or a Protestant or a Baptist receives Acts 2:4 and speaks in tongues, they are then in a position to be taught of the indwelling Spirit, who will teach them and guide them into all truth. (See John 16:13.) The truth that the indwelling Spirit will teach us will agree with men qualified by the Spirit to teach in the church, known as teachers, one of the five ministry gifts of New Testament eldership. Our human spirits will witness to the Holy Spirit working in many different ways in a fully charismatic fellowship, and we shall all recognize the truth, and error will melt away. It will take the bright light from our burning lamps to do it. If our lamps have gone out, we shall only be led by men with their theological darkness, and this will never prepare the bride for the coming of the bridegroom!

Let us be warned not to go off into spiritual comers and ignore the men of God that He is raising up in this day and say we do not need them. We need each other, and every new facet of discovered truth will be shared with the whole body by the Spirit and by each other. We will share with each other rather than teach each other.

The two signs that Moses used will be the two signs that we shall use—miracles and healings, plus a whole catalog of New Testament signs and wonders and miracles of a greater dimension than in the early church. Every day today is an exciting day—it can be for you. Why not start now preparing yourself for His coming, so that you also can be without spot or wrinkle, so that you can have your miracle, your healing and your baptism in the Spirit? What is stopping you? Man or denomination? Husband or wife? Pride?

John saw the bride prepared. *"One of the seven angels…talked with me, saying, Come hither, I will shew thee the bride, the Lamb's wife"* (Revelation 21:9). Inevitably the time is approaching for the coming of Jesus for a perfected church. Will you be one of the wise or foolish members of the church? Will you be ready? John speaks of those who will be ashamed of themselves at His coming (see 1 John 2:28). Some have suggested that the Greek word here is very strong and means they will appear to be paralyzed. They will realize they have not made themselves ready. They did not believe all this teaching about healing, demons, and the baptism in the Spirit. Their churches taught that these signs were not for today. During the war in England, no one ever saw a banana, but it would have been foolish to say they were not for today, because they had a glut of them in Jamaica! There was a time when they were "not for today"—between 1940 and 1945 in Europe, but afterward, bananas came back again. So today, the gifts of the Spirit are available and there is a glut of them. All we have to say is "Come and feed at the Master's table. There is plenty for all."

God help us to be ready on the day He comes for His church. Help me to make myself ready while I have time. Amen.

18

CONCLUSION

If they hear not Moses and the prophets, neither will they be persuaded, though one rose from the dead. (Luke 16:31)

In the present charismatic renewal of the whole church, God is forcing Himself upon an unbelieving people by signs and miracles. These will increase rapidly. There will be mass healings and miracles taking place in huge outdoor meetings that cannot be denied. However, although they cannot be denied, many will not believe because they do not wish to believe. Believing would alter their lifestyles!

The religious Jewish council, led by the high priest Annas, challenged the apostles, saying, *"By what power, or by what name, have ye done this?"* (Acts 4:7). They could not deny the miracle of the healing of the lame man, for they admitted, *"For that indeed a notable miracle hath been done by them is manifest* [or obvious]*...and we cannot deny it"* (Acts 4:16)! This healing was admitted to be notable, and it was intended to be, for this means that God intended the whole of Jerusalem to take note that His Son, Jesus, had indeed risen from the dead and was alive and doing miracles. There is no evidence that Annas or Caiaphas ever accepted the person of Jesus as Savior, but they were given every opportunity to do so. They were without excuse. We believe that this is God's pattern and purpose today, to make it obvious to the whole church that He desires to heal and restore every sick Christian.

From Australia comes an amazing story. It was told by Pastor Leo Harris of Adelaide in his magazine *Impact*. In 1975, three Christian businessmen heard that students in a certain public school were allowed to play with Ouija boards. They were so alarmed that they visited the principal, who ridiculed their protests, saying he did not understand how it worked, but he admitted it did work and it gave the students lots of fun. The three Christian men then walked through the school and discovered where the children played with these boards. They entered the room and again tried in vain to teach them the extreme danger of contacting demon spirits through Ouija boards. The children just laughed at them, and suddenly the wrath of God came upon one of these good men and looking at the board he said, "I rebuke the spirit in that Ouija board in Jesus' name!" Immediately, the board disintegrated into many parts. The resident demon had been expelled from inanimate matter. I told this story to a charismatic minister of an historic church and he said he would not dare to tell it to anyone in his church or denomination! Why not?

This story reminds us of the one where the woman in Medillin, Colombia, threw her holy medal into the fire when she accepted Jesus as Savior, and, at the same instant of time, another holy medal in a box in her home at a distance exploded, and when she opened the box on returning home, there was a pile of dust. Again, a resident demon was cast out violently from inanimate matter. Many just laugh when we warn them that an idol brought from a foreign land may well be the home of an evil spirit living right in their home to visit sickness and trouble upon them. We are awakening today to a greater awareness of the reality of our supernatural God and His Son, Jesus.

I believe that when the emblems of the communion service are prayed over by the minister, they are, in effect, impregnated by the Holy Spirit. The Roman Catholics go a little further and teach that the bread has actually mysteriously changed its state and represents the "real presence of Jesus." The realization that personal evil can dwell in inanimate wood or stone must teach us that the Spirit of God can dwell in consecrated communion bread.

I realize that many will refuse to believe such things, but we need to keep well in mind that Jesus said we would do His works, but we would do *greater* works in our day. (See John 14:12.) Our mind boggles at such a thought that we in our day would do greater works than Jesus. It is hard enough to try to teach people that we can and should do the works that Jesus did, if we exercise enough faith, but to expect miracles of a dimension not compassed by the canon of the Scripture is to invite unbelief and ridicule.

A lady and her husband recently flew from California to Toronto to see me. Her story was strange. From time to time, she was attacked by demons that stiffened her body, and then a terribly icy feeling came over her and her blood felt like ice. She was quite powerless under these attacks and then suddenly strange scratch marks would appear on her arms, about four to six inches in length, although the skin was not broken. She showed these marks to my wife and myself. We prayed for her by rebuking these spirits in Jesus' name, and she began to sob uncontrollably for about one hour as they were progressively cast from her. Her husband looked on in astonishment! How can evil spirits attack a woman and leave visible marks on her body? She was a professing Christian and associated with the charismatic movement in her hometown. It would have been cruel to say, "She could not possibly have a demon," and just shrug off all responsibility as many would do. God is forcing us to realize that things are happening today for which we have no previous theological understanding, and therefore no expertise to deal with the unknown. We are on the verge of the greatest breakthrough of the Spirit of God in the history of the world.

Another case that happened in our experience about the same time concerned a lady who came to us when we were visiting Dallas, Texas. The lady asked for prayer because she had breast cancer that had gone into the lymph glands. In the natural,there was little hope apart from a strange, unexpected remission. My wife and I explained to her that this was probably caused by an evil spirit of infirmity that was trying to destroy her life. She was a Christian, working among young Christian people. As we began to take our authority in Christ over these malign forces, she began to cough deeply and mucous began choking out of her. I tell these things to show that we should not be afraid or appalled. God is trying to get our attention! Suddenly, we heard, "Nein, nein, nein." We listened again, and this time the strange voice said, "Nein, nein, ich komme nicht!" The demon in a southern Texas lady was speaking to us in pure German, refusing to come out. How can we explain these happenings? How can a demon speak German? Quite easily, for it had previously lived in a German-speaking person and was probably liberated at his death, when it would attempt to find another body to inhabit and bring death upon its next victim. Many find it hard to believe in the sign miracle of speaking in other tongues, but when we show that demons also can speak other languages, one can see fear coming on the faces of these we tell. When the Holy Spirit inhabits the human body, He can give many languages to the Spirit-filled Christian in whom He dwells. Satan also counterfeits all the gifts of the Holy Spirit.

It is written of the antichrist that he, energized by Satan, *"doeth great wonders"* (Revelation 13:13). We should remember that the meaning of the word *antichristos* is one who comes in the place of Christ—an imitator of Christ, claiming His authority and ability. By demonic powers, he imitates the power of Christ. We have many antichrists operating in the religious field today. They are active in the midst of the church.

One of the most challenging Scriptures in the Bible is found in Matthew 21:22: *"And all **things**, whatsoever ye shall ask in prayer, **believing**, ye shall receive."* On another occasion, two blind men came to Jesus, and He asked them, *"**Believe** ye that I am able to do this? They said unto him, Yea, Lord. Then touched he their eyes, saying, **According to your faith** be it unto you. And their eyes were opened"* (Matthew 9:28–30). Here we see the simplicity of coming to Him *in faith*. Nothing can be refused if we come in faith, and it seems that whatever our problem, mental or physical, it will constitute a miracle when we experience deliverance from it. Jesus is waiting anxiously for us to stretch out the hands of faith and receive our miracle.

The problem all began in the garden of Eden, when Adam and Eve partook of the fruit of the *knowledge* of good and evil. They did not have this intellectual ability in the garden because they lived solely by faith in God and His Word. The glory of God covered them and they had unbroken fellowship with the Father. It was only when they started to try to use their own wisdom, which of course did not agree with God's revealed wisdom, that they got into very severe trouble and could no longer walk with God in that pure, innocent way. As we educate our children today, they begin to think they know more than God, and so they never expect a miracle, even if they go to some cold, formal, intellectual church every Sunday. Anyone who dares to believe that God works miracles today would be considered an ignoramus, but when they see a miracle, they will ascribe it to the power of the mind. One moment, we change from an ignoramus to one who has super power of the mind able to work "mind miracles." They will not admit that the miracle, which they cannot explain by intellectual means, must be of God if the prayer is made in the name of Jesus. *"By what power and by what name?"* (Acts 4:7), asked the scribes. It is the power of God revealed in answer to the prayer in the name of Jesus. *"There is none other name under heaven given among men, whereby we must be saved"* (verse 12). Here, the word for *"saved"* is *sozo*, which means saved, healed, made whole, delivered, and set free!

Once man is put in the position of having to admit a miracle, he has to make a quick decision about his ideas of God, and human pride is a very strong factor that keeps multitudes chained in ignorance, which they call wisdom. The knowledge of good and evil is too much for mankind. Satan told Eve that when she ate of the fruit of the tree she would *"be as gods"* (Genesis 3:5), and man loves to think of himself as a little god or deity, knowing so much more than his fellows and certainly much more than God Himself.

The evangelical church has basically rejected the miracle of tongues, and many of the classic Pentecostal churches have used the same excuses to reject the ministry of casting out demons; the next wave that is now coming in is of mass miracles, and the charismatic movement must be careful not to make the mistake of rejecting miracles as the norm.

I was talking to a Roman Catholic brother from Ottawa recently, and I asked him how many in his congregation had spoken in tongues. He replied, "Twenty-two! *But* soon they will all have the baptism in the Spirit!" This is expectant faith, and will be rewarded by the whole congregation receiving the sign gift miracle of tongues. Following close after this experience in local churches, we must expect everyone to believe God for a miracle of healing or restoration, and in this way all sick people in our congregations will be made whole (*sozo*). It has come as a great shock to many pastors when some of their people have been prayed for and immediately demons have manifested themselves and come out to the astonishment of all. This is how God means it to be, for we truly believe God is pressing hard for a decision today, first among His children and then among the world. There came a time of decision in Joshua's life when he challenged Israel to *"choose you this day whom ye will serve"* (Joshua 24:15). This challenge is again being forced upon us because of world events. God is intervening in the affairs of men, for He has come down to deliver us out of the hands of our enemies. (See Luke 1:71.) The deliverance of Israel under the old covenant was wrought by miracles by the hand of God alone. There is a Second Exodus taking place today and God's New Testament Israel people in our churches are again being delivered by miracles. The final miracles will take place when once again the whole Christian church understands the power that there is in the blood of Jesus and uses it by sprinkling it on their hearts and homes, and God will see the blood and the great final Passover will take place. The firstborn ones who have been born again of the Spirit will be healed and delivered. The miracle of Holy Spirit fire is now being seen to it run along the ground in our churches and is bringing back healing and life instead of forms and ceremonies. (See Exodus 9:23.) The frogs of the false demons are being seen in our land (see Revelation 16:13; Exodus 8:6), and the darkness that can be felt is evident in every major city of the world—gross darkness of satanic delusion and unbelief (see Exodus 10:22; Isaiah 60:2). Instead of the brook Kidron, being dyed red with the blood of the temple sacrifice, typical of the blood of Jesus, we have had rivers of blood shed in the world wars. (See Exodus 7:21.) The plagues are upon us, but New Testament Israel, the church of the firstborn (see Hebrews 12:23), will be delivered because Jesus made an atonement for us. His shed blood will bring us salvation and healing.

It would seem to me that the more daring the faith of the minister, the more probability of a miracle taking place. I must emphasize the great need for daring faith in commanding a miracle to take place. Sicknesses must be commanded to leave; physical deformities must be commanded to go and bodies to be made whole. Where the nature of a human has been gravely distorted by an incursion of demons, then the evil spirits must be commanded to leave the personality of the sufferer. A man came to see me from Alberta recently. He had been mixed up in the occult and he was extremely depressed to the point of having little interest in life at all. This dangerous state will often lead to chronic melancholia and schizophrenia. The demons causing the trouble were firmly commanded to leave in Jesus' name. They did not move immediately and so we suggested the man start pleading the blood of Jesus to help his deliverance. Within a short time, he suddenly started to speak in tongues as the Holy Spirit came in, and then the deliverance started. The demons were ejected by choking through his throat and continued for about fifteen minutes. The result was amazing. His whole countenance changed from torment to joy, and while he was with us for a few days, his face was beaming. Jesus delivered him by a miracle.

A lady came into church hobbling on an aluminum hand crutch with four feet. She walked with very great difficulty and was assisted by her two daughters. She was driven in from Niagara Falls, Ontario. We ministered to her. The Lord straightened out the back, put the hips back into place and adjusted the shoulders. She walked perfectly, without the hand crutch, and they all wept for joy. Later, she left the church and gave us the crutch for a souvenir. I dared to ask her age. She said she was eighty-three, and she walked *perfectly*.

There is no end to this ministry. It is just beginning. We are learning to *enforce* miracles in the name of Jesus. It seems the more we command them, the more they happen. As faith rises in the church, and especially among the ministers of the church, so will miracles increase. We again remind ourselves that Jesus could do no miracles in His hometown of Nazareth (because of their unbelief).

Many are afraid that if they pray, command, and do their best, nothing will happen! I would suggest that if this is our approach, nothing will ever happen! The more we exercise faith, the more faith we generate, both in ourselves and in those for whom we pray. We must dare to try, and we shall be increasingly satisfied with the results that we shall see. We shall get bolder and bolder in our faith, and miracles will increase in number.

The manifestations of all the gifts of the Spirit (see 1 Corinthians 12:8–10) are miraculous. These gifts should be the normal in our churches today, and the more they operate, the more faith will be generated, and the greater the miracles that will take place. This is an exciting age in which we live. We must attempt great things and expect great things, and they will happen. This is the way of faith.

With God, all things are possible to them that believe.

WHERE IS THE ANTICHRIST?

CONTENTS

PREFACE

This book is written right on time. For years, many sincere evangelical Christians have believed the futurist theory of Bible interpretation. Basically and in short, this teaches that a personal political leader becomes a false Messiah to the Jews. He is the complete fulfilment of all teaching on the Antichrist or the Man of Sin. Before he makes a covenant with the Jews in the Holy Land, the temple of the Jews must be rebuilt, and in this temple he makes his covenant. At the same time there will be a rising of the ten kingdoms in Continental Europe; to fulfill the ten toes of the Gentile image of Daniel.

Those who believe this interpretation are eagerly looking at the European Common Market as prima facie evidence that their understanding is correct, for if there comes a full confederation of ten European kingdoms under the Antichrist, they believe their understanding will be proved to be correct, but if the present nine (not ten) federated States in Europe disintegrate, which seems most likely, then their whole concept will be shattered. We await to see whether indeed these states do break up.

One magazine majoring on this futurist approach recently said that the Antichrist was already overdue, and in fact may already be here! The temple has not been rebuilt; in fact the Jews by their laws would never profane the religious shrine of another faith by pulling down the Dome on the Rock, even if it is built over the sacred rock on which Isaac was offered.

Many of these futurists tell us that "Jesus may come tonight," but, if this is true, no Antichrist has time to appear. It is said that he will wear out the saints of the most high (see Daniel 7:21), which most certainly happened at the time of the dark ages, but does it have to happen in our generation? Events in the present restoration and renewal of the church contradict such a thought.

It is because the teaching of the futurists is not working out that this book has been written to try to give clear teaching on how historical events, already known to us, have demonstrated the perfect fulfilment of so many of these prophecies. The falling away, the Antichrist and the tribulation are already passed into history. They do not have to reappear. We are on the upsurge of the restoration cycle today, as we near the end of the age. We are not on the downgrade. Antichrist is giving way to Christ.

In teaching the identity of the Antichrist in history, we wish to assure our Roman Catholic friends that no insult is intended to them or the members of any denomination. The Priest Savonarola arose in 1490 to protest the degradations and ignorance of his church leaders, but he was put to death. Martin Luther arose to protest the unscriptural teachings of the Pope. Neither was against the Christian church, but they were for Jesus and His Word—the Bible. They wanted to be a blessing to the church.

If we refer to the "errors or pretensions of Rome," we must not forget to keep in mind that many of these errors were transmitted to the Protestant churches born after the Reformation. We are living in a day of total cleansing from sin, iniquity and doctrinal error in the whole church at large. In searching for truth I do not wish to insult anyone, for we are reminded of John the apostle, who was commanded to measure (1) the temple, (2) the altar, and (3) the people. This is exactly what is being done by the Holy Spirit through anointed men today. The church and its members are being measured by God's Word, in order that we may put off the old garments and put on the new. The bride is to be arrayed in glorious garments of righteousness, holiness, and truth.

Tremendous changes are taking place today in all denominations. Is there time for an Antichrist to appear and rule over a world church as some teach? The World Council of Churches appears to be less of a force in the world today than it was at its inception.

Events will show whether the contents of this book are true, and we believe we do not have long to wait.

We beg of our many friends who only know the futurist interpretation to bear with us and consider prayerfully what has been here committed to print.

FOREWORD

No one interested in the fulfilments of Bible prophecy will be indifferent toward H. A. Maxwell Whyte's *Where Is the Antichrist?* His forthright presentation of the historical school of prophetic interpretation will hold the interest of every reader.

In some respects, *Where Is the Antichrist?* may be like the cat let loose in the chicken coop! Those who have held the futurist system of prophetic interpretation as an integral part of their evangelical fabric may well feel rather jolted by Maxwell Whyte's bold bid to take the theory apart. They have my genuine sympathy. I can still remember my own traumatic experience some thirty-two years ago, when the futurist interpretations on which I had been raised as a young man suddenly ceased to be acceptable to me.

The steps I took then to rethink Bible prophecy, I would sincerely recommend to students today. I determined to stand, mentally, with the prophets in their day, then to search diligently through history to find a reasonable fulfilment of their prophecy. The conclusion I came to was that most major prophecies had already had an historical fulfilment, and, as aptly expressed by the author of this book, there is no need for a second fulfilment.

Now, to endorse the historical principle as expressed in this book is not necessarily to accept every detail of interpretation. In this field, there must be room for differences of thought, whether we be historicist or futurist. May I suggest you consider the principle of historical fulfilment, and not be disturbed by any detailed treatment of individual prophecies.

I wish the reader every blessing, even excitement, and indeed, if need be, divine enlightenment as these pages are perused. And to the author I offer congratulations on his bold attempt to call us back to a valid alternative to the modern systems of prophetic interpretation that have proved unsatisfactory to so many.

—*Leo Harris*
Adelaide, South Australia

1

THE FALLING AWAY

During the last 130 years, the evangelical church in general has believed and taught that there would be a great falling away from the truth of the Word of God towards the end of the Christian dispensation. Scary sermons have been preached warning that the days would come when Christians in western lands would be put against the wall and shot in mass massacres, and that the Bible would be taken from them, their children trained in atheism, and that with its last gasp the beaten, battered, bruised, bleeding bride of Christ would say, "Even so, come, Lord Jesus, and rescue me from this position of total defeat."

If such an extreme position has not been taken by some, at least a negative outlook has been held by thousands with the general view that everything would get worse and worse because the great falling away of the church had to occur, and there was very little if anything that the church could do, except wait for the inevitable and the rapture.

Since 1960, the general outpouring of the Holy Spirit upon the whole church has increased tremendously, we dare to suggest with geometric progression, and quite unexpectedly to evangelicals the Spirit of God has been filling many in the "dead historical churches," and thousands of Roman Catholics are gathering in charismatic conventions to rejoice in the newfound liberty of the Holy Spirit, to pray for each other, and to manifest the nine gifts of the Holy Spirit as enumerated in 1 Corinthians 12:8–10, and to lift up Jesus as Lord. The Jesus revolution has started among our young generation, and both these significant trends have upturned many previously held theories about the falling away. It now seems to many that we are on the verge of the greatest revival of the Christian church ever to be imagined in church history. It would seem that a great falling away of the church and a great restoration of the church are two mutually contradictory positions, and that present events are moving so rapidly to a climax that we must reexamine our whole understanding of

Bible prophecy. The fundamentalist churches that have majored on the falling-away concept are now being invaded by the Holy Spirit, and among these people, we have found that there is a new hunger to understand some things that they have been taught that no longer seem to make any sense in view of present happenings. In other words, we find Christians newly baptized in the Spirit in a general state of confusion concerning eschatology.

The whole concept of a falling away is based on Paul's teachings to the Thessalonians 2:3. It is common mistake to try to fit Scriptures into events that are happening in our lifetime. We well remember that before World War II, thousands were trying to find Hitler and Mussolini in the Bible. Many claimed to have done so and preached sermons on their findings! Certain Scriptures in Daniel and Isaiah seemed to fit the picture so exactly that jump interpretations were made, usually without any knowledge of how these Scriptures had already been fulfilled perfectly in history; in fact, church and world history is usually not a strong point with many theologians!

The early Christian church in Thessalonians knew perfectly well that Jesus was going to return to this earth. The Scriptures plainly taught it, Jest emphasized it, and so it would happen one day. We are in agreement with them today. It will happen! The mistake they made was to believe it would happen in their lifetime! It must be supposed that many generations were quite sure that it would happen in their time also, but it did not. With the coming of the Holy Spirit upon the church at the turn of the century, the Lord emphasized through the oral gifts of the Spirit that Jesus was coming back soon, because the very fact of the renewed outpouring of the Spirit upon all flesh was obviously a great sign of the near coming of the Lord. But how near? How soon? It is in the interpretation of "near" and "soon" that thousands have made grievous mistakes.

Paul had the difficult task of persuading an enthusiastic church that the actual return of Jesus was a long way off. There can be little doubt that some resented his slow approach to Bible prophecy. In our lifetime, we have heard many sincere and enthusiastic Christian ministers suggest that the Lord Jesus might come back that very night, but He has not! Altar calls have been based on sermons warning people that the church door might be closed before the next service, and pressing them to make their decisions *now*, not based on sound Bible exegesis, but on fear. What reaction would there be in some of these "converts" when Jesus did not return as suggested by the evangelist? The cliché "if He tarry" can boomerang.

Paul warned the Thessalonians that they should not be shaken in mind or be troubled, because they believed the return of Christ was at hand, but he told them that before this great event would occur, there would be *the* great falling away *first*. We have emphasized the word "the" because the Greek carries this clear meaning. The word "a" in our King James Version is incorrect. Paul is referring to the specific falling away, not several, not a second recurring fulfillment, as some have suggested, but one particular all-important, never-to-be-repeated falling away of the church. After a series of world-shattering events, Jesus would return.

Matthew Henry, in his commentary, states that this falling away would be a general apostasy in matters of sound doctrine, church government, instituted worship, and a holy life. The falling away had no reference to secular governments or leaders. It would be gradual but progressive, leading to the revelation of the Man of Sin, or the Antichrist. History reveals this is exactly what happened, and the early church, full of the graces and gifts of the Spirit, degenerated into an apostate church that controlled the whole of Europe from 600 to 1517, when the Reformation began. During and after these years, such true Christians as existed throughout Europe were hounded like dogs, beaten, starved, and put on the rack. It is reckoned by Dr. Gratton Guiness that fifty million Christians were martyred in the dark ages.

If these tragedies have already been fulfilled to the very letter, why should we expect them to happen again? If the Scripture has been faithfully fulfilled, by what right of exegesis and logic may we expect a secondary fulfillment? The whole purpose of prophecy and its principle is clearly stated by Jesus when He said, "*I go unto my Father.... And **now** I have told you before it come to pass, that, when it is come to pass, ye might believe*" (John 14:28–29). The prophecies that would take place between His ascension from the Mount of Olives and His return to the same place could only be understood in their fulfillment. This disposes at once of clever guesswork, jumping to wrong conclusions, and making Bible prophecy of one's own private interpretation. The Greek word *idios*, meaning "private," as given in 2 Peter 1:20, means "one's own." It is to be regretted that vast numbers of strange Bible interpretations and prognostications are simply from "one's own" mind; and yet books are written, and sometimes sell into a million copies, which contain man-made conclusions that have no bearing on the Bible at all. In fact, the Bible becomes simply an excuse for their interpretations.

When Bible prophecy is fulfilled to the very letter, then there is no room for doubt, and our faith rises to new heights. Can we imagine the searchings that were made in Old Testament times in regard to the "contradictory" prophecies concerning the first advent of Jesus. He would come out of (1) Nazareth, (2) Bethlehem, and (3) Egypt. No doubt, many in those days made learned discourses on how these prophecies would be fulfilled (or not fulfilled), depending on what school of interpretation they belonged to. The events themselves fulfilled the prophecies, not the prognosticators!

During the war years of 1941-42, two full-gospel, fundamental preachers were enabled to travel to Italy by permission of the United States government to inform Mussolini that he was the "king of the north," as recorded in Daniel 11:40, and that he would succeed in taking the Holy Land. Events proved that Mussolini never got into the Holy Land, but this prophecy was fulfilled in every perfect detail when Antiochus defeated the "king of the south," Egypt, in past history. It does not have to be fulfilled again!

Another point of confusion among many has been the meaning of the words *"the last days."* In 2 Timothy 3:1, Paul wrote, *"This know also, that in the last days perilous times shall come."* These carnal men described in verses 2–5 were to appear in the last days. They would be covetous, rebellious, truce-breakers, without natural affection, incontinent (without self-control), fierce, false accusers, traitors, high-minded, lovers of pleasure more than lovers of God, and they would have a form of godliness that would deny the power of God. Believers were warned to turn away from these unprincipled religious men. This is a clear description of the condition of the rulers of the church during the dark ages. Any reading of the history of the church will reveal the truth of this Scripture. The last days simply mean the days of the church age, commonly known as *Anno Domini.* Thus the church age is contrasted with the Before Christ days of the old covenant.

Whereas we agree that wickedness reaches its consummation in the present harvest time of this age, and we still have churches ruled by unprincipled men that deny the power of God, yet the major fulfilment was undoubtedly in the time of the falling away from the Apostolic church into the ignorance and debauchery of the dark ages. In D'Aubigne's *History of the Reformation*, he tells of the journey that Martin Luther took to Rome, and in Northern Italy he stopped over in a monastery of his religious order. One of the priests boasted of how he "fooled" the people by referring to the body of Christ as "the body of a dog," speaking in Latin. He thought it a huge joke, but Luther was not amused.

2

THE ORIGIN OF THE THEORY

The clear inference that *the* falling away would occur after the apostolic age would seem to be obvious to all. To ignore history and to attempt to project these Scriptures of Thessalonians into the indefinite future would seem to us to be a most unsound interpretation. There must be a reason, and of course there is. All schools of interpretation have an originator, and the futuristic interpretation is no exception.

In the early days of the suffering church, between AD 100 and 325, great comfort was drawn from the Scriptures, especially the book of Revelation, which seemed to be so explicit in describing some of the tortures that they endured. Domitian, Nero, Diocletian, and others all seemed to shine out of the Scriptures as the "many antichrists" John refers to in John 2:18. In this verse, the apostle clearly shows us that there would be many antichrists, but one ultimate Antichrist. In his day, there were many antichrists, but it was yet impossible to have any understanding as to the identity of the Man of Sin, the supreme Antichrist of history. He had not been revealed.

In Old Testament times, the Jews reading Daniel's prophecies would soon identify Antiochus IV Epiphanes as a model for antichrist. It was he who, in 20 BC, polluted the Jewish temple by offering a sow on its altar. The Man of Sin is described by Paul as being the *"son of perdition"* (2 Thessalonians 2:3). Jesus called Judas Iscariot "the son of perdition" in John 17:12. John gives the definition of the word *antichrist* by saying that he is one who was with them but went out from then, because they were not truly of the same spirit. (See 1 John 2:19.) In other words, an antichrist is one who was at one time working in the Christian church but became apostate. Judas Iscariot fits this definition. This does not describe a political anti-God ruler yet to come. The prefix *anti-* means "in the place of," or "vice," and although antichrist would be against the children of God, he would only do so by being a false Christ, or a pretending Christ to deceive. He would have a form of religion that would be passed off as Christianity, but would deny the very foundations of New Testament Christianity. He would be a wolf in sheep's clothing.

Jesus made this quite clear when He said to His Jewish disciples, *"If any man shall say unto you, Lo, here is Christ, or there; believe it not. For there shall arise false Christs"* (Matthew 24:23–24). A false Christ is an antichrist. The word comes from the Greek *pseuds*, from which we get the English *pseudo-Christ*. The ultimate of this Man of Sin would be perdition, or perishing as with Judas Iscariot. In 2 Thessalonians 2:8, we read that the Man of Sin would be destroyed by the Spirit coming from the mouth of Jesus, and by the brightness of His coming, surely referring to the final outpouring of the Holy Spirit upon all flesh and the manifestation of the charismatic gifts, culminating in the literal return of Jesus. In the *Encyclopedia Britannica*, we are informed that in times of political excitement during the first centuries of the Christian church, men appealed again and again to the prophecy of antichrist, but as the time for the rise of *the* prophesied Antichrist had not yet come, only the many antichrists could be seen, and suitable comfort obtained from the Bible for the suffering martyr church.

With the completion of the falling away, however, the whole concept changed. Early reformers saw a monstrous organization arising, usurping all the authority of the body of Christ, but revealing none of its graces or gifts. The great apostasy had arrived. The Emperor Phocas announced Pope Innocent III to be supreme pontiff of all the churches in Christendom in AD 606. The protecting power of the pagan Roman Empire had been withdrawn, and the power of the Caesars gave way to the power of the popes. We quote from Matthew Henry:

> Great disputes have been as to who or what is intended by this man of sin and son of perdition: and, if it be not certain that the papal power and tyranny are principally or only intended, yet this is plain.

He further said that "there was something that hindered or withheld, until it was taken away. This is supposed to be the power of the Roman Empire."

In AD 1190, the Abbott Joachim of Fiore and his followers, known as the Joachites, were the first to realize and believe that the new Pontifex Maximus in Rome was the Antichrist and taught Richard I (Coeur de Lion) the Crusade of his beliefs. Later, in 1380, John Wycliffe translated the Bible into the English tongue and quickly identified the pope as the Man of Sin. Early reformers, before and after Martin Luther, identified the pope as the Antichrist, and this became the most terrifying weapon of all reformist preaching. It is true to say that more sermons were preached on the pope being Antichrist than that the true believer was justified by faith. In fact, Martin Luther himself wrote twice to Pope Leo X, informing him with great bluntness that he was Antichrist in his day. Leo did not appreciate this revelation.

The teaching of this revelation of Antichrist was believed universally by all reformers. It gave rise to the Protestant Reformation, and it was loudly proclaimed by such well-known teachers as Peter Waldo, Wycliffe, John Huss of Bohemia, Luther, Calvin, Ridley and Latimer, Bullinger, John Knox, Foxe, Bunyon, John Wesley, Finney, Moody, Grattan Guiness, Spurgeon, F. B. Meyer, among others, and there were no exceptions. They all believed that the pope was the complete fulfillment of Antichrist to arise in "the last days," that is in *Anno Domini* days.

The historical interpretation was incorporated into the doctrines of the Church of England (Westminster Confession 1647), the Church of Scotland (Confession of Faith 1580), the Church of Ireland (Articles 1615), the Dutch Reformed Church, the Lutheran Church, and other Reformed churches.

In the King James Bible, there is a preface containing a letter of thanks and appreciation from all the bishops of the Church of England who had their part in this translation in AD 1611. They congratulated King James for his zeal toward the house of God, by writing in defense of the truth that has given such a blow to that Man of Sin as will not be healed. The letter went on to express the thought that this translation would cause papist persons to traduce them, to speak lies about them, and generally to malign them, because they desired to keep the people in ignorance and darkness. Truly, the translations of the Bible did indeed bring the apostasy to a decline, and in our day, we are seeing its remains destroyed by the coming of the Holy Spirit in power. The papist persons manifested the Man of Sin.

Matthew Henry comments that the Antichrist here mentioned in 2 Thessalonians is a usurper of God's authority in the Christian church who claims divine honors, and to whom can this better apply than to the bishops of Rome, to whom the most blasphemous titles have been given. Our Lord God the Pope, Another God on Earth, the Dominion of God and the Pope is the same.

This teaching and knowledge of the person of the Antichrist was believed by every reformer, bar none, and then, right on through to the nineteenth century. There was not one reformer's voice raised in objection, and there were no alternate schools of interpretation of the prophecies of Daniel and Revelation. The revelation of the Antichrist was the major cause of the Reformation, gaining ground in 1517 at Wittenberg in Eastern Germany. One half of the church in Germany broke with Rome and became Lutherans; from Lutheranism sprang Presbyterianism in Holland and Scotland, and Congregationalism in England.

Such a weapon had to be countered. It was destroying the power of the popes. In 1539, Ignatius Loyola founded the Society of Jesus, or the Jesuits. Their main purpose was to bring Protestants back into the fold of Rome by any means possible; in fact, their motto was "the end justifies the means." From their number arose

Francisco Ribera, a Spanish priest, who wrote a commentary on the apocalypse that was printed in 1593. His thesis was inserted in the form of notes in a Vulgate Bible and put forth the suggestion that the Antichrist was a political ruler who would yet appear on the horizon. This ruler would arise at the end time and would make a covenant with the Jews in a rebuilt temple in Jerusalem and rule for three-and-a-half years. He would become a world ruler of great power and malignity, and would, in fact, rule over the whole world and subdue the church to himself and create a world church. These notes were hidden and forgotten for centuries. No one took them very seriously, at least no Protestant did, even if he knew them; but in 1838, Archbishop William appointed Samuel Roffey Maitland as Librarian and Keeper Manuscripts at Lambeth Palace, where the library of the Church of England was kept. Dr. Maitland discovered the writing of Francisco Ribera and published it. At this time (1831), the Plymouth Brethren were formed, having begun in Dublin, Ireland, six years before. Their object was to enjoy Christian fellowship outside the walls of the tradition churches and so move toward their concept of a primitive Christianity. John Nelson Darby became their unquestioned leader and he accepted the futurist interpretation of the Jesuit priest Ribera as discovered by Dr. Maitland. The Plymouth Brethren were probably the first groups to study the Bible prophecies seriously outside of traditional church, which had become institutionalized after the heat of Reformation had died down. Thus, the evangelicals, as they were called, accepted this strange Jesuit "red herring."

We must not suppose that the Holy Spirit was the motivating power behind Ribera's inventions, which ran completely counter to the emerging revelations of the Reformers, and it is very interesting to note that in spiritist séances in today's present resurgence of occultism, great emphasis is being placed upon their demonic revelations, that indeed, a Great Ruler is coming who will rule the whole earth, and who will be the embodiment of Satan himself. In addition to this, Jean Dixon, the notorious medium, prophesies that the great Antichrist ruler is coming to rule the whole earth. Christians know that the only Ruler who is going to rule this earth is Jesus Christ, the Son of God. The government shall be on His shoulder and He shall be called the Prince of Peace. No Antichrist will usurp this position. If the evil spirits in occultism cause Jean Dixon and Francisco Ribera to agree, what delusion is there but that the spirit of Antichrist is working through these mediums? John explains in 1 John 4:3 that the spirit of antichrist was already in the world, but that should yet be manifest. What is a spirit? It must either be God or the devil, and as this spirit does not agree with the Holy Spirit, it must be a powerful demonic spirit.

Are we to believe what a demon teaches? No wonder Paul wrote to Timothy, warning him that *"in the latter times some shall depart from the faith, giving heed to seducing spirits, and doctrines of devils, speaking lies in hypocrisy"* (1 Timothy 4:1–2).

By "*latter times*," we understand the period known as *Anno Domini*, and it was in the dark ages that the demons took over and the doctrines of the church became anti-Christian.

From 1840 onward, the teaching of the futurist interpretation became the accepted one among fundamental evangelicals. In general, the members of the historic churches knew little or nothing of it, but it can readily be seen that with the renewed outpouring of the Spirit in our day, and the entering into the last generation mentioned by Jesus after the restoration of Jerusalem (see Luke 21:24–32), the whole complexion of Bible prophecy is undergoing radical changes, as we are brought by events to understand that there is not going to be a great falling away of the church into apostasy again, but conversely, a great restoration of the church preparatory to the coming of Jesus, the Bridegroom, for His bride who is now making herself ready.

3

THE GREAT PARENTHESIS

E*very* tree has a root, every doctrine has a proof text, and the root of the futurist interpretation lies in Daniel 9:26. If it can be shown that this root, or proof text, has no relevance to a coming dictator; if we can demonstrate that Scripture has already been perfectly fulfilled, then we that do an honest investigation will show that it does not have to be fulfilled a second time. Of course, if there be those who insist that there must be a second fulfilment, let it be based on sound exegesis, and not on pure guesswork.

The first part of Daniel 9 deals with his prayer for the restoration of Jerusalem, and the Jewish people's answer to this prayer was the appearance of the angel Gat, who informed Daniel that a prophetical period of seventy weeks was determined upon the Jews, and that following the completion of this time period, Jerusalem and the temple would be destroyed, the Jews scattered among all nations, and the Messiah would come, fulfilling the prophecies spoken of. It is understood by all Bible scholars that these seventy weeks represent *weeks* of *years*, that is to say, a period of 490 years. When this period ran out, the Messiah would revealed, rejected, crucified in the midst of the last week, then, afterward, Jerusalem would be utterly destroyed. This period of 490 years was divided 7 plus 62 plus 1. The first seven weeks, or forty-nine years, would see the completion of Jerusalem and the temple under Ezra and Nehemiah, then a long period of sixty-two weeks, or 434 years, would be Jewish history up to the beginning of the final week of seven years that would begin with the anointing of the Most Holy, the Son of God baptized in water in Jordan and anointed of the Holy Spirit in AD 27. This would give the Jews seven years to accept or reject their Messiah. It was God's last call to His people. He came to His own, but they received Him not. (See John 1:11.)

In order to put some substance into the futurist interpretation, it was necessary to build an imaginary bridge, called the Great Parenthesis, which would extend the sixty-ninth week into the seventieth week by a long period of nearly two thousand years. Thus the first sixty-nine weeks would be faithfully fulfilled in sequence, but then a hiatus would be introduced so the final events were postponed into the indefinite future. The very wording of the prophecy in Daniel 9:24–27 precludes any need or possibility of this parenthesis. The whole seventy weeks were determined:

1. To finish the transgression. God had set a time limit of 490 years in which to "finish transgression." Transgression is sin or wrongdoing, but it is more; it is the breaking of a known law. The only people who had the Law given to them in the old Mosaic dispensation were the Israelites. They were the transgressors of the Law. This reminds us of Isaiah 53:8, in which the prophet speaks of the coming Messiah, and says, *"For the transgression of my people was he stricken."* Jesus Christ, as the Lamb of God, was to make an end of transgression by being *"stricken, smitten of God, and afflicted"* (verse 4). In other words, on the cross of Calvary, Jesus died for the sins of the world and the transgression of "my people," Israel. He is the Savior of the world and the Redeemer of Israel. (See John 4:42 and Isaiah 54:5.)

2. To make an end of sins. Not only did Christ atone for transgression, the breaking of known laws of God, but He also atoned for all sins, whether of commission or omission, known or unknown. In Hebrews 9:26, we read, *"But now once in the end of the world hath he appeared to put away sin by the sacrifice of himself."* Again, in John 1:29: *"Behold, the Lamb of God, which taketh away the sin of the world."* And again, in Isaiah 38:17: *"Thou hast cast all my sins behind thy back."* Christ's vicarious death has atoned for all sin; there is but one sin that now stands between God and man, the sin of unbelief: *"of sin, because they believe not on me"* (John 16:9). There is but one thing that will debar a person of eternal life, and that is his or her persisting in unbelief and refusing accept Jesus Christ as Savior.

3. To "make reconciliation for iniquity." We are told in 2 Corinthians 5:19 that *"God was in Christ, reconciling the world unto Himself."* Here, the Scriptures speak of reconciliation iniquity, not transgression; and so, potentially, all mankind is embraced in God's saving grace. Not only Israel who transgressed God's Law, but also those who had not (but are nevertheless sinners) are included here. It is to those who believe that the Lord has given the wonderful ministry of reconciliation, based on the atonement, for in 2 Corinthians 5:18, we read that God *"hath reconciled us to himself by Jesus Christ, and hath given to us the ministry of reconciliation,"* so that as His ambassadors we should carry the news to others, that they too *"be reconciled to God"* (verse 20). Our commission is Mark 16:15–16.

4. To "bring in everlasting righteousness." The Lord tells us in Isaiah 51:6–8 that His salvation shall be forever, and His righteousness shall not be abolished: *"My righteousness shall be for ever, and my salvation from general to generation"* (verse 8). In 1 Corinthians 1:30, we read that Christ *"is made unto us...righteousness."* Man, apart from Christ, has righteousness, for all human righteousness is, in God's sight, filthy rags. (See Isaiah 64:6.) The righteousness of Christ that is imputed to us at conversion must become imparted righteousness, so that the indwelling life of Christ wholly transforms us into His likeness. Christ's kingdom will prevail throughout the whole earth, which shall be filled with the knowledge of the glory of God. (See Habakkuk 2:14.)

5. To "seal up the vision and prophecy." What does this mean? It means that Christ would confirm the message of prophets, and seal, or end, the old dispensation of the Law, opening a new dispensation, that of grace. *"For all prophets and the law prophesied until John"* (Matt. 11:13). John the Baptist came and preached repentance, saying *"the kingdom of heaven is at hand"* (Matthew 3:2). That was to be the new dispensation. The coming of Christ closed the old dispensation and sealed it up, but opened a new one with the message of the "kingdom of heaven." Or, as we read in John 1:17, *"The law was given by Moses, but grace and truth came by Jesus Christ."*

6. To "anoint the Most Holy." The anointing of the Most Holy is wonderful in its fulfillment. It took place, as we know, at the baptism of Christ, when He was anointed with the Holy Spirit. John the Baptist bore record, saying, *"I saw the Spirit descending from heaven like a dove, and it abode upon him"* (John 1:32). He also testified that Christ was *"the Son of God"* (verse 34).

This anointing of Christ with the Holy Spirit at the age of thirty years, reminds us that originally, it was at this age that the priests in Israel were anointed and consecrated for their holy ministry. Upon being anointed with the Holy Spirit, Christ commenced His earthly ministry, declaring that the prophecy of Isaiah 61:1 was fulfilled: *"The Spirit of the Lord GOD is upon me; because the LORD hath anointed me to preach good tidings unto the meek; he hath sent me to bind up the brokenhearted, to proclaim liberty to the captives, and the opening of the prison to them that are bound"* (cf. Luke 4:18).

The anointing of the Most Holy, the Messiah, at the end of the sixty-ninth week, was in wonderful fulfillment of the Scripture, and right on time! This leaves another "week," the seventieth, i.e., the last seven years of the 490-year period. Taking "in the midst of the (seventieth) week" to mean about the middle of the last seven years of the 490 years, this brings us to the crucifixion, which was three years after Christ's baptism and anointing at Jordan. Christ was "cut off" (killed), not for any wrongdoing that He had done, but for the sins of others (cf. Daniel 9:26 and Isaiah 53:8). How remarkable is the fulfilment, both as to its timing and purpose!

7. Confirmation of the Covenant. We read that "*He* [the Messiah] *shall confirm the covenant with many for one week*" (Daniel 9:27), that is, the last "week," seven years of the "seventy weeks" period. Malachi 3:1 speaks of Christ as "*the messenger of the covenant.*" It was during this period of seven years the last seven years of the 490-year period, from the time Christ commenced His ministry until the time of His rejection by the leaders and people of the Jewish nation, that the covenant was confirmed to them, and for a further three or four years until the Jewish nation also rejected the message preached to them by the apostles. Jamieson, Fausset, and Brown's commentary supports this view: "The seventy weeks extend to AD 33,...about three or four years after Christ's death, during which the Gospel was preached exclusively to the Jews. When the Jews persecuted the Church and stoned Stephen (Acts 7:54–60), the respite of grace granted to them was at an end (Luke 13:7–9). Israel, having rejected Christ, was rejected by Christ." In Acts 13:46, Paul says, "*Lo, we turn to the Gentiles.*" The Jews had not only rejected Christ, but also the witness of the Holy Spirit to Him. This commentary then goes on to show how the Prince Titus of verse, the son of the Emperor Vespasian, who came with the Roman army to conquer and destroy the Holy City, was Jesus, who confirmed the covenant with Israel. In Jeremiah 31:31, we read that God would make a new covenant with both houses of Israel, and in Isaiah 42:6, it was prophesied that God would give His Son for a covenant to people, and for a light to the Gentiles. Only Jesus fulfilled this, and no one else will ever make another covenant Israel, in this generation or at any other time. Jesus is the Author of the New Testament, which was sealed in Blood.

In Daniel 9:27, reading of the Messiah, we find that this would confirm the covenant with Israel for one week and seven years, and then in the midst of this week, God causes the sacrifices and oblations of the Jews to cease. The high priest was offering a sheaf of newly ripened wheat before the Lord in the Jewish Temple, just as Jesus was being offered up on the cross as the perfect sacrifice, acceptable unto God. This occurred exactly three-and-a-half years after He was anointed with the Holy Spirit, and midpoint of the last week. During the next three-and-a-half years, the gospel was offered only to the Jews through Holy Spirit, but they rejected the offer of forgiveness. They threw away the offer of the New Covenant made by God, and they stoned God's servant, Stephen. In Acts 13:45-46, it is recorded that the Jews were filled with envy, and against Paul's preaching, contradicting, and blasphemies. Paul and Barnabas waxed bold and said, "*It was necessary that the word of God should first have been spoken to you: but seeing ye put it from you, and judge yourselves unworthy of everlasting life, **lo, we turn to the Gentiles***" (verse 46). Thus the door was closed to the Jews and opened to the Gentiles; the seventy weeks of years had come to an end. The prophecy of Daniel 9:24–27 had been completely fulfilled. It does not have to be fulfilled again.

As we study verse 26 of this prophecy in Daniel 9, we find the "proof text" of the futurists. If this text does not mean what they say it should mean, then the whole framework and structure of their hypothesis falls in ruins. It can no longer be believed if it cannot be substantiated; and appeals to any other portion of the Bible dealing with the Man of Sin or the Antichrist would have no relevance to this verse whatsoever.

We read that after sixty-two weeks, following the reconstruction of the city of Jerusalem and the temple, the Messiah would be cut off, which is easily understood in the light of Isaiah's prophecy in chapter 53, that He would be cut off out of the land of the living. Following this crucifixion, it is recorded that "*the people of the prince*" should come and they would destroy both the city of Jerusalem and the temple. We must be very careful to understand that "*the people of the prince*" is a collective noun and applied to a plurality of people belonging to a prince or ruler. By no stretch of imagination or of grammar can we make "*the people*" apply to an individual, but this is exactly what the futuristic interpretation, invented by a Spanish Jesuit priest, attempts to do. We submit that such an exegesis is impossible. Ribera said this referred to Antichrist! We would repeat that the whole period of 490 years covers the period from the restoration of the temple to the appearing of the Messiah in the midst of that temple, restored by Herod. The context refers to the work of Jesus the Messiah to the Jews and the Christians' Savior. After this program is fulfilled, "*the people of the Prince*" appear and destroy everything.

Matthew Henry, in his commentary, is very explicit about the correct understanding of verses 25–27. Further. Jamieson, Fausset, and Brown confirm that the only one who makes a covenant with the Jews is Jesus, for, in Isaiah 42:6, it is written, "[The Lord will] *give thee for a covenant of the people*"—a clear prophecy of Jesus and His death for His people, Israel. The prince was Titus, the people were the Roman Army.

Jesus makes clear reference to the surrounding of Jerusalem by armies in Matthew 24:15; Mark 13:14; and Luke 21. It was because of His warning that the Christians escaped in AD 68 and 69, when preparatory warning surrounding Roman soldiers were made. The Christian Jews saw that the abomination of desolation was at hand, as Daniel foretold in verse 27, for there could be no need of a temple if the Jews were to be dispersed until 1967, when Jerusalem would again restored to them.

The abomination of desolation was the terrible destruction described as *"the overspreading of abominations he shall make it desolate"* (Daniel 9:27). Prince Titus and the Roman people did a good job in AD 70 and Jerusalem was reduced to desolation. Now that the Jews have been restored to their Promised Land, and Jerusalem given back into their hands again after the miraculous Six-Day War of 1967, there is no need to look for a secondary fulfillment. Jerusalem has been released, and when it is attacked by Russian invasion as described in Ezekiel chapters 38–39, it is He Himself who destroys them in the valley of Armageddon nearly forty miles north of Jerusalem. The Russian armies never reach the gates of the Holy City.

This is why those who hold the futurist interpretation are in confusion today. They have to try to fit an invasion of their imaginary Antichrist into the present time and the destruction of Gog. We are told that Ezekiel 38 and 39 do not apply to the Russian invasion, but to the invasion of the Antichrist. The futurists must believe that Jerusalem will again be surrounded, again be desolated and ruled over by Antichrist, who makes a covenant with them for three-and-a-half years. But Zechariah 13:7 to Zechariah 14:3 was fulfilled in AD 70. Jesus the Messiah already confirmed covenant with them between AD 27 and 34, first in His ministry and then by the Holy Spirit through the church, His body.

We must remember, too, that in the prophecy of the Great Parenthesis, beginning with the head of gold representing Nebuchadnezzar, until its final destruction, there would never be any intervening power arising, because the feet stone of image represented by the ten toes of the Holy Roman Empire under the popes, would be destroyed by the *Stone* (Jesus), and the resulting wind of the Holy Spirit would blow away the dust after the pulverization. The same wind of the Spirit that blows away the dust of the old, blows into the Stone Kingdom, reviving and restoring it, and the Stone that smote the image becomes a great mountain and fills the whole earth. Jesus arises supreme. We are now seeing the beginnings of the greatest restoration of the true body of Christ that has ever been seen. The restoration of the Stone Kingdom follows in sequence the destruction of the Gentile kingdoms. There is no time nor room to fit in an imaginary Antichrist. He is now being destroyed by the brightness of the coming of Jesus.

To attempt to find an imaginary Man of Sin who will yet rule the whole world, including Canada and the United States, in the last generation, and to justify such a strange view from one proof Scripture in Daniel 9:26 that 'the people of the Prince' can be equated with the Man of Sin seems to us to be utterly incredible.

We can only see restoration, not desolation.

4

THREE-AND-A-HALF YEARS

The prophecies of both Daniel in the Old Testament and Revelation in the New Testament are integrated. The prophetical time element in Daniel is that one day equal one year, then we must not force or break this essential face to fit preconceived ideas, for one day will equal one year also in Revelation. The futurists pay no regard to this principle to agree that a day is a year in Daniel, but insist on interpreting a day as a literal day of twenty-four hours in the book of Revelation.

We have endeavored to demonstrate that the 490 years in Daniel started at the time of Artaxerxes (458–58 BC), whose decree to rebuild the temple and the city of Jerusalem finished with the rejection of the gospel by the Jews. Jesus made this so plain when speaking to the Jewish leaders, He said, "*The kingdom of God shall be taken from you, and given to a nation* [in Greek, *ethnos*] *bringing forth the fruits thereof*" (Matthew 21:43). The preaching of the kingdom of God then taken to the Gentiles of Europe, and after their reception, finally nearly disappeared in the Dark Ages until it began to reappear in 1517 with the preaching of Luther. If we reckon the falling away to have started about AD 257, which agrees with history, then 1,260 years later would bring us to Martin Luther. The references in the book of Revelation to "*a time, and times, and half a time*" (Revelation 12:14) and "*a thousand two hundred and threescore days*" (verse 6) agree together that the time of the persecution woman virgin church would be exactly this period of time—1,260 days/years. The references to this 1,260 day/year are found in Revelation 11:13, where it is applied to the two witnesses, and it is truly a wonder what guesses are made as to the identity of these two witnesses. Some say Moses and Elijah, others Enoch and Elijah, but we must never be inconsistent in our approach to the Bible. The angel of the Lord gave the method of interpretation to John in Revelation 1:1 and he signified it, that is, he gave it to him in sign language.

The book of Revelation is a book of symbols that must not be taken literally. The root in the Greek means the same as "signs." A sign is not the substance, but a pointer thereto. A signpost points the way to the fulfilment of our journey. We need not guess about the identity of the two witnesses, for the symbolic language is borrowed from Zechariah 4, where Zechariah saw in a vision a gold candelabra fed by a golden bowl containing oil, which was fed by two branches from two olive trees. The whole vision concerns the future church symbolized in Revelation 1:13, as a golden candelabra with seven candlesticks, with the appearance of Jesus behind. A candlestick in Zechariah means the same as in Revelation; it is the symbol of a local church. In Zechariah, it applied to the building of the temple in Jerusalem for the Jewish church. In Revelation, it is applied to the sevenfold aspect of the Christian church (seven is the number of perfection) throughout the world in its multitude of witnessing congregations. These sevenfold aspects of this witnessing church are described in Revelation 2 and 3 under the names of churches in Asia Minor. In Zechariah 4:11, the question is asked, *"What are these two olive trees…?"* The reply is given is verse 14: *"These are the two anointed ones, that stand by the LORD of the whole earth."*

When we turn into Revelation 11, we find exactly the same symbology used: *"I will give power unto my two witnesses and they shall prophesy a thousand two hundred and three score days…. These are the two olive trees and the two candlesticks standing before the God of the earth"* (verses 3–4). Two is the number of witnesses. *"The testimony of two men is true"* (John 8:17). No one could be put to death under Israel law by the testimony of one person—two were always required, and this stands on our legal statute books today. Two witnesses means complete confirmation and thus the two candlestick witnesses can only be two witnessing Spirit-filled churches, which witnessed in sackcloth for 1,260 years of history and were mostly put to death, and so lay in the streets of the city called Sodom and Egypt, where our Lord was crucified. (See Revelation 11:8.) As Jesus was raised again from the dead, so also was the church raised again by the Spirit of Life, who entered them again in the same area of Continental Europe the Holy Roman Empire, ruled over by the popes. They were not buried. Sodom typified the licentiousness of those ages, and Egypt signified the nature of their religion, full of blasphemy and spiritual idolatry passing off as Christian while persecuting the true Christians and putting them to death. A picture of the work of the Antichrist as seen by all reformers without exception, up to 1840.

In this same chapter we have another mention of three-and-a-half, but this time it is used in the same prophetical context. The two witnesses were to lie as dead bodies for three-and-a-half days, for this would, of course, be equal three-and-a-half years. During the twelfth century, the Hussites of Bohemia, the Albingens of France, and the Wycliffes in England were actively preaching that the papacy was the Antichrist, the Man of Sin, and that the doctrines of the Church of Rome were blasphemous and unscriptural. As a result of this, the papacy declared war against these witnessing "heretics" and the terrible inquisition took place, when these witnesses were hunted down wild dogs and destroyed by every means and torture of their faith. The papacy commanded the armies of the countries in the Holy Roman Empire, the toes of the great beast, to exterminate these martyrs of Jesus, and they did their work so well that in 1400, the Bohe Church sent representatives throughout Europe to try to find any other witnesses of a similar testimony, as they had found none. They had either been exterminated or in hiding in remote mountain regions of Europe, or in islands off the west coast of Ireland. It is interesting to consider that the very word in the Greek for *witness* is *martis*, by which we get the whole interpretation of what Jesus meant when He said that the early church would be witnesses of Him after they had received the baptism in the Spirit on the Day of Pentecost. They would be martyred as witnesses but they would know the resurrection power of Jesus, as stated in Revelation 11:11.

The papal war of extermination had been so successful that a papal bull was issued on December 16, 1513, calling for the remaining Bohemian witnesses to present their cases before the ninth session of the Fifth Lateran Council, which convened in May 1514. Its object was to complete the utter extermination of the Christian witnesses. No witness came, and so, a famous proclamation of triumph was made known in Latin: *Jam nemo reclamat, nullus obsistit.* The voice of the faithful witnessing churches was as silent as the grave. The council was addressed by A. Pucci in 1516, who said, "There is an end of resistance to papal rule and religion, nobody opposes any more." Great jubilation was made at this news, which was celebrated throughout the papal lands by rejoicing, banquets, and making merry. Thus, true to the Bible, from 1514 to 1517, the voice of the two witnesses was silenced; the small remnant remained hidden, as dead but not buried, waiting their resurrection.

Historians of the papacy, such as Roscoe in his work on the life of Pope Leo X, confirm the remarkable accuracy of Revelation 11. Thus, an exact period of three-and-a-half days/years was fulfilled with astonishing accuracy, and was abruptly terminated in 1517, with the publishing by Martin Luther of his ninety-five theses, which he nailed to the door of the church in Wittenberg, Germany. The shock of this tremendous happening sent waves of horror and distress throughout the papacy, for the Spirit of life was beginning to enter into the two-witness church again, and would continue until Jesus Himself would return to gather them to Himself.

We are now in the last generation of the final restoration of this two-witness church, which will yet proclaim the glorious gospel throughout every nation for a witness, and then shall the end come. (See Matthew 24:14.) Note that Jesus said it was a "witness gospel"—there were to be signs following.

If these Scriptures have yet to see a second fulfilment with a personal Antichrist making a covenant with the Jews for three-and-a-half literal years, then we must expect to see almost all true Spirit-filled Christians exterminated in this generation throughout the world. As Christians are today multiplying at an amazing rate in Asia, Africa, and South America, and Mohammedanism in Africa is in retreat, and as the Holy Spirit is being outpoured from on high upon all flesh, and the church is coming together in the power of the Spirit, are we really to see this great renewal brought to a climactic end in persecution, death, and destruction before Jesus comes? In Daniel 7:20–21, we read of the Antichrist, symbolized as a *"horn that had eyes, and a mouth that spake very great things, whose look was more stout than his fellows. I beheld, and the same horn made war with the saints, and prevailed against them."*

The little horn—the papacy—sprang out of the Roman head of the Beast and unquestionably fulfilled this prophecy perfectly. It is truly a terrible picture to believe that the church on earth will shortly be largely exterminated, the work of renewal brought to an untimely end, and our sons and daughters butchered by the Antichrist. Some have even suggested that *"he who now letteth will let, until he be taken out of the way"* (2 Thessalonians 2:7) is none other than the Holy Spirit, which is a very popular interpretation held by the futurist school; but if there is no Holy Spirit, how can the Jews witness during "the great tribulation" without His work of convicting the sinners of sin, righteousness, and judgment? Furthermore, it is a scientific fact not known in 1840 that if the Holy Spirit was withdrawn from the earth, the composition of matter would disintegrate like a huge atomic bomb, for matter is held together by God. (See Colossians 1:16.)

It must be seen that in our day of spiritual renewal, of increase in the charismatic movement of the Holy Spirit and the preparation of the bride for the coming of her Bridegroom, such a picture of gloom, destruction, persecution, and decimation is unrealistic. There has been a great falling away, and we cannot see why there yet has to be another great falling away. History proves the principle of Jesus with all prophecy: *"Now I have told you **before it come to pass**, that, when it is come to pass, ye might believe"* (John 14:29). Bible prophecies, including all of those dealing with the Antichrist, can only be understood in their fulfilment. They have already been fulfilled. Now we are required to believe.

5

SEVEN TIMES

In Leviticus 26, Israel was warned that she would be punished *seven times* if she refused to obey the commandments of her Husband and Lord. This dire warning is repeated three times. (See Leviticus 26:18, 24, 28.) The Lord said that if Israel walked contrary to Him, He likewise would walk contrary to her, and *in fury*, He would chastise them *seven times*. We have already established that *"a time, times, and half a time"* is equal to 1,260 days (see Revelation 12:6, 14), so three-and-a-half times would be 360 + 720 + 180, a time being a complete cycle, or 360 degrees, which is a mathematical constant. Always taking the established principle of one day for a year, then the punishment of Israel would be 7 x 360, or a long period of 2,520 years. History wonderfully demonstrates the truth of this promise of punishment.

Seven is the biblical number of perfection, and as the warning is made three times, it would indicate that the Triune God gave a threefold warning. It could not be ignored. Between 741 and 721 BC, the Assyrians made successive invasions of the northern house of Israel, taking their captives into Assyria, the ruling Gentile world power of those days. The 2,520 years came to an end between AD 1780 and 1800, which saw the emerging of Israel under the new covenant, as the evangelical awakening commenced following the ministry of John Wesley. From 1800 onward, we have seen a progressive return of the church; first, the teaching of justification by faith alone, then the addition of holiness as the hallmark of the rebirth, then the great evangelical awakening in the nineteenth century, followed by the reappearance of the baptism in the Spirit at the beginning of this century. And now, today, the charismatic renewal of the whole church, which is spiritual Israel.

In the parable of the husbandman in Matthew 21:33–44, Jesus made a remarkable prophecy that the kingdom of God would be taken from the Jews and given to a *"nation"* (in Greek, *ethnos*), which would be instrumental in bringing forth the fruits of the kingdom. The pre-Reformation began with John Huss of Bohemia in the fifteenth century, and Wycliffe in England; then the Reformation began with Martin Luther in Germany. This was followed by the arising of John Wesley in England and the general increase in the true born-again church from that time onward. It is evident from history that the church did, in fact, reappear among the Gentiles of Europe, and has then been spread by missionary activity into the farthest parts of the world. Such names as Carey, Livingstone, Taylor, Goforth, and hundreds of early intrepid missionaries all came from among the Gentiles of northwest Europe. The church, thus reappearing, took the gospel to all the other nations. Northern Israel was divorced (see Isaiah 50:1) and therefore lost her identity and name and became "Gentilized." It is only possible to enter the New Covenant in Christ's blood by way of the rebirth. Thus, the believing church is seen as Israel restored.

According to Green's *History of England*, John Wesley was the one man who saved the nation from revolution when France had her revolution. England swung towards the gospel, but France degenerated towards atheism.

Over 120 years after Northern Israel had gone into captivity in Assyria, a new Gentile power had appeared. Babylon was now the ruler on the world's stage. Nebuchadnezzar attacked Jerusalem and the Southern Kingdom of Judah, who had refused the prophecies of Jeremiah and rejected his lamentations over their forthcoming destruction. In 606 BC, the Jews were defeated and began their long night of sorrow. This began their subjugation under the iron hand of the successive Gentile world powers, beginning with Nebuchadnezzar (the head of gold), then under the Medo-Persian empire (the chest and arms of silver), then under Alexander the Great of Greece (the thighs of brass), and finally under the iron kingdom of pagan Rome. The long period of 2,520 years ran out in 1915, the time of the first World War, and it was in 1917 that the famous Balfour Declaration was made, permitting the Jews to return to Palestine to make it their homeland, after *seven times* of punishment. Recent history tells the story of their return, their sufferings, their sorrows and hopes. They became a nation in one day in 1948, and they are now returning to their original possessions. Nothing can overturn God's laws. The Jews are no longer under bondage to the successive Gentile world powers. They are now a sovereign nation. They were never divorced, as was their northern sister, but although they have been restored physically to their land and never lost their national identity, they will yet have to accept the New Covenant in Christ's blood when He comes, for they will *"look upon him whom they have pierced"* (Zechariah 12:10).

The times of the Gentiles have been brought to an end in the restoration of Jerusalem to the Jews. Thus the fury of the Lord has been revealed against His people. (See Luke 21:24.) When we think of the Holocaust, when six million Jews died in concentration camps under Hitler, we can only rejoice with them that we are indeed in the last generation that sees the final downfall of the Gentiles, the full restoration of the church, and the final restoration of the Jews. There is no more falling away for the Jews, because they are now returning to their inheritance.

The Babylonian system, which means confusion, is divided into three parts (see Revelation 16:19), and we believe these are (1) religious, (2) political, and (3) financial. In this last generation, we are seeing tremendous changes in these three parts, unheard of in previous generations. Babylon is falling. (See Revelation 18:2.) At the same time, the Stone Kingdom, God's kingdom, is rising. (See Daniel 2:31–35.)

Paul wrote to the Thessalonians, *"But ye, brethren, are not in darkness, that that day should overtake you as a thief. Ye are all the children of light, and the children of the day"* (1 Thessalonians 5:4–5). Jesus Himself said that we should shine as the sun in His kingdom in this day (see Matthew 13:43), and trample down the wicked because lie, the Sun of righteousness was arising with healing in His wings. (See Malachi 4:2–3.) This is the day of great awakening of the body of Christ, as it is indwelt by His Spirit and fire.

We are beginning to shine and burn.

As we approach the coming of Jesus, the Light of the World, the church will get progressively brighter and brighter, but it will also become darker and darker, for the antichrist religious systems, political chicanery, and monetary misuse. This is why, in the same chapter, we read of the Gentiles: *"Peace and safety; then sudden destruction cometh upon them…and they shall not escape"* (1 Thessalonians 5:3). It was at the beginning of 1973 when we saw the policies of President Nixon bearing fruit. Though many opposed his politics, we believe he was an instrument of God's hands to prepare a way for temporary peace in the world, so that the full gospel could be preached in every nation with evidence (signs following), and then the end of this age would come. (See Matthew 24:14.) The full gospel cannot be preached in mass evangelistic meetings throughout the world while war ravages the countries. It cannot be preached behind the Iron or Bamboo Curtains until the doors of peace are opened to evangelists. All flesh must be at peace if God is to pour out His Spirit upon all nations. (See Joel 2:28.) There was a period of sixty years of peace in the Roman Empire during the ministry of Jesus, and later during the ministry of the apostles throughout Europe, the Middle East, India, and Africa. This would not have been possible if Rome had been at war with surrounding nations. The gospel must be preached in all nations with signs following, which will cause multitudes to turn to Christ because of the miracles of healing and exorcisms that will take place in all lands. This was the pattern of the early church. (See Hebrews 2:3–4.)

We cannot be dogmatic, but we do suggest that this peace will extend to the Battle of Armageddon. What a wonderful time of evangelism this will be as Jesus prepares His bride from every nation and tongue, who will stand before God as a great multitude that no man can number, having come out of great tribulation and had their robes washed in the blood of the Lamb. (See Revelation 7:9.) We believe we are now in this time.

In looking for destruction, we shall not be disappointed, for it is the Babylonian system that is collapsing. Confusion is giving way to order. Chaos gives place to Christ. Have you noticed the developing inflation of money? Many think this will bring nations into poverty, but I believe that God is breaking the power of mammon, which controls governments and big businesses. James makes it quite clear that big businesses will collapse (see James 5:1–5), and this will happen before the outpouring of the latter rain of His Spirit and the ministry of divine healing. The rich financiers and leaders of big businesses find that their riches are corrupted, and the church is told to *"be patient therefore, brethren, unto the coming of the Lord"* (verse 7). Once the restrictive power of money is broken over the peoples, the day of God's plenty will arrive. When we realize that God is the source of all our supply, we will stop looking at bank accounts and turn our eyes upon our Creator.

Let us notice the present destruction of religious systems that have either denied the Son of God or limited the gospel. They have held men in ecclesiastical bondage. The Roman Catholic system is collapsing, and the people and their priests will be liberated to enjoy the fullness of the Holy Spirit and the blessings of God. It is not the believers who form Antichrist. They have been subjected to him. The present outpouring of the Spirit reveals Jesus Christ, who breaks the power of Antichrist.

6

JERUSALEM RESTORED

The fulfillment of the prophecy of the restoration of Jerusalem, spoken by Jesus in Luke 21:24, came as a great surprise to prophetical students. Most of them were looking for a falling away and were not ready for the impact of Jerusalem being restored so soon! Of course, it was recognized that Jerusalem would one day be restored to the Jews, but many believed it would be after the reign of Antichrist! They were quite right, but they thought Antichrist was yet to come, failing to see he had come, and so the Jews could not inherit their Holy City until the Antichrist had reigned for three-and-a-half years. The actual, literal restoration of Jerusalem to Israel after the Six-Day War of June 1967 should change our thinking of much that has passed for Bible prophecy in the past.

No greater miracle has happened in past times. Russia gave to Egypt the dirty work of destroying Israel, and furnished them with two billion dollars' worth of armaments. Egypt is described as the basest of kingdoms which would never again exalt itself above other nations (see Ezekiel 29:14–15), and so the possibility of her winning this war for the Russians was prophetically impossible. God gave to General Dayan of Israel a word of wisdom. He was to send his fighters and destroy the Egyptian planes on the ground at Cairo and Alexandria. This move was so successful that no aircraft could cover the initial advance of Egyptian troops into the Holy Land, and so the war was, in fact, lost before it began. The Egyptian soldiers took off their shoes and ran through the desert sand, leaving behind two billion dollars of unused equipment, which the Israelites picked up as booty. It was then just a matter of mopping up Egyptian positions, which was followed by clearing the Golan Heights from the Syrian guns, and the war was miraculously won in six days.

The purpose of this great miracle, however, was to give back to Israel the city of Jerusalem, and thus were the 2,520 years of Gentile overlordship ended. Jesus said, *"Jerusalem shall be trodden down of the Gentiles, until **the times** of the Gentiles be* *fulfilled*" (Luke 21:24). Unless there is a new captivity of Jerusalem, and a new persecution of the Jews, then we are now seeing the working out of the final prophecies in the final generation. It is our sincere belief that Jerusalem has been finally liberated, and any references to Zechariah 14:1–3 must not be reckoned for future fulfillment, but in the past, in AD 70. The *"all nations"* referred to were those of the Roman Empire, not of the Russian Confederacy of Ezekiel 38 and 39, for these latter are destroyed at Armageddon before they reach Jerusalem. It is because God has already delivered Jerusalem that He will defend the city as Zechariah tells us, *"In that day shall the* LORD **defend** *the inhabitants of Jerusalem"* (Zechariah 12:8). The Lord will stand ready in the Valley of Armageddon and wait for the Russian hordes and defend Jerusalem by destroying these invading armies.

This means that *"blindness in part is happened to Israel, until the fulness of the Gentiles be come in"* (Romans 11:25). The veil is now being taken away, and missionaries are now working in Jerusalem, and Bibles are being distributed, which many of the Jews are reading, trying to find out when their Messiah will come. The times are fulfilled, both for the overlordship of the Gentile Beast system, which has seven heads— Egypt, Assyria, Babylon, Medo-Persia, Greece, Rome Pagan, and Rome Papal—and for the sufferings of the Jews. They are filled up. It is a *"fulness"* deliverance. Now the divine government is being transferred to Israel nationally, and to the body of Christ spiritually, but the end is not yet. It is happening in the last generation.

We can therefore expect to see the collapse of the United Nations as a force in the world, the collapse of communism, now reaching out for a detente with the west, the break-up of religious systems, which have been substituting for the real Spirit-filled body of Christ, the disappearance of the papalhead of the Roman Church, and the overthrow of Mohammedanism, the religion of the false prophet. We are told that both the Beast and the False Prophet end up in the lake of fire, where Satan rightly joins them. (See Revelation 20:10.) In short, all religions, all political systems, and all governments opposed to the kingdom of God are *now* being swept away. We do not wait for this, we are seeing it happen. In the parable of the wheat and tares in Matthew 13:30, we must notice a little word *"first."* Let us consider it:

> Let both [wheat and tares] *grow together until the harvest: and* **in the time of harvest** *I will say to the reapers, Gather ye together* **first** *the tares, and bind them in bundles to burn them: but gather the wheat into my barn.*

We are *now* in the time of the harvest, for this started with the restoration of Jerusalem, and the bringing in of the sheaves. The first act of God is to send reapers, probably angelic, who bind and burn the tares. When the refining has been done, the wheat is safely gathered in, culminating in the return of the Lord for His church.

This agrees perfectly with the words of Jesus found in Matthew 24, that *after* the tribulation of those days, *"He shall send his angels* [messengers] *with a great sound of a trumpet, and they shall gather together his elect from the four winds, from one end of heaven to the other"* (Matthew 24:31). Mark records it *"from the uttermost part of the earth to the uttermost part of heaven"* (Mark 13:27), showing that the final gathering of the wheat will be from those who are with Christ in heaven now, and those who will be changed and caught up to meet Him in the air, exactly as Paul teaches in 1 Thessalonians 4:14–17. That there will be no secret coming is established clearly in 1 Corinthians 15:51–52: *"We shall not all sleep, but we shall all be changed, in a moment, in the twinkling of an eye, at the last trump."* When Jesus breaks through the clouds that will cover the whole earth in that day (see Zechariah 14:7), the archangel blows the trumpet, the graves are thrown open, those alive changed from a mortal body to an immortal body, and both the "quick and the dead" meet Jesus in the clouds; and the Jews will see the whole divine operation. (See Revelation 1:7.) What a spectacle!

Those who believe in a future tribulation must find another Scripture than Matthew 24:21, for this tribulation of the Jews and the church was terminated when Jerusalem was restored. Jesus, however, promised in verse 22 that this period of time would be *"shortened"* (in Greek, *koloboo*), which means to bring to an abrupt end as in amputation. This is exactly what God did in the Six-Day War. Sudden, unexpected fulfillment of prophecy occurred, which fulfilled the seven-time punishment of 2,520 years from the captivities to the restoration.

Some will quickly turn our attention to Daniel 12:1, to the *"time of trouble, such as never was"* and claim that *"at that time thy people shall be delivered."* Can we imagine anything worse than the Holocaust of the Jews under Hitler? Do the futurists really believe this will happen again to the hapless Jews? We are *now* in the time of the end, and knowledge is being increased, and many are running to and fro in jet aircraft and fast automobiles. (See Daniel 12:4.) We do not wait for this in the future; it is being fulfilled before our eyes in this last generation. Then Daniel was shown in vision two angels, who said, in answer to his question, *"How long?"*—*"It shall be for a time, times, and a half* [1,260 years]; *and when he shall have accomplished to scatter the power of the holy people, all these things shall be finished"* (verse 7). This brings us back from 1967 to the beginning of the Dark Ages, which would culminate in a reversal of darkness and suffering to light and deliverance, for both spiritual and national Israel. We must always keep them together in our prophetical sights. The anointing of the Spirit left the early church, and the scattering into the dark night began, but not for ever.

In order that we may not be in ignorance, Jesus told us of other signs that would happen after the big sign of His coming, namely the restoration of Jerusalem. There would be signs in the sun, the moon, and the stars. In August 1972, the biggest solar flare in all history occurred and radio communications were wiped out for several days. This occurred at a time that was least expected by scientists, for the sun spot count was low.

Do we need to remind ourselves of the spectacular landings on the moon by American astronauts since the Six-Day War, when millions of eyes saw men walking on the moon? Who could imagine such a thing a few years ago? Then probes were sent to Mars to take pictures of the terrain, and they found no canals or ships and some scientists were very disappointed. Now probes are being sent to take pictures inside the gaseous envelope of Venus. Truly, knowledge has been increased in this generation, and these are signs of Christ's coming.

From the solar system, Jesus brings us down to the war-torn earth: "*Upon the earth distress of nations, with perplexity*" (Luke 21:25). The word "*Gentiles*" in verse 24 is the same as used for "*nations*" in verse 26. It is *ethnos*, which can be translated as a collection of nations such as we have in the United Nations. The representatives of the nations in UN will find themselves in a state of hopeless confusion and perplexity, meaning there is no way out for them. The reference to the sea and waves roaring speaks of the unstable condition of these nations, for seas in the Bible are a synonym for nations. Men's hearts will fear, because of the conditions of collapse of the Gentile world Beast system. As big business has to let go of the control of money, many will die of heart attacks as they did in the Great Depression of the thirties. When these things *begin* to come to pass, then we are to "look up," to look away from the destruction on earth to the glories of the church renewal and the reappearance of signs, wonders, and miracles in the earth. These come from heaven.

Jesus then gives us a parable of the fig tree and all the trees. It is accepted by all Bible students that the fig tree is a type or picture of the Jewish people. It is now shooting forth, and so we know that summer is nigh, and the coming of Christ is nigh at hand. All the other trees, no doubt, refer to the other nations, now miraculously freed from imperialistic rule by Great Britain, France, Germany, Holland, and Belgium, which controlled large sections of Africa and Asia. In recent years, we have seen the great British Empire literally given away, given back to the native owners. Who could have imagined such a thing in 1945, when the war ended? These are emerging nations, deciding their own destiny, without the interference from imperialistic governments or ecclesiastical hierarchies. They can invite in full-gospel ministries. When the Dutch controlled Indonesia, very few missionaries were allowed in. First, God had to remove the Dutch, and then the communists filled the vacuum; but when they were destroyed, one of the greatest revivals on earth began. France is largely an atheistic country that prevented missionaries from preaching at all in their African colonies, but that has changed. The trees are beginning to bud, preparatory to bringing forth fruit. Summer is nigh.

Jesus finished His discourse by saying, *"When ye see these things come to pass, know ye that the kingdom of God is nigh at hand.... This generation shall not pass away, till all be fulfilled"* (Luke 21:31–32). Our generation is seeing these things coming to pass. There can be no secondary fulfillment. There does not have to be. The time of Jacob's trouble has been fulfilled. *"Alas! for that day is great, so that none is like it: it is even the time of Jacob's trouble, **but he shall be saved out of it**"* (Jerermiah 30:7). Jacob, which means "supplanter," has paid for his rejection of Jesus. He is now being planted instead, back into his homeland and his city, Jerusalem. Will Jacob have another Holocaust? We do not believe so. He has gone through his trouble and he is now emerging and being freed.

7

THE JUBILEE

The Olivet discourse is covered in three chapters, Matt. 24, Mark 13 and Luke 21. While Jesus was seated on the Mount of Olives overlooking the Temple, He was asked two questions: (1) When will the temple be thrown to the ground as You prophesied? (2) What shall be the sign of Thy coming and of the end of the age? (See Matthew 24:1–3). The answer to these two primary questions constituted the Olivet discourse, which covered history from the destruction of the city and temple in AD 70 to their restoration in AD 1967, and the events that would follow in the last generation, culminating in the return of Christ.

In AD 68, Caesar sent an army to surround Jerusalem to warn the Jews because of their political restlessness. Jesus had warned His disciples that this would happen, and that when it did, they were to flee to the mountains of Moab. It was called the abomination of desolation (see Matthew 24:15; Mark 13:14; and Luke 21:20), and this agreed with what Daniel had prophesied would happen after the last of the seventy weeks was fulfilled. *"The people of the prince that shall come shall destroy the city and the sanctuary; and the end thereof shall be with a flood, and unto the end of the war desolations are determined"* (Daniel 9:26). The prince referred to was Titus, the son of the Emperor Vespasian, who was emperor at the time of the final destruction of Jerusalem, and his armies desecrated the temple and destroyed it, which was an abomination in the sight of God and the Jews. When this surrounding army was withdrawn, most of the Christians residing in Jerusalem escaped safely, as Jesus had told them to do, *"Then let them which be in Judaea flee to the mountains"* (Matthew 24:15–16). Again in AD 69, Vespasian sent another expedition that surrounded the city, and after this warning had been given, the rest of the Christians also escaped into the mountains, across the Dead Sea, and the River Jordan. The rest of the Jewish people failed to see this warning because they did not believe on Jesus, and so in AD 70, the final assault began under General Titus, and after a long siege, when one-third of the Jews died of famine and mothers actually ate their children. (See Jeremiah 18:21; Lamentations. 2:20, 4:10). Another third died by the Roman sword, and a third escaped to become the wandering Jew of the diaspora (See Zechariah 14:2).

The Roman soldiers had been forbidden to damage the temple, but in the excitement of the battle, one of them threw a lighted torch through a window. The resultant fire was so intense that the golden and silver vessels melted and ran between the *huge* stones. The soldiers, greedy for spoil, used crowbars to pry each monolithic stone from another to get at the precious metals, and thus was the amazing prophecy fulfilled that every stone would be thrown down. This statement was so extraordinary that it precipitated their two questions.

The year 1917 was a tremendously important year in Bible prophecy, because it was fifty years before the restoration of Jerusalem, and this began the Jubilee of deliverance. The Law of Jubilee is found in Leviticus 25:8–13, and seven sevens of years were to be counted, which is forty-nine years, and the fiftieth year was to be a year of restoration, release, and increase. Every man was to return to his possession, and this is exactly what happened when Jerusalem was restored. In 1917, the First World War was at its peak. German submarines were sinking Allied shipping so fast that these ships could not be replaced, and much needed food and ammunition was failing to arrive. Britain and her allies faced imminent defeat, and the crisis was reached when shipments of cotton from the United States failed to arrive, because this cotton was needed to make gun cotton, the basis of explosives. At this time, God raised up His man, Dr. Chaim Weiseman, who had just invented a cheap substitute for gun cotton using barnyard straw. The British government offered him any price he would ask, for it meant victory or defeat. He refused money and asked that in the event of an Allied victory, Britain would authorize the Jews to make Palestine their homeland. This was agreed to, and Lord Balfour, the Foreign Affairs Minister, got the bill passed through Parliament, and the famous Balfour Declaration was made, permitting the Jews to make a new home in the Holy Land.

At this time, General Allenby was leading an army through the Sinai Desert toward Jerusalem, laying water pipes for water from the Nile, and railway tracks for guns and supplies. When news got through to the Arabs in Jerusalem, they believed that Allenby was a prophet of God, because his name in Arabic was Allah-nebi, and being fatalistic they realized that if Allah was sending his *nebi* (prophet) to take the Holy City, there was no point in resisting, for they would be resisting the will of Allah. General Allenby sent six bombers to fly over the city, dropping pamphlets printed in Arabic calling upon the inhabitants of Jerusalem to surrender. Isaiah had already prophesied of this day, for he wrote, "*So shall the* LORD *of hosts come down to fight for Mount Zion, and for the hill thereof. As birds flying, so will the* LORD *of hosts defend Jerusalem; defending also he will deliver it; and passing over he will preserve it*" (Isaiah 31:4–5). This prophecy was fulfilled exactly, for as soon as the pamphlets started dropping, the mayor of Jerusalem opened one of the city gates and handed the keys to a British sergeant, who immediately delivered them to General Allenby himself. General Allenby thereupon descended from his horse, and with cap in hand, entered before his army and took Jerusalem in the name of the King. The official crest of the bomber squadron of the Royal Air Force who flew over Jerusalem carries a picture of aircraft over the city, and the words: "As birds flying, we deliver Jerusalem." This Scripture has been marvelously fulfilled, but who could have guessed how it could happen until it did? It does not have to be fulfilled again. Jerusalem has been delivered. From 1917 and General Allenby to 1967 and General Dayan is just fifty years. The year of Jubilee had arrived. In this fifty years, Israel grew, often with great frustrations, especially when Great Britain gave up the mandate and handed it to the United Nations. In 1948, Israel became a nation again.

Another monstrous thing arose in 1917. In the October Revolution under Lenin, Russia became the Union of Soviet Socialist Republics, proclaiming the gospel of communism for all the world. It was her avowed intention to make or force every nation into godless, atheistic communism, and crush the church completely out of existence. Khrushchev came to the United States and, in the assembly of the United Nations, told the United States that communist Russia would bury her, they were so sure of ultimate victory; but at the end of a most barbarous fifty years of bloodshed and terror under Stalin and others, the Lord sent frost and rain out of season and ruined their crops. At the same time, God gave the US and Canada their largest grain crops in history, and so Brezhnev was quite ready to talk peace with President Nixon, for he needed the grain to live. If he could not get this grain, then the USSR was finished, communism was defeated, and the Russians would starve to death in their millions. It almost seems like Joseph feeding his brethren all over again! From 1967 onward, communism began to cease being such a source of evil in the world. Now we shall see whole nations liberated from its thralldom, and Asia will get help from the United States, who will pour billions of dollars into Indo-China, Thailand, Philippines, and build these nations back, and the USSR and China will advise them to accept this offer of help, for the communist "giants" can do nothing now to help Asia. Their time is *up*. The fifty Jubilee years are expired; now the church in Asia is going to blossom, and not only in Asia, but every other continent in the world. The Jubilee is on.

There is one more "fifty." *Pentecost*, in Greek, means "fiftieth," and from the Day of Atonement, when the Jews were celebrating the Passover, Jesus shed His blood making an atonement for them. From that dark day, when His blood was poured forth, to the Day of Pentecost, when the Holy Spirit was poured forth, was exactly fifty days. Now the believers in Jesus came into their possession and full inheritance, and the body of Christ was fully manifested to the world in the power of the Spirit.

Israel has yet to be put in possession of all the land from the Nile River to the Euphrates River (See Genesis 15:18), so if Egypt or any other nation attacks her again, Israel will defend her territory. They have entered into their Jubilee of restoration. It seems that the period of peace is coming on the world, but this will finally be shattered when Russia and her confederacy will attack Israel, dwelling safely, without bars or gates, like a cloud to cover the land. (See Ezekiel 38:8–9.) It seems that the aerial invasion of Czechoslovakia was a trial run, when tanks, guns, trucks, and men were landed at the airports of Prague and Bratislava. This time, they will land their supplies on the Plain of Armageddon, and God's wrath will come up in His face and He will destroy them so thoroughly that five-sixths of their army will be decimated, and the rest will be driven into *"a land barren and desolate, with his face toward the east sea* [the Pacific], *and his hinder part toward the utmost sea* [the Arctic], *and his stink shall come up, and his ill savour shall come up, because he has done great things"* (Joel 2:20). In this manner will God remove the Northern Army from the land of Israel.

8

6-6-6

As far as I know, no futurist has ever given a satisfactory explanation of the mystery of the number of a man being 6-6-6. This is obviously a mystery, but one that is supposed to be understood, always bearing in mind a fundamental principle that the book of Revelation is a book of symbols that are supposed to be understood by the Christian church. Let me quote: "And [Jesus] sent and signified it by his angel unto his servant John"; then we read, *"Blessed is he that readeth, and they that hear the words of this prophecy, and keep those things which are written therein: for the time is at hand"* (Revelation 1:1, 3).

From this explanation of the book, we find the following:

1. It was a book of symbols written in sign language.

2. Christians would be blessed in reading (not in a state of confusion because they failed to understand the symbols).

3. They would hear and keep what they read (and understood).

4. The time of the beginnings of fulfillment were at hand, that is about AD 90

As we come to chapter 13, we find that another beast appears who...

1. Causes all to receive a mark in their forehead or right hand.

2. No commerce could take place unless people bore this mark in their forehead or right hand,

3. or did not have the name of the beast,

4. or did not have the number of his name.

We are then told that the number of this beast is the number of a man. This number is 666. In Bible numerology, six is the number of man's works and self-effort. Thus, 666 means the perfection of man's kingdom in a religious sense.

Again, we must remind ourselves that in reading and understanding this mystery intended for us, we shall be blessed by understanding the symbolism. 666 is the number of the beast and the number of a man. It is also the number of the name of the beast and the name of the man. This helps us to interpret the mystery. The beast and the man are therefore equated. They have one number.

We have already explained that the succession of Gentile empires, beginning with Nebuchadnezzar, was to run "seven times," or seven cycles of times of 360 years, a total of 2,520 years. Half of this period was to be occupied by godless pagan governments, and half by ecclesiastical governments. Thus, the first beast of Revelation 13 would represent pagan governments of Europe and the Middle East, and would rule for 1,260 years, and then be replaced by ecclesiastical government for the second half of 1,260 years, taking a day for a year, as in Daniel's seventy-week prophecy. Thus, the other beast of Revelation 13:11 would represent the ecclesiastical power that superseded pagan Rome. Does history record this? Certainly. By permission of the Emperor Constantine, who removed his own seat of government to Constantinople (Istanbul), the Roman Bishop was granted ruling powers of the western part of Europe, which ultimately developed into the Holy Roman Empire, having ten kingdoms represented by the ten toes of the image. The first beast represented by the Caesars in John's day, was replaced by *the* second beast of the popes.

We must never confuse the activities of the Roman Bishop today with his predecessors of the Dark Ages. Those days are past. They are history, never to be repeated. Historically, the period of the rule of Gentile powers has ceased and the times of their end are now running out. There is to be no second falling away or apostasy of the church; there can only be a great restoration. It is happening now. We do not have to wait for it. It is obvious to all. Any church group that will not fall in line with the final move of God in restoring the one true church will be swept away by the power of God's Holy Spirit, be it Protestant or Catholic. It matters not what the name is.

To understand the depths of evil and depravity that occurred in these Dark Ages, one must read church history. I recommend two books from many: D'Aubigne's *History of the Reformation*, and Foxe's *Book of Martyrs*. These history books will show that the church was basically ignorant of both spiritual truths and natural science. It was a period of great darkness, and therefore, great persecution of any, be they a Galileo or a Martin Luther, who dared to propound any truth whatsoever. It was an age governed by superstitions of the basest kind; not by reason but by fear of the absolute power of one man—the pope. He was described as "Lord God the Pope," who was supreme Pontifex Maximus, or ruler of all kings and rulers in the Holy Roman

Empire. He crowned and uncrowned kings, who trembled at his words. Being the supreme pontiff, he claimed to have all power in heaven, on earth, and in hell. Only Jesus was given all power in heaven above and on earth beneath and the regions under the earth. (See Matthew 28:18.) Any man who claims equality with the Son of God is identified as one who comes in the place of Christ, or one who assumes the attributes of Christ. This is basically the meaning of the Greek word *antichristos*.

Only Jesus Christ is infallible, and He is revealed in His Word.

When a pope is crowned, he has placed upon his head a golden crown with three crowns depicted thereon. One crown is for rulership in heaven, one for rulership on earth, and one for rulership of the nether regions (Hades). The keys of loosing and binding are his, and his alone. The popes believed that when Jesus gave His keys to Peter, it meant that He gave them to the series of popes. (See Matthew 16:19.) The doctrinal position of the Roman Church has always been that no priesthood of believers holds those keys, but only the pope. These keys were depicted on ancient postage stamps of the papal states of the last century, before the revolution in Italy when the pope was put in a common Roman jail and all the riches of the papacy were taken and used to build up the kingdom of Italy in 1870. This date may be taken as the time when Rome finally lost its supreme power over the Holy Roman Empire, and with the successive wars of 1914–18 and 1939–45, we have seen a progressive disintegration of this pontifical power, and it is now reduced to a small area in the middle of Rome called the Vatican. From a continent to a one square mile state.

The process of reduction of power is still proceeding, and now God is pouring out His Spirit upon individual Catholics, and the pope has no apparent desire to stop this outpouring. Pope John prayed for it. It will not be long before the Roman Catholic Pontiff will have no power left. It will all come back to the true Corpus Christi, composed of Spirit-filled members from all denominations. It is even possible that the Roman Catholic Church may be taken over by a council of bishops, with no official pope. Time will show whether this is true.

When this golden crown is placed upon the pope's head, and it is a very heavy crown bearing the words *Vicarius Filii Dei*, which basically means Vicarious Son of God. A person who is *vicarious* is one who stands in the place of another; thus, by confession, the pope stands in the place of Jesus Christ for the Roman Church, and this is the meaning of the word *anti*, one who stands in the place of another. Thus, *antichrist* means a religious leader who stands as Jesus, and is therefore a False Christ. (See Matthew 24:24.) The pope claims to be infallible when making pronouncements *ex cathedra*, i.e. from the papal chair above the host in St. Peter's in Rome.

These Latin words can be added mathematically, because certain Roman characters are both letters and numerals; e.g. I is one, V is five, C is one hundred, M is one thousand, etc.

VICARIUS (in old times V and U were equivalent) adds up to 112, FILII adds up to 53, and DEI to 501. These three totals make 666, the number of a man. This is not the number of a church group, assembly, or denomination. It is strictly the number of a man, a man who places himself on an equal with the Son of God. This is what the popes did in the Middle Ages.

In the Greek language, the word LATEINOS means "the Latin man," and again in the Greek letters, we have the same principle. L (30), A (1), T (200), E (5), I (10), N (50), 0 (70), S (200). This again adds up to 666, the number of a man in Greek.

The word ROMITI, in Hebrew letters, adds up as follows: R (200), O (6), M (40), I (10), T (400), I (10) = 666, the number of the Roman man.

It is also strange that the Hebrew word ROMIITH, meaning the Roman kingdom, also adds up to 666, R (200), O (6), M (40), I (10), I (10), TH (400), and as the whole period of the great falling away, or Dark Ages, of 1,260 years, is encompassed in one word APOSTASY, the Greek word APOSTATES, also adds up to 666, as follows: A (1), P (80), O (70), ST (6), A (1), T (300), E (8), S (200). All these proofs help us to identify the Man of Sin, or the Apostate Antichrist, as being a Roman man, taking on titles blasphemously that only belong to the Son of God; sitting in his temple, showing himself to be God (see 2 Thessalonians 2:4) in his Roman kingdom (the papal states). He can also be described as the Latin man, because all masses in the Roman Church were said in Latin.

We are not surprised, then, when the original translators of the King James Bible clearly identified "papal persons" as being identical with the Man of Sin. Thus, a continuing plurality of ruling pontiffs was equated with the man whose number is 666. No Bible scholar believed that any other identification was necessary, from John Wycliffe in 1382, right up to 1840, when John Darby started to propagate the futurist interpretation borrowed from a Jesuit priest. As we read the footnotes of the Amplified Bible in 2 Thessalonians 2:1–9, referring to the power that would hinder the revelation of the Man of Sin, circa AD 600, after the great falling away from apostolic Christianity, "A majority think this refers to the Roman Empire." This means that a minority put this prophecy of the antichrist in the future, and a majority see it fulfilled in past history. The futurist interpretation is of relatively recent innovation, actually from 1840. The whole vast body of eminent Bible scholars from 1383 to 1840 believed the pope was the antichrist. This means a majority. The temporal power of antichristian popes passed away after 1870. They have been relatively benign since that time.

9

THE GREAT TRIBULATION

One of the cardinal beliefs of the futurists is that there will be a great tribulation in the last projected week of Daniel's seventieth week. This unparalleled time of world judgment and suffering under the Antichrist is supposed to spread over three-and-a-half years, or half of the last week.

Apart from the obvious fact that it is impossible to prove this assumption from Scripture, the very use of the word *tribulation* in its settings in the Bible precludes such as far-fetched prophetical conclusion.

Let us consider the setting of the word in Matthew 24. The Holy Spirit gives space in no less than three Gospels to the Olivet Discourse, which took place between Jesus on the one hand and four Jews as His audience. (See Matthew 24; Mark 13; Luke 21.)

The reason for the discourse was because Jesus and these four disciples were admiring the great structure of the temple of the Jews on Mount Moriah in Jerusalem. To the great astonishment of these four men (Peter, James, John, and Andrew), Jesus told them that this temple would be so completely demolished that not even one stone would be left on another. Such a prophecy seemed impossible of fulfillment, because they had no bulldozers or bombs in those days. This led to two major questions recorded in Matthew 24:3: (1) When would the temple be destroyed? (2) What would be the *sign* of His coming and the signs that would appear before the end of the age? Mark and Luke only quote the first question, as this was the one uppermost in their astonished minds. In between these two questions lies the compass of the great tribulation of the Jewish race, and the utter desolation of their Holy City, to be ruled by successive Gentile empires right up to the restoration from the Arabs.

The word *tribulation* is used once in the Olivet Discourse, in Matthew 24:21, and Jesus was answering their first question concerning the destruction of the temple. In

AD 70, General Titus destroyed Jerusalem and the temple was laid in total ruins. The blood-lusty Roman soldiers used crowbars to pry each stone from its neighbor, to get at the molten gold and silver that had flowed between the cracks of the large stones after the great conflagration. Mark does not use the word *tribulation*, but describes this destruction as *"affliction,"* and Luke described this terrible event as *"vengeance,"* distress and wrath coming upon the Jews and their city. The tribulation referred to was restricted in its beginning to the destruction of the temple and city of Jerusalem. The Olivet Discourse had no relevance to any other peoples but the Jews up to the times of the end of the Gentiles and the resultant restoration of Jerusalem to the Jews, which occurred in the Six-Day War of June 1967. This single, prophetical event, told in Luke 21:24, is, we believe, the great sign of the end time, and the coming of Christ, and the beginning of the last generation, which will see the final destruction of the Gentile world system and the rise of the true church of Jesus Christ in all its power and beauty.

Unless one deliberately forces Scripture out of its context, this *"great tribulation"* referred to in only one of the three accounts, is primarily intended for the Jews. Their great tribulation obviously began in AD 70, and continued through the following centuries, culminating in the terrible Holocaust under Hitler.

In Luke 21:25, we then have details of the events that would happen on a worldwide scale *after* Jerusalem was returned to the Jews. Jesus spoke of Jerusalem being encompassed with armies, and it was. He warned Christians to depart, and they did. To attempt to force another tribulation in a mythical period of three-and-a-half years is to seek for the impossible. It will never happen.

In Matthew 24:29, Jesus tells of these worldwide events as being *"after the tribulation of those days."* The catching away of the church occurs after the tribulation of the Jews. (See Matthew 24:31; Mark 13:27). The Scripture has given rise to two divisions among the futurists: the one school believes the church will go through the tribulation and largely be decimated, whereas the second school teaches that the church will be "raptured" before the tribulation. No satisfactory explanation has ever been given to these words *"after the tribulation."*

If the tribulation referred to only has reference to the suffering of the Jews and the down-treading of Jerusalem from AD 70–1967, then the meaning of the Olivet Discourse immediately becomes clear. We are now in the last generation, as the *Amplified Bible* shows us, and God is restoring both natural Israel to the Holy Land, and protecting them, and also restoring His church to its original power and glory.

Coincidentally with the casting off of the Jews, the great falling away of the church began. Even in AD 95, the Emperor Domitian began the first persecution of the church. This was to continue through the reigns of Nero and Diocletian, until the church was finally rescued for a time by Constantine in 325. Rapid degeneration then took place until the church, like Jonah, hit rock bottom for the 1,260 years (three-and-a-half times of prophecy), until Martin Luther arose to turn the tide in 1517. The last 460 years have seen a steady growth of the Bible-believing church, until today, when God is pouring out His Spirit upon the whole church. All the prophecies concerning tribulation, affliction, and vengeance are already past in history. No one can turn the cycle of events back today by a twisted Jesuit-inspired interpretation. It is too late. It just is not working according to their schedule.

There are two relevant references to the word *tribulation* in the book of Revelation. The first is in Revelation 2:10, which speaks of ten days (ten years of Bible prophetical time) of tribulation for the church. Jesus said that the devil would cast some into prison, but they were promised the crown of life if they were faithful unto death. History records that from 303–313, the early church suffered terrible tribulation and affliction under the monster Diocletian, when hundreds of thousands were put to death, thrown to the lions, and burnt in the arenas, as human torches covered with pitch.

The second reference is to the church that came out of their tribulation and had their robes washed white in the blood of the Lamb. This does not refer to a future event, sometimes referred to as "the tribulation of the saints." The number of those who came through their sufferings in the Dark Ages is described in Revelation 7:9 as a great multitude, which no man could number, of all nations. Even today, we have read of sad sufferings of Christians in China, Soviet Russia, Indo-China, and Congo. If God says He is going to pour out His Spirit on *all flesh*, why do we have to anticipate a second decimation of the church?

Both the Jews and the church are now coming into their harvest time. They are emerging from the results of the Great Tribulation. There is restoration in the air today for the church. The stronger the church gets, the greater its power to fulfill Malachi 4:2–3:

> But unto you that fear my name shall the **Sun** of righteousness arise with healing
> in his wings; and ye shall go forth…. And ye shall **tread down the wicked**; for
> they shall be ashes under the soles of your feet in the day that I shall do this.

Instead of the devil throwing Christians into prison again, and causing the death of millions, the table is turned; now the church tramples on the devil and his wicked agents. A very different picture indeed for the utter gloom of the futurist theory.

Jesus told His disciples that they would tread upon serpents and scorpions, and over all the power of Satan. (See Luke 10:19.) Is this promise never to be fulfilled? It is now being fulfilled. The sick are being healed and demons cast out as never before since the days of the early church. Millions are being baptized in the Spirit and receiving the power to tread down the wicked.

If there is going to be a second tribulation, this time it will be for wicked men and nations, especially the Russian bloc that will invade the Holy Land. God then arises to destroy these hordes on the Plain of Armageddon, about forty miles north of Jerusalem. There will be no more surrounding of Jerusalem. It has already happened in history. Jerusalem has been delivered.

Some have taken Zechariah 13:7 to 14:3, which refers to the events of the destruction of Jerusalem and the beginning of the tribulation of the Jews, and applied this to a second destruction of the Holy City, and a second decimation of the Jewish people. It seems that Satan deliberately likes to twist Scripture and try to make it apply to what he would do if Jesus had not defeated him on the cross. Satan would love to rule the world through a man who would be the personification of evil. He would love to destroy the church, and he has tried unsuccessfully over the ages, even to this day. We forget at times, when we look at the evil on the earth, that Jesus has promised to rule and reign and to have the government on His shoulders. He will never allow an Antichrist to rule over this planet, even for three-and-a-half years! This book is not being written with any controversial purpose in mind, to add confusion to those who are already confused by wrong teaching on eschatology, but to state, as firmly and kindly as possible, that there never will be another Antichrist or great tribulation.

> *When a prophet speaketh in the name of the LORD, if the thing follow not, nor come to pass, that is the thing that the LORD has not spoken, but the prophet has spoken it presumptuously: thou shalt not be afraid of him.*
>
> (Deuteronomy 18:22)

If what has been written does not come to pass, then the futuristic interpretation of Scripture may be correct, but if it does come to pass, then a true prophecy has been made. This is the day when true and false prophets must appear, that the true ones may be made manifest among the false.

That is why this book has been written.

10

WHAT ABOUT THE RAPTURE?

The Plymouth Brethren introduced the word *rapture* to describe a secret catching away of the church into heaven before it would return with Jesus after three-and-a-half years, or half the last week of Daniel's prophecy of seventy weeks. Having wrenched this last week out of its proper setting and context, the great tribulation was supposed to happen during this week, and in order that the church would avoid this tribulation, it had to be caught away before this so-called period began, inspite of the fact that both Matthew and Mark quote Jesus as saying the church will be "caught away" *after* the tribulation. The word *rapture* was used to indicate the departure of the church from the earth, and the second phase of the return was called the "appearing" of Jesus with His church. The rapture was *for* the saints, the appearing was *with* His saints. Thus, the second coming of Jesus was strictly divided into two phases. Scary stories were thought up and written about, of drivers of trains suddenly disappearing with the resultant crashes of trains; pilots of aircraft would disappear and jets would crash from the skies with most of their passengers.

The Bible certainly does not teach these things, which can only be referred to as bad fiction. It is true that the coming of Jesus is promised as a thief (see 2 Peter 3:10), but this would not indicate a silent cat-burglar type of approach, for the Bible clearly teaches that the coming of Christ will be as *"lightning cometh out of the east, and shineth even unto the west"* (Matthew 24:27). The whole sky will be lit up with the glory of His presence. There is nothing secret about this. The coming of Jesus to multitudes will be a complete surprise, and an event not expected, as a sudden raid. It will be noisy, too, because there will be heard the great sound of a trumpet of God, the voice of an archangel, and the loud shout of Jesus Himself as He descends for His church! (See 1 Thessalonians 4:16; Matthew 24:30.) Every eye shall see Him and be forced to look up. (See Revelation 1:7.)

I have tried to show that the tribulation is already passed. This is sometimes called the time of Jacob's trouble. As soon as the times of the Gentiles were fulfilled, and their time of world power began to run out, from the restoration of Jerusalem in June 1967, we entered into the post tribulation generation. This is why Matthew writes, "*Immediately after the tribulation of those days…*" (Matthew 24:29). A catalogue of signs are given in Luke 21:24–33, which begin to occur at the conclusion of the tribulation of the Jews and the church. After a tremendous show of cosmic disturbance in verse 29, which heralds the return of Jesus for His church, several consequent events occur. The sign of the Son of Man is seen, then all nations begin to mourn and they will actually see the splendor of His return, but will not be ready for it, to them He comes as a thief. Then the angels are sent ahead, right down to earth, to catch away the true believers, "And He shall send His angels with a great sound of a trumpet, and they shall gather His elect from the four winds, from one end of heaven to the other." Mark describes this tremendous event in chapter 13:27: "*And then shall he send his angels, and shall gather together His elect from the four winds, from the uttermost part of the earth to the uttermost part of heaven.*" In this latter account, the whole church on earth and in heaven is included. Both Matthew and Mark refer to this post tribulation generation as the one that will witness the catching away of the church after the tribulation.

This is a two witness statement to the truth. They both confirm that the church is caught away after the tribulation, not before. This cannot be twisted to suit a predetermined futurist theory. It is self-evident. The word *rapture* is not in the Bible. The events of the return of Christ for the church are clearly recorded for us in Thessalonians and 1 Corinthians 15. Let us see what Paul writes in these two epistles.

In 1 Thessalonians 4:14–17, we have the whole story, and both those who are "asleep," i.e. in heaven, and those on earth are *caught up*, (in Greek, *harpazo*, which means to snatch away). This is the purpose of the angels coming ahead of Jesus, for we could not be caught up into the clouds of the air without their help!

Some have tried to twist these words to suggest that the church will not leave the earth, but rather will be changed on this earth, and be revealed to the unbeliever in clouds of glory. Others have suggested that we are seen by clouds of witnesses, and that the clouds, here referred to, are not water vapor clouds in the sky. The Greek word meaning "to 'snatch away" precludes the thought of a translated church on earth in clouds of glory; in addition, the Greek word for cloud is *nephele*, which is generally used in Scripture to indicate water vapor clouds. The word for "*cloud of witnesses*" in Hebrews 12:1 is *nephos*, which does not necessarily mean a cloud of water. It seems quite clear then that the events are as follows: (1) Jesus descends with a shout, (2) the archangel cries out with a loud voice, (3) God sounds His trumpet, and (4) the angels descend in advance to "snatch away" true believers from every nation instantaneously. Both earthly and heavenly believers will be translated in this great event together) Then, (5) we are caught up to the water vapor clouds *in the air,* that is to say, within the atmosphere of this planet, not beyond in the stratosphere or the cosmic spaces.

As we go into 1 Corinthians 15:51–53, we find the events as follows:

1.　We shall all be changed, both these "asleep" and those on earth.

2.　In the twinkling of an eye, we shall be invested with immortal bodies, a sudden tremendous change.

3.　The trumpet shall sound,

4.　The graves are opened. (See also John 5:28–29.)

There is no record in the Bible of the coming of Jesus being in two phases. Of course, we agree that any school of interpretation may believe and teach this if they feel it is correct, but let them prove it clearly from the Scriptures.

Jesus returns to the atmosphere of this planet, and both the living and the sleeping in Christ will be invested with their immortal bodies, just like His glorified body, and will meet Him in the air. He said He would return *"in the clouds [nephele] of heaven"* (Matthew 26:64), and the angels snatch us away and take us up to Him in the clouds, and then we return with Him to rule and reign on earth.

Unless one forces the rapture into the last week of Daniel, with the church returning to heaven and remaining there for three-and-a-half years, or seven years, which is pure futurism, then there is no Scripture at all to suggest either the church being away from the earth for three-and-a-half years, or for it being in heaven for this supposed period of time. There is, then, no need for a two phase coming!

In history, when mighty conquerors were met returning from battle, they were met at the gates of the city by a welcoming group of chosen citizens, often virgins, and accompanied in triumph into the city. Jesus will return to take over the rule of this planet. That is the purpose of His return—not to go back to heaven. The church meets Him as He enters the gates of this planet, the water vapor cloud gates, and we all return together, the living and the dead in Christ, to rule as His Body on earth for one thousand years.

There is no rapture, but there is a snatching away.

In the last century, there was a move of the Holy Spirit that brought to birth the Catholic Apostolic Church, and one of the pastors was Rev. Edward Irving, of the Church of England. It was an early charismatic church, and in 1832, a woman gave a prophecy in their London, England, church, that there would be a secret rapture. Some believed that this utterance gave the original germ to John Darby of the

Plymouth Brethren, to propagate his theory of a secret catching away before a supposed tribulation period. The doctrine was largely disseminated by the Schofield Reference Bible, but at least two of the contributing editors later changed their views after further study of the Bible, possibly because Jesus said, *"after the tribulation of those days"* (Matthew 24:29; Mark 13:24).

These thoughts began to be spoken in supposed prophecies and teaching sessions at about this time of 1832, owing to the release of the theory of the Father Ribera by Dr. Samuel Maitland, from Lambeth Palace, London. It is very easy to bring forth a prophecy from one's own mind, which has no reference either to the Holy Spirit or evil spirits, and human pride does not permit the speaker to admit it may have been a personal thought and not a divinely inspired utterance. This is why all prophecies must be judged.

Prophecies of gloom and a great falling away from the true faith have previously been learned from teachers of the futurist school, who learned them in their turn from their forefathers. Jesus is the Victor, not the Antichrist!

11

THE NIGHT COMETH

An oft quoted Scripture by the futurists to prove a great falling away and a great persecution of the church is found in the words of Jesus in John 9:4. Jesus had just healed the boy who was blind from birth, and He explained to His disciples that as long as He was with them, being the Light of the world, He would continue to do good and to heal. He said that the night would come and no one would be able to do such works of love and mercy.

He spoke these words in about AD 30. Their fulfillment would have to be after this date. It seems quite clear from history that they were fulfilled in the Dark Ages, so called because spiritual light had gone out. There was no apostle, prophet, or man of God who did the miraculous works of Jesus during this time. The witnesses were lying dead.

If we date Pentecost as being the birth of the church in its full pristine glory and power, when it revealed the very sunshine of Jesus, then in the cycle of the church age from the first Pentecost to Pentecost restored, the opposite of the daylight would be darkness. This great period of darkness extended at its blackest from AD 606 to 1517, when not only spiritual knowledge practically ceased, but general knowledge of the sciences was almost practically exterminated from the earth. It took the Reformation and the Renaissance to bring back progressively some of the light of Jesus.

There are many voices clamoring for our ears today, telling us and openly prophesying to us that the church will go through incredible persecution because of "night coming when no man can work." Visions have been given of this terrible period, but we must remember that no vision or personal revelation must even be considered unless it is backed up with solid Scripture. Visions are not to teach, but to confirm the Word. All prophecies and visions must be subject to judging by the church. If one's mind is thoroughly filled already with futuristic misconceptions, then one's mental pictures and thinking will be colored, and it is so human to say, "the Lord showed me," or "the Lord told me." The gullible find it easier to believe a vision than the Word. We must prove every spirit!

Scripture shows us clearly that there will always be these misguided prophets going through the land, for we read,

> *When a prophet speaketh in the name of the* Lord, *if the thing follow not,* **nor come to pass,** *that is the thing which the* Lord *hath not spoken, but the prophet hath spoken it presumptuously: thou shalt not be afraid of him.*
> (Deuteronomy 18:22)

If a prophet states quite emphatically that there is going to be a great persecution of the church, especially in North America, and it does not come to pass, then it will be proved that he was a false prophet vision or no vision.

In a recent seminar, I spoke positively of the great restoration of the church; of the great desire that God has to bless His people with love and abundance. Inevitably, I was asked about the falling away and the rise of the monster Antichrist. When I showed that all these Scriptures had already been fulfilled in the Dark Ages, and that the church had great blessing to look forward to, not great cursing, the people were overjoyed, and one lady asked for special prayer to be delivered from a spirit of fear of the Antichrist. Negative preaching produces negative results. Negative preaching gives Satan his opportunities and advertises his projected plans. Has it ever occurred to you that prayer can reverse the plans of Satan? God said He would destroy Nineveh, but prayer changed this plan.

Many dislike intensely that a religious leader should be called "antichrist." It upsets them, for surely there must be something good in all leaders, even those of bloodless cults. Paul warned that false Christs, false prophets, would arise from among the church to deceive the elect. If past papal persons have not fulfilled perfectly the prophecies of the Man of Sin, or the Antichrist, then what is the alternative fulfillment? By definition, he is not primarily a political leader; he is a religious leader, a vicarious Christ. He is all-powerful in his day of darkness. He is infallible. He makes and unmakes laws to suit his kingdom. He wears out the saints of the Most High. He sits as God in his temple.

If this historicist interpretation of Scripture is not the correct one, then events rapidly happening in the immediate future will confirm the truth. Either the futurists are right or the majority of us who have believed the teachings as outlined in this book since 1300 are right. The two positions are mutually antagonistic and opposite. They cannot be reconciled. There is not long to wait.

Where is the temple in which Antichrist is to make a covenant with the Jews? Where are the ten toes of the image? Where is the Antichrist?

Supposing Antichrist does not arise? Supposing there is not a great falling away and persecution of the church? Supposing the whole theory of the futurists is proved wrong? Will your faith be upset?

It seems that we have moved a long way from the time when *"the night cometh, when no man can work"* (John 9:4) to a great period of restoration, when the Sun of Righteousness is arising with healing in His wings. It seems that the daylight of His presence is beginning to shine throughout the world in a new way. This is not the night but the day. When Jesus returns, it will be midsummer, not midwinter! (See Luke 21:30.) In the harvest time, the Christian church is to shine like the sun, not be obliterated. (See Matthew 13:43.) If the church began at Pentecost, we are seeing a return to Pentecost—all over the world. What about the prophecy of the Spirit being outpoured on all flesh? Does this indicate darkness, night, and persecution? I am not impressed by any teachings or visions that predict other than what Scripture teaches.

Instead of there being a falling away, there is a coming back. Instead of gross darkness, there is increasing light. The summer is now nigh at hand. Paul says we are all the children of light, and the children of the day. (See 1 Thessalonians 5:5.) The outpouring of the Spirit destroys Antichrist. (See 2 Thessalonians 2:8.)

I do not believe there will be any spluttering out of the present move of God throughout the church or among the young people. This is the time for them to return. The Roman Church will be entirely renewed, as will every Protestant denomination. It was a new generation that had to go into the Promised Land. as we read in Deuteronomy 1:32. The cycle of disobedience of the parents gave way to the renewed obedience of the new generation. This is exactly what Malachi prophesied in chapter 4, verse 6. This onward move among the new generation will go on without hiatus unto crescendo.

So, *"lift up your heads; for your redemption draweth nigh"* (Luke 21:28).

12

THE SPIRIT OF ANTICHRIST

One of the major objections to the statement that the papacy of the Middle Ages was a fulfillment of Antichrist is found in 1 John 4:3: *"And every spirit that confesseth not that Jesus is come in the flesh is not of God: and this is the spirit of antichrist."* The spirit of antichrist is an evil spirit that denies Jesus, who was manifest in the flesh. This does not mean, as some believe, that the antichrist actually taught that Jesus never existed in a mortal body. It means, in simple terms, that the antichrist denied the Christ, who was manifest in the flesh, by being an impostor. The whole ministry of Antichrist, being a false Christ, would deny in every detail the sweet ministry of Jesus, who manifests the grace of God in His life and gave us salvation.

I have already explained that Judas Iscariot is a type of antichrist, for both he (see John 17:21) and the Man of Sin (see 2 Thessalonians 2:3) are described as the son of perdition. Judas was called a disciple, that is, a disciplined follower of Jesus, and a believer (see Luke 6:13–16), and as a believer, he allowed Satan to tempt him to sell his Lord for money (see John 13:2). He accepted the proposition and Satan entered into him (see verse 27), and he sold His Savior for money. This is exactly what Pope Leo X did through the German priest Tetzel, who went throughout Germany selling indulgences for money, with the cry, "He who drops a coin in this box will have his sins forgiven for ever." It was the selling of indulgences that stirred Martin Luther to his depths and precipitated the Reformation. Luther wrote personally to Pope Leo X, naming him as Antichrist. The great basilica of St. Peter's in Rome was built with money obtained by selling salvation for cash salvation, which was purchased by the blood of Jesus and is free to all who believe. The man of sin, the son of perdition, was seen in the activity of the spirit of antichrist working through Leo X.

Pope Leo X denied the salvation of the Christ, who came in the flesh, by selling it for money. The very work of redemption wrought on the cross of Calvary was denied and cancelled out by the blasphemous action of the pope in selling salvation. Truly,

Antichrist denied Jesus Christ, who came in the flesh. He did not say that Jesus had never lived in a mortal body; He simply denied Jesus, who gave that body as a sacrifice for the sins of the world. He was the manifestation of the Antichrist, because he was a false, pretending Christ. He was a phony. His life, ministry, teaching, and practice all denied the finished work of Calvary.

One of the big issues was salvation by faith. This was the rallying cry of the Reformation, "The just shall live by faith," not by works of the church or by obedience to the ordinances of the pope. This simple teaching that Jesus paid it all and gave salvation freely to all the whomsoever, was hotly denied by the whole papal system, from top to bottom, and millions were put to death because they believed this truth. The teachings of the pope in the Middle Ages, from 500 to 1870, simply denied this fact that we are justified by faith alone. It is really only since 1967 that the Roman Catholic Church is teaching again that their members must be born again of the Spirit of God and that Jesus is Lord, because of the present outpouring of the Holy Spirit in the charismatic movement among them. It took the coming of the Spirit in Pentecostal manifestation to bring back to them the simple teachings of the Reformation period. The Roman Church is returning to the Bible, away from traditions of hundreds of years. The spirit of antichrist is being consumed by the word of Jesus's mouth, that is, the return of the charismatic gifts of the Holy Spirit, which are again revealing Jesus as the Head of the church to the Roman Church. God is about to fill the Roman Catholics with His Spirit, because He loves them. He wants to prepare them as well as every other Protestant church group, for His return. His church His bride—will be without spot or wrinkle or any such thing at His coming.

The Spirit of antichrist, referred to in 1 John 4:3, is the same as the spirit that controls the lawless one of 2 Thessalonians 2:8. The word *"Wicked,"* referring to the Man of Sin, or Antichrist, is controlled by a lawless spirit, not governed by the Spirit of God, who reveals Jesus, but by a terrible religious spirit that simulates the Christ. This spirit is *"not of God"* (1 John 4:3), but was already in the world, only to reach its full power after the pagan Roman Empire had been removed.

Again, let us remember that the definition of an antichrist is given by John:

> As ye have heard that antichrist shall come, even now are there many antichrists; whereby we know that it is the last time [i.e., Anno Domini]. **They went out from us**, but they were not of us; for if they had been of us, they would no doubt have continued with us. (1 John 2:18–19)

From this, we find that an antichrist is one who followed with the Lord (as did Judas Iscariot) but finally left the faith and established a false church. This is why the book of Revelation shows us the contrast between the scarlet woman on the seven hills (of Rome) (see Revelation 17:4–5) and the virgin church of Revelation 12.

Thank God that the blood of Jesus is able to cleanse the harlot church, as the power of antichrist is destroyed by the Holy Spirit, the breath of God, and bring it back to the condition of the virgin church. In this, we see Mary the mother of Jesus as a beautiful type of the truly cleansed church, ready for the return of the Savior.

By no stretch of the imagination, or the forcing of Scripture of predetermined hypotheses, can an antichrist ever be made to be a Jew or a political ruler. In the last few days, we have learned that some are teaching that Henry Kissinger of the United States Foreign Office is the Antichrist, and another person told us she expected him to come from outer space at any minute. This is what happens when people are off-track in their understanding of fulfilled prophecy. In attempting to identify any antichrist, in Paul's day or in the Middle Ages, we must look for a man who is a religious apostate from primitive Christianity, and who claims to be the vicarious representative of Christ, but denies the simple teachings of the Savior. Our search will not take us long. He has been manifest in history, which is behind us. If you look for a future Antichrist, you are going to be disappointed. It is to the Christ that we look today, for the government is on His shoulder, and He is already pouring out His spirit upon the whole church, Protestant, Catholic, and Baptist.

Let us not be disturbed by the history of the Roman Church in the Dark Ages. It happened. The Bible prophesied it, and we cannot turn back the clock, but we can all come together in the love of Christ in this final restoration and renewal of the whole church.

I find God has given me a special love for the Catholics, who are emerging from such darkness into the glorious light of the gospel. They are being born again and filled with the Spirit so easily, and few in the Roman Church seem to be opposing God's Spirit, not even the present pope, who may well be the last one. We should pray earnestly that all bishops of the Church of Rome shall soon be baptized in the Holy Spirit, and manifest the gifts of the Spirit. What a wonderful thing it would be if the present pope were to receive the baptism in the Spirit and openly acknowledge that he praised God in tongues daily! Let us pray to this end.

In praying thus, let us also remember that the daughters of Rome are the Reformation churches, the historic churches. May their leaders and members also be likewise filled with the Holy Spirit. May *agape love* be the portion of us all. Amen.

ABOUT THE AUTHOR

ABOUT THE AUTHOR

The picture of a British bulldog, H. A. Maxwell Whyte (1908–1988) had a commanding countenance and a stentorian voice, which was especially awesome when raised against the devil and his demons. He had a big, soft heart, and he loved Jesus. He was a pioneer in this generation in recognizing that *"we do not wrestle against flesh and blood, but against principalities, against powers, against the rulers of the darkness of this age, against spiritual hosts of wickedness in the heavenly places"* (Ephesians 6:12), and he has carried the battle right to the enemy's doorstep. He had faith enough to believe that God would confirm His *"word through the accompanying signs"* (Mark 16:20). In the powerful name of Jesus, he has proclaimed liberty to the captives and opened the prisons for those who were bound. (See Isaiah 61:1.) For more than forty years, he ministered worldwide to the downcast and brokenhearted and led the way in the ministry of the powerful gifts of the Holy Spirit.

Maxwell Whyte was born on May 3, 1908, in London, England. As a child, he was raised in a nominally Christian home in which church attendance was encouraged. Raised as a Presbyterian, Maxwell was strongly influenced by the godly pastor of his boyhood parish, and at age sixteen, he made a commitment to the Lord, although his level of understanding of what this decision meant was meager indeed.

After completing his education at Dulwich College in London, Maxwell entered the business world as a representative of the Anglo-American Oil Company, and even during the Depression years, he enjoyed a measure of success that was the envy of many during those years of economic stress. On June 8, 1934, Maxwell married Olive Hughes in St. Paul's Anglican Church in the London suburb of Beckenham. It was in this peaceful residential area that Maxwell and Olive rejoiced in their comfortable lifestyle, their solid marriage, and the birth of their first two sons, David and Michael.

All was going well for this successful and happy couple until son David became seriously ill. In fear that their son might be taken from them, Olive and Maxwell cried out to the Lord in desperation, and they were both dramatically affected when God restored David to good health. Shortly after this experience, Maxwell was invited by a colleague to attend a small charismatic meeting in Croydon on the outskirts of London. There, for the first time, he witnessed the operation of the gifts of the Holy Spirit and saw a group of people whose relationship with the Lord was one of vitality, not in keeping with religious tradition. Maxwell's life was never the same again as he was truly converted, baptized in water, baptized in the Holy Spirit, and miraculously set free from a smoking habit, all within a few weeks. The year was 1939, and to be a charismatic in those days was not a popular thing for a Christian to be!

At the outbreak of World War II, Maxwell entered the Royal Air Force as a signals officer, where his lifelong interest in amateur radio was put to use in setting up defense communications. During his six and a half years of military service, Maxwell spent many long hours studying the Bible, convinced that one day he would enter into full-time ministry. In 1946, after his discharge from the RAF, Maxwell returned to his business career, only to leave it a few months later to prepare for the ministry. After several months of intensive training and prayer, Maxwell answered the call to emigrate to Toronto, Canada, to be pastor of the United Apostolic Faith Church, a small congregation that had been without a pastor for several years.

So it was, in April 1947, that Maxwell and Olive Whyte and their family of three boys (Stephen was born a few months after the war) arrived in Canada to take up the responsibility of leading a group of a dozen or so believers who made up the fledgling congregation in Toronto. The first few years in Toronto were not easy for the Whytes. They lived in cramped quarters on little income, and in 1952, a fourth son, John, was born. The boys adjusted well to their new environment and soon became full-fledged Canadians. For over three decades, Maxwell faithfully served as pastor to this church. He witnessed the transformation of the small band of worshippers as God built them into a thriving group of believers who held to the charismatic truths of the Bible.

In 1948, while Maxwell was dealing with one of his parishioners who suffered from chronic asthma and another who was suicidal, God sovereignly directed him into an understanding of the reality of spiritual warfare and deliverance. This revelation catapulted Maxwell into a ministry that drew attention from many parts of the globe.

In over forty years of ministry, Whyte ministered in many countries of the world on five continents. At the same time, he authored numerous books dealing with the workings of God in the present charismatic outpourings of the Spirit. Hundreds of letters have told of healings and deliverances of those who have read his writings, believed, and were blessed.

Welcome to Our House!

We Have a Special Gift for You

It is our privilege and pleasure to share in your love of Christian books. We are committed to bringing you authors and books that feed, challenge, and enrich your faith.

To show our appreciation, we invite you to sign up to receive a specially selected **Reader Appreciation Gift**, with our compliments. Just go to the Web address at the bottom of this page.

God bless you as you seek a deeper walk with Him!

WE HAVE A GIFT FOR YOU. VISIT:

whpub.me/nonfictionthx

WHITAKER
HOUSE